Handbook of Radio and TV Broadcasting

Research Procedures
in Audience,
Program and Revenues

Handbook of Radio and TV Broadcasting

Research Procedures in Audience, Program and Revenues

Edited by

James E. Fletcher
University of Georgia

VNR **VAN NOSTRAND REINHOLD COMPANY**
NEW YORK   CINCINNATI   ATLANTA   DALLAS   SAN FRANCISCO
LONDON   TORONTO   MELBOURNE

Van Nostrand Reinhold Company Regional Offices:
New York Cincinnati Atlanta Dallas San Francisco

Van Nostrand Reinhold Company International Offices:
London Toronto Melbourne

Library of Congress Catalog Card Number: 80-19536
ISBN: 0-442-22417-6

Manufactured in the United States of America

Published by Van Nostrand Reinhold Company
135 West 50th Street, New York, N.Y. 10020

Published simultaneously in Canada by Van Nostrand Reinhold Ltd.

15 14 13 12 11 10 9 8 7 6 5 4 2 1

Library of Congress Cataloging in Publication Data
Main entry under title:

Handbook of radio and TV broadcasting.

  Includes index.
  1. Broadcasting—Research—Handbooks, manuals, etc.
2. Radio audiences—Research—Handbooks, manuals, etc.
3. Television audiences—Research—Handbooks, manuals,
etc. I. Fletcher, James E.
HE8689.6.H36   384.54'4'072   80-19536
ISBN 0-442-22417-6

Preface

This project began as CASH—a Comprehensive Assessment Handbook, a project of the Research Committee of the Broadcast Education Association. The early name of the project was no accident. It had been the Committee's intent to produce a research manual for broadcasters which would assist them in reducing the risks of their operations while improving revenue.

At large stations, a station's research represents a substantial expense—rating reports, profiles of special audiences, public surveys for ascertainment, studies of the effectiveness of station promotion campaigns, studies to assist in the development of new programs and formats, cost effectiveness studies of virtually every station undertaking.

Stations in smaller markets, and smaller stations in large markets may not generate revenues enough to finance the excellent commercial research efforts engaged in by more prosperous stations. Yet risk is considerably greater in the day-to-day operation of many small stations. Although research may be needed to reduce risk to station capital and to improve revenues, these stations are often unable to afford it.

In 1976 the Research Committee of the Broadcast Education Association adopted as a goal the development of do-it-yourself research kits which would enable laymen at the local station level to conduct research essential to sound management of these stations. A number of educators across the country have worked with local stations to produce reputable research at bargain rates. In some cases, college and university faculty have recruited their students as journeymen analysts and interviewers in these projects—a pattern referred to as "cooperative research."

The first step in the development of this handbook was a series of discussions among academics and industry professionals at the 1977 annual meetings of the Broadcast Education Association. From these discussions several desirable characteristics for the handbook emerged:

- No research procedure should be included which cannot be properly applied by a well-instructed layman.
- Only research procedures with wide industry acceptance should be included.
- The variety of research recommended should cover the range of management concerns in broadcasting.
- The handbook should be complete in itself. That is, a layman conducting a research project recommended in the handbook should not need to refer to other materials.
- Academic teachers of broadcasting should be available in all parts of the country to advise, audit, and validate the local station research recommended by this handbook.

The contributors to this handbook wish to acknowledge the assistance and encouragement of the Research Directorate of the National Association of Broadcasters, the NAB

Small Market Radio Committee and the NAB 100 Plus Market Television Committee. Each of these provided important influences in the formative stage of this project. Of course, the contributors accept full responsibility for whatever flaws or inaccuracies have crept into their work.

In the summer of 1978, Mr. Ashak M. Rawji, Senior Editor, Professional and Reference Division of Van Nostrand Reinhold offered a contract to the contributors of the CASH project, and this volume was born. Mr. Rawji suggested adding additional pages to discuss the commercially available audience rating systems, and Ms. Constance C. Anthes, Manager, Communications, of the ARBitron Company assisted us in developing the extracts of two market reports included as appendices to this volume. They are used to provide working illustrations connected with our discussion of ratings.

It is our hope as the Research Committee of the Broadcast Education Association that this volume will make an affirmative contribution to both the teaching of broadcasting and its practice in the "real" world.

James E. Fletcher
Athens, Georgia

Contents

Handbook of Radio and TV Broadcasting

Research Procedures
in Audience,
Program and Revenues

1 Why Research ?

James E. Fletcher

For the reader who has chosen this book, the question is probably unnecessary. But, at the risk of belaboring an issue, the purpose of research in telecommunications industries will be reviewed.

Whether commercial or noncommercial, every broadcast station represents a commitment of resources, both public and private. As with any investment, there is some level of risk that there will be a complete loss of these resources, should the undertaking fail to meet its objectives. There is some other risk that the return on investment will not justify continued operation; and there is some likelihood that goals—profit or otherwise—will be met. In each case, resources have been committed with specific though not always stated goals in mind.

Research in the telecommunication industry is primarily directed toward illuminating this relationship between resources committed and desired outcomes.

Consider for a moment the case of a commercial television station. The station must have at least these two goals: (1) to meet commitments in its renewal application in order to qualify for continued renewal, and (2) to produce a profit of a level required by the licensee. To some extent, the second goal is involved with the first, since the Federal Communications Commission expects licensees to use channel allocations in a way which promises a flourishing business with operating funds adequate to meet programming commitments.

The simple statement of these two goals emphasizes that the success of this television station will be determined by the audiences of the station. The size and composition of these audiences establish the value to advertisers of the station commercial time. The needs and preferences of the audience will, to a large extent, influence the variety and content of programs selected for broadcast by the station. Some advertising messages broadcast by the station will be more or less effective, depending on this same audience. It is also true that audience size and composition are not perfectly related to the size of investment in station equipment and programming. Some program investments, in particular, produce disproportionate returns in audience size and loyalty. Other very expensive programs may actually drive audiences away.

If this commercial television station were in a small enough community, research into the relationship between investments and audiences could be done by personal observation, by calling on sponsors and neighbors. But as the size of audiences increases, as the size of required program investments increases, as the competition increases, more exact and far-reaching tools for research are required.

MEASUREMENT

Research involves much more, but the process of assigning numbers to important qualities is crucial in most research; this process is called measurement.

A measure is a protocol or set of rules which define the way in which numbers may be assigned to qualities or quantities of an attribute under study. Ideally a measure is *reliable* and *valid.* If a measure is reliable, then the results of measuring something do not vary with each application of the measure. A measure is valid if there is some credible evidence that the quality which the measure purports to measure is in fact the one being measured. Of the two issues, reliability and validity, reliability must always be considered first, since, if the measure is not reliable—cannot be counted upon to yield the same answer each time it is used to measure the same quality—then the question of validity cannot be addressed. The statistical procedures used to estimate the reliability of a measure are described in detail in Appendix C, Lesson Eight.

The validity of a measure is estimated by three different strategies—face validity, construct validity, and criterion validity. *Face validity* is the process of examining a measure to see whether, from the "face" of it, the measure seems to be reflecting the quality which it is supposed to measure. If, for example, the number of "Country Music Hall" (a popular local program) bumper stickers are counted in the parking lot of the biggest shopping mall in town, the measure may have face validity as a reflection of the popularity of the program. On the other hand, if the measure called for these same bumper stickers to be counted in the same mall parking lot while the program is being broadcast, the face validity of the measure as an index to program popularity would be different.

Construct validity of a measure is the extent to which theory connects the measure to the attribute of concern. For instance, previous research into program selection in the family indicates that when teenagers are present in the home, it is likely that they will select programs to be viewed by the family. This knowledge suggests teenage viewing preferences might be a measure of family viewing preferences as well, and such a measure would have construct validity.

Criterion validity requires that a candidate measure be compared to a measure with an established reputation for validity. Sales figures are used as criteria for measures of advertising effectiveness. A measure of effectiveness which closely follows sales figures would be considered high in validity. Unfortunately in the real world of research reliable criterion measures against which to compare a new measure, are relatively rare. But when they are available criterion validity adds undeniable credibility to a measure.

In addition to reliability and validity, the researcher is interested in the discrimination of a measure—how well it will show as different numbers, different amounts or kinds of an attribute. To illustrate, there is research which shows that taking a course by television is not significantly different in the learning produced from taking the same course taught in the traditional way. The students involved in these research studies were not confused, for they knew when they were taking the course by television and by the traditional methods. But the measure used by the researchers did not *discriminate* between the states of mind of the students in the two different courses. The discriminating ability of a measure is also referred to as *sensitivity.*

Another characteristic of measures is *scale,* the nature of the set of rules by which numbers are assigned in the measurement of the attribute. The simplest measurement scale is a *nominal* scale. In a nominal scale numbers are used as category names. It is not possible to perform arithmetic operations on the numbers resulting from such a nominal scale. For instance, a measure may call for the number, "1," to be used to indicate the survey respondent is male, while the number, "2," is used to indicate that the respondent is female. The numbers in this nominal scale are used as category titles. It is not possible to add these numbers: what would 1 + 2 represent? The results of adding or subtracting, multiplying or dividing the numbers of a nominal scale are absurd. A familiar use of nominal scales in broadcast research is the rating. The basic question asked of a respondent in a rating survey is, "To what station are you listening?" When the respondent answers, "To station XXX," the researcher records a "1" for station XXX and a "0" for stations YYY and ZZZ, the other stations in the market. In other words, listeners are divided into two categories, those who are listening (coded 1) and those who are not (coded 0). After collecting this nominal data from each respondent, the investigator computes the percent of listeners (responses coded 1) which becomes the familiar rating.

Another type of measurement scale, somewhat higher on the dimension of sophistication, is the ordinal scale. In an ordinal system of measurement numbers are assigned to indicate relative magnitude. So the number 2 assigned to an object indicates there is more of it than an object labeled 1. The distance between ordinal numbers is not necessarily equal, but each higher number indicates more of the attribute being measured than the number just smaller. An illustration would be a viewer survey to evaluate local television newscasts. In the community being studied there are three local television stations which broadcast local news. The investigator asks each respondent, "Which of these three stations do you prefer to watch? Which of the three do you like least to watch?" The result is coded 1 for the preferred station, 2 for the station not mentioned by the respondent, and 3 for the station liked least. This sort of task is called *ranking* and results in an ordinal scale. A special set of statistics–rank order statistics–have been developed to deal with the numbers resulting from an ordinal scale.

A third type of measurement scale is *interval*. In an interval system of measurement numbers are assigned so that each number is an equal distance from each adjacent number. This results in a scale with equal *intervals* between. Most of the sensitive statistical routines developed for the researcher can be employed when the measurement scale used is at the interval level of sophistication. A common example of the interval scale is the rating scale in which the investigator askes the respondent, "On a scale of one to ten, with ten being the best possible news program, how would you rate the news of Station XXX?" The responses to this question might be shown graphically as falling on a scale like this:

Worst Possible   1   2   3   4   5   6   7   8   9   10   Best Possible

But, while the interval scale will reflect equal distances among the numbers assigned in measurement, it will not reflect a true zero point for the scale. On the scale above, for instance, the lowest score to be assigned to the response of the individual being interviewed is 1. How many intervals this 1 may be above 0 is not clear, and it is not clear that 10 is 10 times more than 1.

The *ratio* system of measurement provides numbers which are equal intervals apart and are in ratio to the distance between 0 and 1. This is the most sophisticated form of measurement scale. A common illustration of a ratio scale is the Celsius thermometer. Ten degrees Celsius is 10 times warmer than 1 degree; the scale has a 0 point, and all scores are in ratio to the distance between 0 and 1. In spite of the virtues of the ratio scale, it is relatively uncommon in broadcast industry research. It is possible to generate a ratio scale with a series of questions like these: "I am going to name a series of television performers, and I would like you to respond with a number which corresponds in your mind with the excellence of the named individual as a television performer. You can use any number you wish, so long as it is between 1 and 100, and the larger the number, the more excellent you think the performer to be. What number between 1 and 100 would you assign to:

Lili Redford?   _____

George Burnside?   _____

More Gerriford?   _____

Joe Martini? _____

Jill Jones? _____."

The numbers given by any one respondent are converted to ratio scores by dividing each estimate by the average estimate given by that respondent. The result is a set of adjusted estimates which are in ratio to the average estimate given—a ratio scale.

These important matters related to measurement as a tool for research have been discussed to this point—reliability, validity, sensitivity or discrimination, level of scale (nominal, ordinal, interval, or ratio). To make decisions based upon measurements an additional consideration is essential, that of probability.

PROBABILITY AND EXPECTATION

Every gambler is concerned with the risks being taken in a game or competition and with the probability for success when various bets are made. The gambler labels this awareness as "the odds" or "chances," so does the manager. For with every commitment of resources in a new undertaking there is some level of risk and some expectation of gain. For the researcher, these notions are summarized in the concept of *probability*. As a statistician might define the term, probability is the ratio of the relative number of specified outcomes of some process to the total possible number of outcomes from the same process. Consider a clean deck of playing cards, 52 in number, 4 of which are aces. If the cards have been thoroughly shuffled, the probability of drawing an ace from the deck on the first draw is 4 (the number of specified outcomes, aces) in 52 (the total number of cards or possible outcomes). In decimal fraction form, the probability of an ace on first draw from a deck is 4 divided by 52 or .08. In this same deck, the probability of drawing an ace of hearts, of which there is only one in the deck, on the first draw would be 1 in 52, or .02. If the ace of hearts were drawn on the first draw, then the probability of drawing an ace on the second draw, providing the first draw is not replaced, would be 3, the number of remaining aces, in 51, the number of remaining cards, or .06. In sum, probability is the relative likelihood of some specified outcome.

A related concept important in making decisions in business and finance is that of mathematical expectation. In its simplest terms, a mathematical expectation is the product of the probability of some event by the value of that event. Consider the situation of the hungry worker at a coffee break faced by a soft drink machine which is not perfectly reliable. Thirst demands that the worker attempt to get a drink from the machine, but information from coworkers indicates that the machine provides a drink only 9 times out of 10 when the coins are deposited. The probability of getting a soft drink is thus equal to .90, while the possible loss is $.30, the amount required by the machine for each drink, or attempt to purchase a drink. In this case, the mathematical expectation on the loss side of the decision is .10, the probability that a drink will not be delivered after depositing the correct coins, times $ .30, the size of the potential loss, or $ .03. In other words, if a large number of tries are made by the worker to purchase a drink, the average loss per try is likely to be $ .03. This expectation of loss is referred to as *risk*. In the case of the soft drink machine and the thirsty worker, the risk at each purchase of a drink is $ .03.

Most management decision-making will involve both risk and expectation of gains. An informed decision will result from a consideration of risk along with anticipated gains. Consider the decision facing the general manager of a small commercial television station. The station has been offered a weekly program from syndication at an average cost of $25 per program. The program allows four commercial minutes, 1 minute as adjacencies and 3 as participating spots. The least return envisioned from this purchase from syndication would result from the sale of only three 30-second spots in connection with the program, when these spots were part of a contract for run-of-schedule (ROS) announcements. These ROS spots bring the station an average of $5 each, meaning that the worst revenue situation for a typical program from this series purchased from syndication would be a net loss of $10. How likely, or probable, is this worst case? Of the programs scheduled on the station in the same time period over the last 5 years, 5 percent have sold at this low level. The *risk* then of the worst case is .05 (the probability of the worst case) times $10 (the loss involved) or $.50.

On the gain side of the decision, the best any program has done in the same time period is to sell 90 percent of its availabilities with an average price per 30-second spot of $10. Ten percent of the programs purchased from syndication and broadcast in this time period have reached this high level of success. The return per program in this case would be $72 (eight spots times $10 dollars average price times 90 percent sold) less the cost of the program, $25, a net of $47. The expectation of gain would be .10 (the probability of gain) times $47 (the value of gain) or $4.70. Of course, additional computations would be possible for each other possible level of gain or loss.

When levels of risk are compared to levels of gain, it is likely that the general manager will purchase a program from syndication. And to the extent that characteristics of successful programs other than cost have also been measured, the manager will consider them in the decision-making process.

SAMPLING

The economics of broadcast research dictate that only a few of the potential audience of any program or station can be interviewed in any one study. The cost of a professional interviewer interviewing a respondent in a face-to-face setting will today be in excess of $20 per respondent. The cost of a completed telephone interview with one respondent may be well above $5. With the cost of collecting information from only one respondent so high, collecting information from every potential member of a broadcast audience in a community of 50,000 residents would be out of the question (rapid mental calculation: 50,000 residents times $20 per interview equals $1 million). Under these economic circumstances it is not surprising that broadcast researchers elect to talk to selected members of the larger population, these respondents comprising a subgroup or sample selected in a way which increases the likelihood that they will be representative of the larger population.

In most cases the biggest issue in designing an audience survey will be the procedure by which the sample is selected: this process is called *sample design.* Chapters 4 and 5 deal with issues in sample design at some length. One generalization is possible at this point: in most cases, the best sample design will be based on random selection.

Random procedures for selecting a sample of respondents will provide that every member of the population from which the sample is drawn will have an *equal probability* of being selected. If there are 50,000 adults in the market being studied, and if the research calls for a random sample of adults, then each adult in the population must have a probability of 1 in 50,000, or .00002, of being selected into the sample. This procedure requires that sampling be done with *replacement.*

When sampling with replacement, the first person selected into the sample is replaced into the pool of the population. Otherwise, the probability of the remaining adults being drawn into the sample would become 1 in 49,999, then 1 in 49,998, and so on. So, as a conceptual matter at least, each person selected into the sample is thrown back into the pool of those to be selected in order that the equal probability requirement of random selection be met.

The second requirement of a sampling procedure in order for it to be correctly labeled as random is that each selection be made independently of each other selection. To be independent, the selection of the first person into the sample must be unconnected to the selection of the second and subsequent persons into the sample.

It should be noted that there are research situations in which a random sample may not be the best suited to a particular research study, and the following chapters discuss several such situations. But when the sample design does call for a random selection procedure, the researcher cannot compromise the requirements of that procedure without sacrificing the clarity and meaning of the study.

Whenever a sample—no matter how selected—must stand for a larger population, there will be some degree of error produced by the difference in the information collected from the sample as opposed to the information that might have resulted from measuring the entire population. This difference between an answer obtained from a sample and the answer which might have been obtained in a census of the entire population is referred to as *sampling error*. Whenever a study is conducted within a sample, there is some degree of sampling error, and the prudent user of research will not insist that there be no error but that the size of the sampling error be estimated according to the best procedure available. Procedures for estimating sampling error will fill an important number of the pages that follow. In most cases a sample will be designed to produce a sampling error of known dimensions. A common criterion in studies of broadcast audiences is that sampling error have a 95 percent probability of being no more than five rating points for any rating presented in the study. (A rating point is an estimated 1 percent of the available audience; a rating is the percentage of the available audience listening to or viewing a given station or program.)

The size of an audience survey sample is dictated primarily by the size of the acceptable sampling error. If it were known, for instance, that the audiences of two competing stations were different in size by only 2 percent, then the sample design would have to produce a sampling error of 2 percent or less.

It is a fact that smaller sampling errors come from *disproportionately* larger samples. That is, cutting sampling error in half will more than double the size of the sample required. And increasing sample size in this way will increase the cost of the research involved as well. As a consequence, the costs of doing research are continually dictating limits on the accuracy of the research being undertaken.

It may also be apparent that the size of sampling error in any sample design is not a function of the size of the population from which the sample is drawn. To the contrary, sampling error is a direct function of the size of the sample, regardless of the size of the population from which it is drawn. This fact runs counter to the subjective expectation of the average user of broadcast research (in fact, counter to the intuitions of researchers, as well). It is, nevertheless, a fact verified over and over again in actual research.[1] And a little reflection will indicate that sampling error *ought* to be computed from the sample rather than from the population, since the data from the rest of the population has not been collected. The details of computing sampling error will appear at several points in this volume with a basic discussion appearing in Appendix C, Lesson Six.

THE CONTENT OF THIS BOOK

This book has been prepared not as a manual for the researcher but as a manual for the nonresearcher who must understand what a researcher is talking or writing about, and as a manual for the occasional researcher who, because of financial constraints, wishes to undertake a research study without the services of a commercial researcher. To the extent possible, each chapter has been written to be useful without extensive reference to other chapters. Where it may be helpful to the reader who, because of urgent need, begins by reading Chapter 8, for example, references are made in the text to other parts of the book which can provide additional information. Whenever possible, examples have been provided of study questionnaires and data reduction routines, including worked-out mathematical examples where appropriate. The necessary statistical tables and a short self-study course in statistical principles are included as appendices, as well as portions of ARBitron market reports for both radio and television.

The first major topic to be dealt with is that of audience measurement. A thorough discussion reviews the structure, uses and limitations of commercially available rating reports. Every broadcaster should be familiar with the content of these influential reports, and most have at least a passing acquaintance with them. They are influential primarily because national advertising and programming decision-makers use them when buying time and scheduling programs. In short, the ratings cannot be ignored, because some of the most important managers in the industry rely upon them.

At the same time, not every station receives just and equal treatment from the syndicated rating services. The rating services are, after all, commercial operations which must find it profitable to offer their services. For that reason rating surveys are offered more frequently in the largest markets, less frequently in the middle-sized markets and not at all in the smallest. This means that the broadcaster who would like to take advantage of the wealth of information the rating services can provide about station audiences, may not be able to do so because of too few or no rating surveys conducted regularly in the local market.

For such small market broadcasters a chapter on audience measurement is provided with full instructions on how to collect listening and viewing data to supplement the ratings, including a comparison of alternative methods for collecting data on local media habits.

The only form of research actually mandated by the Federal Communications Commission is the Ascertainment of Community Need. A chapter deals with the history of this requirement and the current policies of the FCC with regard to ascertainment. Instructions are provided for the broadcaster who wishes to get more than required from the ascertainment exercise.

The Commission requires the broadcaster to provide to the public in a Public File and as a presentation at license renewal a Problems/Programs List in which programs illustrative of the station's efforts to respond to ascertained problems are enumerated. Most stations will want to know not only that an attempt was made to deal with a problem but how well the problem was dealt with by the broadcast programs involved. For this purpose a chapter on evaluating programs designed to meet community needs has been included.

When a major change in station programming or public image is being considered, a station is well advised to learn about the image of the station currently in the public mind. This and related issues are best addressed with qualitative research, and a chapter deals with the variety and potential of qualitative research.

Message and program testing are those research measures taken to assure the acceptability and popularity of a program or advertising message with a specified audience. This research is undertaken before the materials are broadcast to learn how best to schedule the materials or ways in which they might be improved in post production.

Not every station in a market will be the leader in terms of ratings or other measures of audience popularity. The other stations in the market may be very good buys for some advertisers and may be very profitable to the licensees. If the station cannot sell on the basis of having the largest audiences, it may be able to sell some quality of its special audiences. Such desirable qualities may include the loyalty of the station audience, the presence of large numbers of influential people and opinion leaders in the audience, and so on. These other features of audiences are referred to in a general way as "psychographics." A chapter will explain psychographics and a number of ways to research them.

A chapter on revenue effectiveness examines research procedures which will help to evaluate purchases from syndication, the profitability of locally originated broadcasts, and the point of diminishing returns in spending additional money on program production.

To return to a theme sounded in the opening paragraphs of this chapter, the function of research in broadcasting is to reduce risks while increasing service to the audience and to the advertiser and profitability to the licensee. To that purpose, this book has been prepared.

NOTES—CHAPTER 1

1. The authoritative reference on sampling is William G. Cochran, *Sampling Techniques*, Third Edition (New York:Wiley, 1977).

2 Commercial Sources of Audience Information – the Rating Report

James E. Fletcher

The earliest interest of broadcasters in the dimensions of their audiences was linear. The broadcaster wanted to know how far the transmitted signal reached. In the early twenties, newspapers often included reports that this or that distant station had been received in a local community, and each station displayed with some pride letters and postcards from distant listeners. This same linear interest in audience survives today in the ham radio operator who collects postcards from other distant radio operators with whom contact has been established. In addition, the early interest in widely distributed audiences was reinforced by a desire among some early licensees to sell receivers. Radio receiver manufacturers like RCA, Westinghouse, General Electric, Zenith, and Crossley were among the most enterprising of early broadcasters and wanted to be sure that their signals were heard at great distances, and that audiences liked what they heard enough to buy additional receivers and to persuade their acquaintances of the virtues of the new device.

According to Dr. Sidney Head, the first national radio survey conducted on a systematic basis was underwritten by a baking powder sponsor in 1927. By the 1929–30 radio season a regular program-rating service with routine reports on the audiences of network programs had been instituted.[1] These particular ratings were the "Crossleys," named after innovative broadcaster/manufacturer Archibald Crossley. In 1930 these audience reports became the Cooperative Analysis of Broadcasting (CAB). The CAB conducted surveys intitally in the 33 communities then served by network radio, extracting samples of household listings from telephone directories and conducting *telephone recall* interviews.

In a telephone recall interview a respondent is asked to reconstruct listening or viewing behavior for some period of time prior to the call. The listening reports collected in these telephone interviews were used to compute ratings for each network program. The "Crossley" ratings of the CAB survived until 1946. The CAB was followed by the short-lived Broadcast Measurement Bureau (BMB) which attempted to accumulate circulation figures after the fashion of the Audit Bureau of Circulation which has provided circulation figures for newspapers since 1914.[2, 3] The BMB sent out questionnaires to samples from all counties of the nation to establish the proportion of the audience exposed to the signals of various stations. The BMB went out of business in 1950 due largely to competition from other audience reporting services which better understood the needs of advertisers.

A very influential audience reporting service established in 1934 was Clark-Hooper, Inc. which originally reported magazine and radio audiences. In 1938 C. E. Hooper, Inc. split off from this company and provided monthly ratings of network-sponsored, but not sustaining, programs.[4] The "Hooper" ratings were very influential in the forties and were based upon the *telephone coincidental* method. Samples of telephone households were interviewed by telephone and asked to provide information on the radio programs being heard in the household at the time of the interview. The familiar questions of a telephone coincidental interview include, "Are you listening to the radio? Can you tell me what program you are tuned to?" The Hooper service was important as a source of information on network programs until 1950 when the competition of the A. C. Nielsen Company in particular made selling out to Nielsen very attractive. Nielsen bought out the national rating service of the Hooper Company, leaving Hooper the right to produce reports for individual markets.

The A. C. Nielsen Company entered into the radio audience research business with considerable experience in other forms of marketing research. The first Nielsen Rating Index was issued in 1942 after a period of experimentation with its automatic "Audimeter" audience measuring device. The "Audimeter" in its earliest version was a "black box" which, when connected to a radio receiver, recorded on photographic film the time of day and radio dial position of the household radio receiver. Today the latest version of the Nielson Audimeter is only one of a number of continuous rating devices, although it is not only the oldest but the most respected of the clan. The sample of households used by Nielsen for its Audimeter studies is national in scope, with about 1500 homes hooked up at any moment. This arrangement provides data from about 1200 homes on the average, with 100 of these rotated monthly. The householder is paid a small amount to service the Audimeter, and the Nielsen Company shares in the maintenance cost of the householder's receiver during the time the Audimeter is in use. The very latest in the Audimeter line is the Instant Audimeter which records into a magnetic memory dial position and time of a television receiver. The Instant Audimeter is connected by phone line to a central computer and is dialed by the computer to send its quarter-hour record of viewing. The viewing report from the sample is assembled by the computer and transmitted over other telephone or teletype lines to the offices of Instant Audimeter clients. This service results in very early reports on program performance and is referred to within the broadcast business as the "Nielsen Overnights." In addition to these Audimeter reports, Nielsen today provides regular viewing, diary-based market reports for a large number of markets.

Another significant event of the 1930s was the founding in 1937 of the Office of Radio Research by means of a grant from the Rockefeller Foundation. It was originally located at Princeton University with Paul S. Lazarsfeld as director. His two assistants, Frank Stanton and Hadley Cantril, established independent reputations of their own.

One of the first major publications of the Office of Radio Research was *Social Stratification of the Radio Audience* (1939) by Dr. H. M. Beville, Jr. Dr. Beville was eventually to become the Executive Director of the Broadcast Rating Council (BRC) which is the industry watchdog over audience reporting services. The Office of Radio Research provided the basic detailed groundwork upon which modern audience measurement is based.[5]

In the 1944–45 season The Pulse, Inc. turned in national ratings for the first time. The Pulse had begun as a local market service in the New York City area and employed a data collection method known as the *aided-recall* or *roster* method. The respondent in this case was interviewed face-to-face. The interviewer called upon the respondent and sought to have the respondent reconstruct listening behavior of the previous week. This was done by jogging the memory of the respondent with a *roster* or listing of local programs, stations, or personalities. Pulse also employed *cluster* sampling to identify respondents.

This technique for sampling drew from a telephone directory a geographical location or *sampling point,* rather than a household to be interviewed, which was the start position of a standard pattern of households about the sampling point. The Pulse radio rating services were discontinued in 1978.

In the fifties another rating service entered the field of regular audience measurement. The American Research Bureau (ARB, Arbitron) was a subsidiary of the computer giant, Control Data Corporation. Because of its ready access to large computers, Arbitron chose to employ the diary method for data collection. Sample households were selected from telephone directories for every county of the nation. The selected householders were then recruited to keep a diary of the viewing or listening of an entire week. The television diary asks the householder to report the viewing of every member of the household thus permitting the viewing of a number of people and all day parts to be reported on the same instrument. The result is a large volume of data produced at relatively modest cost.

WHY THE RATINGS?

During the last two decades particularly, the rating services have been under nearly constant attack from some quarter or other. Many within the industry have commented on the shortcomings of the rating services in terms of sample size and of various kinds of error. Disappointed fans blame the cancelation of favorite programs on the ratings. Legislators have felt that the use of ratings as tools for decision-making amounted to conspiracy to frustrate popular taste.

But regardless of the volume or direction of public outcry, and regardless of the variety of shortcomings to which ratings are subject, there is little likelihood in the near future that the ratings will disappear or seriously diminish in influence. Among the more prominent reasons are these: (a) Ratings are the products of relatively small organizations, which (b) provide information otherwise unavailable, (c) at a low cost, (d) in response to stated needs of advertisers, but (e) under the close supervision of the industry.

Rating services are small organizations. In the case of the Nielsen audience measurement services, ratings comprise only a small part of the total research activity undertaken by the company. Arbitron is a subsidiary, only one of several subsidiaries, of a large firm essentially in another business. There are some smaller ratings firms which carry on audience measurement as a principal activity, but when the volume of information output by these organizations is considered, it is apparent that the capital outlay for such a business is relatively modest.

Ratings provide otherwise unavailable information. There may be better ways to collect information from a respondent than the ways used by the ratings services, but none has survived in the marketplace. The reason has been that other methods do not provide so much information at such a low cost.

Ratings are inexpensive. Rating reports are relatively inexpensive especially when contrasted with the cost of custom field surveys of the same scope. The ratings are inexpensive for two important reasons: one has been alluded to in the preceding paragraph—that the data collection methods used by the rating services are unusually efficient. A diary, for example, collects all of the viewing for a week; an aided recall interview collects a week of listening. A telephone coincidental interview, on the other hand, provides information from only one viewer or listener at one point of time, making the telephone coincidental at the other end of the cost spectrum, despite the fact that in other ways this method of data collection is probably superior. The second reason for the relatively low cost of the ratings is the large number of customers who consume these research products. The largest customers of the rating services are national advertisers and advertising agencies, with networks and major production houses also providing major revenues. Reports sold to local stations mean additional revenue to the ratings service. And to the local station, even though the cost of a rating report is considerably higher than another book of equivalent length, the cost is much lower than for any other research package for which the station could pay. This fact explains both the appeal of these market reports to stations and the relatively slow speed at which changes desired by broadcasters are introduced into rating service procedures.

Ratings respond to advertisers. The largest single source of revenue for audience research is the national advertiser and the advertising agency of this advertiser. The necessity of distributing relatively large advertising budgets where they will produce the greatest gains in market position for the product or service involved, has driven national advertising to depend heavily upon research. In addition, the information derived by advertisers from rating reports is very useful to the broadcast industry as a means of stimulating and maintaining advertising expenditures for broadcast time. As a consequence, both broadcasters and the advertisers themselves have a vested interest in seeing the rating services remain responsive to the needs of advertisers. Broadcasters find other uses for the information from rating reports—other than selling time. The ratings are widely used to evaluate programs for retention in the schedule or for rescheduling. Ratings are used as a yardstick of the value of programs purchased from syndication. They are used to suggest the direction of change in radio formats, in local television programs, and in promotional campaigns. The rating reports are not always ideally suited for use as aids to program decisions, but often the reports are the best or only information available.

THE BROADCAST RATING COUNCIL

In 1963 Congress held hearings into the influence and shortcomings of the rating services as they affect the conduct of business in broadcasting. Congress did find certain weaknesses and shortcomings in the audience measurement business. In response to this Congressional pressure, and as a way of shoring up public and industry confidence in the ratings, the Broadcast Ratings Council was organized in January 1964. The stated objectives of the BRC are:

> ...to secure for the broadcasting industry and related users audience measurement services that are valid, reliable, effective and viable, to evolve and determine minimum criteria and standards for broadcast audience measurement services; to establish and administer a system of accreditation for broadcast audience measurement services; to provide and administer an audit system designed to insure users that broadcast audience measurements are conducted in conformance with the criteria, standards and procedures developed.[6]

Under the leadership of the National Association of Broadcasters these organizations joined as members of the BRC with each represented on the Board of Directors:

American Broadcast Company
Columbia Broadcasting System
National Association of Broadcasters
National Broadcasting Company
Radio Advertising Bureau
Station Representatives Association
Television Bureau of Advertising[7]

Full cooperation with the BRC has come from the American Association of Advertising Agencies, the Association of National Advertisers, and the National Association of FM Broadcasters. The BRC fulfills its objectives in three ways: (a) By developing and publishing standards for acceptable audience research; (b) by accrediting audience reporting services; and (c) by auditing audience research organizations.

Nearly anyone regularly using syndicated audience reporting services would benefit from using this basic library recommended by the BRC:

BRC, "Minimum Standards for Broadcast Rating Research," pamphlet (New York, BRC, 1977).

BRC, "Procedures for Accreditation of Broadcast Audience Measurement Services by Broadcast Rating Council, Inc," pamphlet (New York, BRC, 1976).

BRC, "Inside a BRC Audit: A Close-up of the Auditing Procedures of the Broadcast Rating Council including an Illustrative CPA Report," pamphlet (New York, BRC, 1975).

BRC, "Standard Errors and Effective Sample Sizes as Reported for Broadcast Audience Measurement Surveys," (New York, BRC, 1970).

NAB, "Standard Definitions of Broadcast Research Terms," Second Edition, pamphlet (Washington, D.C., National Association of Broadcasters, 1970).

NAB, "Recommended Standards for the Preparation of Statistical Reports in Broadcast Audience Measurement Research," pamphlet (Washington, D.C., NAB, 1969).

Among the BRC standards for accredited rating services are nineteen disclosure standards which "specify the detailed information about a rating service which must be made available to users . . . as well as the form in which the information should be made available."[8] In other words, there are certain matters related to audience research reports which the BRC believes are important for users to know—so important that the accredited services are required to make the information available! Reviewing the most important of these requirements will suggest some of the matters about ratings which most readers of this book should know.

General Standard

Each rating report must include a concise description of the method used by the rating service to collect and present the information contained in the report.

Specifically each report will contain:

1. Statements calling attention to all omissions, errors and biases known to the rating service.

2. Any deviations from standard procedure for these reports.

3. The number of households originally selected for the sample and the number that provided useable data.

4. The base of in-tab and effective sample size used to compute the separate audience data of the report. The in-tab households are the number of households from which useable audience data was received. The effective sample size is the size of a theoretical sample which would have the same level of precision as that actually achieved in the sample reported. The notion of effective sample size is an important one and will be dealt with at greater length later in this chapter.

5. The clear definition of all geographic areas referred to within the report. In actual practice this means that the report will contain a map on which the survey areas are shown.

6. A comparison of the demographic composition of the sample with the demographic composition of the universe—the area from which the sample was drawn. This comparison will reflect any bias the report may contain in the viewing of any particular group.

7. A candid statement of both sampling and nonsampling errors to which the report is subject including the major nonsampling errors believed to affect the audience data reported.

8. The method for developing standard error estimates which can be used with the audience data reported, as well as an interpretation of this error when used in conjunction with information from the report.

9. All weighting or data adjustment procedures used when converting the raw data collected from the audience to the estimates appearing in the report. The most important of these will typically be the weights assigned to various demographic categories which were over- or under-represented in the sample.

10. The minimum number of reports of listening or viewing which the rating service requires in order for a station to be listed at all in the report.

11. Any efforts of which the rating service may be aware by which a station may have attempted to influence the results of a rating. Such efforts by a station are referred to as attempts to "hypo" the ratings.

12. Any unusual circumstances at the time of the data collection for the survey which may have influenced the audience levels reported in the report. Such circumstances might include unusual weather, natural disasters, transmission failures, preemption of regular programs, and so forth.

13. Whether or not the report is part of a regular syndicated series of reports or a special report prepared on the demand of a particular client.

14. The data for each report kept for a period of time adequate to permit full audit by the BRC or by firms engaged by report clients. In addition, the rating service is charged with the responsibility of facilitating the work of auditors in every way.

It should be apparent from the foregoing that the Broadcast Rating Council's minimum standards for accreditation make it easy for any user of rating reports to have access to complete information on the manner in which each report is prepared. In fact, this information is contained in the small type at the beginning or end of every report. No additional publications are necessary to understand the report or how it should be used. The discussion that follows is an attempt to provide the same information, generalizing from the procedures of several rating services and providing some additional explanation when those offered by the rating services do not appear clear enough. The research terms used will be defined according to standard definitions provided by the industry when these definitions exist. Space does not permit the definitive treatment of ratings here, but the most frequently encountered features of this kind of audience report will be included.

SAMPLE DESIGNS

In general, there are three kinds of samples involved in syndicated audience reporting services—national samples, local samples, and sweeps. A national sample is a sample used to generate ratings and other audience estimates for national programs.

For a national sample the *sampling frame* may be the national census. The sampling frame, by definition, is the list of population members from which the sample is drawn. So, for example, a collection of all telephone directories for the national survey might comprise a sampling frame of all listed telephone households. The *sampling unit*, by the way of contrast, is the specific thing drawn into the sample. To continue the example of the national sampling frame of listed telephone directories, the sampling unit for a sample drawn from this frame might be the listed telephone household.

As it happens, national samples used in national ratings such as the Nielsen Audimeter surveys are typically based on Bureau of the Census tracts. The Bureau of the Census, as nearly every public school student knows, conducts a census of the American population every 10 years. This census is updated by samples from the geographic control areas used in the census—the census tracts—during the period between the censuses of the entire population. A census tract is a well-identified geographic area which is charted and numbered by the Bureau of the Census. The first stage of a multi-stage sampling procedure for a national sample might be to draw at random some number of census tracts from which individual households will then be sampled: stage one results in a sample of census tracts; stage two results in a sample of households from those selected census tracts. This is in fact the procedure typically used by the syndicated rating services. The size of these national samples is relatively small, usually fewer than 2000 households representing the viewing of the entire nation. But if the sampling procedure is random, the resulting sample is relatively accurate and precise.

To make sampling random, procedures usually call for the use of random numbers which are either in the memory of a computer or in a table like the one at Appendix D, Table VI. In a list of random numbers the order of numbers is completely unpredictable, yet each number appears with equal frequency if the table is long enough. Since each Census Tract is numbered, numbers corresponding to census tracts to be included in the national sample will be drawn from the list of random numbers. To do this with Table VI pick any point to start. Note the number at this point. Now move in the table in any direction, up, down, right, left. Note the next number found there. Continue moving in the same direction, noting each number encountered. The result is a set of numbers appearing in a random order. When it is desired to draw a random sample of any numbered sampling frame, this procedure produces a set of numbers in random order; matching these numbers to units within the sampling frame produces a random sample.

Within the census tract description of Bureau of the Census data will be a description of the households in each tract. This identification of households can be used as the sampling frame for the second stage of the sample, permitting households to be selected on a random basis within each tract.

Local Samples

Samples from local broadcast markets and upon which local market reports are based are nearly all drawn from telephone directories. These directories are compiled on computer tape by special firms like Metromail Advertising Company. These directories are generally divided by county, so that the rating firm may select the counties which are to be included in the survey of a particular market, then acquire the directories for those counties from the specialized firm. Random samples of these telephone households provide the basic sample selection for the survey.

It might be helpful to review some of the shortcomings and virtues of telephone directory samples, since the matter is perennially one of controversy. The shortcomings of telephone directories are that (a) not every family has a telephone; (b) telephone listings in directories become progressively more out-of-date each month that the directory has been issued (on the average, about 2 percent of the listings become obsolete each month that the directory has been issued); and (c) there are many nonlisted telephone households. This problem of no-telephone households and unlisted telephones was studied by Leuthold and Scheele.[9] Their study dealt with samples from the state of Missouri. They showed the inequitable distribution of no phone and unlisted phones across a variety of community groups. The table on the following page summarizes some of their findings. The figures are for the state of Missouri. The number of no telephone households and unlisted households varies widely from state to state, but the numbers are significant in many cases.

There are at least two methods of overcoming the problems of out-of-date listings and unlisted telephone households. One is a technique called random telephone number generation.[10] In this technique the sampling frame is a theoretic list of all possible telephone numbers in the community, and the sampling unit is a possible telephone number. The prefixes of telephone numbers listed in the community are noted. Then using a Table of Random Numbers or a computer, a set of possible telephone suffixes is generated and matched with the prefixes of telephone numbers for the community. Since every possible telephone number is thus included in the sampling frame, unlisted telephones are in-

SELECTED CHARACTERISTICS	NO PHONE	UNLISTED	TOTAL
Marital Status of Respondent			
Separated	28 %	26 %	54 %
Divorced	12	21	33
Age			
18–29	21	10	31
30–39	10	16	26
Occupation of Head of Household			
Skilled	9	10	19
Semiskilled	17	13	30
Service Workers	12	22	34
Organizational Membership			
Labor Unions	9	15	24
Church Groups	3	5	8
Belongs to no organization	15	10	25
Religion			
Protestant	12	8	20
Catholic	3	14	17

cluded in the sample in roughly the same proportion in which they occur within the community. Disconnected, unconnected, and nonresidential numbers are also included in the sample.

Another technique for compensating the shortcomings of telephone directories is the telephone add-on technique. A number of telephone numbers are drawn from a telephone directory for the sample, and a number added to each, generating a set of telephone numbers which may or may not be in the directory listings. This set of add-on numbers will include unlisted households and households recently connected.

It is also possible to use telephone directories as the frame for a geographic sample. In this case, the listings from the telephone directories are drawn for the addresses they provide rather than for the telephone numbers involved. Each telephone household address drawn into the sample becomes the start point of a cluster of homes that will be interviewed by a face-to-face interviewer.

The areas to be included in a survey of a local market will be made up of counties which may fall into one of three overlapping areas: (a) A metropolitan or Metro area; (b) a set of counties which consist of householders who listen to, or view predominantly, stations from the market being surveyed (predominant counties); and (c) counties in which a significant amount of listening or viewing is to or of home market stations.

Metro Survey Area. The official definition of "Metro Area" is "a Standard Metropolitan Statistical Area, as defined by the U.S. Bureau of the Budget."[11] These areas are defined by the government to guide data reporting regarding the cities by all agencies of government. The same areas are generally used in marketing and advertising research to identify markets. The Metro Area will normally be the smallest of the overlapping survey areas included within the sample design of a local market report. In the Arbitron Radio report for Akron digested in Appendix A, Summit and Portage counties are included within the Metro Area. In the Arbitron Television report of Portland, Oregon, extracted at Appendix B, the Metro Area includes the counties of Clackamas, Multnomah, Washington, and Clark.

Predominant Area. Each county in the United States is assigned to the survey area of some market on the basis of predominant viewing. At some point each year the rating service will review the viewing done in each county to determine to which market the predominance of viewing is dedicated. On that basis the county is assigned to one market only as a predominant county for the following year of rating surveys. In the case of Arbitron, reports like that at Appendix B, the predominant area, is referred to as the Area of Dominant Influence (ADI). It becomes a matter of some importance to a local station which counties are or are not assigned to the home market ADI, since market rank is decided based upon the demographics of the combined ADI counties assigned to a home market. If one or more counties are shifted from one market to another, then the rank of the markets involved changes, giving a higher market rank to the market receiving ADI counties and a lower market rank to the market losing ADI counties. It has happened that the competing stations in a market have collectively mounted advertising campaigns to lure away from another market counties which, when added to the market of the cooperating stations, would give the market a higher rank and, as a consequence, a greater share of national advertising dollars.

In general, the predominant area will include the Metro Area for the same market. But this is not always the case. For example, there are a number of markets which have Metro Areas, but no predominant area at all. This might occur when the predominance of viewing is to out-of-market stations. If there were only one network-affiliated station in a market, the audience would have to tune to an out-of-market station to receive each of the other networks. As a consequence, there may be a predominance of viewing to out-of-market stations. In the 1978 Arbitron ADIs this situation occurred in the Modesto, California, market where the predominance of viewing was to stations in the Sacramento-Stockton market.

Significant Area. This is a survey area which typically includes both the predominant area and Metro Area of the survey. The significant area consists of counties where a significant amount of viewing, although not a predominance, is to the market being surveyed. In the case of Arbitron market reports, these significant counties are referred to as the Total Survey Area (TSA). Arbitron defines this area as "a geographic area comprising those counties in which an estimated 98 percent of the net weekly circulation [viewing] of commercial home market stations occurs."[12] This area is the largest of the three possible overlapping geographic areas included in the survey.

Sample Size. Recall that a Metro county will also be a county of the predominant and significant areas of the survey. Hence the households of this county will be a component of the sample size for each of these three areas. As a consequence, the sample size is usually greatest in these counties and declines in the per county sample size through the predominant counties to the significant counties. In addition, the number of households per county will correspond roughly to the share of that county in the overall population of the area. Counties larger in population are typically providing more households to the sample. This is not always the case, of course, and the prudent user of audience reports carefully examines the in-tab households of each county in interpreting the results of a survey. In Appendix B the county-by-county in-tab sample is listed on page 3. On that page note that the Metro Washington County with a population of nearly 57,000 contributes 83 in-tab households, while the ADI Marion County contributes only 47 diaries despite its more than 59,000 television households.

Sweep Samples

A ratings sweep is an aggregate of local market surveys in which the entire country is surveyed within the same time period. In the United States the November and February-March rating periods are the prinicipal sweep periods. The sample design for each local market as a component of the sweep is the same as if that market were being surveyed in isolation. The sweep report will be available to clients in both an aggregated form and as separate market reports.

DATA COLLECTION—DIARY METHOD

After the sample has been designed, the computer will be used to draw a random sample of the specified counties according to the number of households required in each county. These households are then recruited into the survey. The first step in recruitment is usually to send a letter by first-class mail to the selected households. The letter informs the householder that the household has been scientifically selected into research that will influence what is seen (in the case of television) or heard (in the case of radio) in the local area. In addition, the householder is told to expect a telephone call from the audience research firm. The purpose of the first-class postage is to refine the sample. First-class mail will be returned to the sender if undeliverable. A returned letter tells the research firm that the telephone listing for a particular household was in error and that the household involved should be removed from the sample as not worth the additional expense to recruit into the data collection phase of the survey.

Several days after the letter is delivered the householder receives a telephone call from a worker at the research firm. The telephone worker reviews the purpose of the survey and the fact that diaries will be coming to the household. In the case of a television survey one diary will be delivered to the household. In the case of radio surveys one diary is sent for every potential listener in the household. The telephone worker will also at this time collect some basic information about the household such as number of receivers in the household and demographic composition.

A few days before the diary is to be kept it will arrive in the mail. Typically the rating period is for one week beginning on Wednesday. Just before the family is to begin keeping the diary or diaries (in the case of radio), another call from the telephone worker will remind the family of the obligation to keep the diary and offers to answer any questions the householder may have about the instructions. Several days before the rating period

Thursday					
Time		Station		Place	
Indicate AM or PM		When Listening to FM, Check here (√)	Fill in Station Call Letters, Program, or Personality	Check one (√)	
From	To			At Home	Out of Home
Please check here ☐ if you did not listen to a radio today.					

Figure 2–1. Illustrative Page from a Radio Diary (after Arbitron).

ends a final telephone call reminds the householder to put the diary or diaries in the mail when completed. For the trouble involved the householder receives a small gift or token payment. Examples of radio and television diaries are included at Figures 2-1 and 2-2.

The great appeal of the diary data collection method is that so much viewing or listening information may be collected in a single data collection instrument, thus reducing to a minimum the cost of collecting information about the audience.

There is a price to be paid, of course, in terms of response error, the introduction by a respondent of substantial error. In the case of a television diary one person in the household typically reports the viewing of others, and evidence indicates that a housewife, for example, has a different rate of accuracy when reporting her own viewing and that of her children or husband. In an exploratory study at the University of Kentucky housewives were accurate in reporting the viewing of their husbands as little as 16 percent of the time.[13]

In addition, it is common for a householder to wait until the end of the viewing period to fill out the viewing reports for the entire week, reducing the accuracy of that diary as contrasted with a diary filled out as the viewing reported was going on.

No matter what the shortcomings of the diary method may be, cost effective alternatives, which will produce a richness of data comparable to that of the diary, are simply not available today.

One additional note about data collection in a diary study—the data is not collected in a single week. In a large market the survey may cover four or more weeks. In smaller markets, two or more weeks.

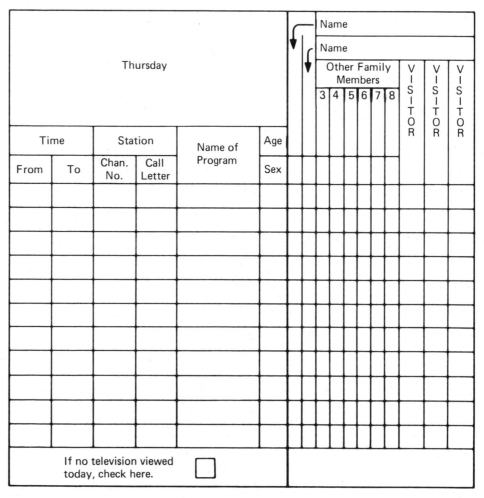

Figure 2-2.   Illustrative Page from a Television Diary (after Arbitron.)

DATA COLLECTION—AIDED RECALL

The aided recall method of data collection has been used in conjunction with a cluster sampling procedure. The sample drawn from a telephone listing frame will be a set of addresses or sampling points which anchor each cluster. The interviewer, who is typically a part-time worker of low status (with deference to the Women's Movement, that often means housewife), then goes to a sampling point drawn from the sampling frame. Then standard instructions—at least standard within any one study—direct the interviewer to respondents in the cluster. For example, the interviewer may be told to face the side of the street opposite to that of the sampling point and select the first single residence to the right. The interviewer is then to solicit interviews from each adult in the household. From there the interviewer is to move across the street and pick one or more houses to the left where all adults and teenagers are to be interviewed, and so on. Again the pattern of the cluster will be the same at each sampling point in the survey. Special instructions will be included to deal with multiple dwellings encountered by the interviewer and with problems such as respondents who do not speak English.

The aided recall interview often requires the respondent to reconstruct the listening of the previous week. This is done by beginning with the day of the interview and working back to a week previous in reverse chronological order. The roster used in these interviews is a list of station call letters, personalities, and features. The respondent is shown the list as a means of jogging memory while reconstructing the week of listening. The information gleaned from the aided recall interview is like that produced by diary-method data collection: the respondents are identified by demographic grouping, and the times during which they listened, and the stations to which they listened, are shown.

It is common that a single interviewer will be able to interview two or three clusters in a single evening, speaking to ten to twenty respondents in the process. At this rate two or three interviewers can conduct a local market audience report survey in as little as two weeks.

DATA REDUCTION AND PRESENTATION

When the raw audience data returns to the offices of the audience research firm it is first checked for completeness. A certain number of diaries or interview schedules are validated as a check on the interviewers or telephone workers. The respondents for these diaries or interviews are telephoned by supervisory personnel to assure that the data was collected substantially as represented. Then the data is fed to computers for preparation of the report seen by users who may subscribe to the rating service in either hardcopy or computer tape forms. The computer tape reports of ratings are for clients who have their own computers and use them to analyze the data contained in a rating report. This practice is nearly universal in large advertising agencies and is becoming more common in the larger broadcast groups.

One of the first analyses performed by the computer in preparing a viewing or listening report is to analyze the sample of respondents whose viewing or listening data provide the information reported. This analysis proceeds from the information about the potential and in-tab samples which appears in the opening pages of the typical audience report.

Demographic Weighting

Due to the differing availability of various demographic groups to the interviewers and telephone workers, it is the rare case that each demographic group will be represented in the sample in exactly the same proportion as in the population from which the sample is drawn. A particular group may be either over-represented in the sample or under-represented. Consider the displays labeled, "Population Estimates and Sample Distribution by Sex-Age Group," on page 3 of Appendix A, the extracted radio report for Akron, Ohio.

In the display for "Total Survey Area" the demographic category, men 18–24, represents, according to the table, 7.9 percent of the estimated population of persons over 12. Yet the same group accounts for only 6.1 percent of the unweighted in-tab sample. The group is under-represented in the survey. This group provided 60 (.061 × 982) in-tab diaries for the Total Survey Area rather than the 76 which would have represented a fair share for this group. As a result the data from this demographic group will be weighted, multiplied by a factor which will bring this under-represented group up to its proportionate share of the population. The basic formula for a demographic weight is this:

$$\text{weight}_{(\text{sex-group})} = \frac{\text{group share of population}}{\text{group share of sample}}$$

In the case of men 18–24 in the Akron study:

$$\text{weight}_{(\text{TSA men 18-24})} = \frac{.079}{.061}$$

$$= 1.295 \ .$$

How should this weight for men 18–24 be interpreted? If the group had been represented equitably in the in-tab sample each sample respondent would have represented 1196 members of the population (90,900 ÷ 76 diaries). Since the in-tab diaries for this group were only 60, then each in-tab diary from this group will have to represent more than 1196 members of the population, will in fact be weighted to represent 1549 members of the population (1196 × weight 1.295 = 1549).

Other groups in the survey will be over-represented. In the Akron study women 25–34 appear to be over-represented in the Metro Area. The demographic weight for this group is:

$$\text{weight}_{(\text{Metro women 25-34})} = \frac{.093 \text{ (share of population)}}{.106 \text{ (share of sample)}}$$

$$= .877.$$

If represented equitably in the in-tab sample, women 25–34 would have been represented in the Metro Area by 59 diaries, each of which would have stood for 4697 members of the population. In fact, since 67 diaries (631 × .106) were in-tab from this group, each diary represented only 4119 members of the population (4697 × weight .877).

The audience information from all diaries will be weighted by a demographic weight like those above before the information becomes the basis of audience estimates in the report.

Data Displays

The audience data is reported for each of the survey samples—Metro Area, predominant counties, and significant counties. In addition, various day-parts are reported. A day-part is a specified period or time of day for which audience information is reported. Several hours and days may be aggregated in reporting a particular day-part, or data may be reported on an hour-by-hour basis. In the case of television reports data will be reported for each program, and both local and network originated programs will be reported.

Rating. Figures which are shown in an audience report as ratings or RTG are "the size of a television or radio audience expressed in relative or percentage terms. A rating represents a percentage of some base. This base must always be stated explicitly."[14] The formulas for rating include:

Average Quarter-Hour Metro Rating for TV households=average number of TV households in Metro area which are tuned to the station reported during this day-part ÷ TV households in the Metro Area × 100.

Program Rating in Total Survey Area for Women 18-24 = average number of women 18-24 in the Total Survey Area who are tuned to the program in question ÷ total women 18-24 in Total Survey Area who live in TV households.

ADI Rating for Total Persons 12+ Monday–Friday 6 A.M.–Midnight = average number of persons 12+ in the ADI tuned to the station specified during the day-part specified ÷ total persons 12+ who live in ADI TV households.

Share. "Generally, the percentage of the aggregate television or radio audience in some specified area at some specified time that is in the audience of a given network, station, or program. A share may be computed on a household basis or on an individual basis. The base for a share on a household basis is normally households using television or radio in a specified geographic area, over a specified time. Thus, a share on a household basis shows the percentage of those households using television or radio that are estimated to be in the audience of a given network, station or program, over a specified time. The base of a share on an individual basis is normally individuals using television or radio in a specified geographic area, over a specified time. Thus, a share on a household basis shows the percentage of those households using television or radio that are estimated to be in the audience of a given network, station or program, over a specified time. The base of a share on an individual basis is normally individuals using television or radio in a specified geographic area, over a specified time .... Thus, a share on an individual basis shows the percentage of these individuals using television or radio that are estimated to be in the audience of a given network, station, or program, over a specified time."[15]

CUME. "Short for 'cumulative audience.' ... A term that refers to the net size of a television or radio audience during two or more time periods. That is, a household or an individual will be counted as part of a cumulative audience only once even though the household or the individual appears in audiences during two or more time periods. Also called 'net audience' or 'unduplicated audience.'"[16] CUME may be clearer with an illustration. Imagine a radio station which has an average of three listeners during the average quarter-hour between 9 A.M. and 10 A.M. on Monday and on Tuesday. But the three individuals on Tuesday are different people from those who listen on Monday. The average quarter-hour figure for 9 A.M.–10 A.M., Monday-Tuesday will show three listeners, while the CUME will be six, the number of unduplicated or different individuals listening in the time period. As a practical matter, in the syndicated reports of today the period of time for which CUME is computed is one week. In sum, the CUME is the number of different individuals during the time period who over one week are estimated to have tuned in the given network, program, or station.

Audience Estimates. These are the estimated number of persons in a given survey area who are members of a specified sex-age group and who are estimated to be in the audience of a specified network, station, or program during a specified time period. It is the convention that in radio reports the estimates will be in terms of hundreds of listeners, while in television reports the estimates are in terms of thousands of viewers. The user of the report is expected to add two zeros (00) to estimates read from a radio report, three zeros (000) to the number read from a television report. Audience estimates are often referred to as projections.

Exclusives. A term used in radio reports, exclusives are members of the audience who listen to one station and one station only.

Out of Home Listening. A term used in radio reports refers to listening at work and in automobiles—not at home.

HUT (Homes using television). A HUT rating is a rating in which the base for computation is the number of homes in the survey area at the time with receivers turned on. A HUT rating is a share. Television reports typically list the total number of TV households using television during each time period.

Trends. Displays of trends compare the audience information from the latest survey period with previous surveys of the same market.

STANDARD ERRORS AND EFFECTIVE SAMPLE SIZES

Lesson Six of the self-study course at Appendix C reports on the sampling distributions involved in rating surveys. The sampling distribution in this case represents the probability distribution of all possible values of a rating from a very large number of samples of the same size. The standard deviation of this sampling distribution is indicated in notation as σ_p where p = rating $\div$ 100. This value, σ_p, is referred to by the BRC as "standard error." It is an index of variation in audience ratings due to sampling. One use of the formula for σ_p is to estimate the confidence interval associated with a rating from a local market report. If one is interested in the 95 percent likely deviation (confidence interval) in a rating due to sampling error, the formula for that deviation is:

$$\frac{p_o - p_t}{100} = \pm 1.96 \sqrt{\frac{p_o(1.0 - p_o)}{N}}$$

where

p_o = rating reported $\div$ 100
p_t = the same rating with no sampling error $\div$ 100
N = the number of respondents in the sample.

To illustrate the application of this formula imagine a survey of 100 households in which it is determined that 20 percent of the households are viewing King Comics, a program broadcast at 9 A.M.–10 A.M. Saturday. The 95 percent confidence interval associated with this rating will be computed:

$$\frac{p_o - p_t}{100} = \pm 1.96 \sqrt{\frac{.2(1.0 - .2)}{100}}$$

$$= \pm 1.96 \sqrt{\frac{.16}{100}}$$

$$= \pm 1.96 \sqrt{.0016}$$

$$= \pm 1.96 (.04)$$

$$= \pm .0784$$

The confidence interval is thus plus or minus 7.84 rating points. It is interpreted in this way: "If a very large number of replications of this survey were made, all with sample size equal to 100 respondents, then 95 out of 100 cases would produce ratings for King Comics within the range, 20 plus or minus 7.84, or between ratings of 12.16 and 27.84."

Confidence intervals may also be computed about audience estimates or projections.

The formula involved may be stated:

$$E_o - E_t = \pm 1.96 \sqrt{\frac{E_o(A - E_o)}{N}}$$

where

E_o = the audience estimate or projection from the audience survey involved

E_t = the same audience estimate or projection if free from sampling error

A = the size of the population from which the sample is drawn

N = the number of respondents in the sample.[17]

Consider this example: An audience survey collects data from 1000 households in a local market which has a population of 10,000 households. Thirty percent of the households reported viewing the 6–7 P.M. news program of Channel 4; hence it is estimated that 3000 households are in the audience of that program. What is the 95 percent likely confidence interval associated with this audience estimate?

$$\begin{aligned}
E_o - E_t &= \pm 1.96 \sqrt{\frac{3{,}000(10{,}000 - 3{,}000)}{1{,}000}} \\
&= \pm 1.96 \sqrt{\frac{21{,}000{,}000}{1{,}000}} \\
&= \pm 1.96 \sqrt{21{,}000} \\
&= \pm 1.96 (144.914) \\
&= \pm 284.031.
\end{aligned}$$

This confidence interval would be interpreted this way: "If a very large number of replications of this audience study were undertaken, each with sample size equal to 1000 and population size stable at 10,000 then in 95 percent of the replications we would expect this audience estimate for the audience of the 6 P.M. Channel 4 News to be 3000 plus or minus 284 or within the range, 2716 and 3284."

At times it may be useful to determine the confidence interval appropriate to the difference between ratings taken in separate surveys. A simple formula for doing this is that below:

$$(p_o - p_{o'}) - (p_t - p_{t'}) = \pm 1.96 \sqrt{\sigma_{po}^2 + \sigma_{po'}^2}$$

where

p_o = rating from the first study $\div$ 100

$p_{o'}$ = rating from the second study $\div$ 100

p_t = theoretic error-free rating from the first study $\div$ 100

$p_{t'}$ = theoretic error-free rating from the second study $\div$ 100

σ_{po} = standard deviation of the sampling distribution of the first rating

$\sigma_{po'}$ = standard deviation of the sampling distribution of the second rating.[18]

Consider this example: During a custom audience survey a year ago, a random sample of 500 television households showed that 30 percent were daily viewing "Aftermag," an afternoon news magazine program. A year later a second custom survey interviewed a random sample of 1000 households and indicated that 28 percent of the sample daily viewed "Aftermag." This shows a 2 percent decline in the rating of this program in a year. When sampling error is considered, what is the difference in ratings after a year? The first step in determining the answer will be to compute σ_{p_o} and $\sigma_{p_o'}$.

$$\sigma_{po} = \sqrt{\frac{.30(.70)}{500}}$$
$$= \sqrt{.21 \div 500}$$
$$= \sqrt{.00042}$$
$$= .020.$$

$$\sigma_{po'} = \sqrt{\frac{.28(.72)}{1000}}$$
$$= \sqrt{\frac{.2016}{1000}}$$
$$= \sqrt{.0002016}$$
$$= .014 .$$

These values are then introduced into the formula for confidence interval for a difference in ratings from independent studies:

$$(p_o - p_{o'}) - (p_t - p_{t'}) = \pm 1.96 \sqrt{(.020)^2 + (.014)^2}$$
$$= \pm 1.96 \sqrt{.0004 + .000196}$$
$$= \pm 1.96 \sqrt{.000596}$$
$$= \pm 1.96 (.0244)$$
$$= \pm .0478.$$

This confidence interval is interpreted in this way: "If each of these two audience surveys were replicated a large number of times, each time with the size sample used initially, then in 95 percent of all comparisons of the results of these studies, the difference between the ratings given the program 'Aftermag' in the two studies would be two plus or minus 4.78 or within the range, – 2.78 to + 6.78." Or, in other words, the confidence interval computed above indicates that the difference in ratings between the two studies is one that could have been due to sampling error.

Effective Sample Size

The formulas above are for computing standard deviation of the sampling distribution and confidence intervals when a simple random sample forms the basis of an audience rating. In the real world of audience research, at least as contained in syndicated audience reports, ratings, shares, and audience estimates are rarely based on simple random samples. An average quarter-hour rating is averaged across the quarter hours which comprise the day-part being reported, and across the weeks of the survey data collection period and perhaps across several demographic groups. Each week of the survey and each demographic group may be represented by a different base of in-tab sample. Each base will have associated with it a unique level of sampling error. In addition, in the case of sex-age groups, demographic weights may have been applied to audience projections. To compute a precise estimate of sampling error in the case of these averages ratings, shares, and projections is virtually impossible, and even to compute an approximation which considers all of these sources of sampling error is difficult enough to be beyond the skills of the average user of rating reports. The research firms which prepare syndicated reports usually assist the user by preparing estimates of effective sample sizes.

An *effective sample size* is "a hypothetical number which is useful as a computational device. It may be defined as the size of a simple random sample which would give the same standard error of an audience measurement as did the actual sampling plan upon which the result is based."[19]

To arrive at effective sample size the research firm computes sampling error by a complicated formula which considers all of the sources of sampling error inherent in averaged reports. Then the formula for standard deviation of the sampling distribution of proportion is solved for sample size of a simple random sample which would produce the same size sampling error. To illustrate let us suppose that for a rating of 50, $p = .50$, the company computes the standard deviation of the sampling distribution of p to be $\pm .015$, the formula for σ_p is then solved for N:

$$\sigma_p = \sqrt{\frac{p(1.0 - p)}{N}}$$

$$.015 = \sqrt{\frac{.5(.5)}{N}}$$

$$\text{squaring } .000225 = \frac{.25}{N}$$

$$\text{multiplying } .000225 \, N = .25$$

$$\text{dividing } N = .25 \div .000225 \text{ or } 1111.111$$

The effective sample size in this case is 1111.

In the case of Arbitron reports like those at Appendix A and B, effective sample size is labeled, "Effective Sample Base," and is provided in order that users may use the standard sampling error formulas substituting ESB for N. To illustrate, consider the extracted Akron radio report at Appendix A. On page 3 the Effective Sample Base for the Metro Area of the survey is given as 615, while that of the Total Survey Area is 782. On page 55 of the same report the Metro CUME rating for Total Persons 12+ for Station WAEZ is given as 9.2. What is the 95 percent confidence interval associated with that rating?

$$p_o - p_t = \pm 1.96 \sqrt{\frac{p_o(1.0 - p_o)}{ESB}}$$

$$= \pm 1.96 \sqrt{\frac{.092(.908)}{615}}$$

$$= \pm 1.96 \sqrt{\frac{.08354}{615}}$$

$$= \pm 1.96 \sqrt{.0001358}$$

$$= \pm 1.96 \, (.011654)$$

$$= \pm .0228.$$

The 95 percent confidence interval associated with the WAEZ Metro CUME rating of 9.2 is plus or minus 2.28, indicating the true value of this rating likely falls within the range, 6.92 and 11.48.

Another example: Consider the average quarter-hour listening estimates on page 54 of Appendix A, Total Survey Area, total person 12+ for Monday–Friday, 6:00 A.M.

until Midnight for station WAKR—11,500 persons. What is the 95 percent probable confidence interval associated with this rating?

$$E_o - E_t = \pm 1.96 \sqrt{\frac{E_o(A - E_o)}{ESB}}$$

$$= \pm 1.96 \sqrt{\frac{11,500\,(1,156,000 - 11,500)}{782}}$$

$$= \pm 1.96 \sqrt{\frac{11,500\,(1,144,500)}{782}}$$

$$= \pm 1.96 \sqrt{\frac{13,161,750,000}{782}}$$

$$= \pm 1.96 \sqrt{16,830,882.35}$$

$$= \pm 1.96\,(4,102.54583)$$

$$= \pm 8040.98984 \text{ or } \pm 8041.$$

The 95 percent probable range of values represented by an audience estimate of 11,500 for the Total Survey Area is 3459 to 19,541.

The foregoing has provided a description of the procedures and bases for the syndicated audience research reports generally available to the advertising and broadcast industries. The following chapter presents the local market report as it is used by broadcast programmers and managers.

NOTES—CHAPTER 2

1. Sydney W. Head, *Broadcasting in America: A Survey of Radio and Television,* Second Edition (Boston: Houghton Mifflin, 1972), p. 292.
2. Harrison B. Summers, "Qualitative Information Concerning Audiences of Network Television Programs," *Journal of Broadcasting,* 5 (1961), 147–160.
3. Sydney W. Head, *Broadcasting in America,* Third Edition (Boston: Houghton Mifflin, 1976), p. 226.
4. Christopher H. Sterling and John M. Kittross, *Stay Tuned: A Concise History of American Broadcasting* (Belmont, California: Wadsworth, 1978), p. 186.
5. Sterling and Kittross, p. 187.
6. Broadcast Rating Council, "Maintaining Rating Confidence and Credibility," pamphlet (New York: BRC, 1975), p. 2.
7. *Ibid.,* p. 5.
8. Broadcast Rating Council, "Minimum Standards for Broadcast Rating Research," p. 2. BRC publications may be ordered from the Broadcast Rating Council, Inc., 420 Lexington Avenue, New York, New York 10017.
9. David Leuthold and Raymond Scheele, "Patterns of Bias in Samples Based on Telephone Directories," *Public Opinion Quarterly,* 35 (1971), 249–257.
10. James E. Fletcher and Harry B. Thompson, "Telephone Directory Samples and Random Telephone Directory Samples and Random Telephone Number Generation," *Journal of Broadcasting,* 18 (1974), 187–191.
11. National Association of Broadcasters, "Standard Definitions of Broadcast Research Terms," Second Edition (Washington, D.C.: NAB, 1970), p. 31.
12. Arbitron Television, "Description of Methodology," pamphlet (New York: American Research Bureau, February 1979), p. 15.

13. James E. Fletcher and Charles Chao-Ping Chen, "Validation of Viewing Reports: Exploration of a Photographic Method," ERIC Document Nr. 50102, 1975.
14. "Standard Definitions," p. 25.
15. *Ibid.*, p. 26.
16. *Ibid.*, p. 20.
17. Broadcast Rating Council, "Standard Errors and Effective Sample Sizes as Reported for Broadcast Audience Measurement Surveys," pamphlet (New York, BRC, 1970), p. 19.
18. *Ibid.*, pp. 20–21.
19. *Ibid.*, p. 21.

3 Reading the Market Report

James E. Fletcher

At Appendix A and B are extracts of a radio report and a television report prepared by Arbitron. It is not the intent of this chapter to promote Arbitron over competing audience reporting services, but the Arbitron reports provide a convenient illustration of features common to reports accredited by the Broadcast Rating Council. In addition, the Arbitron reports, when both radio and television audience reporting services are considered, are available for a greater number of markets than any other accredited service. The lessons learned in studying these extracted reports should prove valuable in working with nearly all other audience reports.

RADIO REPORTS

Some distinctions between radio and television audience reports have already been noted. When data is collected by the diary method, there will be only one diary per household for reporting television viewing, but in a radio sample there will be one diary per listener. It is the convention to report television audience estimates as thousands (000), and radio audience estimates as hundreds (00). And the audiences of radio and television differ in the patterns in which they consume the medium. Many more radio listeners will tune in one station exclusively; in television viewing nearly everyone is a channel switcher. This fact is reflected in radio market reports by separate displays for "Exclusives." There is relatively little television viewing in cars: there is a great deal of radio listening in cars. Office and factory workers may do little television viewing on the job, but many listen to radio constantly. Radio audience reports respond by presenting data on "Out-of-Home listening. Other differences between radio and television audience reports will be apparent as the chapter continues.

Survey Area and Sample Design

The first step in studying any audience report is to review the area surveyed and the sample drawn from that area.

Page 2 of the Arbitron report for Akron (Appendix A) shows the map of the survey areas. The counties in horizontal hatching (Summit and Portage) comprise the Metro Survey Area. These plus the counties in white comprise the Total Survey Area. These areas may not be the same from year to year, and they may not be exactly the same from one audience reporting service to another. As a consequence, wise users study the map in each market report consulted.

In recent radio reports Arbitron is also including ADIs (Areas of Dominant Influence)—predominant counties—even though the ADIs are designated strictly on the basis of television viewing. The new user of radio reports may find this surprising, but reporting radio listening for the television ADIs offers benefits to advertisers and others who buy or sell radio time. Since radio listening in the new Arbitron radio reports is presented for the same areas as television viewing, it is possible to compare the relative efficiency of television and radio in reaching the same audiences. In short, this practice of reporting radio listening for television ADIs helps radio compete with television.

On page 2 of the Akron radio report (Appendix A) is the diary placement by county. Users of radio reports are urged to study diary placement carefully. In this report it is apparent that diaries from 982 persons, 12 years and older, were included in the raw data from which the report was prepared. Of these, 631 (124 + 507) were received from the Metro Survey Area. The table shows that several counties were lumped together in sampling (Coschocton + Holmes + Wayne; Carroll + Tuscarawas). Whether or not this distribution of in-tab diaries is equitable is a judgment that must be made by the user. If the user worked at station WCUE (1000 watts day, 500 watts night in Cuyahoga Falls), there might be some disappointment that listening for Summit County (where Cuyahoga Falls is located just North of Akron) is not presented separately. The WCUE audience will not be distributed over so wide an area as the more powerful stations in the market, and its highly localized audience (at least in terms of Total Survey Area) will be diluted in the report by diaries from many listeners who do not receive the station well. Interpreting this report must involve allowances for this inequity to WCUE.

Additional and important information on sample design for the Akron report is reflected on the next page of Appendix A. The presentations on this page are also important in estimating biases in the data from demographic groups upon which the report is based. Examine the table, "Diary Placement and Return Information." Recall that in the preparation of this report it is telephone households not individuals which were drawn into the sample. Each individual of the households which agree to participate in the survey was sent a diary; only a part of these individual diaries were returned to Arbitron for tabulation.

Considering the Total Survey Area, the "Diary Placement" table reports that 872 households were drawn into the sample. Of these 842 were telephoned by Arbitron. In turn, 744 households with 1796 residents more than 12 years of age agreed to participate in the survey. Of these 982 individuals returned diaries. In other words, only about 55 percent of those receiving diaries returned them in usable form. If one considers noncooperating households as well, less than half of those who might have been in the sample actually contributed to the report. No conclusion as to the nature of the bias introduced by this level of noncooperation is possible. It is likely that cooperators and noncooperators are different in some measurable ways. But the data from this report alone do not provide any clues as to how the audience estimates of the report might have been different had everyone cooperated with the survey. This fact alone would give grounds for interpreting the data of the report with caution. In fairness it should be noted that the level of noncooperation is nearly the same in both Metro and Total Survey Areas, suggesting that there is no urban/rural bias in the level of cooperation.

The "Sample Distribution" tables at the top of the same page of Appendix A permit examination of demographic weighting used in the report. Weights for each demographic group are computed by dividing the figure in the column labeled, "Estimated Population as Percent of Total Persons 12+," by the figure in the column labeled, "Percent of Unweighted In-Tab Sample." Table 3-1 provides weights for the Metro Survey Area. Table 3-2 provides weights for the Metro Survey Area.

Asterisks indicate weights which call for caution when these groups are important to a decision under deliberation.

Table 3-1.   Demographic Weights, Total Survey Area, Akron, October/November 1977.

DEMOGRAPHIC GROUP		A ESTIMATED POPULATION AS PERCENT OF TOTAL PERSONS 12+	B PERCENT OF UNWEIGHTED IN-TAB SAMPLE	A÷B DEMOGRAPHIC WEIGHTS
Men	18–24	7.9	6.1	1.295*
	25–34	9.2	9.9	.929
	35–44	6.6	6.5	1.015
	45–49	3.4	3.3	1.030
	50–54	3.3	3.5	.943
	55–64	5.2	6.1	.852
	65+	4.9	3.7	1.324*
Women	18–24	8.6	6.6	1.303*
	25–34	9.5	11.3	.841
	35–44	6.9	7.4	.932
	45–49	3.5	4.7	.745*
	50–54	3.5	4.4	.795
	55–64	5.6	7.3	.767
	65+	7.1	5.1	1.392*
Teens	12–17	14.6	14.2	1.028

Table 3-2.   Demographic Weights, Metro Survey Area, Akron, October/November 1977.

DEMOGRAPHIC GROUP		A ESTIMATED POPULATION AS PERCENT OF TOTAL PERSONS 12+	B PERCENT OF UNWEIGHTED IN-TAB SAMPLE	A÷B DEMOGRAPHIC WEIGHTS
Men	18–24	8.9	7.6	1.171
	25–34	9.1	9.5	.958
	35–44	6.6	6.7	.985
	45–49	3.4	2.7	1.259
	50–54	5.0	3.3	1.000
	55–64	5.0	6.8	.735*
	65+	4.6	3.5	1.314*
Women	18–24	9.5	7.6	1.250
	25–34	9.3	10.6	.877
	35–44	6.8	7.3	.932
	45–49	3.6	3.6	1.000
	50–54	3.5	4.4	.795
	55–64	5.6	6.7	.836
	65+	6.7	6.0	1.117
Teens	12–17	14.3	13.6	1.051

Sampling Error/Confidence Intervals

The discussion in the preceding chapter regarding sampling error and effective sample size is appropriate to recall here. The basic formula for a 95 percent probable confidence interval about a rating is:

$$p_o - p_t = \pm 1.96 \sqrt{\frac{pq}{N}}$$

This formula establishes the range in which the true value of a rating may fall when sampling error has been considered. When effective sample sizes are provided by the rating service, effective sample size is substituted for N in the formula, yielding:

$$p_o - p_t = \pm 1.96 \sqrt{\frac{pq}{ESB}}$$

Effective Sample Base (*ESB*) is the Arbitron term for effective sample size.

A further refinement is possible in the case of Arbitron reports due to research studies financed by the firm itself. Effective sample size can be made more precise when modified by a factor labeled, "Statistical Efficiency." There is actually more stability in average ratings than the formulas above are able to reflect. This is so, because an average rating is computed for each quarter hour of any time period under consideration. This number of average ratings is then itself averaged to produce the figure recorded in the day-part display of the report. The fact that so many quarter-hour ratings are *averaged* reduces the possible variation due to sampling error. The amount of this *reduced variation in sampling error* is indexed by Statistical Efficiency (SE). An example will make the point clearer.

Consider the data presented on page 10 of Appendix A, "Average Quarter-Hour and Cume Listening Estimates." Note that the day-part covered by this display is Monday–Sunday, 6:00 A.M.–Midnight. The number of quarter hours in this day part is 504 (7 days × 18 hours × 4 quarter-hours per hour). With estimates of Total Men 18+ and 504 quarter-hours, Arbitron reports a Statistical Efficiency (*SE*) of 4.1.[1] The rating for station WGAR in the Total Survey Area will be:

$$\frac{\text{(from page 10) } 4800}{\text{(from page 3) } 468,700} \times 100 \text{ or } .01024$$

The confidence interval associated with this rating for the WGAR audience of men 18+ is thus:

$$p_o - p_t = \pm 1.96 \sqrt{\frac{p(1.0 - p)}{ESB(SE)}}$$

$$= \pm 1.96 \sqrt{\frac{.01024(.98976)}{782(4.1)}}$$

from p. 3 $\nearrow$ $\qquad$ $\nwarrow$ given above

$$= \pm 1.96 \sqrt{\frac{.010135}{3206.2}}$$

$$= \pm 1.96 \sqrt{.00000316}$$

$$= \pm 1.96(.00178)$$

$$p_o - p_t = \pm .00348$$

This confidence interval indicates that the rating for WGAR, TSA Men 18+ is 1.024 ± .348 or that the true rating falls in the range, .676 to 1.372, in 95 percent of the replications of this survey. The true listening estimate falls in the range 3168 to 6431 when sampling error is considered.

Another illustration: On page 54 of Appendix A the day-part being reported is also Monday–Sunday 6:00 A.M. to Midnight. The average quarter-hour listening estimate for Total Persons 12+ in the Total Survey Area for station WAKR is listed as 11,500 persons. The rating corresponding to this estimate is:

$$\frac{11,500}{\text{(from p. 3) } 1,156,000} \times 100 \text{ or } .995$$

The Statistical Efficiency given by Arbitron for a day-part of 504 quarter-hours, Total Persons 12+, is 2.4 (refer to Table 3-3). The confidence interval associated with this rating is:

$$p_o - p_t = \pm 1.96 \sqrt{\frac{p(1.0 - p)}{ESB(SE)}}$$

$$= \pm 1.96 \sqrt{\frac{.00995(.99005)}{782(2.4)}}$$

$$= \pm 1.96 \sqrt{\frac{.009851}{1876.8}}$$

$$= \pm 1.96(.000005249)$$

$$p_o - p_t = .000010287$$

The true value for this rating, when sampling error is considered, has a 95 percent likelihood of falling in the range, .995 ± .0010287 or between .994 and .996. The value of the listening estimate associated with this rating will in 95 percent of the replications of this study fall within the range, 11,491 to 11,514.

Table 3-3   Statistical Efficiencies (SE) for Arbitron Radio reports.

DEMOGRAPHIC GROUP	16–20 QTR-HRS ANY DAY 6–10 A.M. ANY DAY 10 A.M.-3 P.M. ANY DAY 3–7 P.M. ANY DAY 7 P.M.-MID	80 QTR-HRS M-F 6–10 A.M. M-F 3–7 P.M.	100 QTR-HRS M-F 10 A.M.-3 P.M. M-F 7 P.M.-MID	504 QTR-HRS M-SUN 6 A.M.-MIDNIGHT
Men 18–24	1.7	4.3	4.9	9.9
25–34	1.6	3.6	4.2	8.2
35–49	1.5	3.1	3.5	6.2
50–64	1.5	2.9	3.3	5.9
Total Men 18+	1.4	2.5	2.8	4.1
Women 18–24	1.9	3.9	4.3	6.6
25–34	1.7	3.4	3.8	4.6
35–49	1.6	3.1	3.3	4.8
50–64	1.6	2.9	3.2	4.6
Total Women 18+	1.5	2.5	2.7	3.4
Total Teens 12–17	2.0	4.4	4.9	7.9
Total Persons 18+	1.3	2.0	2.1	2.6
Total Persons 18+	1.2	1.9	2.0	2.4

Profiling an Audience

It is often worthwhile to consider various day-parts graphically as a demographic profile. This is a straightforward procedure of translating the figures in the report into a histogram. (Histograms are discussed in detail in Appendix C, Lesson One.) Figure 3-1 presents the demographic profile for Monday–Sunday, 6:00 A.M. to Midnight (page 54 of Appendix A).

Another kind of audience profile will be a profile over time. In making any important decision about programs, for example, it is helpful to consider audience data from several survey periods. In order to further stabilize—or reduce random variations—in reports over time, it may be wise to compute and graph rolling averages. A rolling average would allow the average of the April/May report, the October/November report and the following April/May report to stand for the October/November report. Figure 3-2 contrasts reported and rolling averages for average share trends, Metro Total Persons 12+, Monday 6 A.M. to Midnight, for station WMMS. It should be apparent from the figure that the effect of using the rolling average is to smooth out the influence of any one book in a multireport comparison.

Figure 3-3 shows rolling averages for average share trends, Metro Total Persons 12+ (page six of Appendix A) and Men 18+ over five different day-parts for station WAEZ. This sort of profile may be useful in looking at shifts in audience produced by the "aging" of a format. In the case of station WAEZ, it is apparent that share of Men 18+ and share of Total Persons 12+ are closely associated but that the trends for both are downward.

Time Selling Helps

An important function of audience reports is to permit comparisons of the value of radio or television advertising with newspaper, magazine, outdoor, and other advertising media.

One frequently used index for comparing the value of advertising opportunities is

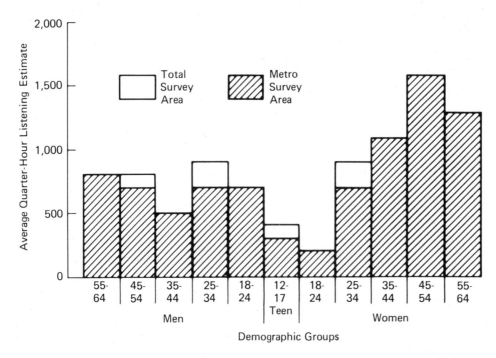

Figure 3–1.   Demographic Profile of Station WAKR, Total and Metro Survey Areas, Monday-Sunday, 6 A.M. to Midnight.

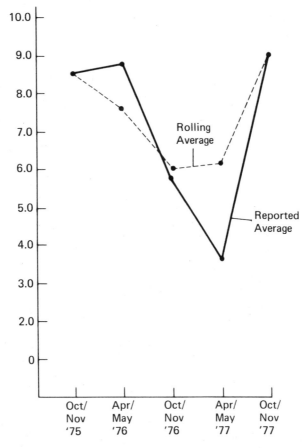

Figure 3–2. Rolling Averages versus Reported Averages, WMMS, Average Share Trends, Metro Total Persons 12+, Monday-Sunday 6 A.M. to Midnight.

cost per thousand (CPM). It represents the cost of reaching 1000 persons one time. If only one commercial spot is considered, CPM is computed:

$$CPM = \frac{\text{Cost of Spot}}{\text{Average Persons in Thousands}}$$

For example, if a one-time 1-minute spot on Kent, Ohio, radio station WKNT-FM during morning drive time costs $20, and the average quarter-hour listening estimate (Monday-Friday, 6–10 A.M.) for TSA Total Persons 12+ is 4100 (see Appendix A, page 62), then the cost per thousand would be:

$$CPM = \frac{\$20.00}{4.1}$$

$$CPM = \$4.88.$$

At the same time, if the one-time 1-minute rate on Akron station WAKR were also $20.00, and the morning drive time, TSA Total Persons 12+ estimated audience were 28,000, the cost per thousand for a spot comparable to that on station WAKR would be:

$$CPM = \frac{\$20.00}{28.2} \quad \text{(from page 62, Appendix A)}$$

$$CPM = \$ \ .71 \ .$$

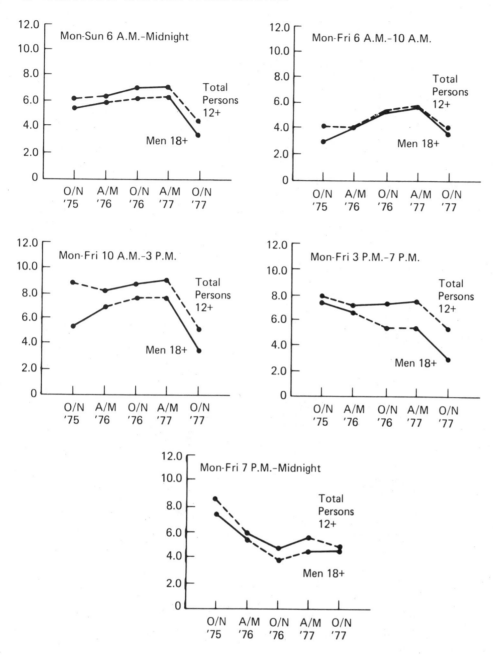

Figure 3-3. Rolling Average Shares, Metro Total Persons 12+ and Men 18+, station WAEZ.

In this fictitious example, it is obvious that the WAKR spot is the better buy. It is also apparent that, if WKNT-FM wants to compete with WAKR on a cost per thousand basis, it will need to set its rates at a level that will produce a CPM closer to $.71. For morning drive time when the average audience of Total Persons 12+ in the Total Survey Area is 4100, the one-time 1-minute rate of WKNT-FM would have to be about 4.1 × $.71, or $2.91, to compete on the CPM basis.

A more common situation in the "real world" is a CPM computation for a schedule of spots, rather than for a single spot. The computation in this case is:

$$CPM = \frac{\text{Cost of Schedule}}{\text{Average Persons in Thousands} \times \text{No. of Spots}}$$

To illustrate, suppose that a metropolitan Akron advertiser has purchased a schedule of 24 30-second spots at a total cost of $150.00 to be run in morning drive time on Cleveland station WMMS-FM. The average quarter-hour listening estimate for morning drive time, Metro Total Persons 12+, is 8500. Therefore the CPM is:

$$CPM = \frac{\$150}{8.5 \times 24}$$

$$= \frac{\$150}{204} \text{ or } \$ .74.$$

A related index of advertising efficiency is *cost per gross rating point* (*CPGRP*). A gross rating point is a single point in audience rating or 1 percent of the potential audience. It is calculated:

$$CPGRP = \frac{\text{cost}}{\text{average rating} \times \text{number of announcements.}}$$

An illustration: A men's shop is considering a campaign of 100 spots rotated through the week and directed toward men 18-49 in the Akron Metro area. The sales manager of Akron station WSLR has quoted a price for this schedule of $500. What is the cost per gross rating point? The average WSLR rating for Metro men 18-49, Monday–Sunday, 6 A.M. to Midnight, is 2.2 (see page 10 Appendix A):

$$CPGRP = \frac{\$500}{2.2 \times 100}$$

$$CPGRP = \$ 2.72 .$$

Analysis for Radio Program Decisions

Two frequently used indices reflect the staying-power of a radio format—how long a listener will stay tuned, and how often the listener will tune in then switch to other stations.

Time spent listening (*TSL*) is a relative index of the average listener's average time with the station for any given day-part.[3]

$$TSL = \frac{\text{average audience} \times \text{number of qtr hrs in day-part}}{\text{CUME}}$$

Table 3-4 compares TSL for Total Survey Area men 18+, Monday–Sunday, 6 A.M. to Midnight for Akron home market stations (see page 10 of Appendix A). It is apparent from the table that, although station WAKR has a greater cume, men who listen to station WSLR listen for a longer time. In addition, station WKNT-FM seems to have developed the strongest listening habit in its male listeners. A more detailed analysis of TSL would include computation for each day-part.

Turnover is the ratio of average quarter-hour listening estimates to cume listening estimates; it is a relative index of the number of different audiences who will be listening during a given day-part over a week's time. The formula for turnover is implied by its definition:

$$Turnover = \frac{\text{CUME audience}}{\text{average audience.}}$$

Again this index will be clearer from an example. Table 3-5 shows turnover for Akron market stations among men 35-64 in the Metro Survey area, Monday–Sunday 6 A.M. to

Table 3-4   Time Spent Listening by TSA Men 18+, Monday-Sunday, 6 A.M. to Midnight, to Akron Home Stations.

STATION CALL LETTERS	AVERAGE PERSONS	X	504 QUARTER-HOURS	÷	CUME PERSONS	=	(TSL) TIME SPENT LISTENING
WAEZ-FM	1,500		756,000		26,600		28.4 qtr-hrs
WAKR	4,200		2,116,800		99,200		21.3
WCUE	400		201,600		16,700		12.1
WHLO	2,800		1,411,200		43,600		32.4
WKDD-FM	2,000		1,008,000		39,800		25.3
WKNT	400		201,600		4,700		42.9
WKNT-FM	1,300		655,200		14,000		46.8
WSLR	4,800		2,419,200		70,300		34.4

Table 3-5   Turnover for Men 35-64, Metro Survey Area, Monday-Sunday 6 A.M. to midnight, Akron Home Market Stations.

STATION CALL LETTERS	CUME AUDIENCE	÷	MEN 35-64 AVERAGE QUARTER-HOUR AUDIENCE	=	TURNOVER
WAEZ	11,800		1,000		11.8
WAKR	45,600		2,000		22.8
WCUE	7,500		100		75.0
WHLO	6,100		300		20.3
WKDD-FM	2,300		100		23.0
WKNT	3,600		200		18.0
WKNT-FM	6,900		1,000		6.9
WSLR	33,700		2,900		11.6

Midnight (page 10 of Appendix A). From the table it appears that WSLR has the soundest format for this audience group. It has the largest average quarter-hour audience and a modest turnover. Generally speaking, if audience levels are high, turnover should be low, indicating great listener loyalty. If average quarter-hour estimates are low, high turnover promises that more audience will learn of the station offerings.

In the case of programs rather than formats, a low turnover and a high time spent listening signify a consistent audience appeal. The kind of program which produces high turnover is a feature with broader appeal than the rest of the format. For example, if only one station provides hourly reports on the condition of local ski slopes, and if skiing is a popular recreation in the community, turnover would be high as skiers switch from their usual station to the station with ski reports. All news stations often have higher turnover and lower time spent listening.

Efficiency

The *efficiency* of a radio format is dealt with at greater length in Chapter 11. In this chapter Efficiency of Target Audience (ETA) is introduced. ETA is the ratio of target audience TSL and total audience TSL:

$$ETA = \frac{\text{target } TSL}{\text{total } TSL} .$$

In Tables 3-6a and 3-6b the ETA of Akron home market stations are reflected as they produce adult male demographics. The larger the figure for ETA the more efficient the format in attracting or recruiting men 18+. From the table it appears that it is station

Table 3-6a   Time Spent Listening, TSA Total Persons 12+, Monday-Sunday, 6 A.M. to Midnight, Akron Home Market Stations.

STATION CALL LETTERS	AVERAGE QTR-HR ESTIMATE	× 504	÷ CUME	(TSL) TIME SPENT = LISTENING
WAEZ	4,800	2,419,200	77,000	31.4
WAKR	11,500	5,796,000	229,600	25.2
WCUE	4,000	2,016,000	93,200	21.6
WHLO	5,200	2,620,800	81,400	32.2
WKDD-FM	5,300	2,671,200	96,400	27.7
WKNT	1,200	604,800	15,700	38.5
WKNT-FM	2,600	1,310,400	40,100	32.7
WSLR	8,300	4,183,200	148,800	28.1

Table 3-6b   Efficiency of Target Audience for TSA Men 18+, Monday-Sunday, 6 A.M. to Midnight, Akron Home Market Stations.

STATION CALL LETTERS	TSL MEN 18+ ÷	TSL PERSONS 12+ =	(ETA) EFFICIENCY OF TARGET AUDIENCE
WAEZ	28.4	31.4	.904
WAKR	21.3	25.2	.845
WCUE	12.1	21.6	.560
WHLO	32.4	32.2	1.006
WKDD-FM	25.3	27.7	.913
WKNT	42.9	38.5	1.114
WKNT-FM	46.8	32.7	1.431
WSLR	34.4	28.1	1.224

WKNT-FM which is most efficient in attracting male demographics. This station also has the lowest turnover in men 35–64 and the greatest TSL for men 18+.

Recycling

Recycling is the proportion of audience for one time period who are also in the audience for another time period. If the proportion of audience for one period that is recycled to another is high, then the material for the second period has greater need for variety and freshness, for example, than otherwise. Percent recycling is computed:

$$\text{Percent Recycling} = \frac{\text{CUME of both periods}}{\text{CUME of one period}} \ .$$

An illustration can be drawn from the January/February 1978 Arbitron radio report for San Jose.[4]

The first step in determining percent recycling of morning drive time audiences to evening drive time audiences is to determine the cume of both periods. To do this it is necessary to add the cumes of each of the two periods (6–10 A.M. and 3–7 P.M.), then subtract the cume of the combined periods (6–10 A.M. + 3–7 P.M.). This is necessary, since many of those listening during 6–10 A.M. are also in the audience at 3–7 P.M. They must be removed from the combined figure. Table 3-7 presents this computation for Total Survey Area, total persons 12+, for the San Jose home market stations during January/February 1978. Several stations—KEEN and KLOK—recycle more than two-thirds of morning drive audiences into evening drive time. This fact, of course, adds to the commercial value of availabilities during the drive time of these stations.

Table 3-7. Percent Recycling of Morning Drive Audience to Evening Drive Time, TSA Total Persons 12+, San Jose Home Market Stations, January/February 1978.

STATION CALL LETTERS	CUME M-F 6 A.M.- 10 A.M.	+	CUME M-F 3 P.M.- 7 P.M.	−	CUME M-F 6 A.M.-10 A.M. AND 3 P.M.-7 P.M.	÷	CUME M-F 6 A.M.- 10 A.M.	=	PERCENT RECYCLING
KARA	59,200		55,300		76,900		59,200		63.5
KBAY	111,600		129,900		169,800		111,600		64.2
KEEN	60,500		66,900		85,600		60,500		69.1
KEZR	39,000		30,400		49,300		39,000		51.5
KFAT	38,800		44,600		62,900		38,800		52.8
KIBE	22,400		15,100		30,400		22,400		31.7
KDFC	23,200		43,400		51,900		23,200		63.4
KLIV	91,800		96,700		144,200		91,800		48.3
KLOK	150,400		165,600		215,700		150,400		66.7
KOME	56,200		81,600		103,600		56,200		60.9
KSJO	74,500		88,000		117,500		74,500		60.4
KXRX	66,700		46,500		77,000		66,700		54.3

Exclusives

An exclusive in a radio audience report is a listener to one and only one station. The proportion of exclusives developed by a station is evidence of long-term loyalty. When a change in format is being considered, it is often desirable to anchor the change in the approval of the station exclusives. The part of the program schedule which accounts for the loyalty of the exclusives may be indicated when the percent of exclusives in the total audience is computed for each of the various day-parts.

Table 3-8 presents the percent exclusives for Akron home market stations in the Total Survey Area for total persons 12+, Monday–Sunday, 6 A.M. to Midnight. Station WAKR has both the largest cumulative audiences and the highest percent exclusives.

Away-from-Home/Out-of-Home

A section of the radio report will deal with out-of-home or away-from-home listening. The bulk of this listening in the average community is in automobiles and at place of work. Experts in radio programming predict that out-of-home listening will increase in the nineteen eighties, particularly radio listening at place of work. Table 3-9 provides a summary of the percent of away-from-home listening for San Jose home market stations as reported for January/February 1978. The percent figures in the table were computed by Arbitron and appear in the report.

The figures in the first column of Table 3-9 represent away-from-home listening during drive time. The next column represents listening away from home during the day and probably reflects listening at work. The final column is percent of away-from-home listening during the evening hours. Note that the figures overall are lower than in the two preceding columns, although some are still quite high. It is interesting to note station KLOK's strong performance in each of these day-parts. In 1978 KLOK listed their format as "MOR/ Personality" in *Broadcasting Yearbook*. Generally strong out-of-home performance in both drive time and other day-parts occurs with a music station which emphasizes personalities, while strong showing in drive time only is likely to occur when the station has a strong and popular information service which commuters and other drivers find valuable.

TELEVISION REPORTS

Television market reports differ from radio audience reports in a number of ways already enumerated. The key difference is probably the amount of money in the television

Table 3-8. Percent Exlusives, TSA Total Persons 12+, Monday Sunday,
6 A.M. to Midnight, Akron Home Market Stations.

STATION CALL LETTERS	EXCLUSIVE CUME	÷	TOTAL CUME	=	PERCENT EXCLUSIVES
WAEZ	3,000		77,000		3.9
WAKR	27,200		229,600		11.8
WCUE	6,300		93,200		6.8
WHLO	—		81,400		—
WKDD-FM	2,900		96,400		3.0
WKNT	—		15,700		—
WKNT-FM	3,700		40,100		9.2
WSLR	15,100		148,800		10.1

Table 3-9. Percent Away-from-Home Listening TSA Total Persons 12+
January/February 1978, San Jose Home Market Stations.

STATION CALL LETTERS	TSA TOTAL PERSONS 12+		
	M-F 6–10 A.M. AND 3–7 P.M.	M-F 10 A.M.-3 P.M.	M-F 7 P.M. MIDNIGHT
KARA	69	64	19
KBAY	50	68	22
KEEN	67	74	32
KEZR	37	46	23
KFAT	47	47	2
KIBE	41	26	—
KDFC	29	33	13
KLIV	42	65	30
KLOK	63	66	46
KOME	44	68	19
KSJO	35	52	20
KXRX	48	89	9

industry. It is not surprising that a television report is longer and offers a greater variety of information and, in many respects, more detail. Appendix B is an extract of the November 1977 Arbitron Television report for Portland, Oregon.

Survey Areas and Sample Design

The second page of the Portland report at Appendix B includes a map of the three overlapping survey areas included in the report—Metro Survey Area (SMSA), Area of Dominant Influence (predominant counties), and Total Survey Area (significant counties).

The fine cross-hatching on the map marks the three counties of the SMSA; the table under the map indicates there are 417,500 households in this Metro area. In the Portland report the Metro counties were sampled—in addition to the usual procedures—according to the Arbitron Expanded Sample Frame (ESF) protocol. This method is similar to the random telephone number generation system described in the preceding chapter. That is, out of all possible telephone numbers that could be connected, a certain number of possible telephone numbers are selected. Known business, institutional, and multiple residence numbers are eliminated, yielding a set of telephone numbers which will enrich the normally selected sample with unlisted and recently connected telephone households.

The Area of Dominant Influence for the Portland Market is marked on the map in coarse cross-hatching and includes 682,200 households. The Metro Survey Area is part of the ADI. It is also worth noting that the ADI includes parts of two states.

The Total Survey Area is indicated in white on the map. Note that the TSA also includes a number of satellite stations indicated by small triangles. A satellite station is a secondary transmitter which rebroadcasts the signal of a primary transmitter, thereby extending the viewing area of the primary station.

Another noteworthy feature of the map page of the report at Appendix B is the schedule of survey dates. The survey reported here is the second of eight scheduled for the program year.

On page 3 of the report at Appendix B is a detailed description of the counties involved in the survey. The columns labeled "CATV Pct" and "ADI Key" are worth studying.

The interesting feature of the CATV penetration of the counties is the relative effect of cable upon home market audiences. The columns below summarize the data presented in the report on cable penetration.

From examination of these figures it appears that the Portland home market stations compete favorably for the attention of viewers in cable homes where out-of-market stations are received as clearly as home-market stations. If it were otherwise, one could

COUNTY	CABLE PENETRATION (CATV PCT)
Portland ADI	
Benton	32.2
Clackamas (Metro)	3.2
Clatsop	79.0
Columbia	11.1
Crook	51.2
Deschutes	59.9
Gilliam	74.7
Harney	78.3
Hood River	36.8
Jefferson	50.4
Lincoln	85.0
Linn	17.0
Marion	2.3
Multnomah (Metro)	1.5
Polk	23.2
Sherman	11.1
Tillamook	71.6
Wasco	74.3
Washington (Metro)	.6
Wheeler	62.8
Yamhill	6.3
Clark (Metro)	—
Cowlitz	48.2
Klichitat	48.0
Skamania	44.7
Wahkiakum	26.2
Average for Portland ADI (less Metro counties)	45.2
Eugene ADI	
Coos	66.0
Douglas	35.4
Lane	45.3
Average for Eugene ADI	48.9
Medford ADI	
Jackson	28.7
Seattle-Tacoma ADI	
Grays Harbor	77.7
King	13.5
Lewis	40.3
Pacific	83.0
Prince	17.3
Average for Seattle-Tacoma ADI	46.4

expect to see that the greater the cable penetration, the more likely the county to fall in an adjacent ADI.

On the following page of the Portland report (page 4 of Appendix B) the demographic composition of the sample is displayed. The "Demographic Characteristics" table does not show the percent of the in-tab sample for each group, a value required for the formula for demographic weights given previously. The formula for demographic weights appropriate to this table is thus:

$$\text{Weight}_{\text{group}} = \frac{\text{proportion of population}}{\text{\# group in-tab/total in-tab.}}$$

Table 3-10 presents the demographic weights for selected groups within the Portland sample. Note that the weights are all close to 1.0, this improvement over the radio market report studied earlier being mainly due to surveying a much larger sample.

The table on page 4 of Appendix B labeled, "Sample Placement, In-Tab and Effective Sample Bases," provides information necessary to estimate sampling error and to compute confidence intervals associated with ratings and audience estimates. According to the table nearly 86 percent of the television households in the original TSA sample accepted diaries. Of these fewer than 62 percent returned usable diaries. It is not possible to know with any surety what influence this noncooperation introduces to the report, but it is likely that the individual user of research from this market will gradually come to have a "feel" for the relative importance of various levels of noncooperation. For example, in communities where the level of functional illiteracy is very high, noncooperation will also be high, for illiterate respondents will typically agree to cooperate (rather than confess to their handicap) then fail to produce usable data. Of course, illiteracy is used here for purpose of illustration; there are many other reasons for noncooperation.

This same display on page 4 of Appendix B provides information on effective sample size (ESB) and Standard Error Weighting Factors (WF). The WF are used for computing sampling error and confidence intervals for areas where the expanded sample frame has been employed. Details on this computation are provided in the discussion on confidence intervals.

Table 3-10. Demographic Weights for Selected Demographic Groups of the November 1977 Television Report for Portland, Oregon.

DEMOGRAPHIC GROUP	GROUP PROPORTION OF POPULATION	÷	GROUP # / TOTAL IN-TAB / IN-TAB	=	WEIGHT
TSA					
Women 18+	.380		2,112/5,498 or .384		.990
Men 18+	.357		1,886/5,498 or .343		1.041
Teens	.116		655/5,498 or .119		.975
Children	.147		845/5,498 or .154		.955
Metro					
Women 18+	.384		910/2,365 or .385		.977
Men 18+	.351		776/2,365 or .328		1.070
Teens	.117		298/2,365 or .126		.929
Children	.148		381/2,365 or .161		.919

Confidence Intervals for Viewing Reports

Sampling error influences all ratings, shares, and estimates appearing in the local market report. Rough estimates of the sampling error assignable to a given rating can be computed by the methods already discussed. By using additional information contained in the television market report it is possible to compute a refined estimate.

Recall the basic formula for a 95 percent probable confidence interval associated with a rating, a formula introduced in connection with radio reports:

$$p_o - p_t = \pm 1.96 \sqrt{\frac{p_o(1.0 - p_o)}{ESB(SE)}}$$

where

$p_o - p_t$ = estimated confidence interval

p_o = rating as presented in the report

ESB = effective sample base (size) found on page 4 of the report

SE = relative efficiency for this demographic group when reported for the number of quarter-hours in the day-part involved. See page v of Appendix B.

Consider an illustration: On page 92 of the Portland Television audience report at Appendix B for the Monday–Friday 11:00–11:15 P.M. time period a rating of 7 is reported for Metro TV households tuned to KATV Eyewitness News over the 4 weeks surveyed. On page 4 of the report note that the ESB for the Metro area TV households is 562. From page v the statistical efficiency for television households and 5 (Monday–Friday) quarter-hours is 1.1. The computation for the 95 percent probable confidence interval associated with this rating is:

$$p_o - p_t = \pm 1.96 \sqrt{\frac{.07(.93)}{562(1.1)}}$$

$$= \pm 1.96 \sqrt{\frac{.06510}{618.2}}$$

$$= \pm 1.96 \sqrt{.000105}$$

$$= \pm 1.96(.01026)$$

$$p_o - p_t = \pm .02.$$

This confidence interval is interpreted, "In 95 percent of the replications of this survey the value for Metro TV HH rating for Monday–Friday, 11:00–11:15 P.M., for KATV will fall between 5 and 9 (7 ± 2)."

In those survey areas where the expanded sample frame protocol was employed the formula for 95 percent probable confidence associated with a rating becomes:

$$p_o - p_t = \pm 1.96 \sqrt{\frac{p_o(1.0 - p_o)}{ESB\left(\dfrac{SE}{WF}\right)}}$$

The new element in this formula is a weighting factor for ESB associated with the survey area where the expanded sample frame was used.

To illustrate note page 107 of Appendix B, the Portland television market report. At 7:30 P.M. Tuesdays station KATU broadcast "The Muppets" which returned a TV household rating in the ADI of 14. According to page v of the report the 2 quarter-hours of this time period call for a statistical efficiency of .9 when TV households are involved. From page 4 of the report the ESB for the ADI is 726, and the Weighting

Factor is 1.07. The 95 percent probable confidence interval about an ADI rating of 14 for "The Muppets" is then:

$$p_o - p_t = \pm 1.96 \sqrt{\frac{.14(.86)}{726\left(\frac{.9}{1.07}\right)}}$$

$$= \pm 1.96 \sqrt{\frac{.1204}{726(.84112)}}$$

$$= \pm 1.96 \sqrt{\frac{.1204}{610.65312}}$$

$$= \pm 1.96 \sqrt{.00019717}$$

$$= \pm 1.96 \, (.01404)$$

$$p_o - p_t = \pm.027518 \, .$$

This result can be interpreted, "It is likely that in 95 percent of a very large number of replications of this survey the value for the ADI TV HH rating for KATU, 'The Muppets,' will be between 11.3 and 16.8 (14 ± 2.7518)."

When the rating or estimate being considered represents a demographic group, the confidence interval is computed in much the same way as indicated above. For example, on page 9 of Appendix B during the period 4:30 to 6:00 P.M., most of the local affiliate schedule is syndicated programming. Many of these programs are targeted to women, because the total audience of women is larger in relative terms during this time period. The formula for computing a 95 percent probable confidence interval for any of the subgroups of women would be:

$$p_o - p_t = \pm 1.96 \sqrt{\frac{p_o(1.0 - p_o)}{n\left(\dfrac{SE}{WF}\right)}}$$

The only unfamiliar element of this formula is n, the number of diaries in-tab for the demographic group in question.

An illustration: During the period from 4:30 to 6:00 P.M. station KVDO on a Monday through Friday basis records an average rating for ADI women 18+ of 11. Page 4 of the report indicates the in-tab sample size for ADI women 18+ is 910. The weighting factor for the ADI is 107. On page v of the report note that the day-part, Monday–Friday, 4:30–6:00 P.M. includes 30 quarter-hours, with a statistical efficiency of 2.2. The computation is then:

$$p_o - p_t = \pm 1.96 \sqrt{\frac{.11(.89)}{910\left(\frac{2.2}{1.07}\right)}}$$

$$= \pm 1.96 \sqrt{\frac{.09790}{910(2.05607)}}$$

$$= \pm 1.96 \sqrt{\frac{.09790}{1871.0237}}$$

$$= \pm 1.96 \sqrt{.0000523}$$

$$= \pm 1.96 (.00723)$$

$$p_o - p_t = \pm.014 \, .$$

This result implies that in 95 percent of a large number of exact replications of this survey, the rating for ADI women 18+, Monday-Friday 4:30-6 P.M., station KVDO, will fall between 9.6 and 12.4.

Confidence Intervals for Audience Estimates

Confidence intervals for audience estimates are computed in the same manner, except that projections are converted to ratings for computation purposes and then back to estimates.

An illustration: On page 16 of the Portland television audience report at Appendix B note the audience for the NBC Nightly News, 6:30 until 7:00 P.M. Monday. In the Total Survey Area an audience of 19,000 men 18-49 are reported. What is the 95 percent probable confidence interval for this audience estimate?

The first step in computation is to convert the estimate into a rating. This is done by dividing the estimate by the estimated total number of men in the TSA (from page 4 of the report) and multiplying by 100 (in further computation this rating will be represented by p, the decimal fraction equivalent of a rating).

$$\text{rating} = \frac{19,000}{933,600} \times 100$$

$$= .02035 \times 100$$

$$\text{rating} = 2.035 .$$

The second step involves finding the other elements required for computation. From page 4 of the report note that 1263 diaries are in-tab from the TSA men 18-49. Note also that the weighting factor (WF) for the TSA is .95. From page v of the report note that the statistical efficiency (SE) for 2 quarter-hours for men 18-49 is .8.

Then the computation of the 95 percent probable confidence interval:

$$p_o - p_t = \pm 1.96 \sqrt{\frac{p_o(1.0 - p_o)}{n\left(\frac{SE}{WF}\right)}}$$

$$= \pm 1.96 \sqrt{\frac{.02035(.97965)}{1263\left(\frac{.8}{.95}\right)}}$$

$$= \pm 1.96 \sqrt{\frac{.01994}{1263(.84211)}}$$

$$= \pm 1.96 \sqrt{\frac{.01994}{1063.5849}}$$

$$= \pm 1.96 \sqrt{.000019}$$

$$= \pm 1.96(.00439)$$

$$p_o - p_t = \pm .009 .$$

This confidence interval of a rating ($p_o - p_t$) is translated to a confidence interval of an estimate ($e_o - e_t$). The translation is accomplished by multiplying the rating confidence interval by the estimated total number of men 18-49 in the TSA (from page 4 of Appendix B):

$$e_o - e_t = \pm.009 \times 933{,}600$$

$$e_o - e_t = \pm 8402 \;.$$

This result indicates that in 95 percent of the exact replications of this survey the audience estimate for TSA men 18–49 to Monday NBC Nightly News will fall in the range 19,000 ± 8402, or from 10,598 to 27,402.

Threshold Estimates

Threshold estimates are used in Arbitron television market reports as a way of displaying the relative sampling error of ratings and estimates in accordance with the stipulated requirements of the Broadcast Ratings Council.

Instead of showing the absolute size of the confidence interval, Arbitron displays the threshold estimate as a relative standard error, one standard error as a proportion of the rating itself. The standard error or standard deviation (see Appendix C, Lesson Two) associated with a rating is computed:

$$\text{standard error} = \sqrt{\frac{p_o(1.0 - p_o)}{n\left(\dfrac{SE}{WF}\right)}}$$

The relative standard error (or deviation) is this standard error in ratio to the rating itself:

$$\text{relative standard error} = \frac{\sqrt{\dfrac{p_o(1.0 - p_o)}{n\left(\dfrac{SE}{WF}\right)}}}{p_o}$$

Sampling error, as reflected in standard error, relative standard error and confidence intervals, varies with the size of a rating. Threshold estimates are the size a rating would have to be for relative standard error to reach 25 percent of the rating or 50 percent of the rating.

Refer to page iv of the Portland television market report at Appendix B, and note the Table of Threshold Estimates there. The first line of the table is labeled, "Households." Under the column headed, "ADI RATINGS, 1–4 Quarter-Hours," is the figure 2. This means that if an ADI rating for TV HH is based on a day-part of 1 to 4 quarter-hours, and the rating is equal to 2, then one standard error is 25 percent of 2 or .5 rating points. If the ADI TV HH rating in question is based upon 1 to 4 quarter-hours, then one standard error will be less than 25 percent of the rating.

Refer to the line in the same table labeled, "Child Total." In this case the threshold estimates for ADI rating and 1 to 4 quarter-hours are 12 (25 to 49 percent of the rating) and 3 (50 percent of the rating). If the ADI Child Total rating were 12, then one standard error would be 3 (25 percent of 12). If the same rating were 3, then one standard error would be 1.5 (50 percent of 3). If the rating were between 12 and 3, then the standard error would be between 3 and 1.5. If the rating were greater than 12, the standard error would be less than 25 percent of the rating.

From the foregoing it may be apparent that threshold estimates are not as precise as the formulae with which this chapter has dealt to this point. They are useful, nonetheless, as order of magnitude estimates which require no computation. For those who prefer, as do the authors, that confidence intervals be standarized at the 95 percent probable level (1.96 standard errors) multiplying the Arbitron threshold estimate by two will produce an approximation.

Some examples: On page 90 of the Portland television market report at Appendix B the average estimated audience, TSA child 2-11, for the ABC Evening News, 6:00–6:15 P.M. for the weeks of November 9 and November 16 was 3000. At the top of column 24 the 50 percent threshold estimate is given as 3000. This means that one standard error of the audience estimate of 3000 is equal to 50 percent of 3000 or 1500. The rough estimate of the 95 percent probable confidence interval for this estimate (e_o - e_t) would be twice that amount or 3000. Based on this rough approximation it might be generalized that in 95 percent of the exact replications of this survey the TSA child 2-11 estimate for the ABC Evening News on station KATU would be between 0 and 6000 (3000 ± 3000).

On the same page of the report and continuing in the TSA child column, note that the 4-week average for the "Odd Couple" on station KOIN, Monday–Friday, 6:45 to 7:00 P.M. is 13,000. From the top of column 24 note that the 25 percent threshold estimate is 13,000. That is, if an estimate in that column is 13,000, then one standard error is equal to 3250 (25 percent of 13,000). A rough approximation of the 95 percent probable confidence interval for the "Odd Couple" TSA children audience is two standard errors or ± 6500 (2 X 3250). This result could be interpreted, "In 95 percent of the exact replications of this survey, the TSA children estimate for Monday through Friday, second half of 'Odd Couple' on KOIN will be between 6500 and 19,500 (13,000 ± 6500)."

These illustrations have been selected, since the figure in the audience estimate coincides exactly with the threshold estimates involved. When the reported rating or estimate does not coincide with the threshold estimate given at the head of the column, the following rules apply:

a. If the rating or estimate is greater than the 25 percent threshold estimate, one standard error is less than 25 percent of the reported rating or estimate.
b. If the rating or estimate is less than the 25 percent threshold estimate but more than the 50 percent threshold estimate, one standard error is between 26 and 49 percent of the reported rating or estimate.
c. If the rating or estimate is less than the 50 percent threshold estimate, then one standard error is more than 50 percent of the reported rating or estimate.

It should be clear that threshold estimates provide only rough approximations at best. If a small calculator is available, the serious user of audience reports will prefer to calculate confidence intervals according to the procedures outlined earlier.

TELEVISION SALES

Profile of a Spot

Because of the greater popularity of television, a wider variety of audiences are available to see commercial announcements than usually hear radio spots. As a consequence, television time tends to be bought more often on the basis of television household ratings and estimates.

Nevertheless the fact that a given television audience for a commercial availability is high in a particular demographic category may make it more or less attractive to a sponsor who knows the demographics of potential customers. A useful sales tool under these circumstances is a demographic profile of station audience.

A histogram for average audiences of KOIN at the 6:00 P.M. station break would reflect the audience composition for the commercial availability adjacent to the CBS Evening News on that station. Figure 3-4 presents such a histogram.

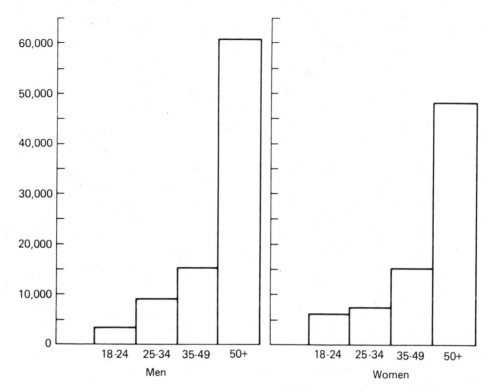

Figure 3–4. Profile of TSA Adult Audience for KOIN Station Break, 6 P.M. Monday-Friday.

The first step in constructing the histogram will be to redivide the demographic categories provided in the report into a set of contiguous and mutually exclusive categories. This is done by following the rules outlined below:

FROM THESE CATEGORIES	THESE ARE DERIVED	BY
Total Women	Women 49+	Subtract Women 18–49 from Women 18+
Women 18–49	Women 18–24	Subtract Women 25–49 from Women 18–49
Women 18–34	Women 25–34	Subtract Women 18–24 from Women 18–34
Women 25–49	Women 35–49	Subtract Women 18–24 from Women 18–49

Comparable sets of categories are also computed for men, yielding figures for a histogram like that at Figure 3-4. A quick review of the figure shows a great predominance of older viewers during this KOIN station break.

Cost per Thousand (CPM)

In contrasting the relative cost of television advertising, the familiar cost per thousand (CPM) is generally used. The usual formula for CPM is:

$$CPM = \frac{\text{cost of spot}}{\text{audience} \div 1000}.$$

To illustrate compare the cost per thousand TV HH of stations reported for the 6:00 P.M. station break on page 91 of the report at Appendix B. Use the 4-week average line for purposes of this computation.

STATION CALL LETTERS	COST PER SPOT (HYPOTHETICAL)	÷	TSA TV HH ÷ 1000	=	CPM
KATU	$175		77		$2.27
KOIN	250		104		2.40
KGW	250		82		3.05
KPTV	125		137		.91

NOTE: the costs per spot above have been invented for purposes of illustration only and have no resemblance to costs of these spots in the Portland market.

This CPM table would look quite different if the objective of the sponsor involved were to reach adults 18–34. In this case the comparative CPM table would be:

STATION CALL LETTERS	A COST PER SPOT (HYPOTHETICAL)	B TSA WOMEN 18–34 ÷1,000	C TSA MEN 18–34 ÷1,000	B + C TSA MEN 18–34 + WOMEN 18–34 ÷1,000	A ÷ (B + C) CPM ADULTS 18–34
KATU	$ 175	12	15	27	$ 6.48
KOIN	250	12	14	26	9.62
KGW	250	11	7	18	13.89
KPTV	125	50	35	85	1.47

Whenever CPMs are computed for demographic groups, the results will be higher costs per thousand than for the comparable TV HH CPMs. CPMs can be computed for every availability for which audience data are reported.

Cost per Gross Rating Point

The cost per gross rating point (CPGRP) was discussed in connection with radio reports. CPGRP is computed in the same way from television spots.

Assume a spot buyer is considering a campaign of 30-second spots to be rotated through the second half of Emergency One broadcast by station KPTV Monday through Friday from 6:00 to 7:00 P.M. The campaign calls for 10 spots per week at an average cost of $105 (a hypothetical figure, not from the KPTV rate card). Half of these spots each week will appear in the 6:30–6:45 P.M. time period, half in the 6:45–7:00 P.M. time period. The buyer is concerned with both television households in the ADI and with women 25–49 in the ADI. CPGRP computations yield:

ADI TV HH	RATING	X	NUMBER OF SPOTS	÷	SPOT COST	=	CPGRP
6:30–6:45	19		5		$ 105		$ 1.11
6:45–7:00	19		5		105		1.11
						Average Campaign CPGRP =	$ 1.11
Women 25–49							
6:30–6:45	15		5		$ 105		$ 1.40
6:45–7:00	15		5		105		1.40
						Average Campaign CPGRP =	$ 1.40

TELEVISION PROGRAMMING

A number of the analyses discussed in Chapter 11 dealing with the revenue effectiveness and value of programs, rely upon information collected from television market reports. In addition, most of the analyses described earlier for data from radio market reports can be used with television market reports as well. The analyses suggested do not represent all of those used widely in the television industry, but will introduce the reader to some of those most frequently referred to.

Audience Flow

Probably no programming concept has had more impact upon program development, acquisition, and scheduling than has the *audience flow criterion*. According to this criterion, the ideal program (a) keeps the audience of the preceding program; (b) adds to that audience; and (c) provides an audience prepared to view the following program.

The most straightforward way of presenting audience flow is by means of a frequency polygon like that at Figure 3-5. This figure presents a view of the TSA estimates for KATU Eyewitness News with TV HH, men 18+ and women 18+ shown. The polygon shows audiences for the period before and after Eyewitness News, Editions 1 and 2. In general, this pattern of audience conforms to the requirements of the audience flow criterion, that is, each subsequent time period accounts for additional audience growth.

Detailed attention can be given to each demographic group if desired in a series of histograms like those in Figure 3-6. For these histograms an interim table like that below is required to convert the demographic categories in the report into mutually exclusive categories.

TIME PERIOD	MEN 18–24	25–34	35–49	50+	WOMEN 18–24	25–34	35–49	50+
5:00–5:15	11	8	10	14	6	3	6	9
5:15–5:30	11	9	9	16	7	4	5	10
5:30–5:45	7	8	10	31	7	6	10	21
5:45–6:00	7	8	9	30	7	8	10	20
6:00–6:15	4	8	12	38	5	10	13	23
6:15–6:30	4	8	11	39	5	10	12	23
6:30–6:45	4	6	13	37	8	12	9	27
6:45–7:00	2	7	12	37	8	9	12	27
7:00–7:15	5	6	12	45	10	16	15	32
7:15–7:30	4	6	11	45	10	16	16	32

From a review of these histograms it is apparent that over the time periods from 5:30 P.M. to 7:30 P.M. the demographics for women become markedly skewed by the addition of many above 50 years of age and the loss of some under 35. Among men there is a slight growth below age 35, and considerable growth in those men over 50 years of age.

Turnover

Turnover in television audiences is much like that in radio audiences. Turnover is the ratio of cume estimates for a given station and day-part to average estimated audience for the same period. If turnover is equal to one, there is no difference between the average and cume audiences: all those who listen typically, listen regularly.

If all else is equal, a Monday through Friday day-part is an excellent buy for advertisers when audience levels are high and turnover is low. For an illustration Table 3-11 compares the turnovers of stations for the period 4:30–6:00 P.M. Monday through Friday based upon TSA data from Appendix B.

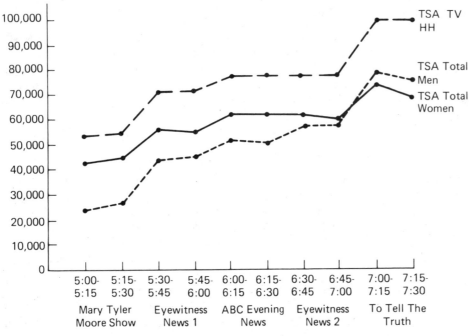

Figure 3–5. Audience, Monday-Friday, TSA station KATU.

Table 3-11. TSA Turnover for Portland Television Stations, Monday through Friday, 4:30-6:00 P.M., November 1977.

STATION CALL LETTERS	TSA TV HH (000) AVERAGE			TSA WOMEN 18+ (000) AVERAGE			TSA MEN 18+ (000) AVERAGE		
	CUME	÷ ESTIMATE	=TURNOVER	CUME	÷ESTIMATE	=TURNOVER	CUME	÷ ESTIMATE	=TURNOVER
KATU	239	53	4.5	207	43	4.8	159	27	5.9
KVD0	4	–	–	3	–	–	2	–	–
KOIN	289	96	3.0	226	83	2.7	226	64	3.0
KOAC	6	1	6.0	1	–	–	–	–	–
KGW	260	56	4.6	179	44	4.1	179	33	5.4
KOAP	29	6	4.8	6	1	6.0	6	–	–
KPTV	282	97	2.9	183	36	5.1	146	28	5.2

More Television Analyses

More analyses of audience data for both programming and management purposes are presented in later chapters. The foregoing, however, suggest some directions for the development of additional applications to benefit the professional user of rating reports.

While it is true that more nearly perfect research could be conducted to reflect the audiences for television, it is also true that to date, none has survived long in the marketplace.

CHAPTER 3—NOTES

1. A complete list of Statistical Efficiencies is available in Arbitron, "Research Guidelines for Programming Decision Makers," pamphlet (New York: Arbitron, 1977), p. 47.
2. *Ibid.*
3. For additional information consult "Research Guidelines for Programming Decision Makers," p. 17.
4. Data for this problem come from pages 63, 67 and 71 for the January/February 1978 San Jose Radio Report of Arbitron.

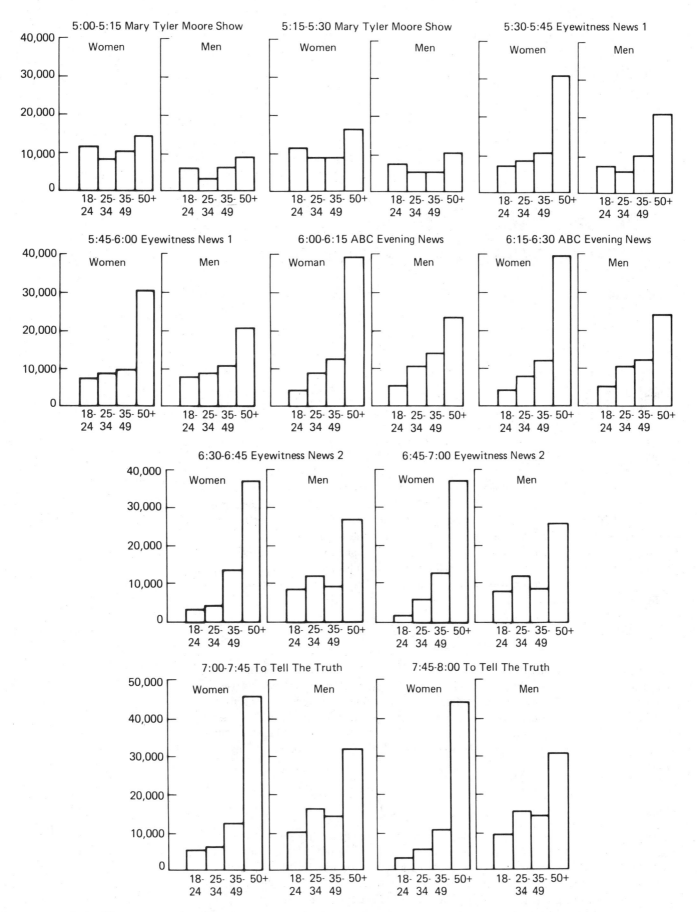

Figure 3-6. Histogram Analysis of TSA Audience Flow, 5:00–7:00 P.M., Monday through Friday, station KATU.

4 Measuring Station Audiences by Telephone

Robert Balon

Among the many unenviable tasks faced by the small market broadcaster are these in particular: (1) Trying to attract local and regional advertisers without the benefit of "numbers" (rating reports) from Arbitron, Media Stat, Birch, and other rating services; (2) basing decisions about programming and personnel on something more scientific than intuition; and (3) ascertaining community needs and wants without credible research tools.

An obvious cure of these ills would be to hire a commercial research service and a programming consultant, but this cure is, for the typical small market broadcaster, prohibitively expensive. This chapter discusses another cure—research plans that can be executed inexpensively and well by station personnel . . . using the TELEPHONE!

The suggestions made in this chapter cannot be adopted haphazardly: if a station elects to conduct these research studies, the procedures must be followed with great care and due attention to quality. Regardless of the size of the market, the requirements of scientific precision are the same.

MEASURING AUDIENCES BY TELEPHONE

The principal reason that a telephone survey is an extremely useful tool for the local broadcaster is that the results may be quantified or put into numerical perspective—statistics, percentages, frequency distributions. Listening and viewing trends in the station ADI or DMA can be measured with an accuracy which will not drive Arbitron or Nielsen from the market but will provide a solid base for local decision-making. And with the assistance of the telephone, the research will be brought in for a *reasonable* amount of money.

USES OF THE SURVEY

The results of a quantitative telephone survey cannot be used as a rating book. There are simply too many differences between the survey which can be mounted by a local station and that of the syndicated rating services. There are a number of uses, however, for which a local survey serves ideally: (1) Building an assessment of station image in the community; (2) better serving the needs of clients and buyers; (3) improving ascertainment procedures; and, probably the critical use, (4) making internal and external programming and promotional decisions based on a sound understanding of the limit of the station audience. If the "do-it-yourself" survey is approached from these perspectives, station management will be pleasantly surprised at the amount of information the survey will yield.

PLANNING THE TELEPHONE SURVEY

Constructing a telephone survey is relatively simple, but the first steps are crucial to the success of the survey.

Defining Problems

Given a limited amount of time in which a respondent can be kept on the phone, the interview must be concise. Accordingly, questions must deal with the problems being addressed by the survey. What is it that the station needs to know? Perhaps some idea of the recognition of local air personalities or the amount of time that people actually spend listening to the station will be important. Or the study may assess the penetration into the marketplace of the station logo. Or the survey may catalog the *reasons* listeners give for tuning to the station. In short, the objectives of the study need to be identified before questions are written. This will save time ... and money. The addition or deletion of each question must be weighed against its ultimate contribution to the study objectives. Will the value of the informaiton gained or lost contribute to the effectiveness and efficiency of the survey?

WHY THE TELEPHONE?

The ultimate justification for the telephone survey is that it can be done quickly and cheaply. Mail surveys are cumbersome, and return rates are rarely above 30 percent. In addition, there are certain losses of control in a mail survey, such as the absence of an opportunity to probe with the respondent answers to key questions—and the critical ability of the interviewer in the phone survey to determine whether the respondent has understood each question and given a relevant and usable response.

For the small market broadcaster in-home surveys are in most cases prohibitively expensive. Shopping mall intercepts (where an interviewer stops a likely respondent who is strolling in the mall), and focus groups (group discussions led by a researcher with likely respondents) are less expensive, but they cannot deliver the amount of high-quality information for the cost of a telephone survey.

In addition to all of the above, the telephone survey can be conducted from the station where management can best supervise the workers involved.

Most broadcasters will find an important benefit from conducting audience measurement surveys is that the same sampling and interviewing experience will be useful in other kinds of research of benefit to the station. Not the least of these is "call-out" research used to evaluate the music programming of the station. More about call-out research will be included later in this chapter and in Chapter 9.

Diaries versus Telephone

Some broadcasters may be misled by arguments they may have heard that the diary method for collecting audience information is superior. The facts are that the telephone survey method is widely used and proven through practice. Research into the issue has shown that there is very little disparity between the results of the telephone recall method and the various diary methods. The reasons are simple enough: (1) Most respondents fill out diaries on a sort of recall basis anyway. Seldom do they log in each night's or each day's listening at the end of the day: in fact, some studies indicate that as many as 75 percent of diary keepers may not fill out diaries on a daily basis. (2) The stations which show up most often in a listener's diary as being listened to over contiguous quarter-hours and in extended cumes agree closely with the respondent's list of favorite stations (a recent CBS study showed that Americans over the age of 18 tend to listen to 2.1 radio stations on a regular basis). As a consequence, when respondents are asked by telephone which two stations they tune to most often, and at what times, acceptable data will generally result. The empirical data supports this statement, but common experience verifies it as well. If a listener is trying to recall a station (whether at the end of a diary-keeping week, such as Wednesday night, or at the end of a short telephone call), it is likely the stations mentioned will be those the listener tunes in most or that are most *familiar*. Hence, if the telephone survey is based upon sound sampling procedures, quarter-hour and cume profiles will not differ markedly from those reported by the syndicated rating services for the same time period.

Nevertheless, the do-it-yourself researcher will not be able to publish telephone survey results in the form of a ratings book, because the information derived from the telephone survey is based upon market percentages culled from relatively broad recall questions. In a rating book like those published by the syndicated services, respondents are assigned weights as described in the preceding chapters, listening data are collected for many more quarter-hours, and procedures which are standard in the ratings business greatly increase the cost of the research.

DRAWING THE SAMPLE

For sake of illustration, imagine a trade area of roughly 100,000 persons. The size of a sample which will give an accurate reflection of station audience will depend upon a number of variables. First, is the station AM or FM? Second, what is its format? These questions are important, because in the sample it is desirable to avoid needless duplication. If the station has an Album Oriented Rock format, there is not much reason to call classical music listeners. If the station is FM, regular AM listeners do not need to be in the sample, and vice versa. In sum, by careful preplanning the survey process can be made more efficient by eliminating from the sample listeners who could not provide usable information.

In the community of 100,000, assume the station in question does have an AOR format and is frequency modulated. The sample does not need to include listeners who never listen to FM. They would not provide information about the sound of an AOR-FM: they are not even likely listeners. Listeners to FM stations with drastically different formats may be eliminated from the sample as well, listeners to classical music, easy listening formats, and so on. In a market of 100,000 this process of eliminating unlikely listeners may reduce the population from which the sample must be drawn to 50,000. This process may not reduce the number of calls which must be made, but it will markedly reduce the number of calls from which survey data must be collected.

QUALIFIERS

Respondents to the telephone survey will be gleaned from the telephone sample by asking a number of *qualifiers*. Qualifiers are questions asked at the beginning of an interview which help to identify the kind of respondent desired for the survey.

Returning to the illustration of the AOR-FM station in the trade area of 100,000, and assuming the market is served by six other stations as well, the interview schedule might include these qualifiers:

"Do you listen to at least 5 hours of radio per week?" This qualifier will eliminate from the survey the casual listener to radio. The casual listener does not, in the typical case, complete Arbitron diaries, and the survey intended to provide important information about the regular audience of an FM station will provide less useful information if the data is diluted by the contributions of the casual listener.

"Do you own an FM radio?" A good question, since it will save the interviewer from interviewing a respondent who could not possibly be in the AOR-FM audience.

"What is your favorite radio station in this area? What is your second favorite?" The responses to these qualifiers identify a radio listener who prefers a station which provides competition for your format or does not. For example, if the respondent indicates a strong preference for classical music stations, it is unlikely that he or she can provide information as to how to improve an AOR format. Getting information about the audiences of quite different formats, on the other hand, may provide good suggestions as to promising directions for change away from an AOR format if audience and business performance of the AOR station are unsatisfactory.

"How old are you?" This qualifier may also be useful in screening respondents who are not potential audience for the station. How important would the views of a 65-year-old who prefers listening to a news-talk station, prove in streamlining the format of an AOR-FM? It is also possible that the views of very young children would be of little interest to the survey.

Depending on the objectives of the survey, qualifiers may screen respondents on the basis of race, income, and lifestyle habits, but in smaller markets the qualifiers enumerated above will usually meet the requirements of audience assessment. Adding additional qualifiers in the small market may reduce the number of potential respondents to an unmanageably low level.

GETTING THE NUMBERS

Once decisions have been made as to the nature of the respondent desired for the survey, the process of drawing a sample of names and telephone numbers can be begun. In the market of 100,000 used here for illustration, the number of calls considered adequate to reflect the population would be about 380. However, the use of the qualifiers given in the preceding section would reduce the population of interest to only a part of the 100,000 total persons in the market. These qualifiers may describe only a part of the 100,000—perhaps 40,000 persons. If so, then a sample of about 150 completed calls could be considered adequate. Note that the use of qualifiers *saves time and money* by eliminating from the study population persons who do not have valuable information to contribute to the research.

In drawing the sample it will be essential that the sampling process be *random*. Otherwise, it will not be possible to generalize from the sample to the state of affairs in the population. It is possible to accumulate valuable information from conversations with friends, calls, and letters from listeners, comments from colleagues, but projecting numbers of listeners in the general population from this sort of information is simply not defensible. A truly random sample will be one in which each and every member of the population has an equal chance of being selected into the sample, and one in which each selection into the sample is made independently of each other selection.

If the random sample is to be drawn from a telephone directory, several facts need to be ascertained in advance: (1) Are there a large number of unlisted telephones in this community? (2) Are there a large number of households without telephones? If it is the case that the proportion of unlisted telephones is small, and the proportion of nontelephone households approaches zero, then the telephone directory will be a good sampling frame.

To insure randomness in the telephone directory sample, selection must rely upon a Table of Random Numbers like that at Table VI, Appendix D. This table and others like it are generated by a computer to eliminate the patterns of repetition in numbers which result when humans select lists of numbers by other procedures. The computer has produced a table in which each number appears with equal frequency and in which the order of numbers is unpredictable. A section of a table of random numbers appears below.

```
40483   12421   10628   51986
34003   90761   33548   14434
17895   04719   67270   61091
97391   31075   09927   79886
97242   42516   79920   96874

87498   75184   93324   83742
42017   53941   45493   87490
55018   42530   60014   77317
73389   40000   79501   17004
48565   86597   82499   15622

67283   64529   81628   09005
12436   31799   78872   87040
00399   34335   02424   05521
03249   36807   91600   18342
58044   36328   95545   46362
```

an arbitrarily selected starting point

In drawing a random sample from a telephone directory the table of random numbers will be used to select the column of the page in which the selected listing will be found, the number of centimeters down the column to the centimeter in which the selected listing will be found. In the case of the illustration for the survey for an **AOR-FM** station in the trade area of 100,000, the researcher may feel confident that if 1000 telephone listings are drawn from the directory, it will be possible to complete 150 calls from the listings drawn.

The directory from which the sample is to be drawn shows residential listings between pages 13 and 214. Each page consists of three columns, and the length of a full column is 28 centimeters. It is apparent that, if five residential listings are drawn from each page containing residential listings, the sample will consist of 1005 listings. The table of random numbers will supply the column number (1, 2 or 3) and the number of centimeters down for each listing.

```
40483   12421   10628   51986        40483   12421   10628   51986
34003   90761   33548   14434        34003   90761   38548   14434
17895   04719   67270   61091        17895   04719   67270   61091
97391   31075   09927   79886        97391   31075   09927   79886
97242   42516   79920   96874        97242   42516   79920   96874

87498   75184   93324   83742        87498   75184   93324   83742
42017   53941   45493   87490        42017   53941   45493   87490
55018   42530   60014   77317        55018   42530   60014   77317
73389   40000   79501   17004        73389   40000   79501   17004
48565   86597   82499   15622        48565   86597   82499   15622

67283   64529   81628   09005        67283   64529   81628   09005
12436   31799   78872   87040        12436   31799   78872   87040
00399   34335   02424   05521        00399   34335   02424   05521
03249   36807   91600   18342        03249   36807   91600   18342
58044   36328   95545   46362        58044   36323   95545   46362
```

Page Number	Column	Centimeters Down	Name	Telephone Number
13	3	17	WM ADAMS	343-1212
13	2	12	JOE ACRES	333-8997
13	1	3	JOYCE AARON	352-1251
13	1	1	ALAN AARON	533-1522
13	3	1	DAN ADAMS	322-5566
14	3	28	ASA ALLEN	888-8888
14	2	24	JILL AEWON	777-9322

The portion of sample worksheet above shows the use of a table of random numbers in drawing a telephone directory sample. In the "page number" column each page of residential listings will appear on five lines, since a decision was earlier made to draw five numbers from each page. The column numbers for those pages are drawn this way: from an arbitrary start point proceed down a single column of digits extracting in order each 3, 2, or 1 and entering it in the column labeled "column" on the sample worksheet. Continue this process until a column has been drawn for each desired listing in the sample.

To draw "Centimeters Down," the location in the directory column for the listings to become part of the sample, pick an arbitrary start point for two digit numbers, two adjacent vertical columns. Continue down these adjacent columns recording on the sample worksheet all two-digit numbers up to 28, until a "Centimeters Down" has been drawn for each listing needed in the sample.

At this point with the first three columns of the worksheet complete, the researcher has the necessary instructions as to the location in the telephone directory of each listing to be part of the sample. For instance, the first entry of the worksheet says to turn to page 13 of the directory, to the third column, and to the listing that appears 17 centimeters from the top of the column. In this directory the name of William Adams, whose telephone number is 343-1212, appears at this location.

COMMUNITIES WITH MANY UNLISTED RESIDENTIAL TELEPHONES

If the community being surveyed is characterized by as much as 30 percent unlisted telephones—and this is not unusual—some additional steps are taken in drawing a telephone sample. Ignoring unlisted telephone residences in the survey runs the risk of producing misleading survey results.

One common way of proceeding is random telephone number generation. First examine the telephone directory noting the three-digit prefixes which identify residential listings in the community. Combine each prefix with a four-digit suffix drawn from four adjacent columns in the table of random numbers. An illustration is provided below. Unfortunately this system will generate a substantial number of unconnected numbers, but it will allow the survey to reach unlisted and recently connected households, some of which may contain heavy media consumers.

It is important to emphasize that once the random procedure has been established for

40483	12421	10628	51986
34003	90761	33548	14434
17895	04719	67270	61091
97391	31075	09927	79886
97242	42516	79920	96874
87498	75184	93324	83742
42017	53941	45493	87490
55018	42530	60014	77317
73389	40000	79501	17004
48565	86597	82499	15622
67283	64529	81628	09005
12436	31799	78872	87040
00399	34335	02424	05521
03249	36807	91600	18342
58044	36328	95545	46362

starting point (pointing to 90761)

Telephone Numbers for Random Number Generation Sample

343-	333-	352-	533-	888-	777-
0761	0761	0761	0761	0761	0761
4719	4719	4719	4719	4719	4719
1075	1075	1075	1075	1075	1075
2516	2516	2516	2516	2516	2516
5134	5134	5134	5134	5134	5134

a survey sample, it must be used throughout the sample selection process. If the sample is *not random*, it is *not generalizable*.

INTERVIEWERS

In telephone survey research, the telephone interviewers must immediately establish with respondents that they are not solicitors. Otherwise, the duration and nature of the co-operation of the respondent will be limited. Investing some time and money in training interviewers will be well worth the investment. In general, it is not a good idea to use personnel of the station as telephone interviewers in audience measurement, since it will be difficult if not impossible for them to avoid influencing the information provided by respondents.

Female teen-agers seem to make excellent interviewers, as do older women. Check the employment rosters of any large surveying organization; both groups are well represented.

Running a newspaper ad to recruit telephone interviewers is often successful in producing a pool of talented interviewers who, with adequate training, will produce excellent data.

The object in conducting a telephone interview is to make the respondent comfortable and, at the same time, to extract *valid* information. Not every person has equal ability at interviewing. Callers must be cordial, attentive, sincere, and *patient*. A telephone interview represents an intrusion upon both the time and privacy of the respondent, and, as might be expected under these circumstances, some respondents upon learning the purpose of the call, will immediately hang up the phone. Nevertheless, if interviewers are well-trained, and the interview schedule has been well-written, the refusal rate will be relatively low. People are interested in media. They are more likely to respond to questions about media than to questions on other topics. To reiterate: the interviewer must not sound as though she is selling something. The questions should be read casually, not as though a "pitch" may follow. The respondent must be given plenty of time to talk. The typical respondent does not spend much time on any day actively thinking about radio. As a consequence, the respondent may have to "shift gears" mentally to respond to a question that would be entirely clear to a broadcaster.

Telephone interviewers should work under supervision. They should be informed that the interviews they report will be *validated*. To validate a telephone interview a second worker calls several of the numbers for which interviews were reported to affirm that the interviews actually did take place as reported. The practice of validation prevents interviewers from turning in data from an imaginary respondent when, in fact, no telephone interview was completed.

When to Call

Calls should be made from 9:00 A.M. to 9:00 P.M. All telephone interviewers should keep a log sheet which lists the number attempted, whether or not the call was received, and the outcome of the call. A log sheet might look like this:

Name of Interviewer _Mary Otis_

Number Called	Time of Call	Completion of call	Response	Outcome	
551-3426	8:24 pm	8:28 pm	CI	CI	CI = completed interview
551-3376	8:29 pm	—	NA	X	NA = not applicable
551-8943	8:30 pm	—	Busy	CB	CB = Callback
557-4732	8:31 pm	—	Refused	X	X = No callback needed
551-4732					
552-9108					

The call placed at 8:29 P.M. was made to a respondent who did not qualify on the basis of screening questions, hence the notation, NA, and X indicating no callback is needed.

Other columns can be added to the log sheet, perhaps a column for each demographic variable important in the study. But most surveys in small markets will need a log sheet no more involved than that above.

Whenever a busy signal is reached, or whenever there is no answer to a ring, three attempts are made to reach the number involved. This will increase the proportion of the numbers in the sample from which usable data can be collected.

COSTS

If the average interview lasts 7 minutes, a single telephone interviewer will be able to complete roughly three interviews per hour. Since there will be respondents who do not answer the qualifiers in the desired way, there may be many completed calls which do not result in completed interviews. If the objective of the survey is to reach 200 respondents, total interviewing time will be from 65 to 75 hours. Assuming all calls are local, the budget for such a survey will run about $400, based on an hourly rate of $4 per interviewer. An additional $100 should be allowed for training of interviewers and validation.

CONSTRUCTION OF THE INTERVIEW SCHEDULE

As noted earlier, the first step in questionnaire design is to define the problem areas for the survey. Then completing a schedule of questions will involve writing questions that produce intelligible responses, can be administered over the telephone, and that optimize useful information.

Validity

Questions asked over the telephone frequently suffer from validity, or lack thereof. If the question is valid, it measures precisely what it is intended to measure. A question lacking in validity produces ambiguous or misleading responses. For example,

> **Question:** *"What do you think is wrong with the programming at KROB?"*
>
> > **Problem**: the question suggests that something *is* wrong.
> >
> > **Solution:** "In general, what do you think of KROB's programming?" Follow-up: "If you were responsible for the programming of KROB (or responsible for the sound of KROB), would you make any changes?"

Write questions that are direct and to the point; avoid excessive verbiage. The simpler the question, the more likely that the respondent will provide a usable answer.

Aided Versus Unaided Recall

The Pulse audience studies used a system known as *roster recall* in which the interviewer would read a list of programs to the respondent and jot down the answers provided. This technique in general is known as *aided recall*. For example, the interviewer might say, "I'm going to read to you the names of stations in your town. Please tell me which ones you listen to on a regular basis." Of course, the wording of this instruction may cause the respondent to name more than one station, even if listening to only one. (The power of suggestion is real, if the interviewer is providing a long list of stations.) On the other hand, there are virtues to the aided recall technique. For example, "I'm going to read you the names of several disc jockeys in the area. Please tell me how well you like each one, if you recognize the name." This sort of question would be virtually impossible for the average listener without some help in jogging memory. If the question had been, "Please tell me the names of your favorite disc jockeys," it would be unusual for a respondent to be able to name more than one or two, depending upon the age of the respondent (presumably young listeners will be more ardent fans, while older listeners will recall old timers well.) If the objective of the survey were to determine the relative popularity of contemporary air personalities, aided recall would be the technique of choice.

Unaided recall places a greater demand on the respondent: "What is your favorite station in Xville?" When the objective of the study is to assess station preference, unaided recall is a good choice, because unaided recall is the same task expected of a respondent who completes a listening diary for a commercial rating service. Hence the unaided recall question will provide an answer comparable to that obtained from a diary survey. And likely sponsors will not miss the similarity.

The balance of the telephone questionnaire or interview schedule could be a combination of aided and unaided recall items. Again reflect the problem areas which the survey is meant to illuminate. Unaided recall items may deal with reasons for listening, station, and format preferences, reasons for tuning out, and general evaluations of programming. Aided recall questions could deal with air personalities, sports, news, weather, and call-letter recognition.

Order of Questions

Once the interview schedule has included the qualifiers, the order of the remaining questions is of great importance. Establish early the time spent listening, favorite musical forms, favorite artists, listening habits, and so on. These are all known as listening "content" questions. "Context" questions should follow. These ascertain the reasons that listening takes place. Finally demographic questions, if time permits, should fill out the questionnaire. Demographics are population characteristics such as age, sex, income, education level, mobility, occupation, marital status, and lifestyle habits. Grouping demographic questions at the end of the interview is preferred to dispersing them throughout. Many respondents will take exception to being asked personal questions—which they interpret the demographic items to be. As a consequence, if the demographic items are dispersed through the questionnaire, the offended respondent may terminate before providing the necessary information about radio listening. Better cooperation with demographic items is possible when the interviewer explains to the respondent that these questions need to be asked to insure that the survey includes a representative sample of the people of the community.

Begin the interview schedule with a salutation—short and to the point. "Hi, my name is ____, and I'm taking a survey on radio listening here in Xville. May I ask you a few quick questions?" If the respondent presses for additional information, explain further, but try to be brief.

Open-ended Questions

An open-ended question is one in which there is no list of set responses for the interviewer to read to the respondent. Example: "What causes you to tune out a particular radio station?" The key to properly asking an open-ended question is to recognize that *probing* by the interviewer may be necessary. Successful probing related to the question above might yield this scenario:

Answer: Well, I'm not sure what you mean?

Question: Well, when you punch out the radio station, either at home or in the car, is there a particular reason?

Answer: Oh, like when I come to a song I don't like?

Question: Yes, that's correct.

Answer: Well, sometimes it'll be a song that I dislike. In fact . . . yeah, that almost always the reason. Yes, it's songs that I don't like.

The key to this scenario was the interviewer's second attempt to phrase the question which helped to clarify it for the respondent. Another example of probing:

Question: Why do you listen to radio?

Answer: Wow! That's a toughie. I guess the music.

Question: Well, what is it about the music that you like?

Answer: Oh, I don't know. I just like it.

Question: Could you try and nail that down for me a bit more?

Answer: Well, I like disco tunes. They get me going in the morning and get me to the office feeling pretty good.

Again, if the interviewer had given up after the first or second response, the respondent would have provided very little information. But proper probing, *without leading the respondent*, can make a great difference with open-ended questions.

As a rule of thumb, about 1½ minutes ought to be allowed for each open-ended question. This is to allow time for probing. For the AOR-FM station in our illustration the finished questionnaire or interview schedule might look like the one in Figure 4–1.

GETTING THE DATA INTO A COMPUTER

The questionnaire or interview schedule at Figure 4–1 is only one of many possibilities that might have been used in this survey. But this questionnaire will do to illustrate the ease with which the resulting data can be analyzed by computer.

Codes

For each question, develop a code. For favorite radio station, for example, give each response a numerical designator:

1 = the ABC affiliate
2 = the NBC affiliate
3 = AOR-FM
4 = country and western FM
5 = clear channel AM in nearby market
6 = public radio FM at nearby college
7 = local FM rocker in adjacent market
8 = local AM all-news in adjacent market
9 = local MBS affiliate in adjacent market
0 = other

As the coder reviews each set of responses the appropriate code is entered in the blank labeled (1). The same coding process is repeated for each response on each questionnaire.

Open-ended questions require a more involved coding process, since the variety of responses is at the greatest for this sort of item. A common way of dealing with an open-

Salutation: Hi. My name is_____and I'm taking a survey on radio listening habits. Do you mind if I ask you a few quick questions?

(ALL ITEMS IN PARENTHESES ARE INSTRUCTIONS TO INTERVIEWERS.)

(QUALIFIERS)

1. Do you spend at least 5 hours per week listening to the radio?
   (IF NOT, TERMINATE.)

2. Are you between the ages of 18 and 40? (IF NOT, TERMINATE.)

3. What is your favorite radio station here in town?
   The one you listen to most often?   (1) _____

4. Do you have a second favorite station?   (2) _____

5. Why do you listen to the radio?   (3) _____

6. What's your favorite kind of music?   (4) _____

7. I'm going to read you some various times during the day. After each time,
   would you please tell me whether you (1) don't usually listen, (2) listen for
   less than an hour, (3) listen from one to two hours, (4) listen more than 2
   hours. (REPEAT IF NECESSARY.)

      1. How about from 6 to 10 A.M.?   (5) _____
      2. And what about from 10 A.M. to 3 P.M.?   (6) _____
      3. What about from 3 to 7 P.M.?   (7) _____
      4. And finally, how about 7 to midnight?   (8) _____

8. Where are you most often when listening to the radio?   (9) _____

9. Would you say the amount of music being played on the air today is just
   about right, too little, or too much?   (10) _____

10. If you received conflicting or different reports of the same news story from
    radio, television, the magazines and newspaper, which of the four versions
    would you be most inclined to believe?   (11) _____

11. Do you agree or disagree that having commercials on radio, is a fair price
    to pay for being able to listen to it?   (12) _____

12. So that we can be sure that we're drawing a true cross-section of the
    community, I'd like to ask a few more questions. What is your
    occupation?   (13) _____

    (CARRY AGE OVER FROM Q. (2) And exactly how old are you? (14) _____

    Sex (DON'T ASK.) 1. male   2. female   (15) _____

Thank you very much for helping us.

Figure 4-1. Example of Telephone Questionnaire or Interview Schedule.

ended question is to draw 20 questionnaires at random from the set resulting from the survey. Each response to the open-ended question is listed. Then by inspection these responses are grouped into categories and a numerical designator assigned. The result is a code like that above. As the questionnaires are then coded, responses which do not fit the coding scheme for the 20 selected respondents are noted, and additional categories with designators are created as necessary. Consider, for example, these responses to Question 5 from the interview schedule at Figure 4-1, "Why do you listen to the radio?" from 20 randomly selected, completed questionnaires:

a. Well, I like to know what's going on in town.
b. The music helps me wake up in the morning.
c. Well, you know those guys on the radio are crazy!
d. It keeps me company now that my dog has died.
e. Oh, I just hum along with my favorite tunes.
f. I listen for the weather report, so I know what kind of coat to wear that day.
g. I just like the music, I guess.
h. I work in a dentist's office, and I play it in the waiting room to relax the patients.
i. It gives me a kind of background while I'm doing my college homework.
j. I want to know what the hits are.
k. I listen for the snow reports, so I know where to ski the next weekend.
l. I play it when being alone gets to me.
m. If I didn't listen for the news and sports and things, I wouldn't know what people were talking about.
n. There's this disc jockey named . . . named DJ Don. He just cracks me up!
o. Well, for one thing I like to hear Paul Harvey.
p. Those country singers get to me right where I'm at.
q. I need sound around me.
r. I'd feel out of touch with the community if I didn't listen.
s. The moods on albums are just right for me in the evenings.
t. I just gotta get the latest game scores.

These responses could be grouped in a number of different ways depending on the objectives of the study. In this case, the useful information from this item is a set of priorities from the listeners as to the program content which most closely defines their attachment to radio listening. The code therefore is in terms of program content listed as a reason for listening. The code might be:

1 = news (items a, m, r, t)
2 = weather (items f, k)
3 = syndicated features (item o)
4 = personalities (items c, n)
5 = latest music (item j)
6 = favorite music (items b, e, g, p, s)
7 = background music (items d, h, i, l, q)
8 = for categories yet to be identified
9 = for categories yet to be identified
0 = other.

After the response to each question from each respondent has been coded, the data are ready to be processed for the computer at a nearby college or university or computer service center.

SPSS

SPSS stands for Statistical Package for the Social Sciences and is the best known and simplest set of computer programs available for processing data from broadcast research.

It is accessible with only a few simple commands and provides a means for reducing data to conclusions that is much cheaper than the same processing by hand.

Accessing the Computer. SPSS runs by a system of coded English-language commands, each punched into a standard machine card. The first set of cards are JOB CARDS which identify the user to the computer: the format of these cards is provided by the computer service where the work is being done. The CONTROL CARDS are the commands which describe to the computer the data to be analyzed and the analysis that is desired. Finally there are the data cards, one or more for each respondent containing the codes corresponding to the answers given.

The basic data card can be punched by the computer center, or a knowledgeable station employee can punch them. Each vertical column of the 80-column standard machine card can contain an item of information. For the survey utilizing the interview schedule at Figure 4-1 the card might contain the information below.

CARD COLUMN	DATUM FROM THE INTERVIEW TO BE PUNCHED HERE
1-3	Respondent Number. Each questionnaire is numbered for control purposes, and this three-digit number is punched here.
4	Blank
5	Code from blank (1)
6	Blank
7	Code from blank (2)
8	Blank
9	Code from blank (3)
10	Blank
11	Code from blank (4)
12	Blank
13	Code from blank (5)
14	Blank
15	Code from blank (6)
16	Blank
17	Code form blank (7)
18	Blank
19	Code from blank (8)
20	Blank
21	Code from blank (9)
22	Blank
23	Code from blank (10)
24	Blank
25	Code from blank (11)
26	Blank
27	Code from blank (12)
28	Blank
29	Code from blank (13)
30	Blank
31-32	Code from blank (14)
33	Blank
34	Code from blank (15)

One card will be required for each respondent. If there are 200 respondents, there should be 200 data cards.

The control cards for SPSS tell the computer to perform analyses on the responses to the 15 questions that would be difficult and very costly otherwise. For the analysis of the data from the survey used as an illustration here the following SPSS control cards would be included in the deck of machine cards going into the computer:

CARD #	CARD COLUMN 1–15	CARD COLUMN 16–80
1	RUN NAME	MY RADIO SURVEY
2,3	VARIABLE LIST	FAVRADA, FAVRADB, WHYLIS, FAVMUS, LISAM, LISMID,LISPM,LISEVE,WHERELI/S,MUSICTDY, CREDIBLE,COMMERCE,OCCUPA,AGE,SEX
		(Note that this is actually two cards; when all when all 80 columns of card #2 are full, card #3 continues beginning with column 16.)
4	N OF CASES	200
5	INPUT MEDIUM	CARD
6,7	INPUT FORMAT	FIXED (F3.0, 1x, F1.0, 1x, F1.0, 1x F1.0, 1x, F1.0, 1x, F1.0, 1x, F1.0, 1x, F1.0, 1x, F1.0, 1x, F1.0, 1x,F1.0, 1x,F1.0, 1x,F1.0, 1x,F2.0, 1x,F1.0)
		(Note that this card continues on to column 16 of card #7. The code in this card says that the input is fixed in that the same variable appears in the same column throughout the set. F3.0 tells the computer that the field it will encounter in the data card is three digits wide with no decimal point. F1.0 describes a one-digit field with no decimal point. 1x tells the computer to ignore a blank column between fields. Most of the problems with SPSS are in this card. Get help from the computer service being used for the analysis.)
8–22	VARIABLE LABELS	FAVRADA, First Favorite Radio Station/
		FAVRADB, 2d Favorite Radio Station/
		WHYLIS, Why Listen to Radio/
		(Continue in this fashion with a card for each variable label.)
23–55	VALUE LABELS	FAVRADA(1)CABC-FM, (2)CABC-AM, (3)CDEF-AM, (4)CDEF-FM,(5)CGHI,(6)CJKL,(7)CMNO/
		(Value label cards tell the computer how to interpret the codes that have been assigned to each variable.)

The next cards tell the computer what statistical products are desired and how the data is to appear in the finished printout.

Crosstabulations. A crosstabulation takes the information from one question and sorts the responses to other questions according to it. For example, crosstabulation might sort the responses to "What is your favorite radio station?" by the responses to "Where are you most often when listening to the radio?" See Figure 4-2 for such a crosstabulation.

Consider CABC-FM in Figure 4-2, and the first column of the table. The figures in the box in that column for the CABC-FM row show that 16 members of the sample listen to the station when they are at home. This represents 57.1 percent of those who listed the station as their first favorite. Of all those who listen at home, CABC-FM is the favorite

```
*  *  *  *  *  *  *  *  *  *  *  *  *  *   C R O S S T A B U L A T I O N   O F * * *
FAVRAD FIRST FAVORITE RADIO STATION                       BY WHERELIS  WHERE LIS
*  *  *  *  *  *  *  *  *  *  *  *  *  *  *  *  *  *  *  *  *  *  *  *  *  *  *  *  *  *
                     WHERELIS
           COUNT I
           ROW PCT IHOME      WORK       CAR       EQUAL       ROW
           COL PCT I                                          TOTAL
           TOT PCT I    1.I      2.I       3.I       4.I
FAVRAD     --------I--------I--------I--------I--------I
              -0  I      1 I      0 I      0 I      0 I        1
                  I  100.0 I      0 I      0 I      0 I       .2
                  I     .3 I      0 I      0 I      0 I
                  I     .2 I      0 I      0 I      0 I
              -I--------I--------I--------I--------I
            1.  I     16 I      5 I      5 I      2 I       28
KOKE FM         I   57.1 I   17.9 I   17.9 I    7.1 I      5.3
                I    4.9 I   11.4 I    4.3 I    4.4 I
                I    3.0 I     .9 I     .9 I     .4 I
              -I--------I--------I--------I--------I
            2.  I      5 I      0 I      7 I      3 I       15
KOKE AM         I   33.3 I      0 I   46.7 I   20.0 I      2.8
                I    1.5 I      0 I    6.0 I    6.7 I
                I     .9 I      0 I    1.3 I     .6 I
              -I--------I--------I--------I--------I
            3.  I     32 I      4 I     12 I      3 I       51
KLBJ AM         I   62.7 I    7.8 I   23.5 I    5.9 I      9.6
                I    9.8 I    9.1 I   10.3 I    6.7 I
                I    6.0 I     .8 I    2.3 I     .6 I
              -I--------I--------I--------I--------I
            4.  I     55 I      2 I     15 I      6 I       78
KLBJ FM         I   70.5 I    2.6 I   19.2 I    7.7 I     14.6
                I   16.8 I    4.5 I   12.8 I   13.3 I
                I   10.3 I     .4 I    2.8 I    1.1 I
              -I--------I--------I--------I--------I
            5.  I     39 I      0 I     11 I      4 I       54
KNOW            I   72.2 I      0 I   20.4 I    7.4 I     10.1
                I   11.9 I      0 I    9.4 I    8.9 I
                I    7.3 I      0 I    2.1 I     .8 I
              -I--------I--------I--------I--------I
            6.  I     17 I      5 I      8 I      4 I       34
KCSW            I   50.0 I   14.7 I   23.5 I   11.8 I      6.4
                I    5.2 I   11.4 I    6.8 I    8.9 I
                I    3.2 I     .9 I    1.5 I     .8 I
              -I--------I--------I--------I--------I
            7.  I     32 I     13 I     19 I     10 I       74
KVET            I   43.2 I   17.6 I   25.7 I   13.5 I     13.9
                I    9.8 I   29.5 I   16.2 I   22.2 I
                I    6.0 I    2.4 I    3.6 I    1.9 I
              -I--------I--------I--------I--------I
       COLUMN      327        44       117        45       533
       TOTAL      61.4       8.3      22.0       8.4     100.0
```

Figure 4-2. Crosstabulation from SPSS Printout of Listener Survey.

of 4.9 percent. And of all those who participated in the survey 3 percent reported listening at home when they also listed KOKE-FM as their first favorite station.

Considering all stations, it is apparent that station CJKL has the greatest proportion of home listeners who list the station as their first favorite—72.2 percent. To summarize, the first figure in the block is row frequency; the second is row percentage; the third is column percentage; and the fourth is total percentage. Some researchers will want to add an OPTIONS card to the processing deck containing a 4,5. For this card the word OPTIONS appears in columns 1-7, while the symbols, "4,5" appear in columns 16-18. This card in the deck will cause the computer to delete from the printout all column percentages and total percentages. The result may be a somewhat easier to read report.

If a university is not nearby, computers are available from other organizations. Banks and other large businesses have data processing units. To use one of these computers the software of SPSS must also be acquired, since this is not a package typically available in a business. If at all available, a university computing center will be the easiest to use of most available computing facilities.

UNDERSTANDING RESEARCH QUESTIONS

Consider the example questionnaire again. When these data have been collected, what will they mean?

From the point of view of the Album Oriented Rock FM station, what would the significance be of finding the station to be number two among the stations listed by the survey respondents? This is the sort of result that must be expected when the respondents have been rather strictly qualified: the survey has not included a sample of the entire market. As a consequence, it is improper to generalize the results to more of the market than those who fit the qualifiers. On the other hand, those who fit the qualifiers are *potential* listeners to the station, and that is the key for program decision-making.

Suppose that the survey reveals that the favorite type of music among FM respondents is softer rock, particularly among those FM listeners in the 25–29 age group, followed by current hits and especially album cuts. Such a finding is of great importance to the station. It suggests to the program director that the playlist needs to be a little broader to include some current releases and some of the "mellower" rock artists, such as Steven Bishop, Robert Palmer, Ricki Lee Jones, Joni Mitchell and others. Such a change will not alienate current listeners but is likely to attract new listeners from the FM audience.

Further suppose that the station is listened to most frequently during drive times. Such a finding suggests that it is morning and afternoon drive times that need to be broadened and mellowed. This is a practice known as *dayparting*. Other dayparts (other than drive times) can include more album cuts, but the largest audience which seems to be available and which prefers greater variety is concentrated in drive time.

What if the survey indicates the station is perceived by the audience as carrying too many commercials and *not enough music*? Recall that this finding reflects only an audience perception. For financial reasons the station may not be in a position to carry fewer commercials, but it may be possible to alter the listener's perception of the commercial load. Perhaps the current practice is twelve commercial minutes per hour organized into nine breaks. Another way to distribute the same commercial load might be to program six stop sets or breaks. Even though the commercial load remains the same, the listener will perceive that he or she is getting more music and fewer commercials, provided the fewer stop sets are well executed.

The survey may also show that the current audience of the station is predominantly young, 18–24. The majority are students and female. This audience composition may mean that the station is seen as the "hip" station in the market and that it appeals primarily to the college students in the market. Such a perception could include the station in the "acid rock," "new wave," or progressive class of stations, which may alienate it from many older adult listeners. Can a station afford to have a narrowly defined audience in a medium-to-small trade area? Usually not: The station may wish to gradually move the format to increase the number of males in the audience and the number of non-students.

Increasing the number of hits and mellower sound may accomplish these ends, for they do in many markets. A careful reading of the trade weeklies will indicate what music items are hot with the demographic groups that are desired as a part of the station audience.

ARE SUCH SURVEY RESULTS SALEABLE?

After thoroughly understanding and using the survey results within the station, the next obvious step is to use the findings externally. This is entirely justifiable. The survey has been conducted in a conservative and scientifically respectable way: the results are generalizable to specified parts of the market. The station would be correct in drawing up a brochure pointing to the characteristics of its audience in relation to the rest of the FM audience. The brochure may meet with skepticism from some corners, because the research has not been done by an "objective" party. But the fact that the research has revealed a portrait of the total market and not an overblown "snapshot" of only one station will ultimately convince the skeptics.

Do not expect that this research will generate huge sums of additional revenue. The survey was undertaken to gain information for programming and internal decision-making. Local sales increases will follow from successful changes made in programming and the station's effort to make the business community aware of the changes.

USING THE TELEPHONE FOR PLAYLIST DEVELOPMENT

To this point the chapter has described a fairly complex market survey, what the industry calls a "one-shot." It would be a pity to ignore the possibilities for using the same system for other purposes. A potentially profitable use is playlist evaluation and development. This kind of research is commonly known as "callout" research. Callout music research is described in some detail in Chapter 9. But some suggestions are offered here as well.

The simplest callout research involves a telephone interview of respondents in which the name of the artist and the name of the records in heaviest rotation on the station are mentioned by the interviewer. The respondent is then asked to report how much he or she likes that recording. The response sought may be yes/no (some programmers prefer this) or it may consist of a scale like:

> 1 = like it very much
> 2 = like it OK
> 3 = no opinion or not sure
> 4 = don't really care for it
> 5 = absolutely hate it
> 6 = like it but tired of hearing it
> 7 = never heard of it at all

When the data from this sort of callout survey is analyzed, it is reported by age group categories. Suppose the station playlist includes "Enough Is Enough" by Barbra Streisand. Research after the first week shows the song averaging 1.5 for men and 2.7 for women. The station decides as a result to use the song in a slightly heavier rotation when men are listening. The song is monitored week by week. When the song slips into the 6.1 category, the record is made a recurrent. Should it go into the 4.5 category it would be removed from the playlist entirely. If the song is going to be disliked, scores of 4.5 will appear very soon after it has been added to the playlist. The usual pattern is for a recording to start off strongly and then later begin to slide into the 6 category. The key to exploiting callout research will be to change the playlist when recordings begin to "burn out."

A frequently encountered problem in callout research occurs when the interview schedule employs aided recall (providing the title of the song and the name of the artist). This *is* the "halo effect." This happens when the name of the artist alone is so well liked that to hear it makes the listener like the recording even before being exposed to it. A way to avoid the halo effect is to include a "placebo" in the interview schedule. Mention an artist followed by an imaginary song title. Should the respondent indicate a strong like for this song that has not been written or recorded, halo effect is occurring, and the respondent's data should be examined very critically.

When the objective of the research is to evaluate a recording that has not yet been released, about 15 seconds of the recording is recorded and played on the telephone for the respondent. Using this system permits study of only a small number of recordings in a single survey, but the number of new recordings which a station would consider adding to the playlist in any week is relatively small.

Sampling is a problem in callout research as it is in all survey research. On the whole, it is better not to rely upon listening panels. Some broadcasters build panels of about 150 respondents who are called weekly for their opinions of music. The panel method does save time and effort, but it runs the risk of the respondent being influenced one week by a response given one or two weeks earlier, badly biasing the survey results. The panel method can be improved somewhat by using a number of panels, each of which is contacted no more than once per month.

Callout research in the radio business is here to stay. When data is collected week after week track records of certain artists and recordings can become important considerations in developing a sound and profitable station playlist.

5 Stratified Samples, Cluster Samples, and Face-to-Face Interviewing

Alan M. Rubin

It has been assumed, as stated in the introduction to this volume, that the reader has a basic knowledge of statistics, including the characteristics of random samples. The preceding chapters have presented the practices of the principal commercial rating services. The reader who needs to review the random sample as a concept is referred to Lesson Six of the Self-Study Course at Appendix C.

This chapter deals with two variations on a simple random sample—the stratified sample and the cluster or area sample. In addition, the chapter includes information on face-to-face interviewing, a data collection method useful regardless of sample design.

THE SIMPLE RANDOM SAMPLE—VIRTUES AND LIMITATIONS

As with all tools, sampling design must be appropriate to the research task. A carpenter would not use a spirit level to hammer a nail or a monkey wrench to turn a screw. And the researcher in broadcasting would not elect to use a simple random sample when another sampling design will better serve the problem being studied. *Simple random sampling* is the basic form of probability sampling. In a simple random sample every member of the population (for example, the local county or households within the coverage area) has an equal opportunity of being selected, or at least a known probability for inclusion in the probability sample. If there are 10,000 households in the market, and a simple random sample of 400 households is drawn, each household has a known probability of one chance in 10,000 of being selected in the sample, assuming that all selections to the sample are made independently. With a properly selected random sample, an investigator is able to generalize from just a few carefully chosen individuals to the entire population. Based upon the simple random sample of 400 households, the broadcast researcher could generalize about the listening habits of the entire broadcast market of 10,000 households. From a sample of a few hundred radio listeners or television viewers, it is possible to conclude that, within specified limits, the broadcast market as a whole would be better served by more frequent or more in-depth local newscasts. The advantage of a sample chosen by random procedures is that it stands the greatest chance of resembling the population from which it is drawn.

But simple random sampling is often a time-consuming and costly procedure. Also, simple random sampling may not provide the answers sought in an equitable fashion. It may not provide specific answers to the programming needs and wants of various community groups. For example, simple random sampling procedures may produce a sample which is 88 percent white and 12 percent black. While this sample composition may be similar to the racial composition of the broadcast market, it may not serve survey objectives. The researcher may be interested in specifically comparing the programming wants and needs of black listeners with those of white listeners. In this case the researcher may want to design a sample in which blacks and whites are represented in equal numbers. If a station were interested in determining how a specific public affairs program was being received by an elderly audience, simple random sampling might not be the best procedure to use. In general, if a specific group-to-group comparison is required, or if the study faces time, money, or personnel limitations (as is often the case), a sample selection procedure other than simple random sampling may be indicated. The two principal alternatives are stratified sampling and cluster or area sampling.

THE STRATIFIED SAMPLE

Stratified sampling is another form of probability sampling. It is essentially random sampling within various strata or subgroups of the population. Stratified sampling requires that the sampling units be classified into various strata according to pre-selected criteria. Strata may be different social groups, geographic locations, or income levels. For purposes of sales research, for instance, a station may be interested in comparing which section of town, age group, or income group listens to a particular program. With this information the station may be able to sell air-time to local businessmen whose products or services are better suited for one or more of these audience groups. A stratified sample can provide the needed information.

Stratification allows the broadcast researcher to use his or her knowledge about the population to increase the precision or accuracy of the sample selected. If there is interest in comparing different groups in the broadcast market, the entire population can be initially divided into two or more homogeneous strata or sub-parts. These may include men and women, or blacks and whites; or low income, middle income, and upper income groups; or the young, the middle-aged, and the elderly; or north-side businessmen and south-side businessmen, and the like. A simple random sample is then taken of each stratum or sub-part to be compared. For example, to stratify by age the population could initially be divided into groups of below 18 years old, 18 to 34 years old, 35 to 49 years old, and over 49 years old. Then a simple random sample of each age group would be taken. The samples of the age groups, with appropriate weighting, could be combined to form the total sample. Chapter 2 presented a description of weighting as it is done by the broadcast rating firms. The *weight* of a demographic sub-part is the proportion which that sub-part represents in the population divided by the proportion the sub-part represents in the sample. A definition of weight in the form of an equation is:

$$\text{Weight}_{\text{sub-sample}} = \frac{\text{Proportion}_{\text{population}}}{\text{Proportion}_{\text{sample}}}$$

An illustration makes this procedure of weighting more understandable. Table 5-1 presents audience shares in a three-radio-station market for each of the four age groups identified above. The figures in the table indicate that Station A received a 50 share among the below 18 age group, a 45 share for the 18 to 34 group, a 30 share in the 35 to 49 year old group, and a 20 share for the over 49 age group. In the actual market population, data obtained from the city's *Statistical Abstracts* indicate the following population distribution for each age group: below 18 years of age, 20 percent; 18 to 34 years of age, 40 percent; 35 to 49 years of age, 30 percent; and over 49 years of age, 10 percent of the city's population. However, since the researcher desires to include each age group in equal proportion for purposes of age group comparison, the stratified sample consists of

Table 5-1.   Audience Shares in a Three-Station Market Stratified by Age Group.

AGE GROUPS	STATION A	STATION B	STATION C
Below 18	50	40	10
18–34	45	40	15
35–49	30	35	30
Over 49	20	30	50

25 percent from each of the four age groups. In order to provide a sample which accurately resembles the actual population distribution of the broadcast market: each subsampled age group must be appropriately *weighted* when combined with the other subsamples. Without weighting, the four age group shares for Station A could be summed and then divided by the total number of sub-samples (four age groups) to produce an average share for Station A:

$$\frac{50+45+30+20}{4} = 36.25 \text{ (average share)}.$$

This procedure would provide a correct audience share for Station A *if* each of the four age groups actually represented 25 percent of the total market population.

However, since *stratified* sampling procedures were used, some age groups were actually over-represented in the selected sample (the below 18 and over-49 age groups), while other age groups were under-represented in the sample (the 18 to 34 and 35 to 49 age groups). Only by appropriately weighting each sub-sample can the four age group sub-samples be combined to provide an accurate assessment of Station A's average share in the market (note that similar procedures would also have to be employed to gauge Station B and Station C's actual average audience share in the broadcast market). In this case, the weight for the subsample of the below 18 year old group can be calculated as follows:

$$\text{Weight}_{(\text{below 18})} = \frac{.20}{.25} = .80.$$

By similar computations, the weights for the three remaining sub-samples can be identified as 1.60 for the 18 to 34 group, 1.20 for the 35 to 49 group, and .40 for the over-49 year old age group. Each age group sub-sample *share* for Station A must be weighted (weight × share), summed with the other *weighted sub-sample shares,* and then divided by the total-number of subsamples (four for this example):

$$\frac{.80\,(50)+1.60\,(45)+1.20\,(30)+.40\,(20)}{4} = 39.0 \text{ (average share)}.$$

Average share, when computed properly from sub-sample weights, is nearly three points higher.

By using stratified sampling procedures specific and often important group comparisons can be made. For example, with the evidence provided by this survey, Station A could sell time to advertisers interested in reaching the 34 and under age groups. At the same time, subsample figures can be combined by using appropriate weighting procedures for a representative sample of the total broadcast market population.

The procedure of taking *simple random samples* of each population subgroup differentiates stratified sampling from a different sampling technique, quota sampling. *Quota sampling* is a form of nonprobability sampling in which quotas are set for the inclusion in the sample of a certain number of individuals from each of several desired subgroups. These subgroups could be, for example, different income levels, races, ages, sexes, and the like. After quotas are determined for each subgroup (in other words, deciding upon just how many individuals are needed to be surveyed within each), interviewers fill the quotas by seeking out the required number of individuals from the appropriate subgroups. In quota sampling, then, samples are not selected on a *random* probability basis. Quota sampling can also be identified as judgment or convenience sampling. It provides no guarantee of accurate and reliable results or generalizability to the population as a whole. Consequently, stratified sampling is the preferred technique of sampling subgroups of the population; it yields reliable and accurate results which may be generalized to the subgroup, and, when sub-samples are combined with appropriate weighting, results which can be generalized to the entire population, such as the broadcast market.

Stratified sampling permits the use of smaller sample sizes, and therefore, reduces the cost of achieving specified levels of accuracy. In other words, simple random sampling procedures may yield numbers of individuals from a certain subgroup insufficient to compare that subgroup (for example, teen-agers) to other subgroups (for example, the middle-aged and the elderly). Stratified sampling is also a probability sampling procedure which ensures sufficient sub-sample sizes. In a simple random sample with insufficient subgroup size, the researcher must expand the sample size and hope that this overall increase will provide substantial representation for the subgroup of interest from which more respondents are required. In stratified sampling the researcher begins with certain knowledge about the population (such as the different towns or communities within the broadcast market) and uses this information to divide the overall population into subgroups for purposes of comparison.

Suppose that station RXYZ desires to determine the needs of each of the four local communities which comprise its coverage area. Based upon available population figures, a simple random sample of 400 households in the market would include 160 households in A-town, 120 households in B-town, 80 households in C-town, and 40 households in D-town. Clearly there are substantial population differences among the four communities. D-town is smaller in population than the others. The simple random sampling procedure would not permit an equal comparison of D-town's broadcast needs with those of A-town. If the station is specifically in need of this comparison, simple random sampling procedures would not provide the best sample design. By using a stratified sample, an equal number of households is selected in each of the four communities. Table 5-2 presents this hypothetical comparison of the number of households in each town which would be represented by these two different sample selection techniques.

The stratified sample in this case achieves greater accuracy. Instead of the different number of sample households in each community provided by the simple random sample, 100 households in each of the four communities are selected in the stratified sample, also a total sample size of 400 households. Each subgroup sample is randomly chosen and is typical or representative of its community.

Table 5-2. Comparison of Simple and Stratified Random Samples.

COMMUNITY	SIMPLE RANDOM SAMPLE	STRATIFIED SAMPLE
	Approximate number of households which would be selected by the different sampling techniques assuming a total sample size of 400.	
A-town	160	100
B-town	120	100
C-town	80	100
D-town	40	100

In most cases, the subgroups of the overall population are not equal in size. In arriving at sub-samples of equal size in the stratified sample, different proportions of each of the four communities were selected. If D-town contained 1000 households, in order to arrive at a subsample size of 100, it would be necessary to select one household in every ten in that town. If B-town had 3000 households, the researcher would have to choose one household in every 300 to produce a sub-sample of 100 households, and so on for C-town and D-town.

Several additional comments about stratified sampling should be made. First, stratified sampling techniques are particularly useful in observing and describing ethnic and cross-cultural differences in the needs, wants, and behaviors of a community. Similarly, stratified sampling can be used to address the question of how broadcast programming meets these needs of various community groups. Quota sampling could also be used for this purpose provided that there is no need to generalize to the market populations. Second, in order to utilize stratified sampling techniques, the researcher must be able to obtain prior information about subgroups within the population. It is imperative that individuals or households which belong to the various subgroups and their relative proportions to the entire population be identified beforehand. Third, a stratified sample is a random probability sample. This is so, because each member of the population has a known chance of being included in the sample, even though only members of the same population group have equal chances of being selected for the sample. Finally, as the earlier discussion of weighting procedures indicates, characteristics of the entire population can be estimated from the stratified sample by appropriately weighting the groups or sub-samples in proportion to their appearance in the population.

CLUSTER SAMPLING

Cluster sampling is another type of probability sample used to reduce the costs of survey sampling, but without measurably increasing sampling error, or, in other words, without increasing the difference between the results found by the sample and those results that would be obtained by a complete census of the population. Cluster sampling is a technique geared to collecting more data at lower costs. It is a technique utilized in order to decrease transportation time and interviewer costs by collecting data from several individuals within the same spatially concentrated area. It is useful to think of cluster sampling as an area probability sample. There is no real gain in using cluster sampling techniques unless the population is spread over a fairly wide geographic area.

The sampling unit of a cluster sample is not the individual person or a single household. It is, instead, a group or cluster of units, such as a group of housing units on the same city block. Populations, then, can be thought of as being composed of an hierarchy of sampling units. For example, if a researcher wants to ascertain the needs or wants of teen-agers in radio listening or television viewing, he or she could randomly select school districts within a state or county, then schools, then classes, and finally the teen-agers. While the teen-agers would be the individual units, the group of classes within the schools would provide a cluster — the sampling unit for cluster sampling procedures. This stage-wise selection process is generally used in cluster sampling technique.

Cluster sampling is the procedure or sampling these selected grouping of units. *Multistage sampling* is the term used for the technique of subsampling parts of the clusters. *Area sampling* is the technique referred to when clusters correspond to separate geographic or territorial units (such as blocks) or when these units are selected from a map rather than a list. Distinctions are sometimes drawn between these three terms; however, the techniques are similar and will be grouped together here under the general label of cluster sampling.

Cluster sampling is probably the most widely used technique for probability sampling. This is particularly true for national samples. It is the successive random sampling of areas (for example, city blocks), clusters (for example, housing units), and individuals (for example, members of households). The cluster sampling technique subdivides the community into smaller groupings which are often more accessible and economical to use in sampling the population. Housing units on selected city blocks often provide natural social clusters. The ultimate subset of units (individual members of households) is arrived at through the successive simple random or stratified samples of larger natural social clusters. For example, it is possible to sample the listening or viewing needs or habits of the broadcast market by first taking a random sample of counties or cities within the Area of Dominant Influence, then a random sample of districts or blocks taken from a city map, then a sample of predetermined clusters of households, and finally, a random or stratified sample of members of these households. The survey would then be administered to this final sample of individual members of households.

Cluster sampling techniques are employed when simple random sampling of individuals is too costly or time-consuming. This means that cluster sampling is generally used when personal interviews are required over a broad geographic area. The clusters are sampling units which contain several individual elements. A brief example may help to clarify clustering procedures.

In order to ascertain the programming needs of its audience, station RXYZ decides that it wants to conduct a personal interview survey of its entire market. The research department of the station decides to draw a sample of clusters of three housing units each and then interview one randomly selected member of each household. Clustering is generally done by housing units rather than by individuals, because it is much simpler to locate the 7th, 8th, and 9th dwelling on a block, for example, than to find the 13th, 14th, and 15th persons on the block. Three housing units are often sampled in a cluster as a sort of compromise between tolerable sampling error and simplicity in administration. Since sampling error increases as the number of housing units in a cluster increases, only three units will be clustered. Three units are also selected, because it would not be economical to sample fewer than that number.

How will RXYZ go about selecting its clusters of sampling units? It could utilize Census Bureau data for cities over 50,000 population, but since RXYZ's market contains fewer than 50,000 persons, the station can consult the records of the electric or gas companies (for their meter connections), water company, tax assessor's office, city clerk, county or state highway departments, telephone company, or school districts. The research department for the station then needs to decide upon levels of tolerable sampling error (such as 5 percent), and confidence limits (that these error estimates are reliable in 95 out of 100 samples). Utilizing the Table for Sample Size (see Table 5-3), they determine that they will have to interview 384 persons. After increasing that amount by 10 percent for respondents who may not wish to cooperate, they arrive at a sample size of 423 (384 + 39 = 423). Dividing this sample size by the three housing units in each sample cluster, they decide that they will require 141 sample clusters (423 ÷ 3 = 141) for their survey.

Table 5-3. Size of Simple Random Sample when Tolerated Sampling Error and Desired Level of Significance is Known.

TOLERATED SAMPLING ERROR	SAMPLE SIZE WHEN DESIRED SIGNIFICANCE LEVEL IS:	
	.05	.01
.01	9,604	16,641
.02	2,401	4,160
.03	1,067	1,849
.04	600	1,040
.05	384	665
.10	96	166
.15	43	74
.20	24	42

Consulting the city directory for RXYZ's market, the researchers note that there are 14,100 housing units. They then divide the total number of housing units (14,100) by the total number of sample clusters (141), providing a "skip interval" of 100. They select a starting point from a Table of Random Numbers (see Table D-VI) and turn to the city directory. They begin with the 8th listing in the directory, and after noting the location of this block, count another 100 listings (the skip interval) and note the block represented by the 108th listing (8 + 100 = 108). They continue to repeat this process utilizing the skip interval until they have identified all 141 blocks needed from which to draw their clusters of three housing units each.

Assuming that the minimum number of housing units per block is 10 for their city, the researchers select a single digit number from the Table of Random Numbers (they happen to locate 5). From this they determine that interviewers will be instructed to proceed to each of the 141 designated blocks, move in a clockwise (or counterclockwise) direction, and locate the 5th, 6th and 7th dwellings on each block. These will be the clusters in which the interviewers will contact one member of each household to interview for the survey. The researchers also need to decide upon a random procedure to be used in order to give the various persons in each household (men and women of various ages) an equal opportunity to be selected for the interview, as well as the number of "call backs" to be allowed in the event that the household member selected for the interview is not home at the time of initial contact. In addition, decisions about vacant housing units and about those who refuse to be interviewed are made beforehand by the project director. (Recall that the sample size was initially increased by 10 percent to account for a certain degree of non-response.)

Several additional observations about cluster sampling should be made. First, time, money, and personnel influence the size of the sample. With too stringent limitations in some or all of these items, smaller sample sizes with greater degrees of sampling error will result. Personal interviews used in clustering procedures should be completed over a relatively short period of several days within realistic limits of money and interviewers available. More money would permit a greater sample size with the potential of producing more accurate and reliable results. Second, clustering procedures are invaluable when there is a need for qualitative, attitudinal information best provided by personal interviewing. Third, estimates generated by clustering procedures will usually result in larger sampling error than the same estimates based upon simple random sampling. The less homogeneous or alike the clusters are in terms of the characteristics being studied (for example, age, education level, income), the greater the sample size needs to be. Finally, cluster sampling procedures are almost always used when face-to-face personal interviews are planned. With mail questionnaires clustering techniques are typically not employed.

At several points during the discussion of sampling techniques, some additional important considerations in survey sampling have been mentioned, such as sampling error, confidence limits, sample size, and personal face-to-face interviewing.

SAMPLING ERROR

Probability sampling is a procedure which allows inferences to a large number of people (a population) based upon surveying relatively few persons (a sample). The premise underlying sampling theory is that one need only talk to a few persons to get an approximate idea of the characteristics, opinions, or behaviors of many people. The principal concern in probability sampling is to reach the *kinds* and *number* of people who are *sufficiently representative* of the entire population in order to be able to generalize from a sample to the population. An efficient sample is one which represents the population and which provides the desired information within tolerable limits of sampling error for the lowest cost in terms of time, money, and personnel.

By its very nature, then, sampling produces some discrepancy between actual (population) values of a characteristic (such as the number of hours a person tunes to station

RXYZ each day) and the estimated (sample) values of that characteristic. *Sampling error* estimates the discrepancy between the sample estimate and the value that would have been discovered by a census of the entire population under identical conditions. Sampling error is the difference between the result of a theoretical measurement of the entire population and the findings from the sample actually surveyed. This accuracy or precision of a sample estimate is influenced by both sampling error and nonsampling errors (such as mechanical or procedural flaws in survey methods).

To a large degree, precision depends on sample size. In random sampling, larger samples provide greater accuracy by reducing chance errors due to sampling. The general rule is to use as large a sample as possible; the smaller the sample size, the larger the sampling error, and vice versa. Generally, statistics calculated from larger samples are more accurate than those computed from smaller samples. There is a smaller range of variation in the means of larger samples, and the means of larger samples are usually closer to the population mean. However, because sampling is also a practical enterprise, a researcher needs only the precision which is "adequate" to make an inference from sample to population.

Some sampling error, therefore, is tolerable. The amount of error tolerated depends on the use intended for the data. For example, in determining which of two popular stations in a broadcast market is the most listened-to, an error of only 2 or 3 percent may be allowed. If it were the case that 46 percent of the audience listen to station A and 54 percent listen to station B, a sampling error of only 3 percent could be tolerated if the results were to be meaningful. This would mean virtual assurance that from 43 to 49 percent of the market listen to station A, while from 51 to 57 percent listen to station B. By tolerating only a 3 percent sampling error, it could be readily determined which of the two is the more listened-to station. The accepted standard of accuracy in broadcast research is a maximum of 5 percent error in no more than 5 replications in 100.

If a population, then, is evenly divided in some characteristic (such as, 50 percent approve of station RXYZ's program format, while 50 percent disapprove), a maximum sample size is needed to give an acceptable sampling error and to provide the best opportunity for an accurate description of the population. This even distribution (in which $p = .5$) is the one of maximum uncertainty. Flipping a coin, for example, yields $p = .5$. As a consequence, the case of $p = .5$ will yield the greatest sampling error for a sample of a given size. To meet the standards of accuracy agreed upon for broadcast audience measurement, sample size is at its greatest when $p = .5$ (even distribution of a characteristic) or when a range of outcomes is anticipated which includes $p = .5$. However, if a survey's only interest is to see how many in the audience can identify the call letters — something not equally divided — a smaller sample size and a somewhat larger sampling error can be tolerated.

CONFIDENCE LIMITS

It is possible to specify beforehand how much discrepancy between the sample estimate and the actual population value (in other words, sampling error) would be acceptable for a particular research project. Although there is no assurance that a population characteristic will fall within the range of tolerated error, it is possible to indicate the degree of confidence a researcher may have in the reliability of an estimate. This degree of confidence is what is referred to as confidence limits.

Generally, *confidence limits* indicate that in either 95 or 99 out of 100 samples like the one that has been selected, the true population value is within the estimated range of tolerated sampling error. In other words, if 100 different random samples of the same size were drawn from the same population, it would be virtually certain that 95 or 99 (depending on the confidence limits selected) of these samples would reflect the same sampling error or less. For example, in a survey with 5 percent sampling error and 95 percent confidence limits, a researcher can be certain that 95 out of 100 different samples of the same size from the same population would contain the equivalent population value plus or minus five percentage points. If in a sample with 5 percent sampling error and 95 percent confidence limits it was found that 40 percent of the listeners of station RXYZ desired shorter newscasts, the researcher could be virtually certain that if he or she would draw 100 different samples from the same broadcast market population, in 95 of these samples the true percentage of listeners in the market who desired shorter newscasts would range from 35 to 45 percent (consult Table 5-3). Or, if a researcher selected a sample size to produce 4 percent sampling error and 99 percent confidence limits, and if he or she found that 25 percent of the sample listen to station RXYZ from 9 A.M. to 10 A.M., the researcher could conclude that in 99 out of 100 different samples selected from the same broadcast market population, the actual percentage of the audience who listened to the station from 9 A.M. to 10 A.M. would vary between 21 and 29 percent.

SAMPLE SIZE

Table 5-3 lists simple random sample sizes needed to produce sampling estimates within limits of tolerated sampling error from one percent to 20 percent at two confidence levels — 95 percent and 99 percent.

The sample sizes in Table 5-3 should be considered minimal for simple random samples. For example, in a broadcast market survey with a tolerated sampling error of 5 percent and confidence limits of 95 samples in 100, a researcher would need a sample size of 384 persons for a simple random sample. Keep in mind that this number would have to be increased by about 10 percent to account for potential nonresponders.

Other factors also affect sample size, and the numbers in Table 5-3 must be adjusted to reflect these elements. First, the type of sampling procedure employed affects sample size. In general, stratified samples require the smallest sample size, simple random samples somewhat larger, and cluster samples even larger. A cluster sample may require sample sizes approximately 1½ times larger than the numbers listed in the table. Second, homogeneity or the degree to which people are alike with regard to characteristics such as age or income level influences sample size. The more the people in the population are unlike, the larger the sample size needs to be. Third, the more categories of data or group characteristics needed for comparison, the larger the sample size needs to be. For example, if it were desirable to compare the broadcast audience on the basis of several categories — age, sex, race, income level, and the like — the sample size would need to be sufficiently large to provide enough respondents within each category. Fourth, the time, money, and personnel available influence how large a sample can be surveyed. The more resources available, the larger the sample size can be. Finally, the actual size of the population has little bearing on the size of the sample, particularly when samples represent less than 5 percent of the population. In deciding the size of a sample it is generally preferable to use as few respondents as possible while preserving the reliability or precision needed in the sample.

Table D-IV presents an alternate means for estimating the size of the sample based upon probable deviation of the results due to sample size. Table D-IV may be used to determine the sample size or the number of interviews needed. A researcher would most likely look at the 50 percent column to determine the number of interviews needed within a certain margin of error. The 50 percent column (p = .50) represents those characteristics which are evenly divided in their estimated occurrence (for example, 50 percent listen to station A, while the remaining 50 percent listen to station B).

Consider this example: From a sample of 400 it is discovered that 40 percent of the respondents prefer shorter newscasts, while 60 percent would rather listen to longer, more in-depth newscasts. The researcher locates the number at the intersection of the horizontal sample size row of 400 and the vertical survey result column of .40 or .60, and notes that with reasonable certainty (odds of 20 to 1) this result is associated with a deviation due to sampling error no greater than plus or minus .049. In other words, in

95 out of 100 samples drawn from the same market population, it is virtually certain that from 35.1 to 44.9 percent desire shorter newscasts, while from 55.1 to 64.9 percent prefer longer newscasts. If the researcher had drawn a sample of half this size (200), the probable deviation of results would be plus or minus .070. If the sample size were doubled (800), the probable deviation would be plus or minus .034. In practical terms for this example, the precision gained in sample estimates would not warrant an increase in sample size beyond the 400 interviews.

The size of the population has little bearing on the size of the sample selected. It is *not* true that larger populations require larger samples. From a statistical standpoint, sample size needed to attain a specific level of reliability or precision is the same for national, state-wide, large market, or small market surveys. The optimum sample size is around 400, and most survey probability samples range from 100 to 500 interviews. Sample sizes of less than 100 should be avoided.

PERSONAL INTERVIEWING

A personal interview is a conversation or dialogue between the interviewer and the respondent with the objective of securing certain information from the respondent. Personal interviews are especially useful in exploring motivations for individual actions or attitudes—*why* a person feels programming to meet a certain community need is important. Personal interviews allow the interviewer to pursue qualitative, attitudinal information in addition to quantitative, demographic and informational data. Personal interviews are employed principally in field research (requiring cluster sampling procedures) and telephone interviewing. Mail questionnaires, of course, do not allow for this dialogue between researcher and those completing the survey.

Personal, face-to-face interviewing is one method of collecting information in broadcast survey research. The other methods are telephone surveys and mail questionnaires. The formal personal interview procedure is one in which a set of questions is asked and answers recorded by the interviewer on a standardized questionnaire form in a face-to-face interaction. The face-to-face context is what differentiates personal field interviews from telephone interviews.

Face-to-face interviewing is often the most appropriate form for collecting audience data, because the personal interview has certain advantages over mail and telephone surveys. Personal interviews can be conducted for longer periods of time as contrasted with telephone interviews or mail questionnaires. Face-to-face interviews provide the interviewer greater flexibility in collecting information than do mail surveys. Personal interviews can probe for more complex responses than either telephone or mail surveys. In addition, sample selection procedures for field interviews often provide better population representation within the sample and response rate as contrasted to both mail and telephone surveys. The comparison of personal interview, mail, and telephone information procedures is presented in Table 5–4. (This table has been adapted from a comparative chart constructed by the University of Illinois Survey Research Laboratory.)

Personal interviews allow for more information to be collected from respondents, because they can last for lengthy periods of time (often 30 minutes or longer). The length of a mail questionnaire must be kept to a maximum of a couple of pages, while telephone surveys should only last for about a quarter of an hour or so. Not only can face-to-face interviews provide more information, they can probe for more complex responses, such as qualitative or attitude and self-perception information in addition to the quantitative data. In a telephone survey, the individual may hang up and terminate the interview if he or she becomes suspicious of questions or motives. Mail surveys often offer more candid replies because of their anonymity, but questions must be kept simple; open-ended questions asking for attitudinal information must be kept to a minimum; and probe or follow-up questions are difficult, if at all possible, to include. Of course the major reason not to include these types of questions on mail surveys is that response rate will be low.

Table 5–4. Comparison of Information Collection Procedures.

SAMPLE	MAIL	TELEPHONE	PERSONAL INTERVIEW
Sample Selection	Relatively Simple (from lists)	Relatively Simple (from telephone directories)	Relatively Simple (from area maps and lists)
Sample Bias	Troublesome (respondents are often higher in interest and education)	Troublesome (under-represents low- and high-income groups)	Controlled (but a potential problem if sample respondents are not located)
Stratifying	Better (lists may contain the needed information)	Poor (information is usually not readily available)	Best (can use census data or statistical profiles)
Clustering	Not Done	Sometimes	Often
QUESTIONNAIRE			
Interview Length	Must be shorter (1 to 3 pages; about 10 minutes)	Short (15 to 30 minutes)	Can be longer (30 minutes or more)
Question Complexity	Simpler (must be straightforward and undemanding of respondents)	Simple (some interviewer flexibility)	More complex and flexible (can use skip patterns, filter questions, and response cards)
Probing For Reasons And Attitudes	Poor (little is possible; danger of nonreturn)	Better (but still a a danger of disconnects)	Best (can obtain more qualitative and complex information)
Sensitive Subjects	Relatively good (offers respondent anonymity)	Risky (a danger of disconnects)	Risky (interviewee unwillingness; possible reply bias)
Question Order Control	Risky (respondent may read ahead)	Excellent control	Excellent control
INTERVIEWING			
Response Rate	Low (15 to 25 percent for a single mailing; higher for several mailings)	Good (can be 70 to 90 percent)	Good (can be at least 80 percent with call backs)
Interviewer Bias	None	Possible (training and supervision can control)	Possible (training, supervision, and verification can control)
Respondent Bias	Low (but possible if another person completes or helps complete the questionnaire)	Possible	Possible (can be influenced by the interviewer's presence)
Respondent Identity	Possible (but identification keys lessen anonymity and possibly response rate)	Identity is known	Identity is known
ADMINISTRATION			
Cost	Economical (particularly if initial response rate is high)	Economical	Costly (three or more times the cost of mail or telephone surveys)
Administrative Demands	Undemanding	Demanding (must hire, train and supervise interviewers)	Demanding (must hire, train, supervise and verify interviewers)

Face-to-face field interviews provide a more flexible means for gathering necessary information. For example, interviewers can more easily control the order of the questions and follow "skip patterns" leading from one "filter question" to another question out of linear sequence. Telephone surveys also provide this interviewer flexibility, but not the potential for interviewers to utilize response cards to ease the flow of the interview. Mail surveys, once again, must be kept rather simple and straight forward so that the person completing the questionnaire can easily follow the logical sequence of questions.

Personal interviews often provide better or more representative samples, as well as increased rates of response. Surveys utilizing personal interview procedures can be designed to be representative of the population, or selective in stratification procedures to survey only specific geographic areas and social or racial groups. Mail survey samples are often limited to available mailing lists, while telephone surveys are often restricted to those numbers listed in telephone directories (although random dialing procedures can be a tremendous aid to overcoming this obstacle). Therefore, both mail and telephone surveys may underrepresent certain income and ethnic groups in the community. In addition, personal interviews provide a good rate of response (often 80 percent or better if appropriate callback, follow-up procedures are followed). This is in contrast to mail surveys which may have a response rate of only 25 percent or less, unless various additional incentives are incorporated to increase the rate of return. These incentives substantially increase the cost of a mail survey and often defeat the economic purpose of conducting a survey by mail. Response rates from telephone surveys are often quite high.

There are, however, disadvantages to employing personal interview methods in survey sampling. First, face-to-face, field interviews require extensive interviewer training, supervision, and control. Simply, personal interviewing presents a heavy administrative load. Training and supervision are also required of telephone interviewers, but the interviewing process itself via the telephone is generally fast and simple. Mail questionnaires are the easiest to administer, since they require no interviewers to be trained or supervised. Second, personal interviewing presents potential dangers of interviewer bias or cheating. In other words, interviewers may not follow the correct procedures for completing the questionnaire, may complete the questionnaire on their own without actually conducting the required interview, or may influence individual responses to questions during the face-to-face interaction. Some of these problems are also potentially present in the telephone survey. In both face-to-face and telephone interviewing, a certain percentage of completed interviews (usually about 10 percent for trained interviewers) must be validated by the research project director. Mail surveys are free of these problems, but not of a related concern. In mail surveys the researcher can never be completely certain that the person to whom the questionnaire was addressed was actually the individual who completed and returned the survey. Finally, the personal interviewing of field surveys involves high costs which are often three times as great as the costs of a mail or telephone survey. Telephone and mail surveys are generally more economical than face-to-face surveys.

Next to the research project director, the interviewer is probably the most important component in the survey method of face-to-face interviewing. Competent interviewing is essential for securing accurate and reliable information. The project director is potentially biased, since he or she possesses knowledge of the survey purposes and objectives; the project director may not be the best interviewer. Once the project is designed and the sample selected, interviewers must be selected, hired, and adequately briefed and trained. Training sessions should be relatively extensive and include such opportunities as interview role-playing exercises. The project director must be convinced that the interviewers know their job and the questionnaire thoroughly *before* they proceed into the field to conduct their interviews. The interviewers must be totally familiar with the question items and instructions in the questionnaire instrument before the training is completed. Any ambiguities must be cleared up during the training sessions.

In designing the questionnaire, the questions should be written in a form which is relatively easy for the interviewer to read. Items must progress in a logical order and be accompanied by reasonable transitions. Questionnaire items need to be precise and convey exactly what is intended in order to secure the appropriate information from the respondents. Instructions provided for the interviewer on the questionnaire need to be specific and simple to follow. The use of instructions printed in bold, capital letters or italics and enclosed in parentheses or boxes, along with the use of vertical lines or arrows to ease following the sequence of questions (particularly if the questionnaire contains skipping instructions and filter questions) makes the interviewer's task much simpler. Figure 5-1 presents a sample questionnaire illustrating several of these points of questionnaire design.

Interviews should be planned and conducted at various times of the day between the hours of 9 A.M. and 9 P.M. when different kinds of people are at home. They should even be conducted on the weekends as well when it is more likely that people are at home. The interviewer must be able to locate the predetermined cluster of households on a block and members of households to interview. During the briefing sessions, clearly marked maps and correct field instructions need to be provided to interviewers (for example, "proceed to the block indicated on the map, turn right, walk in a clockwise direction with the houses on your right, and count housing units until you arrive at the seventh house on the block for your initial interview"). After locating the proper person of the household (and it is best that only that person is present during the interview), the interviewer must be adept at motivating that person to cooperate with the survey. This can be accomplished in several ways — pointing to the importance of the survey information, the personal benefit the respondent will derive from participating in the survey, or justifying the vital need for the information from that particular person. The interviewer must be able to establish a positive, friendly, conversational atmosphere of interaction and rapport at the outset of the interviewing process.

Survey questions must then be asked in a uniform and consistent manner. All items should be presented in the order specified by the questionnaire. Variations in question wording should not occur, although the questions certainly can be repeated twice (but usually not more than twice) if the respondent does not understand them or requests it. If the respondent cannot then answer the question, the interviewer should note "no response" to the appropriate item. The verbal and nonverbal (voice inflections, physical manner, and the like) delivery of the interviewer should be kept as consistent as possible. Interviewers are not machines and absolute uniformity in delivery technique (particularly between two different interviewers) within a personal interaction environment is worth striving for, but relatively uncommon nonetheless. Interviewers, though, must strive for objectivity in their manner of asking questions. All attempts at biasing a response need to be avoided. Interviewers should be neutral and impartial in attitude and should not suggest an answer nor offer a personal opinion. The interviewer task is to absorb and record the information and to relay it back to the research project director in appropriate form on the questionnaire.

Nonresponses and refusals to answer certain questions should be noted by the interviewer. The individual being interviewed should not be pressed too far if he or she refuses to answer a question or the interview may end abruptly and unexpectedly. All complete and partial responses to questions need to be accurately recorded by the interviewer in the appropriate location on the questionnaire. The interviewer should also be neutral, impartial, and accurate in recording answers, and must write the answers as fully and as legibly as possible.

In the event that a selected individual is not at home, a consistent callback procedure must be predetermined by the project director. For example, it may be decided that two callbacks will be permitted if the person is not home at the time of initial contact. Callbacks increase the interviewing cost and the decision about the number of callbacks to allow is a cost effectiveness decision.

WXYZ LISTENER SURVEY

Good morning. I'm _____ from Broadcast Research. We have selected several persons in this area to find out why and when they listen to radio. If you have a few minutes, I would like to ask you a few questions.

1. Do you own a radio? (Circle the appropriate answer)

    Yes 1

    No 2

2. Where do you most frequently listen to the radio? (Circle the appropriate answer)

    Home 1

    Car 2

    Office 3

    Other 4

    Don't Listen (Skip to Q. 5) 5

3. During which of the following hours do you usually listen to the radio? Circle as many answers as provided)

    6 A.M.-12 noon . . 1

    12 noon-6 P.M. . . 2

    6 P.M.-midnight . . 3

    Noon (Skip to Q. 5) . 4

4. Why would you say you prefer to listen to radio during the hours which you indicated?

    _____

    _____

5. What is your favorite radio station? (Circle the appropriate answer)

    RXYZ 1

    RYZX 2

    RZXY 3

Figure 5–1. Sample Questionnaire.

After the interviews are completed for the day, the interviewer should return to the research office and be debriefed by the project director who should check the completed questionnaires. Any problems or questions should be answered at that time, before the next day's interviews. In addition, the project director will also need to verify a certain percentage of the completed questionnaires from all interviews. Generally, this ranges from about 10 percent for experienced interviewers to about 20 percent for inexperienced interviewers.

NOTES—CHAPTER 5

Charles Backstrom and Gerald D. Hursh, *Survey Research* (Evanston: Northwestern University Press, 1963).

Joe Belden, *A Broadcast Research Primer* (Washington, D.C.: National Association of Broadcasters, 1966).

Leslie Kish, *Survey Sampling* (New York: John Wiley and Sons, 1965).

C.A. Moser and G. Kalton, *Survey Methods in Social Investigations,* Second Edition (New York: Basic Books, 1972).

Claire Selltiz, Lawrence S. Wrightman, and Stuart W. Cook, *Research Methods in Social Relations,* Third Edition (New York: Holt, Rinehart and Winston, 1976).

Julian L. Simon, *Basic Research Methods in Social Science: The Art of Empirical Investigation* (New York: Random House, 1969).

Standard Definitions of Broadcast Research Terms, Second Edition (Washington, D.C.: National Association of Broadcasters, 1973).

6 Ascertainment Research

Mary Ann Heller

Broadcasters are familiar with the three words – interest, convenience, and necessity – set forth in 1927 as the public interest standard by which regulatory policies should be designed. Broadcast historians are well aware that this standard tends to shift with the nation's social and political tides. In the early sixties a liberal federal establishment planted seeds for accountability in government and in other institutions: it was natural for the Federal Communication Commission to sow such seeds as well.

In 1960 the FCC issued its "Programming Policy Statement" which drew attention again to the familiar phrase, "public interest, convenience or necessity," and which attempted to give broadcasters an idea of how they could meet their public responsibility. The Commission proposed that future license applications require applicants to state the measures taken by the station to determine the tastes, needs, and desires of the community, as well as the ways in which those needs and desires would be met. The Commission's position was stated: "The principal ingredient of such obligation consists of a diligent, positive and continuing effort by the licensee to discover and fulfill the tastes, needs and desires of his service area. If he has accomplished this, he has met his public responsibility."[1]

During the sixties broadcasters applied the flexible 1960 ascertainment policy to programming decisions. Broadcasters would consult with community leaders concerning the kind of programs the leaders believed the station should present. As Avery has reported, "The predictable responses were either so ambiguous or general, i.e., 'More public affairs,' 'More educational,' etc., that they were of little real value to program decision-makers. Thus for all practical purposes, the initial ascertainment process was regarded as a meaningless exercise by virtually everyone involved."[2]

In the late sixties ascertainment procedures were the basis of FCC actions on several license applications. The Camden Decision in 1969 was one such landmark decision. The McLendon Corporation applied for the license of a station previously licensed to the City of Camden, but the McLendon Corporation was denied. The Commission's denial was based on the failure of the McLendon Corporation to adequately survey the community of intended service. The FCC criticized the applicant, because no research was conducted to determine the demographic composition of the city, and because no effort was made to interview people of foreign extraction or persons representing charitable, educational, or labor organizations. The Commission summarized its action in this way: the steps taken by the McLendons to ascertain Camden's needs and interests were inadequate; their proposed programming cannot be regarded as responsive to properly determined needs.[3]

Six months after the Camden Decision, the FCC presented the "Notice of Inquiry" which was the initial draft of the Ascertainment Primer. As observed by *Broadcasting* the Notice was in response to the Federal Communications Bar Association's request for clarification of the requirements of the ascertainment section of license application forms.[4] The public notice asked applicants to consult with "a representative range" of community leaders on community needs and list each person consulted by name, position, and organization. In addition, broadcasters were required to report on "the significant suggestions" received, whether or not they were adopted, the relative importance of those suggestions, and the relationship of the program service to the needs of the community evaluated in this process.

Attempting to increase the responsiveness of broadcasters to the problems of their communities, the FCC adopted a revised form of the original Notice on February 18, 1971, and entitled it, "Primer on Ascertainment of Community Problems by Broadcast Applicants." The "Report and Order" on ascertainment required commercial broadcasters to exhibit tangible evidence of their concern over community problems, needs, and interests. Since 1971, the procedures mandated by the FCC have been revised several times.[5] A major addition to the original Primer was a 1975 FCC Report and Order which made noncommercial broadcast stations responsible for performing and reporting ascertainment procedures. The Commission stated, "Based on our review of the record in this proceeding, we are convinced that noncommercial broadcasters should be subject to formal ascertainment requirements.[6]" The Commission did, however, allow the noncommercial broadcaster some latitude in designing its leader survey and encouraged the broadcasters to "experiment with a variety of methods and view this freedom, in fact, as a proving ground for methods which might at a later date be applied in the commercial concept."[7]

ASCERTAINMENT REQUIREMENTS

The current ascertainment requirement is designed to identify community problems as they are perceived by (a) leaders and (b) members of the general public. The Commission has stated that it uses the idea of community problems as an interpretation of the interest, convenience, and necessity standard. The ascertainment process is not in any way related to the solicitation of programming ideas, although the Commission does not object to broadcasters including such solicitations in their ascertainment surveys.

Put in simplest terms, the ascertainment requirement includes two surveys: one of community leaders, the other of the general public. The broadcasters need ask nothing more in these surveys than that respondents state their opinions as to the most important community problems. A manual on Ascertainment with a sample questionnaire and instructions for sample selection has been prepared for broadcasters by the National Association of Broadcasters, but licensees are free to engage research firms to conduct the general public survey and to pool their ascertainment efforts with those of other community licensees. In many markets today a leader station arranges with a media research firm to conduct the interviews with members of the general public. Each participating station pays a share of the cost consistent with the relative size of station profits. The result is that all participating stations fulfill the requirement of the public survey at a reasonable cost, and all the stations are provided with the same raw data. The results of the general public survey are community problems listed according to frequency of mention by the respondents.

The stipulated procedures for the leader survey contain more constraints. This survey must be done in person (in most cases) by station staff members which include upper-level management personnel. The Commission has made an important time-saving concession by allowing broadcasters in a number of markets to interview community leaders as a group. Typically this is how it works: One or several larger stations in the market contact all the other broadcasters in the market area to learn whether they care to be included in a collective effort. If a station wishes to participate, it is asked to submit a list of community leaders to be interviewed by the entire group of station representatives.

The leader stations assemble lists of community leaders and arrange for times and places of interview. On designated days representatives from the stations meet as a group to interview a roster of leaders. The leaders are briefed beforehand that the initial question the broadcasters will ask is, "What do you feel are important problems or concerns of your community?" After the leader provides a response to this initial question, the amount of questioning on additional perceptions of problems or of solutions varies, but little additional time for questioning is typically available. It is important to note that broadcasters are not allowed to "lead" the participants in any way; that is, they cannot ask, for instance, whether the leader believes the community suffers from a lack of waste disposal resources.

To summarize, the results of the ascertainment effort yield the following: (a) a random survey of the general public, probably conducted by a research firm which has prioritized the problems according to frequency of mention; (b) from 50 to 200 community leader interview reports (depending on the size of the market) reflecting the problem to which the leader devoted most attention in the interview. Some stations tabulate the number of times a problem is addressed by leaders and construct a list of priorities based upon frequency of mention by the leaders.

In March 1980 the FCC amended ascertainment requirements concerning the adequacy of community leader surveys and affirmed that radio stations in small communities are exempt from the usual ascertainment procedures. In the 1976 *Primer* the FCC had included a community leader checklist suggesting nineteen categories of organizations/ institutions present in many communities whose leaders should be contacted as a part of ascertainment leader surveys. The 1980 amendment requires that the nineteen categories be expanded to include groups who seek out the licensee and who subsequently are determined by the licensee to represent "significant" elements of the community. Radio stations licensed to communities of less than 10,000 population which are not part of SMSAs are relieved of the ascertainment requirement. They are still required, however, to prepare and place in their public files an annual problems list as described below.

For license renewal a station must select the problems which it considers most important and must demonstrate with programming data that those problems were "treated." Because an overwhelming majority of the ascertainment data is gathered within 6 months of filing for license renewal, the problems which a broadcaster decides are most important and deserve treatment are often those to which the station has devoted most programming time over the previous 3-year period. In an effort to make the selection of problems to treat a less retroactive process, the Commission has asked stations to file an annual list of problems that have been treated. The intent of the annual list of problems is twofold. One purpose is to encourage stations to plan their programming *after* formal ascertainment procedures have been conducted. A station is to first ascertain the problems of the community, then select the ascertained problems to treat, and finally develop programs which in some way address these problems. The second reason for the annual list is to motivate broadcasters to meet one of the most recent requirements — that ascertainment be an "on-going" process throughout the license period.

BROADCASTER RESPONSE TO ASCERTAINMENT

The formal ascertainment requirement has sparked much controversy both among broadcasters and special-interest citizen groups. Commercial broadcasters' negative reaction to ascertainment requirements was clearly articulated in a short 1974 statement in *Broadcasting:*

For the conventional, commercial stations, the ratings tell the story along with the sale of product. For the noncommercial outlets, the response is reflected in the support the stations get through subscriptions to logs, contributions and by "feel" of jobs well done. Commerical or public, the marketplace, not the tonnage of local ascertainment surveys, provides the answers.[8]

Noncommercial broadcasters were divided as to whether educational noncommercial stations should be subject to the same ascertainment requirements as commercial stations. The Corporation for Public Broadcasting along with a number of special interest citizen groups believed the noncommercial stations should accept the burden of formal FCC ascertainment filing. The Public Broadcasting Service and the National Association of Educational Broadcasters pleaded to develop their own ascertainment procedures which would place less of a financial burden on the stations. Most noncommercial broadcasters and educators foresaw the Commission's final ruling in 1976 which required noncommercial stations to comply with formal ascertainment procedures.

By the mid-seventies broadcasters' negative feelings toward formal ascertainment had diminished to some extent. Interviews conducted with broadcast managers in Seattle and Yakima, Washington, during the summer of 1977 indicated that a slight majority of the broadcasters in these markets believed: (a) that they understood the FCC ascertainment procedures better than at first; (b) that the requirement should be retained; (c) that the results of the survey were helpful, especially for "other," smaller stations which might neglect informing themselves of community issues; (d) that the Commission should reduce the amount of paperwork necessary to report the execution of prescribed ascertainment procedures. Only two Seattle radio stations revealed strongly negative attitudes toward the ascertainment requirement. The management at these stations felt the ascertainment of community problems was a waste of time for their station staff, since their audiences were not even remotely interested in hearing community problems discussed on the radio.

Several broadcasters volunteered that they had acquired a more positive perspective on ascertainment since it was first prescribed. They attributed their positive shift in attitude to having successfully completed the ascertainment exhibit for license renewal. Once they understood what the FCC required and organized their station staff to execute the procedures, the prospect of compliance with the FCC did not appear so formidable. On the other hand, the ability to comply with the Commission requirement did not necessarily mean that the broadcaster liked the ascertainment requirement.

A more extensive survey of West Coast broadcasters in the summer of 1978 indicated that 63 percent of the 80 broadcasters surveyed by mail did not believe the FCC ascertainment requirement to be useful to their stations. In follow-up interviews with 25 members of the original mail sample, 77 percent again held that the ascertainment requirement was not useful to their station, but 88 percent of the same respondents believed that ascertaining community problems was important. The majority of the broadcasters interviewed preferred designing their own ascertainment methods over having these methods dictated by the Commission. Broadcasters in both small and large markets believed that the reason that the FCC ascertainment policy was not more useful, was that the relatively laborious procedures provided them with no new information regarding community problems. These broadcasters felt that (a) the media set the agenda for public discussion identifying for most of the audience what community problems are, and (b) broadcasters are naturally and necessarily involved with their communities on a day-to-day basis if they are to be successful.[9]

No matter what opinion broadcasters may have of the FCC ascertainment requirement, the requirement stands, and compliance is necessary to insure license renewal. Accordingly, more attention needs to be given to the development of ascertainment procedures which will make ascertainment data more useful to the stations that have collected it.

IMPLEMENTING ASCERTAINMENT DATA

To make ascertainment more than a license application ritual, broadcasters should give some thought to how the data will be used. A wise station staff will decide how the raw data is to be interpreted and how it is to affect program planning, and these staff decisions will be made before interviewing begins. Some stations assign the public affairs or news director the task of interpreting the data and seeing that it is distributed to staff members. At other stations the general manager or corporate vice-president in charge of finance or research assumes these tasks. Several smaller stations relegate the task to the receptionist/ traffic person. But no matter which staff member organizes the material, the person must make a number of initial decisions.

First of all, the person in charge of the ascertainment should consider possible respondent interpretations of the most commonly asked initial question, "What do you think is the most important problem facing your community?" The reference to community is uncertain, unless the interviewer asks the respondent to identify the social or geographic unit that is the respondent's "community." By asking the respondents to identify their referents for community, broadcasters would be able to discern whether, for example, sanitation problems varied throughout the coverage area. If responses concerning sanitation issues were totaled and ranked by frequency of mention with other topics, then sanitation, in spite of the fact that it was the first priority problem of citizens within a particular 100-block area, might be buried in an overall list of problem priorities. Of course, it is a matter of station policy whether or not the station will program to the needs of such small groups within its coverage area.

Another problem related to the initial interview question is that of assuming the first problem named is the one of primary importance to the respondent. A better way of phrasing the question is, "Will you state several community problems of importance to you?" Once the interviewee has generated the problems, the interviewer could ask the respondent to rank the problems mentioned in order of importance. Using this method, the broadcaster will get a more conscious evaluation of a problem's importance.

As for the leader survey, a great deal of care needs to be given to the selection of leaders. It is evident to many broadcasters and researchers that special interest spokespersons who are well-known public figures may not represent the concerns of organized groups. In addition, some groups are not neatly organized, having no easily identifiable leader to contact.[10] To get a better representation of the community the station may interview the obvious community leaders and, in addition, ask group members for recommendations of persons who best represent the group's interests.

Another ascertainment research concern which warrants consideration is the specificity of problem statements. Is the station willing to accept such a generally stated problem as "pollution" as a satisfactory statement of the problem? Research indicates that all issues associated with a problem topic are not necessarily perceived as equally important.[11] For example, one community might perceive water pollution as a primary problem while, at the same time, not perceiving air pollution as an important problem. To illustrate further, respondents who mention water pollution may be referring to industrial wastes being dumped into the water; or, on the other hand, they may have in mind the unusually stringent controls on water pollution for which environmental groups may be lobbying.

If a station decides that problem specificity is important, care should be taken not to lose the specificity of respondent statements during the interpretive stage of the research, so that water pollution and air pollution are not reduced to the same issue when the data are summarized and interpreted. Lumping them together under a common topic like "the environment" could lead to such a distortion. If the station reported the topic of "environment" any program relating to the environment could be used as evidence of the broadcaster's effort to treat the problem. Certainly grouping problems together into broad topics rather than specific issues is expedient for the broadcaster, because it will be easier to find past programming which "treats" the broad problem. But if the broadcaster is concerned with laying meat over the FCC skeleton requirement, the exact issue that is a problem should be clearly specified. Considering the Commission's more recent prescription that ascertainment be an "on-going" process, not to be hurriedly executed 6 to 3 months prior to filing for renewal, broadcasters should think about projecting from their ascertainment data the problem issues to be addressed each forthcoming year. Trends in the relative priorities given particular problems may be apparent, if the data from several ascertainments are compared.[12]

Deciding which problems are worthy of treatment should be a major concern of broadcasters, but often it is given little attention. The most common method of deciding problems to treat is to consult the frequency of mentions from the public survey. Since the research companies prioritize problems according to frequency of mention, the data to support this practice are readily available. One of the problems, however, with using frequency of mention as a criterion for deciding which community problem to treat has already been alluded to — that these surveys are based upon free recall. The fact that respondents recall a problem more frequently does not mean they consider that problem as more important. There is some research to support the notion that prioritizing by frequency of mention yields a different set of priorities than asking a person to rank a number of alternatives generated by that person as well as by others.

It is interesting to note that the majority of broadcasters interviewed in the author's 1978 survey believed that the decision as to which community problems to treat should be based upon criteria other than or in addition to ranking by frequency of mention or current affairs value. One person suggested that the criterion be whether the problem could be presented in an interesting manner; another suggested using, "What's going to do the most people the most good." Several radio stations suggested selecting the problems most relevant to the demographics of a station. But most respondents who believed that additional criteria or procedures for the selection of problems to treat were necessary, were at a loss to suggest any.

Alternatives to ranking problems by frequency of mention do exist. A station might consider asking leaders not only for a list of problems but a set of ranks for problems generated by the public survey. If this technique is adopted, the station will need to specify as clearly as possible the details of the problem issue. Otherwise leaders may not know what dimension of the problem they are ranking. Another technique for intentional ranking asks staff members to rank, perhaps, the top 20 problems identified by frequency of mention in the general public survey. Asking station public affairs and news personnel to participate in the prioritizing of issues may create a commitment in them to develop programs that effectively treat the problems. A final way that group ranking might be used is during or immediately following the collective interviews of the community leaders. The group of broadcast representatives, primarily representing management, could as a group rank the problems which the leaders have generated. This would give each station an idea of how the stations collectively perceived the importance of the issues generated and would give each station an indication of the "most likely to be covered" issues within the market. In addition, this group ranking process might generate among broadcasters discussion that would deal with the substantive aspects of ascertainment — community problems.

Deciding which problems to treat may be easier than deciding how to treat them. The Commission has relegated to the broadcaster the prerogative of selecting the problems to treat, as well as defining the method of treatment. Referring again to the author's 1978 survey, broadcaster's interpretation of "treatment" varied. Thirty-nine percent defined treatment as coverage of or exposure to community problems; thirty-two percent interpreted treatment of a problem as including various points of view with possible solutions; three percent thought it meant not only exposure to the problem but also follow-up exposure of the outcome; three percent responded with "God only knows what the FCC means by treatment." A clear definition of treatment agreed upon before ascertainment data is gathered would obviously be helpful to those responsible for programming.

Identity of "leaders," specificity of problem statements, and the process of selecting problems to treat are areas which the FCC has assumed the broadcaster will deal with in a conscientious manner. The FCC has been careful to avoid any language which might be construed as venturing into the realm of program content — a territory unmistakably forbidden by the Communication Act. But the Act also mandates that the Commission monitor stations' service to the public in terms of public interest programming. What the Commission has designed in the ascertainment requirement is a procedure which is a skeletal shell for helping stations find ways to be more responsive to their community.

REWRITE OF THE COMMUNICATION ACT

The Communication Act of 1934 has been amended many times, each time shading a previously articulated concept or adding a new dimension to broadcast regulation. Because of its progressive and burdensome complexity, and because of new developments in technology, many broadcasters, political figures, and concerned citizens believe that the nation's communication laws need to be rewritten. In 1976, California Democrat Lionel Van Deerlin, Chair of the United States House of Representatives Communication Subcommittee, unveiled H.R. 13015.

Several years may elapse before the final draft and passage of H.R. 13015 or its successors, but its clear direction toward deregulation of the broadcast industry is an important consideration for ascertainment research. The bill as initially proposed eliminated the ascertainment exhibit in license renewal of radio stations and allows television to determine their own methods of ascertaining community problems. According to the summer 1978 survey of West Coast broadcasters, 59 percent of station management believe the change in ascertainment policy would be a positive step. The majority believe that television also should be exempt from filing ascertainment exhibits. The broadcasters reason that all electronic media should be treated equally and that the "marketplace would dispose of those who take advantage of the deregulation policy." The majority of the 41 percent of the broadcasters who expressed negative reactions based their positions on the belief that no broadcasters, especially those in smaller stations, would take the time to conduct interviews.

When the same broadcasters were asked how the change in policy proposed in the Van Deerlin Bill would affect their ascertainment procedures, 58 percent indicated that their procedures would not change and they would continue to adhere to FCC guidelines. The remaining 42 percent gave unique responses. For example, one interviewee said he would ascertain entertainment needs; another said he would pursue ascertainment with the station's advisory council.

Finally broadcasters were asked what changes, if any, they would make in the current FCC ascertainment policy. Only 4 of the 25 said they would make no changes. The two most frequent responses were that the respondent would eliminate the requirement completely for both radio and television stations and minimize the paperwork required by the FCC. Two broadcasters mentioned that the Commission should require greater specificity in the reporting of problem statements.

SUMMARY

The current FCC requirement for ascertainment of community needs has generated much controversy. Most broadcasters readily volunteer their criticism of the ascertainment procedures, yet at the same time they express reservations about the elimination of the requirements. It is doubtful that the Commission will either eliminate or substantially modify a young (relatively speaking) ascertainment policy in the near future, but it is possible that Congress may make major changes in the policy during the eighties by way of a new Communications Act. Particularly if a policy of broadcast deregulation is vigorously endorsed by Congress, ascertainment procedures are likely to be affected.

ILLUSTRATIVE APPROACHES TO ASCERTAINMENT

Sample Design

Sample design, of course, will be an issue only in the survey of the general public. The choices available to the station are basically (a) a simple random sample, and (b) a stratified random sample. The simple random sample would be the method of choice when the community served by the broadcast stations involved is one geographic unit with relatively homogeneous population and economic circumstance. The stratified random sample will be preferred when there are more than one geographic or political entity in the coverage area, and when there are relatively small but important groups within the audience whose needs need to be isolated from those of the area as a whole. For instance, a stratified random sample might be appropriate when the coverage area includes a language minority, such as Spanish-speakers who comprise 10 percent of the population. The researcher would elect to stratify the sample by language group in order that the views of the smaller Spanish-speaking group will be adequately represented. The procedures required to draw such a sample and the weighting factors to be used in interpreting sample data were described at length in Chapter 5. To continue the example of Beeville with its 10 percent Spanish-speaking minority, the researcher decides to draw into the sample 100 respondents from listings in the telephone directory of Spanish-surnamed households. He/she will draw an additional 100 households from the telephone directory — household listings for which surnames are not of Spanish origin. The total sample is thus 200 households in size.

Questionnaire Design and Data Collection

The form of questionnaire to be used will be in part dependent on the data collection technique to be used. One might decide to interview respondents face-to-face, interview them by telephone, or send them questionnaires to be returned by mail. The questionnaires in Figure 6-1, 6-2 and 6-3 are questionnaires for use in the survey of the general public which include the essential question, "What do you think is the most important problem facing your community?" Each questionnaire also includes optional questions suggested by the earlier discussion in this chapter and by a variety of authorities.

Leader Survey Interview

Figure 6-4 is an interview schedule for use during a group interview of community leaders. Each of the broadcast managers who interviews a leader would use this or a similar form which would then be analyzed as part of the entire group of interviews conducted.

Beeville Consolidated Ascertainment Survey of General Public
April/May _____

Interviewer _____

Address of Respondent _____

Time of Interview _____ (DATE) _____ (TIME) _____ (NOT AT HOME)

Hello, my name is _____ and I am a member of a team representing the television stations in Beeville. We are conducting a public opinion survey to help us better understand the communities we serve. I would appreciate it if you will answer just a few questions for me.

1. What do you think is the most important problem facing your community?

    a. _____

2. (Optional) When you refer to your "community" what area do you mean?

    _____

3. (Optional) What other important problems do you see facing your community?

    b. _____

    c. _____

    d. _____

4. (Optional) Let me review each of the problems you have named. I would like you to rate each problem on a scale from one to ten with ten meaning greatest importance and one least importance.

                                                                    a. _____

                                                                    b. _____

                                                                    c. _____

                                                                    d. _____

Interviewer Initials _____ To which of these groups did   Adult _____
the respondent belong?
                                                                  Child _____

                                                                  Male _____

                                                                  Female _____

                                                                  Black _____

                                                                  Caucasian _____

                                                                  Spanish-Speaking _____

Figure 6–1. General Public Interview Schedule for Face-to-Face Interviewing.

Beeville Consolidated Ascertainment Survey of General Public
April/May _____

Interviewer _____

Telephone Number _____

Date and Time of First Call _____ Second Call _____ Third Call _____

Hello, my name is _____. I am a member of a team representing the television stations in Beeville. We are conducting a public opinion survey to help us better understand the communities we serve. I would appreciate your answering a few questions for me.

1. What do you think is the most important problem facing your community?

a. _____

2. (Optional) When you refer to your "community" what area do you mean?

_____

3. (Optional) What other important problems do you see facing your Community?

b. _____

c. _____

d. _____

4. (Optional) Following are some problems mentioned in other surveys in Beeville. As I read them, I would like you to tell me whether you think they are still very important problems here.

Repaving of Broad Street   Yes _____ No _____

Not Enough Jobs for Young People   Yes _____ No _____

Crime in the Streets   Yes _____ No _____

Not Enough Public Swimming Pools   Yes _____ No _____

Racial Problems in the Schools   Yes _____ No _____

5. (Optional) A year from now what do you think will be the most important problem facing your community?

_____

6. (Optional) Can you tell me the occupations of the adults in your household?

_____

_____

_____

Figure 6–2.   General Public Interview Schedule for Telephone Interviewing.

7. Can you tell me which of the following groups you belong to?

Male _____

Female _____

Adult _____

Child _____

Black _____

Spanish-Speaking _____

Thank you very much for helping us. Good-bye. Interviewer/Initials _____

Figure 6-2. (continued)

RKGB-TV RJEF-TV RXYZ-TV RUN-TV RFUN-TV RKGB-TV RJEF-TV RXYZ-TV

Date

Dear Beeviller;

At least annually the television stations of Beeville seek your help in understanding the problems of our community. We want to understand our community better in order to serve it better.

Will you take just a moment to help us by answering the questions at the bottom of this letter? We have included a self-addressed envelope with postage to make it easy for you to give us your views.

Thank you for helping us.

Sincerely,

Joe Doe
Beeville TV Research

1. What in your opinion are the most important problems facing your community?

Most important: _____

Next most important: _____

Next most important: _____

2. (Optional) Looking to the future of your community in the next five to ten years what problem will be most important?

_____

3. (Optional) Considering the entire nation what is the most important problem facing the nation?

_____

4. (Optional) If you could name the one thing which most reduces your personal happiness; what would it be?

_____

Figure 6-3. General Public Mail Questionnaire.

Leader interviewed:	1. What do you think is the most important problem facing your community?
Interviewer:	
Group with which Leader is affiliated:	2. What other important problems face your community?
Race: Black _____ Hispanic _____ Amerindian _____ Oriental _____ Caucasian _____ Other _____	3. (Optional) Over many years what has been the most persistent yet unsolved problem of your community?
Date and Time of interview:	
Address and phone of Leader:	

Figure 6–4.   Community Leader Survey Interview Card.

NOTES—CHAPTER 6

1. "Report and Statement of Policy Re: Commission EnBanc Programming Inquiry," FCC 60–970, July 29, 1960. Reprinted in Frank J. Kahn (Ed.) *Documents of American Broadcasting*, Third Edition (Englewood Cliffs, N.J.: Prentice-Hall, 1978), p. 217.
2. Robert K. Avery, "Access and Ascertainment: A Short History of the Issues," paper presented to annual meeting of the Western Speech Communication Association, November 1975, p. 13.
3. *Camden Decision*, FCC 69–644, Docket No. 18303, June 13, 1969, p. 10.
4. "Community Needs Notice Released by FCC, *Broadcasting*, August 25, 1968, p. 47.
5. As of this writing, the most recent ascertainment guidelines are found in *Federal Register*, Docket No. 19715, January 7, 1976.
6. "Further Notice of Inquiry and Further Notice of Proposed Rulemaking," FCC 75–923, Docket No. 19816, August 14, 1975, p. 13.
7. *Ibid.*, p. 17.
8. *Broadcasting*, February 18, 1974, p. 22.
9. More detailed results of this study may be obtained through the National Association of Broadcasters which funded this research. Write Director of Research, NAB, 1771 N Street, N.W., Washington, D.C. 20036.
10. Stuart Surlin and Tess Bradley, "Ascertainment Through Community Leaders," *Journal of Broadcasting*, **18** (1974), 97–107.
11. Mary Ann Heller, "Problems in Ascertainment Procedures," *Journal of Broadcasting*, **21** (1977), 427.
12. *Loc. Cit.*

7 Effectiveness of Programs to Meet Community Needs

Joseph C. Philport and James E. Fletcher

THE PROBLEM

As emphasized in the previous chapter the requirements to ascertain community needs with community leaders and the general public is likely to stand for the foreseeable future. Programming in response to these needs felt by and identified by the community is not only a prescribed part of license renewal applications but a moral obligation with many broadcast licensees. The success of local magazine and other public affairs programs attests to the fact that programs may respond to the felt needs of the community without completely destroying audience interest.

It is not uncommon that programs designed to respond to ascertainment needs will be relatively expensive when contrasted with some of the less costly titles in syndication. However, these programs are capable (when targeted to the right audiences) of enhancing the image of the station as involved, concerned and active in the community. Surveys of programming effectiveness can serve as important tools in assessing the impact of current ascertainment programming and provide input for the design of future programs. For both reasons of community service and cost efficiency it will be desirable to evaluate the relative success of ascertainment programming at nearly every station. The specific objectives of this evaluation ought to be:

1. Does the programming in fact deal with or influence the solution of the problem to which it is addressed?
2. Does it reach an audience that needs to know about the problem or who can contribute to its solution?
3. In terms of clarity and quality does the program come up to the standards set by other public affairs programs of the station, and does it compare favorably in these terms with comparable programs broadcast by other stations in the market?
4. Does this ascertainment programming contribute to building a strong and enduring relationship between the station and its audience?
5. How can this program be made more effective (a) in cost benefit terms, (b) in terms of reaching the desired audiences, and (c) in terms of addressing the ascertained problems?

A RESEARCH APPROACH

The research design described in some detail in this chapter is addressed to the objectives above and calls for a telephone survey of a random sample of the population in the community(ies) served by the station. In some cases, it will be desirable for several stations to unite for purposes of this research, thus sharing expenses to reduce the cost of the research or to extend its scope, Multiple sponsorship will also add to the credibility of the research.

Questionnaire Construction

The questionnaire suggested here attempts to evaluate a specific public affairs program within the context of the station's overall programming effort. The public affairs offerings of the station, according to station policy, should (1) be concerned with the presentation of local community problems, (2) cover cultural events in the community, and (3) generally serve the community public interest. Receiving an evaluation from the community of excellent or good in any of these areas would be seen as a favorable evaluation of the station effort.

As respondents provide their views on station programming their frame of reference in evaluating programs is likely to be network programs or syndicated programs. Respondents are likely to be quite eager to provide their views on these programs. The wise researcher will allow them to present these views early in the interview by soliciting a global evaluation of the station's *Total Programming Spectrum.* After finding release for a backlog of opinion on progamming, the respondent will then be willing to address the more narrow issues of the programs and programming which are the objective of the evaluation.

Accordingly, the second area of analysis will be *Total Public Affairs Programming.* This data will provide a baseline for comparison of ascertainment programs with other public affairs programming. It will also establish meaningful relationships between audience perceptions of programming overall and public affairs programming in particular. Of course, this area of questioning will not provide a point by point exposition of the strengths and weaknesses of various ascertainment programs.

The final unit of analysis is the *Individual Program.* While to the uninitiated this unit may appear the only one pertinent to the objectives of the research, it has serious limitations when standing apart from the previous two. For one thing, there are very real time limits when conducting a telephone survey. Interviews of twenty minutes or more would be long for the respondents, and it would probably result in a higher level of interviews not completed due to respondent impatience or fatigue. The cost of interviewer time per completed interview schedule becomes expensive at this rate. In a single interview it is practical to collect data on only one program or, at most, on a small number of programs. More importantly, if data are collected only on a specific program from the ascertainment programming menu, there will be no basis for comparison. So, for example, what does it mean when a respondent says that the program, "Mayor's Hotline" is "good"? If the same respondent felt that the typical public affairs program was "just tolerable," then a "good" program would be very highly evaluated. On the other hand, if the typical public affairs program were rated by this respondent as "excellent," then a "good" program needs improvement.

Data Collection by Telephone

In the overall design for this research the decision-maker will be concerned with the method of data collection, sampling procedure, interview schedule, and analysis of data.

The method of data collection recommended for this study is the telephone survey. Arguments for and against telephone and other methods of data collection have been presented in Chapters 4 and 5. In this case, telephone data collection was preferred over face-to-face interviewing in the respondents' homes, because (a) telephone interviewing is cheaper, and (b) telephone interviewing does not require as much training of the interviewers as does face-to-face-interviewing. The telephone method is preferred over mail data collection, because (a) the level of cooperation with the researcher will be higher in telephone interviews (at least in most parts of the country), and (b) the telephone interview gives the researcher control over the time when the respondent provides information. In this study the investigator will likely want to make the telephone interviews during the time period the programs involved are being broadcast (telephone coincidental method). This means that the respondents either are or could be listening to the programs in question as they are being asked questions about them. In the case of mail questionnaires, respondents may be answering questions at any time, and responses during the listening or viewing time of the ascertainment programs would be a matter of coincidence.

Sampling Procedures

Reaching the target population is the first problem to be addressed by the sampling plan. If the objective of the research is to reach the actual listeners and viewers of an ascertainment program, the sample may be very large, since the typical audience for such programs will be small in comparison to the total audience. In addition, the target population may fit a very specific definition cited in the problem being addressed by the population. For example, the ascertained need may be that vocational opportunities are not well understood by a Spanish-speaking minority in the community. This minority may account for 10 percent of the population. The proportion of the Spanish-speaking audience tuned in to any one program will be less than 100 percent. In a random sample of the community, many more households would have to be included within the sample in order to obtain an adequate number of Spanish-speaking respondents who heard the program being evaluated. Of course, in this survey, it will be desirable to include non-listeners as well, if the study is to reflect upon the reasons the program is not being more effective in reaching its intended audience.

While other methods of sampling are possible, as discussed elsewhere in this volume, there are a number of reasons why a simple random sampling strategy is recommended for the survey suggested in this chapter. The first consideration is that one objective of the study is to obtain assessments of the *Total Programming Spectrum* and the *Total Public Affairs Programming* as well. These variables can only be assessed accurately by a sample of the station's total potential audience.

A second reason that a simple random sample is to be preferred is that, under these rules, the probability that the sample will have the same demographic and social makeup as the community will be maximum.

Finally, this sampling method is procedurally simple, requiring the least training to use. The procedure suggested here is random digit add-on in which a random sample of telephone listings is first drawn from the local telephone directory following the procedures outlined in Chapter 4. Then using a table of random numbers like that at Table VI, Appendix D, a single digit random number is drawn for each telephone number drawn in the first step. The two are added, yielding a new telephone number—the one to be called in the survey. The illustration below may make the process clearer.

a NUMBER DRAWN FROM TELEPHONE DIRECTORY	b RANDOM DIGIT FROM TABLE	a + b TELEPHONE NUMBER FOR THE SURVEY
549-4444	3	549-4447
543-3456	9	543-3465
554-6788	0	554-6788
541-2322	7	541-2329
542-3335	4	542-3339

It is the numbers in the last column that will be dialed by the telephone interviewers. The advantage of this system of sampling over merely using the numbers drawn from the directory are (a) the telephone directory is incomplete, since it does not include recent connections and disconnections; (b) the directory does not include unlisted telephone households; but this sampling procedure provides an easy procedure for compensating for some of these shortcomings.

It is a part of the sampling plan that the interviewers will make every reasonable effort to complete calls to the numbers drawn into the sample. "Every reasonable effort" must include a minimum of three callbacks, each in a different part of the day. A callback is another attempt to call the same number; a rule of three callbacks means that attempts to complete the call will be made on four occasions. The reason that the callbacks are made at a different time of day is that the researcher assumes that the reason a family does not answer a call is that they are not typically home at the time of the call. With such an assumption it makes common sense to place the callbacks at other hours of the day.

In terms of procedure, the interviewer will mark on an interview schedule the number from the sample which will be called. When there has been an attempt to complete the call, the appropriate block is checked and the schedule moved to a stack of schedules representing interviews planned for some other time of day.

Distributing calls across time of day is another important part of the sampling plan. Ideally the number of calls in any day-part will be in proportion to the relative importance of that day-part in the total audience of the station. In the case of a network-affiliated television station, the largest audience is likely to be in the evening. In the case of an AM radio station, heaviest listening is likely to be in the daytime, perhaps during morning and evening drive time. Calls are distributed according to listening patterns, because the credibility of a respondent increases when reporting attitudes toward programs broadcast during the same time period as the interview. This is particularly so in the case of television programming. If the respondent is not home to be interviewed at a given time, then it is less likely that the same individual will be home to watch television at that same time. An illustration of the way in which calls might be distributed in a given market follows:

DAY-PART	TOTAL PERSONS USING TV AT THIS TIME	PERCENT USING TV	PERCENT OF SAMPLE CALLS
7-9 A.M.	111,000	16	9
9-noon	151,000	22	13
noon-4	180,000	26	15
4-7 P.M.	330,000	48	28
7-11 P.M.	417,000	61	35
Total Persons CUME 7 A.M.-11 P.M.	683,000	100	100

The percent using television column sums to 173 rather than 100, since many who are in the audience during one day-part are also in the audience during other day-parts. The figures in the last column are percent of the survey sample to be interviewed during the day-part indicated. These figures represent the percent of 173 (the sum of the third column) represented by each item in the third column.

Interview Schedule or Questionnaire

The interview schedule or questionnaire in Figure 7-1 is directed at the evaluation of a weekly discussion program that examines community problems. The title of the program is "Focus on Our Town." The interview schedule is designed to provide an evaluation of the Total Programming Spectrum and of Total Public Affairs Programming. Since "Focus on Our Town" is a relatively popular program, heard by about one third of the adults in the community during any month, we have designed a sample which will deliver 300 completed interviews, one third of which should represent viewers of "Focus on Our

Interviewer: _____ Respondent Phone Nr: _____

---
call record
---

	time of call	completed	male	female	refused	no answer	busy	no TV	other specify
#1									
#2									
#3									
#4									

"Hello. My name is _____. I'm doing a survey of television viewing. I'd like to ask you some questions that will take only a few minutes. First . . ."

1. Do you or your family have a TV set that works?   No _____
                                                          (TERMINATE)

                                                        Yes _____

2. On a typical day, about how many hours do you personally spend watching TV?

                                                        Don't watch _____
                                                          (TERMINATE)
                                                        Less than 1 Hr _____
                                                        1 Hr _____
                                                        2-3 Hr _____
                                                        Over 3 Hr _____

3. Now—thinking about all the channels you watch—how satisfied are you with what you find to watch on TV? Would you say

                                                        Very satisfied? _____
                                                        Somewhat? _____
                                                        Not at all? _____
                                                        Don't know _____

4. Do you watch any shows on WXYZ-TV, Channel 2?   No _____
                                                          (TERMINATE)

                                                        Yes _____

5. How satisfied are you with the things you see on WXYZ, Channel 2?

                                                        Very satisfied? _____
                                                        Somewhat? _____
                                                        Not at all? _____
                                                        Don't know _____

6. Now I would like you to rate the job that WXYZ-TV does in three areas. In each area I will ask you if the station is doing an excellent job, a good job, a fair job or a poor job.

        a. Presenting and discussing local problems   Excellent job _____
                                                        Good job _____
                                                        Fair job _____
                                                        Poor job _____
                                                        Don't know _____

Figure 7-1. Illustrative interview schedule or questionnaire.

b. Covering cultural events in the community

Excellent job _____
Good job _____
Fair job _____
Poor job _____
Don't know_____

c. Generally serving the public of the community

Excellent job _____
Good job _____
Fair job_____
Poor job_____
Don't know _____

7. There are many kinds of local shows on WXYZ-TV, Channel 2. Some people feel there are too many of some kind, not enough of another. Would you tell me for each of the following kinds of shows, does WXYZ have too many or too few, in your opinion, or just about enough?

	don't know	too many	too few	enough
a. Local sports				
b. Local news				
c. Discussion				
d. Children's				
e. Documentaries				
f. Science/nature				
g. Advice				
h. For minorities				
i. Cultural events				
j. Talk on local problems				

8a. Have you watched "Focus on Our Town," WXYZ's local community affairs show during the past month? It's broadcast on Tuesdays at 7 P.M.

Yes _____
(GO TO 9)

No _____
(GO TO 8b)

8b. Are you familiar with "Focus on Our Town?"

Yes _____
(GO TO 9)

No _____
(GO TO 12)

9. Would you say that "Focus on Our Town" is:

One of my favorite local shows _____
Good _____
Average _____
Poor _____

10. I'd like to know if you think that "Focus on Our Town" does:

Excellent job _____
Good job _____
Fair job _____
Poor job _____

Figure 7-1. (continued)

11. Are there any topics you would like discussed on future shows?
   (PROBE IF NECESSARY)

12. Just a few more questions. Stop me when I come to the category which
   represents how far you went in school.

   Less than high school _____
   High school _____
   Some college _____
   College degree _____
   Refused _____

13. Stop me when I come to the category which represents how old you are.

   18-25 _____
   26-35 _____
   36-49 _____
   50+ _____
   Refused _____

14. Stop me when I come to the category which represents your race.

   White _____
   Black _____
   Asian _____
   American Indian _____
   Hispanic _____
   Other _____
   Refused _____

15. What is your occupation?

   Professional & executive _____
   Clerical & sales _____
   Labor (skilled & unskilled) _____
   Other (specify) _____
   Refused _____

16. Stop me when I come to the category that represents your total family income.

   Under $10,000 _____
   $10,000 to $15,000 _____
   $15,000 to $20,000 _____
   More than $20,000 _____
   Refused _____

Thank you very much for your help. Goodbye."

Figure 7-1. (continued)

Town." To complete 300 interviews we have prepared a sample of 600 telephone numbers. The reason that the sample of numbers is so much larger is that the researcher expects to reach some numbers that are not connected, others that are not residences.

Each question will be discussed to clarify objectives and administration:

Questions 1 and 2: Qualifiers

1. Do you or your family have a TV set in working order?
2. On a typical day, approximately how many hours do you personally spend watching TV?

These questions are qualifying questions that determine whether or not an individual is an acceptable respondent. If the respondent does not have a television or does not watch television, we cannot expect that individual to accurately evaluate the programming on WXYZ-TV. If an individual answers "No" to either question 1 or 2, the interviewer should terminate the interview by thanking the respondent for his time and help in the project.

Question 3: Total Programming Spectrum

3. Now, thinking of all channels you watch—how satisfied are you with what is available to watch on TV?

The interviewer asks the respondent to evaluate his overall level of satisfaction with television. The interviewer should read each of the first three responses but should not read the "Don't Know" category. Only one of the four responses should be checked. Sometimes the respondent states that he is unsure as to what is meant by "Satisfied." The interviewer can help by suggesting that "we are concerned with how the respondent generally feels about television and that the respondent should define 'Satisfaction' in his own words." Question 3 is asked at this time to introduce the respondent to the general format of the evaluative questions that will follow. Since it involves a global evaluation of television programming, it is not essential to this study. However, it can be used for a basis of comparison with question 5, "How satisfied are you with the things you see on WXYZ?" to know the respondent's attitude toward TV in general. For example, if the respondent finds TV generally intolerable, it would not be surprising that WXYZ offerings evoke negative responses as well.

Question 4:   Final Qualifier.

4. Do you watch any programs on WXYZ-TV, Channel 2?

This is the final qualifier for the early part of the interview. If the respondent has not watched any WXYZ-TV programming, he/she should not be expected to provide an evaluation of station programs. If the response is "no," then the interview should be terminated.

Question 5:   Total Programming Spectrum.

5. How satisfied are you with the programs available to watch on WXYZ, Channel 2?

This is an evaluative item, in the same form as Question 3. Responses from this item should be interpreted in light of responses to Question 3.

Questions 6a, 6b, and 6c: Total Public Affairs Programming.

6a, b, c: Now I'd like to ask you to rate the job that WXYZ-TV does in three areas. For each item, I'd like to know if you think Channel 2 does an *excellent job,* a *good job,* a *fair job,* or a *poor job.*

a. Presenting and discussing local problems,
b. Covering cultural events in the community.
c. Generally serving the public of the community.

The responses to these items provide insights into the respondent's evaluation of the station public affairs offerings. The researcher may wish to interpret the responses to this item in light of the respondent's responses to Question 5. For example, what do respondents who give a high evaluation of station programming think of the station's coverage of cultural events? If the responses to these three items are added, the result will be a kind of box score for public affairs programming. In dealing with these questions, the interviewer should begin by reading the introductory statement, making certain that the four possible responses are clearly read ("Don't know" is not read). Then each statement is read and the responses recorded separately. Possible responses are repeated whenever necessary.

Questions 7a through 7j: Total Public Service Programming.

7a–7j: There are many different kinds of local programming available on WXYZ. Some people might feel that there is too much or too little programming in some areas. Would you tell me for each kind I mention whether you think WXYZ has *too much, too little,* or *just about enough.*

a. Local sports
b. Local news
c. Discussion
.
.
.
etc.

This question enlarges upon those of Question 6 by asking the respondent to evaluate the relative quantity of public service programs in the station schedule. The interviewer reads the introductory statement along with the three possible responses. With each program type, it may be wise to include the titles of several programs that fall into the category. This will guarantee the correct interpretation of the program category by the respondent. The results of this question will provide insight into the nature of the respondent's replies to Question 6.

Questions 8a and 8b: Individual Program.

8a and 8b: Have you watched "Focus on Our Town?" That's WXYZ's local community affairs program shown on Tuesday evenings during the past month?

Are you familiar with "Focus on Our Town"?

These questions introduce a new part of the interview schedule or questionnaire. This part is directed at an evaluation of a specific program aired by the station. If the answer to question 8a is "yes," then the interviewer should proceed to question 9. If the answer is "no," then the interviewer asks question 8b. If the respondent answers "yes" to question 8b, then the interviewer proceeds to question 9. If the answer is "no," then the respondent is asked questions 12 through 16. If the responses to both questions 8a and 8b are "no," the respondent does not have useful information to contribute to an evaluation of the program in question.

Questions 9 and 10: Individual Program.

9. Would you say that "Focus on Our Town" is: one of *your favorite local programs, good, average* or *poor?*
10. I'd like to know if you think that "Focus on Our Town" does: an *excellent job,* a *good job,* a *fair job* or a *poor job.*

Here the interviewer asks the respondent to evaluate the individual program involved in the research. The responses to these items need to be evaluated in light of the responses given by the respondent to questions 3, 5, 6 and 7.

Question 11: Open-ended.

11. Are there any topics that you would like to hear discussed on future shows?

This is the only open-ended item in the interview. Interviewers will often find it necessary to probe or to ask additional questions in order to draw out the respondent or to make responses clear and interpretable. It should be anticipated that some respondents will be entirely unable to identify subjects for future treatment. These subjects suggested for future programs provide insights into the nature of the image which the program has with the respondents, into directions for the program in the future, and into the actual state of knowledge of the respondent about the program. For example, with regard to this last point, if the respondent states that future programs should deal with gasoline prices, and the program has dealt only with gasoline prices to this date, the researcher would be justified in questioning the usefulness of the data which this respondent can contribute to the survey.

Questions 12 through 16—Demographics. Demographic questions are included at the end of the survey, since they produce a higher refusal rate than the media-related questions. The respondent is advised that there are only a few more questions. If necessary, the interviewer explains that the station is interested in knowing more about the people who watch the station, in order that the viewing audience can be better served. In analysis of the results of the survey, demographic information may be important in deciding whether the program is reaching its target audience. In addition, these demographics may suggest potential sponsors for public affairs programs. Ascertainment programs, for instance, that reach highly paid and highly educated audiences may be attractive to such institutional sponsors as banks and insurance companies

TABULATION OF RESULTS

Simple Frequencies and Percents

If tabulation of the survey data is to be done manually, the first step will be computation of simple frequencies and percents. A simple frequency is the number of respondents who indicated a particular response. The percent of all those who responded to a question who gave a particular response is the simple percent associated with that response. One way to assemble the data for hand tabulation is on accounting sheets with enough columns to allow one column for each possible response (plus about 10 columns to allow for coding of the open-ended question to be discussed later). In the case of the illustrative interview schedule, some 91 columns would be required. Each horizontal line would contain the data for one respondent. A check in a vertical column would indicate that the respondent had selected the response corresponding to that column as his/her response; an empty column would indicate a response the respondent had not selected. The sum of the number of checks in any vertical column would be the simple frequency for the response involved.

The limitation of this method of hand tablulation is the large number of columns required—91. Such a wide sheet is unwieldy. An alternative for hand tabulation which requires fewer columns to tabulate the data is to first code the responses, then record the code corresponding to the respondent's response in a column representing a question in the interview schedule. This method will be illustrated in Figures 7-2 and 7-3.

The first step in hand tabulation is coding; that is, the responses checked on the questionnaire are given the codes indicated in Figure 7-2. The tabulation sheet in Figure 7-3 provides one vertical column for each question in which the coded response of each respondent is recorded, one respondent per horizontal line. At the bottom of the tabula-

	Interviewer:					Respondent Phone Nr:		

call record

	time of call	completed	male	female	refused	no answer	busy	no TV	other specify
#1									
#2									
#3									
#4									

"Hello. My name is _____. I'm doing a survey of television viewing. I'd like to ask you some questions that will take only a few minutes. First . . ."

1. Do you or your family have a TV set that works?   No _____ (0)
   (TERMINATE)

   Yes _____ (1)

2. On a typical day, about how many hours do you personally spend watching TV?

   Don't watch _____ (0)
   (TERMINATE)
   Less than 1 Hr _____ (1)
   1 Hr _____ (2)
   2-3 Hr _____ (3)
   Over 3 Hr _____ (4)

3. Now—thinking about all the channels you watch—how satisfied are you with (3)
   what you find to watch on TV? Would you say

   Very satisfied? _____ (3)
   Somewhat? _____ (2)
   Not at all? _____ (1)
   Don't know _____ (0)

4. Do you watch any shows on WXYZ-TV, Channel 2?   No _____ (0)
   (TERMINATE)

   Yes _____ (1)

5. How satisfied are you with the things you see on WXYZ, Channel 2?

   Very satisfied? _____ (3)
   Somewhat? _____ (2)
   Not at all? _____ (1)
   Don't know_____ (0)

6. Now I would like you to rate the job that WXYZ-TV does in three areas. In each
   area I will ask you if the station is doing an excellent job, a good job, a fair job
   or a poor job.

   a. Presenting and discussing local problems   Excellent job _____ (4)
   Good job _____ (3)
   Fair job_____ (2)
   Poor job_____ (1)
   Don't know _____ (0)

Figure 7–2. Illustrative interview schedule or questionnaire with possible coding indicated.

b. Covering cultural events in the community

Excellent job _____ (4)
Good job _____ (3)
Fair job _____ (2)
Poor job _____ (1)
Don't know _____ (0)

c. Generally serving the public of the community

Excellent job _____ (4)
Good job _____ (3)
Fair job _____ (2)
Poor job _____ (1)
Don't know _____ (0)

7. There are many kinds of local shows on WXYZ-TV, Channel 2. Some people feel there are too many of some kind, not enough of another. Would you tell me for each of the following kinds of shows, does WXYZ have too many or too few, in your opinion, or just about enough?

	don't know (0)	too many (3)	too few (1)	enough (2)
a. Local sports				
b. Local news				
c. Discussion				
d. Children's				
e. Documentaries				
f. Science/nature				
g. Advice				
h. For minorities				
i. Cultural events				
j. Talk on local problems				

8a. Have you watched "Focus on Our Town," WXYZ's local community affairs show during the past month? It's broadcast on Tuesdays at 7 P.M.

Yes _____ (1)
(GO TO 9)

No _____ (0)
(GO TO 8b)

8b. Are you familiar with "Focus on Our Town?"

Yes _____ (1)
(GO TO 9)

No _____ (0)
(GO TO 12)

9. Would you say that "Focus on Our Town" is:

One of my favorite local shows _____ (4)
Good _____ (3)
Average _____ (2)
Poor _____ (1)

10. I'd like to know if you think that "Focus on Our Town" does:

Excellent job _____ (4)
Good job _____ (3)
Fair job _____ (2)
Poor job _____ (1)

Figure 7-2. (continued)

tion sheet the number of responses to each question is represented as N_i and is a count of the number of coded responses in the column above. Then the frequency with which each code number appears in the column is counted and recorded under each question. The percent of the responses to each question for each number code are indicated in parentheses beneath the frequency (f_i) with which the code appears. This percent is computed

11. Are there any topics you would like discussed on future shows?
    (PROBE IF NECESSARY)

(1) Local—city	(5) Nation
(2) Local—county	(6) International
(3) State	(7) Other
(4) Region	

12. Just a few more questions. Stop me when I come to the category which represents how far you went in school.

Less than high school _____ (1)
High school _____ (2)
Some college _____ (3)
College degree _____ (4)
Refused _____ (0)

13. Stop me when I come to the category which represents how old you are.

18-25 _____ (1)
26-35 _____ (2)
36-49 _____ (3)
50+ _____ (4)
Refused _____ (0)

14. Stop me when I come to the category which represents your race.

White _____ (1)
Black _____ (2)
Asian _____ (3)
American Indian _____ (4)
Hispanic _____ (5)
Other _____ (6)
Refused _____ (0)

15. What is your occupation?

Professional & executive _____ (1)
Clerical & sales _____ (2)
Labor (skilled & unskilled) _____ (3)
Other (specify) _____ (4)
Refused _____ (0)

16. Stop me when I come to the category that represents your total family income.

Under $10,000 _____ (1)
$10,000 to $15,000 _____ (2)
$15,000 to $20,000 _____ (3)
More than $20,000 _____ (4)
Refused _____ (0)

Thank you very much for your help. Goodbye."

Figure 7–2. (continued)

by dividing f_i by N_i and multiplying by 100. So, for example, to question #5, there were 100 responses (f_5) coded "1" out of 300 (N_5) total responses to the question:

$$\frac{100}{300} \times 100 = 33\%.$$

These data from any question may then be summarized in the text of a report in this way:

Question # 5: How satisfied are you with the things you see on WXYZ, Channel 2? (With a total of 300 respondents providing answers).

Very satisfied	30% (90 persons)
Somewhat	33% (100 persons)
Not at all	33% (100 persons)
Don't know	3% (10 persons).

RESPONDENT	#1	#2	#3	#4	#5	#6a	#6b	#6c	#7a	#7b	#7c	#7d	#7e
001	0	–	–	–	–	–	–	–	–	–	–	–	–
002	1	3	2	1	3	1	0	0	3	2	3	1	3
003	1	1	0	0	–	–	–	–	–	–	–	–	–
004	1	3	2	1	3	3	2	2	1	2	3	1	2
005	1	3	1	1	2	2	1	1	2	2	3	2	3
006	1	0	–	–	–	–	–	–	–	–	–	–	–
007	1	4	3	1	3	2	2	2	2	2	2	1	3
391	1	2	2	1	1	2	2	1	1	2	1	1	2
392	0	–	–	–	–	–	–	–	–	–	–	–	–
393	1	3	2	1	2	3	2	2	2	2	2	2	3
394	1	3	2	1	2	2	2	2	2	2	2	1	2
395	1	4	3	1	3	2	1	1	2	2	3	1	3
N_i	320	315	310	310	300	300	300	300	300	300	300	300	300

Code

	#1	#2	#3	#4	#5	#6a	#6b	#6c	#7a	#7b	#7c	#7d	#7e
0 f_i	5	5	5	10	10	0	10	15	0	0	0	0	0
(%)	(2)	(2)	(2)	(3)	(3)	(0)	(3)	(5)	(0)	(0)	(0)	(0)	(0)
1 f_i	315	20	20	300	100	90	150	125	120	10	60	225	20
(%)	(98)	(6)	(6)	(97)	(33)	(30)	(50)	(46)	(40)	(3)	(20)	(75)	(7)
2 f_i	–	134	140	–	100	100	115	130	130	270	60	70	140
(%)		(43)	(45)		(33)	(33)	(38)	(43)	(43)	(90)	(20)	(23)	(47)
3 f_i	–	134	145	–	90	100	20	20	50	20	180	5	140
(%)		(43)	(47)		(30)	(33)	(7)	(7)	(17)	(7)	(60)	(2)	(47)
4 f_i	–	22	–	–	–	10	5	10	–	–	–	–	–
(%)		(7)				(3)	(2)	(3)					
5 f_i	–	–	–	–	–	–	–	–	–	–	–	–	–
(%)													
6 f_i	–	–	–	–	–	–	–	–	–	–	–	–	–
(%)													
7 f_i	1–	–	–	–	–	–	–	–	–	–	–	–	–
(%)													

Figure 7-3. Hand Tabulation for Simple Frequencies and Percents.

In general, two out of three respondents had a favorable evaluation of Channel 2 programs (Very satisfied + Somewhat satisfied).

Similar summaries can be prepared for each question.

Demographic Cross-breaks in Hand Tabulation

A very elementary sort of analysis is to examine responses by the demographic group which provided them. For example, when evaluations of "Focus on Our Town" are considered, does any racial group feel better or worse served by the program? The answers to question #10 provide an evaluation of the program, while the responses to question #14 identify the race of the respondent.

In Figure 7-4 the researcher counts the number of respondents who were white (responded to #14 with response coded "1") who also responded to question #10 that the program does "an excellent job" (response code "4"). In similar fashion each cell in the matrix represented by Figure 7-4 is completed. The percents in the parentheses below each of these frequency counts is computed by dividing the number in the cell by the total of the column and multiplying by 100. So, for example, the per-

#7f	#7g	#7h	#7i	#7j	#8a	#8b	#9	#10	#11	#12	#13	#14	#15	#16
-	-	-	-	-	-		-̃	-	-	-	-	-	-	-
1	3	0	2	3	1	-	4	3	1	2	2	1	1	4
-	-	-	-	-	-	-	-	-	-	-	-	-	-	-
2	2	3	2	3	0	1	3	3	2	3	3	3	2	3
1	3	1	2	0	0	0	-	-	-	4	2	2	2	2
-	-	-	-	-	-	-	-	-	-	-	-	-	-	-
1	2	1	2	3	0	1	3	3	1	4	3	1	1	4
1	0	3	2	3	1	-	3	3	2	3	2	1	3	2
-	-	-	-	-	-	-	-	-	-	-	-	-	-	-
2	3	1	2	0	1	-	3	3	2	2	3	1	3	2
1	2	3	2	3	0	0	-	-	-	4	3	3	1	3
1	2	1	2	3	1	-	3	3	2	4	2	1	2	2
300	300	300	300	300	300	150	180	180	180	300	300	300	300	300
0	50	45	0	73	150	120	-	-	-	20	24	23	25	27
(0)	(17)	(15)	(0)	(24)	(50)	(80)				(7)	(8)	(8)	(8)	(9)
180	5	100	10	2	150	30	20	40	74	5	20	93	92	19
(60)	(2)	(33)	(3)	(1)	(50)	(20)	(11)	(22)	(41)	(2)	(7)	(31)	(31)	(6)
100	125	37	280	10	-	-	20	20	57	5	104	99	91	163
(33)	(42)	(12)	(93)	(3)			(11)	(11)	(32)	(2)	(35)	(33)	(30)	(54)
20	120	118	10	215	-	-	100	80	23	70	96	85	92	91
(7)	(40)	(39)	(3)	(72)			(56)	(44)	(13)	(23)	(32)	(28)	(31)	(30)
-	-	-	-	-	-	-	40	40	2	200	56	0	0	43
							(22)	(22)	(1)	(67)	(19)	(0)	(0)	(14)
-	-	-	-	-	-	-	-	-	0	-	-	0	-	-
									(0)			(0)		
-	-	-	-	-	-	-	-	-	20	-	-	0	-	-
									(11)			(0)		
-	-	-	-	-	-	-	-	-	4	-	-	-	-	-
									(2)					

Question #10: I'd like to know if you think that "Focus on Our Town" does: ($N_{10} = 180$)

		White (1)	Black (2)	Asian (3)	Amer. Indian (4)	His- panic (5)	Other (6)	Refused (0)	Row Total
Excellent job (4)	f_i	28	3	1	—	—	4	4	40
	(%)	(38)	(5)	(4)	(0)	(0)	(20)	(100)	(22)
Good job (3)	f_i	35	24	15	—	—	6	—	80
	(%)	(47)	(42)	(65)	(0)	(0)	(30)	(0)	(44)
Fair job (2)	f_i	4	4	4	1	—	7	—	20
	(%)	(5)	(7)	(17)	(50)	(0)	(35)	(0)	(11)
Poor job (1)	f_i	7	26	3	1	—	3	—	40
	(%)	(9)	(46)	(13)	(50)	(0)	(15)	(0)	(22)
Column Total		74	57	23	2	0	20	4	

Figure 7-4. Opinion of "Focus on Our Town" by Race.

cent of blacks who feel the program does a "poor job" is:

$$\frac{26}{57} \times 100 = 46.$$

Other demographic cross-breaks with question #10, which evaluates the program of concern, are similar; and it is possible to report evaluation of the program by education level (question #12), by respondent age groups (question #13), by occupational groups (question #15), and by income levels (question #16).

Program of Interest versus Total Public Affairs Programming

An evaluation of the public affairs programming of the station was provided in the answers to questions #6a, #6b, and #6c. It is desirable to compare responses to these questions with those to question #10, which provided an evaluation of "Focus on Our Town." One approach to making such comparisons for hand tabulation is to average the responses to questions #6a, #6b and #6c, then subtract this averaged response to question #10. A positively signed difference would mean that "Focus on Our Town" was more highly evaluated than the aggregate of public affairs programs on the station, and, if the difference is negatively signed, the program is evaluated as inferior to the aggregate of public affairs programs.

Most researchers, however, will prefer in addition to (or instead of) the analysis just suggested to develop a cross-break or cross-tabulation of question #10 by question #6a, #6b and #6c. The procedure for doing this is illustrated in Figure 7-5.

In Figure 7-5 the 13 vertical columns represented the response codes for the sum of questions #6a, #6b and #6c. These sums range from 0 (don't know) and 1 (2 don't knows plus 1 poor job) to 12 (3 excellent jobs). A review of the resulting cross-tabulation reveals that those who saw public affairs programming as poor also saw "Focus on Our Town" as poor. Those who thought the program did an excellent job were divided among those who had very high and very low evaluations of total public affairs programming of the station. Overall the evaluation of the program seems to have been higher than that of the aggregate of public affairs programs.

Question #10: I'd like to know if you think that "Focus on Our Town" does: (N_{10} = 180)

Sum of responses to 6a + 6b + 6c

			0	1	2	3	4	5	6	7	8	9	10	11	12	Row Total
Excellent job (4)		f_i	0	5	5	15	0	0	0	0	0	0	5	5	5	40
	(%)		(0)	(25)	(31)	(56)	(0)	(0)	(0)	(0)	(0)	(0)	(71)	(83)	(100)	
Good job (3)		f_i	0	5	2	3	5	10	40	3	2	7	2	1	0	80
	(%)		(0)	(25)	(13)	(11)	(50)	(59)	(83)	(43)	(29)	(70)	(29)	(17)	(0)	
Fair job (2)		f_i	0	0	1	2	2	5	5	2	2	1	0	0	0	20
	(%)		(0)	(0)	(62)	(7)	(20)	(29)	(10)	(29)	(29)	(10)	(0)	(0)	(0)	
Poor job (1)		f_i	0	10	8	7	3	2	3	2	3	2	0	0	0	40
	(%)		(0)	(50)	(50)	(26)	(30)	(12)	(6)	(29)	(43)	(20)	(0)	(0)	(0)	
Column Total			0	20	16	27	10	17	48	7	7	10	7	6	5	180

Figure 7-5. Cross-tabulation of Question #10 with Sum of Questions #6a, #6b, and #6c.

Rationale for the Selection of Variables to Be Cross-tabulated

Although cross-tabulations require additional effort, they often provide information that cannot be assumed from a undiscriminated frequency distribution of responses of the total sample. The above example illustrates how cross-tabulations can be used to compare the audience evaluation of a particular program with the general evaluation of the station's public affairs programming effort. Cross-tabulations could also be used to answer these other programming questions:

1. Are the viewers of "Focus on Our Town" light or heavy viewers of television? Does the program reach an audience that does not generally watch television? (Question 2 with Question 8a.)
2. Is the program reaching a special minority audience? (Question 14 with Question 8a.)
3. Do current viewers and nonviewers differ in the topics they want discussed on future broadcasts of the program? (Question 11 with Question 8a.)

The only limit to the number of cross-tabulations that can be conducted is sample size. As the audience is segmented into smaller and smaller units (i.e., Hispanic males or working women) the error associated with their responses increases. Therefore, caution should be urged when interpreting cross-tabulations conducted on small samples. Procedures for determining the error associated with sample size are discussed in other sections of this volume.

Computer Analysis of Data

Chapter Four provided an illustration of computer analysis of audience measurement information. The same sort of analysis is possible with this data reflecting an evaluation of ascertainment programming. A punched card would be prepared for each horizontal line of Figure 7-3. These cards, one per respondent, would become the data cards of the analysis. Additional cards would bear the instructions to the computer as to the analyses desired. Reference to Chapter 4 and to a manual for the particular computer program involved will provide the necessary insight as to procedure. If assistance is required it is available at nearly any computing facility which deals with statistical analysis. Typically consultants on statistical procedures are officed near the computer just to provide such assistance.

Analysis of the Open-ended Question

Question #11, "Are there any topics you would like discussed on future shows?" is an open-ended question. The responses may be coded in two different ways—*a priori coding* or *a posteriori* (after the fact) coding. In a priori coding the researcher, before examining the detailed responses to the item on the interview schedules, decides which dimensions of response are important enough to the study to make quantification important. In the illustrations provided in Figures 7-2 and 7-3 the researcher felt it was desirable to categorize classes of topics by the geographic area where these issues were relevant (local to international). Then as each questionnaire was coded and tabulated the comments of the respondents were classified into these geographic categories.

In a posteriori coding the researcher attempts to allow the comments from the respondents to organize themselves. So, in terms of procedure, the analyst may begin by drawing 20 interview schedules at random from those accumulated for the study. Let the following list be typical of the comments recorded:

Better streets are needed.
Why can't the buses run on time?
Kindergarten teachers should be better trained.
The unions are closing out minority workers.
Discos are really fronts for organized crime.
Why are our property taxes so high?
Federal taxes should be lower.
This town needs more jobs.
It's disgraceful—the state of repair of our courthouse.
If you don't already have training and experience, it's hard to get a job in
our town.
The school lunch program is too expensive.
Why don't they teach scientific creationism in our schools?
Are there American Nazis in our town?
What about the situation of Vietnamese refugees in our town?

These subjects are then grouped according to any system of classification evident in them. For instance, the researcher might group them this way:

1. Issues related to education—teacher training, school taxes, school busing, adult education, vocational training, school lunch, school curriculum.
2. Local government—crime, streets, mass transit, public works, local business, economy.
3. Employment locally—unions, job demand, economic development, population shifts.
4. Federal government—organized crime, farm and economic policies nationwide, politics, federal courts.

The system of categories would be expanded as questionnaires are coded to create new categories for comments which do not fit this scheme. After tabulation this open-ended data may be summarized in frequency counts, percents, and in cross-tabulation much like the other data of the study.

The Finished Report

When analysis of the survey data is complete a written report should be prepared. It should not include all of the tables and charts prepared in the analysis of the data. It should run 5 to 10 typed pages of narrative and seven to eight charts. Including too many percentages will confuse the reader and will have far less impact than such illustrations as pie-charts and bar-graphs.

The report should include a description of the survey area, the sampling procedures, a sample questionnaire, interviewing procedures and the final status of the sample (a statement of the number of people who refused and consented to participate in the survey as-well-as the demographic characteristics of the in-tab sample).

A Last Word

This chapter has provided one illustration only of a procedure for evaluating an ascertainment program. Many other approaches are possible. If, for example, various programs are aimed at particular sub-populations of the community, special sampling procedures and interview schedules may be required. Advice on these matters are available from broadcast and other facilities at nearby universities and through state broadcasting associations.

8 Qualitative Data: The Why of Broadcast Research

Owen S. Rich and Ernest Martin, Jr.

Most broadcast research services provide quantitative research data—primarily identifying how many people of various ages and sex are listening to radio or watching television at given times of day. This quantitative information is useful in buying and selling air time, but it does not usually provide enough insights into the reasons people watch or listen, nor does it aid in predicting future audience reactions. In multiple station markets, programming has become a process of fine tuning where almost imperceptible program variations cause great changes in the composition of station audiences. If a station management is to hold or increase station audiences, it will be necessary to be aware, on a continuing basis, of variations in listening and viewing interests, tastes and trends.

Quantitative audience research alone is not adequate for making decisions about an audience whose listening and viewing preferences are changing. It is essential to know why the audience listens and watches, why one station is preferred over another, and the ways in which listening and watching behavior is maintained or changed.

The study of the whys of audience behavior is usually referred to as *qualitative* research and is often labeled "psychographics." This is a relatively new area of broadcasting research; but as competition intensifies, it is becoming a vital part of the broadcast decision-making process. An increasing number and variety of research firms devote a great deal of effort to qualitative research. These firms do in-depth audience behavior studies utilizing random sampling techniques and in-depth interviews. They maintain a staff of psychologists, sociologists, and communication specialists to interpret the data they gather and to make recommendations to their clients.

Care should be taken not to confuse quantitative and qualitative research. Remember that quantitative research deals primarily with numbers while qualitative research deals primarily with motives. While quantitative research provides ratings and is useful as a sales tool, it does not give adequate information regarding questions such as: Why does the audience do what it does? Who is listening? Why do they tune in? Why do they tune out? What are the music tastes of the audience? Why is a new show popular or unpopular? What are a program's strengths and weaknesses? What is the overall image of the station with the various audiences in its coverage area? Answering these kinds of questions is the prime task of qualitative broadcast research.

QUALITATIVE RESEARCH DATA GATHERING TECHNIQUES

There are a number of methods of gathering qualitative research data. The three most common are mail surveys, telephone surveys and face-to-face interviews.

Mail Survey

The mail survey is used by many small market broadcasters as a means of gathering qualitative data. It permits a wide variety of questions and responses and may sample a good cross section of the target audience. A mail survey is comparatively easy to conduct and does not require large amounts of time from key staff members. If the sample is a true random sample, the mail survey will be reasonably accurate. Sampling error will be low, and correction factors may be used to compensate for the number of responses as a function of age.

There are, however, some difficulties inherent in conducting a mail survey. One of the major problems is the expected sample mortality rate of approximately 75 percent. Sample mortality is the proportion of the sample drawn from whom usable data is not received. In the case of mail surveys, a mortality rate of 75 percent means that only one in four members of the sample can be expected to return questionnaires. Furthermore, those who do return the questionnaire will tend to be in the older age groups of the survey. Consequently, if a sample size of 400 is needed, approximately 1600 questionnaires must be mailed, and the responses of older respondents will be weighted—discounted—in order that their responses will not be given undue consideration in interpreting results of the survey.

How large should the sample in a mail survey be? A reasonable answer to this question is essential, because the validity, reliability and cost of the survey all hinge upon sample size. Many broadcasters feel that the larger a population is, the larger the sample must be. Lesson Six of Appendix C provides self-instruction on this point to the reader who does not recall the reason this belief is incorrect. It might, at first glance, appear reasonable that sampling error is a linear function, that each additional member of the population placed into the sample reduces sampling error an equivalent amount. But such is not the case. In a true random sample, sample size is not a consistent proportion of population size, and sampling error is not a linear function of sample size.

Figure 8-1 dramatically shows the relationship of sampling error, sample size, and sample costs.

Note that on the curve in Figure 8-1 sampling error rises very sharply when sample size drops below 200. Note also that sampling error levels off and shows little change as sample size is increased above 400. Sampling costs, on the other hand, are linear and continue to rise at a constant rate, even though sampling error shows almost no reduction as sample size continues to increase.

Figure 8-1 suggests that a sample size of 400 to 800 will usually provide an adequate sample when the sample is a true random sample. Because there is a possibility of bias in the sample due to reasons other than size, it may be desirable to select a sample size well beyond the knee of the curve where it begins to resemble a straight line function. Many researchers will strive for a sample size of 1000. This larger sample size may increase the cost of the survey and may have little effect on the validity or reliability of the sample responses.

Another major problem with the mail survey is the difficulty in creating a cover letter and questionnaire which will encourage the respondent to provide adequate data but will not bias that data. The rapidly increasing costs of mailing and handling are additional disadvantages of the mail survey.

There are a wide variety of mail questionnaire formats. An example of a questionnaire prepared for a small market survey follows at Figure 8-2. It should be noted that mail questionnairs do not provide insights into shares of audience, quarter CUMES and aver-

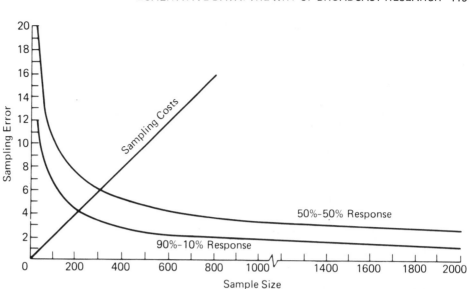

Figure 8–1. Sampling Error Versus Sample Size (prepared by Dr. Owen S. Rich).

age listening/viewing levels. The questionnaires provide audience profiles, demographics, and a variety of qualitative data useful as diagnostic and decision-making tools.

The sample questionnaire at Figure 8-2 which consists of 34 questions is longer than normally recommended. However, it does illustrate the variety of questions that may be included.

As previously noted, the mail questionnaire normally does not provide cumulative audience data or share of audience. Questions two through nine, however, can be processed to yield a cumulative listening index and also an indication of audience share. For example, the mean score for each question could be used as audience share for the station involved, and the sum of responses could be taken as an indicator of audience CUME.

Questions 1, 12, 16, 17, 27, 28, and 29 examine how much and where listening takes place. Questions 13, 14, 15, 18, 25, and 26 address listening preference. Questions 30, 31, 32, and 33 deal with shopping habits, an important consideration in a rural community which is located near an urban area that draws many of the rural buyers. Other questions in the sample questionnaire deal primarily with demographics.

So far as analysis of mail questionnaire data is concerned, cross-tabulation can provide a great deal of valuable information. Cross-tabulation is a simple computer sort of all questionnaires into respondent categories so that the responses to each item may be interpreted in light of the category of respondent. In the case of Figure 8-2 question 23 asks the sex of the respondent. By properly instructing the computer to cross-tabulate based on response to this question, the investigator would see the responses to every other question divided into the responses of males and the responses of females. The same cross-tabulation procedure can provide the basis for a breakdown of responses to any item according to the respondent categories suggested by another item. Cross-tabulation will be described in more detail in a later section on telephone surveys.

The sample mail questionnaire at Figure 8-2 could be improved in a number of ways. For example, return rate could be increased by reducing the total number of questions. It is usually necessary to strike a balance between the amount of information desired in the survey and the respondents' tolerance of questionnaires. Questionnaire tolerance or willingness to respond will vary according to whether the population involved is urban or rural, with level of education, with time of year, among others.

The greatest single challenge of the mail survey is evoking an adequate return rate from the sample. Under the best of conditions, only a relatively small percentage of the sample

MAIL QUESTIONNAIRE

RADIO LISTENING SURVEY

The information which the survey seeks is very important to the study of radio
listening in your area. Your views will be used to represent a number of others
in your community. Please answer the questions as accurately as you can and return
the questionnaire immediately.

EXAMPLE: What is "Utah"
a. City (b.) State c. Country d. Island 3. Nation

Please Circle Only One Answer Per Question

1. How many radios do you have in your home, including auto radios?
a. one b. two c. three d. four e. five or more

2. How often do you listen to KSL?
a. daily b. often c. occasionally d. rarely e. never

3. How often do you listen to KBLW?
a. daily b. often c. occasionally d. rarely e. never

4. How often do you listen to KPST?
a. daily b. often c. occasionally d. rarely e. never

5. How often do you listen to KBUH?
a. daily b. often c. occasionally d. rarely e. never

6. How often do you listen to KVNU?
a. daily b. often c. occasionally d. rarely e. never

7. How often do you listen to KUSU-FM?
a. daily b. often c. occasionally d. rarely e. never

8. How often do you listen to KLUB?
a. daily b. often c. occasionally d. rarely e. never

9. How often do you listen to KCPX?
a. daily b. often c. occasionally d. rarely e. never

10. How often do you listen to OTHER STATIONS? Please list:_____
a. daily b. often c. occasionally d. rarely e. never

11. Which station do you listen to the most?
a. KRGO b. KBLW c. KPST d. KBUH e. KVNU f. KUSU-FM g. KLUB h. KCPX
i. KSL j. other; please list:_____

12. How many hours is your radio turned on each day?
a. 0-1 hour b. 1-2 hours c. 2-3 hours d. 3-4 hours e. 5 or more hours

13. What is your favorite kind of radio listening? (REMEMBER, circle only one)
a. sports b. news c. music d. talk e. other

14. Which northeastern Utah station would you prefer to listen to for national news?
a. KPST b. KBLW c. KBUH d. KVNU e. KVSU-FM

15. Which northeastern Utah station would you prefer to listen to for local news?
a. KPST b. KBLW c. KBUH d. KVNU e. KVSU-FM

Figure 8-2. Questionnaire for a small market survey.

will respond. A modification of Schramm's Fraction of Selection may help to illuminate
the problem:

$$\text{Questionnaire Response} = \frac{\text{Reward}^{1}}{\text{Effort}}.$$

If an individual who has received a questionnaire is to fill it out and return it, the
personal reward must be greater than the effort, according to this formula. It is compara-

16. Do you listen to your radio while driving?
    a. daily b. often c. occasionally d. rarely e. never

17. Where do you listen to your radio the most?
    a. in car b. at home c. in office d. other

18. What is your favorite kind of music? (Choose just ONE, please)
    a. classical (EXAMPLE: Beethoven, Mozart) b. easy listening (EXAMPLE:
    Andy Williams, Henry Mancini, Ray Coniff) c. soft rock (EXAMPLE; Carpenters,
    Association) d. hard rock (EXAMPLE: Three Dog Nite, Chicago) e. soul
    (EXAMPLE: Aretha Franklin, James Brown) f. jazz (EXAMPLE: Dave Brubeck,
    Don Ellis) g. country (EXAMPLE: Buck Owens, Charles Pride, Tammy Wynette)
    h. other (please indicate_____)

19. What is the employment of the head of the household?
    a. farm/ranch b. manufacturing c. professional d. student e. service
    f. sales

20. How many years have you lived in Cache County?
    a. 0-1 year b. 1-5 years c. 5-10 years d. 10-15 years e. 15 or more years

21. May we ask your approximate age?
    a. 13-19 b. 20-29 c. 30-39 d. 40-49 e. 50 or over

22. May we ask your approximate family income?
    a. 0-$5,000 b. $5,000-$10,000 c. $10,000-$15,000 d. over $15,000

23. The sex of the person completing this questionnaire is:
    a. male b. female

24. What is the size of your family?
    a. 1 b. 2 c. 3 d. 4 e. 5 or more

25. Which radio station do you feel is the most involved in Community affairs?
    a. KBLW b. KPST c. KVNU d. KBUH e. KUSU-FM

26. How often would you like to listen to programs of a religious nature?
    a. daily b. often c. occasionally d. rarely e. never

27. In your household, how often do you listen to the radio in the morning?
    a. daily b. often c. occasionally d. rarely e. never

28. In your household, how often do you listen to the radio in the afternoon?
    a. daily b. often c. occasionally d. rarely e. never

29. In your household, how often do you listen to the radio in the evening?
    a. daily b. often c. occasionally d. rarely e. never

30. How often do you shop outside of Cache Valley for food and drugs?
    a. very often b. often c. occasionally d. rarely e. never

31. How often do you shop outside Cache Valley for wearing apparel?
    a. very often b. often c. occasionally d. rarely e. never

32. How often do you shop outside Cache Valley for home furnishings?
    a. very often b. often c. occasionally d. rarely e. never

33. How often do you shop outside Cache Valley for automotive needs?
    a. very often b. often c. occasionally d. rarely e. never

34. Do you live in the City of Logan?
    a. Yes b. No

Figure 8-2. (continued).

tively easy to identify the effort involved in completing and returning the questionnaire,
and every means of reducing that effort should be attempted. The format of the questionnaire should be simple, easy to read, and create as little personal stress as possible.

Identifying some form of reward to increase questionnaire response rate is much more
difficult than identifying effort. Some research firms attempt to raise the level of reward by sending money or offering prizes. A simple but effective way to raise the level
of reward is by promoting a feeling of personal satisfaction and ego boost within the
respondent.

The cover letter may be an important means of promoting personal reward and stimulating questionnaire return. Figure 8-3 provides an illustration.

A comparison of what the letter says and what it means may suggest the rewards in it:

What the Letter Says	*What the Letter Implies*
You are one of a selected few . . .	You are special.
in the Cache Valley area . . .	You live in a special place.
who can do something to help improve radio broadcasting . . .	You can make an important contribution to the community.
Please take a few minutes of your time . . .	Little time is needed.
to complete and return the enclosed questionnaire. A stamped, self-addressed envelope is provided for your convenience.	It's easy and doesn't cost anything.
In no way will you be identified with your response.	No one is trying to sell anything.
This survey selects only a few people to represent the views of your entire community . . .	You are important; you are special in your community.
so your immediate personal response becomes very important.	You should do it now.
Thank you for your help.	We need you.
Sincerely,	
Stevin E. VanLuven	
Research Coordinator	Title is helpful and adds credibility.
P.S. Thanks for your help.	Even a printed personal touch is helpful.

Hopefully, the cover letter will provide enough reward to tip the $QR = \frac{R}{E}$ equation in favor of a response. If the returns to the first mailing of the questionnaire do not provide a sample large enough to bring sampling error within its predetermined limits, a second wave of questionnaires with a second cover letter may be sent to nonrespondents with a plea for response. If the second wave letter does not produce an adequate number of returns, then telephone calls may be made as a final resort. One should not expect more than approximately 30 responses for each 100 mailings. As mailing costs increase, mail surveys become more difficult to justify.

The Telephone Survey

The telephone survey is probably the simplest, least expensive way for the broadcaster to gather data. The telephone survey may take the form of a coincidental survey which must be accomplished within a time frame that coincides with a particular program, block of programs, or time period. The coincidental survey not only provides numbers but provides numbers in reference to specific times of day.

The telephone coincidental survey greatly reduces response errors "in the real world," provides a valid indication of audience behavior as a function of time, and provides data on share of audience for each station. In addition it reduces error due to inaccurate recall or willful distortion.

INTERMOUNTAIN RADIO AND TELEVISON RESEARCH BUREAU
(a Nonprofit Research Organization)
UNIVERSITY STATION BOX A
PROVO, UTAH 84601

February 21, 1972

Dear Radio Listener:

You are one of a selected few in the Cache Valley Area who
can do something to help improve radio broadcasting. Will
you please help us? We need to know what you like to hear
on the radio.

Please take a few minutes of your time to complete and
return the enclosed questionnaire. A stamped, self-addressed
envelope is provided for your convenience. In no way will
you be identified with your response.

This survey selects only a few people to represent the views
of your entire community, so your immediate personal response
becomes very important.

Thank you for your help.

Sincerely,

Stevin E. Van Luven

Stevin E. Van Luven
Research Coordinator

SEV:dm

P.S. Thanks for your help. S.V.L.

Figure 8-3.   Cover letter for a mail survey.

An example of an interview schedule for a simple telephone survey is included as Figure 8-4.

This interview schedule is for a coincidental survey conducted in four separate time periods throughout the broadcast day. Again the schedule has been designed to include a variety of questions for illustration purposes.

This survey was designed to fulfill a diagnostic function for a radio station in a six-station market. Accordingly, the questions specifically relate to problems identified by the station as justifying the expense of a survey.

In this survey, as suggested by the "Time" blank in the heading of the interview schedule, calls were made at various times of day. The times of day were grouped into

INTERMOUNTAIN RADIO AND TV RESEARCH BUREAU
BOX A UNIVERSITY STATION, PROVO, UTAH

Date_____ 1st call_____ 2nd call_____ Telephone_____

Time_____ 1st call_____ 2nd call_____ Name_____

Address_____

1. 1st call a. No answer ( ) b. Answer ( ) c. Busy ( ) d. Other_____ _____ ( )
   2nd call e. No answer ( ) f. Answer ( ) g. Busy ( ) h. Other _____ ( )

2. Hello, this is a radio survey. (No pause.) Is your radio on now?
   a. No ( ) b. Yes ( ) c. No response ( )
   If no to question #2, move on to question 4.

3. What station are you listening to?
   a. KAAA ( ) b. KBBB ( ) c. KCCC ( ) d. KDDD ( ) e. KEEE ( ) f. KEFF ( )
   g. Other_____ ( )

4. What kind of music do you like best? (If necessary read list.)
   a. Country (Buck Owens, Charley Pride ( )   d. Easy Listening (Andy Williams, Henry ( )
   b. Hard Rock (Three Dog Night, Chicago) ( )   Mancini)
   c. Soft Rock (Carpenters, Association) ( )   e. Classical (Bethoven, Mozart)   ( )
                                                f. Other (list_____)   ( )

5. What local radio station do you feel has the best news coverage?
   a. KBBB ( ) b. KCCC ( ) c. KDDD ( ) d. KAAA ( ) f. KFFF ( ) g. Other_____( )

6. What station is your favorite station?
   a. KDDD ( ) b. KCCC ( ) d. KBBB ( ) d. KAAA ( ) f. KFFF ( ) g. Other_____( )

7. I have about three or four more questions. (No pause) Why do you listen to radio?
   (Read list of examples.)
   a. Information ( ) b. Companionship ( ) c. Entertainment ( ) d. Sports ( )
   e. _____ ( ) f. _____ ( )

8. How often do you listen in the morning?
   a. Daily ( ) b. Often ( ) c. Occasionally ( ) d. Never ( )

9. How often do you listen in the middle of the day?
   a. Daily ( ) b. Often ( ) c. Occasionally ( ) d. Never ( )

10. How often do you listen in the evening?
    a. Daily ( ) b. Often ( ) c. Occasionally ( ) d. Never ( )

11. Do you like to hear women announcers on radio?
    a. Positive response ( ) b. Neutral response ( ) c. Negative response ( )

12. Who is your favorite local radio personality? a._____ b. _____

13. One last question. What is your approximate age?
    a. 12 to 19 ( ) b. 20-35 ( ) c. 36-50 ( ) d. Over 50 ( )

----

14. Determine the sex from the voice quality. a. Male ( ) b. Female ( )

15. Time of response.
    a. Morning (7:30-9:00 A.M.) ( )   b. Noon (12:00-1:30 P.M.) ( )
    c. Afternoon (4:30-6:00 P.M.) ( )   d. Evening (8:00-10:00 P.M.) ( )

Figure 8-4. An interview schedule for a simple telephone survey.

four blocks listed as item fifteen of the schedule. The data from item 15 is as follows:

15. Time of response. N (number of respondents) = 649.

	f	%
a. Morning (7:30–9:00 A.M.)	134	20.65
b. Noon (12:00–1:30 P.M.)	160	24.64
c. Afternoon (4:30–6:00 P.M.)	165	25.42
d. Evening (8:00–10:00 P.M.)	190	29.28

Including item 15 in the same format as other items on the interview schedule facilitates computer processing, particularly cross-tabulation.

A summary of the data from item 1 provides information about the success of the survey in collecting data from the sample:

1. Information about the sample.

	f	%
a. Sample size (number of calls attempted)	1058	100.00
b. Out of service, disconnected and no answer	308	29.11
c. Answered but refused to participate	101	9.54
d. Sample response (available audience)	649	61.34

The size of the sample drawn is represented by all questionnaires completed by interviewers, even though a check in item 1 may indicate the sample member was unavailable or provided no data. If the population of the area from which the sample was drawn were 100,000, then each of the individuals in the sample would represent about 100 of the population. Item 1d, "Sample response," represents the number of sample members who provided usable data—the available audience for radio listening. The 649 persons in item 1d collectively represent an available radio audience of 64,900. Throughout the results of this survey, when it may be important to estimate the size of a listening audience, it will be necessary only to multiply the number of sample respondents who reported listening by one hundred. For example, in the summary of data from question 2 below, 489 sample respondents indicated they were not listening to radio. Multiplying by 100, we see that approximately 48,900 persons in the survey area were not listening to radio.

Item 2 of the interview schedule is designed to provide insights into "sets in use" for the survey period:

2. Is your radio on now? N = 649.

	f	%
a. No	489	76.73
b. Yes	145	22.34
c. No response	6	.92

Item 2b shows "sets in use" to be 22.34 percent of the available audience. An estimate of the number of radios in use in the population of the survey area would be 145 multiplied by 100, or 14,500.

The responses to item 3 provide estimates for station share of audience. Audience estimates (CUMES) can also be made from this data.

3. What station are you listening to? N = 145.

	f	%	CUME f × 100
a. KAAA (Rock)	13	8.97	1300
b. KBBB (MOR)	36	24.83	3600
c. KCCC (Rock)	40	27.59	4000
d. KDDD (Country)	33	22.76	3300
e. KEEE (MOR)	7	4.83	700
f. KFFF (Public)	4	2.76	400
g. Other	1	.69	100
h. No response	11	7.59	1100

If one wishes to know how the share of audience varies during the four time periods of item 15, a cross-tabulation will provide the answer. On a computer the sort of audience responses into these categories is almost instant. To make this cross-tabulation manually the investigator sorts the interview schedules into four piles, one representing those who were interviewed in the morning, another for those interviewed at noon, another for those interviewed in the afternoon, and still another for those interviewed during the evening. The responses to item 3 are then summarized for each of these four piles. The results follow:

3. What station are you listening to? N = 145.

	MORNING		NOON		AFTERNOON		EVENING	
	f	%	f	%	f	%	f	%
a. KAAA	5	10.87	3	6.38	2	6.25	3	15.00
b. KBBB	6	13.04	17	36.17	9	28.13	4	20.00
c. KCCC	10	21.74	9	19.15	11	34.38	10	50.00
d. KDDD	18	39.13	8	17.02	6	18.75	1	5.00
e. KEEE	1	2.17	4	8.51	1	3.13	1	5.00
f. KFFF	1	2.17	2	4.26	1	3.13	0	0.00
g. Other	1	2.17	0	0.00	0	0.00	0	0.00
h. No response	4	8.70	4	8.50	2	6.25	1	5.00
	46		47		32		20	

Note that the country station dominates the morning period. The MOR station with its talk and news shows dominates the midday period. A rock station rises in the afternoon and dominates evening listening. This changing share of audience is consistent with the age and music preference data shown in other questionnaire responses.

With that connection between age and music preference in mind, consider a cross-tabulation in which item 4 responses are sorted by age group. Below are the aggregate responses to item 4.

4. What kind of music do you like best?   Age 12–19. N = 67.

	f	%
a. Country	5	7.46
b. Hard Rock	20	29.85
c. Soft Rock	32	47.76
d. Easy Listening	3	4.48
e. Classical	0	0.00
f. Other	1	1.49
g. No response	6	8.96

For the cross-tabulation the computer is instructed to sort sample responses into categories representing responses to item 13 (age). This cross-tabulation will provide music preference by age group.

The age group 12 to 19 is expected to show a marked preference for rock music, since rock is the best-selling category, and this age group accounts for a large proportion of record sales. However, in this relatively conservative rural market soft rock is much preferred over hard rock:

4. What kind of music do you like best? N = 649.

	f	%
a. Country	195	20.05
b. Hard Rock	44	6.78
c. Soft Rock	107	16.49
d. Easy Listening	139	21.42
e. Classical	50	7.70
f. Other	56	8.63
g. No response	58	8.94

The age group 20 to 35 shows an almost equal preference for country and soft rock music with interest in hard rock much lower than that of the next younger age group.

4. What kind of music do you like best?   Age 20–35.   N = 273.

	f	%
a. Country	65	23.81
b. Hard Rock	21	7.69
c. Soft Rock	60	21.98
d. Easy Listening	42	15.38
e. Classical	28	10.26
f. Other	24	8.79
g. No response	33	12.09

The music preferences of the 36 to 50 age group are largely for country and easy listening. Other forms of music do not seem important to this group.

4. What kind of music do you like best?   Age 36–50.   N = 142.

	f	%
a. Country	59	41.55
b. Hard Rock	2	1.41
c. Soft Rock	7	4.93
d. Easy Listening	46	32.39
e. Classical	8	5.63
f. Other	11	7.75
g. No response	9	6.34

Music preferences of those over 50 are very similar to the 36 to 50 age group with country music first and easy listening a more distant second.

4. What kind of music do you like best?   Age 50+.   N = 159.

	f	%
a. Country	66	41.51
b. Hard Rock	1	0.63
c. Soft Rock	4	2.52
d. Easy Listening	46	28.93
e. Classical	14	8.81
f. Other	20	12.58
g. No response	8	5.03

Overall in this survey area the trend of music preference is from rock to country and easy listening as age increases. An unusual feature of the preferences of this market is the dominance of country music in the over 50 age group.

A researcher might also want to ask about a relationship between sex and music preference. The data will yield such answers if another cross-tabulation is performed, one in which the answers to item 4 are categorized by the groups identified in question 14. Still another cross-tabulation, item 4 by item 15, would yield music preference by time of listening.

It should be obvious at this point that a wide variety of tabulations and cross-tabulations of the data from a simple telephone survey can provide a large amount of useful information. This complete view of the data from the survey would provide important insights into radio format with data on music taste, taste for news, influence of air personalities, and others.

Other telephone surveys—not coincidental—may seek information from the past experience of a listener or viewer. Such surveys are much easier to conduct than the coincidental survey and may provide more general information. And much more time may be taken for this type of interview. Hence more questions may be asked. The emphasis of such surveys may be upon qualitative information.

No matter what telephone survey is being employed, the sample ought to be drawn according to a true random sampling procedure. If the sample is not truly random, there is no accurate way to estimate the sampling error inherent in the results.

Proper sample size will depend upon acceptable sampling error, time of day, time of year, geographical location and anticipated mortality. The number of calls placed should be large enough to insure that completed calls bring sampling error within the predetermined limits. Mortality rate will vary with location, time of day, and seasons. It is fair to guess that mortality rate will approximate 50 percent. In other words, one can expect that only one of two telephone calls will normally be answered during the day in most communities.

A telephone interview which will yield qualitative information will be relatively lengthy. As a consequence, the telephone interviewer involved needs to be specially prepared. For example, if the interviewee is allowed to ask questions, the effectiveness of the interview may be impaired. In the well-conducted interview, the interviewee will rarely ask questions. It is desirable to have the interviewee concentrate on answers rather than questions. After identifying themselves, good interviewers immediately ask a simple question. Typically the interviewee responds by answering the question. Other questions from the interviewer then follow quickly without sufficient time for the interviewee to formulate questions. Once the pattern is set and the interviewee is concentrating on responses to questions, the interview proceeds smoothly to its conclusion.

In the radio qualitative study just described 9.54 percent of the sample refused to cooperate. Refusal to cooperate is usually less than 5 percent. In this study an investigation revealed that most of the refusals occurred among respondents to two interviewers. The voice of one of these interviewers sounded rather immature over the telephone. The other seemed apologetic when making requests for information. The interviewer with the immature voice should not have been used. The apologetic interviewer should have been trained to develop a more positive projection of self-concept or be dropped as an interviewer.

Some of the characteristics of the good telephone interviewer are:

1. A mature voice
2. A friendly voice
3. Clear crisp articulation
4. A positive attitude about interviewing
5. Pleasant persistence
6. A willingness to work
7. Honesty
8. Adaptability
9. A strong dialing finger.

The Face-to-Face Interview

The personal face-to-face interview is one of the best methods of obtaining qualitative data. The in-home interview provides reasonably accurate information, broad demographics, possibilities for attitude, and opinion responses in natural environmental settings, and provides insights into socioeconomic conditions. The face-to-face interview will also allow the interviewer to better assess the accuracy of the responses being given by the respondent.

The major disadvantage of the face-to-face in-home interview is that it is usually much more time consuming and expensive than other methods of data collection. The interviewers involved will need special skills; most will need additional training to produce the desired results.

Samples of respondents for face-to-face interviewing should be drawn by a random sampling technique. The sample may be drawn from city directories or, if the number of unlisted numbers is low, from local telephone directories. Any list which contains most of the names of the residents of the community may be the universe from which the random sample may be drawn. It is also possible to use a computer-generated random sample of possible telephone numbers from any specific location.[2] The random telephone number generation technique will include unlisted telephone numbers and the numbers of recently connected residences.

It is often desirable to draw a sample which is a geographical cross-section of the community. This might be done by the grid method. The procedure begins with dividing a map of a community or other geographic area into squares of equal size. This is done by simply ruling on the map a vertical series of equispaced parallel lines and a horizontal series of equispaced parallel lines. The size of the squares will depend upon the number of squares desired. Fifty to one hundred squares is typically adequate, depending upon the size and layout of the community involved.

The next step in the grid method is to decide how many households are to be interviewed and the number of squares of the grid from which they should be drawn. For example, if 200 households are to be interviewed, 10 each might be drawn from 20 randomly selected squares. The 20 squares desired may be drawn with the help of a table of random numbers like that at Appendix D, Table VI, thus reducing to a minimum any bias in selection of the community cross section. Assume that the squares you have drawn on the community map are numbered from 00 to 99: you will be interested in two-digit numbers in the Table of Random Numbers. Start at any point in the table. Write down the two-digit number found there. Then move to the adjacent two-digit number—up, down, right or left. Write the adjacent two-digit number. Continue moving in the table in the same direction until 20 two-digit numbers have been encountered and recorded.

Within each of the 20 squares designated by the selected two-digit numbers from the Table of Random Numbers the households to be designated for interviews may be selected in any scheme which promises a reasonably good mix of the households: for example, every other home, every fifth home, or every home. Ideally, however, the

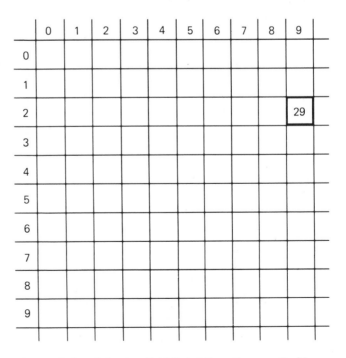

Figure 8–5.   Selection Grid Ruled Over Community Map.

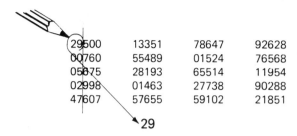

29500	13351	78647	92628
00760	55489	01524	76568
05875	28193	65514	11954
02998	01463	27738	90288
47607	57655	59102	21851

29

Figure 8–6.   Drawing Two-Digit Numbers from the Table of Random Numbers.

scheme by which households are designated in any of the selected squares should be the same scheme of selection in all of the other selected squares.

This grid technique of selecting households for interview is a form of cluster sampling as discussed in Chapter 5.

Acceptance of face-to-face in-home interviewing will vary with respondents according to the size, location, and makeup of the survey area. In small or medium-sized rural communities, door-to-door contacts are usually made with little difficulty. The more metropolitan the community, the greater the reservations of the householder, and in some cases it is possible to interview by appointment only.

Most qualitative data interviews will require an in-home interview time of at least fifteen minutes. Some commercial survey firms doing qualitative research complete very long and complex in-home interviews, some lasting as long as 2½ hours.

Qualitative research usually does not require as many interviews as quantitative research. Since quantitative surveys were designed to provide ratings, share of audience and so on, many more interviews are required, whereas the demands of qualitative research are to reflect behavioral patterns.

QUALITATIVE RESEARCH DESIGN

The success of any survey may depend upon how well the questionnaire is designed. In a telephone survey, the order, content, and complexity of questions will determine the adequacy of the responses and the willingness of the interviewees to participate. In a mail survey the manner in which the questions are worded and printed in the questionnaire as well as its overall layout will play a large part in determining the rate of return or mortality. In the face-to-face interview, the design of the interview schedule as well as the skill of the interviewer may decide whether the interview can be completed.

The format of a questionnaire or interview schedule is important whether the respondent is working directly with it or working with it through an interviewer. In the case of interviews, the performance of the interviewer is enhanced if the interview schedule is easy-to-read, logical, clear, and precise. Data analysis will be facilitated if the questionnaire or interview schedule is easy to score and tabulate.

If the interviewee or respondent is personally reading and marking the questionnaire, it is imperative that the format be attractive, simple, easy to understand, easy to mark, and free of any element which might introduce anxiety into the responses. In most cases, a respondent will not complete a questionnaire or an interview which produces tension or anxiety.

When arranging questions within a questionnaire, simple, easy to answer questions should come first with the more difficult and tension-producing questions last. Once respondents have committed some effort and time to a questionnaire, they will be more willing to answer difficult and personal questions at the end of the period. And, should the respondent break off an interview near the end of the interview schedule, the data that has already been collected to that point can enter the analysis.

Two basic types of questions are commonly used in qualitative research: open-ended and closed-ended. The closed-ended question restricts the response to two or more alternatives which are provided within the questionnaire. The following is an example of a closed-ended question.

16. What kinds of news do you prefer?
    1. National ( )   3. Sports ( )   5. Other ( )
    2. Local   ( )   4. Farm   ( )   _____

Either the respondent or interviewer may merely check the appropriate, predetermined response. The closed-ended question is easy to mark, easy to tabulate and is usually compatible with computer processing. The major disadvantage of the closed-ended question is that it may miss a key concept or idea not considered by the author of the questionnaire.

The open-ended question provides the respondent with unrestricted freedom of choice in response. This freedom enhances the data. The open-ended question offers the respondent an opportunity to react to a question by expressing his attitudes or opinion about the subject or issue. This response may be made in writing by the respondent, or it may be recorded by the interviewer. Open-ended questions may be exploratory in nature and may lead to a series of questions and other comments about the subject at hand. The open-ended question is of great value in identifying and investigating behavioral patterns of the respondent. Care must be taken, however, to insure that the interviewee is not led by the interviewer to make statements which are inaccurate or invalid. The following is an example of the open-ended question.

24. What do you like about Radio Station KEVA?

    _____

    _____

One of the major problems of open-ended questions is the difficulty of tabulation. One of the simplest ways to tabulate the open-ended question is to list each statement and place a tally mark after each repeat. For example, the open-ended question above may produce a number of varied responses which may be listed and tallied as follows.

Statement		f
I like music.	++++ / /	6
The morning news.	/ /	2
I like the announcers.	/ / /	3
Paul Harvey.	/	1
The trading post.	/ / / /	4 .

Most open responses can be forced into less than 10 categories for easy tabulation and recording.

It is imperative that a questionnaire be field-tested before it is adopted. Even the most sophisticated researcher will misjudge the way a respondent will react to or interpret a question. The way to be certain the questions will work is to present them to a smaller sample in the field. A pretest sample of 20 to 30 respondents, who are a cross-section of the later full sample of respondents, will usually be adequate for this pretest.

INFORMATION PROCESSING

Research data is useful only after it is organized in a way that is easy to read and understandable by the decision-maker. Some of the most useful qualitative research information is presented as frequency distributions and cross-tabulations. If only frequency information is required, hand tabulation of the data by totaling responses to each category of each question may be adequate. If, on the other hand, more in-depth analysis such as music preference as a function of age, or station preference as a function of sex is desired, hand tabulation may prove too difficult and time-consuming. In these cases it is strongly recommended that questionnaire data be transferred to computer cards and processed using a standard computer program such as STATO 8 or others which provide relatively complex treatment of data. If trained key-punch operators are not available to produce computer cards for entering the data in the computer, it is possible to code the questionnaire data onto optical scanner sheets, then have the optical scanner automatically read the sheets and cut the computer cards. This additional step is usually worth the time and expense.

When the qualitative data is to be used primarily for diagnostic purposes, it is usually not necessary to test for statistical significance. If results need to be tested for significance, the tests described in Appendix C are applicable.

QUALITATIVE RESEARCH DATA

Some of the questions a radio station manager may ask are: Does the audience really know we are here? Do they listen to our station? Why do they listen? Why don't they listen?

Station Awareness

There are a variety of questions which may help to determine station awareness. One may simply ask the respondent to list the call letters of all of the radio stations in the area. Noting automobile radio push-button setups, overall station preferences, and cumulative listening measures can also indicate station awareness. Here are some sample items.

Station Awareness – Overall Station Recall
1. I'd like you to name all the different radio stations you
   can think of in this area. Please name all you can – even
   if you don't listen to them yourself.

> INTERVIEWER: if respondent cannot recall call
> letters but does know a station's dial position, record
> numbers of dial position and specify AM or FM. Use
> this procedure throughout the questionnaire.

1.	_____	AM	FM
2.	_____	AM	FM
3.	_____	AM	FM
4.	_____	AM	FM
5.	_____	AM	FM
6.	_____	AM	FM
7.	_____	AM	FM
8.	_____	AM	FM
9.	_____	AM	FM
10.	_____	AM	FM

Car Radio Listening Recall
2. Think about the radio stations you may have set on the
   buttons of your car radio. Please name all of the stations
   you can get by pushing one of the buttons.

_____ AM FM
_____ AM FM
_____ AM FM
_____ AM FM
_____ AM FM
_____ AM FM

Overall Station Preference
1. Of all the radio stations you hear which ONE station do you usually spend the most time listening to?
_____ AM FM

2. Now I'd like you to name your overall favorite station in this area. Your first choice?
_____ AM FM

3. How about your second choice? What station would that be?
_____ AM FM

Cumulative Listening Measures
1. What stations do you listen to fairly regularly?
(SPECIFY AM OR FM)

_____   _____   _____

_____   _____   _____

2. Have you listened to KXXX-FM91 during the last month? 1._____YES 2._____NO (GO TO Q.____)
a. What are the things you like or dislike about KXXX. PROBE.

_____

_____

In general, conducting ratings research should be left to firms experienced in rating methodologies. It is possible to construct a rough rating measure. The respondent is asked to "reconstruct" the listening of the previous day. This data is then summarized by time period and demographics.

Station "Rating" — Telephone Reconstruct.
1. Please think back to yesterday. (INTERVIEWER: IF INTERVIEW IS CONDUCTED ON SUNDAY OR MONDAY, SAY: "THINK BACK TO LAST FRIDAY!"). Was it a typical weekday for you? (INTERVIEWER: IF "YES" CONTINUE WITH QUESTIONS. IF "NO" ASK RESPONDENT TO THINK OF A TYPICAL WEEKDAY.) I'd like you to very carefully reconstruct your radio listening. Please take your time. What time was it when you first heard anything on the radio? What station was on? Was it AM or FM? How long did you listen to the station? (Which station was that? Was it AM or FM? How long did you listen to that station?) When was the next time you heard the radio? (REPEAT SERIES OF QUESTIONS FOR ENTIRE

DAY.) (INTERVIEWER: PLACE AN "X" WHERE RESPONDENT BEGAN LISTENING. INDICATE STA-TION – SPECIFY AM OR FM. FROM THE "X" DRAW A WIGGLY LINE DOWN THE COLUMN OF TIMES UNTIL RESPONDENT STOPPED LISTENING. RE-PEAT THIS PROCEDURE THROUGHOUT ENTIRE DAY.)

TIME	"X"	STATION	A.M.	F.M.
Before 6 A.M.	____	_____	____	____
6–6:14 A.M.	____	_____	____	____
6:15–6:29 A.M.	____	_____	____	____
6:30–6:44 A.M.	____	_____	____	____
6:45–6:59 A.M.	____	_____	____	____
7–7:14 A.M.	____	_____	____	____
7:15–7:29 A.M.	____	_____	____	____
7:30–7:44 A.M.	____	_____	____	____
7:45–7:59 A.M.	____	_____	____	____
Continue through 1:59 A.M.				

In addition to awareness and listening behavior, the station management should be interested in what type of image the station projects to its audience. Is the image posi-tive or negative? How does the station image differ across audience age, sex, and per-sonal interest? What is the perceived format of the station, and how does the station format fit into the expressed preference of a stratified audience?

What Is the Image of Stations in My Market?

   A. Open-ended Items.

      1. Now I'm going to name the call letters of some radio stations. As I name each, if you are familiar with the station, I'd like you to describe it in your own words. If you don't know anything about it, just say you don't. The first station is KXXX. Have you heard of it? 1.____ YES   2.____ NO (SKIP TO Q.____)

         a. What kind of music, what kind of program-ming does is have? (PROBE)

         _____

         _____

         b. What kind of people listen to KXXX? (PROBE)

         _____

         _____

   B. *Close-Ended Items.*

      1. Think about all the different radio stations in this area. I am going to read the beginnings of of some sentences. I'd like you to finish the sentence by giving me the name of the first radio station that comes to mind. The station . . .

      Music

         a. Positive

           that plays a nice variety of music . . .

           that plays more of my favorite records than any other station . . .

that really knows about music and musical artists . . .

that plays my favorite oldies . . .

that plays the most music . . .

plays mostly songs I'm familiar with . . .

plays music mostly from albums . . .

b. Negative

that plays music I don't know . . .

that plays a lot of records I'm tired of hearing . . .

that takes just a few records and plays them over and over . . .

that plays music for teenagers . . .

that plays too much unfamiliar music . . .

that plays too many "oldies" . . .

that plays "oldies" that are *too* old . . .

that plays the worst music . . .

that plays a lot of loud, obnoxious records . . .

that is unpredictable – sometimes it plays good music – somtimes bad . . .

that is always interrupting the music with news reports . . .

General Images (Total Station Concept)

a. Positive.

that has changed for the better lately . . .

that I can spend a long time listening to . . .

has a good sense of humor . . .

that gives me really *USABLE* information . . .

where there's always something new and interesting happening . . .

that sounds really exciting . . .

that you were listening to when I called . . .

that is best to wake up to . . .

b. Negative

that has gotten worse lately . . .

that sounded a lot better 5 years ago . . .

that could use the most improvement . . .

that sounds dull . . .

that sounds like it's run by amateurs . . .

that insults my intelligence . . .

that sounds mechanical and impersonal . . .

that sounds outdated . . .

that plays the same commercials over and over again . . .

that is the "teen" station . . .

that would be better if it were on FM in stereo . . .

Announcers

that has the friendliest announcers . . .

that has announcers that don't care about this city . . .

that has announcers who sound dumb . . .

that has announcers who talk too fast . . .

that has boring announcers . . .

that has the silliest announcers . . .

that has announcers who try to be too hip . . .

Contest and Promotion Image

that has annoying contests . . .

that has contests that you have no chance
of winning . . .

that is easist to win a prize on . . .

has contests that are fun to play or listen to . . .

that has annoying jingles singing their call
letters . . .

News, Weather, Traffic, Sports

that gives the news in a way that's easy to
understand it . . .

that has just enough news . . .

that has too much news . . .

that gives newscasts containing information
I don't care about . . .

that I listen to for weather information . . .

has reliable traffic reports . . .

that doesn't devote enough time to sports . . .

Qualitative research data—especially "image" research—can be very enlightening to station management. It would be much more difficult to make decisions affecting the future direction of a station if the manager did not know where the station stood in the minds of the listener. In the final anlaysis, this is the most important contribution of qualitative broadcast research.

NOTES—CHAPTER 8

1. Wilbur Schramm, "How Communication Works, in Schramm (Ed.), Processes and Effects of Mass Communication Urbana: University of Illinois Press, 1954), p. 19.
2. See James E. Fletcher and Harry B. Thompson, "Telephone Directory Samples and Random Telephone Number Generation," *Journal of Broadcasting*, 1974, **18**, 187–191.

9 Message and Program Testing

James E. Fletcher and Ernest Martin, Jr.

Testing telecommunication programs and messages is research that evaluates the likely success of a program or message prior to the time it is broadcast or distributed for broadcast. Favorable audience reactions to broadcast material is nearly always essential to its survival. At the national level, major research expenditures are made in testing pilots and program concepts. Several commercial research firms specialize in this sort of research, evaluating likely audience response to personalities, logos, promotional announcements, and recorded music. In fact, message and program research is one of the fastest growing areas of commercial research in mass communication.

In this discussion, program and message testing procedures will be grouped according to the phase of program development in which they are typically employed—concept, series development, post production, and evaluation of completed material. Many research procedures will be appropriate for all of these levels, but examples will be provided for research at each of these stages of program development.

CONCEPT TESTING

Concept testing involves the solicitation of audience views of a summary or mockup of a proposed message or program. The key to the accuracy and reliability of concept testing lies, as might be expected, in the quality of the summary or mockup—how well it evokes the eventual message or program.

In some cases the program concept for testing might be a short summary paragraph of the program action. For example, "John Kirtland is the outspoken political columnist of the *Beeville Bugle*. Among Beeville luminaries he stands nearly alone as a champion of the common man. Each week he invites to his television interview program Beeville politicians and bureaucrats whose shortcomings have contributed to the general deterioration of the good life in the city. Mr. Kirtland concludes his probing interviews with his own assessment of the problem that has been explored and a summary of the proposed solution which according to Mr. Kirtland is most likely to work."[1]

The concept summary may be shown by a researcher to the respondents of a face-to-face interview who will then be asked to indicate on a scale like the one below how they feel about such a program:

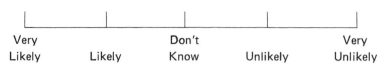

I would watch the Kirtland interview show.

| Very Likely | Likely | Don't Know | Unlikely | Very Unlikely |

When short announcements such as public service announcements or promotional announcements are to be the subject of research, slide/tape storyboards may provide a realistic mockup. The frames of the storyboard from which the announcement is being prepared are shot as 35mm slides. The audio portion of the announcement is recorded by a staff member on the same tape which provides synchronization tones to change the slides in an automatic slide projector. The test audience is then shown this audiovisual storyboard as a representation of the proposed announcement. In this case the researcher might wish to present the mockup announcement to a small group, then conduct a group interview to solicit reactions to the proposed announcement.

To illustrate, consider the research task given to the staff of a local television station concerned over an apparent weakness in the appeal of the sports segment of the daily local news. Responding to this weakness evident in several consecutive rating reports, station management has increased the station investment in sports reporting. A new sports anchor with a reputation as a professional athlete has been engaged; a syndicated series of sports features has been purchased for incorporation into the sports segment. The station news director is concerned that the audience in the market, particularly men 18–35, be made aware of these attractive changes as soon as possible. A set of promotional announcements has been designed to appeal to this audience, and the station plans to schedule these announcements adjacent to entertainment programs that are strong in the desired demographics. The intent of the announcements is to reach men who exclusively watch the sports segment of a competing local station, making them aware of what they are missing when they do not regularly view the sports segment of our station. The storyboards of the new announcements are produced as synchronized slide/tape shows. Respondents are recruited by telephone from a random sample of local telephone households. The recruiter who placed the telephone calls to the telephone household sample asked at each household for residents who were men between 18 and 35. When these men came to the telephone, they were told that they would receive a valuable premium if they would participate in the station study (the premiums were local football tickets). Those men who agreed to participate were invited to attend a group interview where only nonviewers of our sports segment were in attendance, or to another group interview where viewers of our sports segment were in attendance: it is the station's desire to appeal to both groups. When the interview groups (usually about five in size) meet with the research interviewer they will view the audiovisual mockups of the announcements. Then the interviewer will lead a group discussion of the announcements. The discussion will be audiotaped for later analysis. The interviewer will use stimulus questions to get the discussion underway and to keep it going until the full range of respondent comment has been elicited. Some of these stimulus questions might include:

- What do you think is the purpose of this announcement?
- To whom does it seem to be directed?
- Do the announcements describe sports programs that would appeal to you?
- What are some ways that these announcements might be made more interesting?
- If your interest lagged at any point in the announcements, what was it?
- What keeps viewers loyal to the sports programs of the competition?

The audiotape of the group interviews is analyzed later to catalog and count the points made by the respondents. The assertions which are made by the respondents are transcribed then sorted as to the subject of each assertion. Typically a sample size of 20 respondents organized into four groups will provide the variety and depth of comment required to improve announcements represented by audiovisual mockup. However, it is feasible to use very large samples interviewed in this way with assertions summarized by statistics such as mean and standard deviation. With smaller samples the data is adequately analyzed when typical comments are summarized by frequency of occurrence in the group interview.

SERIES DEVELOPMENT

As the production of a campaign or the development of a program series approaches, it may be helpful for research to assess the potential contribution of such program elements as talent or spokesperson. At the national level the controversial Q ratings of Marketing Evaluations, Inc. are of this sort. Marketing Evaluations reports the relative familiarity of the public with programs and performers and the degree to which personalities are the favorites of viewers.[2]

A local broadcaster desiring to know the relative popularity of potential local performers may conduct similar evaluations in the local market. One way of conducting this research with face-to-face personal interviews is to use a response card with photographs of the personalities in question. The response card includes the photographs of the talent being evaluated. If these personalities are on the air in the market, it will pay to use off-monitor shots of the personalities in the settings with which the public is likely to associate them. Photographing them in other settings will cause some confusion in respondents, artificially reducing the number who will recognize the personality. The response card will be shown to the respondent with only one photograph showing at a time. Then the interviewer may ask questions of this sort:

- Do you recognize this personality?
- Who is it?
- Where have you seen the personality?
- On a scale of 1 to 10, with 1 meaning least familiar, and 10, most familiar, how familiar are you with the show on which this personality appears?
- Considering other personalities on this sort of program, how would you rate the performance of this personality? Very good? Good? Poor? Very poor? Don't know?

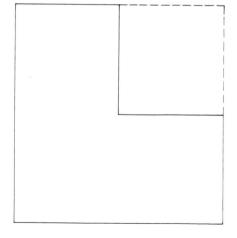

a. Photo card. b. Mask for photo card which exposes one photo at a time.

Figure 9-1.   Response Card for Presenting Photos of Personalities to Respondents.

From each interview a numerical score will be developed for each personality. If the set of questions above were used in the survey, they might be scored according to these rules:

    a. If the respondent answers yes to the first question and correctly answers the next two questions, then assign a familiarity score for that personality equal to the value given by the respondent on the fourth item. If the respondent answers no to the first items and fails to answer the next two items correctly, score the personality zero on familiarity.

    b. On the performance item, score the performance of the personality according to this scheme:

Very Good	= 10
Good	= 8
O.K.	= 6
Poor	= 4
Very Poor	= 2
If familiarity is zero	= 0

To analyze the data, the researcher sums the score of each personality across all respondents to the survey.

In such local surveys it is often helpful to compare local personalities against selected national performers. This may provide a station with information as to the relative appeal of local personalities against competition from national programs.

The same research undertaking may be handled as a mail survey. Figure 9-2 provides a sample mail questionnaire for such a survey. Ideally it would be desirable to split the printing run of the questionnaire so that in one-fourth of the questionnaires each of the four personalities under test appears as the first photograph, since it is possible that the order in which the photographs are presented will affect the responses given by the sample.

Message elements other than personalities may be evaluated in the same comparative ways. And, as implied in the introduction to this chapter, these techniques are appropriate to research into audience reactions to programs and messages at any stage of their development.

MUSIC CALL-OUT RESEARCH

In radio station programming there is probably no element of program more important than the music played by a station. In response to the recognized importance of music to the success of a radio station format, a number of research procedures have been developed to assist the radio program director or music director. Music call-out research is one of these procedures.[3]

There are a number of alternative procedures for assessing the likely popularity and durability of popular recordings. The first was introduced at the 1976 Billboard International Radio Forum by Dr. Ernest Martin, Jr., of Cox Broadcasting Corporation. It is a method of measuring record appeal which has a high potential accuracy.

The first step in this procedure is to record on audiotape the "hooks" of a set of popular recordings proposed for testing. These may be the recordings on the station playlist, or they may be from a list of new releases the station is considering for future play. A "hook" is a representative excerpt of a recorded song. It is important that the researcher select an excerpt that is *representative* of the entire selection. The excerpt should feature

Station RWYZ
Beeville

Dear Viewer;

As indicated in our telephone conversation recently, we appreciate your willingness to assist us in evaluating a number of television personalities. Your responses will be treated with the strictest confidence. The information you provide will be considered seriously and in detail, as we plan our community programming in the future. Thanks to the public spirit of helpful viewers like yourself, we are optimistic about our programs in the coming year.

Thanks again,

John E. Doe

RWYZ News Director

	PHOTO A	PHOTO B	PHOTO C	PHOTO D
Is this person familiar?	Yes__ No__	Yes__ No__	Yes__ No__	Yes__ No__
Write this person's name if you know it.	_____	_____	_____	_____
On what station do you see this person?	_____	_____	_____	_____
Write a "1" under the picture of your favorite.	_____	_____	_____	_____

PLEASE RETURN YOUR ANSWERS IN THE SELF-ADDRESSED
POSTPAID RETURN ENVELOPE. THANKS!

Figure 9–2. Maii Questionnaire for Evaluation of Personalities

the same combination of voices or instruments which characterize the rest of the recording and should contain the more frequently repeated elements of the lyric. In the conventional ballad, a good candidate for "hook" might be the opening lines of the chorus. If the same musical selection is to be studied week after week, the same excerpt should be used as the "hook" of the song each time. The length of a "hook" may vary from 20 to 25 seconds, although 10-second excerpts frequently work quite well.

Particular attention must be given to sample design in this sort of music call-out research. It is desirable that the sample in its demographic profile resemble the audience of the station. The exception will be research which the station hopes to help the format appeal to an audience with a wider range of demographics. In the case of contemporary rock formats, the desirable respondents will include young adult demographics, often the most difficult to recruit into a sample. A telephone sampling technique will be required which includes recently changed telephone numbers, unlisted numbers, etc., if this very mobile segment of the audience is to be sampled. One method for including these numbers is the random telephone number generation technique which produces a sample of all possible numbers in the local exchanges. This system uses a table of random numbers to provide the suffixes for the prefixes corresponding to the available local telephone exchanges. This system will generate numbers for unconnected households and for businesses and institutions. As a result, if this method of sample selection is employed, the interview schedule must begin with the filter question or qualifier, "Is this a household?"[4]

Another method for including unlisted and recently connected households in the sample is a system of telephone number add-ons. In this procedure telephone numbers are drawn from a telephone directory following the procedures described in several of the chapters of this book. Then a random number is added to each telephone number drawn. This procedure is also a way of tapping all the possible numbers for the local telephone exchanges.[5] A filter question or a qualifier like that in the preceding paragraph is also required when "add-on" telephone sampling is used.

At each of the households in the sample, the interviewer will need to interview all household members who fit the demographic requirements of the survey. Typical survey sample sizes range from 50 to 400 households in this sort of research.

The excerpts of the selected songs will be played for the respondents over the telephone. This is done with a phone "patch" or by connecting the output of a tape recorder to the two wires which contact the microphone portion of the telephone handset. This will permit the music to be heard clearly but will allow the interviewer or the respondent to speak above the sound of the music.

The respondent will be asked to rate each musical selection according to a scale given by the interviewer. Two examples of interview schedule items for rating music selections are given in Figure 9-3. The resulting ratings for each song are maintained over time to map the trends up or down in popularity. When the song is on its way up, more frequent play is indicated; on the way down and after "burnout" less frequent play will be the rule.

Example 1. You will hear some short bits of music that you might hear on the radio. Please tell me whether the record is excellent, good, fair or poor, considering what you want to hear on the radio.

	Excellent	Good	Fair	Poor
1. First song	_____	_____	_____	_____
2. Second song	_____	_____	_____	_____
3. Third song	_____	_____	_____	_____
	Etc.			

Example 2. You will hear some short bits of music that you might hear on the radio. I'd like you to rate each song on a scale from "1" to "9," where "9" means that you like the song very much, and "1" means you dislike the song very much. Depending on how you feel about each song, you can give me any number between "1" and "9."

	Dislike								Like	Don't know
	1	2	3	4	5	6	7	8	9	0
1. First song										
2. Second song										
3. Third song										

Figure 9-3. Items for Telephone Interview which Solicit Ratings of Individual Songs.

Another way that music call-out research is done involves the use of listener panels. A panel is a sample which is used repeatedly as a source of information. The station will recruit a panel from the names of those who have made telephone requests for music on the station. This will insure that the panel will be made up of regular listeners to the station. Some members of the call-in audience will be asked by letter if they will participate in the study of radio music. The potential panelist indicates willingness to participate by returning a postpaid postcard which indicates name, phone numbers, and the hours during which the interviewer should call. A portion of the panel is phoned weekly for interview. The data are then summarized as trends. Respondents from the panel may be asked to do more than merely rate the music: they may also be asked to consult with the station as to the best use of the music by commenting on the quality of the performing group involved or on the durability of the music in the foreseeable future. As observed in Chapter 4 the careful researcher will want to use a number of panels in rotation.

The rating data collected in call-out research can be very valuable, since there are many statistical analyses that can be performed on data of this sort. For example, the data can be subjected to factor analysis. Factor analysis is a way of discovering variables which are related to one another in reflecting some common, underlying factor. Factor analysis, in the case of song ratings, begins by computing the product-moment correlations among each of the songs in the study. These correlation coefficients are grouped together by the computer when they indicate a high interrelatedness. The geometric focus of that relatedness is called a factor, and the factor analysis program reports how each song loads on each of the factors discovered in the analysis. The result is a typology of songs which show that particular songs and performers represent similar tastes in music. This typology can be very valuable to the station program director in engineering the appeal of the station. A 1977 study of radio listeners in Kansas found performers grouped in some of these patterns:

Fleetwood Mac – Foreigner, Doobie Brothers, Heart, Boston, Peter Frampton, Steve Miller, Electric Light Orchestra, Boz Scaggs, Waylon Jennings, Eagles, Linda Ronstadt.

Rolling Stones – Ted Nugent, Yes, Thin Lizzy, E. L. O., Kansas, Bob Seger, Grateful Dead.

In planning musical programs for radio it is often helpful to understand the general music preferences of the audience. A telephone survey of a random sample of potential listeners might ask such questions as:

- I know that your music tastes may change at different times of day or night, but, in general, what kinds of music do you especially like to hear on the radio?

- Just to make sure I understand, please give me three artists or groups that represent the type of music you most like to hear on the radio.

    1. ＿＿＿＿＿＿＿
    2. ＿＿＿＿＿＿＿
    3. ＿＿＿＿＿＿＿

- Think back for a moment about the different kinds of music you like to hear. Can you find just about everything you want on the local radio stations, or is there something you miss in the way of music?

    Don't miss anything ＿＿＿＿＿
    (SKIP NEXT ITEM)

    Miss something ＿＿＿＿＿＿

What kind of music can't you find?

Please give me a few examples of the kind of music you're talking about.

It may also be desirable to assess the popularity with a radio audience of specific music groups and performers. These survey items may be helpful in that connection:

- (Open-ended Item)   Please name three (3) musical artists or groups you would most like to hear played often on your favorite radio station.

- (Closed Preference for Groups)   I'm going to read some musical groups and artists. I'd like you to rate the group on a scale from "1" to "9," where "9" means you like the group very much. Depending on how you feel about each group, you can give me any number between "1" and "9."

| | DISLIKE | | | | | | | LIKE | | DON'T KNOW |
	1	2	3	4	5	6	7	8	9	0
Rolling Stones										
Ted Nugent										
Yes										
Thin Lizzy										
E. L. O.										
Kansas										
Bob Seger										
Grateful Dead										

From the open-end item above, data are summarized by frequency of mention, resulting in a relatively crude measure; and the responses to the item tend to be dominated by groups and artists with high recognition. In addition, it will yield three groups per respondent, although nearly every listener wants to hear more than just three groups on a favorite radio station. The second closed-end item does assign a number corresponding to preference of the listener, thus providing insights as to the second, third, and lower choices of the audience. Because it is a measure yielding continuous numbers, it is useful in a wider variety of statistical routines, like the factor analysis discussed in connection with the rating of individual songs.

POST PRODUCTION RESEARCH

At the national program production level, a great deal of money goes into post production research — research that provides insights for the producer into how best to finish off the program or message in question. For example, a rough cut of the pilot of a television series may be shown to a test audience in order to decide whether to make more or less of a particular secondary character in the series.

The specific research requirements of post production include the development of reliable information as to:

- Best scheduling of the new program.
- Ability to compete with programs already on the air.
- Problems in ebb and flow of attention during the program.
- Relative affection or disaffection created in the audience by the program.

- Elements of the program which will violate the prevailing sensibilities of significant parts of the audience.

Each of the national networks has a somewhat different pattern of program testing during post production. They may have an in-house research program — a staff of their own researchers with appropriate facilities. They may use the services of a large commercial research firm such as ASI Marketing Research which operates Preview House, a program testing theater, on the West Coast. Or they may use the services of consultants.

Measures of Interest

Nearly all protocols for measuring audience response to a candidate program involve an assessment of the levels of audience attention throughout the various parts of the program. One method of assessing audience interest level is a series of simple devices called response analyzers. In front of the audience member in a response analyzer system will be a switch or series of switches marked off in segments from "interesting" to "dull." The switches may be push-buttons, toggle switches, or rotary switches with from two to seven positions between "interesting" and "dull." Audiences are asked to adjust these switches to reflect their feelings about what is going on on the screen. The positions of the switches are monitored and recorded by a strip-chart recorder in a room near the theater. From study of the chart record of the response analyzer switches, the researcher can determine the average level of attention on a moment-by-moment basis throughout the program. When attention lags, the producer can endeavor to increase the pace of the action by making a change in editing. If a suspenseful section of the program does not seem to be building to the fever pitch desired, then the musical accompaniment might be reedited to add eerie sensations.[6] Response analyzers have been used in this way since the early 1940s, and considerable folklore has been generated about each of the extant apparatuses. A persistent problem are those audience members at either extreme of attention: a person who is totally engrossed in the program may forget entirely about the necessity of adjusting the analyzer switches. A person whose attention is not engaged at all may go to sleep at the switch.

An alternative to the assessment of interest by response analyzer is the use of graphic interest scales. Each audience member is given a pad of interest scales like this:

At periodic intervals during the program a number appears on the screen. The number signals the audience to complete another interest scale noting beside each the number on the screen. When one scale is completed the audience turns the page to expose a fresh scale. These graphic scales require no maintenance and can be moved easily from one auditorium to another — in contrast to most of the response analyzers. On the other hand, the scales must be coded and averaged separately after the program has ended, a larger expenditure of energy than required with an analyzer which may read out directly in average interest level.

In addition to the moment-by-moment recording of interest level, there are likely to be a series of overall evaluations to be completed by the audience. These may include evaluations of the program, of the characters in the program, or of the situations portrayed. The instruments may be paper-and-pencil self-administered questionnaires or they may be group interviews recorded on audiotape and analyzed assertion-by-assertion as described for concept testing. An important kind of overall evaluation will be attitude toward the program and principal characters. Lesson Nine of the self-study course at Appendix C describes the procedure for designing and refining a Likert-type attitude scale. Another form of attitude measurement receiving wider recognition and use is the semantic differential.[7] Figure 9–4 provides an illustration of a semantic differential suitable for use in post production research.

Even a casual examination of Figure 9–4 reveals one of the great assets of the semantic differential as a tool for measurement — its opacity. It is difficult for a respondent to infer from the appearance of the scales what the investigator is trying to determine. If a respondent does understand what the investigator is looking for, there will be a tendency to give answers that will please.

A caution about the use of semantic differential is that these are not instruments for small samples. The rule of thumb is that about 10 persons should participate for each scale included in the semantic differential. In the case of the semantic differential at Figure 9–4 there are 12 scales. The rule of thumb then would be that the minimum sample include at least 120 respondents.

When using the semantic differential the resulting data are first scored by converting the space checked on each scale to a numeric value. There are a number of different ways of scoring. The scheme shown below is one frequently encountered. The numeric score should be at its largest positive value when the space nearest the more favorable of the opposed adjective pairs has been checked:

fair __7__ : __6__ : __5__ : __4__ : __3__ : __2__ : __1__ unfair

After scoring the data from the semantic differential are routinely subjected to factor analysis. The novice will need assistance at this point. Factor analysis as a statistical procedure is complex enough that only a computer can perform all the required mathematical operations in a reasonable length of time. Nearly any college or university computing center will be equipped to handle this job, and some commercial data services are also prepared to assist with factor analysis. A preliminary step to this factor analysis will be summing scales across concepts for each respondent. This means that one considers the questionnaire completed by Mrs. Brown, adding the scores on the good-bad scale for each program she evaluated and for each performer. The result, if the semantic differential at Figure 9–4 were used, would be 12 sums, one for each scale in the semantic differential, for the aggregate of programs evaluated; another 12 sums for the aggregate of personalities evaluated.

The output of the factor analysis of semantic differentials referring to programs evaluated might look like this:

	FACTOR LOADINGS		
SCALE	FACTOR A (EVALUATIVE)	FACTOR B (POTENCY)	COMMUNALITY
1. nice-awful	.85	−.25	.768
2. sweet-sour	.75	.14	.573
3. heavenly-hellish	.77	.30	.683
4. good-bad	.77	.28	.787
5. mild-harsh	.78	.24	.664
6. happy-sad	.71	.24	.563
7. big-little	loadings too small to interpret		
8. deep-shallow	loadings too small to interpret		
9. strong-weak	.09	.72	.599
10. young-old	loadings too small to interpret		
11. noisy-quiet	.02	.69	.476
12. known-unknown	−.06	.78	.644

The factor of interest here is Factor A (Evaluative), since it coincides with usual interpretations of attitude. The factor loadings represent correlations of each scale with the factors — the degree to which variation on that scale coincides with variation in the factor. It is apparent from studying the factor loadings that the first six scales load

These are the instructions for the following pages.

If you feel that the concept at the top of the page is very closely related to one end of the scale, you should place your checkmark as follows:

fair __X__ : _____ : _____ : _____ : _____ : _____ : _____ unfair

OR

fair _____ : _____ : _____ : _____ : _____ : _____ : __X__ unfair

If you feel the concept is quite closely related to one or the other end of the scale (but not extremely), you should place your check-mark as follows:

strong _____ : __X__ : _____ : _____ : _____ : _____ : _____ weak

OR

strong _____ : _____ : _____ : _____ : _____ : __X__ : _____ weak

If the concept seems only slightly related to one side as opposed to the other side (but is not really neutral), then you should check as follows:

active _____ : _____ : __X__ : _____ : _____ : _____ : _____ passive

OR

active _____ : _____ : _____ : _____ : __X__ : _____ : _____ passive

The direction toward which you check, of course, depends upon which of the two ends of the scale seem most characteristic of the thing you're judging.

If you consider the concept to be neutral on the sacle, both sides of the scale equally associated with the concept, or if the scale is completely irrelevant, unrelated to the concept, then you should place your checkmark in the middle space:

safe _____ : _____ : _____ : __X__ : _____ : _____ : _____ dangerous

IMPORTANT: (1) Place your check-marks in the middle of spaces, not on the boundaries:

	THIS	NOT THIS

_____ : _____ : _____ : __X__ : _____ : _____ : ·X_____

(2) Be sure you check every scale for every concept—do not omit any.

(3) Never put more than one check-mark on a single scale.

"The Boys from Beeville"

nice _____ : _____ : _____ : _____ : _____ : _____ : _____ awful

sweet _____ : _____ : _____ : _____ : _____ : _____ : _____ sour

heavenly _____ : _____ : _____ : _____ : _____ : _____ : _____ hellish

good _____ : _____ : _____ : _____ : _____ : _____ : _____ bad

mild _____ : _____ : _____ : _____ : _____ : _____ : _____ harsh

happy _____ : _____ : _____ : _____ : _____ : _____ : _____ sad

big _____ : _____ : _____ : _____ : _____ : _____ : _____ little

deep _____ : _____ : _____ : _____ : _____ : _____ : _____ shallow

strong _____ : _____ : _____ : _____ : _____ : _____ : _____ weak

young _____ : _____ : _____ : _____ : _____ : _____ : _____ old

noisy _____ : _____ : _____ : _____ : _____ : _____ : _____ quiet

known _____ : _____ : _____ : _____ : _____ : _____ : _____ unknown

Figure 9-4. Instructions and Semantic Differential Suitable for Measuring Attitudes toward Broadcast Programs, Personalities and Ideas.

heavily on the Evaluative factor. As a consequence, if attitude is the variable to be studied, the investigator may add the scores of a respondent on the first six scales to provide an index to the respondent's attitude toward a program or personality.

It is important to perform a factor analysis of semantic differential data as a matter of routine. Typically when measuring attitude toward programs or personalities, factor loadings will not be strikingly different from those above, but on those occasions when factor structure is different, it is often very different.

Of course, when measuring attitudes toward a rough-cut program, there needs almost always to be a standard of comparison within the protocols of the study. One way to provide this comparison is to include in the same visual presentation an existing program with a known track record with audiences. Then it will be possible to make generalizations about the relative performance of the new program when it is scheduled in competition with existing programs.

TEST MARKETS

Test marketing is an esteemed research procedure in marketing and in advertising as well as in broadcasting. In essence test marketing means presenting a program in only one market and evaluating its relative success there prior to releasing it to a larger audience. A network affiliate in Beeville might, for example, be asked to run a pilot program during a specified time period. During the same time period a research effort would be underway to determine the audience appeal of the program. The research method might be telephone coincidental which would tap the views of audience members who had actually experienced making a choice to watch or not watch the pilot program.

Another method of test marketing has received considerable publicity in the last several years. This is the procedure of broadcasting a test program or message on a two-way cable system. Some of these systems are designed to monitor the actual number of connections to the cable system that are tuned to each of the channels carried by the system. The relative popularity of a program against a wide variety of competition can almost instantly be assessed by this means. If more detailed information about audience reaction to various parts of the program is desired, then a sample of respondents can be recruited in advance, each respondent told to view the program on a specific channel and then to respond to it by completing a self-administered questionnaire which has been mailed to the respondent. This latter technique is much like the preview theater in the wealth of data it can produce but has the advantage that the viewer is seeing the test program in a home environment on the same screen where most of the family's programming normally appears. A model self-administered questionnaire for cable viewing of a test program is presented at Figure 9-5. To score the questionnaire at Figure 9-5 count the proportion of times the test program ("Beeville on Parade") is checked as the score for question 1. On items 2 and 3 count the number of adjectives checked as the score for the test program. On item 4 score the spaces on the rating scale according to this scheme:

Excellent   Poor

:   5   :   4   :   3   :   2   :   1   :

Item 5 is an open-ended item. It is usually good insurance to include at least one open-ended item on a self-administered questionnaire of this sort to protect against the possibility that the research has not tapped all of the strong feelings engendered in the audience by the program.

Again it will be important to have some baseline for comparison in a test market study. Item 1 of Figure 9-5 does provide comparative measures, but to evaluate the scores on items 2 through 4, data from another study or from a recent evaluation of another program would be necessary.

Dear Viewer:

I appreciate your willingness to give us your opinion of a new television program, "Beeville on Parade." Please watch the program over the television cable at one of the following times and channels:

Saturday, May 1, 10-11 P.M. — Channel 10

Sunday, May 2, 2-3 P.M. — Channel 6

Monday, May 3, 1-2 P.M. — Channel 2

After you have seen the program, would you answer the questions below? Then mail your completed questionnaire to me in the enclosed stamped envelope.

When I receive your completed questionnaire, I will send you two tickets to the Saturday baseball game. Thanks again.

Jeremy Jones

Research Director

1. Below are several pairs of programs. Indicate with a check (√) the program in each pair which you would prefer to watch.

	Beeville on Parade	_____
OR	Beeville Buzzes	_____
	Vega S	_____
OR	Beeville on Parade	_____
	TV 2 Evening News	_____
OR	Beeville on Parade	_____
	Beeville on Parade	_____
OR	The Tonight Show	_____
	Gilligan's Island	_____
OR	Beeville on Parade	_____

2. Check (√) each of the following words which you feel apply to the host of "Beeville on Parade."

Good-Looking____; Authoritative____; Knowledgeable____; Friendly____;

Wise__; Courteous__; Public-Spirited__; Kind__; Fair__; Honest__;

3. Check (√) all of the words below which you feel describe the guests on "Beeville on Parade."

Interesting____; Outspoken____; Eloquent____; Good-Looking____;

Bright____; Fun____; Witty____; Original____; Friendly____; Unusual____;

4. Rate "Beeville on Parade" on the following scale by marking an X on the scale corresponding to your feelings about the show.

Excellent   Poor

:_____:_____:_____:_____:_____:_____:_____:

5. What suggestions do you have for the producers of "Beeville on Parade?"

Figure 9–5. Self-Administered Questionnaire for Cable Viewer of Test Program.

Some new two-way cable systems provide viewers with a response box on which there are a number of buttons which the viewer can push, causing a signal to be given at the head-end of the cable system. With such a system, the audience using these boxes can provide answers to multiple choice questions which appear on the screen. In such systems it is feasible to present a test program then flash a set of multiple-choice questions on the screen which tap the viewer's reactions to the program.

It is also possible with cable systems to isolate a part of the cable system, under some circumstances, so that only parts of the community are asked about a test program. Particularly in some recent master antenna systems in large apartment complexes, it is possible to present test material to a well-defined subpopulation. The sample size in a program test in a single apartment complex may not be large, but the disadvantages of small sample size may be more than offset by being able to present the program in the viewer's home environment, to have the sample in a compact geographic unit facilitating callbacks and viewer cooperation, and to make it possible to control the technical quality of the video images seen by the sample.

RETENTION AND COMPREHENSION

It is many times the objective of a program producer to educate or inform an audience. The function of news programming is typically said to be to inform the public. The term, "inform," means that some facts will be properly understood, that some will be remembered for future recognition or recall.

Generally speaking, retention measurements deal with what an audience remembers or can recall. Comprehension measurement is concerned with whether the thing recognized or recalled is in the company of appropriate and relevant concepts. In the case of the evening news program on a local television station, retention on the part of the audience would help them to recall the political stance of each candidate in an election, so that they will make a wise choice on election day. Comprehension, on the other hand, might help viewers understand that the office for which the candidates are running is that of alderman, an office in city government.

The simplest and briefest instrument for measuring retention is probably a series of questions about the apparent intent of the test message. In the case of a test commercial, for example:

Who was the sponsor?
Where is the sponsor's place of business?
What products or services does the sponsor provide?

These represent the *minimum* which a sponsor may want to know to be assured of the efficacy of a commercial message. And, because only a minimum is required, instruments made up of questions like these typically do not produce fine discriminations of various levels of retention in the audience. In a laboratory setting, even an unattentive subject will be able to retain this much. When too many respondents in a study are able to answer all the questions, then the reliability coefficient computed from the data (See Appendix C, Lesson 8) will be spuriously low. In order for the retention instrument to discriminate differing levels of retention across the audience, the average score on the retention instrument must be much less than 100 percent correct, and only a few respondents ought to make a maximum score. It is also important that those who remember one announcement more than another should receive higher scores for the announcement best remembered. As a consequence, and in order to identify elements of the message which might be distracting for an audience, it is best to design a measure of retention which recognizes that all parts of a message are capable of producing retention, even though the retention of some parts of the message may not be so desirable from the message producer's point of view. Let us imagine that the message being presented to a test audience promotes a newly refurbished local news-weather-sports program:

Watch News Alive on 5 at 6 P.M. Monday through Friday. Your hosts Shelby Waters and Chuck Abletow are professional journalists who have devoted their careers to getting to the bottom of things and telling it straight. Weatherman Cosmo Parks with Weather Alive Color Radar keeps you up to date on storms, weather watches, and the 5-day outlook. Sports Alive Commentator Red Gatsby provides incisive interpretations of your favorite teams and predictions for professional sports. Don't miss News Alive on 5 at 6.

Begin the design of a retention instrument for this spot by listing questions which contain all the points made by the spot:

What is the name of the evening news program on Channel 5?
At what time is the evening news broadcast on Channel 5?
What are the names of the hosts or anchorpeople on the evening news program on Channel 5?
Which of these is a professional journalist?
What is the name of the weatherperson on Channel 5?
What special devices will the weatherperson on Channel 5 use to present the weather?
How far into the future is the weather routinely predicted on Channel 5?
Who is the sports commentator on Channel 5?
What sports will he predict?

Another way of soliciting recall from this spot would be to ask respondents to reproduce the spot when given a copy in which words are missing:

Watch News — at — P.M. Monday through Friday. Your — Shelby Waters and Chuck — are professional — who have devoted their — to getting to the — of things and telling it —. Weatherman Cosmo Parks with — Alive Color — keeps you up to date on storms, weather — and the five-day —. Sports Alive — Red Gatsby provides incisive interpretations of your — teams and — for professional sports. Don't miss — Alive on 5 at —.

This technique has the advantage of permitting a greater number of items, thereby likely increasing the reliability of the instrument. On the other hand, it also increases the cues or hints provided the respondent, so that the results are more like *recognition* than recall. This method will also be more sensitive to distractions, as the cues for distracting material will operate in the recall instrument as well as in the test message. In the example above, one noun in every set of five consecutive words was eliminated, thus requiring the respondent to reproduce one-fifth of the words of the announcement. The respondent's score would be the proportion of these blanks filled correctly. If after use of the instrument we saw that the instrument was too easy or too difficult, we could increase or decrease the number of blanks which the respondent is required to fill by removing one in every four words or one in every six words.

When recall of words from more than one message are to be measured in a single laboratory session, it will be important to insure that the retention tests used are of approximately equal difficulty, so that, should a difference on the two instruments be reflected in the responses given, it can be assumed that the difference is due to the memorable qualities of the message involved and not to the relative difficulty of the retention instrument used.

Probably the easiest way to assess the relative difficulty of a retention measure is to pretest it with a small group of respondents who respond to it in three laboratory settings:

one without message presentation, one with a single presentation of the test message, one with two or more presentations of the message. There should be marked differences among the retention scores of respondents in each of these three conditions. The proportion of blanks completed in the one presentation condition is taken as indicative of the relative difficulty of the retention test. If the one presentation scores and no presentation scores were the same, we could conclude that the instrument reflects only our ability to guess at the correct responses. If the one presentation and two or more presentation conditions are equal, then we would conclude that the instrument does not discriminate levels of learning—that the difficulty of the unsuccessfully completed items is too great to discriminate relatively high levels of learning from the message. In the comparisons among the pretest results under these three conditions, t tests would be the appropriate tests of significance between pairs of conditions.

As an illustration, two test messages have been recorded on audiotape without the production effects which the eventual completed message will contain—Message A and Message B. One-third of the pretest sample of 15 respondents completed retention questionnaires without hearing either message. Another third heard Message A, then completed questionnaire A, then heard Message B and completed questionnaire B. The remaining third of the respondents heard each message twice before completing the appropriate questionnaire. The data from the pretest groups are shown at Figure 9–6 with

| | Proportion Correct | | | | | |
| | Did Not Hear | | Heard Only Once | | Heard Twice | |
Respondent	Message A	Message B	Message A	Message B	Message A	Message B
1	.40	.42				
2	.38	.39				
3	.40	.40				
4	.39	.38				
5	.30	.30				
6			.60	.54		
7			.57	.61		
8			.55	.58		
9			.61	.63		
10			.63	.63		
11					.71	.72
12					.74	.72
13					.68	.67
14					.55	.54
15					.80	.78

t Test for Independent Means

Did Not Hear vs. Heard Once Message A, $t = -5.21218$, $p < .01$
Message B, $t = -8.21032$, $p < .01$

Heard Once vs. Heard Twice Message A, $t = -1.94255$, $p < .05$
Message B, $t = -2.00310$, $p < .05$

Mean Correct Message A = .56187 (standard deviation = .14375)

Mean Correct Message B = .55400 (standard deviation = .14112)

Figure 9–6. Data from Pretest of Two Retention Instruments.

t tests for independent means between the first and second, and second and third pretest groups.

In a *t* test of independent means (degrees of freedom = 8) the scores of those who had not heard the messages are compared with those who heard the message only once. The significant *t*'s that result indicate that the retention test without the message produces lower scores. The group who heard the messages once when contrasted with those who heard the messages twice produce a significant *t* test. This result indicates that the retention tests can discriminate higher and lower levels of retention. The mean response to both messages is nearly equal, meaning that the tests of these two messages can be considered comparable. The retention instruments involved are now ready to test audience response to television or radio spots or any other form of message which has the same content.

Recognition, on the whole, is an easier task for the respondent. In recognition tasks, the respondent is given cues which are to remind him/her of a message to which he/she has been exposed. This method of measuring memory may also be referred to as aided recall. A common procedure of this sort was the now defunct PULSE survey of radio listening. The respondent was shown a list of programs, call letters, or personalities and asked which he/she recognized. Because of the additional cues provided in the questionnaire or measurement procedure, recognition instruments can extract more memory from the respondents, helping them to report accurately on matters more distant in the past or relatively complex. Another frequently encountered use of recognition instruments today is the evaluation of broadcast news reporters. A respondent would be shown a mosaic of photo portraits. Then the respondent is asked to identify a series of personalities whose names are read by the interviewer. The station which features the greatest number of personalities recognized by the television audience takes some satisfaction in the impression which the station newscasts have left. A personality who is widely recognized throughout the television audience is, of course, more valuable, particularly if he/she is recognized among viewers who normally watch the competition.

Another application of recognition instruments is in the evaluation of slogans. The respondent is shown a list of slogans and asked to select the one properly associated with Channel 13 or Channel 2, etc.

PHYSIOLOGICAL VARIABLES

Probably no other technique of communication research has attracted so much popular attention as the use of human physiological indices as a reflection of interior communication processes. The so-called "lie detector" epitomizes the electronic gadget which provides an unbidden insight into the mind of a speaker who is responding to carefully worded questions. In the polygraph used in lie detection, the variables measured include inspiration volume, electrocardiogram, and "GSR." Inspiration volume refers to the amount of air taken in with each breath and is measured by a tube around the chest of the person being measured; as the chest expands the tube becomes longer, compressing the air inside the tube and moving an air driven pen on a chart recorder. The electrocardiogram of the polygraph records the electrical activity of the heart muscle showing the size and frequency of heart beat. The "GSR" stands for the galvanic skin response and is a measure of the resistance of the skin to a tiny electrical current passed through electrodes usually located on the hands of the person being measured. The theory of lie detection is based upon the fact that all of these indices of response measured by the polygraph are disrupted in a recognizable way when a person has a strong emotional reaction, as to the necessity of deceiving a questioner.

Another electronic gadget said to reflect sincerity is the Voice Stress Evaluator. This is actually a family of instruments which examine the frequency composition of the speaking voice, detecting by changes in the complexity of the sound produced by the voice, changes in anxiety or stress.

In point of fact, these two devices—the polygraph and the voice stress evaluator—are not in significant use in evaluation of broadcast programs and messages, but some close relatives are. In a recent popular article, *TV Guide* reviewed some of the physiological research advertising employs and speculated that "TV commercials, in the future, will be carefully designed to appeal more to our subconscious minds—once the scientists figure out what it is that really turns us on."[8]

Basically physiological measures reflect upon two human activities familiar to all of us. The first is *attention*. Attention has been seen in the practitioner's world as a prelude to information processing: if a person is not paying attention, a message can have little impact. The other behavior of interest to physiological measurement is *state of relaxation*. Some messages make listeners and viewers more or less tense. The resulting tension or lack of it, is seen as a more or less desirable quality, depending on the objective of the message or program under consideration.

Attention is measured by a family of related responses. Attention, in physiological terms, is composed of both general and specific responses, both of which result in increased information flow into the central nervous system related to some outside stimulus. The general attentional response is an increased sensitivity of the perceptual apparatus, increasing the nervous messages sent from all sense organs to the brain. Specific attentional responses are those which direct specific sense organs to provide additional neural information about a stimulus. So the focus of the eyes, in particular may rest upon some part of a televised image then upon another. These specific attentional responses may involve action of the body's muscular system as well, as the head is turned toward a source of stimulation, or a receiver is turned on or off or adjusted. The devices for measuring general attentional responses are cheaper.

The principal ways of measuring general attentional responses are electrodermal conductance, electrodermal potential, photoplethysmography, electroencephalography and pupillometry.[9] The most frequently encountered method is the measurement of electrodermal response, sometimes loosely referred to as GSR. This response is actually a change in the permeability of the skin which results from the activation of the attention center of the midbrain. The increased permeability of the skin in this response is detected, because the resistance of the skin to a tiny current of electricity applied to the skin also changes. The apparatus consists of two electrodes which are attached to the skin of the palm of one hand of the respondent. The electrodes are made of silver and silver chloride and filled at the time of use with a light paste containing potassium chloride (KC1) in about the same dilution as in the fluids of the body. The electrodes are held in place by a doughnut-shaped "collar" which is adhesive on both sides, one side adhering to the skin, the other to the electrode. When working with a respondent, it is important to refer to these electrodes as "contacts" or "sensors" as many are frightened by the word, "electrode." The electrodes are then attached to the recording apparatus. The position of the two electrodes is illustrated at Figure 9-7. Ideally the electrodes will be positioned alternatively on the dominant hand of even-numbered respondents, on the nondominant hand of odd-numbered respondents. This alternating of hands evens out any irregularities in the response due to the differential stimulation of the dominant or nondominant hemispheres of the brain. There are two cautions in electrodermal measurements which protect the safety of the respondent. One is, that like all apparatus with which humans have good electrical contact, physiological apparatus must be well grounded. Most of the commercially available instruments provide for the respondent to be grounded through one of the electrodes. If not, the investigator should provide an independent ground with a large diameter copper wire to a 6-foot or longer copper stake driven into damp soil. Such a ground will also increase the accuracy of measurement, since electrical transients which are common on most domestic power lines, may be smoothed with a good instrument ground.

The second safety concern is current density at the site of the electrodes. If the size of the area of the electrodes in contact with the skin falls below a certain point, or if

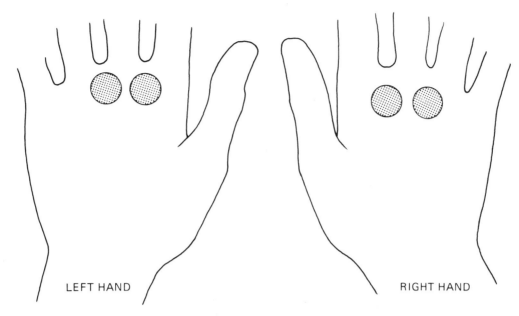

Figure 9-7. Relative Position of the Two Electrodes Required to Measure Electrodermal Conductance.

the amount of current becomes great enough, a burning sensation will be felt by the respondent. This is prevented by dividing the current flowing through the electrode by the area of the electrode to see that the resulting current density is less than 10 microamperes per square centimeter of electrode. The specifications of the measurement will indicate the current which flows to the electrodes as "subject current." In addition, the specifications of the electrodes being used will indicate the area which is in contact with the skin. Once the current density has been computed for a particular combination of instrument and electrodes, it will remain the same so long as that combination is used. All of the equipment recommended here is within the required levels of current density.

Some equipment which can be trusted by the novice to do the necessary work in indexing attention include:

Stoelting #22610 Dermo-Plethysmograph—about $800.

Stoelting Company,
1350 Kostner Avenue,
Chicago, Illinois 60623.
(Area Code 312)522-4500

Lafayette #77010 Single Channel Recorder and Psychogalvanometer—about $900.

Lafayette Instrument Company,
P.O. Box 1279,
Lafayette, Indiana 47902.
(317)423-1505

The recorded trace of electrodermal conductance as a respondent listened to a radio commercial is reproduced at Figure 9-8. In general, the ideal verbal message will have a level to downward pitch, will have a relatively large response at the beginning of the message and a number of smaller ones. A message that is too dull will have very small if any response and a sharp downward trend overall. A message that is irritating or being challenged in the mind of the respondent will have larger responses and an upward trend

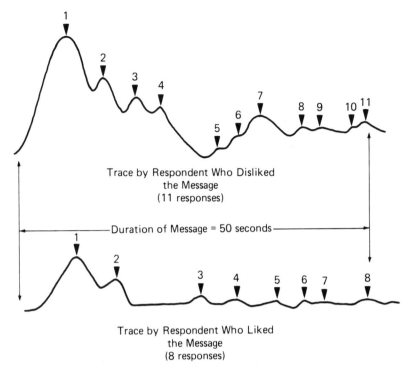

Trace by Respondent Who Disliked
the Message
(11 responses)

Duration of Message = 50 seconds

Trace by Respondent Who Liked
the Message
(8 responses)

Figure 9-8. Electrodermal Conductance Recordings from Respondents Who Liked and Disliked a Fifty Second Message.

overall. In making detailed comparisons between responses to alternative messages count the number of responses that occur after the message has begun and within 2 seconds after the message is completed. This number of responses becomes the measurement which enters into statistical computations.

Typically this measure will be most effectively used when within the framework of a repeated measures design. That is, each subject should hear all the messages being tested. This will reduce the total number of subjects required in the study, and it will use the total variability of any respondent as a control for the responses given to each message, eliminating the need for a control group. It will be important to present the messages in all possible orders, to compensate for any response tendency introduced by the effect of the specific order in which the messages were presented. The statistical analysis will be by repeated measures analysis of variance as discussed in the final lesson of Appendix C.

It is also important when studying any measure of attention to use a collateral variable which reflects the liking or interest of the respondent in the message. The reason for this is that the relationship between attention and retention, for example, is curvilinear.[10]

The person who pays no attention will remember very little. At the same time, he who pays the greatest amount of attention also remembers little. The second point translated to common experience may be clearer. Consider the attention given to the intrusion of some dread thing, such as a spider or a snap quiz at college; the attention given this intrusion is so great that nearly all mental functioning becomes less efficient. So the audience member with the highest interest in a subject is not so likely to remember it well. The highest retention is produced by a moderate level of attention. It is likely that the relationship between liking and attention is similar. Referring to Figure 9-9 consider the two pairs of messages, A & B and C & D. In the first pair B receives more attention; in the second pair C receives more attention. In other words, in the first pair the message with the greater attention value produces the greater retention; but in the second pair the message with the lower attention value produces the higher retention score. The function

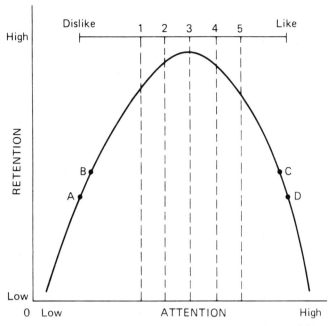

Figure 9-9. Curvilinear Relationship between Attention and Retention.

of a collateral measure such as a scale for like-dislike, or interest-lack of interest, is to identify which part of the circumflex curve of attention the message is on. The reason that the physiological measure should be used is that it is so sensitive to levels of attention: the collateral measure provides a rough index of attention, while the physiological measurement provides a finely tuned measurement of attention.

Other physiological indices of attention include skin potential, alpha-wave and delta-wave electroencephalography, photoplethysmography, pupillometry. Skin potential and electroencephalography will be relatively complex to measure accurately and to interpret for the novice since there is some disagreement among the experts as to exactly how to interpret these measures. Photoplethysmography is a relatively simple measurement to take, is inexpensive and relatively easy to interpret.

Either of the companies listed above can provide the necessary equipment, and costs will be comparable to that for electrodermal conductance measurement. The contact with the respondent is through a transducer which is strapped to the tip of one finger. In the transducer will be a small electric lamp which illuminates the skin below it and a photo-sensitive pickup. Figure 9-10 provides an illustration of the positioning of the transducer.

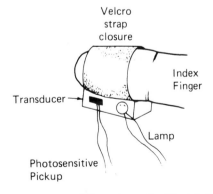

Figure 9-10. Positioning of Transducer for Photplethysmography.

The lamp of the transducer illuminates the capillary bed immediately below. As the capillaries fill with blood, less light is reflected back to the photosensitive pickup. As the capillaries contain less blood, more light is reflected to the photosensitive pickup. The result is a chart recording which reflects each pulse as blood is pushed through the capillaries and which reflects the overall relaxation or constriction of the capillaries, the latter responding both to attention and to the relative tension or relaxation of the respondent. Figure 9-11 shows the recorded trace of the photoplethysmograph. Since the pulse is reflected in the measurement, it is sometimes referred to as blood pulse volume (bpv) or as vasoconstriction. To interpret the record, ignore the valleys in the record and visualize a line connecting or parallel to the hilltops of the record. The attentional response in this record is a rise followed by a depression in the trend of the recording. The number of such responses and their magnitude is the measurement of attention desired by the investigator.

A final index of attention is the pupil response. At the same time that skin conductance increases and the photoplethysmographic record shows an increase in blood pulse volume followed by a decrease, the pupils of the eyes dilate. Because of the relatively small size and responsiveness of the pupils, some researchers feel that pupil response is a particularly sensitive index of attention given to messages. There are two principal ways of measuring pupil response. One is a photographic method in which a motion picture camera is focussed on the eye of the respondent. The size of the pupil in each frame of the resulting film is measured, and the peaks of openness are noted as attentional responses to the message being viewed. The disadvantages of this film system are that it is relatively expensive, tedious in that each frame must be examined, and restrictive to the respondent, as the respondent's head must be held still during the session if the camera is to remain focused on the eye.

An alternative method is television recording of the pupil. In this method a vertically scanning television camera is focused on the eye, and the size of the pupil is electronically measured then recorded on a chart recorder or paper tape. This system is much less trouble for the investigator but considerably more expensive. It is possible also to have a television pupillometer read film recordings of the pupil for more rapid interpretation of film pupillometry.

Some pupillometers are also equipped to record the movements of the eye as a visual image is scanned. The composition of a visual presentation may be studied, with recorded eye movement indicating which part of an image first attracted the eye and how much relative time was spent on each part of the picture. In the case of the television pupillometer, eye movement can be read out on videotape with a white dot superimposed on that part of the image on which the respondent is focussing.

As might be guessed from the foregoing pupillometers can be quite complex and expensive. A small film pupillometer with a Super 8 motion picture camera may cost as little as $2000, but the more complex television pupillometer with eye movement recorder may exceed $20,000 in cost. Two firms which sell pupillometer equipment are:

> G + W Applied Science Laboratories,
> 385 Bear Hill Road,
> Waltham, Massachusetts 02154.

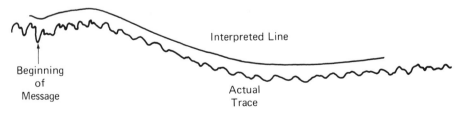

Figure 9-11.   Chart Recording of Photoplethysmographic Response to a Short Promotional Message.

Stoelting Company,
1350 S. Kostner Avenue,
Chicago, Illinois 60623.

The two questions which are best answered by physiological measurement of responses are: (1.) Are the elements of this production presented in the most effective fashion? (2.) Which of a set of possible program elements are best included in a program?

Are the elements of this production presented in the most effective fashion? To answer this question the production would be shown to a number of respondents whose physiological attention levels are monitored. Comparison of these responses to those of the same respondents viewing a competing program will show whether the attentional values of the new program will compete. In addition, because the physiological measures are continuous throughout the period that the respondent views a program, it will be possible to identify which parts of the program are more or less attractive to the respondent's attentional processes.

Which of a possible set of program elements are best included in a program? A common application of physiological measurement in the industry today is the identification of suitable spokespersons and personalities. A comparison videotape is made which includes each of a number of personalities under consideration for inclusion in some program. Each is shown in a comparable situation in the videotapes, and other videotapes show the personalities in every possible order of presentation. Respondents are evenly divided so that an equal number of respondents see each order of presentation. Physiological measures index attention to the various personalities, and the personalities receiving the most favorable attention scores are considered more desirable for production of the eventual program or announcement.

SUMMARY

Message and program testing is near the core motivations of commercial broadcasting, for this research predicts the potential success of programs and messages which will produce the audiences which an advertiser may be willing to buy. In addition, this kind of research can determine the relative effectiveness—in advance—of programs designed to be of significant public benefit, in fulfillment of the broadcasters' obligations under law and in response to the public-spirited motives of the best of American broadcasters.

NOTES—CHAPTER 9

1. Bob Shanks, *The Cool Fire: How to Make It In Television* (New York: W. W. Norton, 1976), pp. 256–7.
2. See Edwin Diamond, "The Mysterious Q: TV's Secret Casting Weapon," *New York*, May 26, 1975; Rowland Barber, "Just a Little List," *TV Guide*, August 10, 1974.
3. See for example Edd Routt, James B. McGrath, and Fredric A. Weiss, *The Radio Format Conundrum* (New York: Hastings House, 1978), pp. 93–8.
4. James E. Fletcher and Harry B. Thompson, "Telephone Directory Samples and Random Telephone Number Generation," *Journal of Broadcasting*, 1974, **18**, 187–191.
5. See also Ernest Martin, Jr., "Programming Research for College Radio Stations," *Journal of College Radio*, 1978, **16**, 10.
6. For a description of a response analyzer consult J. P. Highlander, "Audience Analyzer Measurements and Informational Effects of Speaker Variables in Radio Talks," *Speech Monographs*, 1954, **21**, 188–189; J. V. Irvin and H. H. Brockhaus, "The 'Teletalk Project': A Study of the Effectiveness of Two Public Relations Speeches," *Speech Monographs*, 1963, **30**, 359–368.
7. See C. E. Osgood, G. J. Suci, and P. H. Tannenbaum, *The Measurement of Meaning* (Urbana: University of Illinois Press, 1957); D. R. Heise, "Some Methodological Issues in Semantic Differential Research," *Psychological Bulletin*, 1969, **72**, 406–

422; J. G. Snider and C. E. Osgood (Eds.), *Semantic Differential Technique* (Chicago: Aldine, 1969); James E. Fletcher, "Semantic Differential Type Scales in Communication Research," *Western Speech,* 1972, **36**, 269-275.

8. John Mariani, "Can Advertisers Read—and Control—Our Emotions," *TV Guide,* March 31, 1979; see also "Mind Reading," *Family Weekly,* May 13, 1979, p. 22.

9. These matters are discussed in more detail in James E. Fletcher, "The Orienting Response as an Index of Broadcast Communication Effect," *Psychophysiology,* 1971, **8**, 699-703; "Old Time GSR and a New Approach to the Analysis of Public Communication," *Quarterly Journal of Speech,* 1973, **59**, 52-60.

10. Joseph Trenaman, "Understanding Radio Talks," *Quarterly Journal of Speech,* 1951, **37**, 173-178.

10 Identifying Special Saleable Characteristics of Station Audiences

James E. Fletcher and Joseph C. Philport

The principal business of a commercial broadcast station consists of selling air time to advertisers. Audience measurements—in the form of ratings, CUMES and estimates—provide evidence which the sales staff may use in attracting advertisers. It is often the case that great care is exercised by the station in assembling audience figures by demographics—age and sex. But many advertisers are interested in the quality as well as quantity of audience. And only a handful of stations in a market can accumulate the very large audiences which are attractive to an advertiser because of their sheer size. Other stations in the market must sell time either on the basis of lower rates for smaller audiences or on the contention that their audiences are special in some way other than size.

PSYCHOGRAPHICS—AUDIENCE QUALITY

Many potential sales have been lost because sales people could not alter a client's prejudice about the listeners of album-oriented rock, Top 40 or Country and Western radio formats. In television there are sometimes prejudices on the part of time buyers as to the desirability of various regional or local audiences. The unequivocal remedy to such adverse prejudice is solid research data as to qualities of the station audience which make it especially attractive to advertisers.

For many years it has been the practice of major advertisers to develop qualitative audience research to guide sophisticated media campaigns. In more recent times the stations in large and moderate size markets have made effective use of qualitative research to supplement audience information available from the syndicated rating services. Nevertheless the terms associated with qualitative research—attitude research, life style variables, and psychographics—often evoke negative responses from both broadcasters and their clients. One of the reasons is that the same terms are frequently used to describe characteristics of an audience which were not developed by research at all but were the subjective judgments of a client or advertiser. In addition, it has sometimes been the case that even competently done research on psychographics has been put in question by overly complicated and unclear presentations. Because of such confusion, it is probably wise at this point to introduce some of these terms in detail.

Life-style Patterns

Life style describes people in terms of their activities, interests and opinions along with basic demographics.[1] The various dimensions of life style have been summarized in Table 10-1. Note that three of these dimensions are Activities, Interests, and Opinions. For this reason the items used on life-style pattern questionnaires are sometimes referred to as AIO items.[3]

Research into life-style patterns as conducted by national advertisers, their agencies and commercial research firms typically involves administering a very lengthy questionnaire to a large sample of from 1000 to 5000 respondents. Very few broadcasters could undertake a project of such magnitude. For this reason, it will be necessary for the broadcast station interested in researching life-style pattern to isolate those of special concern to potential advertisers. This focussing of the research will shorten the questionnaire and reduce the number of respondents required, bringing the scope of the project within the capacity of a local station or advertiser.

Activities and Interests

While some academic researchers separate activities and interests as indicated in Table 10-1, the newcomer to life style research may find it convenient to consider the two together, thereby reducing the problems of measurement. For a small market study these are some variables that may be considered.

Media Behavior. What are the media habits of the station audience? Are they light, medium, or heavy consumers of television? Do they read the local newspaper? If so, what sections do they read? A prospective advertiser may learn from such data that advertising on local television or radio supplements print media by increasing exposures or by reaching listeners and viewers who only read out-of-town newspapers.

Recreational Activities. What proportion of the station audience are sports enthusiasts? Participants in sports? Among the fans of professional and college sports? How many travel for recreation? How many weekly or monthly attend the theater? Concerts? Motion pictures? Each of these activities and interests implies a special advertiser with

Table 10–1. Life Style Dimensions as Visualized by Plummer.[2]

Activities	Interests
Work	Family
Hobbies	Home
Social Events	Job
Vacations	Community
Entertainment	Recreation
Club Membership	Fashion
Community	Food
Shopping	Media
Sports	Achievements
Opinions	*Demographics*
Themselves	Age
Social Issues	Education
Politics	Income
Business	Occupation
Economics	Family Size
Education	Dwelling
Products	Geographic
Future	City Size
Culture	Stage in Life Cycle

manifest interest in listeners or viewers with these as part of their life styles. And it is likely that very few other media in the market can deliver these special audiences.

Homebodies versus Social Movers. What proportion of the station audience enjoys puttering in the garden or in do-it-yourself home improvement? What proportion are active in social organizations and clubs? Not only are many advertisers interested in reaching such special audiences with their sales messages, others are concerned with gaining the eyes and ears of influential citizens for their institutional messages.

Major Purchases. Every time salesman's dream is to have data on the number of audience members who have actually purchased an advertiser's products or services. To identify this sort of special audience is money in the bank.

Opinions

In general, soliciting opinions in a systematic way is more difficult than collecting information on activities and interests. In addition, many of the opinion areas indicated in Table 10-1 do not directly relate to the sale of broadcast time. Nevertheless many opinions from the broadcast audience will reflect upon the general reputation or image of the station, and these opinions can contribute mightily to an effective sales presentation. What are the reasons given by the audience for tuning to a particular station? For news? Because station personalities are friendly? To find out about other people in the community? There will be many potential broadcast advertisers who want their messages associated with a station with a friendly and informative image.

Demographics

Demographics are the categories into which a group of people may be divided. In broadcasting, because of the pervasive influence of the ratings, it has become the habit to equate demographics with age and sex, but level of education, income, and occupation are other categories which may have importance.

Psychographics

Psychographics is a general term which refers to all variables other than demographics which can be used to describe an audience for broadcasting or advertising. Psychographics include life-style variables, as well as attitudes, interests, and opinions.

THE PROBLEM OF CREDIBILITY

A major shortcoming of many psychographic studies is lack of credibility. This will be particularly true when the study is either conducted or sponsored by the station that cites it in a sales presentation. Advertisers and advertising agencies look upon this arrangement as an opportunity to produce slanted research results.

One way around this potential problem is to join with other stations in the market in sponsoring or conducting the research. Or it may be possible to link several station studies together under the umbrella of a station representative firm which sponsors the research. An additional benefit of joining with others in the psychographic research undertaking is the possibility of additional research products such as psychographic profiles of the consumers of other mass media in the trade area.

Another route to credibility is to engage independent researchers with a reputation for fairness. Reputable audience or marketing research firms, or university and college research centers will often qualify under this criterion.

If it is the decision of the station to undertake the research with its own staff, then the prudent manager will follow recognized procedures like those in this volume or have the completed research audited by an outside party. The remainder of this chapter is devoted to suggestions for the station undertaking psychographic research of its audiences.

SAMPLE SELECTION

To this point several different methods of drawing a random sample from a community have been described in detail. Again it is difficult to justify any nonrandom sampling procedure when audience measurement is involved. Chapters 4 and 5 provide several detailed models for sample selection that may be used in psychographic research as well. In addition to a random selection of households, the sampling procedure may also specify random procedures for selecting the individual within each household to become the respondent for the survey. Trohldahl and Carter have outlined a procedure of within-household randomization which insures that every category of adult within the household is equitably represented within the sample.[4] It will be important that any formal report of the station's research include a detailed description of sample selection procedures, so that qualified readers may judge for themselves the adequacy of the sample design.

Sample Size. The size of sample that will be considered adequate for the survey will vary according to the same principles as in other field surveys. (This matter is detailed at some length in Lesson Six of Appendix C.)[5] For most purposes, a psychographic survey to identify special, highly saleable audiences will require from 400 respondents up to several thousand, depending on the size and number of special audiences to be assessed in the trade area. For illustration purposes in this chapter, it will be assumed that a random sample of adults numbering 400 will be an adequate sample.

QUESTIONNAIRE

Wording

As pointed out at several times earlier in this volume, the wording of questions will directly affect the answers generated from respondents. "What if" questions should be used only after all other alternatives have proved unsuitable, since these questions seldom bring a realistic response. The more distant in the past is a behavior which the respondent is asked to recall, the less accurate and reliable will be the response. If frequency of some activity is the datum desired, then it may be wise to ask two questions, "How often do you usually go to the motion pictures in one week?" and "How often did you go last week?" The data entering analysis would be the average of these two responses. If words like "frequently participate" are used in a questionnaire (as they are in the examples given in this chapter), then the interpretation of the response should be that it represents relative interest in the activity and not a real index to frequency.

Motivations. Attempts to uncover the reasons why people do the things they do rarely uncover subconscious reasons. More often the response should be interpreted merely as the reasons most frequently talked about. In other words, there are reasons why people do things, and there are reasons that they will give. Nevertheless, the opinions of the respondents on such matters as their image of the station are important, since they do reflect the content of conversations the respondents are likely to have about the station, and hence the reputation given the station by its listeners. In addition, respondents are typically very eager to report their opinions about broadcast stations. Encouraging them to do so in the interview will make them more willing to provide other information when requested. In other words, these questions make for a good interview climate.

A Suggested Questionnaire

The questionnaire at Figure 10-1 was designed to address the psychographics of a station audience—qualitative audience measurement. It was designed for use in a telephone survey in which station personnel have been trained to be the interviewers. Respondents are

Respondent Name _____ Phone Number_____

Date_____ Time of Day: 1st Attempt _____2d_____ 3d _____

Interviewer _____

Hello. I'm_____calling for a local radio station. We are conducting a survey of radio listeners in this area. If it's all right, I would like to ask you a few questions. (If necessary, add: We are not selling anything, and all information will be kept strictly confidential.)

1. a. On the average day, about how many hours do you personally spend listening to radio at home, in your car, and at work? Would you say:

Less than 2 hrs _____
2-3 hrs _____
Over 3 hrs _____
Doesn't listen _____

(If R doesn't listen, then thanks and good-bye.)

b. Yesterday how much time did you personally spend listening to your radio at home, in your car, and at work? Would you say:

Less than 2 hrs _____
2-3 hrs _____
Over 3 hrs _____
Didn't listen _____

2. a. On the average day about how many hours do you personally spend watching television? Would you say:

Less than 2 hrs _____
2-3 hrs _____
Over 3 hrs _____
Never watch _____

b. Yesterday how much time did you personally spend watching television? Would you say:

Less than 2 hrs _____
2-3 hrs _____
Over 3 hrs _____
Didn't watch _____

3. a. About how many times per week do you read any newspaper?

Daily _____
Several Times a Wk _____
Once a Week _____
Less than Once a Week _____

b. How many times did you read any newspaper last week?

Daily _____
Several Times a Week _____
Once a Week _____
Less than Once a Week _____

4. Which of the following sections of the newspaper do you read regularly?

National News _____
Local News _____
Business _____
Editorial _____
Entertainment Section _____
(Radio-Television) _____
Sports _____

5. What is your favoriate radio station in this area? _____

Figure 10-1.　Suggested Questionnaire for Psychographic Audience Survey.

6. Do you listen to DRUZ-FM at least fifteen minutes in the average week?

Yes_____

No_____

7. We are interested in knowing why you listen to your favorite radio station,_____.
Please indicate whether you strongly agree, agree, disagree or strongly
disagree with the following reasons for listening_____.

a. It helps me to find out about things that are happening in my town and
in the surrounding communities.

Strongly Agree_____

Agree_____

Disagree_____

Strongly Disagree_____

b. It informs me of the news events of the day.

Strongly Agree_____

Agree_____

Disagree_____

Strongly Disagree_____

c. The people on the station sound friendly.

Strongly Agree_____

Agree_____

Disagree_____

Strongly Disagree_____

d. The people on the station have good senses of humor.

Strongly Agree_____

Agree_____

Disagree_____

Strongly Disagree_____

e. The people on the station sound like professionals.

Strongly Agree_____

Agree_____

Disagree_____

Strongly Disagree_____

f. I trust/believe the people I hear on the station.

Strongly Agree_____

Agree_____

Disagree_____

Strongly Disagree_____

g. I like the music played by the station.

Strongly Agree_____

Agree_____

Disagree_____

Strongly Disagree_____

8. We are interested in knowing some of the leisure time activities of the people who
live in our community. Please indicate whether you frequently participate in the
following activities.

	Yes	No	Refused
a. Going to theater or films	_____	_____	_____
b. Sports such as bowling, tennis, golf	_____	_____	_____
c. Reading books/magazines	_____	_____	_____
d. Recreational travel/vacations	_____	_____	_____
e. Working around house and in the garden	_____	_____	_____
f. Social organizations and clubs	_____	_____	_____
g. Attending live music presentations—concerts, clubs, discos	_____	_____	_____

Figure 10-1. (continued)

9. In order to know more about the popularity of certain types of products in our community, we would like to know whether you purchased any of the following items during the past year. Please indicate by saying yes or no.

	Yes	No	Refused
a. An automobile	_____	_____	_____
b. Auto tires, batteries or accessories	_____	_____	_____
c. Furniture/carpet/bedding	_____	_____	_____
d. Major appliances	_____	_____	_____
e. Home improvement supplies	_____	_____	_____
f. Lawn & garden supplies	_____	_____	_____
g. A camera or other photo equipment	_____	_____	_____
h. Have you opened a savings or checking account in the past year?	_____	_____	_____

Just a couple more questions. We would appreciate it if you would tell us the following information about yourself.

10. Sex

Male _____
Female _____

11. Please stop me when I mention the age grouping to which you belong.

18-24 _____
25-34 _____
35-49 _____
50-64 _____
65+ _____
Refused _____

12. What was the highest grade of school or degree that you have completed?

High School or less _____
High School Diploma _____
Some college _____
Refused _____

13. What is the occupation of the head of the house?

Professional and Executive _____
Clerical-Sales _____
Labor (skilled and unskilled) _____
Other (specify) _____
Refused _____

14. Please stop me when I mention the income bracket to which your family belongs.

Under $5,000 _____
$5,000-$9,999 _____
$10,000-$14,999 _____
$15,000-$19,999 _____
$20,000+ _____
Refused _____

Thank you for your cooperation. Good-bye.

Figure 10-1. (continued)

adults in households drawn at random from a telephone directory published during the month of the survey.

Questions 1 through 4. These questions provide a thumbnail assessment of the media habits of the respondent. Parts a and b of each question are averaged in accordance with the reasoning above to provide the desired data on media habits.

Questions 5 and 6. Questions 5 and 6 establish where within the listening priorities of the respondent the station being investigated falls. The favorite station is named, and the respondent is asked whether he/she listens to the station of interest 15 minutes or more during an average week. Question 6 determines whether the respondent is a listener or a nonlistener.

Question 8. This question with its parts identifies a number of possible reasons for listening to radio. Respondents are asked to provide their reasons for listening to a favorite radio station. The answers will provide a profile of various listener categories—categories which differ according to their use of radio. The question can be rephrased to solicit reasons for listening to the station being studied. On the other hand, phrased as it is, the question will show audiences with motivations to listen to other stations as contrasted to the motivations of those audiences who listen to the station being studied.

Question 9. A profile of the leisure activities of the audiences in the trading area will directly indicate that certain sponsors with investments in leisure products and services will be good prospects for radio. Indirectly the profile will suggest program undertakings to capitalize or build upon the interests of the audience.

Question 10. Question 10 provides a composite portrait of the buying potential of the market, suggesting ways in which the local buying public differs from national audiences. In addition, trends in product purchases will indicate specific businesses which could profitably use the commercial time of the station.

Questions 10-14. These items solicit information about the demographic dimensions of the survey sample.

Tabulation of Results

Detailed tabulation of the results of a field survey were included in Chapter 7. The tabulation of results from this survey would follow the same procedures.

The first step is the accumulation of the simple frequencies and proportions for responses to each question. Consider the responses to questions 2a and 2b as an example. It will be desirable to average these two responses in interpreting the data. To average the responses to these two items, add the number of responses given in each category under question 2a to the number of responses for the same categories under question 2b; then divide the sum in each category by two. The table below illustrates:

RESPONSE	FREQUENCY 2a	FREQUENCY 2b	AVERAGE FREQUENCY	AVERAGE PROPORTION
Light Viewing (0–2 hrs)	150	250	200	.50
Medium Viewing (2–3 hrs)	145	95	120	.30
Heavy Viewing (3+ hrs)	105	55	80	.20
	400	400	400	1.00

This table of simple frequencies and proportions among responses to questions 2a and 2b presents the relative state of television viewership among the potential radio listeners in the trade area. A relatively large proportion of the local audience is not available to television advertisers more than three hours per day. When this information is put alongside the results to questions 1a and 1b which queried level of radio listening, it should be apparent that adding radio to the media mix in this market significantly extends the possibilities for both reach and frequency.

In tabulating simple frequencies and proportions for responses to question 7, it may be helpful to add together the responses for *strongly agree* and *agree* and for *strongly disagree* and *disagree*. Doing so is called *dichotomizing* the responses, dividing them into only two categories. This will make it easy to report the proportion of listeners who give each possible response to question 7 as a reason for listening to the station being studied. For example, consider this summary of responses to 7b, "listening for news events":

	FREQUENCY	PROPORTION
Strongly Agree	40	.10
Agree	60	.15
Strongly Agree + Agree	100	.25
Strongly Disagree	100	.25
Disagree	200	.50
Strongly Disagree + Disagree	·300	.75
	400	1.00

These results indicate that for three out of four of the station listeners, news is not an important reason for listening. Answers to the other parts of question 7 will provide the reasons that they do listen.

It may also be prudent to comment on the handling of refused responses in tabulating survey results. When a number of respondents have refused to provide responses to a question, the number refusing are subtracted from the total in the survey sample before computing proportions. Consider this example of data received in response to question 8a, "Do you frequently participate in going to theater or films?" Out of the 400 respondents, 60 refused to answer this question yielding an adjusted sample size (total sample of 400 less 60 refusers) of 340. Two hundred respondents indicated that they did frequently participate in attending theater and films.

Frequently participate in going to theater or films	FREQUENCY	PROPORTION
Yes	200	.588
No	140	.412
	340	1.000

Cross-tabulation. The purpose of cross-tabulation in this survey analysis will be to compare various groups within the trade area. One cross-tabulation that will be particularly interesting will be a comparison of listeners to the station being studied versus non-listeners. The station sales manager would find it interesting to compare the relative likelihood of automobile purchase among listeners and nonlisteners to the station. This will require a cross-tabulation of question 6 with question 9a:

	LISTENER FREQUENCY	NONLISTENER FREQUENCY	LISTENER PROPORTION
Purchased an automobile	100	80	.677
Did not purchase an automobile	50	170	.333
	150	250	1.000

Of course, any cross-tabulation that can be interpreted can also be computed.

Other Psychographic Variables

Public Activities

There are a number of relatively familiar psychographic variables not included in the suggested questionnaire but which may be of interest to some specific station. Public activities is a measure of the community and political involvement of potential listeners and viewers. It is based on a series of questions used by the W. R. Simmons Company in their research of network radio audiences. These are the questions asked of respondents in a public activities item:

	YES	NO
a. Has a member of your household ever been involved in public issues?	—	—
b. Has a member of your household ever written a letter to the editor of a magazine or newspaper?	—	—
c. Has a member of your household ever adressed a public meeting?	—	—
d. Has a member of your household ever been active in support of a local issue?	—	—
e. Has a member of your household ever worked in a political campaign?	—	—.[6]

The score of the respondent on this variable is the number of questions answered yes.

Shopper Profiles

The psychographic profile of the composite shopper described below is the result of work reported by Dr. Susan Tyler Eastman of Temple University.[7] The respondent indicates the degree of his/her agreement with each of the statements. In tabulation the total of the respondent's responses on each scale (set of questions) are the numbers entering analysis.

	Strongly Agree	Agree	Disagree	Strongly Disagree
Leader (six items)				
I like to be considered a leader.	3	2	1	0
I think I have a lot of personal ability.	3	2	1	0
I think I have more self-confidence than most people	3	2	1	0
My friends or neighbors often come to me for advice	3	2	1	0
People come to me more often than I go to them for information about brands.	3	2	1	0
I have never really been outstanding at anything.	0	1	2	3
Cash Buyer (four items)				
I buy many things with a credit card or charge card.	0	1	2	3
I like to pay cash for everything I buy.	3	2	1	0
It is good to have charge accounts.	0	1	2	3
To buy anything, other than a house or a car, on credit is unwise.	3	2	1	0
Experimental Shopper (five items)				
I often try new brands before my friends and neighbors do.	3	2	1	0
When I see a new brand on the shelf, I often buy it just to see what it's like.	3	2	1	0
When I find a new brand I like, I usually tell my friends about it.	3	2	1	0
I like to try new and different things.	3	2	1	0

Safe Shopper (three items)

Information I get about a product from a friend is better than what I get from advertising.	3	2	1	0
I like to wait and see how other people like new brands before I try them.	3	2	1	0
I spend a lot of time talking with my friends about products and brands.	3	2	1	0

Bargain Shopper (four items)

A person can save a lot of money by shopping around for bargains.	3	2	1	0
I usually look for the lowest possible prices when I shop.	3	2	1	0
I like to go grocery shopping.	3	2	1	0

Brand-Name Shopper (three items)

Nationally advertised brands are usually worth a few pennies more than a store's own brand.	3	2	1	0
A store's own brand is usually just as good as the nationallly advertised brand.	0	1	2	3
I keep from brands I have never heard of.	3	2	1	0

Messy Housekeeper (five items)

I usually keep where I live very neat and clean.	0	1	2	3
My idea of housekeeping is "once over lightly."	3	2	1	0
I am the kind of person who takes short cuts in cooking.	3	2	1	0
I must admit I really don't like household chores.	3	2	1	0
I take a great deal of pride in my home.	0	1	2	3

Note that in the case of some of the items above, numerical coding is reversed: this means that the item involved is negatively related to the trait to which it is assigned. The last item above, for example, would mark the meticulous rather than messy housekeeper, if the respondent strongly agreed. The respondent's scores on the set of items under any trait are added to yield a composite trait score which is then tabulated.

These shopper profiles can be very important in describing unique features of a broadcast audience, since they indicate not only what advertising appeals are likely to be influential with the audience, but they may imply the level of success that can be predicted from a particular advertising campaign. For example, if the market is dominated by audiences which score high on the "cash buyer" trait, then an advertising campaign based upon easy credit terms will have a difficult time in the market. As might be expected, the sales presentation of a station armed with research information of this sort will be particularly persuasive with advertising agencies, as well as regional and national advertisers.

Summary

Since it is the principal business of broadcasting stations with commercial licenses to sell audiences to advertisers, the availability of audiences with unique qualities can substantially reinforce the profit center of the station. Psychographics, buzz word for this sort of research, is one of the most discussed topics in advertising. The availability of good psychographic research to this point in time has been limited. This chapter has suggested some of the measures, techniques of sample design and data tabulation appropriate to psychographic studies. A recommendation has been made for basic research for the station just beginning to become interested in psychographic assessment of its audience. But the potential for additional important studies will be apparent as soon as the data from the first study becomes available.

NOTES—CHAPTER 10

1. Joseph T. Plummer, "Life Style Patterns: A New Constraint for Mass Communications," *Journal of Broadcasting,* **16** (1971-72), 79-89.
2. Plummer, page 80.
3. Charles King and Douglas Tigert, *Attitude Research Reaches New Heights* (New York: American Marketing Association, 1972).
4. V. C. Trohldahl and R. F. Carter, "Random Selection of Respondents Within Households," *Journal of Marketing Research,* **1** (1964), 71-76.
5. For additional information see Earl Babbie, *Survey Research Methods* (Belmont, California: Wadsworth, 1973).
6. James E. Fletcher, "Commercial versus Public Television Audiences: Public Activities and the Watergate Hearings," *Communication Quarterly,* **25** (1977), 13-16.
7. Susan Tyler Eastman, "Factor Analysis: What It Is and How You Use It," paper presented at the annual meetings of the Broadcast Education Association, Las Vegas, Nevada, April 1978.

11 Effectiveness of Programs in Producing Revenue

James E. Fletcher

The revenue of a radio or television station follows from the size and quality of the audiences which tune to its programs. Advertisers who directly provide this revenue hope to associate their reputations and messages with these programs in order to achieve some selling objective in the audience.

Since programs result in the revenue that keeps a station profitable, management is frequently interested in the "bottom line," how productive is this program in terms of revenue? The question is relevant for nearly every identifiable program effort of every station. This question, in turn, implies two subordinate issues:

1. What is the ratio of the cost of each program effort to the value of the audiences which the program recruits?
2. What is the relative efficiency of the program in producing the specific target audiences sought after by sponsors?

COST/BENEFIT ANALYSIS

In cost/benefit analysis, cost refers to the total of station resources required to air a given program. Benefit to the station is the revenue which can be credited to the audience appeals of the program. These two important data—cost and benefit—ignore the contents of the program and focus on the economic features of the program. The most common way of contrasting cost and benefit is the cost/benefit ratio:

$$\text{cost/benefit ratio} = \frac{\text{value of audience attracted}}{\text{cost of airing the program}} .$$

The cost benefit ratio of a program which produced revenue equal to its cost would be 1.00. A program which returns less than its cost will have a cost/benefit ratio less than 1.00. A profitable program will have a cost/benefit ratio greater than 1.00.

Illustration

The manager of station WOE has invested a considerable amount of money in beefing up the station offerings in morning drive time, hoping to attract more listeners and increase the interest of potential advertisers in purchase of station availabilities.

The manager wants to know how productive his efforts have been in improving the cost/benefit ratio of morning drive time programming. The first step in the necessary cost/benefit analysis is identification of program costs, in this case for the period Monday through Friday, 6:00 A.M. to 9:00 A.M. The figures below show the costs both before and after the beef-up program was initiated by management.

	PREVIOUS PROGRAM	BEEFED-UP PROGRAM
Engineering (the average cost per hour of engineering services at the station multiplied by three, the number of hours of broadcast time occupied by the program)	$ 15.00	$ 15.00
Administration (total annual cost for station adminstration divided by the number of hours which the station broadcasts per year and multiplied by three, the number of hours occupied by the program)	15.00	15.00
Program Department Costs		
Personalities	12.00	23.00
Music Package—Gold	–	2.00
Wire Services	1.00	1.00
Actuality Services	–	1.00
Comedy Service	–	1.00
Syndicated Commentary	2.00	5.00
Toll Charges for Long-Distance Telephone Interviews	–	20.00
News and Traffic Helicopter	–	50.00
TOTAL COST	$ 45.00	$ 133.00

The breakdown above shows that the decision to beef-up morning drive time in this way resulted in an increase in prorgram costs of 196 percent.

The second step in this cost/benefit analysis will be to identify revenues properly associated with morning drive time. Considering agency discounts, discounts for quantity, sales commissions, costs of servicing the accounts and billing, the average yield on an availability during drive time is $4.00 with the station's current rate structure. If 100 percent of availabilities were sold, morning drive time would account for an average revenue of $240.00 per day (60 avails × $4.00).

Prior to the beef-up decision the sales staff was able to sell only about 60 percent of the availabilities in morning drive time, yielding an average daily revenue of $144.00. After 6 weeks of the beefed-up morning drive time programming, the sales staff is averaging 80 percent of availabilities sold during morning drive time, yielding an average daily revenue from morning drive of $192.00. In other words, the new programming has resulted in a 33 percent increase in average daily revenues from morning drive time.

The cost benefit ratio for the previous morning drive program is:

$$\text{cost/benefit} = \$144.00 \div \$45.00$$
$$= 3.20.$$

The cost/benefit ratio for the beefed-up morning drive time program is:

$$\text{cost/benefit} = \$192.00 \div \$133.00$$
$$= 1.44.$$

It is clear from this analysis that the average dollar invested in the previous programming returned $3.20, while the average dollar invested in the beefed-up program is returning only $1.44. It should also be clear that if gross revenue alone were considered, this decline in productivity would not be obvious.

In fairness to the cause of improved broadcast programming, the illustration must be extended to the probable actions of a manager who has made this cost/benefit analysis. If there is any evidence that the improved programming has actually increased the size or quality of audience as well as the average daily revenue, then reverting to the previous program is out of question, of course. Two other feasible alternatives are (1) to increase rates and (2) reduce the cost of the beefed-up program. Increasing rates will be feasible if there has been an increase in audience such that cost per thousand listeners to the advertiser is the same as or lower than the cost per thousand listeners under the previous rate structure. Decreasing the cost of the beefed-up program will be feasible if the appeal of the new program is not adversely affected.

To continue the illustration, the station manager elects to reduce the cost of the beefed-up program by eliminating the helicopter which cost $50.00, opting instead to establish a radio link to the helicopter used by the local police to spot traffic problems. The pilot of the police helicopter is paid $5.00 per day to provide short transmissions on the traffic situation which are recorded and incorporated into the morning program. This change results in a reduction in the average daily cost of the morning drive programming of $45.00. The cost/benefit ratio of the program then becomes:

$$\text{cost/benefit} = \$192.00 \div \$88.00$$
$$= 2.18.$$

From this point the station manager could continue to modify both costs and revenues to improve the cost/benefit ratio in accordance with the objectives of the station.

Cost/benefit analysis can be extended to provide a profile of radio format productivity. "Productivity" in this case would be the cost/benefit ratio itself which can be interpreted as the amount of revenue produced from the average dollar in program investment. Cost estimates can be routinely computed using a worksheet like that at Figure 11-1, while revenues may be identified using a worksheet like that at Figure 11-2.

Cost/benefit ratios can be calculated for each day-part of a radio format to show the relative productivity of the various program efforts of a station. Table 11-1 provides an illustration of the productivity of programs on fictitious station WOE.

DAY-PART	AVERAGE EARNING PER SPOT	% SOLD	AVERAGE DAILY REVENUE	AVERAGE DAILY COST	COST/BENEFIT RATIO
Weekday					
6 A.M.–9 A.M.	4.00	80	192.00	88.00	2.18
9 A.M.–4 P.M.	3.00	60	312.00	85.00	3.67
4 P.M.–7 P.M.	4.00	90	216.00	88.00	2.41
7 P.M.–Midnight	2.00	50	100.00	75.00	1.33
Weekend					
6 A.M.–6 P.M.	3.00	40	288.00	180.00	1.60
6 P.M.–Midnight	2.00	50	120.00	90.00	1.33

Examination of Table 11-1 reveals that there are several time periods in which the average dollar invested in programs is returning much less in revenues than the dollars invested in the programs of other time periods. This is a signal for some remedy from management. One possibility may be to reduce the expenses of these less productive time periods by partially automating the program function of the station during these periods. Or it may be possible to strengthen the programming by additional program investment.

The illustration of station WOE is an instance in which cost/benefit analysis is used to examine the past performance of a program. There are a number of situations in which

WORKSHEET FOR DETAILING PROGRAM COSTS

I. Engineering costs. Engineering costs will be constant for all hours broadcast, if only transmitter and studio equipment is used. First find the total expenditure on engineering at the station during the previous year, less special communication services required for remotes and specials. (a) $ _____ This should include salaries of engineers, replacement equipment, maintenance and spare parts. Next determine the total number of hours broadcast by the station during the year. (b)___hours. Now divide (a) by (b). This dividend is the engineering cost of the average broadcast hour on your station. (a ÷ b) $___per hour. Multiply this figure by the number of broadcast hours occupied by the program under study (c)___hours, to arrive at basic engineering cost of the program (d) $___per program. Add to the basic engineering cost any special engineering costs such as rental of telephone or microwave links, rental of equipment, wages to extra engineering staff (e) $___per program. This total (d + e) is your best estimate of the engineering costs of the program in question (f) $___per program.

II. Administrative costs. Administrative costs represent the fair share of the station overhead which should be borne by every program undertaking of the station. To arrive at this figure first isolate the overall overhead expenses of the station. This should include salaries, fringe benefits, janitorial service, building upkeep, and office expendables among others. For greater detail consult the Accounting Manual for Broadcasters (from the Institute for Broadcasting Financial Management, Inc., 360 North Michigan Avenue, Chicago, Illinois 60601), (g) $___. Divide this figure by the total number of hours broadcast in the year by the station (b) and multiply the resulting dividend by the number of hours in the program under study (c), yielding the administrative cost per program (h) $___per program.

III. Program department costs. These are the costs undertaken directly by the program department in connection with this program. The elements of this cost estimate are many and varied; the list below is suggested for relatively simple program efforts.

(i) Personalities	$ _____
(j) Music royalties and acquisition, performance license	$ _____
(k) Apportioned share of program department overhead	$ _____
(l) Syndicated features	$ _____
(m)Scenery or location lease	$ _____
(n) Telephone expenses	$ _____
(o) Program promotion	$ _____
(p) Other _____	$ _____
_____	$ _____
_____	$ _____
_____	$ _____
(q) Total program department	$ _____

IV. Total Program Cost Estimate (f + h + q) $ _____

Figure 11–1. Worksheet for Estimating Program Costs.

it is desirable to forecast the productivity of a program before it is broadcast. Two examples will be provided here—one in which a local television station is investing in the rights to an off-network rerun being purchased from syndication, the other a purchase of a feature film package from syndication.

EVALUATING AN INVESTMENT IN OFF-NETWORK RERUNS

An off-network series is one that has had a successful run on a commercial network and is subsequently sold for airing by local stations. The rights to off-network series are sold by syndicators who enter into agreements with the program owners which return

	(b)		(d)	(bxcxd)	(e)	(f)	(g)	(exfxg)	Total
(a)	Rate for	(c)	% sold	Yield	Rate for	#	% sold	Yield'	Y + Y'
Program	Adjacency	#			Participation				

WORKSHEET FOR DETAILING REVENUES

Figure 11-2. Worksheet for Detailing Program Revenues.

to the owners a portion of the profits earned by selling the series to individual stations and station groups. One of the complications in the syndication business is the concept of "run." The notion of "run" derives from the practice in theatrical film in which a film is released in first run to all cities in the nation. As soon as the film is shown for a second engagement in any community, then the second run is said to have begun, even though the first run may have been in only one community. In the case of television, this is a significant feature of syndication, since the syndicator must pay all of the residuals to creative people involved in a production in advance of beginning a second and subsequent run. A residual is the payment to a performer or other creative participant in a production for second and later runs of a production. Because the syndicator is obliged to pay residuals at the beginning of each run, there is a tendency to prefer contracts with stations who want the rights to more than one run; and the syndicator is wary of programs series which do not promise to be leased by a large number of stations on each run. The off-network series is therefore a staple in the syndicator's program inventory. Such a series has a reputation in the public mind and in the view of the local broadcaster because of its extensive exposure while playing on the network. When a successful series has appeared for some number of years on the networks, stations may have the opportunity to bid for the rights to showing that series when released as an off-network series, even though the date for availability of the series may be several years away. The amount of money involved to acquire these rights is frequently in the millions of dollars.

Since the money involved in acquiring a program from syndication may be large, considerable study and careful thought are the rule. The person or committee in the broadcast organization responsible for recommending investment in off-network series will have the time and resources to do considerable research into the relative merits of the various series available. Various professionals in the field will examine such matters as nature of the central figure of the series, number of episodes, length, availability date, technical quality (particularly important in the case of series produced on color film, since the quality of color film stock deteriorates over time).

Certainly relevant data will include the ratings for previous runs of the series, whether on the network or in syndication. The series being studied may have been programmed opposite specials, other network series now in syndication, feature films, network series which did not survive, and so forth. The program in each of these competitive situations may have appeared in more than one rating report. The complexity involved in interpreting and assembling this information may be great. The routine that follows is a way of generating a "win rate" from this mass of data—a single figure which estimates the ability of a series in syndication to win out over other series. It is no better, at best, than the information from which it is assembled, but it may be easier to conjure with than a mass of undigested rating figures.

Illustration—"Win Rate." This procedure is an adaptation of Thurstone scaling, used in constructing attitude measurements.[1] It relies upon the assumption that the choice of program to be watched by a television viewer is properly described as a series of dichotomous choices. To illustrate, consider a viewer whose set can receive three television signals — Station A, Station B, and Station C. The receiver can accommodate the signal of only one station at a time. Under the basic "win rate" assumption the viewer in deciding which of the three signals to watch would be choosing between A and B, then A and C, and finally between B and C: hence three dichotomous choices involved in the one decision as to which of three competing signals is to be viewed.

Once that assumption has been made, the first step in computing win rate is to convert reported shares into "win proportions." To continue the illustrations of the three signals, the rating report for November 1976 for the Midvale market reflects these shares for one time period of interest.

Station	Program	Share
A	Bill's House	.40
B	Doctor	.30
C	Hermione	.30

A share is, as noted in Chapter 4, the proportion of those using their television sets who are tuned to a given television station. To find the win proportion of "Bill's House" over "Doctor" divide the share associated with "Bill's House" by the sum of the shares of the two programs.

$$\text{win proportion} = \frac{.40}{.40 + .30}$$
$$= .57.$$

Similarly win proportions can be computed for "Doctor" over "Hermione" and "Bill's

House" over "Hermione." The following represent blocks of shares for time periods in which all network affiliates in the market were scheduling off-network series in several consecutive books (rating reports).

November 1976

Station	Program	Share	Win Proportions

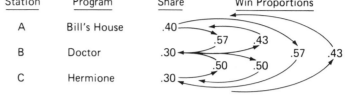

February/March 1977

November 1977

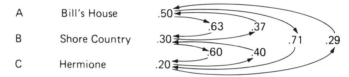

February/March 1978

November 1978

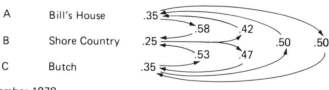

The first of each pair of win proportions is the proportion of bivalent choices in which the more popular program won; the second of each pair of win proportions is the proportion of bivalent choices in which the less popular program won. These win proportions are next distributed as a win matrix, in which the average win proportion of one program over another is computed. This average win proportion is followed by a figure in parentheses which corresponds to the number of rating reports in which the program represented by the vertical column was scheduled opposite the program represented by the horizontal row. The average win proportions from the matrix above are computed as the sum of the column divided by the number of scores in the column. They represent the average competitive success of the program at the head of the column. As additional rating reports enter into the computation these average win proportions can be revised to

WINNERS

Murphy's Den

Fun House

Butch

Shore Country

Hermione

Doctor

Bill's House

LOSERS

LOSERS	Murphy's Den	Fun House	Butch	Shore Country	Hermione	Doctor	Bill's House
Bill's House	**	.43 .38	.43 .47 .33	.37 .42	.50	**	**
Doctor	.57 .62	**	.50 .42	**	**	**	**
Hermione	.57 .53 .71	.50 .58	**	.60	**	**	**
Shore Country	.63 .58	**	.40	**	.53	**	**
Butch	.50	**	**	.47	**	.54	.54
Fun House	**	**	**	**	.46	**	.50
Murphy's Den	**	**	**	**	.46	.50	**
Average Win Proportion for Winners (Number of Comparisons)	.59 (8)	.47 (4)	.43 (6)	.47 (4)	.49 (4)	.52 (2)	.52 (2)

reflect the additional information. The average win proportion itself can be used to compare the relative value of programs being considered for purchase from syndication. They can also be used to compare the likely shares of any set of programs in competition.

To predict shares from average win proportions, apply the following formula:

$$\text{Predicted Share for Program A} = \frac{\text{Average Win Proportion for Program A}}{\text{Sum of Average Win Proportions for all Programs in Competition}}$$

Consider an illustration based upon the average win proportions computed above:

Station	Program	Average Win Proportion	Predicted Share
A	Fun House	.52	.37
B	Doctor	.47	.32
C	Shore Country	.47	.32

$$\text{Predicted Share for Fun House} = \frac{.52}{.52 + .47 + .47}$$

$$= .37$$

$$\text{Predicted Share for Doctor} = \frac{.47}{.52 + .47 + .47}$$

$$= .32$$

$$\text{Predicted Share for Shore Country} = \frac{.47}{.52 + .47 + .47}$$

$$= .32$$

The limitation of such a predicted share, of course, is that it is derived from the available comparisons recorded in rating reports. Where the number of those comparisons is small, great caution is appropriate. But where the number of comparisons is relatively large, the average win proportion may be of some use.

It should be apparent that the win proportion can be used to predict a rating by multiplying predicted share by HUT rating for the time period involved. Predicted audience projections can be estimated by multiplying predicted share by estimate of the total persons viewing during the time period. Having a predicted audience projection will help in establishing rates for participating spots during the program: Multiply the average cost per thousand for this time period by the number of thousands in predicted audience. From the values of participating and adjacent availabilities, cost/benefit ratios can be projected for programs being considered as possible buys from syndication.

EVALUATING A FEATURE FILM PACKAGE

Packages of feature films represent a different problem for the station buying programs from syndication. For one thing, feature film packages rarely have the elements of continuity which connect episodes of a single series: the star, settings, and moods change from one offering of the package to another.

In addition, the films which are grouped together in a package are grouped to satisfy the syndicator's needs more often than to meet those of a particular station buyer. Hence, not all of the films in the package will be of equal value. In some cases, a syndicator may include some very unattractive titles along with the blockbusters of a package, since, otherwise he may not be able to realize any return for his purchase of the rights of the less desirable films. This last possibility is real enough that many buyers of feature film packages will invest in a package expecting not to use some of the titles at all.

Some film packages will include contracts which call for unlimited runs. That is, the contract allows the station buying the package to play any of the titles in the package as often as desired within the life of the contract. Generally this sort of contract will characterize a "library" of films which a station may use to fill time made available by an emergency cancellation of other programming or to fill those quiet hours which follow late fringe programs.

Most of the higher priced feature film packages will be for a limited number of showings (runs). So the contract may read that the station may telecast each title in the package five times during the 5-year life of a contract.

What follows is a method for revenue forecasting of feature film packages being considered for purchase from syndication. It is based upon the income forecast depreciation method used to estimate the value of a syndication contract for depreciation purposes.[2]

As in the example above with evaluation of an off-network series, this method begins with a summary of the revenue experience of the film buyer. Therefore, the buyer prepares a summary like that below of revenue expected according to the number of runs which a given film title receives.

NO. OF RUNS TELECAST	PER CENT OF TOTAL REVENUE RETURNED PER RUN							
	1ST RUN	2D RUN	3D RUN	4TH RUN	5TH RUN	6TH RUN	7TH RUN	8TH RUN
1	100							
2	60	40						
3	50	30	20					
4	50	30	15	5				
5	50	30	15	3	2			
6	50	30	15	3	1	1		
7	50	30	15	2	1	1	1	
8	50	30	15	1	1	1	1	1

This table indicates that a title which is run only once earns 100 percent of the total revenue it will produce in that single run. On the other hand, if a film is run three times, it earns 50 percent of its total revenue on the first run, 30 percent on the second run and 20 percent on its final run.

Given this table of historic percent of total revenue realized for each run of a film title, the film buyer is ready to examine the "deal" which the syndicator is offering in connection with the film package under consideration.

For illustration purposes, let us suppose this is the film package offered by our syndicator:

Term of Contract . . . . five years
Number of Runs per Title . . . . five
Lump Sum Cost of Package $5000
Titles:

1. The Sugargum Tree (195_ Academy Award), 112 min., color, romantic comedy

2. The Rakish Rogue, good box office in first release, 100 min., color, swashbuckler

3. The Sound of Laughter, high budget spectacle, 120 min., color, musical

4. High Mogollon, (Grand Prix of Loire, 196_), 100 min., color, nature documentary

5. The Golden Pheasant, 100 min., color, mixed reviews, Fu Man Chu mystery

6. Mary Hardy, black and white, 75 min., adolescent situation comedy

7. Ten Minutes to Go, 1943, color, 100 min., World War II battle melodrama

8. Troilus and Cressida, British, color, 110 min., film version of the Shakespeare play

9. Grandma Meets Dracula, color, 100 min., adolescent spoof of horror flicks

10. Speckled Death, color cheapy, 80 min., Japanese science fiction

After studying the available information on each of these titles the film buyer estimates his first year use of each film and the likely number of runs each title is going to receive over 5 years. The average revenue of each title for the first year is estimated by the average earnings of other films in the same program slot.

The tables below are the result of the film buyer's study and thought. Based on information in the tables above the expected earnings of each title is now computed.

$$\text{Cost/benefit ratio} = \$8283 \div \$5000$$
$$= 1.66$$
$$\text{Average return per year} = .66 \div 5$$
$$= .13 \ .$$

TITLE NO.	RUNS ANTICIPATED OVER 5 YRS.
1	5
2	5
3	5
4	5
5	5
6	0
7	4
8	4
9	5
10	2

Use of Titles in First Year of Contract

TITLE NO.	PROGRAM SLOT	AVERAGE TITLE EARNS IN THIS SLOT	FIRST YEAR EARNINGS
1	Friday Flick	$500	
	Sunday Sinema	300	$800
2	Sunday Sinema	500	
	Bubblegum Bijou	300	800
3	Friday Flick	500	500
4	Bubblegum Bijou	200	200
5	Friday Flick	500	500
6	Friday Flick	500	500

Title Showing by Contract Year

CONTRACT YEAR	1ST RUN	2D RUN	3D RUN	4TH RUN	5TH RUN
1	1,2,3,4 5,7	1,2			
2	8,9,10	3,4,5,7	1,2,3,4		
3		8,9,10	5,7	1,2	
4			8,9	3,4,5,9	1,2
5				7,8	3,4,5,9

Earnings

TITLE NO.	FIRST YEAR	SECOND YEAR	THIRD YEAR	FOURTH YEAR	FIFTH YEAR
1	1st Run $500 2d Run 300	3d Run $150	4th Run $ 30	5th Run $ 20	
2	1st Run $500 2d Run 300	3d Run 150	4th Run 30	5th Run 20	
3	1st Run 500	2d Run 300 3d Run 200		4th Run 30	5th Run $20
4	1st Run 200	2d Run 120 3d Run 60		4th Run 12	5th Run 8
5	1st Run 500	2nd Run 300	3d Run 150	4th Run 30	5th Run 20
6	—	—	—	—	—
7	1st Run 500	2d Run 300	3d Run 150	4th Run 50	
8		1st Run 500	2d Run 300	3d Run 150	4th Run 50
9		1st Run 500	2d Run 300	3d Run 150 4th Run 30	5th run 20
10		1st Run 500	2d Run 333		
Totals	$3300	$3080	$1293	$492	$118

The average return per year is the yield on the average dollar invested over the life of the contract divided by the number of years over which the contract extends. In this case, while the investment is profitable, it may not be up to the standard of a prosperous television station which may look for an average return per year on the order of .20 or more.

This income forecasting method of evaluating a film package in syndication is merely a way of making a personal estimate of the value of a package in an explicit and routinely disciplined way. It is still a personal estimate with all the strengths and weaknesses implied by such estimates. It may be improved by whatever other analyses are possible from the data available about the films. Certainly ratings and box office information will be helpful.

RECRUITING EFFICIENCY

It is often important in broadcast programming to produce audiences with stipulated composition. For example, it may be the objective of a regional radio station to produce audiences more or less concentrated in the urban or rural areas of that region. Another radio station may wish to sell an audience of young adults or of high income older adults. In television it may be desirable to follow one program successfully reaching children with another also particularly attractive to children.

The ability of a program to produce a given audience segment is called *recruiting efficiency*. Recruiting efficiency may be defined in a formula like this:

$$\frac{\text{Recruiting}}{\text{Efficiency}} = \frac{\text{Estimate of Audience Segment}}{\text{Estimate of Total Audience}}$$

Suppose that a radio station is licensed to a "bedroom community," a suburb of primarily white collar workers who commute to a nearby metropolis. These workers will give the market a higher than average spendable income. The young adults of the community, ages 25–49, will be particularly attractive to advertisers of such high-priced home investments as appliances, furniture and automobiles. At the same time this bedroom community is surrounded by a rural area with a quite different audience of rural families who could listen either to the local station or to stations in the metropolitan area nearby.

For sake of illustration, consider that an audience survey in this area indicated that the local station drew an audience of 16,000 persons, ages 25–49, and an estimated total number of persons of 30,000. The recruiting effiency of this station's programs in producing listeners of ages 25–49 would be:

$$\frac{\text{Recruiting}}{\text{Efficiency}} = \frac{\text{Persons 25–49 (16,000)}}{\text{Total Persons (30,000)}}$$

This recruiting efficiency implies that for every $1.00 spent on station programs, $.53 went to produce young adult audience. In the real world of broadcasting this level of recruiting efficiency is uncommonly good.

Another possible use of recruiting efficiencies may be to identify audience segments that can be exploited by a revised format. If some part of the station's schedule already produces audiences of desirable commercial characteristics, then other parts of the schedule may be revised to focus on this important target group.

When undertaking to revamp a radio format recruiting efficiencies may be valuable inputs when comparing the advantages of programming to this or that audience segment.

An illustration: A local radio station serving one compact community wishes to consider whether it will be better business to direct mid-day programming (1) to the daytime audience at home such as housewives, shut-ins, businessmen home for lunch, or (2) to listeners at work—work radio. The music used in either format might be much the same, although in work radio there may be greater concern about music tempo and its effect upon work tempo. Differences between programs directed to these two audiences at mid-day would be evident in the features used, the way in which news programs are edited and presented, the sponsors carried, and so forth. The audiences recruited would have different values to sponsors. The cost/benefits of the two formats would consider the costs of the different formats, the efficiency of the programming in producing the target audiences, and the sponsor value associated with advertising directed to each of these audience segments.

Value of Audiences

In this illustration the station representative firm estimated the rates that national advertisers might be willing to pay per thousand listeners in various demographic segments. The "station rep" indicates that young adults are in the greatest demand. Based upon the rates paid for each of the two formats nationwide and considering audience composition, the "rep" assembled this table.

DEMOGRAPHIC GROUP	RATE PER THOUSAND		
	PRESENT FORMAT	WORK RADIO FORMAT	% CHANGE
Men 18–49	$ .37	$ .15	– 59
Men 49 +	.51	1.05	+ 95
Women 18–49	.44	.19	– 57
Women 49 +	.65	2.50	+ 285

It should be noted in the table above that the reason the cost of younger groups declines per thousand is that the number of thousands in the audience has grown. In the same way the older age groups become more expensive per thousand, because there are fewer thousands of them in the audience of the work format.

Recruiting Efficiency

Based upon the audience composition of work radio formats in other markets, the following table of recruiting efficiencies for present "at-home" format and proposed "work radio" formats was prepared.

DEMOGRAPHIC GROUP	PRESENT FORMAT	WORK RADIO FORMAT	% CHANGE
Men 18–49	.24	.47	+ 96
Men 49 +	.18	.05	– 72
Women 18–49	.20	.30	+ 50
Women 49 +	.14	.02	– 86

Program Costs

To the extent that estimates are possible these are the average daily costs of the present format and of the proposed work radio format.

PROGRAM ELEMENTS	PRESENT FORMAT	WORK RADIO FORMAT
Engineering	$ 30	$ 30
Administrative Costs	30	30
Personalities	40	40
Music Packages	25	30
News and Features	2	20
Total	$127	$150

The proposed work radio format represents an 18 percent increase in cost of programming.

To perform a cost/benefit analysis, it will be necessary to adjust cost by recruiting efficiency. To get a 96 percent higher recruiting efficiency for men 18–49, the work radio format costs 18 percent more but attracts this audience segment at a cost that is 59 percent lower per thousand than with the present format. For the programmer the cost/benefit ratio is this.

$$\text{Cost/benefit ratio} = \frac{+.96}{+.18}$$
$$= 5.33$$

Considering this analysis, it would appear that each additional dollar spent on the work radio format will return 5.33 times as many men 18–49 as the dollars spent on current programming. Certainly the new format sounds attractive when this valuable audience segment is considered.

From the sponsor's point of view, and with this same audience segment, the cost/benefit ratio of interest would be:

$$\text{Cost/benefit ratio} = \frac{1.96}{1}$$
$$= 1.96$$

The 1.96 is 1.00 for the present recruiting efficiency plus .96 for the improved recruiting efficiency of the new format. The dollar which is currently spent to reach this audience segment by purchase of time with the present format will produce 1.96 as great an audience under the new format. The new format will be attractive to advertisers.

AUDIENCE FLOW

No other program scheduling strategy has received the notoriety of "audience flow" scheduling. This strategy stipulates that when one program follows another, the second and successive programs should attract the audience of the first and then some. The preceding program is referred to as the "lead-in," while the following program is the "follow-on."

The audience flow concept may be clearer after examining a chart of audience projections for a set of stations through the various time periods of the program schedule. When preparing such an audience flow diagram it is always essential to show HUT level on the same diagram. HUT or "homes using television" is the proportion of homes equipped with television which are watching television during the time period in question. Since HUT level goes up and down throughout the viewing day, the ratings of each station are to some extent affected by HUT. A drop in the rating of a given station may not indicate that the follow-on program lost audience from the lead-in: it may only indicate that the total number of people watching television has dropped.

Figure 11-3 shows the audience flow of the television network affiliates in a three-station market from the time local news is broadcast through the first hour of network prime time programs. Note that between 5:30 and 6:30 and between 7:30 and 8:30 there were large gains in HUT level. This will tend to distort upward our view of the follow-on programs in these cases.

Station C has the most consistently upward trend in the audience flow line. It does not have the largest audience, however. The program scheduled by Station C at 6:00 seems to be the problem. The stations each had the same audience for the period 5:30 to 6:00.

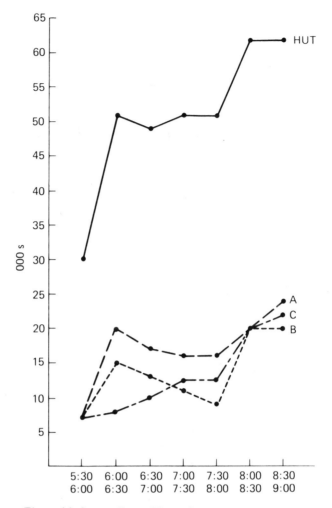

Figure 11-3. Audience Flow of Three Television Stations.

HUT level and the audiences for Stations A and B increased during the next program; the Station C audience did not. According to the audience flow doctrine, if this program could be improved, the audience levels of the remainder of the schedule might be higher.

The pattern of audience for Station A nearly follows the line of the HUT level. This might be the case with a station well-established in the viewing habits of its viewers. It does indicate that the programs in the schedule are popular programs and competitive in every time period, but the follow-on programs do not always build upon the audiences of the preceding programs. In the case of the sharp drop in audience occasioned by the station's 6:30 program, it might be helpful to examine the demographic composition of the audience here to see whether the attraction of the follow-on program is to an audience of entirely different composition.

Station B appears to be in trouble with its audiences. In three consecutive programs, those at 6:30, 7:00, and 7:30 the audience level drops, recovering only when network programming begins at 8:00. This weak lead-in to network programming may adversely affect the audience for the entire network schedule.

Demographics Flow. It may be useful in understanding the overall flow of audience during the broadcast of a particular schedule to chart the demographics over the period in question.

In Figure 11-4 four different demographic groups are represented by ratings for the time period 5:00 until 9:00. The most remarkable feature of this flow is the dramatic

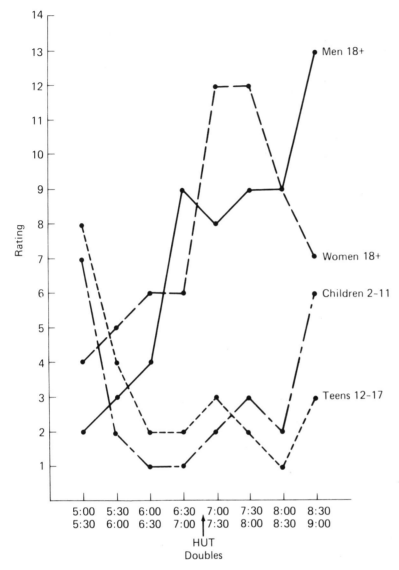

Figure 11-4. Demographic Flow of One Television Station.

drop in the viewing of teens and children accompanied by a marked increase in the viewing of adult men and women. This is sometimes the case when news and public affairs programs are scheduled among a group of off-network series from syndication.

Lead-in and Follow-on Indices. Sometimes it may be desirable to summarize in a single figure the ability of a program to build upon the audience of a preceding program when it is a "follow-on." Or it may be desirable to represent in a single figure the value of a program as a lead-in. An index for lead-in may be constructed by dividing the audience or audience segment of the lead-in by the comparable figure for the follow-on. An index for follow-on may be computed by dividing the audience or audience segment of the follow-on by the audience of the lead-in. The table below is illustrative. As with many other analyses one must be very aware of the HUT levels in using such charts as that in Table 11-2. If HUT were equal for all of the time periods shown, then it would be desirable to schedule programs so that lead-in indexes greater than 1.0 appear in each demographic category important to us in the lead-in show. The follow-on show would ideally show follow-on indexes greater than 1.0 in the same demographic categories. In the case of the program, "Mad Men," lead-in indexes greater than 1.0 appear

Table 11-2.   Lead-In Indexes and Follow-On Indexes of a Local Television Schedule.

Time	Program	Audience Estimate (000)					Lead-in Index/Follow-on Index				
		Children	Teens	Women	Men	Total	Children	Teens	Women	Men	Total
7:30–8:00	Mother	12	6	12	6	36	.80/–	60/–	2.00/–	.75/–	.92/–
8:00–8:30	Chicago Squares	15	10	6	8	39	1.00/ 1.25	.67/ 1.67	.75/ .50	1.00/ 1.33	.85/ 1.08
8:30–9:00	Steam Company	15	15	8	8	46	1.67/ 1.00	1.25/ 1.50	.80/ 1.25	1.00/ 1.00	1.18/ 1.18
9:00–9.30	Blues Concert	9	12	10	8	39	1.29/ .60	.86/ .80	.83/ 1.20	.80/ 1.00	.91/ .85
9:30–10:00	Mad Men	7	14	12	10	43	1.40/ .78	.93/ 1.17	.86/ 1.20	1.25/ 1.20	1.02/ 1.10
10:00–10:30	Witchcraft	5	15	14	8	42	2.50/ .71	5.00/ 1.07	7.00/ 1.17	2.00/ .80	3.82/ .98
10:30–11:00	Boy's Club	2	3	2	4	11	–/ .40	–/ .20	–/ .14	–/ .50	–/ .26

in all but Teens and Women categories, and the Teen lead-in index is nearly 1.0. This sort of program popular with nearly all groups makes an ideal lead-in to prime time viewing. The best program to follow "Mad Men," according to this analysis, would be "Steam Company" which has follow-on indexes greater than 1.0 in every category. Other shifts in scheduling may be made according to the same rationale. Of course, the caveat invoked earlier that the analyst also consider whatever other information is available, should be applied here as well.

FORECASTING

Many decisions must be made about events that have not yet occurred. Certainly the manager must be able to estimate in advance the most likely success or failure of current policies. This may require prediction of trends in audiences or in revenues. It may be useful to project costs and revenues together, since the American economy in recent years has been characterized by cost-push inflation. There are a number of different ways in which such projections can be made. What follows are only a few that are in general use and may be applicable to various broadcast operations.

Rolling Averages

Projecting revenues is far simpler when based upon good dollar figures on past revenues. Figures from the past will reflect the seasonal variations in revenue which characterize virtually every business. There will be other fluctuations which appear to be tied to specific events in the larger economy in which the business functions. There will also be fluctuations which are artifacts of the reporting periods involved. That is, there will be relatively sharp turns in a charted line of revenues due to the fact that they are summarized on a monthly or quarterly basis rather than day-by-day.

To improve upon the realism portrayed by such chart representations it may be helpful to compute rolling averages. A rolling average includes the immediately preceding and following periodic figures at each point in a chart. This may be clearer by representing two revenue records.

Table 11-3 shows the month by month revenues of radio station WOE. Under the column labeled "Rolling Average" the figure for February is listed as $36,333. It was computed by taking the figures for January, February and March from the column "Monthly Revenues 1978-79." The mean of these three months was $36,333, the figure used as the rolling average for February. In similar fashion the rolling average for March is the arithmetic mean of the monthly revenues for the months of February, March, and April. The

Table 11-3.

MONTHLY REVENUES 1978-9	MONTH	ROLLING AVERAGE	PERCENT CHANGE
$45,000	December	$42,333	+ 4
40,000	January	41,000	− 3
38,000	February	36,333	− 11
31,000	March	34,000	− 6
33,000	April	30,333	− 11
27,000	May	30,000	− 1
30,000	June	27,333	− 9
25,000	July	27,333	0
27,000	August	29,000	+ 6
35,000	September	32,333	+ 11
35,000	October	37,000	+ 15
42,000	November	40,667	+ 9

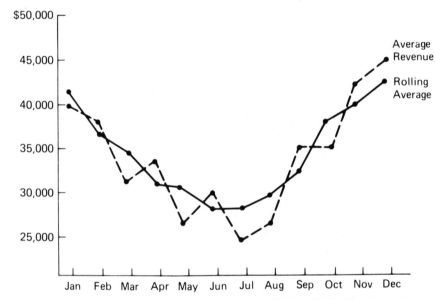

Figure 11-5.   Average Revenues of Station WOE with Rolling Average.

solid line in the chart at Figure 11-5 represents the rolling averages: the line is smoother than that represented by the unadjusted monthly revenue figures. It makes clear that a seasonal slump in revenues occurs in the late spring and summer. Assuming these figures correspond to earlier years we would anticipate that the revenue year 1979-80 will run slightly ahead of the previous year with a seasonal dip bottoming out in May and June. As more data is added to the prediction, the forecast can be made in greater detail.

Note that in Table 11-3 the percent change in rolling average has been computed from one month to the next. This figure can provide a rough monthly projection. If revenues for July 1980, for example, were $32,733, then the revenues for August 1980 might be predicted as $32,733 + .06($32,733) or $34,697. Using the percent of change figures again, the projected revenues for September 1980 would be $34,697 + .11($34,697) or $38,514.

Linear Projections

This method of revenue forecasting—using percent of change figures—is a method of forecasting that might be referred to as linear projection. Such projections assume that growth or decline in revenues will follow past patterns or, at least, bear a fixed relationship to past patterns. It is very well suited to the needs of broadcast stations where the cast of potential sponsors changes only gradually and where the inventory of commercial availabilities is much the same from one year to the next. It is a poor method of forecasting revenues when the percent of availabilities sold varies unpredictably from one year to the next, when the rates charged change wildly or where the commercial inventory changes in size or composition in an irregular fashion. When a station is new in a market or adopts a dramatically new format, revenue figures will also contain a reflection of the penetration of the market by the station, and revenue projections will require some adjustment accordingly.

Exponential Projections

When penetration is an important explanation for the amount of business being done by a station, the projection is no longer linear but exponential. These exponential curves are sometimes also called "growth" curves, since they reflect the rate of change that can be predicted when something is new and comes to be familiar.

Figure 11-6 is an exponential growth curve. That part of the curve labeled A corresponds to the introduction of a station of a market with a relatively slow gain in audience and revenues. The rate of growth accelerates rapidly in the area labeled B, as the popularity of the station reaches critical mass. The rate of growth then slows at C as the station approaches the ceiling of its ultimate penetration of the market. The exact shape of this curve will vary from one situation to another. The point of this discussion is that it is not flat or linear.

The exponential shape of a growth in revenues or audience will be apparent if the percent of change from one period to the next is analyzed as *rate of change*.

Table 11-4 represents CUMES resulting from a telephone survey conducted during each of the first 20 weeks of operation of station WRI. The column labeled "Percent Rate of Change" week #3 is computed this way:

$$\frac{\text{Percent Change for Week \#3} - \text{Percent Change for Week \#2}}{\text{Percent Change for Week \#2}} \times 100$$

$$= \frac{30 - 25}{25} \times 100$$

$$= +20 \ .$$

Each entry in the percent rate of change column was computed in a similar manner. Figure 11-7 provides a graphic representation of this data and confirms the shape of

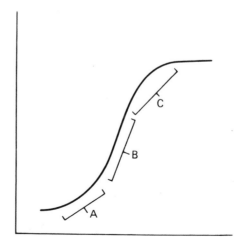

Figure 11-6. Exponential Growth Curve.

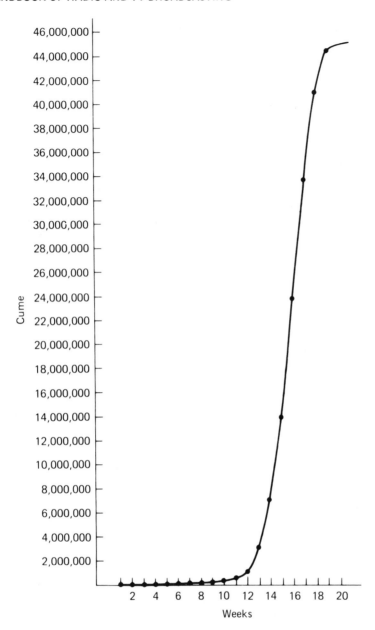

Figure 11-7. Curve of WRI CUMES.

curve also revealed in the percent rate of change column. It is evident from both Table 11-4 and Figure 11-7 that the station audience is nearing its ceiling from about the 15th week. This is an important observation, since it tells us that our objectives in publicity and station promotion need to be changed and our spending priorities reassessed.

CONCLUSION

This chapter has been concerned with the effectiveness of individual station programs and formats in producing the revenue which is the commercial station's lifeblood. The emphasis has been upon describing methods for analyzing data at hand, as opposed to the collection of new data. Each routine described here is useful to the extent it provides a disciplined study of the data at hand for the benefit of more responsive and enlightened decision-making.

Table 11-4.   CUME Levels of New Hypothetical Station WRI for First
20 Weeks of Operation

WEEK	PERSONS CUME	PERCENT CHANGE	PERCENT RATE OF CHANGE
1	2,000	–	–
2	2,500	+ 25	–
3	3,125	+ 30	+ 20
4	4,297	+ 37.5	+ 25
5	6,394	+ 48.8	+ 30
6	10,608	+ 65.9	+ 35
7	19,699	+ 85.7	+ 30
8	40,777	+ 107	+ 25
9	92,972	+ 128	+ 20
10	223,877	+ 140.8	+ 10
11	539,096	+ 140.8	0
12	1,290,596	+ 139.4	- 1
13	3,089,687	+ 139.4	0
14	6,967,244	+ 125.5	- 10
15	13,962,357	+ 100.4	- 20
16	23,777,895	+ 70.3	- 30
17	33,812,166	+ 42.2	- 40
18	40,946,533	+ 21.1	- 50
19	44,386,042	+ 8.4	- 60
20	45,140,605	+ 1.7	- 80

NOTES—CHAPTER 11

1. Allen L. Edwards, *Techniques of Attitude Scale Construction* (New York: Appleton-Century-Crofts, 1957), Chapter Two.
2. Jack S. Levin and Melvin S. Adess, "An Industry-Wide Application of Income Forecast Depreciation," *Broadcast Financial Journal,* **3** (March 1974), 8-14. Reprinted from *The Journal of Taxation,* See also George Dessart, Editor, *Television in the Real World* (New York: Hastings House, 1978), pages 154-158.

Appendix A - Extract of Arbitron Radio Market Report for Akron, October/November 1977

ARBITRON RADIO

Audience Estimates in the
Arbitron Market of

Akron

Survey Period: Oct. 20-Nov. 16, 1977

**Number of Times Per Year
This Market is Surveyed: 2**

Report Contents

1977-78 Schedule of Arbitron Radio Surveys

This report is a compilation of radio audience estimates for this market. All audience estimates are approximations subject to statistical variations related to sample size.

The estimates are based on listening information recorded in diaries by persons 12 years and older. These persons reside in a sample of households systematically selected by computer from telephone directories in the area surveyed. In High Density Spanish areas in which the personal placement and pick-up technique is used, computer-drawn samples are used to specify the key addresses. The actual sample is drawn by taking the starting household adjacent to the key household numbers and systematically proceeding according to Arbitron personal interviewing instructions.

Persons estimates in this report are shown as hundreds (e.g., 141 = 14,100 persons). The symbol (—1) indicates an estimate of less than 50 persons. Total men and total women estimates include estimates for persons 65 +; they do not include Teens.

The survey period covers more than one week. Arbitron has averaged the listening data received and estimates are reported for an "average" week.

This report is intended to furnish radio stations, advertiser and agency clients of Arbitron with an aid in evaluating radio audience size and composition. Arbitron attempts to provide a description of methodology that may be understood by all who use the reports. If any specific details are not completely clear, Arbitron will be happy to provide further explanation on request.

Restrictions on Use of Report

This report which contains data and estimates proprietary to Arbitron is provided to Arbitron clients pursuant to the terms of written contracts between Arbitron and such clients. The data and estimates contained in this report are for the exclusive use of Arbitron clients and their authorized representatives and may be disclosed only to advertisers and/or their agencies who have a bona fide business interest in the data contained herein. For an Arbitron client to divulge the contents of this report to a non-subscribing station, or to lend and/or give a copy to any non-subscriber, including advertisers and/or their agencies constitutes a breach of the license agreement between Arbitron and each of its clients. Quotation by clients of the estimates contained in this report as allowed by the preceding sentence for purposes of advertising or promotion, must identify Arbitron as the source.

Arbitron recommends that the appropriate market, survey period, survey area, time period, and kind of audience estimate (e.g., Boston, October-November 1976 Total Survey Area, Monday-Friday, 8PM-9PM, Average Quarter-Hour Estimates, Men 18-34) be stated and that it be mentioned that the audience estimates are subject to the qualifications given in the Arbitron report.

Users of this report are referred to the current policies of the federal government relating to the use of audience estimates. Neither this report nor any of its contents may be used in any manner by non-clients of Arbitron without written permission from Arbitron.

Tabulated Diaries by Sampling Unit

	In-Tab	Counties in Sampling Unit
MT	124	PORTAGE,OH
MT	507	SUMMIT,OH
T	176	STARK,OH
T	69	COSHOCTON,OH HOLMES,OH WAYNE,OH
T	59	CARROLL,OH TUSCARAWAS,OH
T	47	MEDINA,OH
	982	TOTAL

M METRO SAMPLING UNIT

T TSA SAMPLING UNIT

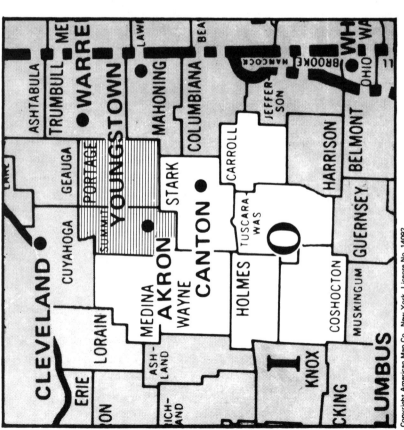

Copyright American Map Co., New York, License No. 14092

Map — The area in which listening data were gathered for this survey in this radio market is shown on the map. The Total Survey Area (TSA) of this market is shown in white. The Metro Survey Area (MSA) is shown by horizontal hatching. (For definitions of TSA and MSA, see Paragraphs 20 and 13 in the back of the report.)

Tabulated Diaries By Sampling Unit — The number of in-tab diaries for each sampling unit is shown. The codes "M" and "T" are used to identify Metro and TSA sampling units, respectively. It is possible for more than one code to appear next to a sampling unit.

Special Interviewing Techniques — Special interviewing techniques are applied in certain sampling units in some markets. Sampling units in which these techniques have been implemented are identified as: "HDBA" - High Density Black Area; "HDSA" - High Density Spanish Area. (For an explanation of these techniques, see Paragraph 33 in the back of the report.)

Population Estimates and Sample Distribution by Sex-Age Group

Total Survey Area

		Estimated Population	Estimated Population as Percent of Tot. Persons 12+	Percent of Unweighted In-Tab Sample	Percent of Weighted In-Tab Sample
Men	18-24	90,900	7.9	6.1	7.9
Men	25-34	106,700	9.2	9.9	9.2
Men	35-44	76,800	6.6	6.5	6.6
Men	45-49	39,300	3.4	3.3	3.4
Men	50-54	38,600	3.3	3.5	3.3
Men	55-64	59,600	5.2	6.1	5.2
Men	65 +	56,800	4.9	3.7	4.9
Women	18-24	99,100	8.6	6.6	8.6
Women	25-34	109,800	9.5	11.3	9.5
Women	35-44	79,700	6.9	7.4	6.9
Women	45-49	40,900	3.5	4.7	3.5
Women	50-54	40,700	3.5	4.4	3.5
Women	55-64	65,300	5.6	7.3	5.6
Women	65 +	82,500	7.1	5.1	7.1
Teens	12-17	169,300	14.6	14.2	14.6
Total Persons	12 +	1,156,000			
Men	18 +	468,700			
Women	18 +	518,000			
Adults	18 +	986,700			

Metro Survey Area

		Estimated Population	Estimated Population as Percent of Tot. Persons 12+	Percent of Unweighted In-Tab Sample	Percent of Weighted In-Tab Sample
Men	18-24	48,300	8.9	7.6	8.9
Men	25-34	49,700	9.1	9.5	9.1
Men	35-44	35,700	6.6	6.7	6.6
Men	45-49	18,500	3.4	2.7	3.4
Men	50-54	17,900	3.3	3.3	3.3
Men	55-64	27,200	5.0	6.8	5.0
Men	65 +	24,800	4.6	3.5	4.6
Women	18-24	51,600	9.5	7.6	9.5
Women	25-34	50,500	9.3	10.6	9.3
Women	35-44	37,100	6.8	7.3	6.8
Women	45-49	19,400	3.6	3.6	3.6
Women	50-54	19,200	3.5	4.4	3.5
Women	55-64	30,400	5.6	6.7	5.6
Women	65 +	36,300	6.7	6.0	6.7
Teens	12-17	78,100	14.3	13.6	14.3
Total Persons	12 +	544,700			
Men	18 +	222,100			
Women	18 +	244,500			
Adults	18 +	466,600			

These population estimates are based upon 1970 U.S. Bureau of the Census estimates updated and projected to January 1, 1978 by Market Statistics, Inc. based on data from Sales Management's 1977 "Survey of Buying Power."

Diary Placement and Return Information

	Metro	TSA
Residential Listings in Designated Sample	527	872
Total Contacts (homes in which telephone was answered)	515	842
Homes in Which Diaries Were Placed	475	744
Individuals Who Were Sent a Diary	1,142	1,796
Individuals Who Returned a Usable Diary (In-Tab)	631	982

	Total Tabulated Diaries	Effective Sample Bases
Total Survey Area	982	782
Metro Survey Area	631	615

PAGE 3

Facilities of Stations Listed in This Report

Information below is obtained from the stations and/or the current issues of Standard Rate and Data Service's "Spot Radio Rates and Data" and "Network Rates and Data." (For an explanation of the criteria for reporting stations, see Pars. 26-28.)

Stations that broadcast on the FM portion of the broadcast frequency spectrum are identified on this page with an FM suffix after the call letters. This suffix is used regardless of whether or not it is included in the official FCC license designation for the station.

	Station	Power (Watts) Day	Night	Frequency (AM in kHz) (FM in mHz)	Network Affiliation	City	County	State
	HOME TO ARBITRON RADIO METRO AREA							
(S)	WAEZ-FM	50,000	50,000	97.5	IND	AKRON	SUMMIT	OH
(S)	WAKR	5,000	5,000	1590	IND	AKRON	SUMMIT	OH
	WCUE	1,000	500	1150	ABC C	CUYAHOGA FALLS	SUMMIT	OH
	WHLO	1,000	1,000	640	IND	AKRON	SUMMIT	OH
	WKDD-FM	50,000	50,000	96.5	IND	AKRON	SUMMIT	OH
	WKNT	1,000	1,000	1520	ABC E	KENT	PORTAGE	OH
	WKNT-FM	3,000	3,000	100.1	ABC E	KENT	PORTAGE	OH
(S)	WSLR	5,000	5,000	1350	ABC E	AKRON	SUMMIT	OH
	OUTSIDE ARBITRON RADIO METRO AREA							
(S)	WDBN-FM	118,000	118,000	94.9	IND	MEDINA	MEDINA	OH
	WDMT-FM	70,000	70,000	107.9	IND	CLEVELAND	CUYAHOGA	OH
	WDOK-FM	50,000	50,000	102.1	ABC E	CLEVELAND	CUYAHOGA	OH
	WGAR	50,000	50,000	1220	ABC E	CLEVELAND	CUYAHOGA	OH
	WGCL-FM	40,000	40,000	98.5	ABC FM	CLEVELAND	CUYAHOGA	OH
	WHK	5,000	5,000	1420	IND	CLEVELAND	CUYAHOGA	OH
	WJW	10,000	5,000	850	CBS	CLEVELAND	CUYAHOGA	OH
	WKSW-FM	50,000	50,000	99.5	IND	CLEVELAND	CUYAHOGA	OH
	WMMS-FM	32,000	32,000	100.7	IND	CLEVELAND	CUYAHOGA	OH
	WQAL-FM	50,000	50,000	104.1	IND	CLEVELAND	CUYAHOGA	OH
	WWWE	50,000	50,000	1100	NBC	CLEVELAND	CUYAHOGA	OH
	WWWM-FM	27,000	27,000	105.7	IND	CLEVELAND	CUYAHOGA	OH
	WZAK-FM	27,500	27,500	93.1	IND	CLEVELAND	CUYAHOGA	OH
	WZZP-FM	50,000	50,000	106.5	IND	CLEVELAND	CUYAHOGA	OH

Footnote Symbols:

(S) Subscribing stations - pre-publication deadline: last day of survey period.

Note: This report is furnished for the exclusive use of network, advertiser, and advertising agency clients, plus subscribing stations.

Network Affiliation Abbreviations:

ABC C	—American Contemporary Radio Network
ABC FM	—American FM Radio Network
ABC E	—American Entertainment Network
ABC I	—American Information Radio Network
CBS	—Columbia Broadcasting System Radio Network

IND	—(Denotes Independent Stations)
MBN	—Mutual Broadcasting System Black Network
MBS	—Mutual Broadcasting System Radio Network
NBC	—National Broadcasting Company Radio Network
NBN	—National Black Network
NIS	—News and Information Service

PAGE 4

200

Special Notices

The information appearing on this page related to Technical Difficulties, Contests, Diary Reference and Station Research Activity is furnished solely for the use of Arbitron clients in making their own evaluations of the audience estimates reported. Such activities or occurrences may have had an affect on listening or the recording thereof and Arbitron makes no attempt to assess their impact.

The information appearing on this page related to Rating Distortion Activities is based upon Arbitron's policy statement dated May 20, 1977.

Technical Difficulties — Time period(s) of five or more consecutive minutes in reported day-parts in which a reported station notified Arbitron of technical difficulties.

Contests, Diary Reference, Station Research Activity — Usually, contests, diary references, and station research activity are brought to Arbitron's attention by stations. When this occurs, Arbitron will contact the station that engaged in any of these activities to obtain complete details. Arbitron will accept information on these activities up to one week after the final date of the survey.

a. Contests — Arbitron will note any contest brought to its attention which covered at least a portion of the survey period and which did not run for at least sixty days prior to the beginning of the survey period and which involved giving away any kind of prizes, cash, merchandise, etc. Even if a contest does not require listening by the par-

ticipants, it will qualify for inclusion in the Arbitron report if it involves any kind of prizes. However, Arbitron will not list a contest conducted during the survey if Arbitron has received a written statement from the station (on a form provided by Arbitron) affirming that the contest involved was not a "contest" but was rather part of the station's regular promotional activities and programs.

b. Diary Reference — Represents any direct or indirect activity on the part of a station in print or on the air, relating to an Arbitron Radio diary survey while the survey is taking place or just prior to the time when the survey is conducted. When a station's activity is considered to meet the diary reference criteria, a sticker will be placed on the front cover of the Arbitron Radio Report calling attention to the station activity.

c. Station Research Activity — "Station Research Activity" refers to any special "on-the-air" activity (e.g., questionnaires), related to programming, news evaluation, listener preference, etc., which is conducted during an Arbitron Radio diary survey. When such activity is considered to be "station research activity," a sticker will be placed on the front cover of the Arbitron Radio Report calling attention to the station activity.

Rating Distortion — ARBITRON WILL DELETE FROM ITS PUBLISHED REPORTS THE AUDIENCE ESTIMATES FOR

STATIONS THAT HAVE ENGAGED IN RATING DISTORTION ACTIVITIES. Rating Distortion is defined as: station activity which may affect the way in which diarykeepers record their listening without causing corresponding changes in actual listening. This includes activities which confuse diarykeepers and which Arbitron believes are likely to cause diarykeepers to:

a. Use their diary as an "entry form" for a contest; or

b. Record radio listening in their diary which exceeds their actual listening.

THIS POLICY OF DELETION OF STATION AUDIENCE ESTIMATES IS IN EFFECT IF RATING DISTORTION OCCURS DURING THE SURVEY PERIOD OR IN THE FOUR WEEKS IMMEDIATELY PRECEDING THE SURVEY PERIOD. When a station's audience estimates are to be deleted for Rating Distortion activities, a sticker will appear on the cover of the Arbitron Radio Report, and the station's activities will be noted on Page 5 of that report.

Arbitron reserves the right to use other means to draw attention to station activity which could affect survey results but which does not meet any of the criteria stated above. Arbitron does not accept complaints of station activities on a confidential basis.

This position reflects our belief that a station is entitled to know what information has been submitted concerning their activity and the source of that information.

The FTC Guidelines Regarding Deceptive Claims of Broadcast Audience Coverage contain language which points out that RADIO STATIONS...

"should not engage in activities calculated to *DISTORT* or *INFLATE* such data — for example, by conducting a *SPECIAL CONTEST*, or otherwise varying ... usual programming or instituting *UNUSUAL ADVERTISING*

or other promotional efforts, *DESIGNED TO INCREASE AUDIENCES ONLY DURING THE SURVEY PERIOD.* Such variation from normal practices is known as '*HYPOING*.'"

It is the opinion of Arbitron that while many stations may engage in promotional activities during a survey period and are not attempting to hypo audiences, some stations may conduct their promotional activity for the specific purpose of increasing audiences artificially during the rating period.

This activity could distort the behavior of the listening audience by making the estimates higher than they would have been if no promotional activity had been conducted during the survey period.

The purpose of this notice is to call attention to the text of the FTC Guidelines and to call attention to report users where there is a possibility that some kind of hypoing might have been conducted during the survey period by one or more stations in the market.

The following stations indicated to Arbitron that they ran one or more contests during the survey period and that these contests were not special contests but were part of the stations' regular promotional activities and programs.

WAKR
WCUE
WHLO
WKDD
WKNT
WKNT-FM
WSLR

- - - - - -

Effective with the population estimates supplied to Arbitron for the 1977-1978 broadcast year, Market Statistics Incorporated (MSI) has revised their updating methodology in order to better account for migration patterns. Changes in population estimates from those of previous reports may be the result of improved methodology as well as any actual year-to-year changes in population. Details are available upon request.

- - - - - -

Average Share Trends—Metro Survey Area

TOTAL PERSONS 12+

STATION CALL LETTERS	MON-SUN 6:00 AM-MID					MON-FRI 6:00 AM-10:00 AM					MON-FRI 10:00 AM-3:00 PM					MON-FRI 3:00 PM-7:00 PM					MON-FRI 7:00 PM-MID				
	O/N 75	A/M 76	O/N 76	A/M 77	O/N 77	O/N 75	A/M 76	O/N 76	A/M 77	O/N 77	O/N 75	A/M 76	O/N 76	A/M 77	O/N 77	O/N 75	A/M 76	O/N 76	A/M 77	O/N 77	O/N 75	A/M 76	O/N 76	A/M 77	O/N 77
WAEZ	6.3	4.4	8.8	8.3	4.2	4.3	2.7	5.9	7.2	3.9	8.8	4.2	11.6	10.5	5.3	7.9	4.5	9.4	8.3	5.2	7.6	2.4	6.7	5.5	5.2
WAKR	15.0	13.9	18.5	22.5	13.8	25.5	24.1	30.0	29.9	23.0	11.3	12.1	15.1	20.7	11.8	10.2	10.8	14.5	20.9	9.1	9.8	8.4	10.0	17.8	9.0
WCUE	5.7	6.7	4.7	4.1	4.4	5.7	6.6	6.3	2.7	5.5	5.1	5.6	4.3	3.5	3.1	5.1	8.6	5.5	5.6	4.5	6.3	6.9	5.8	5.1	5.7
*WHLO	3.2	3.4	3.0	1.8	3.1	5.1	2.7	3.7	2.1	2.8	.9	3.5	3.3	2.7	3.6	3.0	4.1	2.6	2.3	2.9	1.7	3.5	2.0	.4	1.5
WKDD	**	**	2.7	2.4	2.9	**	**	1.4	2.1	2.2	**	**	2.3	3.7	1.9	**	**	3.6	2.6	3.2	**	**	5.6	2.2	6.3
*WKNT	1.4	1.5	1.0	.6	1.5	.6	1.7	.8	.4	1.1	2.2	2.2	1.2	1.4	1.9	.6	.8	.5	.3	.1					
WKNT FM	1.7	2.7	2.1	1.0	3.3	2.2	2.8	2.8	2.1	3.6	2.2	4.3	3.5	1.6	5.1	1.3	1.7	1.4	.1	2.3	1.3	2.4	.9	.8	.8
WSLR	10.1	8.7	7.7	6.4	9.9	14.2	12.4	9.0	8.4	10.7	11.8	9.4	9.8	8.5	11.3	8.3	8.1	6.2	5.7	10.1	3.9	4.7	4.2	3.6	8.4
WDBN FM	7.7	5.7	7.5	5.8	3.7	5.2	3.9	5.5	4.9	2.0	8.9	7.4	8.2	6.0	5.4	7.2	6.6	8.3	5.2	5.0	8.5	4.3	4.4	4.3	1.3
WDMT	**	2.0	.7	2.9	1.5	**	1.4	.6	1.6	1.3	**	1.6	.9	2.9	1.6	**	3.0	.6	3.4	1.4	**	2.9	1.6	3.9	.8
WDOK	1.7	1.2	.9	1.3	1.8	1.1	1.4	.8	1.8	.9	2.6	1.3	1.1	.9	2.1	1.3	1.2	.9	.8	2.2	1.5	.6	.9	.4	2.5
WGAR	8.3	8.0	8.0	9.0	7.9	9.1	9.8	9.7	10.5	10.4	7.0	8.0	6.8	7.7	6.4	9.1	6.1	7.8	9.1	7.1	8.5	7.1	6.0	6.9	5.7
WGCL	5.2	3.7	4.7	2.8	1.8	3.7	2.5	4.3	1.5	1.2	3.8	3.5	3.2	1.5	1.2	6.0	5.1	5.5	4.3	2.4	6.5	4.3	7.1	4.1	1.7
WHK	1.1	1.9	2.0	1.5	1.7	1.3	1.8	2.9	2.3	1.8	.9	1.2	3.2	1.8	1.4	1.7	1.7	1.4	1.1	2.2	2.4	1.8	.9	.6	.2
WJW	2.2	2.0	.9	1.0	1.3	2.2	2.2	.8	1.4	1.8	2.6	2.0	.2	.9	2.0	3.2	3.5	1.1	1.5	1.5	.7	2.2	1.1	1.2	.6
WKSW	.4	.4	1.7	1.2	1.8	.2	.1	.8	.4	1.1	.8	.5	1.9	1.0	2.6	.7	.5	2.4	1.4	3.3	.4	.6	.7	1.6	1.0
WMMS	8.5	8.7	5.7	3.6	9.0	5.3	5.6	3.6	2.4	7.5	7.9	7.2	3.1	2.0	10.3	11.4	9.2	7.3	4.0	10.4	14.3	12.4	11.8	6.3	9.2
WQAL	2.1	3.2	3.7	1.8	3.8	1.3	1.9	2.2	1.6	3.1	4.3	3.0	4.3	2.6	5.2	2.1	4.0	3.5	2.3	4.5	1.7	4.1	2.9	.8	.6
WMME	2.7	3.6	2.8	4.2	2.7	2.2	3.1	2.5	4.4	2.2	1.4	2.3	2.4	3.4	2.0	3.3	2.9	1.8	2.2	2.1	3.7	9.8	7.8	9.5	8.6
WMMM	2.2	3.6	4.3	3.3	4.1	1.5	2.8	2.3	1.8	2.8	2.1	4.8	3.7	2.7	2.5	1.8	2.4	4.5	4.5	4.7	2.8	4.1	8.0	5.5	7.3
WZAK	**	.6	**	**	1.3	**	.3	**	.3		**	.1	**	**	.4	**	1.2	**	**	.7	**	.2	**	**	.4
WZZP	**	**	**	3.5	5.8	**	**	**	2.5	4.1	**	**	**	1.7	3.8	**	**	**	4.1	6.3	**	**	**	6.9	11.7
METRO TOTALS	13.1	14.7	14.8	14.3	14.3	20.1	21.4	21.9	21.5	20.9	13.9	16.7	19.8	16.2	17.4	15.0	15.7	17.4	16.1	16.0	8.4	9.0	8.2	9.3	8.8

Footnote Symbols: (*) means audience estimates adjusted for actual broadcast schedule (**) Station not reported or reported under different call letters this survey (+) means AM-FM Combination was not simulcast for complete time period

ARBITRON

Trends

Average Share Trends—Metro Survey Area

MEN 18+

MON-SUN 6:00 AM-MID

STATION CALL LETTERS	O/N 75	A/M 76	O/N 76	A/M 77	O/N 77
WAEZ	5.4	3.8	9.5	6.2	3.5
WAKR	17.5	12.8	15.4	22.2	12.3
WCUE	3.5	2.9	1.8	3.6	.9
*WHLO	2.7	3.8	5.0	2.9	3.5
WKDD	**	**	3.3	2.6	2.8
**WKNT	.4	1.0	.9	1.0	1.3
WKNT FM	1.2	1.6	1.2	1.0	4.1
WSLR	12.1	9.9	9.2	5.9	14.2
WDBN FM	7.8	7.4	8.0	4.9	2.5
WDMT	**	1.0	.3	4.2	.9
WDOK	1.2	2.2	.9	1.3	1.6
WGAR	8.9	5.4	4.7	11.8	6.9
WGCL	3.9	1.6	3.0	2.0	1.3
WHK	.4	2.2	3.6	2.0	1.9
WJM	1.6	2.2	.9	1.3	2.2
WKSW	.3	1.0	1.8	1.6	2.5
WMMS	15.2	12.5	7.1	3.9	11.3
WQAL	1.6	3.8	4.5	2.0	4.1
WMME	3.1	5.4	2.7	4.6	4.1
WMMM	1.2	4.5	5.6	2.0	4.4
WZAK	**	.6	**	**	1.9
WZZP	**	**	**	1.6	3.1
METRO TOTALS	11.6	14.1	15.2	13.8	14.3

MON-FRI 6:00 AM-10:00 AM

STATION CALL LETTERS	O/N 75	A/M 76	O/N 76	A/M 77	O/N 77
WAEZ	3.0	2.7	7.4	6.8	3.6
WAKR	27.2	22.6	26.0	26.0	19.5
WCUE	4.0	1.8	2.2	2.3	2.0
*WHLO	4.5	4.0	6.6	3.8	3.8
WKDD	**	**	1.8	3.2	2.7
**WKNT	.5	1.6	1.1	.4	.2
WKNT FM	1.5	1.3	1.3	2.3	4.5
WSLR	16.1	14.1	9.2	4.4	15.4
WDBN FM	5.5	6.0	6.8	4.4	.4
WDMT	**	.7	.4	1.9	.9
WDOK	.8	2.7	.7	1.9	.2
WGAR	9.8	8.3	6.3	13.7	9.8
WGCL	3.5	.7	3.9	1.7	.7
WHK	.8	1.6	5.0	3.2	2.2
WJM	1.8	2.9	1.3	1.9	3.8
WKSW	.3	.2	1.1	.6	1.8
WMMS	8.6	8.7	3.9	3.2	10.1
WQAL	1.8	2.2	3.3	1.3	4.0
WMME	2.3	4.0	1.8	4.0	2.0
WMMM	.3	3.1	3.1	1.1	3.1
WZAK	**	.2	**	**	**
WZZP	**	**	**	1.1	2.0
METRO TOTALS	17.9	20.2	20.6	21.3	20.1

MON-FRI 10:00 AM-3:00 PM

STATION CALL LETTERS	O/N 75	A/M 76	O/N 76	A/M 77	O/N 77
WAEZ	5.3	3.5	12.1	7.6	3.8
WAKR	11.3	9.6	10.8	21.1	9.6
WCUE	1.9	3.5	3.0	3.2	.7
*WHLO	1.1	4.1	5.7	3.8	3.1
WKDD	**	**	4.0	5.9	2.9
**WKNT	.4	1.5	.6	1.8	1.4
WKNT FM	1.1	.6	2.3	.9	5.7
WSLR	15.1	10.5	12.1	10.3	15.6
WDBN FM	10.2	9.6	8.0	3.5	2.6
WDMT	**	1.5	.2	2.9	1.0
WDOK	1.1	2.9	1.5	.6	1.2
WGAR	9.1	6.7	3.4	11.4	5.3
WGCL	4.2	2.3	2.7	1.2	1.4
WHK	.8	1.5	4.9	1.8	1.2
WJM	**	1.5	.2	.6	4.1
WKSW	1.2	1.2	2.5	1.2	3.3
WMMS	17.7	11.1	3.8	2.6	12.9
WQAL	3.0	2.3	5.9	3.8	4.8
WMME	1.9	2.6	.8	2.1	2.4
WMMM	.8	6.7	5.3	1.2	3.1
WZAK	**	**	**	**	.5
WZZP	**	**	**	1.5	3.1
METRO TOTALS	12.0	15.4	21.3	15.4	18.8

MON-FRI 3:00 PM-7:00 PM

STATION CALL LETTERS	O/N 75	A/M 76	O/N 76	A/M 77	O/N 77
WAEZ	7.5	3.0	9.7	4.0	2.9
WAKR	13.1	10.3	11.9	23.9	7.8
WCUE	3.4	3.3	2.4	4.3	1.0
*WHLO	2.8	4.3	3.9	4.3	2.9
WKDD	**	**	4.1	2.2	3.1
**WKNT	.3	**	1.0	.3	
WKNT FM	.3	.9	.5		3.1
WSLR	9.4	11.6	8.3	5.6	14.0
WDBN FM	7.2	8.8	9.2	4.0	4.4
WDMT	**	.9	.7	5.0	.5
WDOK	.9	1.8	1.2	.3	1.6
WGAR	10.0	4.3	4.4	13.4	7.0
WGCL	3.1	2.1	1.9	4.0	2.1
WHK	1.3	1.8	2.2	1.2	3.1
WJM	2.8	4.0	1.0	2.5	3.1
WKSW	.3	.6	2.9	2.5	4.9
WMMS	18.4	14.0	9.7	5.0	14.5
WQAL	1.3	5.5	3.6	2.5	4.4
WMME	3.4	5.2	1.2	1.9	2.9
WMMM	.9	3.0	6.3	2.2	4.4
WZAK	**	1.2	**	**	1.3
WZZP	**	**	**	1.6	2.6
METRO TOTALS	14.5	14.9	18.6	14.5	17.3

MON-FRI 7:00 PM-MID

STATION CALL LETTERS	O/N 75	A/M 76	O/N 76	A/M 77	O/N 77
WAEZ	8.9	2.5	6.2	3.3	5.0
WAKR	13.6	8.0	6.2	18.6	7.7
WCUE	3.6	4.5	1.5	2.9	1.1
*WHLO	**	.5	4.6	.5	3.9
WKDD	**	**	5.7	.5	3.3
**WKNT					
WKNT FM	1.8	4.0	.5	.5	
WSLR	3.6	3.5	5.7	3.8	12.7
WDBN FM	6.5	5.0	6.2	3.3	.6
WDMT	**	.5	1.0	7.6	.6
WDOK	2.4	.5	.5	.5	3.9
WGAR	10.1	3.5	3.6	7.1	4.4
WGCL	2.4	2.9	2.6	2.9	1.7
WHK	2.4	4.0	2.1	1.4	.6
WJM		3.0	2.1	1.4	
WKSW		1.0	1.0	2.4	.6
WMMS	22.5	17.5	12.9	6.2	10.5
WQAL	.6	5.0	2.6	1.9	.6
WMME	7.7	16.5	11.3	14.3	16.6
WMMM	2.4	5.5	8.8	4.8	8.3
WZAK	**	**	**	**	.6
WZZP	**	**	**	2.9	5.5
METRO TOTALS	7.6	9.0	8.7	9.5	8.1

Footnote Symbols: (*) means audience estimates adjusted for actual broadcast schedule   (**) Station not reported or reported under different call letters this survey   (+) means AM-FM Combination was not simulcast for complete time period

ARBITRON

Average Quarter-Hour and Cume Listening Estimates

MONDAY–SUNDAY
6.00AM–MIDNIGHT

MEN 18+ / MEN 18-34 / MEN 18-49

STATION CALL LETTERS	MEN 18+ TOTAL AREA AVG PERS (00)	MEN 18+ TOTAL AREA CUME PERS (00)	MEN 18+ METRO AVG PERS (00)	MEN 18+ METRO CUME PERS (00)	MEN 18+ METRO AVG RTG	MEN 18+ METRO AVG SHR	MEN 18-34 TOTAL AREA AVG PERS (00)	MEN 18-34 TOTAL AREA CUME PERS (00)	MEN 18-34 METRO AVG PERS (00)	MEN 18-34 METRO CUME PERS (00)	MEN 18-34 METRO AVG RTG	MEN 18-34 METRO AVG SHR	MEN 18-49 TOTAL AREA AVG PERS (00)	MEN 18-49 TOTAL AREA CUME PERS (00)	MEN 18-49 METRO AVG PERS (00)	MEN 18-49 METRO CUME PERS (00)	MEN 18-49 METRO AVG RTG	MEN 18-49 METRO AVG SHR
WAEZ	15	266	11	180	.5	3.5	2	48		16		1.8	6	118	4	70	.3	1.8
WAKR	42	992	39	883	1.8	12.3	16	275	14	258	1.4	9.0	25	547	22	435	1.4	9.7
WCUE	4	167	3	153	.1	.9	2	78	2	78	.2	1.3	4	134	3	120	.2	1.3
*WHLO	28	436	11	162	.5	3.5	9	180	4	87	.4	2.6	16	303	6	123	.4	2.6
WKDD	20	398	9	197	.4	2.8	19	355	8	174	.8	5.2	20	392	9	191	.6	4.0
*WKNT	4	47	4	47	.2	1.3	2	47	2	47	.2	1.3	1	23	1	23	.1	.1
WKNT FM	13	140	13	140	.6	4.1	2	47	2	47	.2	1.3	4	65	4	65	.3	1.8
TOTAL	17	180	17	180	.8	5.4						2.2	5	88	5	88	.3	2.2
WSLR	48	703	45	570	2.0	14.2	15	243	14	177	1.4	9.0	35	471	33	369	2.2	14.5
WDBN FM	42	636	8	178	.4	2.5	4	82	3	34	.3	1.9	15	239	3	53	.3	1.3
WDMT	3	95	3	79	.1	.9	3	87	1	71	.1	.6	3	95	3	79	.2	.4
WDOK	5	123	5	89	.2	1.6	2	41	1	26	.1	.6	1	88	1	54	.1	.4
WGAR	48	1011	22	461	1.0	6.9	28	703	15	348	1.5	9.7	46	938	21	447	1.4	9.3
WGCL	7	233	4	151	.2	1.3	6	172	3	109	.3	1.9	7	233	4	151	.3	1.8
WHK	10	244	6	133	.3	1.9	6	82	3	52	.3	1.9	8	156	5	89	.3	2.2
WJW	8	185	7	107	.3	2.2	2	27	2	27	.2		8	125	7	88	.5	3.1
WKSW	9	160	8	108	.4	2.5	5	50	4	35	.4	2.6	6	97	5	61	.3	2.2
WMMS	42	537	36	385	1.6	11.3	39	471	34	351	3.5	21.9	42	537	36	385	2.4	15.9
WQAL	16	267	13	159	.6	4.1	6	34	6	18	.6	3.9	14	183	11	98	.7	4.8
WWWE	28	761	13	352	.6	4.1	17	396	8	192	.8	5.2	27	649	12	281	.8	5.3
WWWM	17	308	14	257	.6	4.4	16	265	14	234	1.4	9.0	16	282	14	251	.9	6.2
WZAK	8	105	6	87	.3	1.9							4	46	2	28	.1	.9
WZZP	11	225	10	191	.5	3.1	10	172	9	157	.9	5.8	11	219	10	185	.7	4.4
METRO TOTALS	318	2132			14.3		155	942			15.8		227	1465			14.9	

MEN 25-49 / MEN 25-54 / MEN 35-64

STATION CALL LETTERS	MEN 25-49 TOTAL AREA AVG PERS (00)	MEN 25-49 TOTAL AREA CUME PERS (00)	MEN 25-49 METRO AVG PERS (00)	MEN 25-49 METRO CUME PERS (00)	MEN 25-49 METRO AVG RTG	MEN 25-49 METRO AVG SHR	MEN 25-54 TOTAL AREA AVG PERS (00)	MEN 25-54 TOTAL AREA CUME PERS (00)	MEN 25-54 METRO AVG PERS (00)	MEN 25-54 METRO CUME PERS (00)	MEN 25-54 METRO AVG RTG	MEN 25-54 METRO AVG SHR	MEN 35-64 TOTAL AREA AVG PERS (00)	MEN 35-64 TOTAL AREA CUME PERS (00)	MEN 35-64 METRO AVG PERS (00)	MEN 35-64 METRO CUME PERS (00)	MEN 35-64 METRO AVG RTG	MEN 35-64 METRO AVG SHR
WAEZ	6	118	4	70	.4	2.7	8	144	6	36	.5	3.4	12	150	10	118	1.0	7.4
WAKR	18	428	15	376	1.4	10.2	22	512	19	444	1.6	10.9	21	525	20	456	2.0	14.8
WCUE	2	64	1	50	.1	.7	2	72	1	58	.1	.6	2	89	1	75		.7
*WHLO	15	273	5	93	.5	3.4	21	307	5	93	.4	2.9	15	222	3	61	.3	2.2
WKDD	9	117	2	51	.2	1.4	9	117	2	51	.2	1.1	1	43	1	23	.1	.7
*WKNT	1	23	1	23	.1	.7	1	23	1	23	.1	.6	2	36	2	36	.2	1.5
WKNT FM	3	44	3	44	.3	2.0	9	62	9	62	.7	5.1	10	69	10	69	1.0	7.4
TOTAL	4	67	4	67	.4	2.7	10	85	10	85	.8	5.7	12	98	12	98	1.2	8.9
WSLR	30	373	29	308	2.8	19.7	34	455	32	359	2.6	18.3	31	404	29	337	2.9	21.5
WDBN FM	15	229	2	43	.2	1.4	19	328	1	77	.1	.6	19	394	4	98	.4	3.0
WDMT	2	65	2	49	.2	.7	2	65	2	49	.2	1.1		8		8		
WDOK	1	88	1	54	.1	.7	1	88	1	54	.1	.6	2	60	2	41	.2	1.5
WGAR	39	694	17	314	1.6	11.6	40	719	18	322	1.5	10.3	20	285	7	113	.7	5.2
WGCL	7	183	4	101	.4	2.7	7	183	4	101	.3	2.3	3	61	1	42	.1	.7
WHK	7	146	4	79	.4	2.7	7	154	4	87	.3	2.3	3	107	3	70	.3	2.2
WJM	8	115	7	78	.7	4.8	8	123	8	86	.6	4.0	8	124	7	69	.7	5.2
WKSW	5	87	4	51	.4	2.7	5	103	4	51	.3	2.3	4	88	4	51	.4	3.0
WMMS	14	222	12	174	1.2	8.2	14	222	12	174	1.0	6.9	3	66	2	34	.2	1.5
WQAL	9	173	6	88	.6	4.1	11	198	8	113	.7	4.6	10	199	7	130	.7	5.2
WWME	26	558	11	221	1.1	7.5	27	610	12	273	1.0	6.9	11	343	5	160	.5	3.7
WWWM	7	131	5	100	.5	3.4	7	131	5	100	.4	2.9	1	43		23		
WZAK	4	46	2	28	.2	1.4	4	46	2	28	.2	1.1	5	71	3	53	.3	2.2
WZZP	5	129	4	95	.4	2.7	5	129	4	95	.3	2.3	1	53	1	34	.1	.7
METRO TOTALS	147	1002			14.1		175	1172			14.4		135	965			13.6	

Footnote Symbols: (*) means audience estimates adjusted for actual broadcast schedule (+) means AM-FM Combination was not simulcast for complete time period.

ARBITRON

Average Quarter-Hour Listening Estimates

AVERAGE PERSONS—TOTAL SURVEY AREA, IN HUNDREDS

STATION CALL LETTERS	TOT. PERS. 12+	MEN 18-24	25-34	35-44	45-54	55-64	WOMEN 18-24	25-34	35-44	45-54	55-64	TNS. 12-17
WAEZ	48	1	2	3	3	6	1	3	10	7	6	4
WAKR	115	7	9	5	8	8	2	9	11	16	13	4
WCUE	40	2		1	1		9	4	1	5	2	14
*WHLO	52	1	8	4	9	2		3	2	6	7	
WKDD	53	11	8	1			23	2		1		7
*WKNT	12	1	1	2	1	1		2	1			
WKNT FM	26	1	1	2	6	2		2	2	3	3	
TOTAL	38				7	3			3	3	9	
WSLR	83	5	10	14	10	7	1	5	10	12	3	2
WDBN FM	97	1	4	8	7	4	3	5	9	17	15	31
WDMT	13	1	2		1		3	5	1	1		
WDOK	15		1			2		1	3	4		
WGAR	135	7	21	17	2	1	16	32	4	1	3	31
WGCL	35		6	1			7	5				15
WHK	22	1	5	2		1		2	1	2	1	
WJW	11			3	5					1		1
WKSN	18	1	4	1	1	3		1	1	1		
WMMS	106	28	11	2			46	2				16
WQAL	37	5	1	4	6			3	1	8		
WWWE	40	1	16	6	5	4		2	5	2		2
WWWM	42	9	7			1	6	1			1	17
WZAK	13			3	1	1		1	1	1		
WZZP	56	6	4	1			6	2	4			33

AVERAGE PERSONS—METRO SURVEY AREA, IN HUNDREDS

STATION CALL LETTERS	TOT. PERS. 12+	MEN 18-24	25-34	35-44	45-54	55-64	WOMEN 18-24	25-34	35-44	45-54	55-64	TNS. 12-17
WAEZ	33	1		3	3	6			9	5	6	3
WAKR	108	7	7	5	7	8	2	7	11	16	13	3
WCUE	34	2		1			7	4	1	4	2	12
*WHLO	24	1	3	2	1			1	2	5	1	
WKDD	23	7	1	1			9	2				3
*WKNT	12	1	1	2	1	1		1	1			
WKNT FM	26	1	1	2	6	3		2	3	6	3	
TOTAL	38				7	3			3	7	9	
WSLR	77	4	10	13	9	7	1	5	7	12	3	2
WDBN FM	29			3	1	6	3	4	3	4	4	
WDMT	12	1	2	1			3	4	1	1		
WDOK	14		1			4		1	2	4		
WGAR	62	4	11	6			9	17	3		3	7
WGCL	14		3	1			3	2	1			4
WHK	13	1	2	2		1		2	1	2	1	1
WJW	10			3	5					1		
WKSN	14	1	3	1	1	1		3	1	1	1	
WMMS	70	24	10	2			26	2				6
WQAL	30	5	1	2	5			2	3	7		
WWWE	21	1	5	3	2			1				2
WWWM	32	9	3				6		3			11
WZAK	10			1	1	1		2	1	1		
WZZP	45	6	3	1			5	2				24
TOTAL LISTENING IN METRO SURVEY AREA	781	80	75	49	51	35	79	65	60	75	52	80

SHARES—METRO SURVEY AREA

STATION CALL LETTERS	TOT. PERS. 12+ %	MEN 18-24 %	25-34 %	35-44 %	45-54 %	55-64 %	WOMEN 18-24 %	25-34 %	35-44 %	45-54 %	55-64 %	TNS. 12-17 %
WAEZ	4.2			6.1	5.9	11.4	1.3		15.0	6.7	11.5	
WAKR	13.8	8.8	9.3	10.2	13.7	22.9	2.5	10.8	18.3	21.3	25.0	3.8
WCUE	4.4	2.5		2.0			8.9	6.2	1.7	5.3	3.8	15.0
*WHLO	3.1	1.3	4.0	4.1	2.9			1.5	3.3	6.7	1.9	
WKDD	2.9	8.8	1.3	2.0			11.4	3.1				3.8
*WKNT	1.5	1.3	1.3	4.1	2.0	2.9		3.1	1.7		5.8	
WKNT FM	3.3	1.3	1.3	4.1	11.8	5.7		3.1	3.3		11.5	
TOTAL	4.8				13.8	8.6			5.0		17.3	
WSLR	9.9	5.0	13.3	26.5	17.6	20.0	1.3	7.7	11.7	16.0	5.8	2.5
WDBN FM	3.7				2.0	8.6		6.2	5.0	5.3	11.5	
WDMT	1.5	1.3	2.7				3.8	6.2	1.7	1.3		
WDOK	1.8		1.3			5.7		1.5	3.3	5.3		
WGAR	7.9	5.0	14.7	12.2			11.4	26.2	5.0	1.3	5.8	8.8
WGCL	1.8		4.0	2.0			3.8	3.1	1.7			5.0
WHK	1.7	1.3	2.7	4.1		2.9		3.1	1.7	2.7	1.9	
WJW	1.3			4.1	9.8					1.3		1.3
WKSN	1.8	1.3	4.0	2.0	2.0	8.6		4.6	1.7	1.3	1.9	
WMMS	9.0	30.0	13.3	4.1			32.9	3.1				7.5
WQAL	3.8	6.3	1.3	4.1	9.8			3.1		9.3	7.7	
WWWE	2.7	1.3	9.3	6.1	3.9			1.5	5.0	2.7		2.5
WWWM	4.1	11.3	6.7				7.6		1.7			13.8
WZAK	1.3			2.0	2.0	2.9		3.1				
WZZP	5.8	7.5	4.0	2.0			6.3	3.1	6.7			30.0

Footnote Symbols: (*) means audience estimates adjusted for actual broadcast schedule (+) means AM-FM Combination was not simulcast for complete time period.

PAGE 54

ARBITRON

Cume Listening Estimates

AKRON OCT/NOV 1977

MONDAY-SUNDAY
6:00AM-MIDNIGHT

PAGE 55

CUME PERSONS—TOTAL SURVEY AREA, IN HUNDREDS

STATION CALL LETTERS	TOT. PERS. 12+	MEN 18-24	25-34	35-44	45-54	55-64	WOMEN 18-24	25-34	35-44	45-54	55-64	TNS. 12-17
WAEZ	770		48	33	63	54		50	80	135	76	44
WAKR	2296	119	156	170	186	169	107	220	160	174	185	209
WCUE	932	70	8	42	22	25	201	73	64	40	36	341
*WHLO	814	30	150	83	74	65	11	102	16	53	57	42
WKDD	964	275	80	37		6	268	30	16	26		216
*WKNT	157	21	26	18	23	13		70	25	9	37	40
WKNT FM	401	21	26	18	18	33		70	34	30	67	40
TOTAL	502				41	39			42	39	82	
WSLR	1488	98	145	157	153	94	61	132	186	144	70	144
WDBN FM	1210	10	72	104	152	138		58	96	181	125	
WDMT	311	30	57	8			33	102	24	21		36
WDOK	292		41	36	11	13		50	40	45	15	
WGAR	2698	244	459	169	91	25	394	476	127	54	41	576
WGCL	922	50	122	61			135	116	41	7		380
WHK	512	10	72	63	19	25		40	64	88	40	8
WJW	314	10	17	54	52	18		15	8	35		61
WKSW	328	10	40	47	16	25		59	32	43	15	
WMMS	1510	315	156	52	14	21	336	75	40	7	21	494
WQAL	593	10	24	81	93	25		58	40	88	36	45
WMME	1385	91	305	176	129	38	61	160	112	63	19	171
WWWM	983	151	114	17		26	183	28	8		14	393
WZAK	223			35	11	25		21	8	18	22	11
WZZP	1082	90	82	36	11	6	158	51	64		21	553

CUME PERSONS—METRO SURVEY AREA IN HUNDREDS

STATION CALL LETTERS	TOT. PERS. 12+	MEN 18-24	25-34	35-44	45-54	55-64	WOMEN 18-24	25-34	35-44	45-54	55-64	TNS. 12-17
WAEZ	501		16	33	47	65		7	64	80	65	26
WAKR	2032	119	139	151	154	151	107	149	160	174	173	176
WCUE	801	70	8	42	8	25	172	59	64	31	36	276
*WHLO	414	30	57	25	11	25	11	45	16	37	36	29
WKDD	444	140	34	17		6	96	30	16	7		88
*WKNT	157	21	26	18	23	13		70	25	9	37	40
WKNT FM	401	21	26	18	18	33		70	34	30	67	40
TOTAL	502				41	39			42	39	82	
WSLR	1140	61	116	136	107	94	32	106	121	97	58	108
WDBN FM	447	10	24	8	45	45		30	32	93	66	
WDMT	236	30	41	8			33	60	24	21		19
WDOK	185		26	17	11	13		23	8	31	15	
WGAR	1265	133	215	77	30	6	205	225	81	37	29	208
WGCL	520	50	59	42			76	60	41	7		175
WHK	281	10	42	26	19	25		15	33	44	29	8
WJW	216	10	17	17	52			15	8	15		61
WKSW	234	10	25	26		25		31	32	29	15	
WMMS	939	211	140	34	7	21	195	75	24	7	21	232
WQAL	360	10	8	26	79	25		31	24	65	36	26
WMME	646	60	132	68	73	19	32	68	65	39	8	82
WWWM	726	151	83	17		6	183	15	8		14	239
WZAK	181			17	11	25		7	8	8	22	11
WZZP	823	90	67	17	11	6	129	38	64		21	370
TOTAL LISTENING IN METRO SURVEY AREA	5228	463	479	349	344	272	516	482	355	371	304	743

CUME RATINGS—METRO SURVEY AREA

STATION CALL LETTERS	TOT. PERS. 12+ %	MEN 18-24 %	25-34 %	35-44 %	45-54 %	55-64 %	WOMEN 18-24 %	25-34 %	35-44 %	45-54 %	55-64 %	TNS. 12-17 %
WAEZ	9.2		3.2	9.2	12.9	14.0		4.3	17.3	20.7	21.4	3.3
WAKR	37.3	24.6	28.0	42.3	42.3	55.5	20.7	29.5	43.1	45.1	56.9	22.5
WCUE	14.7	14.5	1.6	11.8	2.2	9.2	33.3	11.7	17.3	8.0	11.8	35.3
*WHLO	7.6	6.2	11.5	7.0	3.0	9.2	2.1	8.9	4.3	9.6	11.8	3.7
WKDD	8.2	29.0	6.8	4.8		2.2	18.6	5.9	4.3	1.8		11.3
*WKNT	2.9	4.3	5.2	5.0	6.3	4.8		6.7	9.2	2.3	12.2	5.1
WKNT FM	7.4	4.3	5.2	5.0	4.9	12.1		13.9	11.3	7.8	22.0	5.1
TOTAL	9.2				11.3	14.3		13.9	11.3	10.1	27.0	
WSLR	20.9	12.6	23.3	38.1	29.4	34.6	6.2	21.0	32.6	25.1	19.1	13.8
WDBN FM	8.2	2.1	4.8	2.2	2.2	16.5		5.9	8.6	24.1	21.7	
WDMT	4.3	6.2	8.2	2.2			6.4	11.9	6.5	5.4		2.4
WDOK	3.4		5.2	4.8	3.0	4.8		4.6	2.2	8.0	4.9	
WGAR	23.2	27.5	43.3	21.6	8.2		39.7	44.6	21.8	9.6	9.5	26.6
WGCL	9.5	10.4	11.9	11.8			14.7	11.9	11.1	1.8		22.4
WHK	5.2	2.1	8.5	7.3	5.2	9.2		3.0	8.9	11.4	9.5	1.0
WJW	4.0	2.1	3.4	4.8	14.3				2.2	3.9		7.8
WKSW	4.3	2.1	5.0	7.3		9.2		6.1	8.6	7.5	4.9	
WMMS	17.2	43.7	28.2	9.5	21.7	9.2	37.8	14.9	6.5	1.8	6.9	29.7
WQAL	6.6	2.1	1.6	7.3	21.7			6.1	6.5	16.8	11.8	3.3
WMME	11.9	12.4	26.6	19.0	20.1	7.0	6.2	13.5	17.5	10.1	2.6	10.5
WWWM	13.3	31.3	16.7	4.8		2.2	35.5	3.0	2.2		4.6	30.6
WZAK	3.3							1.4	2.2	2.1	7.2	1.4
WZZP	15.1	18.6	13.5	4.8	3.0	2.2	25.0	7.5	17.3		6.9	47.4
	96.0	95.9	96.4	97.8	99.5	99.9	99.9	95.4	95.7	96.1	99.9	95.1

Footnote Symbols: (*) means audience estimates adjusted for actual broadcast schedule (+) means AM-FM Combination was not simulcast for complete time period.

ARBITRON

206

Average Quarter-Hour Listening Estimates

AVERAGE PERSONS—TOTAL SURVEY AREA, IN HUNDREDS

STATION CALL LETTERS	TOT. PERS. 12+	MEN 18-24	MEN 25-34	MEN 35-44	MEN 45-54	MEN 55-64	WOMEN 18-24	WOMEN 25-34	WOMEN 35-44	WOMEN 45-54	WOMEN 55-64	TNS. 12-17
WAEZ	54	2	3	4	5	7	2	5	9	10	8	
WAKR	282	16	19	12	17	19	2	26	30	37	38	15
WCUE	65	4		4	4	1	18	11			6	16
*WHLO	70	2	22	3	7	5		1		4	10	
WKDD	57	10	9	2			25	3		3		5
*WKNT	13	1		2	5	3			2	5		
WKNT FM	41	1		2	10	3		2	4	5		
TOTAL	54			6	15				6			
WSLR	132	6	17	21	18	4	2	11	14	21	7	1
WDBN FM	74	2	5	9		5	2	3	11	19		
WDMT	17	1	3				2	8	1	2		
WDOK	16		2	1		3		2	6	4		
WGAR	232	17	48	33	3		36	48	9	1		30
WGCL	40		7	4			2	7	1	1		19
WHK	31	2		2	3	2		4	3	3	2	
WJM	27			9	13					4		
WKSM	17	3						6	1	2		
WMMS	124	41	14	1			47	4	1	1		15
WQAL	47	6	1	6	12	3	1	3	1	13		
WWWE	38	1	9	6	1		1	7	7	5		
WWWM	38	6	7	1			4	1				19
WZAK	3											
WZZP	60	5	3	2			6	4	4			36

AVERAGE PERSONS—METRO SURVEY AREA, IN HUNDREDS

STATION CALL LETTERS	TOT. PERS. 12+	MEN 18-24	MEN 25-34	MEN 35-44	MEN 45-54	MEN 55-64	WOMEN 18-24	WOMEN 25-34	WOMEN 35-44	WOMEN 45-54	WOMEN 55-64	TNS. 12-17
WAEZ	44			4	5	7	2	5	9	8	7	8
WAKR	261	16	13	12	15	19	2	18	30	37	38	11
WCUE	63	4	5	4		1	16	11		4	6	16
*WHLO	32	2	5	2		3		1		4	3	
WKDD	25	6		2			7	3		1		2
*WKNT	13	1		2	10	3		2	2	5	5	
WKNT FM	41	1		2	10	3		2	6	5	5	
TOTAL	54											
WSLR	122	5	17	21	15	4	1	11	10	21	6	1
WDBN FM	23		3		1	1		3	5	5	1	
WDMT	15	1	3					6	1	1	2	
WDOK	10		2	2		1	2	1	6	4		
WGAR	118	8	21	12	3		26	24	9	1	5	9
WGCL	14		2	1			2	1	1	1		7
WHK	21	2		2		2			3	3		
WJM	21		5	4	13					4		
WKSM	12					3		1	1	2		
WMMS	85	31	14	3			32	4	1			3
WQAL	35	6		3	9		1	4	1	10		
WWWE	25	1	4	3	1			4	7	4		
WWWM	32	6	7	1			4	1	2			14
WZAK	3											
WZZP	47	5	2	2		2	5	2	4			27
TOTAL LISTENING IN METRO SURVEY AREA	1136	98	105	79	85	46	104	103	97	127	93	92

SHARES—METRO SURVEY AREA

STATION CALL LETTERS	TOT. PERS. 12+ %	MEN 18-24 %	MEN 25-34 %	MEN 35-44 %	MEN 45-54 %	MEN 55-64 %	WOMEN 18-24 %	WOMEN 25-34 %	WOMEN 35-44 %	WOMEN 45-54 %	WOMEN 55-64 %	TNS. 12-17 %
WAEZ	3.9			5.1	5.9	15.2	1.9		9.3	6.3	8.6	
WAKR	23.0	16.3	12.4	15.2	17.6	41.3	1.9	17.5	30.9	29.1	40.9	12.0
WCUE	5.5	4.1		5.1			15.4	10.7		3.1	6.5	17.4
*WHLO	2.8	2.0	4.8			6.5		1.0		3.1	3.2	
WKDD	2.2	6.1	3.8	2.5			6.7	2.9		.8		2.2
*WKNT	1.1	1.0		2.5	11.8	6.5		1.9	2.1	3.9	5.4	
WKNT FM	3.6	1.0		2.5	11.8	6.5		1.9	4.1	3.9	10.8	
TOTAL	4.7								6.2		16.2	
WSLR	10.7	5.1	16.2	26.6	17.6	8.7	1.0	10.7	10.3	16.5	6.5	1.1
WDBN FM	2.0				1.2	2.2			5.2	3.9	2.2	
WDMT	1.3	1.0	2.9				1.9	5.8	1.0	1.6		
WDOK	.9					2.2	1.0	1.0	4.1	3.1		
WGAR	10.4	8.2	20.0	15.2	3.5		25.0	23.3	9.3	.8	5.4	9.8
WGCL	1.2		1.9	1.3			1.9	1.0	1.0			
WHK	1.8	2.0	1.9	2.5		4.3			2.1	2.4	2.2	7.6
WJM	1.8		5.1	15.3						3.1		
WKSM	1.1		4.8			6.5		1.0	1.0	1.6		
WMMS	7.5	31.6	13.3				30.8	3.9	1.0			3.3
WQAL	3.1	6.1		3.8	10.6	1.2		1.0	1.0	7.9	3.2	
WWWE	2.2	1.0	3.8	3.8	1.3		1.0	3.9	7.2	3.1		
WWWM	2.8	6.1	6.7	1.3			3.8					15.2
WZAK	.3											
WZZP	4.1	5.1	1.9	2.5			4.8	1.9	4.1			29.3

Footnote Symbols: (*) means audience estimates adjusted for actual broadcast schedule (+) means AM-FM Combination was not simulcast for complete time period.

ARBITRON

Cume Listening Estimates

Day Parts Avg & Cume

CUME PERSONS—TOTAL SURVEY AREA, IN HUNDREDS

STATION CALL LETTERS	TOT. PERS. 12+	MEN 18-24	25-34	35-44	45-54	55-64	WOMEN 18-24	25-34	35-44	45-54	55-64	TNS. 12-17
WAEZ	339	70	24	17	38	32	22	29	32	81	43	11
WAKR	1578	70	82	92	139	113	43	148	119	137	173	133
WCUE	432	20	20	25	25	6	115	37	8	26	36	149
*WHLO	444	20	118	28	45	38	145	23	8	31	35	8
WKDD	398	91	48	9		6	145	15	9	17	6	67
*WKNT	63	11	9	9	18	20	11	39	17	14	20	19
WKNT FM	220	11	9	9	18	20	11	39	17	14	20	19
TOTAL	259								25	14		
WSLR	855	58	59	86	133	32	50	84	122	88	40	50
WDBN FM	557		31	18	102	32		15	47	109	58	
WDMT	139	21	41	27		6	11	36	16	14		
WDOK	140		16	27		6		29	40	15	7	
WGAR	1497	155	338	101	23	25	232	302	41	14	15	251
WGCL	343	10	58	36		19	22	56	17			144
WHK	236	10	55	18	42			13	32	37	22	
WJW	139			45	42					18		
WKSW	97		25			13	254	21	16	22		172
WMMS	748	168	66	27	14			15	32			8
WQAL	307	10	16	54	85	6	10	51	8	45	14	
WMME	394	10	96	53	17	.26	21	101	24	30		16
WMMH	389	91	24	8		19	54	7				153
WZAK	38		32	8		6		7	8			
WZZP	506	50	32			6	104	44	24		7	244

CUME PERSONS—METRO SURVEY AREA IN HUNDREDS

STATION CALL LETTERS	TOT. PERS. 12+	MEN 18-24	25-34	35-44	45-54	55-64	WOMEN 18-24	25-34	35-44	45-54	55-64	TNS. 12-17
WAEZ	257	22	8	17	38	32	22	29	32		43	11
WAKR	1462	70	65	92	124	113	43	104	119	137	173	116
WCUE	394	20	25	25		6	86	37	8	17	36	149
*WHLO	223	20	41	8		19	23	23	8	31	14	8
WKDD	175	60	17	9		6	32	15	7			29
*WKNT	63	11	9	9	18	20		39	17	14	15	19
WKNT FM	220	11	9	9	18	20		39	17	14	52	19
TOTAL	259								25		52	
WSLR	668	21	59	86	86	32	22	84	72	74	29	50
WDBN FM	156				9		13	15	16	41	22	
WDMT	109	21	25				11	22	16	14	14	
WDOK	60		9				6	15	8	15	7	
WGAR	750	81	157	43	8	15	129	157	41	14	14	99
WGCL	164	10	26	17	17		22	15	17			57
WHK	176	10	24	18	18	19			16	37	22	
WJW	69			8	42					8		
WKSW	84		25		8	13	141	8	16	22		60
WMMS	437	131	66	17				15	16		14	
WQAL	199	10	33	34	71	6	21	24	8	31		8
WMME	206	10	24	8	17		46	46	24	15		
WMMH	295	91	17			6	54	7	8			118
WZAK	38			8				7				
WZZP	399	50	17	8		7	75	31	24			194

CUME RATINGS—METRO SURVEY AREA

STATION CALL LETTERS	TOT. PERS. 12+ %	MEN 18-24 %	25-34 %	35-44 %	45-54 %	55-64 %	WOMEN 18-24 %	25-34 %	35-44 %	45-54 %	55-64 %	TNS. 12-17 %
WAEZ	4.0		1.6	4.8	10.4	11.8	4.3		8.6	11.4	14.1	1.4
WAKR	26.8	14.5	13.1	25.8	34.1	41.5	8.3	20.6	32.1	35.5	56.9	14.9
WCUE	7.2	4.1		7.0		2.2	16.7	7.3	2.2	4.4	11.8	19.1
*WHLO	4.1	4.1	8.2	2.2		7.0		4.6	2.2	8.0	4.6	1.0
WKDD	3.2	12.4	3.4	2.5		2.2	6.2	3.0		1.8		3.7
*WKNT	1.2	2.3	1.8	2.5	4.9	7.7		7.7	4.6	3.6	4.9	2.4
WKNT FM	4.0	2.3	1.8	2.5	4.9	7.4		7.7	6.7	3.6	1.7	2.4
TOTAL	4.8										1.7	
WSLR	12.3	4.3	11.9	24.1	23.6	11.8	4.3	16.6	19.4	19.2	9.5	6.4
WDBN FM	2.9	4.3	5.0		2.5	4.8		3.0	4.3	10.6	7.2	
WDMT	2.0			2.5			2.1	4.4	4.3	3.6	3.6	7.7
WDOK	1.1							3.0	2.2	3.9	2.3	1.0
WGAR	13.8	16.8	31.6	12.0	2.2	2.2	25.0	31.1	11.1	3.6	4.9	12.7
WGCL	3.0	2.1	5.2	4.8			4.3		4.6	9.6	7.3	7.3
WHK	3.2	2.1	4.8	5.0	11.5	7.0		4.3		2.1		
WJW	1.3			2.2	2.2					2.1		
WKSW	1.5		5.0			4.8		1.6	4.3	5.7		
WMMS	8.0	27.1	13.3	2.2			27.3	3.0	4.3			7.7
WQAL	3.7	2.1		4.8	19.5	2.2		4.8	2.2	8.0	4.6	1.0
WMME	3.8	2.1	6.6	9.5	4.7	2.2	4.1	9.1	6.5	3.9		
WMMH	5.4	18.8	4.8	2.2			10.5					15.1
WZAK	.7	.7						1.4	2.2		2.3	
WZZP	7.3	10.4	3.4	2.2			14.5	6.1	6.5			24.8

Totals:

	TOT. 12+	M 18-24	25-34	35-44	45-54	55-64	W 18-24	25-34	35-44	45-54	55-64	TNS 12-17
TOTAL LISTENING IN METRO SURVEY AREA	4403	413	430	271	297	202	418	416	322	349	260	589
Cume Ratings %	80.8	85.5	86.5	85.9	81.6	74.3	81.0	82.4	86.8	90.4	85.5	75.4

Footnote Symbols: (*) means audience estimates adjusted for actual broadcast schedule (+) means AM-FM Combination was not simulcast for complete time period.

ARBITRON

Average Quarter-Hour Listening Estimates

MONDAY–FRIDAY
7.00AM–8.00AM

METRO SHARES

STATION CALL LETTERS	TOT. 12+ %	MEN 18+ %	WM. 18+ %	TNS. 12-17 %
WAEZ	3.5	3.6	4.3	.5
WAKR	24.7	20.8	30.4	16.1
WCUE	8.5	5.0	8.6	18.8
*WHLO	1.0	1.4	.7	.5
WKDD	2.8	2.9	2.3	4.2
*WKNT	.5		1.0	
WKNT FM	4.2	6.2	3.6	.5
+WKNT FM TOTAL	4.7	6.2	4.6	.5
WSLR	10.3	15.1	8.6	1.6
WDBN FM	1.1	.5	1.9	
WDMT	1.3	1.2	1.7	
WDOK	.5		1.1	
WGAR	11.3	9.6	13.0	10.4
WGCL	.7	.7		3.6
WHK	1.5		1.1	
WJW	2.3	4.5	1.1	
WKSW	.3	.9		
WMMS	6.5	8.1	5.7	4.2
WQAL	2.8	5.3	1.3	.5
WMME	2.4	1.9	3.4	
WMMH	3.1	1.7	.6	16.7
WZAK	.1		.1	
WZZP	4.3	1.4	2.1	20.8

AVERAGE PERSONS — TOTAL SURVEY AREA, IN HUNDREDS

STATION	TOT. PERS. 12+	MEN 18-34	MEN 18-49	MEN 25-49	MEN 25-44	MEN 35-44	MEN 45-54	MEN 18+	WOMEN 18-34	WOMEN 18-49	WOMEN 25-49	WOMEN 25-44	WOMEN 35-44	WOMEN 45-54	WOMEN 18+	TNS. 12-17
WAEZ	75	13	20	20	15	2	8	33	11	26	25	21	11	11	41	1
WAKR	406	40	79	58	41	22	25	131	40	109	106	82	45	55	232	43
WCUE	125	12	27	15	15	15		29	38	43	24	20	1	4	60	36
*WHLO	54	27	39	37	25		12	47						2	6	1
WKDD	75	21	23	12	12	2		24	38	40	9	7		3	41	10
*WKNT	7															
WKNT FM	62	6	15	10	10	9	9	36	1	9	9	9	8	6	25	1
+WKNT FM TOTAL	69	6	15	10	10	9	9	36	1	9	9	9	8	6	32	1
WSLR	156	29	69	64	45	21	24	88	12	39	35	22	14	20	65	3
WDBN FM	56		4	4			18	25	2	16	16	4	2	17	31	
WDMT	19	7	7	6				7	11	11	7	7		1	12	
WDOK	20	4	7	7	3	3		7	8	9	9	9	1	4	13	
WGAR	302	73	108	102	102	35	3	118	109	123	80	80	14	3	130	54
WGCL	50	13	22	21	21	9		22	8	8	8	8			8	20
WHK	37	19	23	17	17	4		26	3	8	8	6	3	2	11	
WJW	47		32	32	18	18	21	39	2	8	8	8			8	
WKSW	5	1	1	1	1	1		5	2	2	2	2			2	
WMMS	146	62	62	14	14			62	56	56	2	2			56	28
WQAL	47	7	32	27	9	7	19	33	3	9	9	3			13	1
WMME	58	14	22	20	20	5		25	13	28	26	26	15	10	31	2
WMMH	52	10	10	5	5			10	4	4					4	38
WZAK	1														1	
WZZP	92	6	8	4	4		2	8	10	18	13	13	8		18	66

AVERAGE PERSONS — METRO SURVEY AREA, IN HUNDREDS

STATION	TOT. PERS. 12+	MEN 18-34	MEN 18-49	MEN 25-49	MEN 25-44	MEN 35-44	MEN 45-54	MEN 18+	WOMEN 18-34	WOMEN 18-49	WOMEN 25-49	WOMEN 25-44	WOMEN 35-44	WOMEN 45-54	WOMEN 18+	TNS. 12-17
WAEZ	52	1	8	8	3	2	8	21	1	15	14	11	11	10	30	1
WAKR	364	36	69	48	37	22	19	121	20	89	86	62	45	55	212	31
WCUE	125	12	27	15	15			29	38	43	24	20	1	4	60	36
*WHLO	14	5	5	3	3			8						2	5	1
WKDD	41	14	16	6	6	2		17	15	15	7	7		1	16	8
*WKNT	7															
WKNT FM	62	6	15	10	10	9	9	36	1	9	9	9	8	6	25	1
+WKNT FM TOTAL	69	6	15	10	10	9	9	36	1	9	9	9	8	6	32	1
WSLR	151	29	69	64	45	21	24	88	12	35	31	18	10	20	60	3
WDBN FM	16						3	3	2	2	2			3	13	
WDMT	19	7	6	6				7	11	7	7	4		1	12	
WDOK	8		6	6				7	4	4	4				8	
WGAR	167	42	52	46	46	10	3	56	70	84	48	48	14	3	91	20
WGCL	11	4	4	3				4	4						8	7
WHK	22	7	11	5	5			8		5	5	3		2	8	
WJW	34	7	19	19	19	4	8	26	5	8	8				8	
WKSW	5	1	1	1	1	1		5								
WMMS	95	47	47	14	14			47	40	40	2	2			40	8
WQAL	41	5	30	25	7	7		31	2	8	8	2			9	1
WMME	35	6	8	6	6	2		11	6	21	19	19	15	7	24	
WMMH	46	10	10	5	5			10	4	4					4	32
WZAK	1														1	
WZZP	63	6	8	4	4		2	8	7	15	10	10	8		15	40
TOTAL LISTENING IN METRO SURVEY AREA	1472	257	432	309	242	108	120	582	252	443	312	244	123	141	698	192

Footnote Symbols: (*) means audience estimates adjusted for actual broadcast schedule (+) means AM-FM Combination was not simulcast for complete time period.

ARBITRON

Average Quarter-Hour Listening Estimates

AKRON OCT/NOV 1977

MONDAY-FRIDAY 8.00AM-9.00AM

AVERAGE PERSONS—TOTAL SURVEY AREA, IN HUNDREDS

STATION CALL LETTERS	TOT. PERS. 12+	MEN 18-34	MEN 18-49	MEN 25-49	MEN 25-44	MEN 35-44	MEN 45-54	MEN 18+	WOMEN 18-34	WOMEN 18-49	WOMEN 25-49	WOMEN 25-44	WOMEN 35-44	WOMEN 45-54	WOMEN 18+	TNS. 12-17
WAEZ	70	10	10	10	6	6	4	17	12	24	18	18	12	13	53	
WAKR	241	26	35	21	16	16	16	70	24	66	50	64	28	28	171	
WCUE	42								29	34	9	9		5	37	5
WHLO	66	25	33	31	30	7	4	45	2	2	2	2			21	
WKDD	55	28	28	20	20			28	23	25		2		4	27	
WKNT	14							1							13	
WKNT FM	39		3	3	3		9	17	3	5	5	5	3	6	22	
TOTAL	53						9	18	3	8	8	8	6	6	35	
WSLR	116	18	53	48	34	21	16	71	26	26	16	16	7	20	45	
WDBN FM	84	9	33	33	27	18	6	34	3	36	24	36	21	24	50	
WDMT	19	5	5	3	3			5	12	13	10	1	1	5	14	
WDOK	23						2	2	17	17	16	17	16	5	21	
WGAR	201	74	108	81	80	33	3	111	66	78	54	54	12	3	88	2
WGCL	32	9	11	11	11	2		11	7	8	7	5	1	1	8	13
WHK	35	8	12	10	10	4		19	5	7	7	7	5	1	16	
WKJN	32	21	21	21	10	9	14	25	3	7	7	7		7	7	
WKSW	22	9	9	9	9	9		13	8	8	8		1	1	9	
WMMS	128	51	51	15	15	1		51	67	71	7	7	4		71	6
WQAL	47	10	16	6	6	6	4	20	1	6	1			19	27	
WMME	29	12	19	19	19	7	1	20	4	5	6	6	2	3	9	
WMMM	32	20	24	15	15	4		24	5	5	6	3			5	3
WZAK	4							1	1	3	3	3	2		3	
WZZP	60	16	18	6	6	2		18	14	22	13	13	8		22	20

AVERAGE PERSONS—METRO SURVEY AREA, IN HUNDREDS

STATION CALL LETTERS	TOT. PERS. 12+	MEN 18-34	MEN 18-49	MEN 25-49	MEN 25-44	MEN 35-44	MEN 45-54	MEN 18+	WOMEN 18-34	WOMEN 18-49	WOMEN 25-49	WOMEN 25-44	WOMEN 35-44	WOMEN 45-54	WOMEN 18+	TNS. 12-17
WAEZ	61		10	10	6	6	4	17	6	18	12	12	12	10	44	
WAKR	228	22	30	16	12	4	15	62	19	61	59	45	28	28	166	
WCUE	40								27	32	14	9		5	35	5
WHLO	28	6	6	4	4			15	2	2	2	2			13	
WKDD	22	14	14	8	8			14	6	6	2	2		2	8	
WKNT	14							1							13	
WKNT FM	39		5	3	3		9	17	2	3	3	3	3	6	22	
TOTAL	53						9	18	2	8	8	8	6	6	35	
WSLR	116	18	53	48	34	21	16	71	9	26	26	16	7	20	45	
WDBN FM	23	5	5	3	3		1	1	3	13	13	13	10	24	22	
WDMT	15	5	5	3	3			5	8	9	6	1		1	10	
WDOK	14						2	2	8	8	8	7	7	5	12	
WGAR	122	36	49	36	36	13	2	51	39	61	39	39	12	3	71	2
WGCL	9	2	4	4	4			4	2	4	4	1	1		5	13
WHK	30	6	10	8	8	4		17	4	5	4	4	1	1	13	
WKJN	26	6	17	8	5	4	14	19		4	4	4		7	7	
WKSW	14	9	9	5				13	9					1	1	
WMMS	84	43	43	15	15			43	38	39	4	4	1		39	2
WQAL	35	10	11	1	1	1	4	15	4	5	5	5	4	13	20	
WMME	13	4	4	4	4		1	5	3	5	5	5		3	8	
WMMM	31	20	24	15	15	4		24	5	5	3	3	2		5	2
WZAK	4							1	1	3	3	3	2		3	
WZZP	47	13	15	3	3	2		15	12	22	13	11	8	3	20	12
TOTAL LISTENING IN METRO SURVEY AREA	1089	211	316	213	179	71	77	440	201	359	248	197	107	130	626	23

METRO SHARES

STATION CALL LETTERS	TOT. 12+ %	MEN 18+ %	WM. 18+ %	TNS. 12-17 %
WAEZ	5.6	3.9	7.0	
WAKR	20.9	14.1	26.5	
WCUE	3.7	3.4	5.6	21.7
WHLO	2.6	3.4	2.1	
WKDD	2.0	3.2	1.3	
WKNT	1.3	.2	2.1	
WKNT FM	3.6	3.9	3.9	
TOTAL	4.9	4.1	5.6	
WSLR	10.7	16.1	7.2	
WDBN FM	2.1	.2	3.5	
WDMT	1.4	1.1	1.6	
WDOK	1.3	.5	1.9	
WGAR	11.2	11.6	11.3	
WGCL	.8	.9	.8	
WHK	2.8	3.9	2.1	
WKJN	2.4	4.3	1.1	
WKSW	1.3	3.0	.2	
WMMS	7.7	9.8	6.2	8.7
WQAL	3.2	3.4	3.2	
WMME	1.2	1.1	1.3	
WMMM	2.8	5.5	.8	8.7
WZAK	.4	.2	.5	
WZZP	4.3	3.4	3.2	52.2

Footnote Symbols: (*) means audience estimates adjusted for actual broadcast schedule (+) means AM-FM Combination was not simulcast for complete time period.

ARBITRON

Exclusive Cume Listening Estimates— Metro Survey Area, In Hundreds

MON.-SUN. 6:00 AM - MID.

STATION CALL LETTERS	TOTAL PERS. 12+	MEN 18+	WOMEN 18+	TEENS 12-17
MAEZ	30	11	19	
MAKR	272	113	159	
MCUE	63	6	46	11
*MHLO	-1			
MKDD	29		18	11
*MKNT	-1			
MKNT FM	37	22	15	
TOTAL	45	22	23	
MSLR	151	85	55	11
MDBN FM	40	26	14	
MDMT	7		7	
MDOK	7		7	
MGAR	99	63	36	
MGCL	37	8		29
MHK	16	16		
MJM	-1			
MKSW	22	6	16	
MMMS	102	83	19	
MQAL	44	19	25	
MME	8		8	
MMM	50	39	11	
MZAK	11	11		
MZZP	51	17	15	19

MON.-FRI. 6:00 AM - 10:00 AM

STATION CALL LETTERS	TOTAL PERS. 12+	MEN 18+	WOMEN 18+	TEENS 12-17
MAEZ	51	21	30	
MAKR	677	282	355	40
MCUE	161	27	71	63
*MHLO	43	25	18	
MKDD	47	18	18	11
*MKNT	-1			
MKNT FM	36	22	14	
TOTAL	44	22	22	
MSLR	271	122	123	26
MDBN FM	17		17	
MDMT	15	8	7	
MDOK	15		15	
MGAR	255	123	106	26
MGCL	29			29
MHK	33	26	7	
MJM	46	38	8	
MKSW	16		16	
MMMS	194	103	83	8
MQAL	86	29	49	8
MMME	32	8	24	
MMM	84	65		19
MZAK	-1			
MZZP	146	35	34	77

MON.-FRI. 10:00 AM - 3:00 PM

STATION CALL LETTERS	TOTAL PERS. 12+	MEN 18+	WOMEN 18+	TEENS 12-17
MAEZ	66	29	37	
MAKR	353	144	201	8
MCUE	97	27	47	23
MHLO	65	36	29	
MKDD	50	16	34	
*MKNT	18		18	
MKNT FM	75	21	54	
TOTAL	101	21	60	
MSLR	216	101	115	
MDBN FM	80	26	54	
MDMT	26	8	18	
MDOK	19	11	8	
MGAR	168	55	105	8
MGCL	-1			
MHK	7		7	
MJM	19	19		
MKSW	39	31	8	
MMMS	222	94	94	34
MQAL	77	29	48	
MMME	32	16	16	
MMM	114	38	32	44
MZAK	6	6		
MZZP	141	18	35	88

MON.-FRI. 3:00 PM - 7:00 PM

STATION CALL LETTERS	TOTAL PERS. 12+	MEN 18+	WOMEN 18+	TEENS 12-17
MAEZ	60	29	31	
MAKR	292	101	183	8
MCUE	170	17	59	94
MHLO	46	22	24	
MKDD	39	11	28	
*MKNT	-1			
MKNT FM	47	9	38	
TOTAL	47	9	38	
MSLR	272	184	77	11
MDBN FM	83	31	52	
MDMT	26		26	
MDOK	71	22	49	
MGAR	235	98	129	8
MGCL	42	8	7	27
MHK	48	26	22	
MJM	40	30	10	
MKSW	30	22	8	
MMMS	197	110	79	8
MQAL	90	57	33	
MMME	8		8	
MMM	138	48	32	58
MZAK	6	6		
MZZP	141	25	34	82

MON.-FRI. 7:00 PM - MID.

STATION CALL LETTERS	TOTAL PERS. 12+	MEN 18+	WOMEN 18+	TEENS 12-17
MAEZ	61	17	44	
MAKR	305	135	151	19
MCUE	74		45	29
*MHLO	8		8	
MKDD	66	19	36	11
MKNT FM	41	19	22	
MSLR	178	78	89	11
MDBN FM	50	26	24	
MDMT	42	8	34	
MDOK	55	22	33	
MGAR	203	92	111	
MGCL	25	17	14	8
MHK	14		14	
MJM	11			11
MKSW	16		16	
MMMS	115	86	21	8
MQAL	42	28	14	
MMME	84	57	16	11
MMM	138	54	50	34
MZAK	34	17	17	
MZZP	134	34	45	55

Footnote Symbols: (*) means audience estimates adjusted for actual broadcast schedule (+) means AM-FM Combination was not simulcast for complete time period.

ARBITRON

Glossary of Selected Terms as Used in This Arbitron Report

1. AM-FM Totals—A figure shown for AM-FM affiliates in time periods when they are predominantly simulcast. *(See Pars. 22 - 25.)*

2. Area of Dominant Influence (ADI)—Where applicable, Arbitron Television's geographic market design which defines each Television market exclusive of others based on measurable viewing patterns. Every county in the United States (excluding Alaska and Hawaii) is allocated exclusively to one ADI.

3. Average Quarter-Hour Persons—The estimated number of persons who listened at home and away to a station for a minimum of five minutes within a given quarter hour. The estimate is based on the average of the reported listening in the total number of quarter hours the station was on the air during a reported time period. This estimate is shown for the MSA, TSA and ADI.

4. Average Quarter-Hour Rating—The Average Quarter-Hour Persons estimate expressed as a percentage of the universe. This estimate is shown in the MSA and ADI.

5. Average Quarter-Hour Share—The Average Quarter-Hour estimate for a given station expressed as a percentage of the Average Quarter-Hour Persons estimate for the total listening in the MSA within a given time period. This estimate is shown only in the MSA.

6. Away-From-Home Listening—Estimate of listening for which the diary keeper indicated listening was done away from home.

7. Cume Persons—The estimate number of *different* persons who listened at home and away to a station for a minimum of five minutes within a given day-part. (Cume **estimates** may also be referred to as "cumulative," "unduplicated" or "reach" estimates.) This estimate is shown in the MSA, TSA and ADI.

8. Cume Rating—The estimated number of Cume Persons expressed as a percentage of the universe. This estimate is shown for the MSA only.

9. Day-Part—A given part of a day (e.g. 6-10 AM, 7 PM-Midnight.)

10. Effective Sample Bases (ESB)—The sample size to be used for estimating the statistical variance of these audience estimates. *(See Par. 38.)*

11. Exclusive Cume Listening—The estimated number of Cume Persons who listened to one and only one station within a given day-part.

12. In-Tab Sample—The number of usable diaries returned and actually tabulated in producing the report.

13. Metro Survey Area (MSA)—Metro Survey Area generally correspond to Standard Metropolitan Statistical Areas (SMSA's) as defined by the U.S. government's Office of Management and Budget (OMB) subject to exceptions dictated by historical industry usage and other marketing considerations.

In New England, SMSA's are definded on a "town" rather than a county basis. Where the SMSA represents 65% or more of the SRDS full-county definition for the market Arbitron uses the SRDS full-county definition to define the Metro Survey Area; where the SMSA represents less than 65% of the population of the SRDS full-county definition for the market, Arbitron uses the SMSA to define the Metro Survey Area.

14. Metro Totals and ADI Totals (Total listening in Metro Survey Area or Total listening in the ADI)—The Metro Total and ADI Total estimates include estimates of listening to reported stations as well as to stations that did not meet the Minimum Reporting Standards plus estimates of listening to unidentified stations.

15. Minimum Reporting Standards (MRS)—Specific Minimum Reporting Standards are applied to determine the stations listed in this report. *(See Pars. 26 - 27.)*

16. Rating—(See Average Quarter-Hour Rating and Cume Rating.)

17. Sampling Unit—A geographic area consisting of a single county, a group of counties or a part of a county. *(See Par. 30.)*

18. Share—(See Average Quarter-Hour Share.)

19. Simulcast—The broadcasting of the same program at the same time by AM-FM affiliated stations.

20. Total Survey Area (TSA)—Where applicable, a geographic area that includes the Metro Survey Area plus certain counties located outside the MSA. (For explanation of the criteria used in establishing the TSA, *See Par. 29.)*

21. Universe—The estimated number of persons in the sex-age group and geographic area being reported.

For additional information, the reader is directed to "Standard Definitions of Broadcast Research Terms," published by the National Association of Broadcasters, 1771 N Street, N.W., Washington, D.C. 20036.

Description of Methodology

AM-FM Totals

22. Criteria—When AM-FM affiliates are simulcast during an entire given day-part a Total line will appear following the AM and FM lines. When AM-FM affiliates are separately programmed during a given day-part, no Total line will be shown. When the AM-FM affiliates both simulcast and program differently during a given day-part, a Total line will be shown if:

1. The amount of separate programming during the day-part **does not** exceed **an average of one hour per day,** and;
2. The amount of simulcasting during the day-part **does** exceed **an average of one hour per day.** (e.g. Day-Part: Monday-Sunday, 6 AM-Midnight; Separate Programming—6 AM-7 AM. Simulcast—7 AM-Midnight. A Total line would be shown for the entire day-part.)

There are two exceptions to this rule. In the combined 6 AM-10 AM and 3 PM-7 PM day-parts the total line will be shown only if the affiliates have a total line in each of the separate day-parts. If only the Saturday or Sunday 6 AM-10 AM day-part is simulcast and no other day-parts qualify for a total line then each station may or may not request a total line for Saturday or Sunday 6 AM-10 AM due to the public service nature of programming by most stations in these day-parts.

In one-hour time periods, the Total line will be shown only when the stations are entirely simulcast during the time both are on the air.

When the above criteria are met, Total lines will be shown although one or both stations may not have been on the air during the entire given day-part. For example, if stations XXXX and XXXX-FM are simulcast, and station XXXX signs off the air at 8 PM and XXXX-FM signs off the air at midnight, the Total line in the 7 PM-Midnight day-part will reflect the audience of XXXX from 7 PM to 8 PM, and the audience of XXXX-FM from 7 PM to Midnight. (Stations broadcasting for less than an entire reported day-part are indicated by an asterisk next to the station call letters.)

23. Average Quarter-Hour Listening—The AM-FM Total line is the summation of the estimated number of persons who listened to the AM station plus the estimated number of persons who listened to the FM station during a given time period.

24. Cume Persons—The AM-FM Total line represents the estimated number of *different* persons who listened to either the AM station, the FM station or both stations during a given day-part. The Total line provides an estimate of the unduplicated audience to the AM-FM combination during the given day-part. if the Total line *equals* the sum of the individual AM and FM estimates, there is no reported duplication of listening between the two stations. If the Total is *less* than the sum of the individual figures, there is reported duplication (persons listening to both stations in the same time period.)

25. Exclusive Cume Listening—The Total line represents the estimated number of different persons who listened to either the AM station only, the FM station only or both stations only during the given day-part. Persons who listened to both the AM and FM stations are reported only in the Total line and are not shown in the estimates for the AM and FM individually. If the Total line *equals* the sum of the AM and FM estimates, there is no reported duplication of listening between the two stations. If the Total line is *more* than the sum of the individual figures, there is reported duplication of listening.

Criteria for Reporting Stations

26. Minimum Reporting Standards (MRS) for AM-Only and FM-Only Stations—Non-commercial radio stations are not listed in Arbitron market reports and therefore are not considered in the Minimum Reporting Standard evaluation. A Commercial AM-only or FM-only station is included in this report if it has met **both** of the following Minimum Reporting Standards for Metro or ADI:

a. The station must have received five or more minutes of listening in at least ten metro diaries or 1% of the metro in-tab diary quota, whichever is greater, during the current survey of the market. (Ten ADI diaries or 1% of the ADI in-tab diary quota for ADI markets.)

b. The station must have an Average Quarter-Hour MSA rating of at least 0.1% among persons 12 + for the time the station is on the air during the Monday-Sunday 6 AM-Midnight period. (Average Quarter-Hour ADI rating of 0.1% for ADI markets.)

27. Minimum Reporting Standards (MRS) for AM-FM Combination Stations—

a. AM-FM affiliates which simulcast for less than 10% of the total number of quarter hours when both stations are on the air simultaneously (Monday-Sunday, 6 AM-Midnight) are considered to be **separately programmed** stations. Thus, each will be treated independently, and each must meet the same criteria used for AM-only or FM-only stations. *(See Par. 26.)*

b. AM-FM affiliates which are simulcast from 10% to 90% of the total number of quarter hours when both stations are on the air simultaneously (Monday-Sunday, 6 AM-Midnight) are considered to be **simulcast** stations. Provided that one of the two stations meets both MRS criteria described in Paragraph 26 above, the second station is included in the report if (a) it meets the criteria of Paragraph 26a, and (b) it achieves the average quarter-hour requirement described in Paragraph 26b for any one of the four basic Monday-Friday day-parts (6 AM-10 AM, 10 AM-3 PM, 3 PM-7 PM, 7 PM-Midnight).

c. AM-FM affiliates which are simulcast more than 90% of the total number of quarter hours when both stations are on the air simultaneously (Monday-Sunday, 6 AM-Midnight) are regarded as totally simulcast stations and therefore will be treated as a single station in both phases of the MRS criteria described in Paragraph 26. If the **combined** audience of the two stations is sufficient to meet both criteria of Paragraph 26, then both stations will be listed in the report even though one (or both) stations might not meet the MRS criteria individually.

28. Home and Outside Stations—Any Station licensed to cities located within the Metro Survey Area of this market is a "home" station. (However, some Canadian and Mexican stations are assigned as home stations to United States markets, even though they are not licensed to a city within the Metro Survey Area.) All other stations are considered "outside" stations. For ADI markets, outside stations are further reclassified into: (a) "outside the Metro Survey Area but home to the ADI", and (b) "outside the Metro and the ADI". The Minimum Reporting Standards for inclusion in this report are the same for all stations.

29. Total Survey Area—When a market is surveyed for the first time, the TSA will generally include every county which is covered by the 0.5 MV/M signal of at least two AM stations licensed to the metro area of the market. Where available, diary results are used in lieu of, or in addition to, signal contours. Survey area definitions are reviewed following the market's initial survey. Reviews are conducted at least once a year. (Generally, these are based upon combined diary returns from the Spring and Fall surveys.) Counties are added to or subtracted from a TSA whenever home stations are mentioned in a specified percentage of the total diaries returned from the county. The TSA does not necessarily include all counties in which all home stations have coverage. Neither does the TSA definition indicate that all home stations have equal coverage in all non-metro counties. Further, Arbitron reserves the right to exercise its best professional judgment by modifying and/or waiving certain procedures described above when strict adherence to these procedures would result in a county addition or deletion which would appear unreasonable or illogical in light of known topographic, geographic, or other exceptional conditions.

PAGE i

Total Survey Area audience estimates for stations may be reported in more than one Radio Market. A station may be reported as a "home station" in its own Metro and Total Survey Area and as an "outside station" in the Metro and Total Survey Area of some other market. Due to market definition overlap, Total Survey Area audience estimates for outside stations are not additive to the Total Survey Area audience estimates reported in that station's home market.

Sampling and Calculation Techniques

30. Sampling Methodology—Surveys for Arbitron Radio Market Reports are accomplished through the use of a geographic unit called an Arbitron sampling unit. A sampling unit can consist of one county, a group of counties or part of a county.

Sample base goals, expressed in terms of Total Persons 12 +, are established for the MSA, TSA and the ADI, if applicable. The number of homes required to achieve each sample base goal is determined by dividing the Total Persons 12 + by total homes and applying this ratio to the sample.

Diary return quotas are established for each sampling unit with a probability proportional to population in the survey area. The diary return quota is then converted to a home quota based on the estimated number of persons 12 + in a home.

The actual number of diaries placed in each sampling unit is determined by the quota established for the sample base goals and the rate of return which Arbitron can reasonably expect based on past placement experience. The total sample is divided into approximately equal weekly segments for placement.

For each survey, a complete new sample of households is computer-selected for each sampling unit through the use of a systematic interval selection technique. These samples of households are drawn from lists of subscribers appearing in current telephone directories, supplied by Metro-Mail Advertising Company. This sample selection, like all other processes used in developing Arbitron Radio estimates, is audited by the Broadcast Rating Council.

If a need for additional sample names arises after the original sample has been selected by the computer, that sample may be drawn manually using a technique wherein Arbitron randomly selects the telephone directories from which the sample is to be drawn, then randomly selects from the names listed in those directories.

In High Density Spanish areas in which the personal placement and pick-up technique is used, computer-drawn samples are used to specify the key addresses. The actual sample is drawn by taking the starting household adjacent to the key household number and systematically proceeding according to Arbitron personal interviewing instructions.

31. Arbitron Radio Listening Diary—Arbitron uses one-week individual diaries to gather listening information. Bilingual (Spanish-English) diaries are printed for placement with persons who indicate a preference for a Spanish-language diary.

32. Data Retrieval—Initially, Arbitron sends a letter to the sample households, informing them of their selection by the computer, and stating that an interviewer will be calling to request their cooperation in the survey. Arbitron interviewers are instructed to contact selected sample households by telephone to gain acceptance of the diaries and to determine the number of persons 12 + living in the home at the time of the placement call. Explicit instructions are provided to each interviewer, and independent checks are regularly conducted by Arbitron interviewer coordinators and the Arbitron Field Operations Department. Diaries are then mailed directly to the consenting sample households from Arbitron headquarters in Beltsville, Maryland. Cash incentives are included with diaries as a means of stimulating respondent cooperation. Arbitron sends a diary for each person 12 + reported in the sample household.

Interviewers are instructed to make at least five attempts to reach every household selected in the sample so that everyone in the sample has a reasonable chance of being contacted. These attempted calls are made at different hours during the day and evening. After the initial contact, the interviewer's directions are to make two additional contacts with the sample households: (1) the day before the survey begins to make sure the diary has been received, to assist members of the household in understanding the diary's purpose, and how to keep it; and (2) several days later to make sure that no difficulties have developed, to remind the diary keepers to return their diaries, and to thank them for cooperating in the survey. In cases where sample households are so remotely located that substantial toll charges are incurred, follow-up is made by letter rather than by telephone.

Although explicit instructions are provided each interviewer, and independent checks are regularly conducted by interviewer coordinators and the Arbitron Field Operations Department, there may be instances where such instructions are not followed.

33. Special Interviewing Techniques—Special interviewing techniques and processing procedures are employed in certain markets to improve representation of certain ethnic groups. These techniques have been developed to aid in obtaining radio listening information from persons who may have language and/or writing problems and who otherwise might not be fully represented in the in-tab sample. Two types of Special Interviewing Techniques are employed. The first consists of daily telephone interviewing for a seven-day period, with the interviewer recording the listening information as received from the respondent. This technique is used in certain geographic areas having a high-density Black population. These areas are identified as "HDBA" (High Density Black Area). In markets where Metro Survey Area data are weighted proportionately for Black and non-Black populations, the daily telephone interviewing technique is also used for all Metro Survey Area Black households, regardless of their location. The second technique, used in certain high-density Spanish-language geographic areas ("HDSA"-High Density Spanish Area), involves three personal visits to place, to sustain interest in, and to pick up the standard seven-day listening diary in either the English or bilingual format. The latter technique allows for the inclusion in this sample of persons who live in non-telephone households or in households with unlisted phone numbers. Listening data gathered in this manner are projected against the estimated number of persons living in geographic areas in which these special interviewing procedures were implemented.

34. Tabulation of Diaries—All diaries returned to Arbitron are not necessarily tabulated. Only those with seven usable days are processed. Among those not used are diaries which are obviously incomplete or inaccurate and those which arrive after the production cut-off date. The total number of in-tab diaries may or may not reach or exceed the designated in-tab quota.

35. Returned-Sample Weighting—Returned diaries are weighted to reflect the estimated proportion of sex, age, geographic population and race (where ethnic weighting is employed), based on the characteristics of the survey area. Geographic area and sex-age control is maintained for diary returns by partitioning the survey area into sampling units and then subdividing the population of each sampling unit into the reported sixteen sex-age groups. The number of strata formed by this procedure equals sixteen times the number of sampling units. In computing the results, the value of each diary returned from a stratum is a result of weighting the returned sample in an attempt to compensate for disproportionate returns from any sampling unit or sex-age group. In certain markets with high ethnic population groups, weighting to compensate for disproportionate returns of ethnic diaries is used in addition to those mentioned above. With this value established for each diary, listening is estimated by adding the values of each diary in which listening is recorded to a particular station at a given time. Local time differences within a market that overlaps time zones, and time differences caused by seasonal time changes, are accounted for in the results by adjusting diary entries to the time zone observed by the stations located in the market being measured.

36. Tabulation of Cume Listening Estimates for Day-Part Combinations—The criterion for tallying listening in those day-parts which have been combined is five or more minutes of listening at any time in any of the day-parts. (e.g., a person who listened in the Monday-Friday, 6-10 AM and 3-7 PM day-parts would be counted only once in the Cume Persons tabulation for the entire eight-hour period. The same procedure would apply if the person listened in only one of the day-parts.)

37. Sampling Error—Arbitron estimates are subject to the statistical variance associated with all surveys using a sample of the universe, and all the factors described in paragraph 39 of this report entitled "Limitations". Approximations of the sampling error can be developed by use of the NOMOGRAPH (on the inside rear cover) and the Effective Sample Base *(See Par. 38)* based on two standard deviations, provided the user of this report keeps in mind that, due to the factors discussed in Paragraph 39 of this report entitled "Limitations", the accuracy of Arbitron measurements, data and reports and their statistical evaluators cannot be determined to any precise mathematical value or definition.

38. Effective Sample Bases (ESB)—Estimates of Effective Sample Bases indicate the size of simple random samples (in which all diaries have equal value) that would be required to provide the same degree of reliability as the samples actually used to produce the estimates in this report. The statistical reliability of such estimates depends on the ESB and only indirectly on the number of diaries tabulated, and is also subject to all of the factors described in paragraph 39 of this report entitled "Limitations". Bases are reported for the purpose of estimating sampling variation. The Arbitron formula to estimate ESB's takes into account the disproportionate sampling of Metro areas, and differences in return rates among sampling units and among the individual sex-age categories. (Total tabulated diaries and ESB's for this report are listed on Page 3.)

Limitations

39. Limitations—In addition to the sources of possible errors which are described elsewhere in this book, the user should be aware of the limitations described below:

a. The sample is drawn only from households listed in telephone directories. This eliminated non-telephone households and telephone households not listed in the directory. Commercial establishments listed in the directory are specifically excluded from the sample. Households on military installations may or may not be listed in the local telephone directory. Further, all possible telephone directories may not be available in the lists prepared by Metro-Mail Advertising Corporation and used as Arbitron's sample frame.

b. Non-responding persons may have listening habits which differ from those of respondents. Similarly, the listening habits of persons residing in non-telephone households or those not listed in telephone directories may vary from those of persons who own phones and are listed in directories.

c. Non-responding persons in the original designated household sample prevent the "in-tab sample" from being a perfect probability sample.

d. The sample design and/or response patterns (including those markets where special diary placement and/or listening data retrieval are utilized) may preclude proper representation of certain groups within the population such as ethnic groups and persons in certain low-income or low-education groups, or individuals whose primary language is other than English. Such persons, whose listening habits may differ from other persons, may not be fully represented in the audience estimates because usable diaries may not be obtained from them. These factors may be significant to the extent that radio listening of these groups differs from those of other groups.

e. Population data from Bureau of the Census and Market Statistics, Inc., which are used in this report, are subject to defects and limitations such as sampling, processing and recording errors. In addition, for those years between decennial census dates, Census data are based upon a sample which is significantly smaller in most regions that are employed by Arbitron; and Market Statistics, Inc. utilizes published government figures in estimating population for individual counties. These defects and limitations in data from Bureau of the Census and Market Statistics, Inc. are inherent in Arbitron estimates based thereon.

f. Diaries, or portions thereof, may be completed improperly if the diary instructions are not understood or are not followed. Such diaries may thereby be excluded from the survey. Some diary entries may have been made on the basis of hearsay or recall, the estimates of the diary keeper or could have been influenced by comments made by the interviewer to survey participants.

g. Human and computer processing errors may occur after the diaries are received at Arbitron headquarters. Consequently the degree of variance in the data may be greater than that expected from sampling variance alone.

h. The data upon which Arbitron has based its Returned Sample Weighting may not be precise.

i. Logical analysis and pre-processing preparation of the data may affect some of the diary listening entries before the data are projected.

j. Arbitron conducts research involving new methods of improving cooperation from diary keepers and/or securing additional information from such persons. Occasionally, a portion of this research may be performed in conjunction with the actual surveys, and when so done, may cause the degree of variance in the data to be greater than that expected from sampling variation alone.

k. Certain data, such as when the station was on and off the air and time, periods when AM-FM affiliates were simulcast or separately programmed, are based on data supplied by the stations and/or the current issue of Standard Rate and Data Service's "Spot Radio Rates and Data." These data may not be precise.

l. Situations in which AM/FM affiliates have the same call letters may result in respondent confusion in correctly identifying the station to which the listening occurred.

m. To the extent that any provisions contained in this section "Limitations", are inconsistent or conflict with any provisions contained in the "Special Notices" on Page 5 of this report, such special notices should be deemed to supersede and/or amend this section of the report.

Retention of Raw Materials

40. Retention Schedule—In-tab Arbitron listening diaries used for the computation of the audience estimates published in this report will be stored and used for cross-tabulations for eleven months from the closing date of the survey and then destroyed along with all unusable diaries. Subscribers to this report are advised that if special cross-tabulations of the reported estimates are desired, they should be ordered before the retention period has expired. Upon proper appointment, subscribers to this report may examine the in-tab Arbitron listening diaries (prior to the destruction thereof) at Arbitron's Beltsville offices.

Appendix B-Extract of Arbitron Television Market Report for Portland, Oregon, November 1977

ARBITRON TELEVISION

Audience Estimates in the
Arbitron Market of

Portland, OR

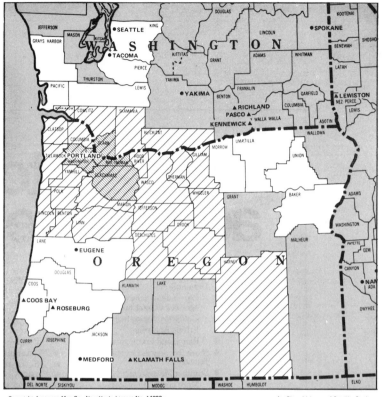

Copyright American Map Co., New York, License No. 14092.

▲ City of License of Satellite Station

The "Total Survey Area" of this market is shown in white on the accompanying map. Where appropriate, the "Area of Dominant Influence" is indicated by coarse cross-hatching and the Arbitron "Metro (or Home County) Rating Area" by fine cross-hatching.

Survey Period: November 2-November 29, 1977
Survey Months:

OCT NOV FEB MAY JUL
This report is furnished for the exclusive use of network, advertiser, advertising agency, and film company clients, plus these subscribing stations—

KATU   KVDO   KOIN   KOAC

KGW   KOAP   KPTV

Schedule of Survey Dates 1977-78

October	Sept. 28-Oct. 25, 1977
November	Nov. 2-Nov. 29, 1977
December	Nov. 30-Dec. 27, 1977
January	Jan. 4-Jan. 31, 1978
February	Feb. 1-Feb. 28, 1978
March	March 1-March 28, 1978
May	May 3-May 30, 1978
July	July 5-Aug. 1, 1978

Estimates of Households in Market

	TSA	Pct TV HH	ADI	Pct TV HH	Metro Rating Area	Pct TV HH
TOTAL HOUSEHOLDS	1,557,600		682,200		417,500	
TV HOUSEHOLDS	1,483,500	100	649,200	100	400,500	100
COLOR TV HH	1,211,000	82	532,500	82	328,200	82
MULTI-SET TVHH	622,200	42	300,300	46	209,000	52
CATV SUBSCRIBERS	288,500	19	84,100	13	5,600	1
UHF TV HH	1,245,400	84	551,800	85	336,600	84

Television Stations

Call Letters	Channel Number	Affiliation	Identification Authorized by FCC
KATU	2	ABC	PORTLAND, OR
KVDO	3	ETV	SALEM, OR
KOIN	6	CBS	PORTLAND, OR
KOAC	7	ETV	CORVALLIS, OR
KGW	8	NBC	PORTLAND, OR
KOAP	10	ETV	PORTLAND, OR
KPTV	12	IND	PORTLAND, OR

Counties Included in Survey Area

Key	ADI Assignment		TV HH In Adjacent ADI	Adjacent ADI Market
A	COUNTY IS IN HOME MARKET ADI			
1	COUNTY IS IN ADJACENT ADI 1		132,200	EUGENE
2	COUNTY IS IN ADJACENT ADI 2		94,900	MEDFORD
3	COUNTY IS IN ADJACENT ADI 3		863,100	SEATTLE-TACOMA
0	COUNTY IS IN OTHER ADI MARKET			

ADI Key			CATV Pct	County	State	TV HH Estimates	TV HH In-Tab	ADI Key			CATV Pct	County	State	TV HH Estimates	TV HH In-Tab
0			59.5	BAKER	OR	5,600	12	A	C		23.2	POLK	OR	14,600	16
A	C		32.2	BENTON	OR	20,300	25	A			11.1	SHERMAN	OR	900	4
A	M		3.2	CLACKAMAS	OR	70,800	96	A			71.6	TILLAMOOK	OR	6,400	17
A	C		79.0	CLATSOP	OR	11,000	18	0	C		52.1	UMATILLA	OR	16,700	34
A			11.1	COLUMBIA	OR	10,800	19	0	C		65.3	UNION	OR	7,900	11
1	C		66.0	COOS	OR	19,100	47	A			74.3	WASCO	OR	6,900	7
A			51.2	CROOK	OR	4,300	5	A	M			WASHINGTON	OR	67,200	115
A			59.9	DESCHUTES	OR	14,600	14	A			6.3	YAMHILL	OR	15,700	9
1	C		35.4	DOUGLAS	OR	27,500	63	A	M		.6	CLARK	WA	56,700	83
A			74.7	GILLIAM	OR	600	3	A	C		48.2	COWLITZ	WA	25,800	17
A			78.3	HARNEY	OR	2,300	5	3	C		77.7	GRAYS HARBOR	WA	21,700	23
A			36.8	HOOD RIVER	OR	5,400	5	3	C		13.5	KING	WA	435,700	491
2	C		28.7	JACKSON	OR	43,100	125	A			48.0	KLICKITAT	WA	4,700	2
A			50.4	JEFFERSON	OR	3,200	4	3	C		40.3	LEWIS	WA	18,200	17
1	C		45.3	LANE	OR	85,600	177	3			83.0	PACIFIC	WA	6,100	4
A			85.0	LINCOLN	OR	10,200	9	3	C		17.3	PIERCE	WA	145,400	152
A			17.0	LINN	OR	28,200	21	A			44.7	SKAMANIA	WA	1,900	7
A			2.3	MARION	OR	59,100	47	A			26.2	WAHKIAKUM	WA	1,300	8
0			42.8	MORROW	OR	1,700	4								
A	M		1.5	MULTNOMAH	OR	205,800	284								

M=METRO COUNTY
C=CATV CONTROL IMPLEMENTED

TOTALS 1,483,500 2,006

Demographic Characteristics

Under Arbitron's Stabilized Demographic Characteristics Procedure, each market's demographic characteristics remain constant throughout the entire broadcast year, except in cases of market definition changes or reports including counties with no in-tab households.

Population estimates are shown for each market's TSA and ADI, and include all sex-age categories for which audience estimates are reported in the Television Market Report. These Arbitron estimates include *only* persons living in Television Households, and are based on total households projections and population estimates provided by Market Statistics, Inc. For a description of the Stabilized Demographic Characteristics Procedure, please see the section of this report entitled *Projection of*

Audiences or see separate publication provided to all television report subscribers entitled *Description of Methodology.*

The user should be aware that there are no existing Census data which are directly comparable to the projections shown on this page. The Bureau of the Census issues reports within *all* households, including those without television sets. Census estimates have been updated and projected to January 1, 1978 by Market Statistics Inc.

The *In-Tab Sample Sizes* for all reported audience categories may be used with the Standard Error and Percentage of Error formulas (on the last page of this report) for a determination of an estimate of sampling error.

| | | Total Survey Area | | | | | ADI | | | |
| | | MSI Est* Pct of Total | Distribution in TV HH | | | In-Tab Sample Sizes | MSI Est* Pct of Total | Distribution in TV HH | | In-Tab Sample Sizes |
			Projections	Pct of Total	Pct of Group			Projections	Pct of Total	
PERSONS 2+		100.0	3,910,100	100.0	100.0	5,498	100.0	1,717,200	100.0	2,365
ADULTS 18+		73.7	2,880,800	73.7	100.0	3,998	73.5	1,263,200	73.6	1,686
PERSONS 15-24		20.3	792,200	20.3	100.0	928	19.4	332,800	19.4	409
PERSONS 12-34		42.9	1,682,100	43.0	100.0	2,196	41.8	716,900	41.7	1,000
WOMEN	TOTAL	38.0	1,485,600	38.0	100.0	2,112	38.4	660,100	38.4	910
	18-49	24.0	938,900	24.0	63.2	1,377	23.6	406,100	23.6	608
	15-24	10.1	395,000	10.1	26.6	478	10.0	171,500	10.0	227
	18-34	15.6	611,700	15.6	41.2	820	15.3	263,200	15.3	384
	25-49	16.9	659,600	16.9	44.4	1,064	16.7	286,200	16.7	457
	25-54	19.7	771,700	19.7	51.9	1,225	19.6	336,600	19.6	526
	25-64	24.6	961,100	24.6	64.7	1,541	24.7	424,800	24.7	659
	WRKNG	NA	429,200	11.0	100.0	632	NA	193,100	11.2	288
MEN	TOTAL	35.7	1,395,200	35.7	100.0	1,886	35.1	603,100	35.1	776
	18-49	23.9	933,600	23.9	66.9	1,263	22.8	390,900	22.8	535
	18-34	15.7	615,100	15.7	44.1	721	14.8	253,300	14.8	318
	25-49	16.8	656,800	16.8	47.1	990	16.5	282,700	16.5	424
	25-54	19.6	766,400	19.6	54.9	1,132	19.2	330,400	19.2	469
TEENS	TOTAL	11.6	455,300	11.6	100.0	655	11.7	200,400	11.7	298
	GIRLS	5.7	222,700	5.7	48.9	322	5.7	98,200	5.7	150
CHILDREN	TOTAL	14.7	574,000	14.7	100.0	845	14.8	253,600	14.8	381
	6-11	9.6	375,300	9.6	65.4	548	9.5	163,400	9.5	241
HOUSEHOLDS BY AGE OF HEAD OF HOUSEHOLD										
	TOTAL	100.0	1,483,500	100.0			100.0	649,200	100.0	
	UNDER 35	32.2	477,700	32.2			30.6	198,400	30.6	
	35-54	32.5	481,700	32.5			31.7	205,900	31.7	
	55+	35.3	524,100	35.3			37.7	244,900	37.7	

*Census estimates updated to January 1, 1978 by Market Statistics, Inc., based on estimates from Sales Management's 1977 "Survey of Buying Power."

NA = Updated Census data not available.

Sample Placement, In-Tab and Effective Sample Bases

The columns below show: the estimated number of television households in the original computer-drawn sample; the number of those households accepting diaries; the number of households returning usable (in-tab) diaries; an estimate of the television households Effective Sample (ESB); the Standard Error Weighting Factor; the number of ADI in-tab diaries for each week of the survey; and the ADI weekly rating ESB.

| | Est TV HH in Original Sample | TV HH Accepting Diaries | TV HH In-Tab | Est TV HH ESB | Standard Error Weighting Factor | Weekly ADI TV HH Ratings | | |
							In-Tab	ESB
METRO RATING AREA-STD. SAMPLE	562	507	328					
METRO RATING AREA-ESF	464	403	250					
METRO RATING AREA-TOTAL	1,026	910	578	562		WEEK 1	211	181
ADI (INCLUDING METRO)	1,512	1,327	846	726	1.07	WEEK 2	205	174
BALANCE OF SURVEY AREA	2,285	1,929	1,160			WEEK 3	224	194
TOTAL SURVEY AREA	3,797	3,256	2,006	1,742	.95	WEEK 4	206	179

Average Quarter - Hours Viewed Per Week in the TSA and in the ADI

Estimates of the average number of quarter-hours viewed in the average week within sample households in the Total Survey Area and in the ADI are shown: by Household, the average number of quarter-hours per household in which there was viewing of one or more sets; by Women, the average number of quarter-hours viewed by all women age 18 + within the household; by Men, the average number of quarter-hours viewed by all men age 18 + within the household.

VIEWED PER WEEK IN TSA	BY HOUSEHOLDS	166.2	BY WOMEN	94.8	BY MEN	80.4
VIEWED PER WEEK IN ADI	BY HOUSEHOLDS	169.2	BY WOMEN	95.0	BY MEN	80.1

Special Notices

1. Notices in this column are of a specific nature, applying only to this Television Market Report.

The information appearing on this page related to Technical Difficulties is furnished solely for the use of Arbitron clients in making their own evaluation of the audience estimates reported. Such occurrences may have had an affect on viewing or the recording thereof and Arbitron makes no attempt to assess their impact. For details on the Arbitron policy of reporting Technical Difficulties, see the separate publication provided to all television report subscribers entitled *Description of Methodology.*

The information appearing on this page related to Rating Distortion activities is based upon Arbitron's policy statement dated May 20, 1977.

Special notices relating to a station appear only in the station's home market report.

THE EXPANDED SAMPLE FRAME (ESF) TECHNIQUE HAS BEEN IMPLEMENTED IN THE METRO RATING AREA OF THIS MARKET. ADDITIONALLY, THE TSA OF THIS MARKET CONTAINS ONE OR MORE COUNTIES IN THE METRO RATING AREA OF SEATTLE-TACOMA, WHERE THE ESF TECHNIQUE HAS ALSO BEEN IMPLEMENTED. ESF IS DESIGNED TO SUPPLEMENT THE STANDARD ARBITRON SAMPLE SELECTION PROCEDURES AND TO INCLUDE HOUSEHOLDS WITH UNLISTED TELEPHONE NUMBERS. TELEVISION HOUSEHOLDS ACCEPTING DIARIES WERE MEASURED IN ACCORDANCE WITH STANDARD ARBITRON PROCEDURES. TELEPHONE RETRIEVAL WAS IMPLEMENTED FOR ESF HOUSEHOLDS LOCATED IN HIGH DENSITY BLACK AREAS.

STATIONS KOAC-TV (ETV), KOAP-TV (ETV) AND KVDO-TV (ETV) ARE NOW CLIENTS TO THIS REPORT. CLIENT ETV STATIONS WHICH QUALIFY ACCORDING TO NORMAL MINIMUM REPORTING STANDARDS APPEAR IN THE TIME PERIOD AVERAGES SECTION AS WELL AS THE DAY-PART SUMMARY OF THIS REPORT.

DURING THE PERIOD COVERED BY THIS SURVEY, STATION KVDO-TV WAS OFF THE AIR AT THE FOLLOWING TIMES:

```
 1:50 PM  TO   2:22 PM   THURSDAY    NOVEMBER   3
10:47 PM  TO  11:00 PM   FRIDAY      NOVEMBER   4
 7:30 AM  TO   8:06 AM   TUESDAY     NOVEMBER   8
 2:08 PM  TO   2:44 PM   WEDNESDAY   NOVEMBER  23
```

DURING THE PERIOD COVERED BY THIS SURVEY, STATION KOAC-TV WAS OFF THE AIR FROM 10:30 AM TO 1:30 PM ON THURSDAY, NOVEMBER 17.

DURING THE PERIOD COVERED BY THIS SURVEY, STATION KGW-TV EXPERIENCED TECHNICAL DIFFICULTY FROM 10:37 AM TO 10:44 AM ON THURSDAY, NOVEMBER 17.

2. The following notices are of a general nature, applying to the methods and procedures used in all Television Market Reports.

> **RATING DISTORTION** — ARBITRON WILL DELETE FROM ITS PUBLISHED REPORTS THE AUDIENCE ESTIMATES FOR STATIONS THAT HAVE ENGAGED IN RATING DISTORTION ACTIVITIES. Rating Distortion is defined as station activity which may affect the way in which diarykeepers record their viewing without causing corresponding changes in actual viewing. This includes activities which confuse diarykeepers and which Arbitron believes are likely to cause diarykeepers to:
> a. Use their diary as an "entry form" for a contest; or
> b. Record television viewing in their diary which exceeds their actual viewing.
> When a station's audience estimates are to be deleted for Rating Distortion activities, a sticker will appear on the cover of the Television Market Report, and the station's activities will be noted on Page 5 of that report.

THANKSGIVING DAY DELETION — Arbitron has deleted all viewing estimates for Thanksgiving Day, Thursday, November 24, 6:00 AM to 3:30 PM.

Audience estimates for this time period have been deleted from all sections of this report, including Day-Part Summary, Network Program Averages, Time Period Averages and Program Audiences.

As a result, week 4 audience estimates for Monday-Friday before 3:30 PM are 4 day averages. Monday-Friday averages do not include audience estimates for the deleted time period, except PVT's. Both PVT's and average quarter-hours viewed per week (Page 4) are full four-week estimates.

This deletion enables Arbitron to provide Monday-Friday program audience estimates, prior to 3:30 PM, which include up to 19 days.

Symbols Used in this Report

3. Index to symbols used in Television Market Reports:

Day-Part Audience Summary
    ٭٭ = Estimates based on less air time than unmarked stations.
    + = Parent plus Satellite estimates.

Weekly Programming and Time Period Averages
    — = Station did not achieve a reportable rating.
    ٭ = Sample below minimum for reporting weekly ratings.
    ≠ = Station experienced technical difficulty (see notice this page).
    < = In the M-F Section this indicates program was aired less than five days in M-F Period.
    + = Parent plus Satellite audience estimates.
    (DP) = Parent and Satellite carried different programs during part or all of marked time period.

    (SP) = Parent and Satellite carried same programming during entire marked time period.
    N.O.A. = Not On Air

Program Audiences
    ٭ = Program estimates included in an average.
    ≠ = Station experienced technical difficulty (see notice this page).
    Letter code following Parent + Satellite = fourth and eighth characters of Program Title of Parent Station. Usually two letters will follow on the "Parent + Satellite" line (e.g., TELL TRUTH = LU). However, if either the fourth or eighth character is a blank space, only one letter will appear (e.g., TONIGHT SHOW = I). This letter code allows the user to determine which Parent + Satellite average goes with which program title.

ADI Market Data

TV Net Weekly Circulation

The estimated number of unduplicated Television Households in the ADI which viewed a station for at least five continuous minutes, at least once during a survey week, is reported for each home commercial station. To be reported, a station must have had a Net Weekly Circulation of at least 500 Television Households. Circulation of stations with satellites is the combined circulation of the Parent and its Satellites. Such stations are indicated by a plus (+) sign next to the *PARENT* station call letters. Based on Arbitron nationwide surveys of May and November 1976 and February 1977, these estimates have been compiled according to 1977-78 ADI definitions and projected to January 1, 1978 Television Households. Arbitron is unable to report estimates for stations operational since February 1977.

Station	Circulation	Pct	Station	Circulation	Pct
KATU	585,000	90	KGW	572,000	88
KOAC	19,000	3	KOAP	180,000	28
KOIN	602,000	93	KPTV	508,000	78
KVDO	21,000	3			

Chain Grocery Stores

The number of stores within the ADI owned or operated by each chain company is furnished by Progressive Grocer Co., based on information from its files current to September 1977. A chain company is defined as an operator of 11 or more retail stores. Supermarket, superette and convenience store chains are included. Progressive Grocer defines supermarket as any grocery store with an annual sales volume of $1,000,000 or more, and superette as any grocery store with sales from $500,000 to $1,000,000 per year. It defines a convenience store as a small, compact, self-service store, open long hours and featuring a limited line of brands and sizes, with an annual sales volume of about $225,000.

Company Name	Number	Company Name	Number
ALBERTSONS INC	24	BIG C MARKET	2
DARI MART STORES INC	3	DISCO FOODS	6
KEIL'S FOOD STORES	7	KIENOWS FOOD STORES	13
MARKET BASKET STORES	26	MAYFAIR MARKET	6
MC KAYS MARKETS	87	PLAID PANTRY MARKET	87
QUICK SHOP MINIT MARTS	43	ROSAUERS SUPER MARKETS	1
ROTH'S IGA FOODLINERS	6	SAFEWAY STORES INC	60
SEVEN ELEVEN STORES	71	SWIFT MART INC	12
TRADEWELL STORES INC	25	UDDENBERGS THRIFTWAY I	1
WAREMART INC	7		

Magazine and Newspaper Circulation

Circulation and percent penetration figures for magazines and newspapers were furnished by American Newspaper Markets, Inc., as published in CIRCULATION '77/'78. Most circulation figures are adjusted by American Newspaper Markets, Inc. and represent a 12-month net paid average. Newspaper circulation is total daily circulation (excluding Sunday) with a breakout of morning and evening circulation figures of 2-buy newspapers. Circulation for once per day newspapers is reported in the PM column. Newspapers shown are limited to those published within the ADI. These figures do not necessarily represent unduplicated households within the ADI.

Further information about the data reported here, or additional information about magazine or newspaper circulation is available from American Newspaper Markets, Inc., Box 182, Northfield, Illinois 60093, (312) 446-6200.

Magazine	Circulation	Pct	Magazine	Circulation	Pct
AM HME	23,787	3.5	PET HO	88,402	13.2
COSMO	19,745	2.9	F CIRC	115,421	17.2
FARM J	10,142	1.5	FORTN	4,622	.7
GDHSK	52,169	7.8	LHJ	59,939	8.9
MCCL	61,100	9.1	N GEO	102,158	15.2
NWSWK	29,346	4.4	NWYRKR	3,369	.5
OTDR L	24,848	3.7	PEOPLE	21,285	3.2
PLAY B	58,167	8.7	R DGST	219,254	32.7
RED BK	44,843	6.7	17	14,583	2.2
SPTILL	24,322	3.6	TTMF	42,847	6.4
TV GUI	238,227	35.5	USNEWS	24,997	3.7
VOGUE	4,152	.6	WO DAY	112,039	16.7

Paper	AM Circ	Pct	PM Circ	Pct
ALBANY DEMOCRAT-HERALD			18,897	3
ASTORIA ASTORIAN			7,609	1
BEND BULLETIN			13,733	2
CORVALLIS GAZETTE-TIMES			12,775	2
LONGVIEW NEWS			23,868	4
OREGON CITY ENTRPRS-COURIER			7,567	1
PORTLAND OREGONIAN, OREGON J	207,928	31	99,107	15
SALEM ORE STATESMN, CAPITL J	42,299	6	21,900	3
THE DALLES CHRONICLE			5,235	1
VANCOUVER COLUMBIAN			34,906	5

ADI Market Data

Sales Data

Effective Buying Income, Total Retail Sales, and seven categories of store sales have been compiled by Market Statistics, Inc., and furnished to Arbitron. These data, based on SALES MANAGEMENT'S "1977 Survey of Buying Power" updated to January 1977, were rearranged according to Arbitron's 1977-78 ADI definitions. For further information on MSI's demographic and socioeconomic data, contact: SALES MANAGEMENT, 633 Third Avenue, New York, New York 10017, (212) 986-4800.

ADI Households		Per Cent of U.S.	ADI Rank
Total Households	682,200	.91	22
Television Households	649,200	.89	24

	$ AMOUNT (000)	
Effective Buying Income	10,068,906	27
Total Retail Sales	5,632,261	26
Food Store Sales	1,538,084	17
Supermarket Sales	1,464,196	18
General Merchandise Store Sales	564,122	43
Department Store Sales	445,733	39
Furn-Household-Appliance Store Sales	281,372	28
Automotive Store Sales	1,134,309	23
Drug Store Sales	166,016	28

Census Data

Westat, Inc. has extracted the reported items for Arbitron from the 1970 Census Supplementary Report HC (S1-7), Fourth Count Housing and Population Summary Tape Files. This Census information has been rearranged according to Arbitron's 1977-78 ADI definitions.

For further information about the data reported here, or additional statistical census information, contact: Westat, Inc., 11600 Nebel Street, Rockville, Maryland 20852, (301) 881-5310.

Years School Completed (Number of Persons 25+)		Occupation (Number of Persons 16+)	
Elementary		White Collar	308,624
(1-8 Years)	184,854	Blue Collar	215,118
High School		Farm Workers	19,606
(1-4 Years)	485,168	Service Workers	76,140
College		Occupation Not	6,544
(1 Year or More)	235,354	Reported	

Value of Housing (Number of Owner Occupied Units)		Second Home (Number of Households With)	
		Yes	24,399
Less Than $10,000	52,671	No	522,768
$10,000-$14,999	79,974		
$15,000-$19,999	73,842	Farm Residents	
$20,000-$24,999	42,252	(Percentage of ADI	
$25,000-$34,999	32,561	Population Residing	
$35,000-$49,999	12,261	On Rural Farms)	4%
$50,000 and Over	4,634		
Median Value	$ 16,114	Automobiles Available (In Occupied Housing Units)	

Family Income (Number of Families)			
		None	69,451
		1	258,588
		2	181,140
Under $5,000	76,118	3 or More	37,988
$ 5,000-$ 9,999	141,110		
$10,000-$14,999	126,153	Means of Transportation	
$15,000-$24,999	65,711	To Work	
$25,000 and Over	17,319		
		Private Vehicle	509,620
Median Income	$ 9,856	Public Conveyance	25,241
		Other	80,940

Passenger Car Registrations

ADI Share of New Private Passenger Car Registrations is supplied by the Motor Statistical Division of R. L. Polk and Co. Polk prepares monthly reports (actual census) of new cars registered in each state. Fleet, other commercial or government registrations are not included. Figures shown are for the entire 1977 model year.

Further automotive statistical information may be obtained from the Motor Statistical Division, R. L. Polk and Co., Polk Building, 431 Howard Street, Detroit, Michigan 48231, (313) 961-9470.

Manufacturer	1977 Model Year Pct
American Motors Corporation	1.4
Chrysler Corporation	11.2
Ford Motor Company	16.0
General Motors Corporation	29.2
Other	42.2
Total	100.0

Chain Drug Stores

The National Association of Boards of Pharmacy, through Medical Mailing Services, Inc., has furnished Arbitron with Chain Drug Store information current to August 1976. NABP defines a chain drug company as one having four or more stores. In addition, NABP includes only those company stores with licensed pharmacies in its list of chain drug stores. In the event of store name change, the parent company is not identified.

Further information regarding chain drug stores may be obtained from Medical Mailing Services, Inc., One IBM Plaza, Chicago, Illinois 60611, (312) 467-9500, or the National Association of Boards of Pharmacy.

Company Name	Number	Company Name	Number
BI MART DRUGS	2	CENT-WISE DRUG STORE	4
DISCO MART PHCY	1	ECONOMY DRUGS	1
FRED MEYER INC	24	OLYMPIC DRUG	1
OREGON RETIRED PERSONS PHCY	1	PAY LESS DRUG STORE	15
PAY N SAVE DRUGS	4	PAY N TAKIT STORES INC	3
PERMANENTE SERV PHAR	2	SAV-RITE INC	1
VALU MART DRUG	1	WALGREENS	1
WHITE CROSS PHARMACY	1		

SPECIAL NOTICE

MAGAZINE CIRCULATION DATA WERE INCORRECTLY REPORTED FOR SEVEN MAGAZINES IN THIS MARKET'S OCTOBER 1977 REPORT. SEE PAGE 6 OF THIS REPORT FOR CORRECTLY REPORTED CIRCULATION FOR THE FOLLOWING MAGAZINES:

PEOPLE

PLAYBOY

READER'S DIGEST

RED BOOK

17

SPORTS ILLUSTRATED

TIME

PLEASE NOTE THAT AMERICAN NEWSPAPER MARKETS, INC. NOW PROVIDES CIRCULATION DATA FOR PEOPLE MAGAZINE, REPLACING TRUE MAGAZINE.

ADI Market Data

Day-Part Audience Summary

DAY-PART AND STATION	ADI RTG (1)	ADI SH (2)	METRO RTG (3)	METRO SH (4)	TV HH (5)	2+ (6)	18+ (7)	15-24 (8)	12-34 (9)	W TOT 18+ (10)	W 18-49 (11)	W 15-24 (12)	W 18-34 (13)	W 25-49 (14)	W 25-54 (15)	WKG WMN 18+ (16)	M TOT 18+ (17)	M 18-49 (18)	M 18-34 (19)	M 25-49 (20)	M 25-54 (21)	TEENS TOT (22)	GIRLS (23)	2-11 (24)	6-11 (25)
MON-FRI 7.00A -9.00A																									
KATU	5	26	5	29	33	41	39	5	10	26	12	3	6	9	10	3	13	7	4	5	5			2	1
** KVDO																									
KOIN	2	9	2	11	12	18	14		2	7	2		1	2	3	1	7	3	1	3	4			4	1
** KOAC																									
KGW	4	23	4	23	28	37	36	2	5	21	6	1	3	5	9	5	15	4	2	3	5			1	1
** KOAP																									
KPTV	6	35	6	38	45	67	14	6	18	9	8	3	6	6	6	2	5	4	4	2	2	8	3	45	24
HUT/PVT/TOT	18		16		118	163	103	13	35	63	28	7	16	22	28	11	40	18	11	13	16	8	3	52	27
9.00A -NOON																									
KATU	5	29	5	29	37	48	41	11	19	28	17	8	11	10	11	4	13	6	5	3	3	3	2	4	2
KVDO																									
KOIN	4	23	4	23	30	34	33	2	7	26	10	2	6	8	10		7	3	1	3	3			1	
KOAC					2	2																		2	
KGW	4	23	4	24	28	36	31	7	13	19	10	4	6	7	8	4	12	5	4	2	3	3	2	2	1
KOAP	1	5	1	6	6	6																		6	1
KPTV	3	15	3	18	20	23	18	5	11	15	10	4	7	7	8	1	3	2	2	1	1	2	1	3	1
HUT/PVT/TOT	18		17		123	149	123	25	50	88	47	18	30	32	37	9	35	16	12	9	10	8	5	18	5
NOON -4.30P																									
KATU	5	19	5	20	34	36	33	9	15	27	18	8	12	11	12	3	6	3	2	2	2	1	1	2	1
KVDO					1																				
KOIN	6	22	5	21	40	48	47	4	10	34	13	3	7	11	13	3	13	3	2	3	2	1	1		
KOAC																									
KGW	6	24	7	29	41	56	46	12	25	33	20	8	14	14	17	6	13	8	5	5	5	6	4	4	3
KOAP					1	1																		1	
KPTV	7	29	7	31	51	73	45	15	31	25	16	8	11	10	11	5	20	13	10	7	8	10	5	18	11
HUT/PVT/TOT	25		23		168	214	171	40	81	119	67	27	44	46	53	17	52	27	19	16	18	18	11	25	15
4.30P -6.00P																									
KATU	7	16	8	17	53	86	70	17	33	43	24	10	15	16	19	10	27	16	10	10	12	8	4	8	6
KVDO																									
KOIN	13	29	13	29	96	153	147	10	20	83	24	4	9	21	29	14	64	20	8	15	22	3	1	3	2
KOAC					1	1																		1	1
KGW	8	18	9	20	56	89	77	13	28	44	19	8	12	13	19	10	33	14	8	11	14	8	4	4	3
KOAP	1	2	1	2	6	7	1		1	1	1		1	1	1									6	2
KPTV	14	31	15	33	97	168	64	35	77	36	29	17	21	17	19	9	28	21	16	12	14	40	18	64	45
HUT/PVT/TOT	46		45		309	504	359	75	159	207	97	39	58	68	87	43	152	71	42	48	62	59	27	86	59
5.00P -7.30P																									
KATU	11	19	10	19	75	122	106	17	38	57	24	8	13	18	22	15	49	27	16	20	23	9	4	7	5
KVDO					1																				
KOIN	14	25	14	25	99	160	149	13	30	82	29	6	13	24	32	18	67	26	12	20	28	5	2	6	5
KOAC					1																				
KGW	11	20	12	23	75	114	107	10	25	61	22	6	12	17	25	14	46	17	9	14	18	4	2	3	2
KOAP	1	1	1	1	4	5	2		1	2	1		1	1	1									3	1
KPTV	18	32	18	34	120	230	123	51	109	72	56	29	40	35	39	19	51	39	28	25	29	41	20	66	46
HUT/PVT/TOT	56		55		375	631	487	91	203	274	132	49	79	95	119	66	213	109	65	79	98	59	28	85	59
6.00P -7.30P																									
KATU	12	20	11	19	84	141	123	17	39	63	23	6	10	19	24	16	60	33	19	25	29	10	4	8	6
KVDO					1	1																		1	1
KOIN	13	22	13	22	90	149	133	16	36	73	30	8	14	24	32	18	60	26	14	20	27	8	3	8	6
KOAC					1	1											1				1			1	
KGW	13	22	14	25	86	134	125	14	32	70	25	8	14	19	27	17	55	21	12	17	22	6	3	3	2
KOAP			1	1		2											1							1	
KPTV	19	32	20	35	130	254	151	56	120	87	68	33	49	43	47	24	64	47	33	31	37	38	19	65	44
HUT/PVT/TOT	58		57		395	683	536	103	227	295	146	55	87	105	130	75	241	127	78	93	116	62	29	85	59
7.00P -7.30P																									
KATU	14	24	13	22	98	164	139	21	48	67	22	7	11	17	21	17	72	41	25	31	33	12	4	13	9
KVDO					1	2																		2	1
KOIN	12	21	12	21	87	136	125	14	27	72	27	6	10	23	31	16	53	20	11	14	23	6	3	5	4
KOAC					1																				
KGW	11	20	14	24	78	128	112	18	42	66	33	11	19	24	29	18	46	25	15	20	23	8	4	8	5
KOAP	1	1	1	2	4	7	7	1	3	3	1		1	1	1		4	2	2	1	2				
KPTV	17	30	19	33	120	237	148	49	108	86	66	31	46	42	47	25	62	45	29	31	37	33	18	56	40
HUT/PVT/TOT	58		57		389	674	531	103	228	294	149	55	87	107	129	76	237	133	82	97	118	59	29	84	59
7.30P -8.00P																									
KATU	14	26	14	26	100	183	134	32	77	62	35	14	23	25	29	15	72	49	33	37	40	21	9	28	19
KVDO					2	3																		3	2
KOIN	13	23	13	23	90	146	131	15	30	72	29	7	10	25	33	18	59	24	12	18	27	8	4	7	5
KOAC					1																				
KGW	11	20	12	21	77	124	105	18	37	63	28	11	17	20	25	16	42	20	12	14	17	8	5	11	8
KOAP	1	1	1	1	5	3	3			3															
KPTV	15	27	17	30	105	196	132	35	76	72	47	20	30	32	37	21	60	38	24	26	32	22	12	42	31
HUT/PVT/TOT	56		54		380	655	505	100	220	272	139	52	80	102	124	70	233	131	81	95	116	59	30	91	65

** ESTIMATES BASED ON LESS AIRTIME THAN UNMARKED STATIONS
+ PARENT/SATELLITE RELATIONSHIP

Day-Part Audience Summary

DAY-PART AND STATION	TV HOUSE-HOLDS (26)	WOMEN 18-49 (27)	WOMEN 18+ (28)	MEN 18+ (29)	TSA HH PER ADI RTG PT (00) (30)	ADI TV HH RTG (1)	SH (2)	PERSONS 15-24 (31)	12-34 (32)	WOMEN TOT 18+ (33)	WOMEN 18-49 (34)	WOMEN 15-24 (35)	WOMEN 18-34 (36)	WOMEN 25-49 (37)	WOMEN 25-54 (38)	WKG WMN 18+ (39)	MEN TOT 18+ (40)	MEN 18-49 (41)	MEN 18-34 (42)	MEN 25-49 (43)	MEN 25-54 (44)	TNS TOT 12-17 (45)	CHILD 2-11 (46)	CHILD 6-11 (47)	METRO (48)	HOME ADI (49)	ADJ #1 (50)	ADJ #2 (51)	ADJ #3 (52)	ADJ RTG #1 (53)	ADJ RTG #2 (54)	ADJ RTG #3 (55)
MON-FRI 7.00A-9.00A																																
KATU	99	44	78	53	69	5	26	2	1	4	3	2	2	3	3	2	2	2	1	1	1				55	94	1		4			
** KVDO																																
KOIN	60	13	38	31	77	2	9			1				1	1	1	1	1		1	1		2	1	55	88	9			1		
** KOAC	1		1	1																							89	10				
KGW	93	28	82	63	67	4	23	1	1	3	1	1	1	2	3	2	2	1	1	1	1				53	99	1					
** KOAP	4	1	2	1																					26	100						
KPTV	156	39	45	37	71	6	35	1	2	1	2	1	2	2	1	1	1	1	1	1	1	4	16	13	53	93	7			2		
HUT/PVT/TOT						18		4	5	10	7	4	6	8	8	6	7	5	4	4	5	5	19	15								
9.00A-NOON																																
KATU	237	121	195	115	71	5	29	3	3	4	4	4	4	3	3	2	2	2	2	1	1	1	2	1	54	93	2		5			
KVDO	7	1	1																							77	21	2				
KOIN	183	74	174	71	71	4	23	1	1	4	2	1	2	3	3		1			1	1				53	91	8			2	1	
KOAC	15	2	2	1																					11	51	49					
KGW	169	77	144	85	68	4	23	2	2	3	2	2	2	2	2	2	2	1	2	1	1	1	1	1	60	98	1		1			
KOAP	44	11	16	5	66	1	5																2		75	100						
KPTV	132	65	97	45	72	3	15	1	1	2	2	2	2	2	2	1	1	1	1		1	1	1	1	61	91	6	1	2	1		
HUT/PVT/TOT						18		8	8	13	11	9	11	11	11	5	7	5	6	5	5	5	9	6								
NOON-4.30P																																
KATU	199	117	175	97	71	5	19	3	2	4	4	5	5	3	3	1	1	1	1	1	1	1	1		55	92	1	1	6			
KVDO	9	3	6	5																						86	13	1				
KOIN	266	117	258	141	72	6	22	1	1	5	3	2	3	4	1		2	1	1	1	1	1			49	91	6		3	2		
KOAC	8	3	4	1																					18	82						
KGW	255	136	231	151	68	6	24	3	3	5	4	4	5	4	4	2	2	2	2	2	1	3	2	2	66	96	1		1			
KOAP	36	9	15	9																					75	99						
KPTV	289	132	187	149	72	7	29	5	4	3	4	5	4	3	3	2	3	3	4	2	2	5	7	6	57	91	5		4	2		
HUT/PVT/TOT						25		13	12	18	16	16	17	15	15	8	10	8	9	6	6	11	11	10								
4.30P-6.00P																																
KATU	239	124	207	159	72	7	16	5	4	6	5	6	5	5	5	5	4	4	3	3	3	3	3	3	58	90	1		6	1		
KVDO	4	2	3	2																					34	96		3				
KOIN	289	102	273	226	72	13	29	3	3	11	6	2	3	7	7		9	5	3	5	6	1	1	1	54	91	7		1	5		
KOAC	6	1	1	1																					67	33						
KGW	260	122	230	179	69	8	18	4	4	6	4	4	4	4	5	5	5	3	3	3	4	3	2	2	65	95	1		1			
KOAP	29	9	9	6	71	1	2																2	1	83	100						
KPTV	282	149	183	146	68	14	31	10	10	5	7	10	8	6	5	4	4	5	6	4	4	19	24	26	62	95	3		2	2		
HUT/PVT/TOT						46		23	22	30	23	24	22	23	24	21	24	18	17	16	18	29	34	37								
5.00P-7.30P																																
KATU	399	175	328	343	71	11	19	5	5	8	5	4	5	6	6	7	7	7	6	7	7	4	2	3	55	91	1		5	1		
KVDO	11	2	4	2																					23	65	33	2				
KOIN	385	174	358	312	71	14	25	4	4	11	7	4	5	8	9	9	10	6	5	6	7	3	2	2	56	92	6		1	5		
KOAC	12	3	7	5																					44	53	3		1			
KGW	303	147	290	248	67	11	20	3	4	9	5	4	5	6	7	7	8	4	4	5	5	2	1	1	66	97			1			
KOAP	44	14	25	25	68	1	1																1	1	79	100						
KPTV	378	255	340	282	69	18	32	15	15	10	13	16	15	11	11	9	8	10	11	8	8	20	24	26	61	95	4		2	3		
HUT/PVT/TOT						56		28	29	40	32	29	30	32	34	33	35	28	27	28	30	30	33	36								
6.00P-7.30P																																
KATU	356	136	277	309	71	12	20	5	5	9	5	3	4	6	6	7	9	8	7	8	8	4	3	3	53	92	1		5	1		1
KVDO	10	2	4	1																					12	62	38					
KOIN	341	151	310	275	71	13	22	4	5	10	7	4	5	8	9	9	9	6	5	7	8	3	3	3	56	92	6		1	4		
KOAC	8	2	5	5																					34	61	5		1			
KGW	271	127	258	214	67	13	22	4	4	10	6	4	5	6	8	9	9	5	4	6	6	3	1	1	67	97			1			
KOAP	28	10	20	22																					70	100						
KPTV	345	239	320	256	69	19	32	17	16	13	16	19	18	14	13	12	10	12	13	11	11	18	24	25	61	95	4		2	4		
HUT/PVT/TOT						58		31	32	44	36	32	34	36	38	38	39	33	32	33	35	30	33	36								
7.00P-7.30P																																
KATU	287	90	202	238	71	14	24	6	6	9	5	4	4	5	6	8	11	10	9	10	9	6	4	5	51	92	2		4	1		
KVDO	7			1																			1	1	19	72	28					
KOIN	206	79	178	145	71	12	21	4	4	10	6	4	4	8	9	8	8	5	4	5	7	3	2	3	54	92	7			5		
KOAC	4	1	2	2																					8	79	14		1			
KGW	181	94	171	131	68	11	20	5	6	10	8	6	7	8	8	9	7	6	6	7	7	4	3	3	71	95	1		1	1		
KOAP	20	8	14	17	74	1	1										1	1	1	1	1				82	100						
KPTV	273	176	228	188	69	17	30	14	14	12	16	18	17	14	13	13	10	11	11	10	10	16	20	23	62	94	3		3	3		
HUT/PVT/TOT						58		32	33	44	36	33	34	36	37	38	39	35	34	35	36	30	33	37								
7.30P-8.00P																																
KATU	329	145	243	279	70	14	26	9	10	9	8	7	8	8	8	7	11	12	13	13	12	10	10	10	55	93	1		4	1		
KVDO	9	1	1	1																			1	1	13	67	26	7				
KOIN	219	86	192	158	71	13	23	4	4	10	7	4	4	8	9	9	9	6	5	6	7	3	3	3	57	92	8			5	1	
KOAC	3		2	2																					95	5						
KGW	216	95	190	152	69	11	20	5	5	9	6	6	6	7	7	8	7	5	5	5	4	4	4	4	61	95	1		3			
KOAP	18	3	14	6	67	1	1			1															59	100						
KPTV	259	135	203	179	69	15	27	10	10	10	11	11	11	10	10	10	9	9	9	8	9	11	15	17	63	94	4		2	3		
HUT/PVT/TOT						56		31	32	41	34	30	31	35	36	35	39	34	33	34	35	31	35	39								

Day-Part Summary

Network Program Averages

DAY-PART AND NETWORK	NO. OF ¼ HRS NTWK PRO-GRAMS T'CAST	ADI TV HH RTG	ADI TV HH SH	METRO TV HH RTG	METRO TV HH SH	TV HH	PERSONS 2+	PERSONS 18+	PERSONS 15-24	PERSONS 12-34	WOMEN TOT 18+	WOMEN 18-49	WOMEN 15-24	WOMEN 18-34	WOMEN 25-49	WOMEN 25-54	WOMEN 25-64	WKG WMN 18+	MEN TOT 18+	MEN 18-49	MEN 18-34	MEN 25-49	MEN 25-54	TEENS 12-17 TOT	TEENS 12-17 GIRLS
		1	2	3	4	5	6	7	8	9	10	11	12	13	14	15	56	16	17	18	19	20	21	22	23
MONDAY-FRIDAY 9.00A -12 NOON																									
ABC	152	6	35	6	35	42	56	46	14	24	31	19	9	13	11	12	15	5	15	8	7	4	4	4	2
CBS	114	3	17	3	19	21	20	18	2	6	17	9	2	6	7	8	12	1	1					3	2
NBC	228	4	22	4	24	28	37	31	7	13	19	10	4	6	7	8	10	4	12	5	4	2	3	3	2
12 NOON -4.30P																									
ABC	268	5	22	5	22	36	40	37	10	18	30	20	9	14	12	14	16	3	7	4	3	3	3	1	1
CBS	228	5	22	4	21	36	42	40	4	10	31	18	3	7	11	13	16	3	9	2	2	1	2	1	1
NBC	193	5	23	6	27	35	41	37	7	16	31	18	6	13	13	16	20	4	6	2	1	1	1	2	2
4.30P -7.30P																									
ABC	57	13	23	13	23	93	153	132	21	49	64	27	8	14	21	26	37	17	68	41	24	32	36	11	3
CBS	41	14	24	14	25	102	164	156	11	32	81	28	4	13	24	33	49	21	75	30	15	24	33	4	1
NBC	43	14	24	16	28	93	145	139	12	31	75	24	7	14	18	26	44	17	64	22	13	18	24	4	2
11.00P -1.00A																									
ABC	72	2	18	3	20	15	22	22	6	11	12	7	3	5	4	5	6	2	10	7	6	4	6		
CBS	102	3	25	3	25	20	24	24	6	11	14	9	4	6	5	7	9	5	10	6	5	4	5		
NBC	120	5	46	7	51	37	53	51	9	19	29	15	4	10	11	14	19	5	22	12	8	8	11	1	
SATURDAY 8.30A -1.00P																									
ABC	72	10	43	10	44	67	91	63	13	27	19	7	4	5	4	6	8	4	44	20	11	15	19	11	3
CBS	72	7	31	7	34	53	83	27	16	34	16	12	9	10	6	6	7	5	11	10	8	5	6	16	7
NBC	58	3	12	3	13	19	30	11	5	12	7	6	4	4	4	4	4		4	3	3	2	2	5	4
SAT + SUN 10.00A -2.00P																									
ABC	88	9	32	9	33	59	75	63	10	21	19	6	2	4	4	6	9	7	44	21	11	16	20	6	1
CBS	110	11	40	10	41	75	113	81	26	48	26	16	8	10	10	12	14	7	55	34	24	20	23	14	4
NBC	78	5	18	5	19	34	51	41	10	21	16	10	5	7	6	7	9	6	25	15	10	11	14	4	2
MON-SAT 7.30P-11P + SUN 6P-11P																									
ABC	342	18	31	18	32	120	221	162	52	108	82	56	27	37	37	42	50	22	80	58	39	40	45	32	16
CBS	350	16	28	16	28	114	199	163	34	79	89	51	18	31	38	47	59	24	74	45	29	33	40	19	10
NBC	348	15	26	17	30	101	178	146	29	70	81	47	14	28	37	43	54	20	65	43	27	32	36	15	7
SUN-SAT 6.00P -11.00P																									
ABC	403	17	30	18	31	117	213	160	48	100	80	52	24	34	35	40	49	21	80	56	37	39	44	29	14
CBS	399	16	27	16	28	111	195	161	32	74	89	48	17	29	36	45	58	23	72	42	27	31	38	18	9
NBC	397	15	26	17	29	100	173	145	27	65	82	45	14	27	35	42	54	20	63	39	25	29	33	13	7

TOTAL SURVEY AREA, IN THOUSANDS (000)

Network Program Averages

DAY-PART AND NETWORK	NO. OF ¼ HRS NTWK PROGRAM T'CAST	TSA (000) CHILD 2-11	TSA 6-11	ADI TV HH RTG	SH	PERS 15-24	PERS 12-34	W TOT 18+	W 18-49	W 15-24	W 18-34	W 25-49	W 25-54	W 25-64	WKG WMN 18+	M TOT 18+	M 18-49	M 18-34	M 25-49	M 25-54	TNS TOT 12-17	CHILD 2-11	CHILD 6-11	METRO	HOME ADI	ADJ #1	ADJ #2	ADJ #3	RTG ADJ #1	RTG ADJ #2	RTG ADJ #3
		24	25	1	2	31	32	33	34	35	36	37	38	57	39	40	41	42	43	44	45	46	47	48	49	50	51	52	53	54	55
MONDAY-FRIDAY 9.00A - 12 NOON																															
ABC	152	6	3	6	35	4	3	4	4	5	5	3	3	3	2	2	2	3	1	1	2	2	1	53	93	2		4	1	1	
CBS	114	2	1	3	17	1	1	2	2	1	2	2	2	3	2	2	1	2	1	1	1	1	1	61	94	5		4	1		
NBC	228	3	2	4	22	2	2	3	2	2	2	2	2	2	2	2	1	2	1	1	1	1	1	60	98	1		1			
12 NOON - 4.30P																															
ABC	268	2	1	5	22	3	2	4	4	5	5	4	3	3	1	1	1	1	1	1	1	1		53	92		1	6	1		
CBS	228	1	1	5	22	1	1	4	3	1	2	3	3	4	1	1	1	1	1	1	1			50	91	5		4	1		
NBC	193	2	1	5	23	2	2	4	4	3	5	4	4	4	2	1	1	1	1	1	1			66	97	1					
4.30P - 7.30P																															
ABC	57	10	8	13	23	6	7	9	6	4	5	7	7	9	8	11	10	9	11	10	6	3	4	56	94	1		4	1		
CBS	41	4	3	14	24	3	4	11	7	2	4	8	9	11	10	11	7	5	8	9	2	1	1	56	92	5		2	4		
NBC	43	2	1	14	24	4	4	11	6	4	5	6	8	10	9	10	5	5	6	7	2	1		67	98						
11.00P - 1.00A																															
ABC	72			2	18	2	2	1	1	2	2	1	1	1	2	1	2	2	1	1				70	87	3		12			
CBS	102			3	25	2	1	2	2	2	2	2	2	2	2	1	1	2	1	1				63	91	3		6			
NBC	120	1	1	5	46	2	3	4	4	2	4	4	4	4	3	4	3	3	3	3	1		1	73	97			2			
SATURDAY 8.30A - 1.00P																															
ABC	72	17	12	10	43	4	4	3	2	2	2	1	2	2	2	7	5	4	5	5	5	6	7	57	96			2			
CBS	72	40	25	7	31	5	4	2	3	5	3	2	2	2	2	2	2	3	1	1	8	13	13	56	89	7		3	3		
NBC	58	14	9	3	12	1	2	1	1	2	1	1	1	1		1	1	1	1	1	3	5	5	59	93	2		3			
SAT + SUN COMBINED 10.00A - 2.00P																															
ABC	88	6	5	9	32	3	3	3	2	1	1	2	2	2	2	7	5	4	6	6	3	2	3	59	96	4		2	2		
CBS	110	18	12	11	40	8	6	4	4	5	4	3	3	3	3	9	8	9	7	7	7	6	6	54	92			2	2		
NBC	78	6	4	5	18	2	3	2	2	2	2	2	2	2	3	4	3	3	4	4	2	2	2	59	95			2			
MONDAY-SATURDAY 7.30P-11.00P PLUS SUN 6.00P-11.00P																															
ABC	342	27	20	18	31	15	15	12	13	15	14	13	12	11	11	13	14	15	14	13	16	10	11	62	96			2			
CBS	350	17	12	16	28	9	10	12	12	10	11	12	13	13	11	11	10	10	11	11	9	6	7	57	90	7		2	6		
NBC	348	17	12	15	26	9	10	12	11	8	11	13	12	12	10	10	11	11	11	11	8	6	7	66	97			2			
SUNDAY-SATURDAY 6.00P - 11.00P																															
ABC	403	24	18	17	30	14	14	12	12	13	12	12	11	11	10	13	14	14	14	13	14	9	10	61	96	1		3	1		
CBS	399	16	11	16	27	9	9	12	11	9	10	12	12	12	11	11	10	9	10	11	8	6	6	57	91	7		2	6		
NBC	397	15	11	15	26	8	9	12	11	8	10	12	12	12	10	10	10	10	10	10	7	6	6	66	97			2			
		24	25	1	2	31	32	33	34	35	36	37	38	57	39	40	41	42	43	44	45	46	47	48	49	50	51	52	53	54	55

Weekly Programming — Time Period Averages

STATION	PROGRAM	WK1 11/2 (58)	WK2 11/9 (59)	WK3 11/16 (60)	WK4 11/23 (61)	RTG (1)	SH (2)	OCT 77 (62)	MAY 77 (63)	FEB 77 (64)	NOV 76 (65)	RTG (3)	SH (4)	TV HH (5)	W TOT 18+ (10)	W 18-49 (11)	W 15-24 (12)	W 18-34 (13)	W 25-49 (14)	W 25-54 (15)	WKG WMN 18+ (16)	M TOT 18+ (17)	M 18-49 (18)	M 18-34 (19)	M 25-49 (20)	M 25-54 (21)	TEENS 12-17 (22)	CHILD 2-11 (24)
▲RELATIVE STD-ERR 25-49%		8	8	7	8	2						3		12	13	13	17	15	11	12	13	14	14	16	12	12	17	25
(1S.E.) THRESHOLDS 50+%		2	2	2	2	-						-		3	3	3	4	4	3	2	3	3	3	4	3	3	4	6
MONDAY 4.00P-4.30P																												
KATU	MEDICAL CNTR	4	5	5	2	4	13	14	22	23	15	4	14	28	24	14	6	9	9	9	5	6	3	2	1	2	6	4
KVDO	N A	1	-	-	-			**	**	**	**			2													2	
KOIN	MIKE DOUGLAS	10	8	6	10	8	27	32	22	23	24	7	25	61	52	15	6	7	13	17	5	30	4	4	1	4	6	
KOAC	N A	-	-	-	-																							
KGW	AFTERNOONER	10	3	6	5	6	20	23	15	20	18	7	25	45	34	25	13	15	17	19	7	17	13	9	8	8	13	9
KOAP	N A	1	1	-	-	1	3	5	**	**	**	1	3	4	3	2		2	2	2		1	1	1	1	1	2	4
KPTV	MICKEY MOUSE	6	8	14	11	10	33	23	33	27	36	9	32	68	11	8	4	6	5	6	1	11	7	5	4	4	15	65
	HUT/PVT/TOT	31	26	34	30	30		22	27	30	33	28		208	124	64	29	39	46	53	18	65	28	21	15	19	44	82
4.30P-5.00P																												
KATU	LUCY SHOW	3	7	6	4	5	14	13	21	18	22	5	16	36	24	15	6	8	11	12	6	13	9	5	6	6	12	12
KVDO	N A	1	-	-	-			**	**	**	**			2													2	
KOIN	MIKE DOUGLAS	11	8	7	10	9	26	30	24	21	22	8	25	67	55	17	6	6	15	19	7	35	7	4	4	7	6	2
KOAC	N A	-	-	-	-																							
KGW	AFTERNOONER	9	3	8	4	6	17	22	10	18	22	8	25	45	37	27	14	17	18	20	8	18	11	7	8	10	11	10
KOAP	N A	1	2	-	1	1	3	4	**	**	**	1	3	6	2	2		2	2	2		3	1	1	1	1		5
KPTV	FLINTSTONES	9	10	13	12	11	31	30	34	23	22	10	31	77	17	14	7	12	8	9	3	13	7	6	3	6	23	68
	HUT/PVT/TOT	36	33	36	35	35		23	29	33	36	32		233	135	75	33	45	54	62	24	82	35	23	22	30	54	97
5.00P-5.30P																												
KATU	MARY T MOORE	6	11	9	6	8	16	14	19	16	20	10	21	57	46	30	14	22	19	20	12	24	13	6	11	13	13	6
KVDO	N A	1	-	-	-			**	**	**	**			1														
KOIN	NEWSROOM 6-E	14	17	14	15	15	31	32	30	34	29	15	31	110	97	27	3	9	25	35	11	74	22	8	17	26	2	3
KOAC	N A	-	-	-	-									1														1
KGW	NEWS EXTRA	9	5	6	9	7	14	16	16	20	18	8	17	52	42	13	4	6	10	20	12	25	6	2	6	9	7	2
KOAP	N A	1	1	1	1	1	2	3	**	**	**	1	2	5	2	2		2	2	2		1	1	1	1	1		5
KPTV	GILLIGANS IS	15	13	18	16	16	33	27	30	23	24	15	31	109	33	23	18	20	14	15	8	28	20	15	13	14	49	80
	HUT/PVT/TOT	47	50	51	47	49		37	37	44	45	48		334	220	95	39	59	70	92	43	152	62	32	48	63	71	97
5.30P-6.00P																												
KATU	EYWTNS NWS 1	7	10	13	12	10	18	14	23	20	20	10	19	77	57	25	6	16	21	26	16	49	24	13	20	26	6	5
KVDO	N A	-	-	-	-			**	**	**	**																	
KOIN	NEWSROOM 6-E	15	18	14	15	15	27	27	25	30	25	16	30	109	95	27	4	10	23	34	17	77	27	8	22	29	5	3
KOAC	N A	-	1	-	-									2	1	1			1	1		1	1					1
KGW	530 NW TNGHT	15	9	9	9	12	21	23	23	28	25	11	20	81	60	19	5	10	16	26	17	49	13	6	11	16	8	1
KOAP	N A	1	2	1	-	1	2		**	**	**	1	2	5	1	1		1	1	1		1	1	1	1	1		6
KPTV	BEWITCHED	14	16	20	14	16	29	30	20	16	25	17	31	113	46	38	25	29	24	25	14	32	25	18	15	17	48	72
	HUT/PVT/TOT	51	57	57	58	56		44	44	50	55	54		387	260	111	40	66	86	113	64	208	90	46	69	89	67	88
6.00P-6.30P																												
KATU	ABC EVE NEWS	9	9	12	13	11	18	17	23	21	20	11	19	78	60	20	5	9	17	22	16	52	23	10	20	23	6	3
KVDO	N A	-	-	-	-			**	**	**	**																	
KOIN	CBS EVE NEWS	15	14	14	14	14	23	24	25	29	23	14	25	99	78	23	2	7	22	35	21	72	26	9	25	32	4	4
KOAC	N A	-	-	-	-																							
KGW	530 NW TNGHT	15	9	9	18	13	22	24	25	29	27	13	23	85	67	21	6	10	17	28	18	53	16	6	14	20	10	1
KOAP	N A	-	-	-	-				**	**	**																	
KPTV	EMERGENCY 1	19	24	22	17	20	33	28	25	21	27	21	37	139	87	66	37	53	40	44	18	57	43	30	31	37	48	79
	HUT/PVT/TOT	58	59	60	63	60		54	53	56	60	57		401	292	130	50	79	96	129	73	234	108	55	90	112	68	87
6.30P-7.00P																												
KATU	EYWTNS NWS 2	9	11	12	12	11	18	17	25	19	24	11	20	79	61	25	6	10	21	27	17	62	31	16	23	28	8	2
KVDO	N A	-	-	-	-			**	**	**	**																	
KOIN	ODD COUPLE	16	11	9	11	12	20	22	21	26	19	11	20	84	63	30	10	17	22	28	16	53	27	11	24	28	15	13
KOAC	N A	-	-	-	-									2	1			1	1	1		1						1
KGW	NBC NGHT NWS	14	10	12	22	14	23	28	29	32	29	15	27	95	76	22	5	11	18	30	17	64	19	8	17	24	5	
KOAP	N A	1	1	1	1	1	2		**	**	**			6	6					1		4						4
KPTV	EMERGENCY 1	17	23	19	16	19	32	28	23	21	27	20	36	128	87	66	33	50	42	47	20	58	44	30	33	39	43	69
	HUT/PVT/TOT	58	59	57	64	60		54	52	57	59	56		394	294	143	54	88	103	134	71	242	121	65	97	121	71	84
7.00P-7.30P																												
KATU	NFL MON FTBL	23	24	22	24	23	37	37	28	18	38	23	39	159	63	34	12	18	26	31	22	143	95	60	75	82	26	23
KVDO	N A	-	1	-	1			**	**	**	**			4														7
KOIN	MERV GRIFFIN	15	14	11	13	13	21	18	19	27	22	11	19	94	83	26	7	9	23	32	16	42	10	6	7	16	7	7
KOAC	N A	-	-	-	-									2								1						
KGW	BIRTHDY MASS	7				7	11					7	12	47	51							17						
	EVENING		8		8	13	10	16					11	18	69	60	23	8	11	18	21	14	39	19	11	15	17	10	4
	--4 WK AVG--			9	14	18	30	30	23	10	17	64	57	24	8	13	19	23	14	34	16	9	13	14	8	4		
KOAP	N A	-	-	-	-			2	**	**	**			2	2	1			1	1		1	1		1	1		1
KPTV	I LOVE LUCY	14	17	15	15	15	24	21	19	21	16	16	27	105	75	57	29	41	35	40	20	49	35	20	28	30	29	50
	HUT/PVT/TOT	62	63	58	69	63		62	53	56	64	59		430	280	142	56	81	104	127	72	270	157	95	124	143	70	92
7.30P-8.00P																												
KATU	NFL MON FTBL	26	24	22	26	25	41	41	30	18	38	24	41	169	66	36	13	20	27	33	21	150	101	65	78	84	27	27
KVDO	N A	-	1	-	1			**	**	**	**			4														7
KOIN	MERV GRIFFIN	12	14	11	11	12	20	19	23	29	23	12	21	88	79	29	6	10	25	33	16	43	12	7	8	17	6	6
KOAC	N A	-	-	-	-									1														
KGW	BIRTHDY MASS	6				6	10					6	11	40	39							11						
	25000 PYRAMD		6	7	15	9	15					10	17	65	59	30	9	17	23	24	20	32	15	10	11	11	9	8
	--4 WK AVG--			9	15	14	26	29	21	9	16	59	54	27	9	16	20	23	17	27	12	8	9	9	7	6		
KOAP	N A	-	-	-	-			2	**	**	**			2	2	2		1	2	2		2	1	1	2	2		2
KPTV	ADAM 12	13	14	13	13	13	21	21	17	20	15	14	24	95	63	42	18	30	28	31	16	51	30	18	22	26	19	42
	HUT/PVT/TOT	62	59	57	67	61		63	53	55	66	58		418	264	136	46	77	102	122	70	273	157	99	119	138	59	90
8.00P-8.30P																												
KATU	NFL MON FTBL	28	24	21	25	25	37	35	29	25	33	24	38	166	65	34	13	21	22	27	19	149	95	59	72	79	21	20
KVDO	N A	-	1	-	-			**	**	**	**			3	1													

TECHNICAL DIFFICULTY
< M-F PROGRAM AIRED LESS THAN FIVE DAYS
+ PARENT/SATELLITE RELATIONSHIP
* SAMPLE BELOW MINIMUM FOR WEEKLY REPORTING
▲ SEE TABLE ON PAGE iv

Time Period Averages

DAY, TIME, AND STATION	CHILD 6-11 (25)	PERS 18+ (7)	PERS 15-24 (8)	PERS 12-34 (9)	PERS 15-24 (31)	PERS 12-34 (32)	W TOT 18+ (33)	W 18-49 (34)	W 15-24 (35)	W 18-34 (36)	W 25-49 (37)	W 25-54 (38)	WKG WMN 18+ (39)	M TOT 18+ (40)	M 18-49 (41)	M 18-34 (42)	M 25-49 (43)	M 25-54 (44)	TNS 12-17 (45)	CHD 2-11 (46)
THRESHS 25-49%	21	17	20	19	6	2	2	3	9	5	4	3	7	2	3	6	4	4	8	10
THRESHS 50+%	5	3	5	3	1	–	–	–	2	1	1	1	1	–	1	1	1	1	2	2
MON 4.00P																				
KATU	2	30	10	17	3	2	3	3	3	4	3	3	1	1	1	1			3	1
KVDO			2	2	1															
KOIN		81	9	17	2	2	7	3	3	2	4	5	3	4	1	1		1	3	
KOAC																				
KGW	7	51	20	37	5	4	4	4	6	4	4	4	3	3	3	3	2	2	5	2
KOAP	3	4	1	5		1				1	1			1					1	2
KPTV	42	21	8	26	2	3	1	2	2	2	2	2		1	2	2	1	1	7	24
H/P/T	54	187	50	104	15	14	17	14	15	13	14	14	8	10	8	9	5	5	22	31
4.30P																				
KATU	8	37	12	25	3	3	3	4	3	4	4	2	1	2	1	2	1		5	4
KVDO			2	2	1														1	
KOIN	1	90	9	16	2	2	7	4	3	2	5	5	3	5	1	1	1	1	3	
KOAC																				
KGW	8	54	19	35	5	4	5	5	6	5	5	4		3	3	3	3	3	5	3
KOAP	2	5		3						1	1									1
KPTV	41	30	15	40	4	5	2	3	4	4	3	2	1	2	2	2	1	2	11	25
H/P/T	60	216	57	121	18	17	19	17	18	16	18	18	11	13	9	10	7	8	29	38
5.00P																				
KATU	5	70	18	41	5	5	6	7	8	8	6	5	5	3	1	3	3		5	2
KVDO																				
KOIN	2	171	9	18	2	2	13	6	2	3	8	9	6	11	5	3	5	7	1	1
KOAC	1																			
KGW	2	67	7	15	2	2	6	2	2	2	3	5	6	4	1		2	2	3	
KOAP	2	3		3																2
KPTV	57	61	35	84	11	11	4	5	11	7	4	4	3	4	5	6	4	4	23	29
H/P/T	69	372	69	161	22	22	32	23	24	22	23	25	20	24	16	13	16	17	34	36
5.30P																				
KATU	3	105	12	35	3	4	7	5	3	5	6	7	7	7	6	4	6	7	3	1
KVDO																				
KOIN	3	172	11	23	3	3	13	6	3	4	7	9	8	12	6	3	7	8	2	1
KOAC	1	1																		
KGW	1	108	10	24	3	3	9	4	3	3	5	7	8	8	3	2	3	4	4	
KOAP	3	2		2																2
KPTV	55	77	44	95	13	12	6	9	14	11	8	7	7	5	6	6	5	5	23	25
H/P/T	66	465	77	179	23	24	37	25	23	24	27	31	30	33	22	17	24	26	33	31
6.00P																				
KATU	2	112	11	25	3	3	8	4	2	3	5	6	7	8	6	4	6	7	3	1
KVDO																				
KOIN	4	150	2	20		2	11	5	1	2	7	9	10	11	6	3	8	9	1	1
KOAC																				
KGW	1	120	11	25	3	3	10	5	3	4	6	8	8	8	4	2	5	6	4	
KOAP																				
KPTV	54	144	58	130	17	17	13	15	20	19	13	13	9	9	11	11	11	11	23	29
H/P/T	61	526	82	200	25	28	43	31	28	29	32	37	36	39	28	23	32	34	34	33
6.30P																				
KATU	2	123	16	33	4	4	8	5	3	4	7	9	9	9	7	5	8	8	4	1
KVDO																				
KOIN	9	115	17	43	5	6	9	7	5	6	8	8	8	8	7	4	8	8	7	5
KOAC		2																		
KGW		140	8	24	3	3	11	5	3	4	6	8	9	10	5	3	6	7	2	
KOAP		9					1													
KPTV	45	145	51	122	15	16	13	15	18	18	14	13	10	9	11	11	11	12	21	25
H/P/T	56	534	92	222	27	31	44	34	30	33	35	38	34	41	32	27	35	37	35	33
7.00P																				
KATU	18	206	42	103	12	14	9	8	7	7	8	9	11	22	23	22	25	22	13	8
KVDO	3																			2
KOIN	6	125	10	21	3	3	11	6	4	3	8	9	7	6	2	2	2	4	3	3
KOAC		1																		
KGW					8								3							
4 WK	2	99	14	31	4	4	8	5	4	4	6	6	5	5	4	3	4	4	4	1
KOAP	1	3																		
KPTV	35	124	37	90	11	12	11	14	16	15	12	11	10	8	8	7	9	9	14	19
H/P/T	65	550	102	242	32	35	42	35	33	31	35	36	34	44	40	37	43	42	36	34
7.30P																				
KATU	21	216	48	112	14	15	10	8	8	7	9	9	10	24	25	24	26	23	13	9
KVDO	3																			2
KOIN	5	121	11	22	3	3	11	4	4	4	8	9	7	6	2	2	2	4	3	2
KOAC																				
KGW					6								2							
4 WK	5	90	14	36	4	5	8	7	5	6	7	8	5	5	4	3	4	3	4	3
KOAP	1	4		2																2
KPTV	31	113	27	66	8	9	9	10	10	11	9	8	8	8	7	7	8	8	10	16
H/P/T	65	534	98	232	31	33	39	33	28	30	34	35	33	45	40	39	41	41	30	32
8.00P																				
KATU	15	213	45	100	13	14	10	8	8	8	7	8	10	24	23	23	24	23	10	6
KVDO		1																		

Station Break Averages

TOTAL SURVEY AREA, IN THOUSANDS (000)

TIME / STATION	ADI TV HH RTG (1)	MET TV HH RTG (3)	TV HH (5)	W TOT 18+ (10)	W 18-49 (11)	W 18-34 (13)	W 25-49 (14)	M TOT 18+ (17)	M 18-49 (18)	M 18-34 (19)	M 25-49 (20)	CHILD TOT 2-11 (24)
THRESHS 25-49%	2	3	12	13	13	15	11	14	14	16	12	25
THRESHS 50+%	–	–	3	3	4	3	3	3	3	4	3	6
4.00P												
KATU	4	4	27	23	13	8	9	8	5	4	1	3
KVDO			2									
KOIN	8	7	60	50	16	7	15	25	4	4	1	
KOAC												
KGW	6	7	45	32	24	15	15	17	13	9	8	8
KOAP	1	1	2	2	1	1	1	1	1	1	1	2
KPTV	9	9	65	12	9	7	5	13	9	7	5	60
H/P/T	29	27	201	119	63	38	45	64	32	25	16	73
4.30P												
KATU	5	5	32	24	15	9	10	10	6	4	4	8
KVDO			2									
KOIN	9	8	64	54	16	6	14	32	5	4	2	1
KOAC												
KGW	6	8	45	36	26	16	18	17	13	9	9	9
KOAP	1	1	5	3	2	2	2	2	1	1	1	5
KPTV	11	10	73	14	11	9	7	12	7	6	3	67
H/P/T	33	30	221	131	70	42	51	73	32	24	19	90
5.00P												
KATU	7	8	46	35	23	15	15	18	10	5	8	9
KVDO			1									
KOIN	12	12	88	75	23	8	21	54	14	6	10	2
KOAC			1									
KGW	7	8	48	39	19	11	13	21	8	4	7	7
KOAP	1	1	6	2	2	2	2	2	1	1	1	5
KPTV	14	13	93	25	19	16	11	20	14	11	8	75
H/P/T	42	40	283	176	86	52	62	115	47	27	34	99
5.30P												
KATU	10	11	68	52	28	19	20	37	19	10	16	6
KVDO												
KOIN	15	16	110	97	28	10	25	78	25	7	20	3
KOAC			2									1
KGW	10	10	66	51	16	8	13	36	9	4	8	1
KOAP	1	1	5	1	1	1	1	1	1	1	1	6
KPTV	16	16	111	39	30	24	19	30	22	16	14	76
H/P/T	53	51	362	240	103	62	78	182	76	38	59	93
6.00P												
KATU	11	11	76	57	22	12	19	49	23	11	20	4
KVDO												
KOIN	15	15	105	86	24	9	21	74	26	9	24	4
KOAC			1	1		1	1					1
KGW	13	13	83	64	21	10	17	52	15	6	13	1
KOAP	1	1	3	1	1	1	1	1	1	1	1	3
KPTV	19	19	127	68	53	41	32	44	34	24	23	77
H/P/T	59	56	395	277	122	73	91	220	99	51	81	90
6.30P												
KATU	11	11	79	61	23	10	19	57	27	13	22	3
KVDO												
KOIN	13	12	91	69	26	12	22	62	26	10	24	8
KOAC			1	1				1				
KGW	14	14	90	71	21	10	17	59	18	7	16	
KOAP	1	1	3	3				2				
KPTV	20	21	133	86	65	51	41	57	43	30	32	73
H/P/T	60	57	397	291	135	83	99	238	114	60	94	84
7.00P												
KATU	17	17	119	63	30	14	24	103	63	38	48	13
KVDO			2									4
KOIN	13	11	88	73	29	14	23	46	18	8	16	10
KOAC			2	1								
KGW												
4 WK	12	13	80	66	22	11	18	48	17	8	15	2
KOAP	1		4	3	1		1	2			1	
KPTV	17	18	117	82	62	46	39	54	40	25	31	61
H/P/T	61	58	412	288	144	85	105	254	139	79	111	90
7.30P												
KATU	24	24	163	62	34	18	26	146	99	63	77	25
KVDO			4									7
KOIN	13	12	92	81	27	9	24	44	11	6	8	7
KOAC			2									
KGW												
4 WK	9	10	61	55	25	14	19	30	14	9	11	4
KOAP			2	2	2	2	1	2	2	1	2	2
KPTV	15	15	99	69	50	36	32	50	32	19	25	45
H/P/T	62	59	423	269	138	78	103	273	158	98	123	90
8.00P												
KATU	25	24	169	66	35	21	25	151	99	63	75	24
KVDO			4	1								4

Daily

DAY AND TIME / STATION — PROGRAM	WK1 11/2 (58)	WK2 11/9 (59)	WK3 11/16 (60)	WK4 11/23 (61)	ADI B/G (1)	ADI SH (2)	OCT 77 (62)	MAY 77 (63)	FEB 77 (64)	NOV 76 (65)	MET B/G (3)	MET SH (4)	TV HH (5)	W TOT 18+ (10)	W 18-49 (11)	W 15-24 (12)	W 18-34 (13)	W 25-49 (14)	W 25-54 (15)	WKG WMN 18+ (16)	M TOT 18+ (17)	M 18-49 (18)	M 18-34 (19)	M 25-49 (20)	M 25-54 (21)	TEENS 12-17 (22)	CHILD 2-11 (24)
▲RELATIVE STD-ERR 25-49%	8	8	7	8	2							3	12	13	13	17	15	11	12	13	14	14	16	12	12	17	25
(1 S.E.) THRESHOLDS 50+%	2	2	2	2	-							-	3	3	3	4	4	3	2	3	3	3	4	3	3	4	6
SATURDAY																											
3.30P- 4.00P																											
KATU NCAA FOOTBLL	10		11	11	11	42					11	44	71	22	7	2	3	6	8	5	46	18	7	13	16	6	4
ABC SAT NEWS	10				10	45					10	53	65	17							49						
J WAYNE THTR		6			6	26					6	29	40	19							25						
--4 WK AVG--					9	36	48**	36**	29**	48**	9	39	62	21	9	4	5	7	9		41	16	8	11	15	9	5
KVDO N A	-	-	-	-																							
KOIN SP SPT SPECT	7				7	32					7	37	49	16							34						
SPTS SPECTLR		6	5	6	6	23					5	20	45	20	3		1	3	4	3	23	13	5	9	11	3	8
--4 WK AVG--					6	24	17	36**	19**	19**	5	22	46	19	5	1	3	4	5	5	26	16	7	12	13	2	7
KOAC N A	-	-	-	-																							
KGW STR TREK	1	4	3	4	3	12	9	14**	29**	11**	4	17	23	8	4	5	3	3	4	2	9	7	5	4	5	7	11
													1								1	1		1	1		
KOAP N A	-	-	-	-																							
KPTV SA VIRGINIAN	4	5	5	6	5	20	26	14	19	15	5	22	41	27	17	10	14	10	12	7	23	10	6	8	11	8	8
HUT/PVT/TOT	22	23	26	28	25		23	14	21	27	23		173	75	35	20	25	24	30	20	100	50	26	36	45	26	31
4.00P- 4.30P																											
KATU SN PDRO BUMS	9			6	8	31					6	25	54	31	18	15	13	10	10	8	25	14	9	9	11	16	13
LNDSY WAGNER		7			7	30					9	35	45	16							10						
NCAA FOOTBLL			7		7	22					7	23	48	17							16						
SUGAR TIME			6		6	19					6	19	41	19							10						
--4 WK AVG--					7	27	32**	21**	27**	38**	7	27	49	24	13	12	10	8	10	5	18	12	9	6	7	16	12
KVDO N A	-	-	-	1									2								2						
KOIN SPTS SPECTLR	7	6	8	7	7	27	26	26**	20**	29**	8	31	56	23	11	2	6	9	10	9	45	24	9	20	24	5	6
KOAC N A	-	-	-	-																							
KGW TRUTH-CONSEQ	1	2		3	2	8					3	12	15	10	4	2	1	3	4	1	10	4	2	1	2	3	4
E SDE W SDE			-								1	3	2	2							6						
--4 WK AVG--					2	8	11	16**	23**	25**	3	12	12	8	3	2	1	2	4	1	9	3	1	2	4	2	3
KOAP N A	-	-	-	-									1														1
KPTV SAT SHOW	7	8	16	6	9	35	26	32	27	8	9	35	66	42	31	17	25	19	22	10	40	32	25	23	23	18	28
HUT/PVT/TOT	27	23	32	24	26		19	19	30	24	26		186	97	58	33	42	38	46	25	114	71	44	51	58	41	50
4.30P- 5.00P																											
KATU SN PDRO BUMS	8			5	7	23					5	18	49	33	18	15	14	10	10	6	22	14	9	9	11	14	9
LNDSY WAGNER		7			7	28					9	33	47	21							14						
FISH			8		8	23					8	23	54	27							17						
--4 WK AVG--					7	23	30**	21**	28**	42**	7	24	50	29	16	13	13	11	13		19	13	10	8	10	15	16
KVDO N A	-	-	-	1									2								2						
KOIN SPTS SPECTLR	9	7	9	9	8	27	25	26**	19**	27**	9	31	64	28	14	3	7	11	13	10	55	29	13	23	27	10	9
KOAC N A	-	-	-	-																							
KGW WRLD ANIMALS	4	1		5	3	11					3	11	23	8	2	2	1	1	1	2	16	6	2	4	5	3	3
E SDE W SDE			1		1	3					3	5	5	2							6						
--4 WK AVG--					3	10	15	21**	25**	27**	3	10	19	7	2	2	1	2	2	2	14	5	2	4	5	2	3
KOAP N A	-	-	-	-																							
KPTV SAT SHOW	8	9	17	7	10	33	25	32	28	8	10	34	75	50	37	21	30	22	26	12	48	38	31	25	27	18	28
HUT/PVT/TOT	32	25	35	29	30		20	19	32	26	29		210	114	69	39	51	45	54	29	138	85	56	60	69	45	56
5.00P- 5.30P																											
KATU TV 2 SPECIAL	8		5		7	18					7	18	45	29	19	4	8	16	19	7	33	19	11	17	22	7	7
WDE WRLD SPT		10			10	29					10	29	72	35							52						
TV 2 MV SPC				5	5	14					5	17	33	25							22						
--4 WK AVG--					7	19	27**	24**	31**	35**	7	20	48	30	19	5	8	16	18	10	35	21	12	17	21	9	7
KVDO N A	-	-	-	-																							
KOIN SPTS SPECTLR	10				10	28					10	29	81	28							63						
NEWSROOM 6-W		6	15	15	12	32					12	33	87	78	23	7	9	17	24	13	62	16	6	13	20	5	1
--4 WK AVG--					11	30	27	32**	23**	35**	11	31	86	65	20	6	8	15	21	14	63	22	10	19	25	7	3
KOAC N A	-	-	-	-									2	2	2	1	2	1	1							4	17
KGW J COUSTEAU	7	6	6	7	7	19	20	12**	21**	19**	6	17	45	27	15	5	10	11	14	6	30	16	9	14	17	4	17
													1	1	1		1	1	1		1	1	1				
KOAP N A	-	-	-	-																							
KPTV SAT SHOW	9	12	13	8	11	30	23	24	23	11	11	31	78	50	38	23	29	22	27	13	54	45	36	26	28	26	32
HUT/PVT/TOT	36	35	40	36	37		30	30	37	35	35		260	176	96	41	59	66	82	44	183	105	68	76	91	46	59
5.30P- 6.00P																											
KATU TV 2 SPECIAL	10		5		7	18					7	18	49	26	17	2	6	16	19	8	35	21	13	20	25	9	7
WDE WRLD SPT		12			12	32					11	31	85	35							67						
TV 2 MV SPC				5	5	13					5	18	35	26							25						
--4 WK AVG--					8	21	31**	28**	41**	32**	8	23	55	28	18	4	7	16	18	12	41	27	17	22	26	11	7
KVDO N A	-	-	-	-																							
KOIN NEWSROOM 6-W	12				12	31					13	34	87	58							66						
NEWS CONF 6		6	9	10	8	21					7	21	60	56	15	5	6	10	13	9	39	9	5	6	10	2	1
--4 WK AVG--					9	24	21	28**	15**	24**	9	26	67	57	16	5	6	11	14	11	46	14	7	11	15	3	1
KOAC N A	-	-	-	-									3	2	2	1	2	1	1		2	1	1	1	1		
KGW J COUSTEAU	6	7	10	12	8	21	24	16	18	22	8	23	59	38	20	6	12	16	20	10	36	17	8	16	20	6	18
KOAP N A	-	-	-	-									1	2	2	1	2	1	1	1	1	1	1	1	1		1
KPTV SAT SHOW	9	10	14	9	11	29	21	24	23	19	11	31	77	53	39	23	29	23	28	13	57	47	37	26	28	25	32
HUT/PVT/TOT	39	37	39	38	38		29	25	39	37	35		262	180	97	40	58	68	82	47	183	107	71	76	90	45	59
6.00P- 6.30P																											
KATU NORTON-YOUNG	19				19	38					21	40	132	72							136						
WDE WRLD SPT		11			11	29					11	31	75	23							62						
TV 2 SPECIAL			6		6	14					6	14	39	26							29						
TV 2 MV SPC				4	4	10					4	11	30	18							24						
--4 WK AVG--					10	23	25**	21**	35**	22**	10	24	69	35	23	6	10	19	23	14	63	41	24	32	37	17	11
KVDO N A	-	-	-	-																							
KOIN CBS NEWS-SAT	8	8	9	10	9	21	19	18	12	18	8	20	64	59	15	4	7	11	16	12	46	14	9	12	16	1	1
KOAC N A	-	-	-	-									1								1						
KGW SA 6 NW TNGT	10	10	11	14	11	26	31	36	28	36	12	29	77	65	25	3	11	23	29	11	53	22	12	21	26	2	7
KOAP N A	-	-	-	-									1	1	1		1	1	1		2	2	2				
KPTV SAT MOVIE	12	9	16	12	12	28	22	21	19	22	12	29	90	62	47	27	38	27	33	14	68	57	43	33	37	29	31
HUT/PVT/TOT	50	38	44	42	43		36	33	43	45	41		302	222	111	40	67	81	102	52	233	136	90	98	116	49	50
	58	59	60	61	1	2	62	63	64	65	3	4	5	10	11	12	13	14	15	16	17	18	19	20	21	22	24

\# TECHNICAL DIFFICULTY
< M-F PROGRAM AIRED LESS THAN FIVE DAYS
+ PARENT/SATELLITE RELATIONSHIP
* SAMPLE BELOW MINIMUM FOR WEEKLY REPORTING
▲ SEE TABLE ON PAGE iv

Time Period Averages

DAY, TIME, AND STATION	CHILD 6-11 (25)	18+ (7)	15-24 (8)	12-34 (9)	P15-24 (31)	P12-34 (32)	W TOT 18+ (33)	W 18-49 (34)	W 15-24 (35)	W 18-34 (36)	W 25-49 (37)	W 25-54 (38)	WKG WMN 18+ (39)	M TOT 18+ (40)	M 18-49 (41)	M 18-34 (42)	M 25-49 (43)	M 25-54 (44)	TNS 12-17 (45)	CHD 2-11 (46)
THRESHS 25-49%	21	17	20	19	6	2	2	3	9	5	4	3	7	2	3	6	4	4	8	10
THRESHS 50+%	5	3	5	3	1	–	–	–	2	1	1	1	1	–	1	1	1	1	2	2
SAT 3.30P																				
KATU	3	68	8	16	2	2	3 (3,3,4)	2	1	1	2	3	3	7 (8,4)	5	3	5	4	3	1
4 WK	3	62	11	22	3	3	3	2	2	2	2	3	3	7	4	3	4	4	5	2
KVDO																				
KOIN	6	42	5	9	1	1	3 (2)	1			1	1	1	5					1	3
4 WK	5	44	6	12	1	1	2	1		1	1	1	2	3	3	2	3	3	1	3
KOAC																				
KGW	9	17	9	15	2	2	1	1	3	1	1	1	1	1	2	2	1	2	4	4
KOAP		1																		
KPTV	6	49	13	28	4	4	3	4	5	5	3	3	3	3	2	3	2	3	3	3
H/P/T	23	173	39	77	11	11	11	8	11	9	8	8	9	16	13	11	13	13	13	12
4.00P																				
KATU	11	56	22	38	5	4	4 (2,2,3)	3	5	4	3	2	4	4 (2,3,2)	4	4	3	3	6	5
4 WK	9	42	19	34	5	4	3	2	6	3	2	3	2	3	3	3	2	2	7	5
KVDO		2																		
KOIN	4	68	8	19	2	2	3	2	1	2	3	3	3	6	5	3	6	6	2	2
KOAC																				
KGW	2	20	3	5	1	1	1	1	1		1	1	1	1 (1)	1		1	1	1	1
4 WK	2	17	2	4	1	1	1	1	1		1	1	1	1	1	1	1	1	1	1
KOAP	1																			
KPTV	18	81	29	68	8	9	6	7	9	9	6	6	4	6	7	8	7	6	8	10
H/P/T	34	210	58	125	16	16	14	13	17	15	13	13	11	17	16	16	16	16	18	19
4.30P																				
KATU	7	55	22	37	5	4	4 (3,4)	3	6	4	3	2	4 (2,3)	4	4	4	3	3	6	3
4 WK	13	47	19	36	5	4	3	4	6	4	3	3	2	3	4	4	3	3	6	6
KVDO		2																		
KOIN	7	83	12	30	4	4	3	3	2	2	3	3	4	8	6	4	7	7	5	3
KOAC																				
KGW	1	24	5	5	1	1	1	1	1			1		2 (1)	1	1	1	1	1	1
4 WK	1	21	4	5	1	1	1		1		1		1	2	1	1	1	1	1	1
KOAP	1																			
KPTV	19	97	36	79	9	10	7	8	11	10	7	7	5	7	8	10	8	7	8	11
H/P/T	40	250	71	150	18	19	16	16	20	18	15	15	13	21	20	20	20	20	20	21
5.00P																				
KATU	6	62	8	26	2	4	4 (5,4)	5	2	3	6	4	4	5 (8,3)	5	4	6	6	4	3
4 WK	5	64	13	29	3	4	4	4	2	3	5	5	5	5	5	4	5	6	5	3
KVDO																				
KOIN		140	10	20	3	3	10 (4)	5	4	3	5	7	5	9 (8)	4	2	4	5	2	
KOAC		2	1	2																
4 WK	1	128	9	25	3	3	9	4	3	3	4	5	5	9	5	3	5	6	3	1
KGW	14	57	10	23	3	3	4	4	3	4	4	4	3	5	4	3	5	5	2	6
KOAP		3	2	3																
KPTV	23	104	46	90	12	11	7	8	12	10	7	7	6	7	10	12	8	7	12	12
H/P/T	43	358	81	172	21	22	24	22	20	20	22	23	20	28	24	24	25	25	22	22
5.30P																				
KATU	6	61	5	28	2	4	4 (5,4)	4	2	6	6	4	4	5 (10,4)	5	5	7	7	4	3
4 WK	6	69	12	33	4	4	4	4	2	5	5	5	5	6	6	6	7	7	5	3
KVDO																				
KOIN		95	8	13	2	2	8 (8)	3	3	2	3	3	3	10 (10)	6	2	2	3	1	
KOAC																				
4 WK		102	8	16	2	2	8	3	2	2	4	4	4	6	3	2	3	4	1	
KGW	13	74	10	26	3	3	5	5	3	5	5	5	5	5	4	3	5	6	3	6
KOAP	1	3	2	3																
KPTV	24	110	47	90	12	11	7	9	12	10	7	7	6	8	10	12	8	7	12	11
H/P/T	44	362	80	171	21	22	26	22	20	20	23	23	22	28	25	25	25	25	22	21
6.00P																				
KATU									10 (3,4,3)				22 (10,5,4)							
4 WK	8	98	24	50	7	7	5	5	3	4	6	6	7	10	10	9	11	11	8	4
KVDO																				
KOIN	1	104	6	17	2	2	8	3	2	2	3	4	5	7	3	3	4	4		
KOAC		1																		
KGW	6	118	5	24	1	3	9	6	2	4	7	8	5	8	5	5	7	7	1	2
KOAP		3	2	3	1								1							
KPTV	22	129	58	110	17	14	8	10	15	13	8	8	6	10	13	15	10	9	14	11
H/P/T	37	453	95	204	28	27	32	26	22	24	26	28	24	36	33	33	32	32	24	19
(col #)	25	7	8	9	31	32	33	34	35	36	37	38	39	40	41	42	43	44	45	46

Station Break Averages

TIME / STATION	ADI TV HH RTG (1)	MET TV HH RTG (3)	TV HH (5)	W TOT 18+ (10)	W 18-49 (11)	W 18-34 (13)	W 25-49 (14)	M TOT 18+ (17)	M 18-49 (18)	M 18-34 (19)	M 25-49 (20)	CHILD TOT 2-11 (24)
THRESHS 25-49%	2	3	12	13	13	15	11	14	14	16	12	25
THRESHS 50+%	–	–	3	3	3	4	3	3	3	4	3	6
3.30P												
(4 WK)	11	11	70	24	11	6	8	47	21	9	15	5
(KOIN 4 WK)	6	5	40	19	9	5	8	22	16	10	9	8
(KOAC)				1								
(KGW)	3	3	17	7	3	3	2	7	5	4	3	8
(KOAP)				1				1	1		1	
(KPTV)	6	6	45	31	19	15	12	24	10	7	8	8
H/P/T	26	24	174	81	42	29	30	101	53	30	36	29
4.00P												
(4 WK)	8	8	56	21	10	8	6	30	14	8	9	8
(KVDO)			1					1				
(KOIN)	7	7	52	22	8	4	7	37	21	8	16	7
(4 WK)	3	4	18	9	4	2	3	9	5	4	3	7
(KOAP)								1	1		1	1
(KPTV)	7	7	53	33	24	20	14	30	20	15	15	18
H/P/T	26	25	181	85	46	34	30	108	61	35	44	41
4.30P												
(4 WK)	7	7	49	27	15	11	10	18	11	8	7	13
(KVDO)			2					2				
(KOIN)	8	9	59	25	12	6	10	50	26	11	21	7
(4 WK)	3	3	15	9	3	1	2	12	4	3	3	2
(KOAP)			1					1				1
(KPTV)	10	10	70	45	34	28	21	44	35	28	24	29
H/P/T	28	28	196	106	64	46	43	126	76	50	55	52
5.00P												
(4 WK)	7	7	49	29	16	10	13	27	17	10	13	12
(KVDO)			1					1				
(4 WK KOIN)	10	11	74	46	18	9	14	59	25	12	20	6
(KOAC)				1	1	1	1	1	1	1	1	
(KGW)	5	5	32	18	9	6	7	21	10	6	9	11
(KOAP)			1	1	1	1	1	1	1	1	1	
(KPTV)	10	11	76	50	37	26	22	50	41	33	26	30
H/P/T	33	33	234	145	82	56	58	159	94	62	68	59
5.30P												
(4 WK)	8	8	51	29	19	8	16	37	24	14	19	7
(4 WK KOIN)	11	11	78	62	17	6	13	54	18	10	14	2
(KOAC)			3	2	2	2	1	1	1	1	1	
(KGW)	8	7	51	32	17	10	13	33	16	9	15	16
(KOAP)			1	2	2	2	1	1	1		1	1
(KPTV)	11	11	79	52	39	29	23	57	47	37	27	32
H/P/T	38	36	263	179	96	57	67	183	107	72	76	58
6.00P												
(4 WK)	9	10	62	31	19	7	17	52	33	20	26	10
(KOIN)	9	8	65	58	16	7	11	46	15	9	12	1
(KOAC)			2	1	1	1	1	2	1	1	1	
(KGW)	10	10	68	51	23	12	20	45	20	10	19	13
(KOAP)			1	2	2	2	1	2	2		2	1
(KPTV)	12	12	83	56	42	33	24	62	52	40	30	33
H/P/T	41	38	281	199	103	62	74	209	123	82	88	58
(col #)	1	3	5	10	11	13	14	17	18	19	20	24

Daily

Weekly Programming

Time Period Averages

DAY AND TIME / STATION	PROGRAM	WEEK-BY-WEEK ADI TV HH RATINGS WK 1 11/2	WK 2 11/9	WK 3 11/16	WK 4 11/23	ADI TV HH RTG	ADI TV HH SH	ADI TV HH SHARE TRENDS OCT 77	MAY 77	FEB 77	NOV 76	METRO TV HH RTG	METRO TV HH SH	TV HH	WOMEN TOT 18+	WOMEN 18-49	WOMEN 15-24	WOMEN 18-34	WOMEN 25-49	WOMEN 25-54	WKG WMN 18+	MEN TOT 18+	MEN 18-49	MEN 18-34	MEN 25-49	MEN 25-54	TEENS TOT 12-17	CHILD TOT 2-11
		58	59	60	61	1	2	62	63	64	65	3	4	5	10	11	12	13	14	15	16	17	18	19	20	21	22	24
▲RELATIVE STD-ERR	25 - 49%	8	8	7	8	2						3		12	13	13	17	15	11	12	13	14	14	16	12	12	17	25
(1S.E.) THRESHOLDS	50 + %	2	2	2	2	-						-		3	3	3	4	4	3	2	3	3	3	4	3	3	4	6
SATURDAY																												
6.30P- 7.00P																												
KATU	NORTON-YOUNG	21				21	41					22	42	147	68							159						
	EYWTNS NWS 4		7	8	7	7	18					8	22	50	43	20	4	10	16	19	10	37	22	12	18	20	4	6
	--4 WK AVG--					11	26	25	20	27	24	12	29	74	49	25	6	13	20	25	14	67	40	24	31	36	11	11
KVDO	N A	-	-	-	-			**	**	**	**																	
KOIN	THIS LAND	5	6	6	8	6	14	14	17	18	17	6	15	47	42	12	4	5	9	15	8	36	15	10	9	15	4	2
KOAC	N A	-	-	-	-				**	**	**			1														
KGW	NBC NGHT NWS	10	12	14	12	12	28	33	34	33	35	12	29	81	68	23	4	11	21	27	14	54	20	11	17	22	3	8
KOAP	N A	-	-	1	-				**	**	**			1	1	1		1	1	1	1	2	2	2				
KPTV	SAT MOVIE	14	10	16	12	13	30	22	23	18	24	13	32	96	72	53	31	43	30	36	18	75	62	45	40	44	29	36
	HUT/PVT/TOT	51	37	44	40	43		36	35	45	46	41		300	232	114	45	73	81	104	55	234	139	92	97	117	47	57
7.00P- 7.30P																												
KATU	NORTON-YOUNG	24				24	42					23	43	166	86							185						
	LAWRNCE WELK		16	14	20	17	35					14	32	111	118	32	7	16	26	36	22	65	14	9	10	18	4	12
	--4 WK AVG--					18	35	38	50	43	39	16	35	125	111	36	9	18	28	38	24	95	37	24	27	37	10	17
KVDO	N A	-	-	-	-			**	**	**	**			1														
KOIN	HEE HAW	13	9	8	9	10	20	21	14	14	18	10	22	73	56	28	9	13	23	28	16	50	26	13	21	26	13	23
KOAC	N A	-	-	-	-				**	**	**			2	1		1					1	1		1	1	2	
KGW	CORAL JUNGLE	7	8	10	9	8	16	21	10	24	21	9	20	57	37	21	4	10	19	22	7	46	31	21	22	24	10	18
KOAP	N A	-	-	1	-				**	**	**	1	2	2	2	1	1	1	1	1	1	2	1		1	1	1	1
KPTV	SAT MOVIE	13	9	15	13	13	25	17	19	14	19	12	26	94	68	51	27	39	32	38	20	71	57	40	36	40	29	35
	HUT/PVT/TOT	57	46	50	53	51		48	42	51	57	46		354	275	137	51	81	103	127	68	265	153	98	108	129	65	94
7.30P- 8.00P																												
KATU	NORTON-YOUNG	24				24	43					24	44	167	93							184						
	LAWRNCE WELK		15	15	20	17	33					15	33	111	111	28	8	14	23	31	22	60	14	7	9	13	7	11
	--4 WK AVG--					19	37	36	50	44	38	17	35	125	107	34	11	18	26	34	25	91	37	23	25	32	12	13
KVDO	N A	-	-	-	-			**	**	**	**			1														
KOIN	HEE HAW	13	10	8	10	10	19	22	17	16	19	10	21	76	62	33	10	16	26	32	20	54	30	16	25	31	12	24
KOAC	N A	-	-	-	-				**	**	**			1														
KGW	CORAL JUNGLE	6	9	9	9	8	15	22	7	22	21	9	19	58	39	22	4	10	20	24	9	46	31	20	22	26	10	14
KOAP	N A	-	1	2	-	1	2		**	**	**	1	2	6	5	3	1	3	2	3	4	5	3	2	2	2	1	
KPTV	SAT MOVIE	13	8	14	13	12	23	18	19	14	17	12	25	90	69	50	27	35	30	36	19	69	55	39	34	38	27	32
	HUT/PVT/TOT	56	47	51	55	52		50	42	50	58	48		357	282	142	53	82	104	129	77	265	156	100	108	129	62	83
8.00P- 8.30P																												
KATU	NORTON-YOUNG	24				24	41					25	42	168	97							182						
	TABITHA		12	13	12	13	25					12	25	87	67	44	23	27	29	31	13	52	38	27	27	29	41	50
	--4 WK AVG--					16	30	24	21	31	23	16	31	107	75	46	22	27	31	34	19	85	53	38	37	42	38	41
KVDO	N A	1	-	-	-			**	**	**	**			2	2						1	1						
KOIN	SNPY CME HME	16				16	27					17	29	116	79							74						
	BOB NEWHART		14	10	16	14	27					14	29	98	85	33	15	22	21	35	24	64	30	19	22	29	8	11
	--4 WK AVG--					14	26	31	36	33	37	14	27	103	84	37	16	24	25	38	23	67	36	26	21	29	17	22
KOAC	N A	-	-	-	-				**	**	**			3	2	1	1	1			1	1						
KGW	BIONIC WOMAN	9	11		8	10	19					11	22	65	41	22	3	11	21	23	10	38	24	13	19	19	8	21
	NBC SAT MOV			16		16	31					19	37	114	96							86						
	--4 WK AVG--					11	21	28	21	25	32	13	25	78	55	30	3	14	29	31	11	50	28	15	23	24	7	20
KOAP	N A	1	2	2	1	1	2	2	**	**	**	1	2	10	10	4	1	2	3	5	3	5	2	1	1	2	1	
KPTV	SAT MOVIE	9	6	9	14	10	19	9	15	5	7	9	18	73	58	42	21	31	25	28	16	54	45	32	29	32	20	25
	HUT/PVT/TOT	59	47	51	56	53		54	47	55	60	51		376	286	160	64	99	113	136	74	263	164	112	111	129	83	108
8.30P- 9.00P																												
KATU	NORTON-YOUNG	26				26	43					26	45	178	135							180						
	ABC SAT MOV		10			10	20					12	26	71	47							59						
	OPRTN PETICT			18	18	18	33					17	34	122	86	65	34	35	44	53	34	93	74	44	53	62	59	56
	--4 WK AVG--					18	33	27	22	27	16	18	35	123	89	57	27	30	39	47	29	107	75	48	49	58	44	32
KVDO	N A	1	-	-	-			**	**	**	**			2	2						1							
KOIN	SNPY CME HME	17				17	28					16	28	129	78							69						
	GOT ECH OTHR		15	7	10	11	21					11	22	79	67	28	10	21	20	31	11	54	29	21	24	26	7	17
	--4 WK AVG--					12	22	25	35	32	35	12	24	91	70	31	11	22	23	35	14	58	34	27	22	26	21	27
KOAC	N A	-	-	-	-				**	**	**			2	1						1	1						
KGW	BIONIC WOMAN	10	15		8	11	20					12	24	71	45	28	5	15	26	29	10	41	32	19	24	24	16	37
	NBC SAT MOV			16		16	31					19	34	110	93							87						
	--4 WK AVG--					12	22	25	22	25	32	14	27	81	57	34	4	16	33	36	12	52	37	21	28	30	13	32
KOAP	N A	1	2	3	1	2	4	4	**	**	**	2	4	11	10	3		1	3	4	3	5	1	1		1	1	
KPTV	WRESTLING	7	6	6	15	8	15	13	14	13	13	8	16	67	45	21	8	14	16	18	9	56	24	16	15	17	5	12
	HUT/PVT/TOT	60	49	52	55	54		56	51	56	62	51		377	274	146	50	83	114	140	69	279	171	113	114	132	84	103
9.00P- 9.30P																												
KATU	LAWRNC WLK 1	17				17	30					16	28	114	95							102						
	ABC SAT MOV		13			13	22					14	25	87	65							66						
	STRSKY-HUTCH			16	16	16	30					15	28	109	84	64	38	41	41	47	18	77	64	43	39	46	44	41
	--4 WK AVG--					16	29	32	24	25	27	15	27	105	82	50	27	29	33	39	16	80	57	39	32	37	31	24
KVDO	N A	-	-	-	-			**	**	**	**			1	1	1	1	1	1	1		1	1		1	1	1	1
KOIN	SNPY CME HME	19				19	33					19	33	145	86							85						
	JEFFERSONS		17	14	15	15	27					16	29	107	89	44	17	25	32	42	21	65	35	18	29	37	11	24
	--4 WK AVG--					16	29	27	33	42	34	16	29	117	89	45	17	26	33	46	20	70	41	26	26	34	26	33
KOAC	N A	-	-	-	-				**	**	**			1							1	1						
KGW	NBC SAT MOV	13	22	15	10	15	27	22	20	19	23	17	31	100	81	53	9	29	45	52	24	66	48	29	38	41	10	8
KOAP	N A	-	2	3	1	1	2	2	**	**	**	1	2	10	11	3		2	3	3	2	5	2	2	1	1	1	
KPTV	WRESTLING	8	5	6	15	8	14	14	13	12	13	8	15	65	41	17	5	9	14	16	6	58	23	14	15	19	6	10
	HUT/PVT/TOT	57	59	53	56	56		59	54	57	62	55		399	305	169	59	96	129	157	69	281	172	110	113	133	75	76
9.30P-10.00P																												
KATU	LAWRNC WLK 1	18				18	34					17	33	119	89							74						
	ABC SAT MOV		14			14	25					14	26	96	64							66						
	STRSKY-HUTCH			16	17	17	34					15	30	112	84	65	36	41	44	50	18	79	64	43	42	51	43	42
	--4 WK AVG--					16	30	34	26	26	29	15	29	110	81	50	29	29	34	39	15	75	52	36	29	36	36	25
		58	59	60	61	1	2	62	63	64	65	3	4	5	10	11	12	13	14	15	16	17	18	19	20	21	22	24

TOTAL SURVEY AREA, IN THOUSANDS (000)

TECHNICAL DIFFICULTY
< M-F PROGRAM AIRED LESS THAN FIVE DAYS
+ PARENT/SATELLITE RELATIONSHIP
* SAMPLE BELOW MINIMUM FOR WEEKLY REPORTING
▲SEE TABLE ON PAGE iv

Time Period Averages   Station Break Averages

Time Period Averages

DAY, TIME, AND STATION	CHILD 6-11 (25)	PERS 18+ (7)	15-24 (8)	12-34 (9)	PERS 15-24 (31)	12-34 (32)	W TOT 18+ (33)	W 18-49 (34)	W 15-24 (35)	W 18-34 (36)	W 25-49 (37)	W 25-54 (38)	WKG WMN 18+ (39)	M TOT 18+ (40)	M 18-49 (41)	M 18-34 (42)	M 25-49 (43)	M 25-54 (44)	TNS 12-17 (45)	CHD 2-11 (46)
THRESHS 25-49%	21	17	20	19	6	2	2	3	9	5	4	3	7	2	3	6	4	4	8	10
THRESHS 50+%	5	3	5	3	1	-	-	-	2	1	1	1	1	-	1	1	1	1	2	2
SAT 6.30P																				
KATU (prog)							10							25						
KATU	3	79	11	25	3	3	6	5	2	3	5	6	5	6	6	5	6	6	2	2
4 WK	7	116	22	47	6	6	7	6	3	5	7	7	7	11	10	9	11	10	5	4
KVDO																				
KOIN	2	78	11	19	2	2	5	3	2	2	3	4	3	5	3	2	3	4	2	1
KOAC											1									
KGW	6	121	7	25	2	3	10	5	2	4	7	8	6	8	5	4	6	6	1	2
KOAP		3	2	3							1			1	1	1	1	1		
KPTV	23	147	59	116	16	14	9	11	16	14	9	9	7	11	14	16	12	11	13	12
H/P/T	38	465	101	210	28	28	33	26	24	25	27	28	24	36	33	34	33	33	23	21
7.00P																				
KATU (prog)							12							29						
KATU	7	183	12	29	3	4	18	8	4	6	9	10	11	10	3	3	3	5	2	5
4 WK	9	205	23	52	7	7	16	8	5	6	9	11	12	15	9	9	9	10	5	6
KVDO																				
KOIN	16	106	15	39	4	5	7	6	4	4	7	7	7	6	4	4	7	7	5	12
KOAC		2	2	2							1									
KGW	13	82	15	41	4	6	5	5	2	3	6	6	4	7	8	8	8	7	5	6
KOAP	1	4	1	2							1			2	2	1	2	2	1	
KPTV	23	139	53	107	15	13	9	11	14	13	9	9	8	10	13	14	11	10	13	12
H/P/T	62	538	109	243	32	33	41	32	28	29	34	35	31	41	37	37	36	36	32	36
7.30P																				
KATU (prog)							14							28						
KATU	8	171	14	28	4	4	17	7	4	5	8	9	11	9	3	2	3	4	3	4
4 WK	8	198	27	53	7	7	16	8	5	6	9	10	12	14	9	9	8	9	6	5
KVDO											1									
KOIN	17	115	17	44	4	6	8	7	5	5	9	9	9	8	7	5	8	8	6	9
KOAC											2				1		1			1
KGW	10	85	15	39	4	5	5	5	2	3	7	7	5	7	8	8	8	7	5	5
KOAP		10	2	6	1	1	1			1			1	1	1	1	1	1		1
KPTV	20	137	54	101	15	12	9	10	14	11	9	9	8	10	12	13	10	9	12	10
H/P/T	55	545	115	243	33	34	42	34	29	30	36	38	35	42	39	39	37	37	33	33
8.00P																				
KATU (prog)							14							28						
KATU	38	119	38	94	10	12	10	10	12	9	10	9	5	8	9	9	8	8	20	18
4 WK	31	159	45	102	12	13	11	11	11	9	10	10	8	13	13	14	12	11	19	15
KVDO		3																		
KOIN (prog)							11							12						
KOIN	6	149	25	48	7	6	12	8	8	7	9	12		9	7	7	7	8	4	4
4 WK	13	150	35	66	10	9	11	8	9	8	10	11	10	8	9	7	8	8	8	8
KOAC		3	1	1																
KGW	12	79	10	32	3	4	6	5	2	4	7	6	5	6	6	5	6	6	4	8
KGW (prog)							13							13						
4 WK	13	104	10	35	3	5	8	7	2	5	9	9	5	7	7	5	8	7	4	7
KOAP		15	2	4	1	1	1	1		1	1	2	1	1	1	1	1			
KPTV	15	112	41	83	11	9	7	8	10	9	7	7	6	8	8	10	11	8	8	8
H/P/T	72	546	134	291	38	39	41	37	35	35	37	39	34	41	40	41	37	37	42	42
8.30P																				
KATU (prog)							20 / 7							28 / 8						
KATU	45	179	66	138	18	18	12	15	18	12	15	15	16	15	18	16	18	18	29	21
4 WK	25	194	61	121	17	16	13	13	15	10	13	13	13	16	18	17	16	16	22	12
KVDO		2																		
KOIN (prog)							10							11						
KOIN	11	121	15	48	4	6	9	6	5	7	6	8	5	8	6	6	7	6	3	5
4 WK	17	128	28	69	8	8	9	7	6	7	9	9	6	8	7	9	6	6	9	8
KOAC		2																		
KGW (prog)							13							13						
KGW	22	86	15	50	4	6	6	6	3	5	8	5	6	8	7	8	7	8	8	14
4 WK	20	109	15	49	4	6	8	8	2	6	11	10	5	8	9	7	9	8	6	12
KOAP		15	1	3		1	1	1		1	1	1	2	1	1		1	1		
KPTV	8	101	17	35	4	4	5	4	4	5	4	4	4	7	5	6	4	4	1	5
H/P/T	70	551	122	277	36	38	41	36	29	33	39	41	32	43	41	42	39	38	41	40
9.00P																				
KATU (prog)							14 / 10							16 / 9						
KATU	32	160	71	128	18	16	12	15	21	15	14	14	9	11	14	13	13	14	22	15
4 WK	19	162	56	98	14	12	12	12	15	10	11	11	8	12	13	13	11	11	15	9
KVDO		2	1	2																
KOIN (prog)							11							13						
KOIN	18	154	24	54	7	7	12	10	9	9	10	11	10	10	8	6	9	10	6	9
4 WK	24	158	39	78	11	10	12	10	10	9	11	12	9	11	10	10	9	10	12	11
KOAC		1																		
KGW	7	147	23	68	7	9	12	13	5	11	15	15	11	11	12	11	13	12	5	3
KOAP		16	1	5		1	2	1		1	1	1	1	1		1				1
KPTV	7	99	13	28	3	3	5	4	3	3	4	4	3	8	5	5	4	4	2	3
H/P/T	57	585	133	279	37	39	44	41	34	37	44	45	34	44	43	43	41	41	37	29
9.30P																				
KATU (prog)							13 / 10							12 / 9						
KATU	34	163	66	126	16	16	12	15	19	14	15	15	9	11	14	13	14	15	21	16
4 WK	21	155	57	100	14	12	12	12	16	10	11	11	7	11	11	11	10	10	17	10

Station Break Averages — TOTAL SURVEY AREA, IN THOUSANDS (000)

TIME	ADI TV HH RTG (1)	MET TV HH RTG (3)	TV HH (5)	W TOT 18+ (10)	W 18-49 (11)	W 18-34 (13)	W 25-49 (14)	M TOT 18+ (17)	M 18-49 (18)	M 18-34 (19)	M 25-49 (20)	CHILD TOT 2-11 (24)
THRESHS 25-49%	2	3	12	13	13	15	11	14	14	16	12	25
THRESHS 50+%	-	-	3	3	3	4	3	3	3	4	3	6
6.30P												
4 WK	11	11	71	42	24	11	20	63	39	22	30	11
KOIN	8	7	55	50	13	6	10	40	14	10	10	2
KOAC								1				
KGW	12	12	80	68	24	11	22	55	21	12	19	8
KOAP	1	1		1	1	1	1	2	2	2	2	
KPTV	13	13	93	67	50	41	29	71	59	44	36	32
H/P/T	43	41	301	228	112	70	82	232	135	90	95	53
7.00P												
KATU	15	14	100	78	30	15	24	83	40	25	30	13
KVDO			1									
KOIN	8	8	59	48	19	8	15	43	20	11	15	12
KOAC			2	1				1	1			1
KGW	10	11	69	51	21	10	19	49	26	16	20	14
KOAP	1	1		2	1	1	1	2	2	1	1	
KPTV	13	13	95	71	53	41	32	73	60	43	39	35
H/P/T	47	44	327	251	124	75	91	251	149	96	106	74
7.30P												
KATU	19	17	125	109	35	18	27	92	37	23	26	15
KVDO			1									
KOIN	10	10	75	60	32	16	25	52	27	14	22	24
KOAC			2	1				1	1			1
KGW	8	9	57	38	21	10	19	46	31	21	22	15
KOAP	1	1	4	3	2	2	1	4	2	1	2	1
KPTV	12	12	92	68	50	37	30	69	56	39	34	33
H/P/T	52	47	356	279	140	83	102	264	154	98	107	88
8.00P												
KATU	18	16	116	92	40	22	28	86	44	30	30	28
KVDO			2	1								
KOIN 4 WK	12	12	89	71	34	19	25	60	34	21	23	24
KOAC			2	1	1		1					
KGW 4 WK	10	11	67	46	25	11	23	47	29	17	22	16
KOAP	1	1	8	7	3	3	2	5	3	2	2	
KPTV	9	9	84	66	48	34	30	64	51	37	32	29
H/P/T	53	50	368	284	151	90	108	263	161	107	109	97
8.30P												
KATU 4 WK	17	17	116	82	52	29	36	95	64	42	43	36
KVDO			2	2				1				
KOIN 4 WK	13	14	98	78	36	24	30	62	35	26	22	24
KOAC			3	2	1		1					
KGW 4 WK	12	14	80	55	31	15	30	51	33	18	26	27
KOAP	2	2	11	10	4	2	3	5	2	1	1	
KPTV	9	9	68	49	30	22	18	53	34	24	22	18
H/P/T	54	52	378	278	154	93	112	268	168	111	114	105
9.00P												
KATU 4 WK	17	17	114	83	52	29	34	94	67	44	40	28
KVDO			1	1								
KOIN 4 WK	14	15	105	78	39	24	28	63	37	26	24	30
KOAC			2	1				1				
KGW	14	16	90	69	43	23	39	58	42	24	33	20
KOAP	2	2	11	11	3	2	3	5	2	2	2	1
KPTV	14	16	66	43	18	11	15	56	22	14	14	11
H/P/T	55	53	389	286	155	89	119	277	170	110	112	89
9.30P												
KATU 4 WK	16	15	107	81	48	28	33	76	53	36	30	25

Weekly Programming — Time Period Averages

STATION	PROGRAM	WK1 11/2	WK2 11/9	WK3 11/16	WK4 11/23	ADI TV HH RTG	ADI TV HH SH	OCT 77	MAY 77	FEB 77	NOV 76	METRO RTG	METRO SH	TV HH	W TOT 18+	W 18-49	W 15-24	W 18-34	W 25-49	W 25-54	WKG WMN 18+	M TOT 18+	M 18-49	M 18-34	M 25-49	M 25-54	TEENS 12-17	CHILD 2-11
(col #)		58	59	60	61	1	2	62	63	64	65	3	4	5	10	11	12	13	14	15	16	17	18	19	20	21	22	24
▲RELATIVE STD-ERR (1S.E.) THRESHOLDS	25-49%	5	5	5	5	1						2		7	6	7	8	7	6	6	6	7	7	9	7	6	9	13
	50+%	1	1	1	1	-						-		1	1	1	2	2	1	2	2	1	1	2	1	2	2	3
MON-FRI 3.30P-4.00P																												
KATU	MEDICAL CNTR	4	4			4	14					4	15	27	22	14	7	9	8	8	2	5	5	5	1	1	2	1
	MEDICAL CNT<			4	3	4	13					4	14	27	22	12	6	7	8	8	5	11	5	3	3	4	6	4
	--4 WK AVG--					4	14	20	15	22	19	4	14	27	22	13	7	8	8	8	4	8	5	4	2	3	4	3
KVDO	N A	1	-	-	-			**	**	**	**			2														1
KOIN	MIKE DOUGLAS	9	6	6	7	7	24	35	30	26	19	6	21	50	44	13	3	6	11	15	4	21	6	4	3	4		2
KOAC	N A	-	-	-	-																							
KGW	AFTERNOONER	7	6		8	7	25					8	30	50	35	25	13	18	15	18	6	19	14	10	8	8	14	12
	AFTERNOONER<			6	8	7	23					8	28	45	28	19	12	14	11	12	6	28	19	13	12	13	11	11
	--4 WK AVG--					7	24	15	20	22	19	8	29	48	32	22	13	17	14	16	6	23	16	11	9	10	13	12
KOAP	N A	-	-											1														
KPTV	BUGS BUNNY	8	8	13	10	10	34	30	30	26	41	10	36	71	19	15	10	11	9	10	2	17	11	9	6	7	21	55
	HUT/PVT/TOT	29	26	31	28	29		20	20	23	27	28		199	117	63	33	42	42	49	16	69	38	28	20	24	41	70
4.00P-4.30P																												
KATU	MEDICAL CNTR	3	4			4	13					4	13	27	21	14	6	9	8	8	3	5	3	3		1	2	3
	MEDICAL CNT<			5	3	4	13					4	13	30	25	14	8	8	9	9	6	11	5	4	2	3	7	8
	--4 WK AVG--					4	13	17	20	24	16	4	13	29	23	14	7	9	9	9		8	4	4	1	2	5	5
KVDO	N A	1	-	-	-			**	**	**	**			2														1
KOIN	MIKE DOUGLAS	10	7	7	9	8	26	30	28	24	23	7	23	60	53	15	5	7	12	17	7	28	7	4	4	6	3	1
KOAC	N A	-	-	-	-																							
KGW	AFTERNOONER	8	6		7	7	23					8	28	51	37	24	15	17	14	18	8	23	16	11	10	11	16	11
	AFTERNOONER<			6		6	18					9	27	43	29							28						
	--4 WK AVG--					7	23	13	16	17	16	8	27	49	35	23	14	17	14	17	8	24	17	12	11	12	14	10
KOAP	N A	-										1	3	5	1	1		1	1	1		1						5
KPTV	MICKEY MOUSE	9	9	13	9	10	32	26	28	28	39	10	33	69	14	11	6	9	7	8	1	12	7	6	4	5	19	60
	HUT/PVT/TOT	32	29	33	30	31		23	25	29	31	30		214	126	64	32	43	43	52	21	72	35	26	20	25	42	81
4.30P-5.00P																												
KATU	LUCY SHOW	4	5			4	11					5	14	33	26	19	7	11	12	13	5	5	4	4	1	1	8	10
	LUCY SHOW<			7		7	19					8	21	52	39							16						
	VARIOUS				4	4	12					8	28		25							16						
	--4 WK AVG--					5	14	16	19	19	24	5	15	36	29	20	9	11	13	14	8	11	6	5	3	3	10	11
KVDO	N A	1	-	-	-			**	**	**	**			1														1
KOIN	MIKE DOUGLAS	11	8	8	10	9	26	28	27	25	21	8	24	65	56	17	5	7	14	19	8	33	9	5	6	9	4	2
KOAC	N A	-	-	-	-			**	**	**	**			1														1
KGW	AFTERNOONER	7	6		7	7	21					8	24	49	37	24	14	17	14	18	7	23	16	11	10	11	14	10
	AFTERNOONER<			7		7	19					9	24	47	31							31						
	--4 WK AVG--					7	20	16	15	16	21	8	24	49	36	24	14	17	14	17	8	25	18	12	11	13	13	10
KOAP	N A	1	2	1	1	1	3	4	**	**	**	1	3	6	1	1		1	1	1		1						6
KPTV	FLINTSTONES	11	10	13	11	11	31	28	31	31	24	12	35	78	20	16	9	12	9	10	5	15	9	7	4	6	26	63
	HUT/PVT/TOT	36	34	37	33	35		25	26	32	34	34		236	142	78	37	48	51	61	29	85	42	29	24	31	54	93
5.00P-5.15P																												
KATU	MARY T MOORE	7	9	8		9	17					9	18	60	49	33	15	22	20	22	13	27	15	10	9	12	10	9
	MARY T MOOR<				5	5	11					5	12	33	26							16						
	--4 WK AVG--					7	15	26	14	16	19	8	17	53	43	29	14	19	18	20	11	24	15	9	9	12	9	8
KVDO	N A	-	-	-	-			**	**	**	**																	
KOIN	NEWSROOM 6-E	14	17	17	16	16	34	26	31	35	31	16	33	113	98	29	4	10	26	35	16	79	24	10	18	27	2	3
KOAC	N A	-	-	-	-			**	**	**	**			1														1
KGW	NEWS EXTRA	8	6	5	8	7	15	21	20	21	17	8	17	46	37	13	5	7	9	15	9	25	9	5	7	10	4	3
KOAP	N A	1	1	1	-	1	2	3	**	**	**	1	2	3	1	1		1	1	1		1						5
KPTV	GILLIGANS IS	14	14	17	14	15	32	23	29	28	26	16	33	103	35	27	18	20	15	17	8	29	22	16	13	15	47	71
	HUT/PVT/TOT	45	51	50	44	47		39	35	43	42	48		321	214	99	41	57	69	88	44	157	70	40	47	64	62	91
5.15P-5.30P																												
KATU	MARY T MOORE	7	10	8		9	18					10	20	61	51	34	16	23	20	23	14	29	17	12	9	12	9	9
	MARY T MOOR<				5	5	11					5	12	32	27							15						
	--4 WK AVG--					7	15	25	14	14	19	8	16	54	45	29	14	20	18	20	12	26	16	11	9	12	8	8
KVDO	N A	-	-	-	-			**	**	**	**																	
KOIN	NEWSROOM 6-E	14	17	18	16	16	33	25	33	34	33	16	33	116	98	28	3	10	25	34	16	82	25	10	19	28	1	4
KOAC	N A	-	-	-	-			**	**	**	**			1														1
KGW	NEWS EXTRA	8	6	6	8	7	15	20	19	20	16	8	16	47	38	13	5	7	9	15	9	26	9	5	7	10	1	2
KOAP	N A	1	1	1	-	1	2	3	**	**	**	1	2	5	1	1		1	1	1		1						5
KPTV	GILLIGANS IS	14	14	17	15	15	31	23	28	27	26	16	33	104	35	27	17	19	16	18	9	31	23	17	13	15	48	69
	HUT/PVT/TOT	45	52	52	45	48		40	36	44	43	49		327	217	98	39	57	69	88	46	165	73	43	48	65	60	89
5.30P-5.45P																												
KATU	EYWTNS NWS 1	10	9	12		10	18					10	18	74	59	26	8	14	19	24	16	45	24	13	17	22	8	6
	EYWTNS NWS <				9	9	17					7	14	61	48							42						
	--4 WK AVG--					10	19	26	17	20	20	10	19	71	56	25	8	15	18	23	15	44	23	13	16	21	7	6
KVDO	N A	-	-	-	-			**	**	**	**																	
KOIN	NEWSROOM 6-E	13	17	15	16	15	28	22	27	29	25	15	28	110	93	27	4	11	24	33	17	77	26	10	20	29	3	5
KOAC	N A	-	-	-	-			**	**	**	**			1														1
KGW	530 NW TNGHT	11	9	11	12	11	20	24	27	25	25	12	22	73	56	19	5	10	15	23	12	46	16	8	14	18	4	1
KOAP	N A	1	2	1	1	1	2					1	2	6	1	1		1	1	1		1						7
KPTV	BEWITCHED	15		18	14	16	30					16	30	106	49	40	24	27	24	25	13	39	32	24	18	21	46	60
	BEWITCHED<		17			17	30					20	36	117	60							35						
	--4 WK AVG--					16	30	24	22	18	24	17	31	109	52	43	25	30	26	28	14	38	30	23	17	21	46	62
	HUT/PVT/TOT	51	56	57	53	54		46	41	51	51	54		370	258	115	42	67	84	108	58	205	95	54	67	89	60	82
5.45P-6.00P																												
KATU	EYWTNS NWS 1	9	10	12		10	18					10	18	74	57	25	8	14	18	23	17	45	25	14	18	23	8	6
	EYWTNS NWS <				9	9	17					7	14	62	46							44						7	5
	--4 WK AVG--					10	19	28	19	20	22	9	17	71	54	24	8	15	17	22	16	45	25	15	18	22	7	5
KVDO	N A	-	-	-	-			**	**	**	**																	
KOIN	NEWSROOM 6-E	13	17	15	16	15	28	21	26	29	25	15	28	109	94	27	4	11	24	33	17	77	27	11	21	30	3	4
KOAC	N A	-	-	-	-			**	**	**	**			1														1
KGW	530 NW TNGHT	12	10	11	12	11	20	23	26	27	25	12	23	75	59	20	5	11	16	24	12	47	15	7	13	18	4	2
(col #)		58	59	60	61	1	2	62	63	64	65	3	4	5	10	11	12	13	14	15	16	17	18	19	20	21	22	24

* TECHNICAL DIFFICULTY
< M-F PROGRAM AIRED LESS THAN FIVE DAYS
+ PARENT/SATELLITE RELATIONSHIP
* SAMPLE BELOW MINIMUM FOR WEEKLY REPORTING
▲ SEE TABLE ON PAGE IV

Time Period Averages   Station Break Averages

Time Period Averages

DAY, TIME, AND STATION	CHILD 6-11 (25)	PERSONS 18+ (7)	PERSONS 15-24 (8)	PERSONS 12-34 (9)	PERS 15-24 (31)	PERS 12-34 (32)	W TOT18+ (33)	W 18-49 (34)	W 15-24 (35)	W 18-34 (36)	W 25-49 (37)	W 25-54 (38)	WKG WMN 18+ (39)	M TOT18+ (40)	M 18-49 (41)	M 18-34 (42)	M 25-49 (43)	M 25-54 (44)	TNS 12-17 (45)	CHD 2-11 (46)
THRESHS 25-49%	11	9	11	8	3	1	1	1	4	2	2	2	3	1	2	3	2	2	5	5
THRESHS 50+%	3	-	2	2	-	-	-	-	1	-	-	-	-	-	-	-	-	-	1	1
M-F 3.30P																				
KATU		26	11	16	3	2	3	3	4	3	2	2	1	1	1	2			1	
	3	33	10	16	2	2	3	3	2	2	3	2	2	1	1	1	1	1	3	1
4 WK	2	30	11	16	3	2	3	3	3	3	3	2	1	1	1	1		1	2	1
KVDO			1	1															1	
KOIN		65	6	12	2	2	6	3	2	2	4	4	2	3	1	1	1	1	1	
KOAC																				
KGW	9	54	22	42	6	6	5	6	8	7	5	5	3	3	4	4	3	3	6	4
	8	56	21	38	6	5	4	4	6	5	3	3	2	4	5	5	4	4	5	4
4 WK	9	55	21	41	6	5	4	5	7	6	4	4	3	4	4	4	3	3	6	4
KOAP				1																
KPTV	34	36	19	41	6	5	2	3	5	4	3	3	1	2	3	3	2	2	9	19
H/P/T	45	186	58	111	17	15	17	15	18	15	14	14	7	11	10	11	7	7	20	26
4.00P																				
KATU	2	26	9	14	3	2	3	3	4	3	3	2	1	1	1	1			1	1
	6	35	12	19	3	2	3	3	3	3	2	2	2	1	1	1		1	3	3
4 WK	4	31	11	17	3	2	3	3	4	3	2	2	2	1	1	1			2	2
KVDO			1	1																
KOIN		81	8	14	2	2	7	3	3	2	4	4	3	4	2	2	1	2	1	
KOAC																				
KGW	9	59	24	44	7	6	5	5	8	6	4	5	3	3	4	4	3	3	7	4
									4					4						
4 WK	8	59	23	43	7	6	5	5	8	6	4	4	3	4	4	4	3	3	6	3
KOAP		1	1																	2
KPTV	38	25	12	34	4	5	2	3	4	3	2	2	1	1	2	2	1	1	9	22
H/P/T	51	197	55	110	17	16	18	15	19	15	14	14	9	12	9	10	7	7	22	32
4.30P																				
KATU	7	31	12	22	3	3	4	4	4	4	3	3	2	1	1	1			3	3
									5					2						
									3					2						
4 WK	9	40	15	25	4	3	4	4	5	4	4	3	3	2	2	2	1	1	4	4
KVDO			1	1																
KOIN	1	89	8	16	2	2	8	4	2	2	4	5	3	5	2	2	2	2	2	1
KOAC																				
KGW	8	60	23	42	7	6	5	5	8	6	4	4	4	4	4	4	3	3	7	3
									4				5							
4 WK	8	61	23	42	7	6	5	5	7	6	4	4	4	4	4	4	3	3	6	3
KOAP	1	2		1																3
KPTV	41	35	20	45	6	6	3	4	5	4	3	3	2	2	2	3	1	2	13	23
H/P/T	60	227	67	130	20	18	20	18	22	18	17	17	13	14	11	12	8	9	27	37
5.00P																				
KATU	6	76	22	42	6	5	7	8	9	8	6	6	5	4	4	4	3	3	4	3
									4					3						
4 WK	5	68	20	38	6	5	6	7	8	7	5	5	5	3	4	3	3	3	3	2
KVDO																				
KOIN	2	177	11	22	3	3	13	7	2	4	8	9	8	12	5	4	6	7	1	1
KOAC	1																			1
KGW	2	62	8	16	3	2	5	3	3	3	4	4	4	4	2	2	3	3	2	1
KOAP	1	1		1																6
KPTV	50	64	38	83	11	11	5	7	10	7	5	5	4	5	5	6	4	4	22	26
H/P/T	61	372	77	160	24	23	31	24	25	23	23	25	21	25	18	17	16	18	30	35
5.15P																				
KATU	6	80	25	44	7	6	7	9	9	8	6	6		4	4	4	3	3	4	3
									4					2						
4 WK	5	71	22	39	6	5	6	7	8	7	5	5	5	4	4	4	3	3	4	2
KVDO																				
KOIN	3	180	10	21	3	3	13	7	2	4	8	9	8	12	4	4	6	7	1	1
KOAC	1																			1
KGW	1	64	8	15	2	2	5	3	3	3	4	4	4	2	2	3	3	2	2	
KOAP	1	1		1																2
KPTV	50	66	38	84	11	11	5	7	10	7	5	5	4	5	6	6	4	4	23	26
H/P/T	61	382	78	160	24	23	31	24	25	23	23	25	21	26	18	17	17	19	31	35
5.30P																				
KATU	4	104	17	35	5	4	8	6	5	5	6	6	7	7	6	5	6	6	3	2
							6						6							
4 WK	4	101	16	34	5	4	8	5	4	5	6	6	7	7	6	5	6	6	3	2
KVDO																				
KOIN	4	170	11	24	3	3	13	6	2	4	8	9	8	12	6	4	7	8	1	1
KOAC	1																			1
KGW	4	102	8	22	2	3	8	5	3	4	5	7	6	7	4	3	4	5	2	1
KOAP	3	1		1																3
KPTV	46	88	48	97	14	13	7	10	14	10	8	7	6	8	9	6	6	6	22	22
							8						5							
4 WK	46	90	47	99	14	13	7	10	14	11	9	8	7	6	7	8	6	6	22	22
H/P/T	59	464	82	180	24	25	38	28	24	25	29	31	29	33	24	21	23	25	29	32
5.45P																				
KATU	4	102	17	36	5	5	8	6	5	6	6	7	7	7	6	5	6	6	4	2
							6						7							
4 WK	4	99	16	36	4	4	7	5	4	5	6	6	7	7	6	5	6	6	3	2
KVDO																				
KOIN	3	171	11	25	3	3	13	6	2	4	8	8	8	11	6	4	7	8	1	1
KOAC	1																			1
KGW	1	106	8	22	2	3	9	5	3	4	5	7	6	7	3	3	4	5	2	1
	25	7	8	9	31	32	33	34	35	36	37	38	39	40	41	42	43	44	45	46

Station Break Averages

TIME / STATION	ADI TV HH RTG (1)	MET TV HH RTG (3)	TV HH (5)	W TOT18+ (10)	W 18-49 (11)	W 18-34 (13)	W 25-49 (14)	M TOT18+ (17)	M 18-49 (18)	M 18-34 (19)	M 25-49 (20)	CHD TOT 2-11 (24)
THRESHS 25-49%	1	2	7	6	7	7	6	7	7	9	7	13
THRESHS 50+%	-	-	1	1	1	2	1	1	1	2	1	3
3.30P												
KATU												
	4	4	26	22	12	7	9	5	3	3	1	2
KVDO			2									
KOIN	7	5	45	39	13	7	11	18	4	3	2	1
KGW												
	7	8	46	30	21	16	13	21	15	10	10	10
KOAP			1									
KPTV	9	9	61	18	15	11	9	16	10	8	4	42
H/P/T	26	25	181	109	61	41	42	60	32	24	17	55
4.00P												
KATU												
	4	4	27	22	13	9	8	8	4	4	1	3
KVDO			2									
KOIN	8	7	54	48	14	7	12	24	6	4	3	
KGW												
	7	8	48	33	23	17	13	23	17	12	11	11
KOAP	2	2	3	1	1	1	1	1				2
KPTV	10	10	70	17	13	10	8	14	9	7	5	58
H/P/T	30	29	204	121	64	44	42	69	36	27	20	74
4.30P												
KATU												
	5	5	33	26	17	10	10	10	6	5	2	8
KVDO			2									
KOIN	9	8	63	55	16	7	13	31	8	5	5	2
KOAC			1									1
KGW												
	7	8	48	34	23	17	13	24	17	12	11	10
KOAP	1	1	6	1	1	1	1	1				6
KPTV	11	11	73	17	14	10	8	14	8	7	4	61
H/P/T	34	33	226	133	71	45	45	80	39	29	22	88
5.00P												
KATU												
	6	7	45	37	24	15	15	18	11	7	6	9
KVDO			1									
KOIN	13	12	89	77	23	9	20	56	17	8	12	3
KOAC												1
KGW	7	8	48	36	18	12	11	25	13	8	9	7
KOAP	1	1	6	1	1	1	1					6
KPTV	14	14	91	28	22	16	12	22	16	12	9	68
H/P/T	41	42	281	179	88	53	59	121	57	35	36	94
5.15P												
KATU												
	8	8	54	44	29	20	17	24	15	10	9	8
KVDO												
KOIN	16	16	115	98	29	10	26	81	25	10	19	4
KOAC			1									1
KGW	7	8	47	38	13	7	9	26	9	5	7	3
KOAP	1	1	5	1	1	1	1					5
KPTV	15	16	104	35	27	20	16	30	23	17	13	70
H/P/T	48	49	326	216	99	58	69	161	72	42	48	91
5.30P												
KATU	9	9	62	50	27	17	18	35	20	12	14	7
KVDO												
KOIN	16	16	113	96	28	11	25	80	26	10	20	5
KOAC			1									1
KGW	9	10	60	47	16	9	12	36	13	7	11	2
KOAP	1	1	6	1	1	1						6
KPTV	16	17	107	43	35	25	21	35	27	20	15	66
H/P/T	51	52	349	237	107	63	77	186	86	49	60	87
5.45P												
KATU	10	10	71	55	24	14	18	47	26	15	19	6
KVDO												
KOIN	15	15	110	94	27	11	24	77	27	11	21	5
KOAC			1									1
KGW	11	12	74	58	20	11	16	47	16	8	14	2
	1	3	5	10	11	13	14	17	18	19	20	24

Weekly Programming / Time Period Averages

DAY AND TIME / STATION — PROGRAM	WK1 58	WK2 59	WK3 60	WK4 61	ADI RTG 1	ADI SH 2	OCT 77 62	MAY 77 63	FEB 77 64	NOV 76 65	METRO RTG 3	METRO SH 4	TV HH 5	W TOT 18+ 10	W 18-49 11	W 15-24 12	W 18-34 13	W 25-49 14	W 25-54 15	WKG WMN 18+ 16	M TOT 18+ 17	M 18-49 18	M 18-34 19	M 25-49 20	M 25-54 21	TEENS 12-17 22	CHILD 2-11 24
▲RELATIVE STD-ERR 25-49%	5	5	5	5	1						2		7	6	7	8	7	6	6	6	7	7	9	7	6	9	13
(1S.E.) THRESHOLDS 50+%	1	1	1	1	-						-		1	1	1	2	1	1	2	2	1	1	2	1	2	2	3
MON-FRI																											
5.45P- 6.00P																											
KOAP N A					1	2	2	**	**	**	1	2	6	1													6
KPTV BEWITCHED	15		18	14	15	28					16	30	105	53	44	27	30	26	28	15	40	33	25	18	21	48	61
BEWITCHED<		17			17	30					21	38	119	61							36						
--4 WK AVG--					16	30	23	21	20	24	17	32	109	55	46	27	33	27	30	16	39	31	23	17	21	47	63
HUT/PVT/TOT	50	57	57	54	54			47	42	51	51	53	371	263	118	44	71	85	110	61	209	99	57	70	92	61	81
6.00P- 6.15P																											
KATU ABC EVE NEW<	10			12	11	19					10	18	80	62	23	5	13	19	26	16	60	30	16	24	30	7	6
ABC EVE NEWS		10	11		10	17					12	20	74	61	24	6	10	20	23	15	41	25	13	21	22	9	3
--4 WK AVG--					11	19	26	17	21	21	11	19	77	62	24	6	12	20	25	16	51	28	15	23	26	8	5
KVDO N A	-	-	-	-			**	**	**	**			1														
KOIN CBS EVE NEW<	15				15	25					18	32	108	76							69						
CBS EVE NEWS		15	15	15	15	25					14	24	102	83	25	4	12	21	29	21	76	26	14	20	28	2	5
--4 WK AVG--					15	25	22	27	28	23	15	26	104	81	27	4	12	23	32	22	74	28	14	23	31	3	4
KOAC N A	-	-	-	-			**	**	**	**			1														
KGW 530 NW TNGH<	13				13	22					12	21	83	74							52						
530 NW TNGHT		11	12	14	12	20					13	22	82	62	21	4	10	18	26	14	50	15	7	13	20	5	2
--4 WK AVG--					12	20	24	29	26	27	13	22	82	65	20	5	11	17	26	15	51	15	7	12	18	4	2
KOAP N A	-	-	-	-			**	**	**				1														
KPTV EMERGENCY 1	19		21	17	19	32					19	33	131	82	66	35	48	41	45	21	62	46	34	27	34	45	70
EMERGENCY 1<		22			22	37					24	42	155	109							66						
--4 WK AVG--					20	34	24	25	21	27	20	34	137	89	69	35	50	44	48	22	63	48	35	30	36	44	71
HUT/PVT/TOT	59	59	60	59	59			54	48	57	56	58	402	297	140	50	85	104	131	75	239	119	71	88	111	59	82
6.15P- 6.30P																											
KATU ABC EVE NEWS	10	10	11		10	17					11	19	72	59	23	5	10	19	23	15	43	24	12	20	23	7	4
ABC EVE NEW<				13	13	22					11	20	69	69							72						
--4 WK AVG--					11	19	27	17	21	21	11	19	76	62	23	6	12	19	24	16	50	27	15	22	26	7	5
KVDO N A	-	-	-	-			**	**	**	**																	
KOIN CBS EVE NEW<	15				15	26					18	32	108	76							71						
CBS EVE NEWS		14	14	14	14	24					13	22	100	81	25	4	12	21	29	19	74	26	15	20	28	3	5
--4 WK AVG--					14	24	22	27	28	23	14	24	102	80	28	4	13	24	32	21	73	29	15	23	32	3	4
KOAC N A	-						**	**	**				1														
KGW 530 NW TNGHT	13	11	13	14	13	22	25	29	28	27	13	22	83	66	21	5	11	17	26	16	52	15	7	12	17	5	2
KOAP N A	-	-	-	-			**	**	**				1														
KPTV EMERGENCY 1	20		21	17	19	32					19	33	131	85	69	35	50	43	47	22	64	48	36	29	36	43	69
EMERGENCY 1<		22			22	37					24	43	154	108							67						
--4 WK AVG--					20	34	25	23	21	27	20	34	137	91	71	35	52	45	50	23	65	49	36	31	37	42	70
HUT/PVT/TOT	58	59	60	59	59			55	48	57	56	58	399	299	143	50	88	105	132	76	240	120	73	88	112	57	81
6.30P- 6.45P																											
KATU EYWTNS NWS <	10			14	12	20					10	18	87	66	24	6	12	20	28	18	67	34	21	24	33	8	7
EYWTNS NWS 2		10	8		9	16					10	17	66	53	21	6	7	18	21	14	44	23	11	17	18	7	2
--4 WK AVG--					11	19	27	19	21	21	10	18	77	60	23	6	10	19	25	16	56	29	16	21	26	8	5
KVDO N A	-	-	-	-			**	**	**	**			1														1
KOIN ODD COUPLE<	15				15	25					14	25	104	83							58						
ODD COUPLE		11	11	10	11	19					13	22	75	59	30	13	17	21	26	16	50	25	13	19	24	13	13
--4 WK AVG--					12	21	16	23	26	21	11	19	82	65	33	13	19	24	30	18	52	28	14	22	27	13	12
KOAC N A	-						**	**	**				2	1						1	1				1		
KGW NBC NGHT NWS	13	12	17	16	15	26	29	33	30	28	16	28	97	78	24	6	14	19	28	18	65	21	12	17	23	4	2
KOAP N A	-	-	-	1	1	2	**	**	**				4	3							2						
KPTV EMERGENCY 1	19		21	16	19	32					19	33	126	85	68	35	50	41	45	23	63	47	35	29	36	40	67
EMERGENCY 1<		22			22	38					25	45	152	108							76						
--4 WK AVG--					19	33	25	23	21	28	20	35	133	91	71	34	52	44	49	24	66	50	37	33	38	39	69
HUT/PVT/TOT	59	58	58	58	58			56	48	57	57	57	396	298	151	59	95	106	133	77	242	128	79	93	115	64	89
6.45P- 7.00P																											
KATU EYWTNS NWS 2	10	10	9		10	17					10	18	70	53	21	4	7	19	25	14	50	27	15	19	24	7	3
EYWTNS NWS <				14	14	24					10	19	97	72							75						
--4 WK AVG--					11	19	16	21	27	20	11	20	80	58	21	5	9	19	25	15	56	29	17	21	26	7	4
KVDO N A	-	-	-	-			**	**	**	**			1														1
KOIN ODD COUPLE<	14				14	24					13	23	99	76							57						
ODD COUPLE		11	11	10	11	19					11	20	74	57	31	14	18	21	26	17	47	25	13	19	24	14	14
--4 WK AVG--					11	19	16	21	27	20	11	20	80	62	33	13	19	23	30	19	50	27	14	22	27	14	13
KOAC N A	-						**	**	**				2	1						1	1				1		
KGW NBC NGHT NWS	13	12	16	16	14	24	27	32	30	29	16	29	95	79	25	7	15	19	28	18	64	21	12	18	24	3	2
KOAP N A	-		1	1	1	2	**	**	**				4	3							1						
KPTV EMERGENCY 1	19		20	16	19	33					19	33	126	87	70	35	51	43	47	23	65	49	36	31	38	40	66
EMERGENCY 1<		22			22	39					24	44	149	106							76						
--4 WK AVG--					19	33	25	23	21	27	20	36	132	92	72	35	52	45	49	24	68	52	38	34	40	39	67
HUT/PVT/TOT	58	57	58	58	58			55	47	56	56	56	391	295	151	60	95	106	133	77	240	129	81	95	118	63	87
7.00P- 7.15P																											
KATU TELL TRUTH<	12	13	12		12	21					12	21	89	60	20	6	9	16	20	17	63	35	21	27	29	11	13
VARIOUS				19	19	32					16	29	127	92							104						
--4 WK AVG--					14	24	33	26	25	28	13	23	99	68	23	8	11	18	22	18	73	41	26	31	33	13	13
KVDO N A	-	-	-	-			**	**	**	**			1														2
KQIN MERV GRIFFIN	16	11	10	12	12	21	17	19	23	25	12	21	87	72	27	6	10	23	31	17	53	21	11	15	23	6	5
KOAC N A	-	-	-	-			**	**	**				1														
KGW EVENING<	13			11	12	20					14	25	82	73	34	9	20	26	32	19	53	25	16	18	23	4	7
EVENING		9	13		11	19					14	24	77	62	32	13	18	22	27	18	46	29	16	25	27	11	9
--4 WK AVG--					12	21	24	32	29	25	14	25	80	68	33	11	19	24	30	19	50	27	16	22	25	8	8
KOAP N A	1	-		1	1	2	2	**	**	**	1	2	4	2	1			1	1	1	4	2	2	1	2		
KPTV I LOVE LUCY	15		20	15	17	29					17	30	115	81	61	31	42	38	43	21	60	42	28	29	36	33	53
I LOVE LUCY<		21			21	37					25	45	141	98							66						
--4 WK AVG--					18	31	22	21	21	19	19	33	122	85	66	31	46	42	47	25	62	44	29	31	37	33	56
HUT/PVT/TOT	58	57	58	59	58			58	47	56	57	57	394	295	150	56	87	108	131	79	242	135	84	100	120	60	84

\# TECHNICAL DIFFICULTY
< M-F PROGRAM AIRED LESS THAN FIVE DAYS
+ PARENT/SATELLITE RELATIONSHIP
* SAMPLE BELOW MINIMUM FOR WEEKLY REPORTING
▲ SEE TABLE ON PAGE iv

Time Period Averages   /   Station Break Averages

DAY, TIME, AND STATION	CHILD 6-11	PERS 18+	15-24	12-34	PERS 15-24	12-34	W TOT 18+	W 18-49	W 15-24	W 18-34	W 25-49	W 25-54	WKG WMN 18+	M TOT 18+	M 18-49	M 18-34	M 25-49	M 25-54	TNS 12-17	CHD 2-11	TIME	ADI TV HH RTG	MET TV HH RTG	TV HH	W TOT 18+	W 18-49	W 18-34	W 25-49	M TOT 18+	M 18-49	M 18-34	M 25-49	CHILD 2-11
col #	25	7	8	9	31	32	33	34	35	36	37	38	39	40	41	42	43	44	45	46		1	3	5	10	11	13	14	17	18	19	20	24
THRESHS 25-49%	11	9	11	8	3	1	1	1	4	2	2	2	3	1	2	3	2	2	5	5		1	2	7	6	7	7	6	7	7	9	7	13
THRESHS 50+%	3	–	2	2	–	–	–	–	1	–	–	–	–	–	–	–	–	–	1	1		–	–	1	1	1	2	1	1	1	2	1	3
M-F 5.45P																					5.45P												
KOAP	2	2		2																2		1	1	6	1	1	1	1	1	1	1	1	7
KPTV	47	93	53	103	15	14	8	10	16	11	9	8	8	6	8	9	6	6	23	22													
4 WK	47	94	51	103	15	14	8	11	15	12	9	8	8	6	8	9	6	6	22	23		16	17	109	53	44	31	27	38	30	23	17	63
H/P/T	58	472	86	188	25	26	38	28	25	26	29	31	29	33	24	22	24	26	30	31		54	54	371	261	116	68	86	210	100	58	72	84
6.00P																					6.00P												
KATU	6	122	13	36	4	5	9	5	3	4	6	7	9	7	6	8	9		3	2													
	2	102	13	32	4	5	8	6	3	4	7	6	6	6	5	7	8		3	1													
4 WK	4	112	13	34	4	4	9	5	3	4	6	7	7	8	7	6	8	8	3	2		11	10	74	58	24	13	19	49	27	15	21	6
KVDO																																	
KOIN	4	159	11	28	3	4	12	6	2	4	7	8	10	12	6	5	7	8	1	1													
4 WK	3	156	11	29	3	4	11	6	2	4	8	9	11	11	7	5	7	9	1	1		15	15	107	88	27	12	24	76	28	13	22	4
KOAC																				1													1
KGW	1	112	8	22	2	3	11→9	5	2	4	6	7	8	8	4	3	5	6	3	1													
4 WK	1	116	9	21	3	3	10	5	3	4	5	7	7	8	4	3	4	5	2	1		12	13	79	62	20	11	16	50	16	8	13	2
KOAP																						1	1	4	1	1	1	1	1	1	1	1	3
KPTV	48	144	64	127	19	17	12	16	20	17	14	13	11	10	11	13	9	10	22	26													
4 WK	48	152	62	129	18	17	13	16	19	18	14	13	11	10	12	13	10	10	21	26		18	19	123	72	57	41	36	51	39	29	24	67
H/P/T	56	536	95	213	28	30	44	34	28	32	35	38	36	39	30	28	31	33	29	31		57	56	388	281	129	78	96	227	111	66	81	83
6.15P																					6.15P												
KATU	3	102	11	29	3	4	8	6	3	4	7	7	7	6	6	5	7	7	4	2													
4 WK	4	112	13	33	4	4	9	5	3	4	6	7	7	8	7	6	7	7	4	2		11	11	77	62	23	11	19	50	28	15	23	5
KVDO																																	
KOIN	4	155	11	30	3	4	11	6	2	4	7	8	10	11	6	5	6	8	1	2													
4 WK	3	153	11	31	3	4	11	7	2	4	8	9	10	11	7	6	8	9	2	1		15	15	103	81	28	13	24	75	29	15	23	4
KOAC																				1													
KGW	1	118	10	23	3	3	10	5	3	4	6	8	7	8	4	3	4	5	2	1		13	13	83	66	21	11	17	52	16	8	13	2
KOAP																				1													
KPTV	46	149	64	129	19	17	12	16	20	18	14	13	11	10	12	14	10	10	21	25													
4 WK	46	156	62	130	18	17	13	17	19	19	15	14	11	10	12	14	10	10	20	25		20	20	137	89	70	51	44	65	49	36	31	71
H/P/T	54	539	96	217	28	30	44	34	28	32	36	38	37	39	30	29	31	33	29	31		59	58	402	298	142	86	104	242	122	74	90	82
6.30P																					6.30P												
KATU	6	133	18	41	5	5	9	5	3	4	6	7	9	10	8	8	8	9	4	2													
	1	97	13	25	4	4	7	5	3	3	6	6	6	6	5	6	6	7	4	1													
4 WK	4	115	16	33	5	4	8	5	3	3	6	7	7	8	7	6	7	7	4	2		11	11	76	61	23	11	19	52	28	16	22	5
KVDO	1																			1				1									1
KOIN	10	109	22	43	6	6	8	7	6	7	7	8	9	8	6	5	6	7	5	5													
4 WK	9	117	22	46	6	6	9	8	7	7	8	9	9	8	7	5	7	8	6	5		13	13	92	73	31	16	24	63	28	15	22	9
KOAC		2																						1					1				1
KGW	1	143	12	30	3	4	12	6	4	5	6	8	11	9	5	5	6	7	2	1		14	15	90	72	23	13	18	59	18	10	15	2
KOAP		5							1															1					1				
KPTV	45	148	62	125	18	17	12	16	19	18	14	13	12	10	12	13	10	10	19	24													
4 WK	45	157	60	128	17	17	13	17	19	19	15	14	11	12	14	11	11		19	25		20	20	135	90	70	51	44	66	50	37	32	70
H/P/T	60	539	110	237	32	33	44	37	34	36	37	39	38	40	33	32	33	35	31	34		59	58	398	299	147	91	105	242	124	78	91	87
6.45P																					6.45P												
KATU	2	103	13	29	4	4	7	5	3	3	6	7	11	7	6	6	6	6	4	1													
4 WK	3	114	14	33	4	4	8	5	3	3	6	7	8	7	7	7	7	7	4	2		11	10	77	59	23	10	19	55	29	17	21	4
KVDO	1																			1				1									1
KOIN	11	104	23	45	7	6	8	7	8	7	7	8	9	7	6	5	6	7	6	5													
4 WK	9	111	22	46	6	6	9	8	7	7	8	9	9	8	7	5	7	7	6	5		12	11	81	64	34	19	24	51	27	14	21	13
KOAC		2																		1				2		1			1				
KGW	1	143	11	30	3	4	12	6	4	5	6	8	9	10	5	5	6	7	2			15	16	96	79	25	15	19	65	21	12	18	2
KOAP		4							1													1	1	4	3				2				
KPTV	46	152	62	127	18	17	12	16	19	18	14	13	12	10	12	13	10	11	19	24													
4 WK	45	160	60	128	17	17	13	17	19	19	15	14	11	12	14	11	11		18	25		19	20	133	91	71	52	44	67	51	37	34	68
H/P/T	59	534	107	237	32	33	44	37	34	36	36	38	38	40	33	32	33	35	30	34		58	57	394	297	153	96	106	241	128	80	94	88
7.00P																					7.00P												
KATU	9	123	17	41	5	5	8	5	3	3	5	5	8	9	8	7	9	8	5	4													
4 WK	9	141	22	49	6	6	9	5	4	4	5	6	11	10	9	10	9	6	4			13	12	88	63	22	10	18	64	35	21	26	9
KVDO	1																		1					1									2
KOIN	4	125	14	27	4	4	10	7	4	4	8	9	8	8	5	4	5	7	3	2		12	12	84	67	31	15	24	51	24	13	18	9
KOAC																								2		1			1				
KGW	4	126	18	40	5	5	10	8	5	7	8	9	10	8	6	6	6	6	2	2													
	7	108	18	45	5	5	6	9	8	7	7	8	9	7	6	7	7	8	6	3													
4 WK	6	117	19	43	5	6	10	8	6	7	8	9	7	7	6	7	7	9	4	3		13	15	87	73	29	17	22	57	24	14	20	5
KOAP		6	1	3															1	1		1	1	4	3	1	1	1	3	1	1	1	
KPTV	39	141	47	103	14	14	12	14	18	16	13	12	11	9	10	11	10	10	16	19													
4 WK	40	147	47	107	14	14	12	15	17	17	14	13	12	10	11	11	10	10	16	21		19	20	127	89	69	49	43	64	47	33	32	62
H/P/T	60	536	103	229	32	33	44	37	33	34	37	38	39	39	35	34	35	36	30	33		58	57	393	296	152	92	108	240	131	82	97	87

Weekly Programming — Time Period Averages

MON-FRI   NOV 1977   PAGE 92   PORTLAND, OR

STATION	PROGRAM	WK1 11/2	WK2 11/9	WK3 11/16	WK4 11/23	ADI RTG	ADI SH	OCT 77	MAY 77	FEB 77	NOV 76	METRO RTG	METRO SH	TV HH	W TOT 18+	W 18-49	W 15-24	W 18-34	W 25-49	W 25-54	WKG WMN 18+	M TOT 18+	M 18-49	M 18-34	M 25-49	M 25-54	TEENS 12-17	CHILD 2-11
	(col #)	58	59	60	61	1	2	62	63	64	65	3	4	5	10	11	12	13	14	15	16	17	18	19	20	21	22	24
▲RELATIVE STD-ERR	25-49%	5	5	5	5	1							2	7	6	7	8	7	6	6	6	7	7	9	7	6	9	13
(1 S.E.) THRESHOLDS	50 + %	1	1	1	1	-							-	1	1	1	2	2	1	2	2	1	1	2	1	2	2	3
MON-FRI																												
7.15P- 7.30P																												
KATU	TELL TRUTH<	12	13	13		12	21					11	19	89	59	19	6	8	15	19	16	63	36	21	28	30	11	14
	VARIOUS				19	19	32					16	30	129	88							105					12	14
	--4 WK AVG--					14	24	33	26	23	28	13	23	99	66	21	7	10	17	21	17	74	42	26	32	34	12	14
KVDO	N A	-	-	-										1														2
KOIN	MERV GRIFFIN	16	11	10	12	12	21	17	19	25	25	12	21	87	72	27	6	10	23	31	16	53	20	11	14	23	6	6
KOAC	N A	-	-	-	-				**	**	**			1														
KGW	EVENING<	13			11	12	20					13	24	81	72	34	9	20	26	32	19	51	24	16	17	22	3	7
	EVENING		9	12		11	19					14	24	73	62	33	15	20	22	27	17	42	28	16	24	26	13	8
	--4 WK AVG--					11	19	22	30	29	23	13	23	77	67	34	12	20	24	30	18	47	26	16	21	24	8	8
KOAP	N A	1	1	1	1	1	2	2	**	**	**	1	2	5	3	1		1	1	1	1	4	2	1	2	2		
KPTV	I LOVE LUCY	15		19	15	16	28					17	30	112	81	62	31	42	39	44	22	61	43	29	29	36	32	51
	I LOVE LUCY<		21			21	37					24	44	142	98							69						
	--4 WK AVG--					17	29	22	21	21	19	18	32	120	85	66	31	45	42	47	25	63	45	30	31	37	32	55
	HUT/PVT/TOT	58	57	57	59	58		58	47	56	57	56		390	293	149	56	86	107	130	76	241	135	85	99	120	58	85
7.30P- 7.45P																												
KATU	VARIOUS	14	13	12	18	14	25	33	23	24	28	14	26	99	61	34	14	23	24	28	14	73	50	34	37	40	20	27
KVDO	N A	-	-	-	-			**	**	**	**			2														3
KOIN	MERV GRIFFIN	15	12	11	12	13	23	17	19	25	25	13	24	90	72	29	7	10	25	33	18	59	24	12	18	27	8	6
KOAC	N A	-	-	-	-				**	**	**			1								1						
KGW	VARIOUS	12	9	12	12	11	20	22	31	29	25	12	22	77	64	28	11	17	20	25	16	43	20	12	14	17	8	11
KOAP	N A	-	1	1	-	1	2	2	**	**	**	1	2	5	3													1
KPTV	ADAM 12	14		16	13	15	26					15	27	101	69	45	20	27	30	36	19	59	35	22	23	31	20	41
	ADAM 12<		18			18	33					21	40	122	81							65						
	--4 WK AVG--					15	27	21	21	20	19	17	31	106	72	47	19	29	33	38	21	61	38	24	26	33	22	43
	HUT/PVT/TOT	57	55	56	57	56		58	48	55	57	54		380	272	138	51	79	102	124	69	237	132	82	95	117	58	90
7.45P- 8.00P																												
KATU	VARIOUS	14	13	13	18	14	25	33	23	24	28	14	26	101	63	36	14	24	26	30	15	72	49	33	37	40	22	28
KVDO	N A	-	-	-	-			**	**	**	**			2														3
KOIN	MERV GRIFFIN	15	12	11	12	13	23	18	19	25	25	13	24	90	73	30	6	11	26	34	18	59	24	13	17	26	7	7
KOAC	N A	-	-	-	-				**	**	**			1								1						
KGW	VARIOUS	12	8	12	12	11	20	23	32	29	25	11	20	76	63	28	11	17	20	25	17	42	20	12	14	17	8	11
KOAP	N A	-	1	1	-	1	2	2	**	**	**	1	2	5	3													1
KPTV	ADAM 12	14		16	13	14	25					15	27	100	67	44	20	28	29	34	19	59	35	22	23	31	20	39
	ADAM 12<		17			17	31					19	37	115	80							60						
	--4 WK AVG--					15	27	21	21	20	19	16	30	104	70	46	20	29	31	36	21	59	38	24	26	32	21	41
	HUT/PVT/TOT	57	54	56	57	56		57	47	55	57	54		379	272	140	51	81	103	125	71	233	131	82	94	115	58	90
11.00P-11.15P																												
KATU	EYWTNS NWS 3	7	5	7		6	21					8	26	45	33	23	8	13	17	18	6	26	16	10	12	14	4	2
	EYWTNS NWS <				5	5	16					6	19	37	25							31					3	2
	--4 WK AVG--					6	21	19	23	29	23	7	23	43	31	21	7	12	15	17	7	27	17	11	13	15	3	2
KVDO	N A	-		-				**	*#	**	**																	
KOIN	NEWSROOM 6-L	8		11	12	10	33					11	34	73	58	25	7	14	19	26	12	43	19	11	16	22	3	1
	VARIOUS		7			7	27					7	26	46	40							25					3	1
	--4 WK AVG--					9	31	31	27	29	30	10	32	66	54	26	8	15	19	25	11	39	19	11	15	20	3	1
KOAC	N A	-	-	-	-				**	**	**			1														
KGW	1100 NW TNGT	9	10	9	9	9	31	31	35	29	30	11	35	62	49	24	5	13	20	24	8	38	21	12	17	20	3	1
KOAP	N A	1	3	4		1	3	4	**	**	**	1	4	5	5	2	1	2	1	1	2	4	2	2	1	2		
KPTV	FREVR FERNWD	4	2	3	3	3	10	12	12	13	17	3	10	21	14	10	7	9	5	6	2	10	9	7	7	7	5	1
	HUT/PVT/TOT	30	26	30	31	29		26	26	31	30	31		198	153	83	28	51	60	73	30	118	68	43	53	64	14	5
11.15P-11.30P																												
KATU	EYWTNS NWS 3	6	4	6		6	23					7	25	40	32	22	7	12	16	17	5	23	15	9	11	13	3	1
	EYWTNS NWS <				4	4	14					6	19	34	25							31					3	1
	--4 WK AVG--					5	19	17	26	25	22	6	21	39	30	20	6	11	15	16	6	25	16	10	12	14	3	1
KVDO	N A	-		-				**	**	**	**																	
KOIN	NEWSROOM 6-L	8		10	11	10	36					11	37	68	52	20	5	11	15	22	10	40	17	10	14	20	1	1
	VARIOUS		5			5	23					5	22	36	28							18					1	1
	--4 WK AVG--					8	30	29	26	29	26	9	32	60	46	20	5	12	15	21	9	35	16	9	13	17	1	1
KOAC	N A	-	-	-	-				**	**	**			1	1	1	1	1										
KGW	1100 NW TNGT	8	9	9	9	9	33	33	35	29	33	10	36	57	44	21	5	12	17	21	7	34	18	11	15	18	3	1
KOAP	N A	1		1		1	4	4	**	**	**	1	4	5	4	2	1	2	1	1	2	3	2	2	1	2		
KPTV	FREVR FERNWD	4	2	3	2	3	11	13	9	14	15	3	11	20	14	11	7	10	5	6	2	9	8	7	6	6	3	1
	HUT/PVT/TOT	28	22	28	28	27		24	23	28	27	28		182	139	75	25	48	53	65	26	106	60	39	47	57	10	4
11.30P-11.45P																												
KATU	VARIOUS	4	2	3	3	3	19	23	14	19	19	3	18	22	15	9	4	7	5	6	5	15	9	7	6	8		1
KVDO	N A	-		-																								
KOIN	CBS LT MOVI<	3		5	5	4	24					5	25	30	21	12	4	9	8	11	5	17	9	7	7	9		2
	VARIOUS		2			2	20					2	20	17	12							5						
	--4 WK AVG--					4	25	15	21	25	19	4	24	27	19	11	4	8	7	10	4	14	8	6	6	8		2
KOAC	N A	-	-	-				**	**	**				2	2						1							
KGW	TONIGHT SHOW	8	5	8	8	7	44	46	43	50	44	9	53	49	39	21	5	14	16	20	7	31	16	10	13	17	1	1
KOAP	N A	1		-				**	**	**				2							1							
KPTV	DRAGNET<	2	1	1	1	1	6	8	14	13	13	2	12	9	7	4	3	4	2	2		4	3	2	2	2	2	1
	HUT/PVT/TOT	17	10	17	18	16		13	14	16	16	17		109	82	45	16	33	30	39	19	64	36	26	27	35	3	5
11.45P-MDNGHT																												
KATU	VARIOUS	3	1	3	3	3	21	17	17	13	14	3	20	19	14	8	4	6	4	5	3	14	9	7	5	7		1
KOIN	CBS LT MOVI<	3		4	4	4	25					4	22	27	17	10	3	7	7	10	5	14	7	6	6	8		1
	VARIOUS		2			2	25					2	22	14	9							3						
	--4 WK AVG--					3	21	17	17	20	21	3	20	24	15	9	3	7	6	8	4	11	6	5	5	7		1
KOAC	N A	-	-	-				**	**	**				2	2						1							
KGW	TONIGHT SHOW	7	5	8	8	7	50	50	50	47	50	8	53	45	36	19	5	13	14	17	5	28	14	9	11	15	1	1
KOAP	N A	1		-				**	**	**				2	2						1							
KPTV	DRAGNET<	2	1	1	1	1	7	8	8	7	7	1	7	8	5	2	2	2	1	2		5	3	2	2	3	2	1
	HUT/PVT/TOT	16	8	15	16	14		12	12	15	14	15		98	72	38	14	28	25	32	15	55	31	23	22	30	4	3
	(col #)	58	59	60	61	1	2	62	63	64	65	3	4	5	10	11	12	13	14	15	16	17	18	19	20	21	22	24

TECHNICAL DIFFICULTY
< M-F PROGRAM AIRED LESS THAN FIVE DAYS
+ PARENT/SATELLITE RELATIONSHIP
* SAMPLE BELOW MINIMUM FOR WEEKLY REPORTING
▲ SEE TABLE ON PAGE iv

Time Period Averages

TIME PERIOD AVERAGES — TOTAL SURVEY AREA (000) / ADI RATINGS

DAY, TIME, AND STATION	CHILD 6-11 (25)	PERS 18+ (7)	15-24 (8)	12-34 (9)	PERS 15-24 (31)	12-34 (32)	W TOT 18+ (33)	18-49 (34)	15-24 (35)	18-34 (36)	25-49 (37)	25-54 (38)	WKG WMN 18+ (39)	M TOT 18+ (40)	18-49 (41)	18-34 (42)	25-49 (43)	25-54 (44)	TNS 12-17 (45)	CHD 2-11 (46)
THRESHS 25-49%	11	9	11	8	3	1	1	1	4	2	2	2	3	1	2	3	2	2	5	5
THRESHS 50+%	3	–	2	2	–	–	–	–	1	–	–	–	–	–	–	–	–	–	1	1
M-F 7.15P																				
KATU	10	122	17	40	5	5	8 (12)	4	3	3	5	5	7	9 (17)	8	8	9	8	5	4
4 WK	10	140	21	48	6	6	9	5	4	4	5	6	8	11	10	10	10	9	6	4
KVDO	1																			1
KOIN	5	125	14	27	4	4	10	6	3	3	7	8	8	8	5	4	5	7	3	2
KOAC																				
KGW	4	123	17	39	5	5	10	8	5	7	8	9	9	8	6	6	8	7	2	2
	6	104	21	49	6	7	9	8	8	7	7	7	8	7	6	6	8	7	6	3
4 WK	5	114	19	44	5	6	10	8	7	7	8	8	9	7	6	6	7	7	4	3
KOAP		7	1	3										1	1	1	1	1		
KPTV	38	142	48	103	14	14	12 (14)	15	18	16	13	12	11	10	11	11	10	10	16	19
4 WK	40	148	48	107	14	14	12	15	17	17	14	13	13	10	11	11	10	10	16	20
H/P/T	61	534	103	229	32	33	43	36	33	33	36	37	38	39	35	34	35	36	31	33
7.30P																				
KATU	18	134	33	77	9	10	9	8	8	8	8	7	11	11	12	13	13	12	10	10
KVDO	2																			1
KOIN	5	131	15	30	4	4	10	7	4	4	8	9	9	9	6	5	6	7	4	3
KOAC		1																		
KGW	8	107	18	37	5	5	9	6	6	6	7	7	8	7	5	5	5	5	4	4
KOAP		3					1													
KPTV	31	128	34	69	10	9	10 (12)	11	12	10	10	9	10	9 (10)	8	8	7	8	10	14
4 WK	32	133	34	75	10	10	10	11	11	11	11	10	10	9	9	9	9	9	11	15
H/P/T	65	509	100	219	31	32	41	34	30	31	35	36	35	39	34	33	34	35	31	35
7.45P																				
KATU	19	135	33	79	9	10	9	8	8	9	8	8	7	11	12	12	13	11	11	10
KVDO	2																			1
KOIN	5	132	15	31	4	4	10	7	4	4	9	9	9	9	6	5	6	8	3	3
KOAC																				
KGW	8	105	18	37	5	5	9	7	6	6	7	7	8	7	5	5	5	5	4	4
KOAP		4					1													
KPTV	30	126	34	70	10	9	10 (11)	10	11	10	10	9	9	9 (9)	9	8	7	8	10	14
4 WK	30	130	34	74	10	10	10	11	11	10	10	10	10	9	9	9	8	9	10	15
H/P/T	64	506	100	221	31	32	40	34	30	31	35	36	35	38	34	33	34	35	31	35
11.00P																				
KATU	2	59	13	27	3	4	5 (3)	5	4	5	5	5	3	4 (4)	4	4	4	4	2	1
4 WK	2	58	12	26	3	3	4	5	3	4	5	4	3	4	4	4	4	4	1	1
KVDO																				
KOIN	1	101	11	28	3	4	8 (6)	6	4	5	6	7	6	6 (4)	5	4	6	6	1	1
4 WK	1	92	12	29	3	4	7	6	4	5	6	7	5	6	5	4	5	6		1
KOAC																				
KGW	1	87	11	28	3	4	7	6	3	5	7	7	4	6	5	4	6	6	2	1
KOAP		9	2	4			1		1	1			1	1		1	1	1		
KPTV	1	24	10	21	2	3	2	2	3	2	2	2	2	2	2	3	2	2	2	
H/P/T	5	270	47	108	13	15	23	21	16	20	21	22	17	19	18	17	20	20	7	3
11.15P																				
KATU	1	55	12	24	3	3	5 (3)	5	4	4	5	4	2	4 (4)	4	3	4	3	2	1
4 WK	1	55	11	23	3	3	4	4	4	4	4	4	3	4	4	3	4	4	1	
KVDO																				
KOIN	1	92	9	22	3	3	7 (4)	5	4	5	6	5	5	6 (3)	4	4	5	5	1	1
4 WK	1	81	9	22	3	3	6	5	3	4	5	5	4	5	4	3	4	5	1	
KOAC		1	1	1																
KGW	1	78	10	26	3	3	7	5	3	4	6	6	4	5	4	4	5	5	1	1
KOAP		7	2	4			1	1	1	1			1	1	1		1	1		
KPTV	1	23	9	20	2	2	2	2	3	3	2	2	1	1	2	2	2	2	1	
H/P/T	4	245	42	96	11	13	20	18	13	17	18	19	14	17	15	15	17	18	6	2
11.30P																				
KATU	1	30	7	14	2	2	2	2	2	2	2	2		2	2	3	2	2	1	
KVDO																				
KOIN	2	38	6	16	2	2	3 (2)	3	2	3	3	3	2	2 (1)	2	2	2	2		1
4 WK	2	33	5	14	1	2	2	2	2	3	2	3	2	2	2	2	2	2		
KOAC																				
KGW	1	70	9	25	3	3	6	5	3	5	5	6	3	5	4	4	4	5	1	
KOAP		2							1				1							
KPTV	1	11	4	9	1	1	1	1	1	1	1	1	1	1	1	1	1	1	1	
H/P/T	5	146	25	62	8	9	11	11	9	12	11	12	10	10	9	10	10	10	3	2
11.45P																				
KATU		28	8	14	2	2	2	2	2	2	2	2		2	2	2	2	2	1	
KOIN	1	31	4	13	1	2	2 (1)	2	2	3	2	3	2	2 (1)	2	2	2	2		
4 WK	1	26	4	12	1	2	2	2	2	2	2	2	2	2	1	2	2	2		
KOAC																				
KGW	1	64	9	23	2	3	5	4	3	5	5	5	3	4	3	3	4	4	1	
KOAP		2											1							
KPTV	1	7	3	6	1	1	1	1	1	1	1	1		1	1	1	1		1	
H/P/T	3	127	24	55	7	8	10	9	8	10	9	10	9	9	8	9	9	9	3	1

STATION BREAK AVERAGES — TOTAL SURVEY AREA, IN THOUSANDS (000)

TIME / STATION	ADI TV HH RTG (1)	MET TV HH RTG (3)	TV HH (5)	W TOT 18+ (10)	18-49 (11)	18-34 (13)	25-49 (14)	M TOT 18+ (17)	18-49 (18)	18-34 (19)	25-49 (20)	CHILD 2-11 (24)
THRESHS 25-49%	1	2	7	6	7	7	6	7	7	9	7	13
THRESHS 50+%	–	1	1	1	1	2	1	1	1	2	1	3
7.15P												
KATU / 4 WK	14	13	99	67	22	11	17	72	41	25	31	14
KVDO		1										2
KOIN	12	12	87 (1)	72	27	10	23	53	21	11	15	6
KGW / 4 WK	12	14	78	67	34	20	25	48	26	16	21	8
KOAP	1	1	5	3	1	1	1	4	2	2	1	
KPTV / 4 WK	18	19	121	85	66	46	42	62	44	29	31	56
H/P/T	58	57	392	294	150	88	108	239	134	83	99	86
7.30P												
KATU	14	14	99 (2)	64	28	17	21	73	46	30	34	21 (3)
KOIN	13	13	89 (1)	72	28	10	24	56	22	12	16	6
KGW	11	13	77	66	31	19	23	45	23	14	18	10
KOAP	1	1	5	3	1	1	1	2	1	1	1	
KPTV / 4 WK	16	18	113	79	57	38	37	63	42	27	29	49
H/P/T	57	55	386	284	145	85	106	240	134	84	98	89
7.45P												
KATU	14	14	100 (2)	62	35	24	25	73	50	34	37	28 (3)
KOIN	13	13	90 (1)	73	30	11	26	59	24	13	18	7
KGW	11	12	77	64	28	17	20	43	20	12	14	11
KOAP	1	1	5	3				1				
KPTV / 4 WK	15	17	105	72	47	30	32	61	39	24	27	43
H/P/T	56	54	380	274	140	82	103	238	133	83	96	92
11.00P												
KATU / 4 WK	9	10	60	43	30	20	20	36	25	17	17	4
KVDO		1						1	1			1
KOIN / 4 WK	12	13	81 (1)	67	37	23	27	51	29	18	23	2
KGW	12	13	77	63	35	20	28	49	30	18	23	2
KOAP	1	1	5	4	2	2	1	4	2	2	1	
KPTV	3	4	22	16	8	6	5	11	7	5	5	1
H/P/T	37	39	247	193	112	71	81	152	94	60	70	11
11.15P												
KATU / 4 WK	6	7	41	30	19	11	14	25	16	10	12	1
KOIN / 4 WK	9	10	63	50	23	14	17	37	18	10	14	1
KOAC			1	1	1							
KGW	9	11	60	47	23	13	19	36	20	12	16	1
KOAP	1	1	5	3	2	1		4	2	2	1	
KPTV	3	3	21	14	11	10	7	10	9	7	7	1
H/P/T	28	30	191	147	79	51	56	112	65	41	50	4
11.30P												
KATU	4	5	30	22	14	9	10	20	12	8	9	1
KOIN / 4 WK	6	7	44	32	16	10	11	24	12	8	9	1
KOAC			1	1	1							
KGW	8	10	53	42	21	13	17	33	17	11	14	1
KOAP	1	1	5	3	2	1	2	4	2	1	1	
KPTV	2	3	15	11	8	7	4	7	6	5	4	1
H/P/T	22	23	148	113	62	41	43	86	48	33	37	4
11.45P												
KATU	3	3	21	15	9	7	5	15	9	7	6	1
KOIN / 4 WK	4	4	25	18	10	7	7	12	7	6	5	1
KOAC			1	1	1							
KGW	7	9	47	38	20	14	15	30	15	10	12	1
KOAP	1		4	5	1		1					
KPTV	1	2	9	6	3	3	2	3	3	3	2	1
H/P/T	15	16	106	82	43	31	30	60	34	26	25	4

Mon.-Fri.

Program Audiences

STATION / PROGRAM	NO. OF WK	NO. OF ¼ HRS	ADI TV HH RTG	ADI TV HH SH	METRO TV HH RTG	METRO TV HH SH	TV HOUSE-HOLDS	WOMEN TOT 18+	18-49	15-24	18-34	25-49	25-54	25-64	WKG WMN 18+	MEN TOT 18+	18-49	18-34	25-49	25-54	TEENS TOT	GIRLS
col	1	2	1	2	3	4	5	10	11	12	13	14	15	56	16	17	18	19	20	21	22	23
▲RELATIVE STD-ERR 25-49% (1S.E.) THRESHOLDS		2			3		12	13	13	17	15	11	12	12	13	14	14	16	12	12	17	15
50+%							3	3	3	4	4	3	2	3	3	3	3	4	3	3	4	4
5.00P KATU																						
MON *MARY T MOORE	4	8	8	16	10	21	57	46	30	14	22	19	20	25	12	24	14	6	12	14	13	8
TUE *MARY T MOORE	4	8	7	15	8	17	50	43	26	12	19	16	17	20	8	23	15	10	9	10	6	3
WED *MARY T MOORE	4	8	8	15	8	16	57	47	33	16	21	20	23	25	12	23	14	11	5	8	9	6
THU *MARY T MOORE	4	8	7	15	8	18	52	44	30	16	20	17	21	24	13	27	18	13	10	12	8	4
FRI *MARY T MOORE	3	6	9	18	8	17	58	44	30	15	19	17	20	22	12	28	19	12	13	17	8	3
SAT TV 2 SPECIAL	2	10	7	17	7	17	45	27	17	4	7	14	18	20	8	33	19	11	18	23	9	3
SUN EYWTNS NWS 6	4	8	6	16	7	18	45	38	20	7	11	16	23	27	12	33	17	10	11	15	6	4
AVG MARY T MOORE		38	8	16	9	17	55	45	30	15	20	18	20	23	12	25	15	10	9	11	4	5
KOIN																						
MON *NEWSROOM 6-E	4	16	15	29	15	30	109	96	27	4	10	24	35	58	14	76	25	8	20	28	3	1
TUE *NEWSROOM 6-E	4	16	17	32	16	31	118	97	31	5	12	27	34	58	14	81	23	9	17	26	2	1
WED *NEWSROOM 6-E	4	16	17	32	17	32	125	102	24	1	7	24	36	61	18	89	28	11	24	34	3	1
THU *NEWSROOM 6-E	4	16	15	31	14	29	106	96	31	5	12	26	34	53	20	73	28	11	20	28	1	
FRI *NEWSROOM 6-E	4	16	14	29	15	30	102	89	25	3	11	22	29	50	15	74	23	13	16	25	1	1
SAT *NEWSROOM 6-W	4	8	12	32	12	33	87	72	21	6	8	16	22	34	14	64	20	8	16	22	5	2
SUN *NEWSROOM 6-W	4	8	14	34	14	34	105	87	17	3	7	15	23	42	11	68	20	8	17	23	3	2
AVG NEWSROOM 6-W		16	13	33	13	34	96	78	18	4	7	15	22	37	13	64	18	7	15	21	4	2
AVG NEWSROOM 6-E		80	16	31	16	31	112	95	27	4	10	24	33	55	17	78	25	10	19	28	3	1
KGW																						
MON *NEWS EXTRA	4	8	7	15	8	16	51	41	12	4	5	9	19	24	12	23	5	2	5	8	7	3
TUE *NEWS EXTRA	4	8	7	13	7	15	44	31	8	3	4	6	10	19	8	32	11	6	6	10	3	1
WED *NEWS EXTRA	4	8	7	14	8	16	49	40	13	5	7	10	15	25	9	28	10	5	8	10	5	3
THU *NEWS EXTRA	4	8	7	15	8	17	46	42	21	8	13	14	21	26	7	30	13	10	11	16	3	1
FRI *NEWS EXTRA	4	8	6	13	7	16	43	36	12	5	7	7	12	16	9	22	9	4	8	10	1	
SAT J COUSTEAU	4	16	8	20	7	20	52	31	17	5	10	13	16	23	9	32	16	8	15	18	5	2
AVG NEWS EXTRA		40	7	14	8	16	47	38	13	5	7	9	15	22	9	26	9	5	7	10	4	2
KPTV																						
MON *GILLIGANS IS	4	8	16	32	15	32	108	33	23	18	20	13	14	16	8	27	20	15	12	13	48	20
TUE *GILLIGANS IS	4	8	15	31	17	35	102	37	30	18	20	18	19	21	10	35	25	17	18	22	44	24
WED *GILLIGANS IS	4	8	17	32	17	33	112	31	27	16	18	17	19	21	8	28	22	16	12	14	52	21
THU *GILLIGANS IS	4	8	13	29	15	32	91	29	23	15	17	12	15	17	7	29	23	18	10	11	48	20
FRI *GILLIGANS IS	4	8	15	33	16	34	104	45	34	19	24	19	21	24	9	30	22	17	13	15	41	17
SUN HOLYWOD BEST	4	44	11	21	10	22	77	50	33	14	22	21	27	30	15	70	55	39	37	39	15	3
AVG GILLIGANS IS		40	15	32	16	33	103	34	26	17	19	15	17	19	8	30	22	16	13	15	47	21
5.30P KATU																						
MON *EYWTNS NWS 1	4	8	11	19	10	19	76	57	25	6	16	21	26	37	16	48	24	13	20	26	6	3
TUE *EYWTNS NWS 1	4	8	10	19	10	17	73	60	26	9	18	17	20	29	16	47	27	13	22	25	4	
WED *EYWTNS NWS 1	4	8	10	18	10	18	73	55	23	5	12	18	25	34	14	44	22	16	13	17	4	2
THU *EYWTNS NWS 1	4	8	9	17	10	19	68	54	26	9	13	19	24	33	17	43	23	13	17	21	8	4
FRI *EYWTNS NWS 1	3	6	9	19	9	17	68	55	21	11	12	14	20	29	13	48	28	15	19	24	12	6
SUN SPCL EDITION	4	8	8	18	8	21	53	42	26	9	17	20	26	30	10	35	23	13	19	23	7	3
AVG EYWTNS NWS 1		38	10	18	10	18	72	55	24	8	14	18	23	32	15	46	25	14	18	22	8	4
KOIN																						
SAT NEWS CONF 6	3	6	8	22	7	21	60	55	14	4	5	10	13	16	8	38	9	5	6	10	2	
SUN FACE NATION	4	8	11	26	10	25	80	76	13	2	5	11	16	31	9	51	13	6	8	12	1	1
KGW																						
MON *530 NW TNGHT	4	16	12	21	12	22	82	64	21	6	10	17	27	40	17	51	15	6	13	18	9	4
TUE *530 NW TNGHT	4	15	11	19	11	20	76	56	17	4	6	15	23	37	11	48	12	6	11	19	6	4
WED *530 NW TNGHT	4	16	12	21	14	23	83	66	21	5	11	17	26	42	16	53	17	8	14	19	3	1
THU *530 NW TNGHT	4	16	11	21	12	22	74	63	24	5	15	19	27	40	13	46	17	10	13	17	1	
FRI *530 NW TNGHT	4	16	11	21	12	24	76	61	19	5	11	14	22	37	13	47	15	7	13	16	1	
AVG 530 NW TNGHT		79	12	21	12	22	78	63	21	5	11	17	26	40	15	49	15	7	13	18	4	2
KPTV																						
MON *BEWITCHED	4	8	16	29	17	32	113	46	39	25	30	24	25	27	14	31	24	17	15	17	48	23
TUE *BEWITCHED	3	6	15	27	16	29	103	60	49	27	31	30	31	35	14	51	38	29	24	30	43	21
WED *BEWITCHED	4	8	16	29	17	30	114	51	46	24	32	30	32	34	14	37	31	22	17	19	56	25
THU *BEWITCHED	4	8	15	29	17	32	103	48	37	25	27	19	23	26	14	37	32	28	13	14	45	20
FRI *BEWITCHED	4	8	15	29	15	29	103	58	48	31	35	26	28	29	12	32	27	20	17	20	37	19
AVG BEWITCHED		38	16	29	16	30	107	52	44	26	31	26	28	30	14	38	31	23	18	21	46	21
6.00P KATU																						
MON *ABC EVE NEWS	4	8	11	18	11	19	78	60	19	5	8	16	21	35	16	53	24	10	20	23	6	2
TUE *ABC EVE NEWS	4	8	11	17	11	18	74	62	26	7	16	20	24	34	15	47	30	15	26	29	8	3
WED *ABC EVE NEWS	4	8	10	17	10	17	71	57	17	3	10	14	21	32	16	40	19	12	15	18	3	1
THU *ABC EVE NEWS	4	8	10	18	11	19	74	60	23	4	9	21	25	36	18	47	27	14	22	24	6	3
FRI *ABC EVE NEWS	4	8	9	17	9	17	64	54	30	6	10	19	22	30	14	41	22	12	17	20	8	4
FRI *NCAA FOOTBLL	1	13	24	39	20	35	157	108	46	13	20	38	48	70	20	168	108	71	70	84	33	6
SUN TOWN HALL NT	3	12	5	11	6	12	34	25	15	4	6	12	13	18	8	20	14	8	11	12	2	2
AVG NCAA FOOTBLL		102	13	43	13	44	88	34	13	4	7	11	13	20	7	73	37	21	26	32	12	3
AVG ABC EVE NEWS		40	10	17	10	18	72	60	22	5	11	18	23	34	16	46	24	12	20	23	6	2
KOIN																						
MON *CBS EVE NEWS	4	8	14	23	14	24	99	77	23	1	7	22	34	52	21	72	25	8	25	32	3	1
TUE *CBS EVE NEWS	4	8	15	24	15	25	104	85	29	7	16	23	30	51	19	67	28	11	25	30	5	2
WED *CBS EVE NEWS	4	8	15	24	16	26	108	86	34	5	16	30	39	55	23	76	29	18	22	32	4	2
THU *CBS EVE NEWS	4	8	16	27	15	27	109	84	32	6	14	26	36	51	23	82	34	18	24	34	2	
FRI *CBS EVE NEWS	4	8	13	22	12	22	89	74	22	4	12	18	26	34	19	69	26	17	19	30	3	
SAT CBS NEWS-SAT	4	8	9	20	8	19	64	59	14	4	6	10	16	24	11	45	14	9	12	16	1	
SUN *ODD COUPLE	4	8	12	26	11	24	86	59	34	14	21	24	29	41	19	46	27	16	20	22	19	9
AVG ODD COUPLE		46	12	25	11	20	82	64	35	14	20	25	31	43	19	50	27	15	20	25	14	6
AVG CBS EVE NEWS		40	14	24	14	25	102	81	28	4	13	24	33	49	21	73	28	15	22	31	4	1
KGW																						
SAT SA 6 NW TNGT	4	8	11	26	12	28	76	63	24	3	10	22	28	45	11	53	22	11	21	26	2	2
SUN SU 6 NW TNGT	4	8	14	29	15	34	96	78	24	5	12	20	32	43	15	66	28	16	21	28	4	2
col	1	2	3	4	5		10	11	12	13	14	15	56	16	17	18	19	20	21	22	23	

* TECHNICAL DIFFICULTY
+ PARENT/SATELLITE RELATIONSHIP
▲ SEE TABLE ON PAGE iv
* INCLUDED IN AVERAGE

Program Audiences

DAY AND TIME / STATION PROGRAM	WK	¼HR	CH 2-11 (24)	CH 6-11 (25)	P 2+ (6)	P 18+ (7)	P 15-24 (8)	P 12-34 (9)	RTG (1)	SH (2)	15-24 (31)	12-34 (32)	W TOT18+ (33)	W18-49 (34)	W15-34 (35)	W18-34 (36)	W25-49 (37)	W25-54 (38)	W25-64 (57)	WKG WMN (39)	M TOT18+ (40)	M18-49 (41)	M18-34 (42)	M25-49 (43)	M25-54 (44)	TEEN 12-17 (45)	CH 2-11 (46)
▲RELATIVE STD-ERR 25-49%			25	21	27	17	20	19	2		6	2	2	3	9	5	4	3	3	7	2	3	6	4	4	8	10
(1 S.E.) THRESHOLDS 50+%			6	5	4	3	5	3			1		2	1	1	1			1		1	1	1	1	1	2	2
5.00P KATU																											
MON *MARY T MOORE	4	8	6	5	89	70	18	41	8	16	5	5	6	7	8	8	6	5	5	5	3	3	1	3	3	5	2
TUE *MARY T MOORE	4	8	7	5	79	66	18	35	7	15	5	5	6	7	7	7	5	5	5	4	4	4	4	3	3	5	3
WED *MARY T MOORE	4	8	7	4	86	70	25	41	8	15	7	5	6	7	8	7	6	6	5	4	3	3	4	2	2	4	1
THU *MARY T MOORE	4	8	10	8	89	71	25	41	7	15	7	5	6	7	10	7	5	5	5	6	4	5	5	4	4	3	3
FRI *MARY T MOORE	3	6	10	6	90	72	22	39	9	18	7	5	6	7	9	7	5	5	5	6	5	5	5	4	5	3	4
SAT TV 2 SPECIAL	2	10	6	5	75	60	8	27	7	17	2	4	4	4	2	3	5	5	5	.4	5	5	4	6	7	4	2
SUN EYWTNS NWS 6	4	8	9	7	86	71	14	27	6	16	4	4	5	5	4	4	5	6	6	6	6	4	4	4	5	2	3
AVG MARY T MOORE		38	8	6	87	70	22	39	8	16	6	5	6	7	8	7	6	5	5	5	4	4	4	3	3	4	3
KOIN																											
MON *NEWSROOM 6-E	4	16	2	2	177	172	10	21	15	29	3	3	13	6	2	4	8	9	12	7	11	6	3	6	7	2	1
TUE *NEWSROOM 6-E	4	16	6	5	186	178	12	23	17	32	3	3	13	7	3	5	9	9	13	7	12	5	3	6	7	1	2
WED *NEWSROOM 6-E	4	16	2	2	196	191	6	21	17	32	2	3	13	5	1	2	8	9	13	9	13	7	4	8	8	2	1
THU *NEWSROOM 6-E	4	16	3	2	173	169	13	24	15	31	4	3	13	8	3	5	9	9	12	10	11	7	4	6	7	1	1
FRI *NEWSROOM 6-E	4	16	5	4	169	163	10	25	14	29	3	3	12	5	2	4	7	8	11	8	11	5	4	5	6	1	1
SAT *NEWSROOM 6-W	4	8	1		142	136	10	21	12	32	3	3	10	5	3	3	5	6	8	6	9	4	3	5	6	2	
SUN *NEWSROOM 6-W	4	8	1	1	159	155	6	18	14	34	2	2	11	4	1	3	5	6	8	6	9	5	3	6	6	2	
AVG NEWSROOM 6-W		16			146	142	7	18	13	33	2	2	10	4	2	3	5	6	8	5	9	5	3	5	6	2	
AVG NEWSROOM 6-E		80	4	3	180	173	11	23	16	31	3	3	13	6	2	4	8	9	12	8	12	6	4	6	7	1	1
KGW																											
MON *NEWS EXTRA	4	8	1	1	72	64	7	14	7	15	2	2	6	3	2	2	3	5	5	6	4	1		2	2	3	
TUE *NEWS EXTRA	4	8			66	63	10	13	7	13	3	2	4	2	2	2	2	3	4	4	5	2	2	2	3	1	
WED *NEWS EXTRA	4	8	4	2	77	68	8	17	7	14	2	2	6	3	3	3	4	6	5	5	4	2	2	3	3	2	1
THU *NEWS EXTRA	4	8	4	2	79	72	11	26	7	15	3	3	6	5	5	5	4	6	6	3	5	3	4	4	5	1	1
FRI *NEWS EXTRA	4	8	1	1	60	58	6	12	6	13	2	2	5	3	3	3	2	3	3	4	3	2	2	3	3		
SAT J COUSTEAU	4	16	17	13	85	63	9	23	8	20	3	3	4	4	3	4	4	5	5	4	5	4	3	5	5	3	6
AVG NEWS EXTRA		40	2	1	70	64	8	16	7	14	2	2	5	3	3	3	3	4	5	4	4	2	2	3	3	2	1
KPTV																											
MON *GILLIGANS IS	4	8	79	56	187	60	36	83	16	32	11	11	5	6	11	7	4	4	4	4	4	5	6	4	4	23	29
TUE *GILLIGANS IS	4	8	65	44	181	72	33	81	15	31	10	11	5	7	10	7	6	5	5	5	5	6	6	6	6	22	24
WED *GILLIGANS IS	4	8	79	60	190	59	40	86	17	32	12	12	5	7	9	7	6	6	5	4	5	6	7	4	4	25	30
THU *GILLIGANS IS	4	8	62	44	168	58	42	83	13	29	12	11	4	6	9	6	4	4	4	4	5	6	7	3	3	23	23
FRI *GILLIGANS IS	4	8	63	45	179	75	37	82	15	33	10	11	6	8	11	9	6	5	5	4	4	5	6	4	4	19	24
SUN HOLYWOD BEST	4	44	19	13	154	120	39	76	11	21	11	10	7	7	8	8	7	7	6	7	10	13	15	12	11	7	7
AVG GILLIGANS IS		40	70	50	181	64	37	82	15	32	11	11	5	7	10	7	5	5	4	4	5	6	6	4	4	22	26
5.30P KATU																											
MON *EYWTNS NWS 1	4	8	5	3	116	105	12	35	11	19	3	4	8	5	3	5	6	7	8	7	7	6	4	6	7	3	1
TUE *EYWTNS NWS 1	4	8	9	7	120	107	15	35	10	19	4	5	8	6	5	6	6	6	7	7	7	7	5	7	7	2	4
WED *EYWTNS NWS 1	4	8	5	4	108	99	15	32	10	18	4	4	7	5	2	4	6	7	7	6	6	5	6	4	4	2	2
THU *EYWTNS NWS 1	4	8	3	2	108	97	16	34	9	17	5	4	7	6	5	5	6	7	7	7	6	6	5	5	6	4	2
FRI *EYWTNS NWS 1	3	6	7	5	122	103	22	39	9	19	6	5	8	5	6	4	4	5	7	6	7	7	6	6	7	5	2
SUN SPCL EDITION	4	8	14	10	98	77	15	37	8	18	4	5	6	6	4	6	6	7	6	5	6	6	5	7	7	3	5
AVG EYWTNS NWS 1		38	6	4	115	101	17	36	10	18	5	4	8	5	4	5	6	6	7	6	7	6	5	6	6	3	2
KOIN																											
SAT NEWS CONF 6	3	6	1		96	93	7	12	8	22	2	2	8	3	3	2	3	3	3	3	6	2	2	2	3	1	
SUN FACE NATION	4	8			128	127	7	12	11	26	2	2	10	3	1	2	3	4	6	3	7	3	2	2	3		
KGW																											
MON *530 NW TNGHT	4	16	1	1	125	115	11	25	12	21	3	3	9	6	3	4	5	8	9	8	8	3	2	4	5	4	
TUE *530 NW TNGHT	4	15	1	1	111	104	7	18	11	19	2	2	8	4	2	2	5	6	8	5	8	3	2	4	6	3	
WED *530 NW TNGHT	4	16	2	1	124	119	9	22	12	21	2	3	10	5	3	4	6	8	10	8	8	4	3	4	5	2	1
THU *530 NW TNGHT	4	16	5	3	115	109	9	26	11	21	3	4	9	6	3	5	6	8	9	7	8	4	4	5	5	1	2
FRI *530 NW TNGHT	4	16			109	108	7	19	11	21	2	3	9	5	3	4	5	6	8	6	8	4	2	4	5	1	
AVG 530 NW TNGHT		79	2	1	118	112	8	22	12	21	3	3	9	5	3	4	5	7	9	7	8	4	3	4	5	2	1
KPTV																											
MON *BEWITCHED	4	8	71	55	196	77	44	95	16	29	13	12	6	9	14	11	8	7	6	7	5	6	6	5	5	23	25
TUE *BEWITCHED	3	6	46	32	200	111	51	103	15	27	15	14	8	12	16	12	10	9	8	8	8	10	11	8	9	21	18
WED *BEWITCHED	4	8	72	54	216	88	49	110	16	29	15	15	8	11	14	12	10	9	8	7	6	8	11	6	6	27	25
THU *BEWITCHED	4	8	62	45	192	85	56	100	15	29	16	14	7	9	15	10	6	7	6	7	6	8	11	5	6	22	23
FRI *BEWITCHED	4	8	60	45	187	90	47	92	15	29	14	12	8	11	17	12	8	8	6	7	6	5	7	5	6	18	23
AVG BEWITCHED		38	63	47	199	90	49	100	16	29	14	13	7	10	15	11	8	8	7	7	6	7	9	6	6	22	23
6.00P KATU																											
MON *ABC EVE NEWS	4	8	3	2	122	113	11	24	11	18	3	3	8	4	3	5	6	8		7	8	6	4	7	7	3	1
TUE *ABC EVE NEWS	4	8	6	5	123	109	13	39	11	17	4	5	9	6	4	6	7	7	8	7	7	7	6	9	8	4	3
WED *ABC EVE NEWS	4	8	4	3	104	97	8	25	10	17	3	3	8	4	2	4	5	6	7	7	6	4	5	5	5	2	1
THU *ABC EVE NEWS	4	8	2	2	115	107	11	29	10	18	3	4	8	6	2	4	7	7	8	7	7	5	3	5	7	3	1
FRI *ABC EVE NEWS	4	8	6	4	109	95	12	30	9	17	3	4	8	5	3	4	6	6	7	7	6	5	5	5	5	3	2
FRI *NCAA FOOTBLL	1	13	20	17	329	276	67	124	24	39	20	17	16	11	8	8	13	14	16	10	27	27	28	25	25	17	8
SUN TOWN HALL NT	3	12	2	1	49	45	7	16	5	11	2	2	4	4	2	4	4	4	4	4	4	4	3	4	4	1	1
AVG NCAA FOOTBLL		102	8	7	127	107	20	40	13	43	6	6	5	3	3	3	4	5	6	4	12	9	8	9	9	6	3
AVG ABC EVE NEWS		40	4	3	116	106	11	29	10	17	3	4	8	5	3	4	6	6	8	7	7	6	5	7	6	3	2
KOIN																											
MON *CBS EVE NEWS	4	8	4	4	156	149	1	18	14	23		2	11	5	1	2	7	9	11	10	11	6	3	8	9	1	1
TUE *CBS EVE NEWS	4	8	6	5	163	152	11	32	15	24	3	4	12	7	3	5	8	9	11	10	10	6	4	8	8	2	1
WED *CBS EVE NEWS	4	8	3	2	169	162	13	38	15	25	3	5	11	8	2	5	10	10	11	11	11	7	7	7	8	1	1
THU *CBS EVE NEWS	4	8	4	3	172	166	16	34	16	27	4	4	12	7	4	5	8	10	11	12	13	8	7	9	9	1	1
FRI *CBS EVE NEWS	4	8	3	2	149	143	13	32	13	22	4	4	11	5	2	5	6	7	8	10	11	6	7	6	8	1	1
SAT CBS NEWS-SAT	4	8			105	104	6	16	9	20	2	2	8	3	2	2	3	4	5	5	7	3	3	4	4		
SUN *ODD COUPLE	4	8	24	20	148	105	25	56	12	26	7	7	8	7	7	7	8	9	9	7	9	7	6	7	7	9	9
AVG ODD COUPLE		46	15	11	143	114	24	49	12	21	6	6	9	8	7	7	8	8	9	9	8	7	6	7	7	6	6
AVG CBS EVE NEWS		40	4	3	162	154	11	32	14	24	3	4	11	6	2	4	8	9	11	10	11	7	5	7	9	2	1
KGW																											
SAT SA 6 NW TNGT	4	8	7	6	125	116	4	23	11	26	1	3	9	6	2	4	7	8	10	5	8	5	5	7	7	1	2
SUN SU 6 NW TNGT	4	8	6	5	157	144	15	35	14	29	3	5	11	6	3	4	7	9	10	7	10	7	6	7	8	4	1
			24	25	6	7	8	9	1	2	31	32	33	34	35	36	37	38	57	39	40	41	42	43	44	45	46

Program Audiences

DAY AND TIME / STATION PROGRAM	NO. OF WK	NO. OF ¼ HRS	ADI TV HH RTG (1)	SH (2)	METRO TV HH RTG (3)	SH (4)	TV HOUSE-HOLDS (5)	WOMEN TOT 18+ (10)	18-49 (11)	15-24 (12)	18-34 (13)	25-49 (14)	25-54 (15)	25-64 (56)	WKG WMN 18+ (16)	MEN TOT 18+ (17)	18-49 (18)	18-34 (19)	25-49 (20)	25-54 (21)	TEENS 12-17 TOT (22)	GIRLS (23)
▲RELATIVE STD-ERR 25-49% (1S.E.) THRESHOLDS 50+%			2		3		12 / 3	13 / 3	13 / 3	17 / 4	15 / 4	11 / 3	12 / 2	12 / 3	13 / 3	14 / 3	14 / 3	16 / 4	12 / 3	12 / 3	17 / 4	15 / 4
6.00P KPTV																						
MON *EMERGENCY 1	4	16	20	33	20	36	133	86	65	34	51	41	45	49	19	57	43	29	32	38	44	22
TUE *EMERGENCY 1	3	12	20	33	20	34	139	91	75	37	54	47	50	55	27	73	56	43	33	40	40	19
WED *EMERGENCY 1	4	16	21	34	21	35	141	90	71	30	49	48	51	57	23	67	53	39	35	40	44	20
THU *EMERGENCY 1	4	16	18	31	18	33	121	88	68	39	49	38	43	47	21	59	45	35	23	28	40	20
FRI *EMERGENCY 1	4	16	18	32	19	34	122	77	63	31	49	38	42	46	20	57	40	29	26	32	34	15
SAT SAT MOVIE	4	40	12	24	11	25	88	66	49	27	37	29	34	39	17	68	55	40	34	38	27	15
AVG EMERGENCY 1		76	19	33	20	34	131	87	68	34	50	42	46	51	21	62	46	34	29	35	40	19
6.30P KATU																						
MON *EYWTNS NWS 2	4	8	11	18	11	19	79	60	24	6	9	20	26	36	17	63	32	16	24	29	8	5
TUE *EYWTNS NWS 2	4	7	9	14	8	13	62	48	17	6	10	13	16	24	10	40	21	10	16	18	8	4
WED *EYWTNS NWS 2	4	8	11	18	9	15	78	62	21	5	10	17	24	34	15	55	23	15	16	21	2	2
THU *EYWTNS NWS 2	4	8	10	17	9	17	70	55	19	3	7	18	25	36	15	47	26	16	19	23	5	3
FRI *EYWTNS NWS 2	3	6	10	19	10	18	72	57	25	7	9	22	26	36	18	50	26	17	17	23	10	7
SAT EYWTNS NWS 4	3	6	7	18	8	22	50	41	19	4	9	15	18	23	9	37	22	12	18	20	4	
AVG EYWTNS NWS 2		37	10	17	9	17	73	57	21	5	9	18	24	34	14	50	25	14	18	22	6	4
KOIN																						
MON *ODD COUPLE	4	8	12	20	11	20	83	64	31	10	18	23	29	46	15	52	26	11	23	27	15	4
TUE *ODD COUPLE	3	6	13	21	14	23	91	78	43	18	26	29	35	49	21	48	26	12	23	26	13	6
WED *ODD COUPLE	4	8	11	19	11	19	81	58	34	14	17	25	31	43	17	50	25	12	20	28	14	6
THU *ODD COUPLE	4	8	13	23	12	22	92	75	41	17	23	28	34	48	25	69	41	27	25	30	15	6
FRI *ODD COUPLE	4	8	8	15	8	16	59	50	23	9	14	17	24	30	16	36	18	11	13	18	7	3
SAT THIS LAND	4	8	6	15	6	13	47	41	12	4	5	9	14	21	8	36	15	10	9	15	4	1
SUN ASK MANAGER	4	8	7	13	7	15	47	31	10	5	7	7	10	18	8	31	14	8	11	13	5	3
AVG ODD COUPLE		46	12	21	11	20	82	64	35	14	20	25	31	43	19	50	27	15	20	25	14	6
KGW																						
MON *NBC NGHT NWS	4	8	14	24	15	27	95	75	21	5	11	17	29	45	17	63	19	8	17	23	4	2
TUE *NBC NGHT NWS	4	8	14	24	15	25	94	67	16	3	6	14	22	41	19	58	17	9	16	22	3	1
WED *NBC NGHT NWS	4	8	15	26	19	32	104	89	30	9	20	22	31	54	23	73	22	13	20	27	3	1
THU *NBC NGHT NWS	4	8	14	25	15	28	94	76	28	9	18	21	31	48	16	60	21	13	17	24	4	2
FRI *NBC NGHT NWS	4	8	14	26	15	28	94	81	25	8	16	18	23	42	16	70	28	17	21	23	5	2
SAT *NBC NGHT NWS	4	8	12	28	12	30	80	69	24	4	11	22	28	42	14	53	20	11	17	22	3	3
SUN WILD KINGDOM	4	8	21	42	22	46	146	113	45	17	27	32	44	62	21	95	45	28	33	44	25	11
AVG NBC NGHT NWS		48	14	25	15	28	94	76	24	6	14	19	27	45	17	64	22	12	19	25	3	1
7.00P KATU																						
MON NFL MON FTBL	4	49	23	35	22	36	153	59	32	12	19	22	26	36	18	138	90	57	70	76	21	4
TUE *TELL TRUTH	4	8	11	19	11	19	82	63	17	6	10	13	15	31	16	47	22	14	17	18	8	5
WED *TELL TRUTH	4	8	11	19	10	16	82	70	14	4	6	12	15	32	16	47	19	9	13	13	5	4
THU *TELL TRUTH	4	8	10	18	8	15	71	63	21	7	9	16	20	31	14	51	26	18	18	19	8	3
FRI *TELL TRUTH	3	6	10	19	8	15	74	64	19	4	7	15	19	30	15	43	22	11	18	18	6	4
SAT LAWRNCE WELK	3	12	17	33	14	32	111	115	30	8	15	24	33	56	22	61	13	7	9	15	5	2
SUN HARDY/DREW	4	16	11	17	13	20	78	45	36	19	25	25	28	32	13	37	27	18	16	21	35	18
AVG TELL TRUTH		30	11	19	9	17	77	64	17	5	8	13	16	30	15	48	22	13	16	17	6	3
KOIN																						
MON *MERV GRIFFIN	4	16	13	20	11	19	91	81	28	6	9	25	33	52	16	44	11	6	8	17	6	4
TUE *MERV GRIFFIN	4	16	12	21	13	22	84	69	27	6	9	24	35	49	16	52	23	12	16	24	7	4
WED *MERV GRIFFIN	4	16	14	25	14	23	100	80	34	6	13	30	39	57	22	69	30	16	23	34	5	3
THU *MERV GRIFFIN	4	16	12	22	11	23	86	68	25	8	10	18	26	44	19	63	26	15	17	25	6	2
FRI *MERV GRIFFIN	4	16	12	22	12	23	81	68	29	7	11	26	32	44	15	54	23	12	17	25	9	5
SAT HEE HAW	4	16	10	19	10	21	74	58	30	9	14	24	29	39	19	52	27	14	22	27	13	6
SUN 60 MINUTES	4	16	26	41	28	43	192	170	69	15	37	57	74	106	53	148	79	46	62	74	10	5
AVG MERV GRIFFIN		80	13	22	12	22	88	72	28	6	10	24	32	48	17	56	22	12	16	25	7	3
KGW																						
MON *EVENING	3	6	10	15	12	19	68	60	24	8	11	19	21	30	14	38	18	11	14	16	9	5
TUE *EVENING	4	8	12	20	14	24	78	61	33	10	18	25	28	40	20	48	30	18	24	27	13	6
WED *EVENING	4	8	12	21	15	26	85	70	38	14	23	26	31	45	19	53	28	17	22	26	6	3
THU *EVENING	4	8	13	24	15	28	88	74	36	13	22	26	35	48	19	54	29	19	23	30	7	3
FRI *EVENING	3	6	12	23	15	29	81	78	41	15	26	29	35	49	22	53	29	17	23	24	10	5
SAT CORAL JUNGLE	4	16	8	16	9	19	57	37	21	4	9	19	22	28	9	46	31	20	22	25	10	5
SUN WORLD DISNEY	3	16	17	27	15	25	117	82	56	23	36	40	44	49	18	77	55	37	41	47	39	17
AVG EVENING		36	12	20	14	25	81	69	35	13	20	25	30	43	18	51	28	17	22	26	10	5
KPTV																						
MON *I LOVE LUCY	4	8	15	24	16	27	104	74	57	29	41	35	39	44	20	49	35	20	28	30	29	19
TUE *I LOVE LUCY	3	6	19	32	18	31	126	92	67	29	44	45	51	55	24	69	48	32	37	45	34	19
WED *I LOVE LUCY	4	8	18	30	20	34	123	83	65	32	48	40	44	51	26	54	40	27	27	32	32	17
THU *I LOVE LUCY	4	8	19	34	19	37	127	94	70	35	48	43	50	56	28	70	50	36	27	34	41	22
FRI *I LOVE LUCY	4	8	15	27	16	30	104	77	60	31	44	36	42	45	23	52	35	23	25	33	27	14
AVG I LOVE LUCY		38	17	29	18	32	117	82	63	31	45	39	44	49	24	58	41	27	28	34	32	18
7.30P KATU																						
TUE MUPPETS	4	8	14	23	15	27	98	57	45	13	33	38	39	44	17	49	40	27	34	36	28	14
WED MATCH GME PM	4	8	12	22	11	20	88	69	24	12	18	15	18	32	13	48	24	18	16	19	10	7
THU GONG SHW	4	8	9	18	9	18	66	58	42	21	32	26	31	34	14	50	39	27	32	33	23	8
FRI NW CAND CMRA	3	6	7	14	7	14	53	45	23	9	12	15	20	24	10	32	20	12	12	12	15	9
KGW																						
MON 25000 PYRAMD	3	6	9	15	10	17	65	59	30	9	17	23	24	35	20	32	15	10	11	11	8	5
TUE *HLYWD SQUARE	4	8	12	21	12	21	81	65	22	10	12	15	21	32	17	51	21	10	14	19	10	6
WED THATS HLYWD	4	8	10	17	12	20	68	51	30	12	18	22	27	32	12	40	26	17	18	21	12	6
THU *HLYWD SQUARE	4	8	13	24	12	25	88	72	29	11	18	21	27	36	17	54	27	18	16	22	5	3
FRI 100000 TUNE	3	6	13	26	14	28	89	82	41	17	25	28	32	43	21	48	26	14	22	23	10	7
AVG HLYWD SQUARE		16	12	22	12	23	85	69	26	11	15	18	24	34	17	52	24	14	15	20	8	5
KPTV																						
MON *ADAM 12	4	8	13	22	14	24	94	63	41	17	29	28	31	36	15	50	29	17	22	26	19	12
TUE *ADAM 12	3	6	14	25	14	25	99	66	41	17	22	28	32	39	13	60	34	19	25	32	20	11
			1	2	3	4	5	10	11	12	13	14	15	56	16	17	18	19	20	21	22	23

TECHNICAL DIFFICULTY
+ PARENT/SATELLITE RELATIONSHIP
▲ SEE TABLE ON PAGE iv
* INCLUDED IN AVERAGE

Program Audiences

DAY AND TIME / STATION PROGRAM	NO. OF WK	NO. OF ¼ HRS	CHILD 2-11 (24)	CHILD 6-11 (25)	PERS 2+ (6)	PERS 18+ (7)	PERS 15-24 (8)	PERS 12-34 (9)	RTG (1)	SH (2)	P15-24 (31)	P12-34 (32)	W TOT 18+ (33)	W 18-49 (34)	W 15-24 (35)	W 18-34 (36)	W 25-49 (37)	W 25-54 (38)	W 25-64 (57)	WKG WMN 18+ (39)	M TOT 18+ (40)	M 18-49 (41)	M 18-34 (42)	M 25-49 (43)	M 25-54 (44)	TEENS 12-17 (45)	CHILD 2-11 (46)
RELATIVE STD-ERR 25-49% (1 S.E.) THRESHOLDS			25	21	27	17	20	19	2		6	2	2	3	9	5	4	3	3	7	2	3	6	4	4	8	10
THRESHOLDS 50+%			6	5	4	3	5	3	1		1			2	1	1	1		1		1	1	1	1	2	2
6.00P KPTV																											
MON *EMERGENCY 1	4	16	74	49	261	143	53	124	20	33	16	17	13	15	19	18	14	13	11	10	9	11	11	11	11	22	27
TUE *EMERGENCY 1	3	12	78	49	282	164	71	137	20	33	21	19	13	18	22	20	16	14	13	14	12	14	17	11	12	20	28
WED *EMERGENCY 1	4	16	84	57	285	157	59	132	21	34	17	17	13	17	17	18	16	14	13	11	11	13	15	12	12	20	30
THU *EMERGENCY 1	4	16	55	38	242	147	69	124	18	31	19	16	13	16	21	18	13	12	11	11	9	11	13	7	8	18	20
FRI *EMERGENCY 1	4	16	64	40	232	134	52	112	18	32	15	15	11	15	18	18	13	12	10	10	9	10	11	8	9	16	24
SAT SAT MOVIE	4	40	32	21	193	134	54	104	12	24	15	13	9	10	14	12	8	8	8	7	10	12	14	10	9	12	11
AVG EMERGENCY 1		76	70	46	259	149	60	124	19	33	18	17	12	16	19	18	14	13	11	11	10	12	13	10	10	19	26
6.30P KATU																											
MON *EYWTNS NWS 2	4	8	2	2	133	123	16	33	11	18	4	4	8	5	3	3	6	7	8	7	9	8	5	8	8	4	1
TUE *EYWTNS NWS 2	4	7	5	4	101	88	13	28	9	14	4	4	6	4	3	3	5	5	5	5	6	5	4	5	5	4	2
WED *EYWTNS NWS 2	4	8	4	3	123	117	12	27	11	18	4	4	8	5	2	3	6	7	8	7	8	5	6	5	5	1	2
THU *EYWTNS NWS 2	4	8	2	2	109	102	11	28	10	17	3	4	7	4	2	2	6	6	8	7	7	6	6	6	6	3	1
FRI *EYWTNS NWS 2	3	6	5	3	122	107	16	36	10	19	5	5	8	6	4	3	7	7	8	7	8	7	7	6	6	5	2
SAT EYWTNS NWS 4	3	6	6	3	88	78	11	25	7	18	3	3	6	5	2	4	5	6	6	5	6	6	5	6	6	2	2
AVG EYWTNS NWS 2		37	4	3	117	107	13	29	10	17	4	4	7	5	3	3	6	6	7	7	7	6	6	6	6	3	1
KOIN																											
MON *ODD COUPLE	4	8	13	9	144	116	17	44	12	20	5	6	9	7	5	6	8	8	10	8	8	7	4	8	8	7	5
TUE *ODD COUPLE	3	6	21	16	160	126	24	51	13	21	6	6	11	10	9	9	10	10	11	10	7	6	4	8	8	6	8
WED *ODD COUPLE	4	8	9	5	131	108	21	43	11	19	6	6	8	8	6	8	8	9	9	8	7	6	5	6	7	6	3
THU *ODD COUPLE	4	8	15	11	174	144	36	65	13	23	10	9	11	10	9	9	9	9	11	12	11	10	10	8	9	7	6
FRI *ODD COUPLE	4	8	12	9	105	86	16	32	8	15	4	4	7	5	5	5	6	6	6	6	6	4	4	4	5	3	4
SAT THIS LAND	4	8	2	2	83	77	11	19	6	15	2	2	5	3	2	2	3	4	4	3	5	3	2	3	4	2	1
SUN ASK MANAGER	4	8	8	6	75	62	8	20	7	13	2	2	4	2	3	2	2	3	4	3	4	3	3	4	4	2	3
AVG ODD COUPLE		46	15	11	143	114	24	49	12	21	6	6	9	8	7	7	8	8	9	9	8	7	6	7	7	6	6
KGW																											
MON *NBC NGHT NWS	4	8			142	138	8	23	14	24	3	3	11	5	3	4	6	8	10	9	10	5	3	6	7	2	
TUE *NBC NGHT NWS	4	8	2	1	130	125	6	18	14	24	2	3	10	4	2	2	5	6	9	9	10	5	4	6	7	2	1
WED *NBC NGHT NWS	4	8	2	1	167	162	12	36	15	26	3	5	13	6	4	7	7	9	12	11	11	5	7	7	8	2	
THU *NBC NGHT NWS	4	8	4	1	144	136	14	35	14	25	4	5	12	7	5	7	7	9	11	8	10	5	5	6	7	2	2
FRI *NBC NGHT NWS	4	8	1	1	157	151	17	38	14	26	5	5	12	6	5	6	6	7	10	8	11	7	7	7	6	2	
SAT *NBC NGHT NWS	4	8	8	6	133	122	7	25	12	22	2	3	10	5	2	4	7	8	9	6	8	4	4	6	6	1	2
SUN WILD KINGDOM	4	8	34	24	267	208	39	80	21	42	11	10	16	10	10	9	9	11	13	10	15	10	10	10	12	11	11
AVG NBC NGHT NWS		48	3	2	146	140	10	29	14	25	3	4	11	6	3	5	6	8	10	8	10	5	5	6	7	2	1
7.00P KATU																											
MON NFL MON FTBL	4	49	17	13	235	197	41	97	23	35	12	13	9	8	7	7	7	7	8	9	22	22	21	23	21	11	5
TUE *TELL TRUTH	4	8	14	8	132	110	12	32	11	19	4	4	8	4	3	4	4	4	7	7	7	5	5	5	5	3	4
WED *TELL TRUTH	4	8	6	4	128	117	10	20	11	19	3	3	9	3	2	2	4	4	7	7	7	5	4	4	4	2	2
THU *TELL TRUTH	4	8	13	9	135	114	17	35	10	18	5	5	8	5	4	3	5	5	7	6	7	6	7	6	5	4	5
FRI *TELL TRUTH	3	6	8	5	121	107	9	24	10	19	3	4	9	4	3	4	4	4	6	6	5	4	5	5	5	3	2
SAT LAWRNCE WELK	3	12	12	8	193	176	13	27	17	33	4	4	17	7	4	5	8	10	13	11	10	3	3	3	4	2	4
SUN HARDY/DREW	4	16	40	30	157	82	37	78	11	17	10	10	6	9	10	9	9	8	7	7	6	6	6	6	6	16	15
AVG TELL TRUTH		30	11	7	129	112	12	27	11	19	4	4	9	4	3	3	4	5	7	7	7	5	5	5	5	3	3
KOIN																											
MON *MERV GRIFFIN	4	16	7	6	138	125	10	21	13	20	3	3	11	6	4	3	8	9	11	7	6	2	2	2	4	3	2
TUE *MERV GRIFFIN	4	16	3	3	131	121	14	28	12	21	4	4	10	7	4	3	8	10	11	7	8	6	5	6	7	3	1
WED *MERV GRIFFIN	4	16	8	4	162	149	14	34	14	25	4	5	11	8	4	5	10	10	12	11	10	7	6	8	9	3	3
THU *MERV GRIFFIN	4	16	6	6	143	131	20	31	12	22	5	5	9	6	4	4	6	7	9	10	9	6	5	5	7	3	3
FRI *MERV GRIFFIN	4	16	7	5	138	122	15	32	12	22	4	4	10	7	4	9	9	9	10	7	8	5	4	5	7	3	3
SAT HEE HAW	4	16	23	16	146	110	16	41	10	19	4	5	8	7	5	5	8	8	8	8	7	6	5	7	7	6	9
SUN 60 MINUTES	4	16	5	3	333	318	36	93	26	41	10	12	23	15	8	13	18	20	23	24	22	18	16	20	20	5	2
AVG MERV GRIFFIN		80	6	5	141	128	14	29	13	22	4	4	10	7	4	4	8	8	11	9	8	5	5	5	7	3	2
KGW																											
MON *EVENING	3	6	3	2	110	98	13	31	10	15	4	4	8	5	4	4	6	6	7	6	5	4	5	4	4	5	1
TUE *EVENING	4	8	12	8	134	109	19	49	12	20	6	7	9	8	6	7	9	8	9	9	8	8	7	8	8	6	4
WED *EVENING	4	8	10	6	139	123	21	46	12	21	6	6	9	8	7	8	8	8	10	9	8	7	7	8	8	3	4
THU *EVENING	4	8	8	6	143	128	21	48	13	24	7	7	11	9	7	8	9	10	11	9	9	7	7	8	8	5	4
FRI *EVENING	3	6	5	4	146	131	23	53	12	23	7	7	11	10	8	9	10	10	11	11	8	7	6	8	7	5	3
SAT CORAL JUNGLE	4	16	16	11	109	83	15	39	8	16	4	5	5	5	2	4	5	5	6	6	8	8	7	7	7	5	4
SUN WORLD DISNEY	3	16	69	42	267	159	45	112	17	27	13	16	12	14	14	14	14	13	11	9	13	14	14	14	14	19	27
AVG EVENING		36	9	6	139	120	21	47	12	20	6	6	10	8	7	7	8	8	10	9	8	7	6	7	7	4	3
KPTV																											
MON *I LOVE LUCY	4	8	50	35	202	123	37	90	15	24	11	12	11	14	16	15	12	11	10	10	8	8	7	9	9	14	19
TUE *I LOVE LUCY	3	6	56	44	251	161	44	110	19	32	13	15	13	16	17	16	15	14	12	12	11	12	13	13	14	16	21
WED *I LOVE LUCY	4	8	67	50	236	137	50	107	18	30	14	14	12	15	18	17	13	12	11	13	9	10	10	9	9	15	23
THU *I LOVE LUCY	4	8	54	39	259	164	62	125	19	34	18	17	14	17	20	18	14	14	12	14	11	13	14	9	10	19	19
FRI *I LOVE LUCY	4	8	55	34	211	129	43	94	15	27	13	13	11	14	18	17	11	12	11	9	8	8	9	8	9	13	21
AVG I LOVE LUCY		38	56	40	228	140	47	104	17	29	14	14	12	15	18	16	13	12	11	12	9	10	10	10	10	15	21
7.30P KATU																											
TUE MUPPETS	4	8	68	39	202	106	26	88	14	23	8	12	8	11	8	12	13	11	10	9	7	10	10	12	10	13	24
WED MATCH GME PM	4	8	12	9	139	117	22	46	12	22	6	6	10	6	7	5	5	7	9	6	7	6	7	6	5	4	4
THU GONG SHW	4	8	25	18	156	108	34	82	9	18	9	11	8	9	10	11	8	8	7	7	8	10	10	11	10	11	9
FRI NW CAND CMRA	3	6	6	4	98	77	19	39	7	14	6	5	6	5	5	4	5	5	5	4	4	5	5	4	3	7	2
KGW																											
MON 25000 PYRAMD	3	6	7	4	106	91	14	35	9	15	4	5	8	7	5	6	7	6	9	9	5	4	4	4	3	4	3
TUE *HLYWD SQUARE	4	8	9	7	135	116	18	32	12	21	5	4	9	5	4	6	5	6	7	8	5	5	5	4	6	4	4
WED THATS HLYWD	4	8	14	11	117	91	23	47	10	17	6	6	7	6	6	7	7	7	6	6	6	6	6	5	5	6	5
THU *HLYWD SQUARE	4	8	9	6	140	126	23	41	13	24	6	6	10	7	5	6	7	8	8	8	6	7	5	6	7	2	4
FRI 100000 TUNE	3	6	20	15	160	130	22	49	13	26	7	7	12	9	10	9	9	9	9	10	8	7	6	8	7	5	8
AVG HLYWD SQUARE		16	9	7	138	121	21	37	12	22	6	5	10	6	5	5	6	7	8	8	6	6	5	5	6	3	4
KPTV																											
MON *ADAM 12	4	8	42	31	174	113	26	65	13	22	8	9	9	10	10	11	9	8	8	8	8	7	7	8	8	10	16
TUE *ADAM 12	3	6	39	31	185	126	27	61	14	25	8	8	9	9	10	8	9	8	8	7	10	8	7	9	9	9	12
			24	25	6	7	8	9	1	2	31	32	33	34	35	36	37	38	57	39	40	41	42	43	44	45	46

Program Audiences

DAY AND TIME / STATION PROGRAM	TELE-CASTS NO. OF WK	NO. OF ½ HRS	ADI TV HH RTG	SH	METRO TV HH RTG	SH	TV HOUSE-HOLDS	WOMEN TOT 18+	18-49	15-24	18-34	25-49	25-54	25-64	WKG WMN 18+	MEN TOT 18+	18-49	18-34	25-49	25-54	TEENS 12-17 TOT	GIRLS
			1	2	3	4	5	10	11	12	13	14	15	56	16	17	18	19	20	21	22	23
▲RELATIVE STD-ERR 25-49% (1S.E.) THRESHOLDS 50+%			2		3		12 / 3	13 / 3	13 / 3	17 / 4	15 / 3	11 / 3	12 / 3	12 / 3	13 / 3	14 / 3	14 / 3	16 / 4	12 / 3	12 / 3	17 / 4	15 / 4
7.30P KPTV																						
WED *ADAM 12	4	8	17	30	20	35	115	80	49	24	33	31	37	46	22	61	39	25	25	31	24	13
THU *ADAM 12	4	8	15	29	16	33	105	78	49	20	29	35	42	49	24	58	37	24	21	28	22	14
FRI *ADAM 12	4	8	14	26	15	29	93	57	41	19	28	27	32	36	19	53	33	23	22	30	18	9
AVG ADAM 12		38	15	26	16	29	101	68	44	19	28	30	35	41	19	56	34	22	22	28	21	12
8.00P KATU																						
TUE HAPPY DAYS	4	8	33	51	34	54	223	160	126	64	91	83	88	101	52	144	114	79	78	83	82	45
WED EIGHT ENOUGH	4	20	34	23	36	148	104	75	35	51	54	59	68	28	66	49	34	32	40	56	34
THU KOTTER	4	8	17	26	17	28	115	80	59	29	40	37	43	47	17	71	58	36	41	45	43	18
FRI DONNY-MARIE	3	12	21	37	20	36	141	109	59	22	42	42	48	64	24	71	47	35	33	36	29	15
SAT TABITHA	3	6	13	25	13	26	86	67	44	22	26	29	31	35	13	51	37	27	26	28	40	25
SUN 6 MILN $ MAN	3	12	13	20	15	23	89	56	38	13	22	29	35	43	18	68	47	30	29	32	25	8
KOIN																						
MON LOGANS RUN	2	8	10	16	12	21	73	45	37	14	21	28	33	35	13	45	39	23	25	27	33	12
TUE FITZPATRICKS	3	12	7	11	7	11	48	36	17	5	5	15	20	27	9	26	14	7	7	12	16	9
WED GOOD TIMES	3	6	10	15	9	14	69	46	27	12	17	17	21	30	15	40	20	12	15	20	19	7
THU WALTONS	3	16	28	44	27	41	202	186	108	43	71	77	92	115	39	104	53	34	39	48	36	23
FRI NEW WNDR WMN	2	8	12	21	13	24	82	56	43	23	28	29	35	38	15	58	47	33	33	36	28	14
SAT BOB NEWHART	3	6	14	26	14	28	98	86	34	15	22	22	36	51	24	63	29	18	21	28	8	4
SUN RHODA	2	4	24	36	22	36	169	138	79	29	54	58	71	95	49	89	48	34	33	43	24	18
KGW																						
MON HOUSE PRARIE	3	14	20	30	19	30	140	117	55	20	33	42	47	61	19	60	31	17	25	26	23	14
TUE MAN ATLANTIS	2	8	5	8	7	10	34	22	17	5	9	14	17	17	9	18	16	8	14	14	7	4
TUE *BIG EVENT	1	12	19	32	27	43	127	92	77	19	51	64	67	76	33	97	81	57	54	57	15	7
WED GRZZLY ADAMS	3	12	23	35	24	38	148	121	54	20	28	39	52	72	28	97	54	35	38	44	19	9
THU CHIPS	3	12	12	18	11	18	77	59	34	11	19	27	32	37	12	55	40	30	25	31	19	11
THU *BIG EVENT	1	8	19	33	19	30	133	100	64	30	37	43	52	58	39	92	53	33	37	44	32	16
FRI CPO SHARKEY	3	6	10	18	11	20	71	60	24	7	12	17	22	30	11	42	20	11	12	17	4	2
SAT BIONIC WOMAN	3	12	10	19	12	23	68	42	24	5	13	22	24	31	10	39	28	16	22	22	13	8
AVG BIG EVENT		53	18	31	21	35	119	96	66	21	43	51	58	67	30	84	65	46	48	52	18	9
KPTV																						
MON *THE MOVIE	4	32	8	12	8	13	55	45	25	10	17	19	20	28	14	29	17	13	11	13	8	8
TUE *THE MOVIE	3	24	9	14	10	15	64	47	24	10	12	16	19	25	14	40	23	11	19	22	4	3
WED *THE MOVIE	4	32	8	12	8	13	58	36	17	5	12	14	16	22	9	47	31	21	22	27	6	3
THU *THE MOVIE	4	32	7	11	7	12	49	32	14	4	6	12	17	24	13	40	21	10	14	18	7	3
FRI *THE MOVIE	4	32	7	12	8	15	47	34	23	8	15	18	20	24	10	31	20	14	14	15	7	5
AVG THE MOVIE		152	7	12	8	14	54	39	21	8	13	16	19	25	11	37	22	14	15	18	7	5
8.30P KATU																						
TUE LAVRNE-SHRLY	4	8	30	48	32	50	204	157	121	66	87	77	80	95	48	123	92	63	66	73	74	44
THU WHTS HAPNING	4	8	15	23	16	26	101	79	57	26	39	35	42	46	17	60	46	29	33	39	33	14
SAT OPRTN PETICT	3	6	15	31	15	32	102	70	51	28	29	34	41	48	26	73	55	32	40	46	47	21
KOIN																						
WED BUSTNG LOOSE	3	6	8	12	8	13	57	41	29	12	19	19	21	27	8	38	22	13	16	21	14	5
SAT GOT ECH OTHR	3	6	11	20	11	22	78	66	27	10	20	19	30	44	11	52	27	20	23	25	7	3
SUN ON OUR OWN	3	6	16	24	16	25	119	84	45	17	30	34	45	59	30	60	34	24	23	32	20	13
KGW																						
FRI CHICO-MAN	3	6	10	18	11	20	70	58	24	8	11	17	22	30	11	40	15	8	10	16	7	3
KPTV																						
SAT WRESTLING	4	24	8	15	8	15	64	42	19	6	11	15	17	21	7	55	23	15	14	17	6	3
SUN IN SEARCH OF	4	8	6	10	7	11	44	34	16	7	9	11	15	20	5	37	26	17	16	18	8	3
9.00P KATU																						
TUE 3 COMPANY	4	8	18	28	18	27	123	102	78	37	56	53	56	62	25	64	49	30	40	44	42	26
WED CHARLS ANGLS	4	16	20	36	23	39	138	95	72	39	48	48	53	59	21	74	56	41	35	42	55	30
THU BARNY MILLER	3	6	16	27	19	31	110	80	53	26	39	28	36	46	19	83	55	41	35	47	21	6
THU *LOVE BOAT	1	4	21	40	20	38	141	125	86	39	47	64	74	79	28	90	76	38	58	63	76	41
SAT STRSKY-HUTCH	2	8	16	31	15	29	110	83	63	37	40	41	47	54	17	78	64	43	40	48	43	25
SUN ABC SN NT MV	3	29	17	29	18	31	109	83	64	31	43	41	45	52	25	83	67	44	46	48	27	15
AVG LOVE BOAT		12	20	42	20	40	137	118	81	41	50	54	64	71	27	97	78	48	54	63	57	32
KOIN																						
MON BETTY WHITE	2	4	11	18	12	20	78	66	39	12	21	30	36	45	14	36	23	11	19	19	10	6
TUE MASH	4	8	26	39	26	40	183	144	87	42	51	61	78	97	44	138	87	58	61	78	47	23
WED CBS WD NT MV	3	26	15	29	15	28	104	78	51	12	31	41	49	58	28	76	55	31	47	56	6	2
THU HAWAII 5-0	2	8	16	29	17	31	110	90	51	21	40	32	41	48	16	64	32	21	22	25	6	5
FRI CBS FR NT MV	2	16	13	26	13	24	89	58	47	27	36	26	26	31	16	67	53	42	35	37	25	10
SAT JEFFERSONS	4	8	15	26	15	27	107	85	45	14	23	34	45	60	20	68	39	22	29	37	23	7
SUN ALL IN FAMLY	3	6	23	33	22	33	166	137	62	20	33	50	68	90	36	102	52	30	38	51	33	17
KGW																						
MON NBC MON MOV	3	24	19	34	23	43	127	98	63	16	40	51	61	75	36	82	64	42	43	47	8	5
TUE MULLIGN STEW	2	8	5	9	5	8	37	28	16	9	9	12	15	21	9	16	13	6	10	10	10	6
WED *NBC MOV WEEK	2	16	15	27	17	32	101	83	46	13	20	39	47	63	23	86	49	30	33	41	19	7
THU JAMES AT 15	3	12	9	15	10	17	56	44	32	16	21	24	26	31	12	27	20	16	14	16	21	13
FRI ROCKFRD FILE	4	16	16	28	18	31	105	86	52	18	33	39	44	54	21	70	45	25	35	42	17	11
SAT NBC SAT MOV	4	38	14	28	17	34	94	77	51	8	28	44	50	60	20	63	45	27	35	38	8	2
SUN *BIG EVENT	4	33	17	30	20	34	113	97	64	19	42	50	57	67	28	77	61	44	48	52	15	8
AVG BIG EVENT		53	18	31	21	35	119	96	66	21	43	51	58	67	30	84	65	46	48	52	18	9
AVG NBC MOV WEEK		22	17	31	19	35	115	98	51	13	23	44	51	66	27	82	45	26	33	39	20	9
KPTV																						
SUN *COLUMBA CRSD	3	12	2	2	1	1	12	10	2	2	2			2		6	3	2	1	1		
AVG COLUMBA CRSD		28	1	2	1	2	6	5	1	1	1			1		3	1	1				
			1	2	3	4	5	10	11	12	13	14	15	56	16	17	18	19	20	21	22	23

TECHNICAL DIFFICULTY
+ PARENT/SATELLITE RELATIONSHIP
▲ SEE TABLE ON PAGE IV
* INCLUDED IN AVERAGE

Program Audiences

DAY AND TIME / STATION PROGRAM	WK	¼HR	2-11	6-11	2+	18+	15-24	12-34	RTG	SH	15-24	12-34	TOT 18+	18-49	15-24	18-34	25-49	25-54	25-64	WKG WMN 18+	TOT 18+	18-49	18-34	25-49	25-54	TEENS 12-17	CHILD 2-11
(col code)			24	25	6	7	8	9	1	2	31	32	33	34	35	36	37	38	57	39	40	41	42	43	44	45	46
▲RELATIVE STD-ERR (1 S.E.) THRESHOLDS 25-49%			25	21	27	17	20	19	2	6	2	2	2	3	5	4	3	3	3	7	2	3	6	4	4	8	10
50+%			6	5	4	3	5	3		1				2	1	1	1			1		1	1	1	1	2	2
7.30P KPTV																											
WED *ADAM 12	4	8	51	38	216	141	41	82	17	30	12	11	11	11	13	12	10	10	10	11	10	10	10	9	9	11	17
THU *ADAM 12	4	8	40	27	198	136	38	75	15	29	11	10	11	12	11	10	12	12	11	12	9	9	9	6	7	10	14
FRI *ADAM 12	4	8	42	29	170	110	32	69	14	26	9	9	8	10	11	10	9	9	8	10	9	8	9	8	9	9	16
AVG ADAM 12		38	43	31	188	124	33	71	15	26	10	9	10	10	11	10	10	9	9	10	9	9	8	8	8	10	15
8.00P KATU																											
TUE HAPPY DAYS	4	8	99	69	485	304	115	252	33	51	32	34	23	30	36	34	28	26	23	25	22	27	28	27	24	41	38
WED EIGHT ENOUGH	4	20	57	43	283	170	59	141	22	34	16	19	15	17	18	18	18	17	15	14	10	12	13	11	11	27	20
THU KOTTER	4	8	40	32	234	151	57	119	17	26	17	16	12	14	17	15	13	12	11	9	11	15	14	14	13	20	14
FRI DONNY-MARIE	3	12	65	43	274	180	42	106	21	37	12	15	16	14	13	16	14	14	15	11	11	11	13	11	10	15	25
SAT TABITHA	3	6	49	37	207	118	37	93	13	25	10	12	10	10	12	9	10	9	8	6	8	9	9	8	8	20	18
SUN 6 MILN $ MAN	3	12	35	25	184	124	41	77	13	20	12	10	8	9	8	9	10	10	10	9	11	12	12	10	10	11	13
KOIN																											
MON LOGANS RUN	2	8	34	23	157	90	36	77	10	16	10	9	6	8	8	8	9	8	7	6	6	8	7	7	7	15	12
TUE FITZPATRICKS	3	12	2	1	80	62	13	28	7	11	4	4	5	4	2	5	6	6	5	4	4	3	2	4	9	8	1
WED GOOD TIMES	3	6	19	14	124	86	24	48	10	15	7	7	6	6	7	6	6	7		6	5	5	5	6		9	7
THU WALTONS	3	16	42	24	368	290	61	141	28	44	18	19	26	25	25	25	25	25	24	19	16	13	12	13	14	17	16
FRI NEW WNDR WMN	2	8	40	22	182	114	43	89	12	21	11	11	8	10	13	10	9	9	8	7	8	10	11	10	10	13	15
SAT BOB NEWHART	3	6	11	5	168	149	25	48	14	26	7	6	12	8	8	7	9	10		12	10	7	7	7	8	4	4
SUN RHODA	2	4	12	8	263	227	47	112	24	36	13	14	19	18	15	18	19	20		23	13	11	12	10	12	10	3
KGW																											
MON HOUSE PRARIE	3	14	42	29	242	177	32	73	20	30	10	10	17	13	12	13	14	13	14	7	9	8	6	9	8	11	16
TUE MAN ATLANTIS	2	8	11	11	58	40	7	24	5	8	2	3	3	4	3	3	4	4	5	4	3	4	3	2	4	2	4
TUE *BIG EVENT	1	12	3	3	207	189	50	123	19	32	15	17	14	19	11	19	22	20	18	17	16	20	22	19	17	7	1
WED GRZZLY ADAMS	3	12	34	25	271	218	40	82	23	35	11	11	17	12	9	9	13	15	17	15	16	14	14	14	13	9	14
THU CHIPS	3	12	18	13	151	114	29	68	12	18	9	10	8	9	8	7	9	8	9	6	9	10	12	9	9	10	7
THU *BIG EVENT	1	8	24	21	248	192	52	102	19	33	15	14	14	16	17	14	15	15	13	16	14	14	13	13	13	15	9
FRI CPO SHARKEY	3	6	8	7	114	102	15	27	10	18	5	4	9	6	4	5	6	7	7	6	7	5	4	4	5	3	3
SAT BIONIC WOMAN	3	12	29	17	123	81	13	42	10	19	4	5	6	6	2	4	7	7	7	5	6	7	6	7	6	6	11
AVG BIG EVENT		53	12	9	210	180	42	107	18	31	12	15	14	16	12	16	18	17	15	15	14	16	18	17	16	9	5
KPTV																											
MON *THE MOVIE	4	32	7	6	89	74	16	38	8	12	5	5	6	5	6	6	6	5	6	6	4	4	5	4	3	5	3
TUE *THE MOVIE	3	24	5	3	96	87	15	27	9	14	4	4	7	6	5	5	5	6	6	6	6	5	4	6	6	2	2
WED *THE MOVIE	4	32	5	4	94	83	15	39	8	12	4	5	5	4	3	4	4	5	5	4	7	7	8	7	7	2	2
THU *THE MOVIE	4	32	3	3	82	72	12	23	7	11	3	3	4	3	2	2	4	5	5	4	6	4	3	4	5	3	1
FRI *THE MOVIE	4	32	5	4	77	65	15	36	7	12	4	4	5	5	5	6	6	5		5	5	5	5	4	4	3	1
AVG THE MOVIE		152	5	4	88	76	16	34	7	12	4	4	5	5	4	5	5	5	5	5	6	5	5	5	5	3	2
8.30P KATU																											
TUE LAVRNE-SHRLY	4	8	74	51	428	280	101	224	30	48	29	30	23	29	37	32	26	23	22	23	20	23	25	23	22	36	27
THU WHTS HAPNING	4	8	28	23	200	139	46	101	15	23	14	14	11	14	15	14	12	12	10	8	9	11	11	11	11	16	10
SAT OPRTN PETICT	3	6	40	32	230	143	55	108	15	31	15	14	10	12	15	10	12	12	11	12	12	14	12	13	13	23	15
KOIN																											
WED BUSTNG LOOSE	3	6	16	15	109	79	24	46	8	12	7	6	5	7	7	6	6	6		6	6	5	5	5	6	7	6
SAT GOT ECH OTHR	3	6	17	11	142	118	15	47	11	20	4	6	9	6	5	7	6	8	9	5	8	6	6	7	6	3	5
SUN ON OUR OWN	3	6	11	9	175	144	31	74	16	24	9	10	11	10	10	10	11	12	12	15	9	8	9	7	9	9	3
KGW																											
FRI CHICO-MAN	3	6	8	5	113	98	14	26	10	18	4	4	9	6	5	4	6	6	7	5	7	4	3	4	5	4	3
KPTV																											
SAT WRESTLING	4	24	10	7	113	97	15	32	8	15	4	4	5	4	3	4	4	4	4	3	8	5	5	4	4	2	4
SUN IN SEARCH OF	4	8	2	1	81	71	20	34	6	10	6	5	5	4	3	4	4	4	2	6	7	6	5	5	5	4	1
9.00P KATU																											
TUE 3 COMPANY	4	8	22	16	230	166	52	128	18	28	15	17	15	18	21	20	17	15	14	12	10	12	12	14	13	20	8
WED CHARLS ANGLS	4	16	30	26	254	169	70	144	20	36	20	19	14	17	22	18	16	15	14	11	11	13	15	11	11	26	11
THU BARNY MILLER	3	6	17	17	201	163	51	101	16	27	15	14	12	13	15	15	10	10	10	9	13	14	16	12	13	9	7
THU *LOVE BOAT	1	4	17	17	308	215	77	161	21	40	23	22	19	21	23	18	22	21	18	14	15	19	15	20	19	37	6
SAT STRSKY-HUTCH	2	8	41	33	245	161	68	126	16	31	17	16	12	16	20	14	14	14	13	9	14	17	14	14	13	22	16
SUN ABC SN NT MV	3	29	9	6	202	166	61	114	17	29	18	16	12	16	18	16	14	13	12	12	14	17	17	16	15	13	3
AVG LOVE BOAT		12	27	25	299	215	77	155	20	42	22	21	17	19	22	18	18	19	17	14	15	19	18	18	18	28	10
KOIN																											
MON BETTY WHITE	2	4	4	4	116	102	19	42	11	18	5	6	9	9	7	8	10	10	10	7	6	6	4	6	5	5	1
TUE MASH	4	8	16	12	345	282	78	156	26	39	22	20	20	20	23	18	20	21	21	22	21	21	22	20	21	22	6
WED CBS WD NT MV	3	26	5	3	165	154	23	68	15	29	7	9	11	12	7	11	13	13	12	13	12	13	12	16	16	3	2
THU HAWAII 5-0	2	8	9	4	169	154	32	67	16	29	9	12	11	12	14	9	10	9	7	7	10	7	7	6	6	2	3
FRI CBS FR NT MV	2	16	28	22	178	125	52	103	13	26	14	13	8	11	15	13	9	7	7	7	10	12	14	12	11	12	10
SAT JEFFERSONS	4	8	22	16	198	153	31	68	15	26	9	9	11	10	8	10	11	12		9	10	9	8	9	10	10	8
SUN ALL IN FAMLY	3	6	7	7	279	239	43	96	23	33	12	12	19	14	10	12	17	19	20	18	16	13	11	13	14	15	3
KGW																											
MON NBC MON MOV	3	24	3	2	191	180	38	90	19	34	12	13	14	16	10	15	18	18	17	18	13	16	17	15	14	4	1
TUE MULLIGN STEW	2	8	4	2	58	44	13	25	5	9	4	3	4	4	5	3	4	4	5	4	3	3	2	4	3	4	2
WED *NBC MOV WEEK	2	16	14	13	202	169	36	69	15	27	10	9	12	11	7	13	14	14		12	14	12	12	11	12	10	5
THU JAMES AT 15	3	12	9	6	101	71	25	58	9	15	7	8	6	8	10	8	7	7		6	4	5	6	5	5	11	3
FRI ROCKFRD FILE	4	16	19	15	192	156	30	75	16	28	9	10	13	13	10	12	14	13	13	11	11	11	10	12	12	9	7
SAT NBC SAT MOV	4	38	7	6	155	140	21	63	14	28	6	9	11	12	5	11	15	15	14	9	10	11	10	12	11	4	3
SUN *BIG EVENT	4	33	13	9	202	174	35	101	17	30	11	14	14	15	11	16	17	16	15	14	13	16	17	17	16	8	5
AVG BIG EVENT		53	12	9	210	180	42	107	18	31	12	15	14	16	12	16	18	17	15	15	14	16	18	17	16	9	5
AVG NBC MOV WEEK		22	10	10	210	180	32	69	17	31	10	10	14	12	7	9	15	15	15	12	13	12	10	12	12	10	4
KPTV																											
SUN *COLUMBA CRSO	3	12			16	16	4	4	2	2	1	1	2	1	1	1				1	1	1	1				
AVG COLUMBA CRSO		28			8	8	2	2	1	2	1		1														
(col code)			24	25	6	7	8	9	1	2	31	32	33	34	35	36	37	38	57	39	40	41	42	43	44	45	46

Program Title Index

PROGRAM	TIME	DAY	STATION	PROGRAM	TIME	DAY	STATION	PROGRAM	TIME	DAY	STATION	PROGRAM	TIME	DAY	STATION
ABBOT-COSTLO	2.30P	SUN	KATU	COLUMBA CRSD	9.00P	SUN	KPTV	HAWAII 5-0	9.00P	THU	KOIN	MISSION IMP	10.00P	SUN	KPTV
ABC EVE NEWS	6.00P	MON	KATU	CORAL JUNGLE	7.00P	SAT	KGW	HEE HAW	7.00P	SAT	KOIN	MLN $ MV FEA	11.30P	SAT	KATU
ABC EVE NEWS	6.00P	TUE	KATU	CPO SHARKEY	8.00P	FRI	KGW	HLYWD SQUARE	7.30P	TUE	KGW	MOD SQUAD	MDNGHT	MON	KPTV
ABC EVE NEWS	6.00P	WED	KATU	CPT KANGAROO	8.00A	M-F	KOIN	HLYWD SQUARE	7.30P	THU	KGW	MOD SQUAD	MDNGHT	TUE	KPTV
ABC EVE NEWS	6.00P	THU	KATU	DAVY GOLIATH	6.45A	SUN	KGW	HOLYWOD BEST	5.00P	SUN	KPTV	MOD SQUAD	MDNGHT	WED	KPTV
ABC EVE NEWS	6.00P	FRI	KATU	DAY DISCOVRY	10.00A	SUN	KPTV	HOLYWOD SQRE	9.30A	M-F	KGW	MOD SQUAD	MDNGHT	THU	KPTV
ABC SN NT MV	9.00P	SUN	KATU	DAYS LIVES	12.30P	M-F	KGW	HOT FUDGE	8.00A	SAT	KPTV	MOD SQUAD	MDNGHT	SUN	KPTV
ABC WKND NWS	11.00P	SAT	KATU	DINAH	9.00A	M-F	KPTV	HOUSE PRARIE	8.00P	MON	KGW	MOD SQUAD	12.30A	SAT	KPTV
ABC WKND NWS	11.00P	SUN	KATU	DIRECTIONS	1.00P	SUN	KATU	HOW COME	NOON	SAT	KGW	MON NIGHT MV	11.30P	MON	KATU
ADAM 12	7.30P	MON	KPTV	DOCTORS	1.30P	M-F	KGW	HOW TO PETE	10.00A	SAT	KPTV	MOV SPECTLR	1.00P	SAT	KOIN
ADAM 12	7.30P	TUE	KPTV	DONNY-MARIE	8.00P	FRI	KATU	I AM GREATST	6.30A	SAT	KGW	MOVIE OF WK	12.15A	SUN	KATU
ADAM 12	7.30P	WED	KPTV	DOXOLOGY/NWS	6.00A	SUN	KGW	I LKE MYSELF	3.00P	SAT	KGW	MOVIE 12	11.30P	FRI	KPTV
ADAM 12	7.30P	THU	KPTV	DRAGNET	11.30P	MON	KPTV	I LOVE LUCY	7.00P	MON	KPTV	MULLIGN STEW	9.00P	TUE	KGW
ADAM 12	7.30P	FRI	KPTV	DRAGNET	11.30P	TUE	KPTV	I LOVE LUCY	7.00P	TUE	KPTV	MUPPETS	7.30P	TUE	KATU
AFTERNOONER	3.00P	M-F	KGW	DRAGNET	11.30P	WED	KPTV	I LOVE LUCY	7.00P	WED	KPTV	MYSTRY OF WK	12.30A	WED	KATU
AFTERNOONER	3.30P	M-F	KGW	DRAGNET	11.30P	THU	KPTV	I LOVE LUCY	7.00P	THU	KPTV	NASHVILLE RD	MDNGHT	SAT	KPTV
AFTERNOONER	3.30P	MON	KGW	DRM JEANNIE	3.00P	M-F	KPTV	I LOVE LUCY	7.00P	FRI	KPTV	NASHVL MUSIC	11.30P	SAT	KPTV
AFTERNOONER	3.30P	TUE	KGW	EARLY BIRD	6.45A	M-F	KGW	IDEA THING	6.00A	SAT	KATU	NAT GEOGRPHC	4.00P	SUN	KATU
AFTERNOONER	3.30P	WED	KGW	EDGE OF NGHT	3.00P	M-F	KATU	IMPACT	9.00A	SUN	KOIN	NBC MON MOV	9.00P	MON	KGW
AFTERNOONER	3.30P	THU	KGW	EIGHT ENOUGH	8.00P	WED	KATU	IN SEARCH OF	8.30P	SUN	KPTV	NBC MOV WEEK	9.00P	WED	KGW
AFTERNOONER	3.30P	FRI	KGW	EMERGENCY 1	6.00P	MON	KPTV	INSIGHT	12.30A	SUN	KGW	NBC MOV WEEK	9.30P	MON	KGW
ALICE	9.30P	SUN	KOIN	EMERGENCY 1	6.00P	TUE	KPTV	INTNL ZONE	8.30A	SUN	KOIN	NBC NGHT NWS	6.30P	MON	KGW
ALL FAMILY-D	2.30P	M-F	KOIN	EMERGENCY 1	6.00P	WED	KPTV	IRONSIDE	1.30P	SUN	KATU	NBC NGHT NWS	6.30P	TUE	KGW
ALL IN FAMLY	9.00P	SUN	KOIN	EMERGENCY 1	6.00P	THU	KPTV	ISSUE ANSWRS	NOON	SUN	KATU	NBC NGHT NWS	6.30P	WED	KGW
ALL MY CHILD	NOON	M-F	KATU	EMERGENCY 1	6.00P	FRI	KPTV	IT IS WRITTN	10.30A	SUN	KPTV	NBC NGHT NWS	6.30P	THU	KGW
AM NORTHWEST	9.00A	M-F	KATU	EVENING	7.00P	MON	KGW	J COUSTEAU	5.00P	SAT	KGW	NBC NGHT NWS	6.30P	FRI	KGW
ANIMALS 3 X	9.00A	SUN	KATU	EVENING	7.00P	TUE	KGW	JABBERJAW	8.00A	SUN	KATU	NBC NGHT NWS	6.30P	SAT	KGW
ANOTHER WRLD	2.00P	M-F	KGW	EVENING	7.00P	WED	KGW	JAMES AT 15	9.00P	THU	KGW	NBC PRO FTBL	1.00P	SUN	KGW
ARCHI-SABRNA	9.00A	SAT	KGW	EVENING	7.00P	THU	KGW	JEFFERSONS	9.00P	SAT	KOIN	NBC PRO FTBL	3.30P	THU	KGW
ARCHIES	8.30A	M-F	KPTV	EVENING	7.00P	FRI	KGW	JIM SWAGGART	11.00A	SUN	KPTV	NBC RELIG SR	8.00A	SUN	KGW
AS WRLD TRNS	12.30P	M-F	KOIN	EYWTNS NWS 1	5.30P	MON	KATU	JOY IN SOUL	1.00A	SUN	KGW	NBC SAT MOV	9.00P	SAT	KGW
ASK MANAGER	6.30P	SUN	KOIN	EYWTNS NWS 1	5.30P	TUE	KATU	KIDS WORLD	12.30P	SAT	KGW	NCAA FOOTBLL	9.30A	SAT	KATU
BAGGY PANTS	8.30A	SAT	KGW	EYWTNS NWS 1	5.30P	WED	KATU	KNOCKOUT ≠	10.30A	M-F	KGW	NCAA FOOTBLL	6.00P	FRI	KATU
BARETTA	10.00P	WED	KATU	EYWTNS NWS 1	5.30P	THU	KATU	KOIN KITCHEN	10.00A	M-F	KOIN	NEW MR MAGOO	8.00A	SAT	KOIN
BARETTA LATE	11.15P	SUN	KATU	EYWTNS NWS 1	5.30P	FRI	KATU	KOJAK	10.00P	SUN	KOIN	NEW WAY LIVE	8.00A	SUN	KPTV
BARNBY JONES	10.00P	THU	KOIN	EYWTNS NWS 2	6.30P	MON	KATU	KOTTER	8.00P	THU	KATU	NEW WNDR WMN	8.00P	FRI	KOIN
BARNY MILLER	9.00P	THU	KATU	EYWTNS NWS 2	6.30P	TUE	KATU	LAFF-A-LYMPC	7.30A	SAT	KATU	NEWS CONF 6	5.30P	SAT	KOIN
BATMAN-TARZN	10.30A	SAT	KOIN	EYWTNS NWS 2	6.30P	WED	KATU	LAMP UNTO FT	7.00A	SUN	KOIN	NEWS EXTRA	5.00P	MON	KGW
BETTER SEX	11.00A	M-F	KATU	EYWTNS NWS 2	6.30P	THU	KATU	LATE MOVIE-W	11.30P	FRI	KOIN	NEWS EXTRA	5.00P	TUE	KGW
BETTY WHITE	9.00P	MON	KOIN	EYWTNS NWS 2	6.30P	FRI	KATU	LATE MOVIE-W	11.30P	SAT	KOIN	NEWS EXTRA	5.00P	WED	KGW
BEWITCHED	5.30P	MON	KPTV	EYWTNS NWS 3	11.00P	MON	KATU	LAVRNE-SHRLY	8.30P	TUE	KATU	NEWS EXTRA	5.00P	THU	KGW
BEWITCHED	5.30P	TUE	KPTV	EYWTNS NWS 3	11.00P	TUE	KATU	LAWRNCE WELK	7.00P	SAT	KATU	NEWS EXTRA	5.00P	FRI	KGW
BEWITCHED	5.30P	WED	KPTV	EYWTNS NWS 3	11.00P	WED	KATU	LIFE TO LIVE	1.30P	M-F	KATU	NEWS HILITES	6.45A	SAT	KPTV
BEWITCHED	5.30P	THU	KPTV	EYWTNS NWS 3	11.00P	THU	KATU	LITL RASCALS	10.00A	SUN	KATU	NEWS HILITES	6.45A	SUN	KPTV
BEWITCHED	5.30P	FRI	KPTV	EYWTNS NWS 3	11.00P	FRI	KATU	LOGANS RUN	8.00P	MON	KOIN	NEWS REVIEW	1.00A	SUN	KPTV
BIG EVENT	8.00P	TUE	KGW	EYWTNS NWS 4	6.30P	SAT	KATU	LOOK UP LIVE	7.30A	SUN	KOIN	NEWSROOM 6-D	11.30A	M-F	KOIN
BIG EVENT	8.00P	THU	KGW	EYWTNS NWS 5	11.15P	SAT	KATU	LOU GRANT	10.00P	TUE	KOIN	NEWSROOM 6-E	5.00P	MON	KOIN
BIG EVENT	9.00P	SUN	KGW	EYWTNS NWS 6	5.00P	SUN	KATU	LOVE BOAT	9.00P	THU	KATU	NEWSROOM 6-E	5.00P	TUE	KOIN
BIONIC WOMAN	8.00P	SAT	KGW	FACE NATION	5.30P	SUN	KOIN	LOVE BOAT	10.00P	SAT	KATU	NEWSROOM 6-E	5.00P	WED	KOIN
BOB NEWHART	8.00P	SAT	KOIN	FAITH TODAY	6.00A	SUN	KOIN	LOVE OF LIFE	10.30A	M-F	KOIN	NEWSROOM 6-E	5.00P	THU	KOIN
BOLD ONES	11.00P	SUN	KPTV	FAMILY	10.00P	TUE	KATU	LUCY SHOW	4.30P	MON	KATU	NEWSROOM 6-E	5.00P	FRI	KOIN
BRADY BUNCH	7.30A	SUN	KATU	FAMILY FEUD	11.30A	M-F	KATU	LUCY SHOW	4.30P	TUE	KATU	NEWSROOM 6-L	11.00P	MON	KOIN
BRUNCH THTR	NOON	SAT	KPTV	FAMLY AFFAIR	7.00A	SUN	KATU	LUCY SHOW	4.30P	WED	KATU	NEWSROOM 6-L	11.00P	TUE	KOIN
BRUNCH THTR	NOON	SUN	KPTV	FAT ALBERT	12.30P	SAT	KOIN	LUCY SHOW	4.30P	THU	KATU	NEWSROOM 6-L	11.00P	WED	KOIN
BUGS BUNNY	3.30P	MON	KPTV	FISH	4.30P	SAT	KATU	LUCY SHOW	4.30P	FRI	KATU	NEWSROOM 6-L	11.00P	THU	KOIN
BUGS BUNNY	3.30P	TUE	KPTV	FITZPATRICKS	8.00P	TUE	KOIN	M $ MV FEA 2	1.00A	SAT	KATU	NEWSROOM 6-L	11.00P	FRI	KOIN
BUGS BUNNY	3.30P	WED	KPTV	FLINTSTONES	4.30P	MON	KPTV	MAN ATLANTIS	8.00P	TUE	KGW	NEWSROOM 6-L	11.00P	SAT	KOIN
BUGS BUNNY	3.30P	THU	KPTV	FLINTSTONES	4.30P	TUE	KPTV	MARCUS WELBY	10.30A	M-F	KPTV	NEWSROOM 6-L	11.00P	SUN	KOIN
BUGS BUNNY	3.30P	FRI	KPTV	FLINTSTONES	4.30P	WED	KPTV	MARY T MOORE	5.00P	MON	KATU	NEWSROOM 6-W	5.00P	SAT	KOIN
BUGS-RD RUNR	8.30A	SAT	KOIN	FLINTSTONES	4.30P	THU	KPTV	MARY T MOORE	5.00P	TUE	KATU	NEWSROOM 6-W	5.00P	SUN	KOIN
BUMPITY	9.30A	SUN	KATU	FLINTSTONES	4.30P	FRI	KPTV	MARY T MOORE	5.00P	WED	KATU	NFL FOOTBALL	10.00A	SUN	KOIN
BUSTNG LOOSE	8.30P	WED	KOIN	FREVR FERNWD	11.00P	MON	KPTV	MARY T MOORE	5.00P	THU	KATU	NFL MON FTBL	7.00P	MON	KATU
C B BEARS	7.00A	SAT	KGW	FREVR FERNWD	11.00P	TUE	KPTV	MARY T MOORE	5.00P	FRI	KATU	NFL PRE GAME	9.30A	SUN	KOIN
CALL MCARONI	7.30A	SUN	KGW	FREVR FERNWD	11.00P	WED	KPTV	MASH	9.00P	TUE	KOIN	NOT WMN ONLY	6.30A	M-F	KPTV
CAMERA 3	8.00A	SUN	KOIN	FREVR FERNWD	11.00P	THU	KPTV	MATCH GME PM	7.30P	WED	KATU	NW AT NOON	NOON	M-F	KGW
CAROL BURNET	10.00P	SAT	KOIN	FREVR FERNWD	11.00P	FRI	KPTV	MATINEE 12	1.00P	M-F	KPTV	NW CAND CMRA	7.30P	FRI	KATU
CARTER CNTRY	9.30P	THU	KATU	GARDENING	9.00A	SAT	KPTV	MAUDE	9.30P	MON	KOIN	NWS HEADLINE	1.00A	TUE	KATU
CARTN CASTLE	7.00A	M-F	KPTV	GD MORN AMER	7.00A	M-F	KATU	MAVERICK	2.30P	SAT	KOIN	ODD COUPLE	6.00P	SUN	KOIN
CATHEDRL TMW	9.00A	SUN	KPTV	GEN HOSPITAL	2.15P	M-F	KATU	MEDICAL CNTR	3.30P	MON	KATU	ODD COUPLE	6.30P	MON	KOIN
CBS EVE NEWS	6.00P	MON	KOIN	GET TOGETHER	8.30A	SUN	KGW	MEDICAL CNTR	3.30P	TUE	KATU	ODD COUPLE	6.30P	TUE	KOIN
CBS EVE NEWS	6.00P	TUE	KOIN	GILLIGANS IS	5.00P	MON	KPTV	MEDICAL CNTR	3.30P	WED	KATU	ODD COUPLE	6.30P	WED	KOIN
CBS EVE NEWS	6.00P	WED	KOIN	GILLIGANS IS	5.00P	TUE	KPTV	MEDICAL CNTR	3.30P	THU	KATU	ODD COUPLE	6.30P	THU	KOIN
CBS EVE NEWS	6.00P	THU	KOIN	GILLIGANS IS	5.00P	WED	KPTV	MEDICAL CNTR	3.30P	FRI	KATU	ODD COUPLE	6.30P	FRI	KOIN
CBS EVE NEWS	6.00P	FRI	KOIN	GILLIGANS IS	5.00P	THU	KPTV	MEET PRESS	9.00A	SUN	KGW	ON OUR OWN	8.30P	SUN	KOIN
CBS FR NT MV	9.00P	FRI	KOIN	GILLIGANS IS	5.00P	FRI	KPTV	MERV GRIFFIN	7.00P	MON	KOIN	ONE DAY TIME	9.30P	TUE	KOIN
CBS LT MOVIE	11.30P	MON	KOIN	GONG SHOW	11.30A	M-F	KGW	MERV GRIFFIN	7.00P	TUE	KOIN	OPEN LINE	11.15P	SUN	KGW
CBS LT MOVIE	11.30P	TUE	KOIN	GONG SHW	7.30P	THU	KATU	MERV GRIFFIN	7.00P	WED	KOIN	OPRTN PETICT	8.30P	SAT	KATU
CBS LT MOVIE	11.30P	WED	KOIN	GOOD NEWS	11.30A	SUN	KPTV	MERV GRIFFIN	7.00P	THU	KOIN	ORAL ROBERTS	8.30A	SUN	KPTV
CBS LT MOVIE	11.30P	THU	KOIN	GOOD TIMES	8.00P	WED	KOIN	MERV GRIFFIN	7.00P	FRI	KOIN	PERRY MASON	NOON	M-F	KPTV
CBS LT MOVIE	11.45P	SUN	KOIN	GOSPEL HOUR	7.00A	SUN	KPTV	MICKEY MOUSE	4.00P	MON	KPTV	PHIL DONAHUE	9.00A	M-F	KOIN
CBS MNG NEWS	7.00A	M-F	KOIN	GOT ECH OTHR	8.30P	SAT	KOIN	MICKEY MOUSE	4.00P	TUE	KPTV	POLICE STRY	11.30P	THU	KATU
CBS NEWS-SAT	6.00P	SAT	KOIN	GRDNING HUME	8.00A	SUN	KGW	MICKEY MOUSE	4.00P	WED	KPTV	POLICE WOMAN	10.00P	TUE	KGW
CBS SUN NEWS	11.30P	SUN	KOIN	GRZZLY ADAMS	8.00P	WED	KGW	MICKEY MOUSE	4.00P	THU	KPTV	POP GO CNTRY	11.00P	SAT	KPTV
CBS WD NT MV	9.00P	WED	KOIN	GT ARMSTRONG	11.00A	SAT	KPTV	MICKEY MOUSE	4.00P	FRI	KPTV	PRAYER/NEWS	6.15A	SAT	KGW
CHARLS ANGLS	9.00P	WED	KATU	GT GRAPE APE	8.30A	SUN	KATU	MIDNIGHT SPC	1.00A	FRI	KGW	PUBLIC AFFRS	6.30A	M-F	KATU
CHICO-MAN	8.30P	FRI	KGW	GUIDING LGHT	1.30P	M-F	KOIN	MIKE DOUGLAS	3.30P	MON	KOIN	QUINCY	10.00P	FRI	KGW
CHIPS	8.00P	THU	KGW	HAPPY DAYS	8.00P	TUE	KATU	MIKE DOUGLAS	3.30P	TUE	KOIN	RAFFERTY	10.00P	MON	KOIN
CHRISTOPHERS	6.30A	SUN	KATU	HAPPY DAYS-D	10.00A	M-F	KATU	MIKE DOUGLAS	3.30P	WED	KOIN	RAMBLIN ROD	7.30A	M-F	KPTV
COLLEGE FB	12.30P	SUN	KATU	HARDY/DREW	7.00P	SUN	KATU	MIKE DOUGLAS	3.30P	THU	KOIN	RED HND GANG	11.30A	SAT	KGW
COLUMBA CRSD	7.00A	SAT	KPTV	HAROLD LLOYD	11.30A	SUN	KGW	MIKE DOUGLAS	3.30P	FRI	KOIN	REDD FOXX	10.00P	THU	KATU

PROGRAM TITLE INDEX   NOVEMBER 1977   PAGE 114   PORTLAND, OR

Program Title Index

PROGRAM	TIME	DAY	STATION	PROGRAM	TIME	DAY	STATION	PROGRAM	TIME	DAY	STATION	PROGRAM	TIME	DAY	STATION
RHODA	8.00P	SUN	KOIN	WRLD ANIMALS	4.30P	SAT	KGW								
ROCKFRD FILE	9.00P	FRI	KGW	YNG-RESTLESS	11.00A	M-F	KOIN								
ROSETTI-RYAN	10.00P	THU	KGW	10 OCLCK NWS	10.00P	MON	KPTV								
RYANS HOPE	1.00P	M-F	KATU	10 OCLCK NWS	10.00P	TUE	KPTV								
SA VIRGINIAN	2.30P	SAT	KPTV	10 OCLCK NWS	10.00P	WED	KPTV								
SA 11 NW TN	11.00P	SAT	KGW	10 OCLCK NWS	10.00P	THU	KPTV								
SA 6 NW TNGT	6.00P	SAT	KGW	10 OCLCK NWS	10.00P	FRI	KPTV								
SANFRD-SON-D	9.00A	M-F	KGW	10 OCLCK NWS	10.00P	SAT	KPTV								
SAT FLM FEST	7.30A	SAT	KOIN	100000 TUNE	7.30P	FRI	KGW								
SAT MOVIE	6.00P	SAT	KPTV	1100 NW TNGT	11.00P	MON	KGW								
SAT NGT LIVE	11.30P	SAT	KGW	1100 NW TNGT	11.00P	TUE	KGW								
SAT SHOW	4.00P	SAT	KPTV	1100 NW TNGT	11.00P	WED	KGW								
SCND CITY TV	10.00P	MON	KATU	1100 NW TNGT	11.00P	THU	KGW								
SECRETS ISIS	NOON	SAT	KOIN	1100 NW TNGT	11.00P	FRI	KGW								
SERCH-RESCUE	11.00A	SAT	KGW	12 IN AM	10.30A	SAT	KPTV								
SGN OFF NWS	1.00A	MON	KPTV	20000 PYRAMD	10.30A	M-F	KATU								
SGN OFF NWS	1.00A	TUE	KPTV	25000 PYRAMD	7.30P	MON	KGW								
SGN OFF NWS	1.00A	WED	KPTV	3 COMPANY	9.00P	TUE	KATU								
SGN OFF NWS	1.00A	THU	KPTV	530 NW TNGHT	5.30P	MON	KGW								
SIGN OF LIFE	6.30A	SUN	KGW	530 NW TNGHT	5.30P	TUE	KGW								
SINISTR CINE	11.30P	FRI	KATU	530 NW TNGHT	5.30P	WED	KGW								
SKATEBIRDS	8.00A	SAT	KOIN	530 NW TNGHT	5.30P	THU	KGW								
SN PDRO BUMS	4.00P	SAT	KATU	530 NW TNGHT	5.30P	FRI	KGW								
SND TRUMPETS	6.15A	SUN	KGW	6 MILN $ MAN	8.00P	SUN	KATU								
SOAP	9.30P	TUE	KATU	60 MINUTES	7.00P	SUN	KOIN								
SPACE ACADMY	10.30A	SAT	KOIN	8 LIVELY ART	9.30A	SUN	KGW								
SPCE SENTNLS	10.30A	SAT	KGW												
SPCL EDITION	5.30P	SUN	KATU												
SPR FRNDS HR	6.30A	SAT	KATU												
SPTS SPECTLR	3.30P	SAT	KOIN												
SRCH FOR TMW	11.30A	M-F	KPTV												
STAR TREK	4.00P	SUN	KPTV												
STR TREK	3.30P	SAT	KGW												
STR-HTH LATE	11.30P	WED	KATU												
STRSKY-HUTCH	9.00P	SAT	KATU												
SU 11 NW TN	11.00P	SUN	KGW												
SU 6 NW TNGT	6.00P	SUN	KGW												
SUN MATINEE	2.00P	SUN	KPTV												
SUNDAY MORN	10.30A	SUN	KATU												
SUNRSE SMSTR	6.30A	M-F	KOIN												
SUNRSE SMSTR	6.30A	SAT	KOIN												
TABITHA	8.00P	SAT	KATU												
TATTLETALES	3.00P	M-F	KOIN												
TELL TRUTH	7.00P	TUE	KATU												
TELL TRUTH	7.00P	WED	KATU												
TELL TRUTH	7.00P	THU	KATU												
TELL TRUTH	7.00P	FRI	KATU												
THATS HLYWD	7.30P	WED	KGW												
THE MOVIE	8.00P	MON	KPTV												
THE MOVIE	8.00P	TUE	KPTV												
THE MOVIE	8.00P	WED	KPTV												
THE MOVIE	8.00P	THU	KPTV												
THE MOVIE	8.00P	FRI	KPTV												
THIS IS LIFE	6.30A	SUN	KOIN												
THIS LAND	6.30P	SAT	KOIN												
THNK P PNTHR	8.00A	SAT	KGW												
THRILLER	1.00A	SAT	KGW												
THUNDER	10.00A	SAT	KGW												
THURS NT SPC	12.30A	THU	KATU												
TLK ABT PIC	11.30A	SAT	KPTV												
TO SAY LEAST	11.00A	M-F	KGW												
TODAY SHOW	7.00A	M-F	KGW												
TOMORROW SHW	1.00A	MON	KGW												
TOMORROW SHW	1.00A	TUE	KGW												
TOMORROW SHW	1.00A	WED	KGW												
TOMORROW SHW	1.00A	THU	KGW												
TONIGHT SHOW	11.30P	MON	KGW												
TONIGHT SHOW	11.30P	TUE	KGW												
TONIGHT SHOW	11.30P	WED	KGW												
TONIGHT SHOW	11.30P	THU	KGW												
TONIGHT SHOW	11.30P	FRI	KGW												
TONY RANDALL	9.30P	SAT	KOIN												
TOWN HALL NT	6.00P	SUN	KATU												
TOWN-COUNTRY	6.00A	M-F	KGW												
TRUTH-CONSEQ	4.00P	SAT	KGW												
TUE MOVIE WK	11.30P	TUE	KATU												
TV 2 SPECIAL	5.00P	SAT	KATU												
UNTAMED WRLD	4.00P	SUN	KOIN												
VIEWPOINT	9.30A	SUN	KGW												
VISION ON	7.00A	SUN	KGW												
WACKO	7.00A	SAT	KOIN												
WALTONS	8.00P	THU	KOIN												
WEEKEND MAT	1.00P	SAT	KGW												
WEEKEND MAT	4.00P	SUN	KGW												
WHEEL FRTUNE	10.00A	M-F	KGW												
WHTS HAPNING	8.30P	THU	KATU												
WILD KINGDOM	6.30P	SUN	KGW												
WILDLIFE TH	8.30A	SAT	KPTV												
WORLD DISNEY	7.00P	SUN	KGW												
WRESTLING	8.30P	SAT	KPTV												

Program Title Index

ADI Rating Trends

```
MON/FRI
TIME AND ADI RATINGS
STATION OC NO FE MA OC NO FE MA JU OC
        75 75 76 76 76 76 77 77 77 77

7:00 AM TO 9:00 AM
KATU     1  2  2  3  4  4  4  4  5  4
KVDO       ***********       *********
KOIN     3  3  2  3  2  3  2  2  2  2
KOAC                            ***
KGW      5  4  5  4  4  4  5  4  4  4
KOAP                            ***
KPTV     5  5  4  4  6  7  6  6  3  4
HUT     15 15 15 14 17 18 17 15 15 14

9:00 AM TO NOON
KATU     3  3  3  2  4  4  4  4  5  4
KVDO       ***********       *********
KOIN     4  4  5  4  5  4  6  3  5  4
KOAC                            ***
KGW      5  5  5  5  4  5  4  3  5  4
KOAP     1  1  1  1  1  1  1  2*** 1
KPTV     3  3  3  2  2  3  2  2  3  2
HUT     17 16 18 14 16 18 19 15 19 14

NOON TO 4:30 PM
KATU     5  5  5  4  5  4  6  4  6  4
KVDO       ***********       *********
KOIN     5  4  6  5  5  6  6  5  5  6
KOAC
KGW      7  6  7  5  6  7  6  5  5  5
KOAP
KPTV     5  5  6  4  5  6  5  4  4  4
HUT     23 22 25 19 22 24 23 19 21 20

4:30 PM TO 6:00 PM
KATU    10  9  9  8  8  9  8  6  6  9
KVDO          ******       *********
KOIN     9  9 11  9 12 11 12 10 10  9
KOAC
KGW     11 12 11  8  8  9  9  7  8  8
KOAP     2  3  3  2  1  2  2  1  1  1
KPTV     8 10 11  7  7 10 11  9  6  9
HUT     41 44 46 37 38 42 42 35 31 37

5:00 PM TO 7:30 PM
KATU    12 12 12 11 11 12 11  8  8 14
KVDO          ******       *********
KOIN    11 12 13 10 13 13 15 11 11 10
KOAC
KGW     15 15 15 11 13 13 14 12 11 12
KOAP     1  1  1  1  1  1  1  1
KPTV    10 13 14 10 10 13 11 10  8 12
HUT     51 56 57 45 48 53 53 44 40 51

6:00 PM TO 7:30 PM
KATU    13 14 13 13 12 14 12 10  9 16
KVDO          ******       *********
KOIN    13 14 14 11 13 13 15 11 11 10
KOAC
KGW     16 16 16 13 15 15 16 15 12 14
KOAP
KPTV    12 15 16 11 10 14 12 11 10 14
HUT     55 61 61 49 52 56 56 48 43 56

7:00 PM TO 7:30 PM
KATU    16 18 17 13 14 16 13 12 11 19
KVDO          ******       *********
KOIN    14 14 13 10 12 14 13  9  9 10
KOAC
KGW     14 14 14 13 15 14 16 15  8 13
KOAP              1  1  1              1
KPTV    10 12 14 10 10 11 12 10 10 13
HUT     56 61 61 48 53 57 56 47 39 58

7:30 PM TO 8:00 PM
KATU    14 16 12 11 15 16 13 11  9 19
KVDO          ******       *********
KOIN    13 13 13  9 13 14 14  9  8 10
KOAC
KGW     17 16 17 14 14 14 16 15 11 13
KOAP     1  1  1  1  1  1  1           1
KPTV    10 12 13 10  9 11 11 10  7 12
HUT     56 59 58 47 55 57 55 48 37 57

7:30 PM TO 11:00 PM
KATU    17 17 20 16 18 19 21 14 13 16
KVDO          ******       *********
KOIN    17 17 17 13 16 17 16 17 13 15
KOAC
KGW     14 17 15 14 14 16 14 13 12 13
KOAP     1  1  1  1  2  2  1  1  1  1
KPTV     5  5  5  6  5  4  5  6  5  7
HUT     56 60 61 51 56 58 57 52 45 53
```

```
MON/FRI
TIME AND ADI RATINGS
STATION OC NO FE MA OC NO FE MA JU OC
        75 75 76 76 76 76 77 77 77 77

10:30 PM TO 11:00 PM
KATU    13 14 19 14 13 15 20 11 12  9
KVDO          *****       *********
KOIN    13 14 13 10 12 13 13 14 12 14
KOAC
KGW     11 15 13 12 11 14 10 12 11 12
KOAP     1  1     1  1  1     1  1  1
KPTV     4  3  3  3  4  3  3  3  4  4
HUT     43 49 49 41 43 47 47 43 41 41

11:00 PM TO 11:30 PM
KATU     6  6  6  6  4  7  8  6  6  5
KVDO    ***       *********       ************
KOIN     7  7  8  7  6  8  8  7  7  8
KOAC
KGW      9 11  9  8  9  9  8  9  9  8
KOAP                            1
KPTV     2  2  5  5  5  4  4  3  3  3
HUT     25 27 30 26 24 29 29 25 26 25

11:30 PM TO 1:00 AM
KATU     2  2  2  2  1  2  2  1  2  2
KVDO    ***       *********       ************
KOIN     3  3  3  3  3  2  3  2  3  2
KOAC    ***                ************
KGW      4  5  7  5  5  6  4  5  4  5
KOAP    ***    1  1  1*********
KPTV     1  1  1  1  1  1  1  1  2  1
HUT     11 12 13 10 10 11 12  9 12  9
```

```
SATURDAY
TIME AND ADI RATINGS
STATION OC NO FE MA OC NO FE MA JU OC
        75 75 76 76 76 76 77 77 77 77

8:30 AM TO 1:00 PM
KATU     4 10  6  4  9 12  5  4  4  8
KVDO   **********************************
KOIN     8  8  8  4  7  8  6  5  5  6
KOAC    ***              ***
KGW      8  4  3  5  7  4  3  4  5  5
KOAP     1  1  1  1
KPTV     2  2  3  1  1  1  2  2  2  1
HUT     23 25 21 15 26 26 17 15 16 21
```

Glossary of Arbitron Terms

ADI (Area of Dominant Influence)—An exclusive geographic area consisting of all counties in which the Home Market Stations receive a preponderance of total viewing hours. (See separate publication provided to all television report subscribers entitled *Description of Methodology.)*

Adjacent ADI—Areas of Dominant Influence which are adjacent to the home market's ADI and which are serviced by the home-market stations. Where more than three adjacent ADI's lie within the home market's TSA, selection of the three to be reported is based on an analysis of home station circulation in each adjacent ADI. The ADI's to which each county in the TSA has been assigned are identified by codes which appear above the county listing; counties with the code "O" lie within the ADI of a market which is not reported in this publication.

Average Quarter-Hour Audience—(See Quarter-Hour Audience)

Color-Set Penetration—Arbitron reports estimates of color television households penetration for each survey area within the market, based on information obtained during the diary placement interview.

Controls—Arbitron weighting techniques are used in all sampling units to establish proportionate representation of viewing by sampling unit, by age of head of household and by week. The weighting techniques are also used in certain sampling units containing CATV households, and in certain sampling units where special interviewing techniques are used. The County list on Page 3 indicates the CATV households controls. In certain markets which meet Arbitron criteria, racial and/or ethnic characteristics are also considered when establishing weights.

Cume Households—For each reported Home Market Station, an estimate of the number of different Television Households that view at least once during the average week for five continuous minutes or more during the reported day-part. This is an unduplicated or cumulative estimate of circulation. The estimate is based on viewing within the TSA only.

Effective Sample Base (ESB)—The sample size to be used for estimating the statistical variance of audience estimates when used in conjunction with Statistical Efficiencies. The statistical reliability of audience estimates depends only indirectly on the number of diaries tabulated and is also subject to all of the factors described in the section of this report entitled *Limitations.* (See separate publication provided to all television report subscribers entitled *Description of Methodology.)*

Home County—The county in which a station's city of license is located. (See Metro Rating Area.)

Households Using Television (HUT)—The estimated percent of television households with at least one television set turned on for five minutes or more during an average quarter hour, as reported for the ADI, Metro or Home County.

In-Tab Sample—The number of Television Households, or persons within those households, whose reported viewing is tabulated in producing the report. In-Tab Sample includes television households which returned diaries and selected Planned-No-Viewing Households.

Metro (Or Home County) Rating Area (MRA)—Metro Rating Areas, where applicable, generally correspond to Standard Metropolitan Statistical Areas as defined by the U.S. Government's Office of Management and Budget, subject to exceptions dictated by historical industry usage and other marketing considerations such as channel allocations. (Home-market MRA counties are indicated in the listing by an "M" preceding the county name.) Where there is no defined ADI, ratings may be shown for the Home County of the station's city of license. The Home County is indicated in the listing by an "H" preceding the county name.

Multi-Set Penetration—Arbitron reports penetration estimates of households with more than one television set for each survey area within the market, based on information obtained in the diary placement interview.

Net Weekly Circulation—An estimate of the number of unduplicated Television Households which viewed a station for at least five continuous minutes at least once during the week. This estimate is reported as Cume Households in Column 26 of the Sign-on/Sign-off day-part.

Network Averages—The average weekly audience to network programming reported for eight day-parts. These estimates are based on network carriage by home-market stations only.

Original Sample Size—The number of estimated Television Households originally drawn for the survey.

Planned-No-Viewing Households—Television households which indicated at the time of the diary placement interview that no television viewing would occur during the survey week, and which did not return a usable diary. (See separate publication provided to all television report subscribers entitled *Description of Methodology.)*

PVT (Persons Viewing Television)—The total number of persons by sex-age group viewing *all* television in the ADI, reported as a percent of the total number of ADI persons in each demographic category. This estimate includes viewing to both reported stations and to non-reported stations, which include stations whose audiences were below the minimum reporting standards and stations which were not tested.

Percentage Distribution—The share of Television Households viewing a home-market station, reported for each day-part within specified survey areas.

Projection—The expansion of sample statistics to household or population information in the respective universe. Estimates of persons viewing in a specific sex-age group are projected and then rounded to the nearest thousand. A projection of less than 500 persons for a specific category will not be printed; this blank is not intended to imply that no viewing occurred.

Quarter-Hour Audience—A projected estimate of the unduplicated audience having viewed a station for a minimum of five minutes within a specific quarter-hour. These quarter-hour total audiences when combined into larger time periods become Average Quarter-Hour Audiences.

Rating—The estimated percent of television households, or persons within those households, tuned to a particular station for five minutes or more during an average quarter hour of the reported time period for the ADI, Metro or Home County. If the rating is estimated to be less than 0.5% for a time period, the space is left blank; this blank is not intended to imply that no viewing occurred.

Relative Standard Error Thresholds—The thresholds indicate the approximate degree of sample variations in the audience estimates reported. Thresholds are shown for two levels of relative error: 25-49 percent and 50 percent plus. One Standard Error (1SE) is used in the calculation of thresholds. (See separate publication provided to all television report subscribers entitled *Description of Methodology.)*

Satellite Station—A station that duplicates some or all of the programming of a parent station in order to serve an area not normally reached, and which is assigned separate call letters and channel number by the FCC. In its regularly issued Television Market Reports, Arbitron combines the audiences of "satellite" stations with those of the "parent" station under certain conditions. (See separate publication provided to all television report subscribers entitled *Description of Methodology.)*

Share—The percentage of the total Households Using Television (HUT) reached by a station during a specified time. It is possible for the sum of the shares to exceed 100%. All shares of 100% or greater will appear as "99".

Television Households (TV HH)—An Arbitron estimate of the number of households having one or more television sets.

TOT (Totals)—The sum of estimated viewing in the Total Survey Area to all *reported* stations, by households and by demographic categories. This "Total" does not include viewing to stations whose audiences were below the minimum reporting standards or to stations which were not tested.

Total Households—An updated estimate based on 1970 census provided by Market Statistics, Inc. These estimates are projected to January 1, 1978 and include households on military installations.

Total Survey Area (TSA)—A geographic area comprising those counties in which, by Arbitron estimates, approximately 98% of the net weekly circulation of commercial home market stations occurs. All TSA estimates are reported in thousands.

UHF Penetration—Arbitron reports estimates of UHF penetration in the TSA, the ADI and Metro of all Metro markets, TSA and ADI of all non-Metro markets, and the TSA of all non-ADI markets. These estimates are based on the in-tab diary sample.

Universe—All television households located in the specified area.

Working Woman—A female age 18+ who works outside the home 30 or more hours per week.

For additional information, the reader is directed to "Standard Definitions of Broadcast Research Terms," published by the National Association of Broadcasters, 1771 N Street, N. W., Washington, D.C. 20036, and Arbitron's "Description of Methodology."

An Arbitron Report of Television Audience Estimates

This report is a compilation of television audience estimates for this market. The estimates are based on information supplied by television households over the period of the sample survey. The households were selected by computer from local telephone directory sources. All television audience estimates are approximations subject to statistical variations related to sample sizes.

Arbitron uses one-week family viewing diaries to gather information for television audience reports. Information, such as color-set and multi-set ownership, is also gathered by telephone at the time of the diary placement interview. Diaries are printed in Spanish for placement with families who indicate preference for a Spanish language diary.

A methodology description is provided in this report. A more detailed description of Arbitron methodology may be found in a separate publication, *Description of Methodology*. If any specific details are not completely clear, further explanation will be furnished on request.

Arbitron clients who also receive survey data on EDP tape should note that the estimates on the tape are in somewhat different form than reported in this book.

Estimates Reported by Section

Day-Part Audience Summary—Average quarter-hour audience estimates are summarized for each station by standard day-part segments. The day-part groupings in Central and Mountain time zone markets differ slightly from those in Eastern and Pacific time zones to better represent those times which are normally devoted to network and local programming. Station estimates in this summary are based on the quarter-hour periods that each station was on the air during the specified day-part. Periods in which off-air technical difficulties occur are not included in station averages. Estimates for stations on the air for less time than the station telecasting the most quarter-hours during the period are so designated by a double asterisk (**). Because Arbitron viewing estimates are tabulated only for those time periods between 6:00 AM and 2:00 AM, "Sign-on" and "Sign-off" day-parts do not include telecasts prior to or after these hours. (See separate publication provided to all television report subscribers entitled *Description of Methodology.)*

Network Program Averages—These averages include *only* network program quarter-hour audiences carried on home stations with all local or syndicated programming eliminated.

Weekly Programming and Time Period Averages—Average quarter-hour audience estimates are reported for each station for each night of the week, from 4:00 PM to 2:00 AM (local time), and for all day Saturday and Sunday. For the Monday-Friday period, estimates are reported as five-day averages. Station estimates are based on the quarter-hour periods that each station was on the air during the specified time period. Periods in which off-air technical difficulties occur are not included in station averages.

The Weekly Programming and Time Period Averages section is arranged as follows: The time period is listed, followed by the station call letters and the first week's first quarter-hour program title. If the title is the same for any other quarter-hour in any week of the survey it will not be repeated. Different program titles appear on the lines following with a maximum of eight title lines per station. If there is more than one title for a station during a time period a four-week average line follows the title lines. The weekly ADI rating(s) for a given program appear in the appropriate week's rating column. If the first and second quarter-hour of a half-hour time period have different programming, two ADI weekly ratings are shown for the appropriate week, one representing each quarter-hour.

Wednesday	WK 1	WK 2	WK 3	WK 4
6:30-7:00 PM				
WAAA				
Brady Bunch	6			
News		6	8	
Basketball			10	11
—4 Wk Avg—				

A dash (—) in one of these weekly rating columns indicates that the program did not achieve a reportable rating. A blank in one of these weekly rating columns indicates that the station was not on the air. To qualify for individual weekly reporting, a minimum of 70 in-tab households must be achieved in each of the survey weeks. In markets with smaller sample only multi-week average estimates are reported and an asterisk (*) will appear in the weekly columns. On each title line, after the weekly rating(s), the time period averages are reported. For those programs telecast two or more weeks during a time period, complete household and demographic information is reported. For those programs telecast only once in a time period, in those markets with weekly ADI ratings, the following is reported:

ADI TV Household Ratings and Shares
ADI Ratings for Total Men and Total Women
Metro TV Household Ratings and Shares
TSA TV Households, Total Men and Total Women

For those programs telecast only once in a time period in markets without weekly ratings, no estimates are reported. The four-week average line includes complete household and demographic estimates which are averages for all weeks of the survey.

Program titles are requested on a time-formatted, pre-printed log form from each commercial station. See separate publication provided to all television report subscribers entitled *Description of Methodology.*

Station Break Averages—Audiences reported are averages of two quarter-hours. The time listed is the station break time between the two quarter-hours included in the average. Periods in which off-air technical difficulties occur are not included in station averages.

Program Audiences—Average quarter-hour estimates are reported for those programs which meet certain qualifications. All quarter-hours of a qualifying program telecast by Home Market or outside Class I station during the multiple week survey are included. The number of quarter-hours on which the averages are based is shown in the report. To qualify for inclusion a program must have been telecast *at least one* quarter-hour on the *same day* during each of *two* survey weeks. The program is reported in the Program Audiences section even if it was carried at different times, as long as the program was on the *same calendar day* of the weeks involved (e.g., first Wednesday at 5:00 PM and third Wednesday at 8:00 PM). Only full program quarter-hours are included.

Accumulation of quarter-hour estimates is based on program title. Programs of one quarter-hour duration shown two or more times during the same day and also on different weeks will be averaged together and reported in the section.

Time Periods and Programs Reported—Since Arbitron does not have individual day titles for programs telecast prior to 3:30 PM Monday through Friday, programs must qualify within the Arbitron time frames. Thus, a movie telecast each day, Monday-Friday 2:30 PM-4:30 PM is reported as two programs with a weighted average of the two programs. The first is a Monday-Friday average of the 2:30-3:30 portion of the movie. The second is an average of the individual days (Monday through Friday) from 3:30 to 4:30 combined with the Monday-Friday 2:30 to 3:30 portion of the program. The resulting final program average (see example below) includes all quarter-hours the program was telecast, even though it began prior to the 3:30 PM break for individual day reporting and averaging. The Monday-Friday average must be contiguous to the 3:30 PM time period to be included in the weighted average.

2:30 PM WAAA		No. of Wks.	No. of ¼ Hrs.
*M-F	Movie	4	80
3:30 PM WAAA			
*M-F	Movie	4	80
*Mon.	Movie	4	16
*Tue.	Movie	4	16
*Wed.	Movie	4	16
*Thu.	Movie	4	16
*Fri.	Movie	4	16
Avg.	Movie		160

Programs scheduled more than once weekly *after* 3:30 PM are reported as daily estimates and as a weekly average. If a program is telecast seven days a week during the survey, *two* averages are provided. The first is a five-day average of the Monday through Friday telecasts and the second is a seven-day average including the Monday through Friday telecast, as well as the Saturday and Sunday telecasts. A 6:00 PM newscast would be reported for each individual day Monday through Friday with a five-day average (5 AV) followed by the Saturday and Sunday individual days and a seven-day average (7 AV) which includes all telecasts of the program.

6:00 PM WAAA		6:00 PM WAAA	
*Mon.	News	*Sat.	News
*Tue.	News	*Sun.	News
*Wed.	News	7AV.	News
*Thu.	News		
*Fri.	News		
5AV.	News		

The weekly average of programs telecast more than once weekly, but with varying start times appears *each time* the program title appears. The average represents all time periods in which the program was telecast. An asterisk (*) preceding a program title indicates that the estimates for the program are included in an average.

Because viewing estimates are tabulated only for those time periods between 6:00 AM and 2:00 AM, the Program Audience estimates do not include viewing to programs prior to 6:00 AM and after 2:00 AM (e.g., a program that begins at 12:30 AM and continues to 3:00 AM would be reported only for the 12:30 AM-2:00 AM period). No program averages are reported for programs which begin after 1:00 AM (local time) during the survey period.

No single title of a multi-titled quarter-hour can be exclusively credited to a quarter-hour time period. Therefore, no single title of a multi-titled quarter-hour appears in the Program Audiences Section. For the reporting of program averages of Parent + Satellite combinations, the Parent and Satellite are assumed to be telecasting the same programs.

Sampling and Calculations

Sampling Methodology—Surveys for Arbitron Television Market Reports are accomplished through the use of a geographic unit called an Arbitron Sampling Unit. A sampling unit is normally one county, although some counties have been divided into two or more sampling units because of population distribution, terrain, or areas in which special interviewing techniques are used. (There are no instances in which an Arbitron Television Sampling Unit consists of more than one county.) The actual number of diaries placed in each Sampling Unit is determined by the quota established for the unit and the rate of return which Arbitron can reasonably expect based on past placement experience. The total sample is divided into approximately equal weekly segments for diary placement, and the returns are tabulated separately for each survey week. For each survey a complete new sample of families is computer-selected for each sampling unit through the use of a systematic interval selection technique. These samples of households are drawn by Metromail. This sample selection, like all other processes used in developing Arbitron television estimates, is audited by the Broadcast Rating Council. Instances of hand drawn samples are outlined in Arbitron's separate publication provided to all television report subscribers entitled *Description of Methodology.*

Diary Placement and Return—Arbitron initially sends a letter to sample households informing them of their selection by computer, and stating that an interviewer will call to request their cooperation in the survey. Interviewers are instructed to contact the selected sample households by telephone to place the diaries. Interviewers are instructed to make at least five attempts to reach every household selected in the sample in order that everyone in the sample has a reasonable chance of being contacted. These attempted calls are made at different hours during the day and evening. Diaries are then mailed directly to the sample households from Arbitron headquarters in Beltsville, Maryland. Arbitron sends a diary for each television set in the known multi-set households. Following the survey, respondents are asked to mail their diaries back to Arbitron in Beltsville.

Although explicit instructions are provided each interviewer, and independent checks are regularly conducted by interviewer coordinators and the Arbitron Field Operations Department, there may be instances where such instructions are not followed. Special interviewing techniques and processing procedures are employed in certain markets to improve representation of certain ethnic groups. See separate publication provided to all television report subscribers entitled *Description of Methodology*.

Tabulation of Diaries—All diaries returned to Arbitron are not necessarily used in tabulating television audience estimates. Among those not used are diaries which are incomplete or inaccurate, and those which arrive after the production cut-off date. The total number of in-tab diaries may not reach the original quota. On the other hand, the total may exceed the quota.

Entries in diaries returned from multi-set households are edited so as to provide unduplicated viewing information for a given household. Local time differences within a market which overlaps time zones and time differences caused by seasonal time changes are accounted for in the results by tabulating all viewing by a station's local time relative to the time zone of the market being tabulated.

Arbitron has developed other special editing procedures for situations where a CATV system is required to protect a local station against duplication of its programs brought in by the CATV system from other sources. These special editing procedures are described in Arbitron's separate publication provided to all television report subscribers entitled *Description of Methodology*.

Projection of Audiences—Diary data for basic viewing categories are projected for each quarter-hour by a technique which assigns a value in terms of households and/or persons to each in-tab diary. The value assigned is referred to as the households-per-diary-value or HPDV. Selected planned-no-viewing households are included in the calculation of HPDV.

Projections derived using the HPDV are then summed across weighting cells and sampling units in each survey area (Metro, ADI and TSA) and gathered by various time periods for reporting. Individual survey variations in projected sex/age populations are stabilized for all survey periods for each year ending in September. Audiences thus calculated may be reported for basic data categories or for combinations thereof; depending on the survey area, they may be reported as projections or converted into ratings. See separate publication provided to all television report subscribers entitled *Description of Methodology*.

Returned-Sample Weighting—Arbitron exercises sample controls by calculating HPDV's taking into account the following: county, special interviewing technique areas, survey week, CATV households, and the age of the head of the household. In certain markets which meet Arbitron criteria, racial and/or ethnic characteristics of the household are also considered. See separate publication provided to all television report subscribers entitled *Description of Methodology*.

Criteria for Reporting Stations

In order to report the maximum amount of viewing in any given Arbitron-defined television market, the criteria for reporting stations are applied each time the market is surveyed. The viewing levels of stations located outside of the market, as well as home stations, are examined to determine whether any qualify for inclusion in the report. Arbitron normally tests more stations than usually qualify.

Criteria are established according to station location and audience size. The minimum reporting standards are:

A. **Home Station:** any station located within the Metro, Home County and/or ADI of the market being reported.
   1. A Home Station is included in the report if it delivers a 1% Net Weekly Circulation based on the Total Survey Area and also has a minimum of 500 households per average quarter-hour; or
   2. If it delivers 1% of the Metro television households (or Home County television household in a non-ADI market) for at least 30 reported quarter-hour segments; or
   3. If it delivers 1% of the Metro television households (or Home County television households in a non-ADI market) for at least 8% of its broadcast time.
   These criteria are applied to data encompassed

from sign-on to sign-off, Sunday through Saturday, for each station. Qualified ETV Stations appear in the Day-Part Summary section only.

B. **Outside Station:** any station which is reported as a Home Station in another television market is an Outside Station and is classed according to different minimum reporting criteria:
   1. Class I Outside Station
      a. Must attain a 10% share of total ratings for 4:00 PM to 1:00 AM, Sunday through Saturday, based on the ADI (or Home County in a non-ADI market); or
      b. Must attain a Metro rating of 5 for at least 100 quarter-hours, or for at least 20% of its programmed air time.
      If a station qualifies for Class I, all data related to the Metro and ADI will be reported in all sections of the report except the ADI Rating Trends.
   2. Class II Outside Station
      a. Must attain an average rating of "one" for 4:00 PM to 1:00 AM, Sunday through Saturday, based on the ADI (or Home County in a non-ADI market); or
      b. Must attain an average ADI (or Home County in a non-ADI market) rating of 1.5 for the early and late fringe time periods (Monday-Friday 5:00-7:30 PM and 11:00 PM-1:00 AM, Eastern Time).
      If a station qualified for Class II, Metro and ADI data will be reported in the Day-Part Summary section only.
For complete data on outside stations, see the respective home market reports.

C. **Satellite Station**—Arbitron recognizes two classes of satellites:
   1. S-1 Satellites—These are satellites which duplicate the programming of the parent station in its entirety, carry no other programming from any other source, and at all times telecast programming which is identical to that of the parent.
      Audiences of such satellites are always reported in combination with those of the parent in the parent's market report.
   2. S-2 Satellites—These are satellites that duplicate most, but not all, of the parent station's programming. Audiences of such satellites and the parent are shown on two lines in the parent's market report. The first line shows the audience of the parent alone, and the second line shows the combined audience of parent and satellite(s) together. When programming is identical on both stations, the symbol (SP) will appear as part of the program title to represent Same Progamming. When programming differs, the symbol (DP) will appear as part of the program title to represent Different Programming. However, (a) when an S-2 satellite is located in a market other than the home market of the S-2's parent station, and (b) when at least one non-satellite station is located in the same market as the S-2 satellite, the audience of the satellite alone is shown in the market report of the non-satellite station. In these instances, the audiences of such satellites are not combined with those of the parent in the parent's home market report.

Limitations

In addition to the sources of possible errors which are described elsewhere in this book, the user should be aware of the limitations described below:

A. The sample is drawn only from households listed in telephone directories which eliminates non-telephone households and telephone households not listed in the directory. Commercial establishments listed in the directory are specifically excluded from the sample. Households on military installations may or may not be listed in the local telephone directory. All telephone directories may not have been located and included in the list prepared by Metromail, which is used as Arbitron's sample frame.

B. Non-responding households may have some effect on the survey results to the extent that the television viewing habits of non-respondents differ from those of respondents. Similarly, the viewing habits of non-telephone households or those not listed in telephone directories may vary from those of households which have telephones and are listed in directories.

C. Non-responding households in the original designated sample prevent the "in-tab TV households" from being a probability sample.

D. The sample design and/or response patterns (including those markets where special diary placement and/or viewing data retrieval are utilized) may preclude proper representation of certain groups within the population such as ethnic groups, households in certain low-income or low-education groups or households whose primary language is other than English. Such households may not be fully represented in reported audiences because usable diaries may not be obtained from them. These factors may be significant to the extent that television set ownership and/or viewing habits of these groups differ from those of other groups.

E. Data from Bureau of the Census, Advertising Research Foundation, and Market Statistics, Inc. are subject to defects and limitations such as sampling, processing, and recording errors. In addition, for those years between decennial census dates, Census data are based upon a sample which is significantly smaller in most regions than that employed by Arbitron; and Market Statistics, Inc. utilizes published government figures in estimating population for individual counties. These defects and limitations in data from Bureau of the Census, Advertising Research Foundation and Market Statistics, Inc. are inherent in Arbitron estimates based thereon.

F. Diaries, or portions thereof, may be completed improperly if the diary instructions are not understood or are not followed. Such diaries may thereby be excluded from the survey.

G. Some diary entries may have been made on the basis of hearsay, recall, the estimates of the diary keeper, or could have been influenced by comments made by the interviewer to survey participants.

H. It is possible that human and computer processing errors may occur after the diaries are received at Arbitron headquarters. Consequently, the degree of variance in the data may be greater than that expected from sampling variation alone.

I. The population data upon which Arbitron has based its Sample Weighting may not be precise.

J. Logical analysis and pre-processing preparation of the data may affect some of the diary viewing entries before the data are projected.

K. Arbitron conducts research involving new methods of improving television household cooperation and/or securing additional information from sample households. Occasionally a portion of this research may be performed (on very limited basis) in conjunction with the actual surveys, and when so done, may cause the degree of variance in the data to be greater than that expected from sampling variation alone.

L. To the extent that any provisions contained in this section, "Limitations," are inconsistent or conflict with any provisions contained in the "Special Notices" on page 5 of this report, such special notices should be deemed to supersede and/or amend this section of the report.

Retention of Raw Materials

Retention Schedule—In-tab Arbitron viewing diaries used for the computation of the audience estimates published in this report will be stored and used for cross-tabulations for eleven months from the closing date of the survey and then destroyed along with all unusable diaries. Subscribers to this report are advised that if special cross-tabulations of the reported estimates are desired, they should be ordered before the retention period has expired. Upon prior appointment, subscribers to this report may examine the in-tab Arbitron viewing diaries (prior to the destruction thereof) at Arbitron's Beltsville office.

Threshold Estimates Table

The degree of sampling error as a percentage of reported *four-week* Program Audiences estimates can be determined from the table below. Threshold estimates for commonly occurring quarter-hour combinations are provided in the form of ADI Ratings and TSA Projections (in 000's). By comparing an estimate from the Program Audiences section of the report with the appropriate threshold estimate in the Table, the percentage range of sampling error may be estimated at one Standard Error (1 S.E.). If the reported estimate is *less than or equal to* the estimate found in the table, it has a corresponding percentage range of sampling error.

Use this table by finding the demographic category and the number of quarter-hours included in a program average estimate, and comparing the reported audience estimate with the threshold in the table for an estimation of the range of sampling error as a percentage of the reported estimate. See the last page of this report and the Glossary of Terms for a further discussion of Sampling Error as it relates to audience estimates in Arbitron Television Reports. Also, see the separate publication provided to all television report subscribers entitled *Description of Methodology*.

In using the table below to find the threshold estimates, the user should keep in mind that, due to the factors discussed in the "Limitations" section of this report, the accuracy of Arbitron measurements, data or reports cannot be determined to any precise mathematical value or definition.

Table of Threshold Estimates for the Determination of Relative Standard Error

RELATIVE STD-ERROR (1 S.E.) THRESHOLDS		ADI RATINGS 1-4	8-12	16-28	32-48	49-56	60-77	78-98	100-136	140-176	TSA PROJ 1-4	8-12	16-28	32-48	49-56	60-77	78-98	100-136	140-176
HOUSEHOLDS	25-49%	2	2	1	1	1	1	1			12	12	9	7	7	6	6	4	3
	50+%										3	3	1	1	1	1	1		
PERSONS 2+	25-49%	1	1	1	1	1					27	27	20	16	16	12	12	8	4
	50+%										4	4	4	4	4				
15-24	25-49%	7	6	4	3	3	2	2	1	1	22	20	15	11	11	8	8	6	5
	50+%	1	1	1							6	5	3	2	2	2	2	1	1
12-34	25-49%	3	2	1	1	1					22	19	12	8	8	5	5	3	3
	50+%										5	3	2	2	2				
ADULTS 18+	25-49%	1	1	1							20	17	12	9	9	6	6	3	3
	50+%										3	3	3						
WOMEN TOTAL	25-49%	2	2	1	1	1					16	13	9	6	6	4	4	4	4
	50+%										3	3	1	1	1				
18-49	25-49%	4	3	2	1	1	1	1	1	1	16	13	9	7	7	6	6	5	4
	50+%	1									4	3	2	1	1	1	1	1	1
15-24	25-49%	11	9	6	4	4	3	3	3	2	21	17	12	8	8	6	6	5	5
	50+%	3	2	1	1	1					5	4	3	2	2	2	2	1	1
18-34	25-49%	6	5	4	2	2	2	2	1	1	18	15	10	7	7	6	6	5	4
	50+%	1	1	1							4	4	2	2	2	1	1	1	1
25-49	25-49%	5	4	3	2	2	2	2	1	1	13	11	9	6	6	5	5	4	4
	50+%	1	1								3	3	2	1	1	1	1	1	1
25-54	25-49%	4	3	2	2	2	1	1	1	1	13	12	8	6	6	5	5	4	4
	50+%	1	1								3	2	2	2	2	1	1	1	1
25-64	25-49%	3	3	2	1	1	1	1	1	1	13	12	8	6	6	5	5	4	4
	50+%										3	3	2	1	1	1	1	1	1
WORKING WOMEN	25-49%	8	7	5	3	3	3	3	2	2	15	13	9	6	6	5	5	4	4
	50+%	2	1	1							4	3	2	2	2	1	1	1	1
MEN TOTAL	25-49%	3	2	1	1	1					15	14	10	7	7	4	4	3	3
	50+%										3	3	1	1	1				
18-49	25-49%	4	3	2	2	2	1	1			16	14	9	7	7	5	5	3	3
	50+%	1	1								4	3	2	1	1	1	1		
18-34	25-49%	7	6	5	3	3	2	2	1	1	18	16	12	9	9	6	6	4	3
	50+%	1	1	1							4	4	3	2	2	1	1	1	1
25-49	25-49%	5	4	3	2	2	1	1	1	1	13	12	9	7	7	5	5	3	3
	50+%	1	1								3	3	2	1	1	1	1	1	1
25-54	25-49%	4	4	3	2	2	1	1	1		14	12	9	6	6	5	5	3	2
	50+%	1	1								3	3	2	2	2	1	1	1	
TEENS TOTAL	25-49%	9	8	6	5	5	3	3	2	2	19	17	13	9	9	7	7	5	4
	50+%	2	2	1	1	1					5	4	3	2	2	1	1	1	1
GIRLS	25-49%	17	14	10	7	7	5	5	4	4	18	15	10	7	7	6	6	4	4
	50+%	5	4	2	2	2	1	1	1	1	5	4	2	2	2	1	1	1	1
CHILD TOTAL	25-49%	12	10	7	5	5	3	3	3	2	30	25	18	13	13	9	9	7	6
	50+%	3	2	1	1	1	1	1			7	6	4	3	3	2	2	2	1
6-11	25-49%	15	13	9	7	7	5	5	3	3	24	21	15	11	11	8	8	6	5
	50+%	4	3	2	1	1	1	1	1	1	6	5	4	3	3	2	2	2	1
METRO 1 HH	25-49%	3	3	2	2	2	1	1	1	1									
	50+%																		

What BRC Accreditation Means

The Arbitron Service has been accredited by the Broadcast Rating Council since September 1965. To merit continued BRC accreditation Arbitron: (1) adheres to the Council's Minimum Standards for Broadcast Research, (2) supplied full information to the BRC regarding all details of its operation (3) conducts its measurement service substantially in accordance with representations to the subscribers and the Council and (4) submits to, and pays the cost of, thorough on-going audits of Arbitron operations by CPA firms engaged by BRC. In addition to sizable annual audit charges, Arbitron provides office and file space for BRC auditors as well as considerable staff and computer time involved in various aspects of these inspections.

Further information about BRC's accreditation and auditing procedures can be obtained from Executive Director, Broadcast Rating Council, 420 Lexington Avenue, N.Y.C. 10017.

Restrictions on Use of This Report

Estimating the Degree of Sampling Error

The first step in approximating the degree of sampling error in relative percentage terms of an Arbitron audience estimate is calculating the statistic standard error of the estimate. A standard error (σ) simply reflects the extent to which a survey result is subject to sampling error; that is, a standard error suggests whether it is likely that an attempted complete canvass of the population surveyed, conducted in the same manner and with the same care as the sample, would produce a much different result than the one available. An approximation of the standard error (based on one standard deviation) for estimates in this report can be calculated from the following formula:

$$\text{A.} \quad \sigma = \sqrt{\frac{p(100-p)}{n\left(\dfrac{SE}{WF}\right)}}$$

where p = audience estimate expressed as a rating, n = in-tab count for the demographic category, SE = Statistical Efficiency for a given time period and demographic category as determined from the Chart of Statistical Efficiencies, and WF = Standard Error Weighting Factor from Page 4. Statistical Efficiencies shown in the chart have been derived from the *Arbitron Replication* studies which analyze the empirical standard error about the types of data Arbitron produces.

The percentage of sampling error may be defined as the ratio between the calculated standard error (as determined above) and the estimate itself.

An approximation for the percentage of error of an Arbitron estimate may be calculated from the following formula:

$$\text{B.} \quad r = \frac{\sigma}{p} = \frac{\sqrt{\dfrac{p(100-p)}{n\left(\dfrac{SE}{WF}\right)}}}{p}$$

where r = an approximation of sampling error in relative percentage terms, p = audience estimate expressed as a rating, n = in-tab count for the reported demographic category, SE = Statistical Efficiency for a given period of time and demographic category, and WF = Standard Error Weighting Factor from Page 4.

The Standard Error and Relative Percentage of Error calculations above are both based upon one standard deviation (as specified by the Broadcast Rating Council). These calculations indicate that we can be 68% certain that the Arbitron estimate falls within ± range of the standard error calculation or has a relative percentage of error as calculated from the Relative Percentage of Error calculation provided the user keeps in mind that due to the factors discussed in the "Limitations" section of this report, that the accuracy of Arbitron measurements, data or reports and their statistical evaluators cannot be determined to any precise mathematical value or definition. Note that this procedure applies only to ratings. To calculate the Standard Error of projections, the projections must first be converted to a percentage (or rating) basis.

Arbitron has performed the required calculations necessary to approximate the degree of sampling error in relative percentage terms through threshold estimates on Page iii for Program Audiences estimates.and in the Weekly Programming and Time Period Averages section of this report at the top of each page. For Program Audience estimates these Threshold values are valid only for programs telecast all four weeks. An approximation of the relative sampling error for programs telecast less than four weeks can be computed using Formula "B" above by adjusting the in-tab count for the demographic category (n) to reflect the number of weeks covered. The threshold estimates approximate the degree of sampling error at levels specified by the Broadcast Rating Council. (See also Glossary of Terms.)

Table of Statistical Efficiencies

This Table was derived from *Arbitron Replication* study. Copies of the study have been distributed to most commercial television and radio stations. The statistical efficiencies displayed in this Table are used as an input to the percentage of sampling error formula and were developed in the *Arbitron Replication* book. The statistical efficiencies presented in the accompanying Table were approximated from a national sample of television households. The Standard Error Weighting Factor (ADI or TSA as appropriate for the estimate) is used to bring the SE's originally developed from the national sample into alignment with the actual conditions affecting each market and each survey. To determine an individual market SE, simply divide the SE from the Table below by the Standard Error Weighting factor.

Statistical efficiencies (SE) are determined by the audience category for which an estimate is produced and the number of quarter-hours averaged to calculate the estimate. To use this Table, find the population group in question in the left-hand column of the Table. Then, follow the row of numbers to the right of this column until you reach the column for the number of quarter-hours in the time period or day-part in question. A listing of the number of quarter-hours included in time period and day-part estimates is provided for your convenience in using the Table. The proper quarter-hour figure for use *in this Table* when examining Program Audiences estimates can be determined by dividing the number of quarter-hours listed in the report by the number of weeks the program was telecast. For further information concerning the sampling error of estimates based on less than four week sample sizes see the separate publication provided to all television report subscribers entitled *Description of Methodology*.

Number of quarter-hours in time period and day-part estimates published in Arbitron Television Market Reports

Quarter-Hours	Time Period or Day-part	Quarter-Hours	Time Period or Day-part	Quarter-Hours	Time Period or Day-part
1	All single day quarter-hour time periods e.g.,11-11:15 pm, Tuesday	18	8:30 am-1 pm, Saturday day-part	84	7-10 pm, Sunday-Saturday day-part 8-11 pm, Sunday-Saturday day-part
2	All single day half-hour time periods e.g., 9-9:30 pm, Thursday	30	3:30-5 pm, Monday-Friday day-part 4:30-6 pm, Monday-Friday day-part	90	11 am-3:30 pm, Monday-Friday day-part Noon-4:30 pm, Monday-Friday day-part
5	All Monday-Friday quarter-hour time periods e.g., 5-5:15 pm, Monday-Friday		5-6:30 pm, Monday-Friday day-part 6-7:30 pm, Monday-Friday day-part	98	6:30-10 pm, Sunday-Saturday day-part 7:30-11 pm, Sunday-Saturday day-part
10	All Monday-Friday half-hour time periods e.g., Noon-12:30 pm, Monday-Friday		10:30 pm-Midnight, Monday-Friday day-part 11:30 pm-1 am, Monday-Friday day-part	104	7:30-11 pm, Monday-Saturday + 6-11 pm, Sunday day-part
	6-6:30 pm, Monday-Friday day-part	32	1-5 pm, Saturday-Sunday day-part		6:30-10 pm, Monday-Saturday + 5-10 pm, Sunday day-part
	7-7:30 pm, Monday-Friday day-part	40	7-9 am, Monday-Friday day-part	140	6-11 pm, Sunday-Saturday day-part
	6:30-7 pm, Monday-Friday day-part		9-11 am, Monday-Friday day-part		5-10 pm, Sunday-Saturday day-part
	7:30-8 pm, Monday-Friday day-part	50	4-6:30 pm, Monday-Friday day-part	420	9 am-Midnight, Sunday-Saturday day-part
	9:30-10 pm, Monday-Friday day-part		5-7:30 pm, Monday-Friday day-part	560	6 am-2 am, Sunday-Saturday (Sign-on/Sign-off) day-part
	10:30-11 pm, Monday-Friday, day-part	60	9 am-Noon, Monday-Friday day-part		
	10-10:30 pm, Monday-Friday day-part	60	7-10 pm, Monday-Friday day-part		
	11-11:30 pm, Monday-Friday day-part		8-11 pm, Monday-Friday day-part		

Statistical efficiencies for population groups by number of quarter-hours in a time period or day-part during the average week

	1	2-3	4-7	8-14	15-24	25-34	35-44	45-54	55-64	65-74	75-91	92-300	301-560
Households	.9	.9	1.1	1.4	1.8	2.3	2.8	3.2	3.6	4.0	4.4	4.9	10.7
Persons 2+	.4	.4	.5	.6	.8	1.1	1.4	1.7	1.9	2.2	2.5	2.9	11.0
Persons 15-24	.6	.6	.8	1.1	1.6	2.1	2.5	2.8	3.0	3.3	3.5	3.8	5.5
Persons 12-34	.5	.6	.9	1.4	2.0	2.8	3.4	3.9	4.3	4.6	5.1	5.5	8.5
Adults 18+	.5	.6	.8	1.1	1.6	2.2	2.7	3.1	3.6	3.9	4.5	4.9	9.9
Total Women	.6	.8	1.1	1.5	1.9	2.2	2.4	2.5	2.6	2.6	2.7	2.7	3.0
Women 15-24	.6	.7	1.0	1.4	1.9	2.3	2.5	2.6	2.8	2.8	2.9	3.0	3.4
18-49	.6	.8	1.0	1.5	1.8	2.1	2.3	2.4	2.5	2.6	2.6	2.7	3.0
18-34	.6	.8	1.1	1.4	1.8	2.2	2.4	2.5	2.6	2.7	2.8	2.9	3.2
25-49	.7	.8	1.1	1.4	1.8	2.1	2.3	2.4	2.5	2.6	2.7	2.7	3.0
25-54	.7	.8	1.1	1.4	1.8	2.1	2.3	2.4	2.5	2.6	2.6	2.7	3.0
25-64	.7	.8	1.1	1.5	1.9	2.2	2.4	2.5	2.6	2.6	2.7	2.8	3.1
Total Working Women	.6	.8	1.1	1.5	1.9	2.2	2.4	2.5	2.6	2.6	2.7	2.7	3.0
Total Men	.7	.8	1.1	1.6	2.3	3.2	3.8	4.4	4.9	5.3	5.9	6.4	10.7
Men 18-49	.7	.8	1.1	1.6	2.3	3.2	4.0	4.7	5.3	5.9	6.7	7.4	15.0
18-34	.7	.8	1.0	1.5	2.1	3.0	3.6	4.2	4.8	5.3	5.9	6.5	12.8
25-49	.7	.8	1.1	1.5	2.1	3.0	3.7	4.4	5.1	5.7	6.6	7.3	18.4
25-54	.7	.8	1.0	1.5	2.1	3.0	3.7	4.4	5.0	5.6	6.4	7.1	16.3
Total Teens	.5	.6	.8	1.1	1.5	2.0	2.4	2.7	3.0	3.2	3.5	3.7	5.4
Girl Teens	.5	.7	1.0	1.4	1.8	2.2	2.4	2.6	2.7	2.8	2.8	2.9	3.3
Total Children	.3	.4	.6	.8	1.1	1.4	1.6	1.7	1.8	1.9	2.0	2.1	2.5
Children 6-11	.4	.5	.7	.9	1.3	1.7	2.0	2.2	2.4	2.6	2.8	2.9	4.0

Appendix C - Basic Statistical Routines: A Self-Study Course

Appendix C - Basic Statistical Routines: A Self-Study Course

INTRODUCTION

The lessons that follow are intended as a brief introduction for beginners—or as a hurried review for the more experienced—to the statistical routines most frequently encountered in research conducted in or for the broadcast industry. The lessons are designed to build from the simplest concepts to the more complex. The presentation is intuitive as opposed to mathematical. In other words, the statistics are presented as ways of problem-solving which grow out of the nature of the problem faced by the researcher. Algebraic proofs and derivations, which are important to the advanced student, are not included here. At the end of this appendix is a list of references which will be useful to the reader who prefers the mathematical approach to statistical subjects.

This course has been included to provide the necessary background for those who will want to understand the statistical concepts discussed in the body of this book but who have not the academic training or work experience which makes these subjects commonplace.

Each of the lessons that follows is bite-sized, designed to be consumed at one sitting before proceeding to the next lesson. Those with prodigious appetites for numbers may consume more than one lesson at a time, but the average reader will want each to digest in order to make the following lesson more palatable.

At the end of each lesson is one or more problems for the reader to solve, using the principles taught in the lesson. A step-by-step solution for each of these problems is provided. As one might expect, more is learned by the reader who attempts to solve the problems on his/her own before consulting the solution.

We have included at the head of each lesson the principles and notations covered by the lesson. As an additional check on learning refer back to the lesson heading after completion of a lesson to assure that all elements of the heading are now understood.

Good Luck!!

Lesson One   What is Typical?—Summary Statistics

FREQUENCY DISTRIBUTIONS
Frequency Tables
Histograms
Frequency Polygons

MEASURES OF CENTRAL TENDENCY
Median
Mode
Mean
Notations—$\Sigma, X, N, f, \overline{X}$

In the language of the researcher, a *distribution* is a collection of measurements which have been ordered to reflect the relative frequency or proportion of various scores. A *frequency distribution* is a species of this genus, a collection of measurements arranged to show the frequency with which each score category appears in the collection.

Let us consider an example. The program director has invited a representative group of listeners into a radio station to preview the new station jingle. The P.D. has played the jingle for the sample and asked them to assign a score of 1 through 15 to the jingle, according to how attractive they find it. The list below represents the names of the respondents with the attractiveness score each has assigned to the new jingle (the higher score, the more attractive the jingle as perceived by the respondent).

NAME	ATTRAC-TIVENESS SCORE
John	12
Alice	15
Mary	6
Joe	7
Herb	9
Gertrude	15
Mike	9
Frank	8
Lea	8
Lee	7
Lynn	8
Lauri	10
Sherm	11
Jim	12
Ray	8
Monique	7
Marsha	9
Spiro	9
Bill	7
Dick	6

As it stands, this list is a collection of measures; it will become a *frequency distribution* when it has been rearranged to reflect the frequency (shown in notation as "*f*") of each score in the collection. The table below shows one way of constructing a frequency table which represents the measurements above. The left-hand column represents each possible score which a respondent could have assigned to the new jingle for its attractiveness. In the center of the table a tally mark corresponds to each respondent who actually recorded a score of the value indicated for attractiveness. The number of tally marks for each possible score is then entered in the right column. If the P.D. were to include this frequency table in a report any possible score value for which the frequency (*f*) is zero would be left out of the table.

POSSIBLE SCORE VALUE FOR ATTRACTIVENESS	TALLY MARKS	f
15	//	2
14		0
13		0
12	//	2
11	/	1
10	/	1
9	////	4
8	////	4
7	////	4
6	//	2

In order to simplify the description of scores, many researchers will refer to the measurements as X_i or Y_i. In the frequency table above the left-hand column could be labeled X_i. The scores in that column actually represent score categories with the numbers in the X_i column representing the midpoint of each category. It might be desirable in our report of the attractiveness of the new station jingle to prepare a frequency table which occupied less space on the page. That could be done by including in the X_i column categories that included more possible score values. The frequency table below represents the same collection of measurements with the frequency of wider score categories shown. In this case each score category has a width of three.

X_i	TALLY MARKS	f
14 (12.5–15.5)	//	2
11 (9.5–12.5)	////	4
8 (6.5–9.5)	////////////	12
5 (3.5–6.5)	//	2

The score values in parenthesis would not be printed in the table as published, because the experienced reader would understand what had been done to construct the table. Likewise the tally marks would not appear in the published version of this table. The advantage of this shorter table with wider score categories is principally that it is shorter and easier to understand at a glance.

The frequency table is one way of representing a frequency distribution. Another is the *histogram*—sometimes called a bar graph. The histogram is a graphic representation of the information in our collection of measurements. In the histograms below the same information from the study of the attractiveness of the new station jingle are presented.

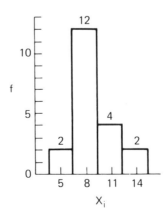

The conventions for drawing histograms dictate that the taller a bar, the larger the frequency or proportion; the more to the right the bar, the larger the score values represented by the bar. If adjacent bars represent score categories which are contiguous, then the bars are shown touching. If the score categories are not contiguous, then the bars are not shown touching. In the histogram below the sex of our respondents is summarized. In this case the score categories (men, women) are not contiguous, and the bars of the histogram do not touch.

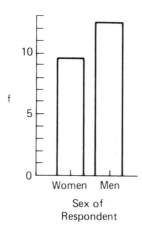

Still another way to represent a frequency distribution is a *frequency polygon,* sometimes called a "fever" chart. The frequency polygon below presents the same frequency distribution from our study of the attractiveness of the new station jingle.

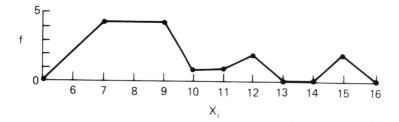

Construct this frequency polygon by first drawing a chart much like that for the histogram in which the vertical dimension is frequency (f) and the horizontal dimension represents score categories (X_i). The higher a point on the chart, the greater the frequency. The more right on the chart, the larger the value for X_i. From the frequency table plot a point for each score category which represents the frequency with which each score category appears in the distribution. Then these points are connected in order to complete the frequency polygon.

Measures of Central Tendency

A measure of central tendency is a single number, or statistic, which summarizes the prevailing feature of a distribuition. Several measures of central tendency are commonly used, each with its own name and computational routine. They are the median, mode, and arithmetic mean.

The *median* represents the midpoint of a set of scores. To determine the median, rearrange the measurements in the distribution so that there is a single progression of numbers from large to small, or vice versa. Then determine what score value would divide this distribution ordered as to magnitude, into two parts, each of which includes the same number of scores. This score value in the middle is the *median.* To illustrate, consider again the measurements of the attractiveness of the new station jingle. If these measurement scores are arranged from large to small, a list like this results.

```
        15
        15
        12
        12
        11                    10 scores lie
        10                     above 8.5
         9
         9
         9
         9
    ──────────── 8.5
         8
         8
         8
         8
         7                    10 scores lie
         7                     below 8.5
         7
         7
         6
         6
```

The list includes 20 scores. We identify a score value above and below which fall 10 scores. In this case that score value is 8.5: it is the median of this distribution of attractiveness scores.

The *mode* is the most frequently appearing measurement in a distribution. A distribution may have more than one mode. There may be a primary and a secondary mode in a distribution. Examine the frequency polygon drawn from the responses to the new station jingle. Note that the most frequently appearing scores in the distribution are 7, 8, and 9, each of which appears four times. Since 8 is the middle of these scores, we will use it to represent the distribution as the primary *mode*. Note also that there is a small peak separated from the rest of the frequency polygon which represents two scores of 15. A researcher might designate 15 as a secondary mode, since it represents a second peak in the frequency polygon.

The *arithmetic mean* is sometimes referred to as an "average" and routinely called the *mean*. It is computed from this general formula.

$$\overline{X} = \frac{\Sigma X_i}{N}$$

Expressed in words rather than notation, this formula says, the arithmetic mean, $\overline{X}$, is equal to (=) the sum of all (Σ) scores (X_i) divided by the number of scores (N).

The computation below is for the mean for the distribution of responses to the new station jingle.

X_i	f	$f(X_i)$
15	2	30
14	0	0
13	0	0
12	2	24
11	1	11
10	1	10
9	4	36
8	4	32
7	4	28
6	2	12
	20 = N	183 = ΣX_i

$$\bar{X} = \frac{\Sigma X_i}{N}$$

$$\bar{X} = \frac{183}{20} \text{ or } 9.15.$$

The left and center columns of the table above represent a frequency table with a score category width of one. The right-hand column is the product of frequency by score value for each line of the table. The sum of the right-hand column is the sum of all scores in the distribution, ΣX_i. The total of the center or f column is the number of scores in the distribution, N. When these values are entered into the formula for the mean, we learn that $\bar{X} = 9.15$.

Of the three measures of central tendency the mode is probably the easiest to determine. The mode will be a relatively useful measure when the frequency polygon for the distribution is quite peaked, least useful when the frequency is flat. The median is also rapidly computed but tells us more about the extremes of the distribution than does the mode. At the same time the median is at its poorest when few scores fall at the median. This might be the case in a bimodal distribution with a frequency polygon like that below.

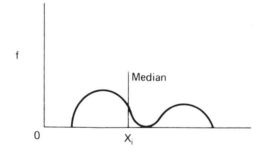

These disadvantages of the mode and median tend to make the mean an ever more attractive measure of central tendency for the researcher.

Considering the mode, median, and mean together in frequency polygons representing different shaped distributions may make these distinctions among measures of central tendency clearer.

Symmetrical Distribution. In a symmetrical distribution, represented by the frequency polygon immediately below, mode, median, and mean all fall at the same score value.

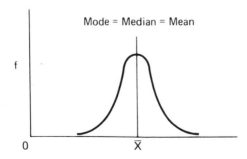

In a symmetrical distribution that is unimodal, the mean divides the distribution into two equal parts, hence is also the median. And the mean also represents the most frequently appearing score, the mode.

Skewed Distribution. A distribution is skewed when it is not symmetrical when drawn as a frequency polygon. If the less bulky part of the skewed frequency polygon is to the right (pointing toward the higher score values on the horizontal dimension), then the distribution is said to be *positively skewed*. If the less bulky part of the skewed frequency polygon is to the left (pointing toward the lower score values on the horizontal dimension), then the distribution is said to be *negatively skewed*. To understand the relationships among the three measures of central tendency in skewed distributions, it will be necessary to review notation for inequalities.

SYMBOL	MEANING
>	greater than
<	less than
≤	equal to or less than
≥	equal to or greater than
=	equal to
≠	not equal to
≈	approximately equal to

Now examine the frequency polygons below representing both positively and negatively skewed distributions.

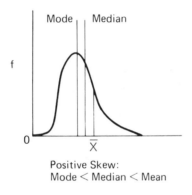

Positive Skew:
Mode < Median < Mean

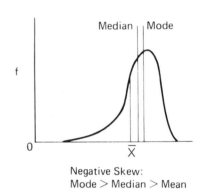

Negative Skew:
Mode > Median > Mean

Consider the illustration of a distribution of scores received by a sample of respondents who attempted to recall the content of a television commercial. The resulting scores are summarized in the frequency polygon below.

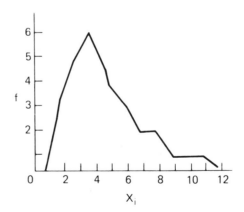

To determine the median of this distribution first order the scores according to magnitude and then select that score value which divides the distributions into two equal sets of scores. This process yields a median of 4.5.

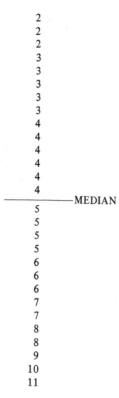

```
                2
                2
                2
                3
                3
                3
                3
                3
                4
                4
                4
                4
                4
                4
        ─────────────── MEDIAN
                5
                5
                5
                5
                6
                6
                6
                7
                7
                8
                8
                9
               10
               11
```

To find the mode and mean of the distribution construct a frequency table. From examination of the table, it is apparent that the mode, or most frequently appearing value, is 4.

The mean is computed according to the routine outlined above.

X_i	f	$f(X_i)$
2	3	6
3	5	15
mode — 4	6	24
5	4	20
6	3	18
7	2	14
8	2	16
9	1	9
10	1	10
11	1	11
	28 = N	143 = ΣX_i

$$\overline{X} = \frac{\Sigma X_i}{N}$$

$$\overline{X} = \frac{143}{28}$$

$$\overline{X} = 5.10714.$$

This distribution of recall scores is positively skewed as evident from the appearance of the frequency polygon and the relationship among measures of central tendency: mode of 4 < median of 4.5 < mean of 5.10714.

Another illustration. The Research Department has asked a sample of children to give a score to the early fringe cartoon show which represents on a scale of 1 to 12 how much they like the show. The resulting scores are summarized in this frequency polygon.

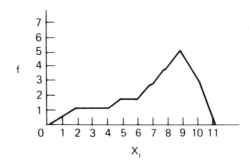

To determine the median, X_i measurements are first reordered according to magnitude, and the score which divides the distribution into equal parts—in this case 8.5—is taken as median.

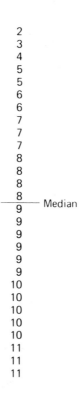

2	
3	
4	
5	
5	
6	
6	
7	
7	
7	
8	
8	
8	
8	Median
9	
9	
9	
9	
9	
9	
10	
10	
10	
10	
10	
11	
11	
11	

The mode and mean of this distribution are determined from the frequency table below. The mode, the most frequently appearing score, is 9.

	X_i	f	$f(X_i)$
	2	1	2
	3	1	3
	4	1	4
	5	2	10
	6	2	12
	7	3	21
	8	4	32
mode —	9	6	54
	10	5	50
	11	3	33
		$28 = N$	$221 = \Sigma X_i$

$$\overline{X} = \frac{\Sigma X_i}{N}$$

$$\overline{X} = \frac{221}{28}$$

$$\overline{X} = 7.89286.$$

This distribution of children's liking scores is negatively skewed as revealed by the appearance of the frequency polygon of the distribution and the relationship among the measures of central tendency: mode of 9 > median of 8.5 > mean of 7.89286.

These illustrations have been drawn from unimodal distributions. The same procedures for examining skew hold for multimodal distributions.

Assignment #1—Frequency Distributions and Measures of Central Tendency

The following scores represent the performance of a group of adults on a retention test following a videotaped instructional presentation.

.30	.50	.46	.28	.50
.40	.56	.33	.73	.33
.10	.56	.44	.07	.05
.35	1.00	.40	.40	.61
.45	.83	.44	.60	.00
.30	.20	.61	.67	.60
.94	.73	.10	.72	.25
.30	.74	.93	.73	.30
.67	.67	.94	.67	.85
.44	.33	.65	.44	.21

a. Construct a frequency table from the above. Assign the scores to 10 score categories.
b. Construct a frequency polygon from the same data.
c. Construct a histogram from these data.
d. Determine the mode, median, and arithmetic mean of these data.
e. How would you describe the shape of this distribution?

Lesson Two. How Typical Is Typical?—Dispersion

MEASURES OF DISPERSION

Range
Percentile
Standard Deviation
Definitional and Computational Formulae
  for Variance and Standard Deviation
Notation – $\sqrt{}, S^2, S$

There is a great necessity for measures of central tendency to be accompanied by measures of dispersion whenever research is reported. That necessity will be clear from examining the following three frequency polygons corresponding to three distributions with equal means but different dispersions.

Distribution A represents a *rectangular distribution,* one in which all values for variable X_i occur with equal frequency. Distribution B is symmetrical and unimodal. Distribution C is bimodal and symmetrical; no scores occur at the mean value, and frequencies increase as score values approach the extremes of the distribution.

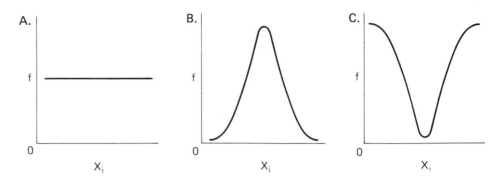

Clearly the mean is most representative of the entire collection of measurements in the case of Distribution B and least representative in the case of Distribution C. It is apparent that, despite the fact that the means of these three distributions are equal, there are important differences among them that are concealed when only the means are considered.

Range

A better way to describe these distributions might be to report the range of measurements along with the mean of the distribution. In the set of scores—1, 2, 2, 3, 3, 3, 2, 2, 1—scores range from 1 to 3. The range of scores, as a consequence, is 3 - 1, or 2. Using the range with the mean improves the picture given of the distribution involved, but the range alone does not make it clear whether these scores are distributed at the extremes or clustered about the mean. In fact, in the distributions above, all have the same values for range as well as the same value for means.

Percentile

Percentiles locate individual scores with respect to the remainder of a distribution of scores. If a person receives a score at the 92nd percentile, 92 percent of all other scores in the distribution fall at or below this score. (Question: Which measure of central tendency would fall at the 50th percentile? Answer: The median.)

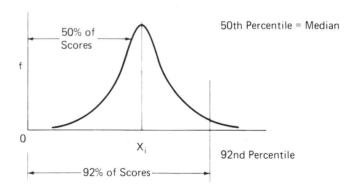

Variance

Another way of summarizing data about the dispersion in a distribution might be to compute the difference between each score and the mean of scores. The resulting differences are called *deviations*. To summarize them they might be added. The total deviation from the mean of the distribution would then be represented as a single figure. To illustrate:

X_i	$X_i - \overline{X}$
1	$1 - 1.8 = -.8$
2	$2 - 1.8 = .2$
3	$3 - 1.8 = 1.2$
2	$2 - 1.8 = .2$
1	$1 - 1.8 = -.8$
$\Sigma X_i = 9$	$0 = \Sigma(X_i - \overline{X})$

$$\overline{X} = \frac{\Sigma X_i}{N}$$

$$= \frac{9}{5}$$

$$\overline{X} = 1.8$$

It will always be the case that a simple sum of deviations from the mean of a distribution will equal zero (regardless of the shape of the distribution). This procedure obviously does not provide a measure of dispersion which is sensitive.

Since the deviation of each score shows its dispersion from the mean, the statistician sums them after first squaring them. The square of any number is always positive. The sum of squared deviations must always be a value that is greater than zero. This sum which is larger as squared deviations from the mean are greater is a useful index of dispersion called *variance*. The notation for the variance of a distribution is S^2. Algebraically variance can be defined in this formula:

$$S^2 = \frac{\Sigma(X_i - \overline{X})^2}{N}$$

This formula in words says: Variance (S^2) is equal to (=) the mean squared deviation from the mean $[(X_i - \overline{X})^2]$. It is a definition of this measure of dispersion.

To facilitate computation of variance, however, streamlined computational formulae are used:

$$S^2 = \frac{\Sigma X_i^2}{N} - \overline{X}^2$$

–or–

$$S^2 = \frac{\Sigma X_i^2}{N} - \left(\frac{\Sigma X_i}{N}\right)^2.$$

These computational formulae and the definitional formula are equivalents and produce exactly the same answers when used to determine variance. This fact will be clear from the following computations of the variance in a set of liking scores, determined first according to the definitional formula, then by a streamlined, computational formula.

X_i	$X_i - \overline{X}$	$(X_i - \overline{X})^2$	X_i^2
1	$-.8$	.64	1
2	.2	.04	4
3	1.2	1.44	9
2	.2	.04	4
1	$-.8$	.64	1
$9 = \Sigma X_i$		$\Sigma(X_i - \overline{X})^2 = 2.80$	$19 = \Sigma X_i^2$

Definitional Formula:

$$S^2 = \frac{\Sigma(X_i - \overline{X})^2}{N}$$

$$= \frac{2.8}{5}$$

$$S^2 = .56$$

Computational Formula:

$$S^2 = \frac{\Sigma X_i^2}{N} - \left(\frac{\Sigma X_i}{N}\right)^2$$

$$= \frac{19}{5} - \left(\frac{9}{5}\right)^2$$

$$= 3.8 - (1.8)^2$$

$$= 3.8 - 3.24$$

$$S^2 = .56$$

If the same distribution is presented as a frequency table, the computational routine is slightly different:

X_i	f	$f(X_i)$	(X_i^2)	$f(X_i^2)$
1	2	2	1	2
2	2	4	4	8
3	1	3	9	9
	5	9		19

$$S^2 = \frac{\Sigma X_i^2}{N} - \left(\frac{\Sigma X_i}{N}\right)^2$$

$$= \frac{19}{5} - \left(\frac{9}{5}\right)^2$$

$$= 3.8 - 3.24$$

$$S^2 = .56$$

Standard Deviation

Variance provides a relative measure of the dispersion in a distribution, but the measure is expressed in terms of *squared deviations* rather than in terms of the units in which the original measurements were taken. In order to have an index of dispersion in the same units as the original measurements, the square root of variance is used. This square root of variance is called *standard deviation*. In terms of notation, the standard deviation of a sample is S. The definitional and computational formulae for standard deviation are the same as those for variance with the exception that each side of the equation is represented by the square root of the comparable term from the variance formulae.

Definitional: $S = \sqrt{S^2}$

$$S = \sqrt{\frac{\Sigma(X_i - \overline{X})^2}{N}}$$

Computational: $S = \sqrt{\dfrac{\Sigma X_i^2}{N} - \left(\dfrac{\Sigma X_i}{N}\right)^2}$

-and-

$$S = \sqrt{\frac{\Sigma X_i^2}{N} - \overline{X}^2} \, .$$

Visualize these notions of variance and standard deviation. In the frequency polygons that follow which of each pair has the larger variance and standard deviation?

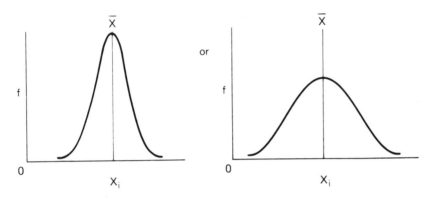

In the first pair of frequency polygons the right polygon has the larger variance and standard deviation, as the frequency of measurements at the mean is smaller. As the mean becomes less representative of the distribution as a whole, variance, and standard deviation take on larger values.

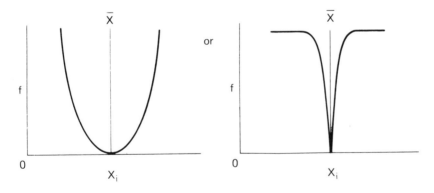

In the second pair of frequency polygons there are no measurements at the mean in either case. But in the right distribution there are more measurements that fall close to the mean. As a result the mean is more representative of the distribution on the right, and variance (and standard deviation) is larger for the distribution on the left.

The third pair of distributions are bimodal. If one examines the frequency with which measurements fall between the modes in each of the distributions, it is apparent that more measurements fall near the mean in the distribution on the right. Hence, the distribution on the left will have the greater variance and standard deviation.

The variance and standard deviation of a distribution when considered along with the mean provide useful information as to the degree to which the mean is representative of

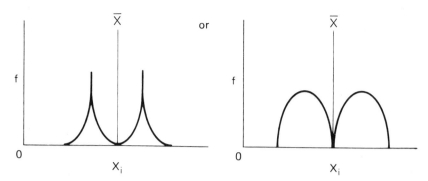

the distribution as a whole. It should not be surprising that variance, standard deviation and mean provide the basic building blocks from which nearly all statistical procedures proceed.

Assignment #2–How Typical is Typical?

The following scores were received by a group of housewives on an attitude instrument designed to reflect attitude toward a modern washday detergent.

11	7	9	12	13
8	5	14	7	2
3	13	2	15	1
5	2	14	9	3
10	6	4	14	1

a. Compute the variance of this distribution of attitude scores using the definitional formula for variance.

b. Compute the variance of this distribution of attitude scores using the computational formula for variance.

c. What is the standard deviation of the distribution of scores?

d. How many standard deviations is a score of 10 above or below the mean of this distribution of attitude scores?

e. How many standard deviations is a score of 3 above or below the mean of this distribution of attitude scores?

Lesson Three: Comparing Apples and Oranges– Standard Scores and Normal Distributions

> Statistic vs Parameter
> Random Sample
> Sample Distribution
> Population Distribution
> Sampling Distribution
> Probability Distributions
> Normal Distribution
> Standard Scores
> Standard Error of the Mean
> Notation–μ, σ^2, $\sigma_{\bar{x}}$, Z, prob.

The researcher will use samples—representative subgroups—rather than entire populations for studies as a means of reducing the cost of research. A sponsor desiring to know the attractiveness of a commercial to housewives will talk to a small group of housewives whose views he hopes resemble the larger population of all housewives, because he cannot afford to speak to all housewives.

Statistic versus Parameter

A *statistic* is an attribute of a *sample* drawn from some larger population of persons, stimuli, responses or contexts. A statistic provides an economical description of the distribution of scores from the sample.

A *parameter* is an attribute of a *population* from which samples may be drawn. So, for example, the population of concern may be ladies-of-the-house in Clarke County, Georgia. The parameter of interest may be degrees of liking for Johnny Carson. Collectively these ladies-of-the-house are so large a group that the researcher cannot measure the degree each likes Johnny Carson without exceeding the research budget.

In the interests of economy, the researcher elects to represent this large population of ladies-of-the-house by a selected subgroup—a sample.

To differentiate between degree of liking in the sample and degree of liking in the population, different sets of symbols are used. For population parameters summary indices are represented as small Greek letters; for sample statistics the comparable indices are represented by capital Roman letters.

CHARACTERISTIC	SAMPLE STATISTIC	POPULATION PARAMETER
Arithmetic Mean	$\overline{X}$	μ (mu)
Variance	S^2	σ^2 (sigma squared)
Standard Deviation or Standard Error	S	σ (sigma)

Random Sampling

The most important consideration in drawing a sample from a population is that the sample be representative of the population from which it is drawn. The method of sampling most frequently used in studies of broadcasting is that of *random selection*. Random selection of a representative subgroup of a population results in a *random sample*. The selection of a sample has been random when the following two criteria are met:

a. Every member of the population has an equal likelihood of being selected for the sample, and
b. Every selection into the sample is made independently of every other selection into the sample.

If these two conditions are met, the likelihood that the sample will be representative of the population has been optimized. Hence, the continuing popularity of the random sample.

Sample Distributions, Population Distributions and Sampling Distributions

A sample distribution is a distribution of scores taken from a sample. The views of ladies-of-the-house above would be a sample distribution. The mean of the sample distribution is $\overline{X}$ in notation, while sample variance is denoted S^2. These sample statistics are used to estimate, or infer, the parameters of the population from which the sample is drawn. This use of sample statistics is a branch of statistical study known as *inferential statistics*.

A population distribution is a distribution of measurement scores which represent all members of a population. A population distribution might result from a census of the population. In most research in broadcasting, such a census is prohibitively expensive. For that reason, the best information available is likely to be a series of estimates based upon samples from a population.

A *sampling distribution* results from a large number of samples being drawn from a population. The sampling distribution is the distribution of sample statistics from this large number of samples. As a sample of size N is drawn from a population, the mean of the sample ($\overline{X}$) will differ by some amount from the mean of the population (μ). The amount of that difference ($\overline{X} - \mu$) might be referred to as "sampling error." If many other samples of the same size (N) were drawn it is likely that the mode of the sampling distribution would be equal to the mean of the population (μ). In the sampling distribution of sample means it would be possible to estimate "sampling error" ($\overline{X} - \mu$). This fact explains the importance of the sampling distribution in inferential statistics. The statistical "tests" to be discussed later in these lessons are all based upon some use of sampling distributions.

Probability Distributions

The discussion of distributions in Lessons One and Two dealt exclusively with frequency (f) distributions. Probability distributions are close relatives. Instead of representing the frequency of various score categories, the probability distribution represents the probability of those score categories. To better understand probability distributions it will be prudent to review some characteristics of probability in general. A common way of doing this is to consider the outcome of rolling dice.

Problem: What is the probability or likelihood of a composite score of seven when two honest dice are rolled?

Solution: First recognize the 6 possible outcomes on each die, and the 36 possible outcomes when 2 dice are rolled. A 7 could result as follows:

DIE A	DIE B	COMPOSITE SCORE
3	4	7
4	3	7
5	2	7
2	5	7
1	6	7
6	1	7

The likelihood of a composite score of 7 is thus 6 in 36. Simplifying 6/36 yields 1/6, the *probability* of an outcome of seven when casting two honest dice.

In the example above and in general, a probability may be defined as the ratio of the number of events of interest (combinations of two dice which sum to seven) to the total possible events (all combinations of two dice).

Continuing the example of two honest dice it would be possible to compute the probability (prob.) of each sum (X_i) of two dice. From those probabilities a *probability polygon* could then be constructed.

	X_i	Prob. (X_i)
	2	1/36
	3	2/36
	4	3/36
	5	4/36
Probability	6	5/36
Table	7	6/36
	8	5/36
	9	4/36
	10	3/36
	11	2/36
	12	1/36

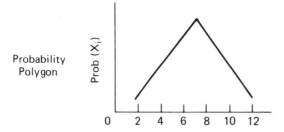

Probability
Polygon

Normal Distribution

The normal distribution is a well catalogued probability distribution of considerable importance in statistical work. It is important because (1) it is frequently a workable approximation for naturally occurring probability distributions and (2) it is mathematically convenient inasmuch as it is determined by only two parameters, mean and variance (or standard deviation). Tables of the probability dimensions of the normal distribution are readily available in reference works and one short table (Table II) is included at Appendix D.

Standard Scores (Z)

Standard scores are measurements which have been converted into numbers of standard deviations above or below the mean of a distribution. This conversion permits comparisons of measurements which have been taken in different measurement units.

With standard scores, it is literally possible to compare apples and oranges. For example, one could determine whether this year's apple crop is as good as the orange crop. To do this, the standard score of this year's apple crop would be computed within a distribution of the values of each annual apple crop (assume this standard score is +1.0). Then the standard score of the orange crop would be computed within a distribution of annual orange crop values (assume this standard score is +.5). It would be possible then to conclude that while this was a good year for both crops—to have a year this good in apples was more unusual.

The key characteristic of standard scores which makes such magic possible is that they equalize the mean and variance of different distributions of measurements. Standard scores are shown with the notation, Z. The definitional formula for a standard score is:

$$Z_i = \frac{X_i - \mu}{\sigma}$$

Consider first the numerator of this formula. Since μ, the population mean, is subtracted from each score (X_i), the mean of a set of standard scores will always be zero. Examine the denominator. Since the population standard deviation (σ) is the denominator, the standard deviation of a distribution of standard scores will always be one. As a consequence, the variance of a distribution of standard scores will also be one.

ILLUSTRATION: If $\mu = 2$ and $\sigma^2 = .25$, what is the standard score equivalent of a measurement of 4?

$$Z_4 = \frac{4 - 2}{.5}$$

$$= \frac{2}{.5}$$

$$Z_4 = +4$$

ILLUSTRATION: In a normal distribution of measurements, $\mu = 5$ and $\sigma^2 = 25$, what is the standard score equivalent of a measurement of 10?

$$Z_{10} = \frac{10 - 5}{5}$$

$$\underline{\underline{Z_{10} = +1}}$$

Standardized Normal Scores

Standard scores may be computed for the scores in any distribution. When they are computed from a sample distribution that can be assumed to resemble the well-cataloged normal distribution, the relative probability of the sample standard scores can be speedily determined.

For example, if the standard score computed from a sample score is +1.0, Table II of Appendix D is consulted. That table reports that a standard score of +1.0 is at the 84.1. percentile. Formally stated, the probability of a standard score of +1.0 in a normal distribution is equal to or less than .841. In notation:

$$\text{prob. } (Z_{10} = +1.0) \leqslant .841$$

If sampling error is the relative likelihood—probability—that a sample statistic differs from its equivalent population parameter by some amount, it might be possible to use standard scores to estimate the probability of various sizes of sampling error. This is the basic process of statistical inference.

In the case of the mean of a sample, the sampling distribution of means is a probability distribution of all possible values for sample means of a given size sample. If this sampling distribution of means is normal in its shape, then it will be possible to use a table like that at Table II, Appendix D, to report the probability of a given sample mean as it differs from the estimated mean of the population from which the sample is drawn.

To determine the standard score equivalent of a sample mean in the sampling distribution of means, the mean and standard deviation of the sampling distribution must be estimated.

The mean of the sample or the mean of past samples from the population is usually taken as the best available estimate of the mean of the population (μ).

The standard deviation of the sampling distribution of sample means, sometimes called the standard error of the mean and indicated in notation as $\sigma_{\overline{X}}$, is estimated by the following formula:

$$\text{est. } \sigma_{\overline{X}} = \frac{S}{\sqrt{N - 1}}$$

The verbal equivalent of this formula reads, the estimated standard deviation of the sampling distribution of the mean is equal to the standard deviation of the sample in question divided by the square root of one less than the sample size.

Problem: A simple random sample of 10 U.S. households was drawn and the householders involved asked to report the average number of hours television viewed in their households on Mondays. The amount of viewing on Mondays is the variable of interest, X_i. From many previous surveys of this sort, we know that the average daily viewing per household—*all* days considered—is 6.25 hours. This long term, all-days-considered average is estimated to be the mean of the population distribution, $\mu = 6.25$ hrs. When we compute the mean for Monday viewing from our sample, we discover $\overline{X} = 7.0$ hours, and that the standard deviation of the sample (S) is 3. It would seem that TV is viewed more on

Mondays than on the average day, but sampling error $(\bar{X} - \mu = .75)$ could account for some or all of this difference. The question for statistical analysis becomes, what is the relative likelihood (probability) that a sample of 10 $(N = 10)$ from a normally distributed population with $\mu = 6.25$ will yield a sample mean of 7 $(\bar{X} = 7)$?

Answer: The first step in solving this problem is to recognize that the probability involved will be sought in Table II of Appendix D. For this problem Table II becomes the sampling distribution of the mean. The first step in using this table will be to compute the standard score equivalent of $\bar{X} = 7.0$.

Recall the formula for computing standard scores:

$$Z = \frac{X_i - \mu}{\sigma}$$

In this case, $\bar{X} = 7.0$ and $\mu = 6.25$ are given. The standard deviation of the sampling distribution of means is:

$$est.\ \sigma_{\bar{X}} = \frac{S}{\sqrt{N-1}}$$

Substituting the values from the sample,

$$est\ \sigma_{\bar{X}} = \frac{3.0}{\sqrt{10-1}}$$

$$= \frac{3}{\sqrt{9}}$$

$$est\ \sigma_{\bar{X}} = \frac{3}{3}\ or\ 1.0\ .$$

Then using these values to compute $Z_{\bar{X}}$,

$$Z_{\bar{X}} = \frac{\bar{X} - \mu}{\sigma_{\bar{X}}}$$

$$= \frac{7.0 - 6.25}{1}$$

$$Z_{\bar{X}} = \frac{.75}{1}\ or\ .75\ .$$

Referring to Table II read down the standard score column to +.75. Note that the corresponding percentile $(Z_{\bar{X}} = +.75)$ is .773. This means that the relative likelihood of a sample of size 10 producing a mean of 7.0 and standard deviation of 3.0 when the sample has been drawn from a population with a mean of 6.25 is 77.3 percent or less. In other words, it appears quite likely that Monday viewing reported by these householders is not different from viewing on average days by an amount that could not be explained as anything but sampling error.

The experienced reader will recognize that this process is exactly that involved in tests of hypotheses, a subject for the following lesson.

Assignment #3—Standard Scores and Normal Distributions

1. For an opinion survey an investigator intended to select into his sample every other house on a given street by flipping a coin. Heads, he would visit houses with even numbers; tails, he would visit houses with odd numbers. Would this method of sample selection rightly be labeled random selection? Explain.

2. The following scores are drawn from a population with a mean of 24 and a variance of 100. What are the standard score equivalents of the following measurements?

15	18
20	21
24	25
28	29.5
32.4	40
34	

3. If the scores above are drawn from a normal distribution, 84 percent will fall at or below which of the above measurements?

4. What is your estimate of the standard deviation of the mean for the following distribution?

X_i	f
4	2
5	3
6	1

Lesson Four: What Did It Prove—Hypothesis Testing.

Hypothesis—null, research
Significance (alpha) level
- rejection region
- critical value
- significance

One and two tailed tests
Notation—H_o, H_R, α

Even a casual reader of research reports becomes aware of the language of hypothesis tests—significance, probability, rejection. These terms and the procedures in which they are involved answer this perplexing question for the investigator, "Could the measurement from this sample reflect a result which could be explained as sampling error (chance), or were the processes suspected really at work?" In order to answer this question the investigator will rely upon his understanding of probability distributions, especially the sampling distribution of means.

The Null Hypothesis

In a *null hypothesis* the investigator states the question addressed by his research as if sampling error (chance) alone could account for the difference between sample mean and anticipated population mean. These are some of the algebraic forms which null hypotheses may take.

H_o: $\mu = .85$. This formula is read, "The null hypothesis is that the population mean is equal to .85." Implied is that the sample mean will differ from .85 only as might be predicted by the relative probabilities of sampling error recorded in the sampling distribution of means.

Another frequently encountered form of the null hypothesis is H_o: $\mu_1 = \mu_2$. This formula is saying, "The null hypothesis is that the mean of the population from which the first sample is drawn is equal to the mean of the population from which the second sample is drawn." Another way of looking at this second sort of null hypothesis would be to observe that it holds that two samples were drawn from the same population or from equivalent populations.

The Research Hypothesis

Research hypotheses are really the more exciting of the two major categories of hypotheses involved with hypothesis testing. They are the theoretical statements which provide alternatives to the assertion of the null hypothesis that sampling error (chance) could explain the study results. Research hypotheses may be designated H_R, or as H_1, H_2, H_3, etc., if more than one research hypothesis is to be entertained. Like the null hypothesis, the research hypothesis may deal with one sample or more but is always stated as an inequality. Here are some examples with verbal equivalents.

H_R: $\mu \neq .85$—the mean of the population from which the sample was drawn is not equal to .85. It may be a larger or a smaller value; this is called a *bidirectional* research hypothesis.

H_R: $\mu_1 \neq \mu_2$—the mean of the population from which the first sample was drawn is not equal to the mean of the population from which the second sample was drawn. This is a bidirectional research hypothesis involving two samples.

H_R: $\mu > .85$—the mean of the population from which the sample is drawn is larger than .85.

H_R: $\mu < .85$—the mean of the population from which the sample is drawn is less than .85. This and the preceding research hypothesis are *unidirectional* hypotheses involving only one sample.

H_R: $\mu_1 > \mu_2$—the mean of the population from which the first sample was drawn is larger than the mean of the population from which the second sample was drawn.

H_R: $\mu_1 < \mu_2$—the mean of the population from which the first sample was drawn is less than the mean of the population from which the second sample was drawn. This and the preceding research hypothesis are unidirectional research hypotheses involving two samples.

The Relative Probability of Various Sample Means

The research hypothesis becomes a better explanation than the null hypothesis when, by study of the sampling distribution of the mean, it is determined that it is unlikely—improbable—that the sample mean differs from the population mean by some amount that could be explained by sampling error alone. *Exactly how unlikely* or *improbable* a sample mean must be in the sampling distribution of means (in order for the research hypothesis rather than the null hypothesis to be a better explanation of the sample data) is a matter of convention. Within the behavioral sciences the most frequently encountered conventions for defining exactly how unlikely or improbable, are 5 chances in 100 (.05 level), 1 chance in 100 (.01 level) and 1 chance in 1000 (.001 level). The most frequently encountered convention in radio and television audience research is 5 chances in 100 (.05 level). This is commonly referred to as "a significance level of .05" or "significance at the .05 level." Significance level is also referred to as alpha level after the Greek letter alpha, α, which denotes it algebraically. Again, the alpha or significance level is the relative probability that a sample mean is distant enough from the hypothesized population mean that the research hypothesis becomes a better explanation of the sample data than the null hypothesis. This probability will be assessed in the sampling distribution of the mean.

Depicting this hypothesis testing process graphically in the sampling distribution of means may be helpful.

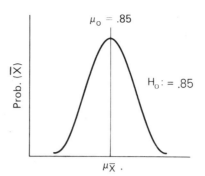

For the sake of illustration assume that the shape of this distribution—this sampling distribution of means—is normal, that it represents the relative probability of all possible values for sample means from samples of size N. The mean of this sampling distribution is the most probable value for means of samples of size N, the mean of the population from which the samples are drawn. Since it is the null hypothesis that is being tested, the mean of the sampling distribution of means is taken to be the value of the population mean given in the null hypothesis—.85 in the example of the single sample null hypotheses discussed above.

It will be necessary to show on the probability polygon of the sampling distribution of means the improbable portions of the sampling distribution of means which will indicate that the research hypothesis is a better explanation for the sample data than is the null hypothesis. Inspecting the polygon above should reveal that the least probable values for the sample means are on the tails of the distribution. The research hypothesis provides the clue as to which tail. If the research hypothesis is bidirectional, then both tails will be of interest. If unidirectional, then only one tail—that indicated by the direction of the inequality sign—will be of interest. To illustrate:

H_R: $\mu \neq .85$—of interest are improbable sample means that are smaller than $\mu_o = .85$, *and* improbable sample means that are larger than $\mu_o = .85$. The researcher will perform a *two-tailed test* of the null hypothesis.

H_R: $\mu > .85$—of interest are those improbable sample means that are larger than $\mu_o = .85$. The researcher will perform a *one-tailed test* on the upper tail.

H_R: $\mu < .85$—of interest are those improbable sample means which are smaller than $\mu_o = .85$. The researcher will perform a one-tailed test on the lower tail.

To continue the illustration of H_R: $\mu \neq .85$, requiring the two-tailed test, assume that convention dictates a significance level, or alpha level, of .05. This means that if the entire probability polygon of the sampling distribution of means were thought of as 100 percent, 5 percent divided between the upper and lower tails would represent the values for sample means which were so improbable as to cause us to "reject" the null hypothesis and to prefer the explanation of our sample data suggested by the research hypothesis. These portions of the tails of the distribution are appropriately called "regions of rejection."

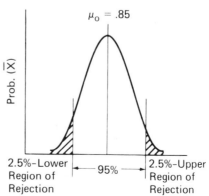

Since the shape of the sampling distribution of means has been assumed to be normal, we can refer to our cumulative normal distribution table (Table II in Appendix D) to find the standard scores at the 2.5th and 97.5th percentiles. These will be standard scores of -1.96 and +1.96. In order to compare these standard scores to sample data it will be necessary to describe the boundaries of the regions of rejection in terms of measurement units. To convert standard scores to measurement units multiply the standard scores by the standard deviation of the sampling distribution of means. Assume that in our example, $\sigma_{\bar{X}} = 2$. The boundary of the upper region of rejection then is $+1.96 \times 2$, or 3.92 above the mean. Since the mean (taken from the null hypothesis) is equal to .85, this upper critical value becomes $.85 + (1.96 \times 2)$, or 4.77. In the same way the critical value or boundary of the lower region of rejection becomes $.85 - (1.96 \times 2)$, or -3.07.

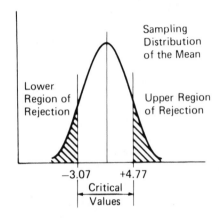

If the sample mean were $\bar{X} = .932$, this value would fall short of the upper critical value: this sample mean *could* have been drawn from a population with a mean of .85. Hence, we say that this sample mean is *not significant* at the .05 level, and the null hypothesis is a better explanation of our sample data than is the research hypothesis.

If, on the other hand, the sample mean were $\bar{X} = -4.0$, this sample mean would fall within the lower region of rejection: it would be unlikely that a population from which a sample could be drawn producing this sample mean would have a population mean of .85. It would be said that this sample mean has a probability of .05 or less (prob. $\leqslant$ .05); it is *significant* at the .05 level. And the research hypothesis appears to be a better explanation of the sample data than is the null hypothesis.

Look at the same example with a different research hypothesis—$H_R: \mu > .85$. The tail of interest in this instance is the upper tail only. It will be necessary to locate a single region of rejection amounting to 5 percent of the sampling distribution on the upper tail only. Consulting the cumulative normal distribution table (Table II in Appendix D), note that a standard score of +1.65 is at the ninety-fifth percentile. To convert to measurement units multiply by $\sigma_{\bar{X}} = 2$ and add $\mu_o = .85$, yielding +4.15. This is the single critical value for a one-tailed test on the upper tail. Any sample mean larger than +4.15 will fall

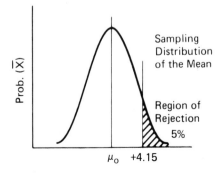

within the region of rejection, labeling it as significant at the .05 level (prob. ≤ .05). The null hypothesis, under these circumstances, would have to be rejected, as the research hypothesis provides a better explanation of the sample data.

Whenever called upon to perform hypothesis tests, the prudent researcher may wish to draw a probability polygon like those above representing the sampling distribution of the mean. Doing so will help to make the process clearer.

Assignment #4–Hypothesis Testing

1. Assume that you have drawn a sample from a normal population. You have taken a measurement from each member of the sample.
   a. If H_o: $\mu = 10$ and H_R: $\mu \neq 10$, and if $\bar{X} = 20$ and est. $\sigma_{\bar{X}} = 10$, perform the required hypothesis test. Set $\alpha = .05$. Sketch the sampling distribution of the mean showing rejection regions and critical values.
   b. If H_o: $\mu = 10$ and H_R: $\mu > 10$, and if $\bar{X} = 27$ and est. $\sigma_{\bar{X}} = 10$, perform the required hypothesis test. Set $\alpha = .05$. Sketch the sampling distribution of the mean showing rejection regions and critical values.
2. Assume that the following sample is drawn from a normal population.

X_i	f
4	2
5	3
6	1

   a. Compute $\bar{X}$ and est. $\sigma_{\bar{X}}$.
   b. Test hypotheses H_o: $\mu = 2$ and H_R: $\mu > 2$ at the .05 level of significance.

Lesson Five: Working with Small Samples–The t Test

> Student's Distribution of t
> Degrees of Freedom
> Use of the t Table
> t Tests
>   Single means
>   Two independent means
>   Two correlated means
> Notation–df, t

In Lesson Three it may have been clear to the careful reader that scores drawn from a normally distributed population–if drawn at random–will also be normally distributed. Theoretically such is the case. But in the real world of measurement when *small samples* are drawn from normally distributed populations, there is a consistent bias in the dis-

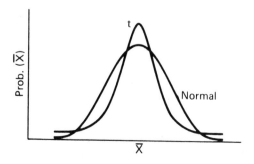

tribution of the sample. This small sample bias is also reflected in the sampling distribution of the mean. This biased sampling distribution for small samples drawn from normal populations is well-cataloged and known as the *t distribution,* or the Student's *t* distribution. In general, the *t* distribution is more peaked and fatter in the tails than the normal distribution, something like the sketch below.

A *t* statistic from the mean of a single sample resembles a standard score for that sample mean, except that the denominator of the standard score formula becomes the estimated standard deviation of the sampling distribution of means. In algebraic terms:

$$Z_{\bar{X}} = \frac{\bar{X} - \mu_o}{\sigma_{\bar{X}}} \quad \text{and} \quad t = \frac{\bar{X} - \mu_o}{\text{est.}\,\sigma_{\bar{X}}} \,.$$

Note that the illustration given at the end of Lesson Three was actually a *t* statistic rather than a standard score equivalent of a sample mean.

In a table of the sampling distribution of the *t* statistic, critical values of *t* are shown for both one- and two-tailed tests at the .05, .01 and .001 levels of significance. A *t* table is included as Table III in Appendix D.

Degrees of Freedom

The notation, *df,* when it appears in a statistical context, indicates "degrees of freedom." The definition of degrees of freedom is "that number of measurements in a collection of measurements which are free to take on any value when some statistic is known." To illustrate, imagine a collection of three scores with a mean equal to four. Only two of the three scores is free to take any value: for when two scores are named, the third is wholly determined if the mean of the three is to equal four. If two of this set of three scores were 2 and 2, then the third must be eight, so that $\bar{X} = 4$. And again if two of the scores were –3 and 5, then the third score must be 10 so that $\bar{X} = 4$.

The degrees of freedom associated with a *t* statistic computed from a single sample, *df,* will always equal $N - 1$, one less than the size of the sample.

t Test of a Single Mean

The *t* test of a single mean is the test implied by the discussion to this point. From the tabled values for *t,* the researcher reads out the critical value(s) for *t* for a one- or two-tailed test at the appropriate level of significance and at $N - 1$ degrees of freedom. Then the sample *t* is computed as described earlier and compared with the critical values to determine whether or not it falls into the region(s) of rejection.

Example: $H_o: \mu = 0$

$H_R: \mu \neq 0$

$\bar{X} = 3$

$N = 10$

$S^2 = 100$

Set $\alpha = .05$

Step 1. Enter the *t* table at the two-tail, .05 level, and $9(N - 1)$ degrees of freedom. Read out 2.262 and –2.262 as critical values. Sketch the sampling distribution of *t*.

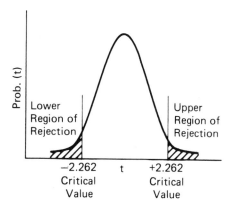

Step 2. Compute *t*.

$$t = \frac{\overline{X} - \mu_o}{\text{est.} \, \sigma_{\overline{X}}}$$

$$= \frac{3 - 0}{10 / \sqrt{9}}$$

$$t = \frac{3}{10/3}$$

$$= \frac{3}{3.33333}$$

$$t = .9000 \, .$$

Step 3. Compare *t* computed from the sample with the critical values from the *t* table. The sample *t* is not in a region of rejection. Hence, H_o cannot be rejected.

t Test for Two Independent Means

The *t* test for two independent means is called for when the data represent the same measurements taken from two different samples of respondents. The procedures for locating the critical value(s) for *t* in the table is the same discussed above, except that in this case, df are $N_1 + N_2 - 2$ (two less than the number of scores in both samples combined). The *t* statistic is computed as:

$$t = \frac{\overline{X}_1 - \overline{X}_2}{\sqrt{\dfrac{N_1 S_1^2 + N_2 S_2^2}{N_1 + N_2 - 2} \left(\dfrac{1}{N_1} + \dfrac{1}{N_2} \right)}}$$

where

$\overline{X}_1$ = the mean of the first sample

$\overline{X}_2$ = the mean of the second sample

S_1^2 = the variance of the first sample

S_2^2 = the variance of the second sample

N_1 = the number of scores in the first sample

N_2 = the number of scores in the second sample.

Example:

$$H_o: \mu_1 = \mu_2$$

$$H_R: \mu_1 > \mu_2$$

$$S_1^2 = 100; S_2^2 = 144$$

$$N_1 = 10; N_2 = 10$$

$$\overline{X}_1 = 12; \overline{X}_2 = 10$$

Set $\alpha = .05$.

Step 1. $df(N_1 + N_2 - 2) = 18$.

Step 2. Enter t table at one-tail, .05 level and 18 df. Read out critical value of +1.734.

Step 3. Compute t statistic using the formula above:

$$t = \frac{12 - 10}{\sqrt{\frac{10(100) + 10(144)}{18}\left(\frac{2}{10}\right)}}$$

$$= \frac{2}{\sqrt{\frac{2(1000 + 1440)}{180}}}$$

$$= \frac{2}{\sqrt{\frac{4880}{180}}}$$

$$= \frac{2}{\sqrt{27.11111}}$$

$$= \frac{2}{5.26683}$$

$t = .38411$, N.S.

(N.S. means "result not significant at the required alpha level.")

Step 4. Compare the t computed from the sample with the critical t located in the t table. Note that this sample t is not in the region of rejection, hence H_o cannot be rejected, and we say the sample t is not significant at the .05 level.

t Test for Correlated Means

The t test for correlated means is indicated when only one sample is involved, but two measurements from the sample are to be compared. The appropriate degrees of freedom are $N - 1$. The t statistic is computed according to the following formula:

$$t = \frac{(\overline{X}_1 - \overline{X}_2)}{\frac{S_{Diff}}{\sqrt{N - 1}}}$$

In this case the computation is from difference scores, the difference between the first and second measurements for each respondent. The numerator of the formula is the mean (average) difference score. The S_{Diff} in the denominator is the standard deviation of difference scores.

Example: The following data are from a study of the impact of educational television upon attitude toward school work.

Respondent	X_1 Attitude Score Before TV	X_2 Attitude Score After TV	$(X_1 - X_2)$ Difference Score	$(X_1 - X_2)^2$
1	9	4	5	25
2	7	3	4	16
3	8	2	6	36
4	6	1	5	25
5	2	0	2	4
			$\Sigma(X_1 - X_2) = 22$	$106 = \Sigma(X_1 - X_2)^2$

$$H_o : \mu_1 = \mu_2$$

$$H_R : \mu_1 \neq \mu_2$$

Step 1. Find mean difference score, $\overline{(X_1 - X_2)}$

$$\overline{(X_1 - X_2)} = \frac{\Sigma(X_1 - X_2)}{N}$$

$$= \frac{22}{5}$$

$$\overline{(X_1 - X_2)} = 4.4$$

Step 2. Find standard deviation of difference scores, S_{Diff}.

$$S_{Diff}^2 = \frac{\Sigma(X_1 - X_2)^2}{N} - \overline{(X_1 - X_2)}^2$$

$$= \frac{106}{5} - (4.4)^2$$

$$= 21.2 - 19.36$$

$$S_{Diff} = 1.84$$

$$S_{Diff} = \sqrt{S_{Diff}^2} = 1.35647 .$$

Step 3. Compute t using the formula given.

$$t = \frac{\overline{(X_1 - X_2)}}{S_{Diff} / \sqrt{N - 1}}$$

$$= \frac{4.4}{1.35647 / \sqrt{5 - 1}}$$

$$= \frac{4.4}{1.35647 / 2}$$

$$= \frac{4.4}{.67823}$$

$$t = 6.48745 .$$

Step 4. Consult table for critical values of *t*. Note H_R requires a two-tailed test. Degrees of freedom, *df,* are $N - 1$ or 4. Level of significance is .05. Find critical values of *t* to be +2.776 and –2.776.

Step 5. Compare sample *t* with critical values. Note that sample t falls within upper region of rejection. Hence, the sample t is significant at the .05 level, and $H_o: \mu_1 = \mu_2$ can be rejected. $H_R: \mu_1 \neq \mu_2$ seems to be a better explanation of the sample data.

A Short-Cut Version of the *t*-Test of Correlated Means—the Unique Sample Test

The unique sample test is the creation of A.E. Brandt.[1] It is a rapid, although rough, way of performing a *t* test of correlated means; that is, it is a way of determining that the mean differences between two measures taken from the same sample of respondents are different enough that something other than sampling error accounts for that difference.

To perform the unique sample test, the sign of the difference between measure *a* and measure *b* is determined for each respondent. If measure *a* is larger than measure *b* in the case of respondent #1, then "+" is the sign of the difference. If measure *b* is larger than measure *a* in the case of respondent #2, then the sign of the difference is " – ". If measure *a* and *b* for a respondent are the same, then "*0*" is the sign of the difference. After the sign of difference has been determined for each respondent, then U_{diff}, the test statistic, is computed according to this formula.

$$U_{diff} = \frac{a + .5c}{a + b + c}$$

where

a = the frequency of the more frequently appearing directional sign (+ or –)

b = the frequency of the less frequently appearing directional sign (+ or –)

c = the frequency of "*0*" differences.

U_{diff} is computed from the sample data, then compared to the critical values given in the following table to assess significance.

If a test at the .05 level is desired, and the number of respondents is:	If a test at the .01 level is desired, and the number of respondents is:	Then U_{diff}, to be significant, must be equal to or greater than:
4	7	1.00
5	8	.95
6	11	.90
8	13	.85
10	17	.80
15	28	.75
25	46	.70
45	78	.65
100	175	.60
390	660	.55

Illustration 1. A broadcast problem that can be addressed using this test is that of the combination discount in broadcast time sales. From a sponsor's point of view a combination discount is attractive, if it promises to deliver two audiences at a lower unit price when purchased together than when purchased separately. For instance, a children's combination for a television station might mean a reduced cost to a sponsor who purchased a combination of one spot in the morning children's program with a second spot in the afternoon children's program. The combination would be a very poor buy in terms

of reach, if it could be shown that exactly the same audience watched the afternoon show as watched the morning show, for it would imply that we could reach that audience by purchasing a single spot in either of the shows.

The researcher assigned to solve this problem elects to travel to Beltsville, Maryland, to examine the diaries collected in the most recent ARBitron survey of the market. These diaries (for the sake of illustration) show that twenty households in the sample reported viewing either or both of the morning and afternoon children's shows, as summarized below.

WATCHED MORNING KIDVID 1 = YES; 0 = NO	WATCHED AFTERNOON KIDVID 1 = YES; 0 = NO	SIGN OF DIFFERENCE
1	0	+
0	0	0
1	0	+
1	0	+
1	0	+
1	1	0
1	0	+
1	0	+
1	0	+
0	0	0
1	1	0
0	0	0
1	0	+
1	1	0
1	0	+
1	0	+
1	1	0
1	1	0
1	0	+
1	0	+

The first step in performing the unique sample test is to establish the sign of differences as in the third column above. Then U_{diff} is computed.

$$U_{diff} = \frac{12 \ (\text{no. of +s}) + .5 \ (8 - \text{no. of } 0\text{s})}{20}$$

$$= \frac{16}{20} \text{ or } .8 \ .$$

Consulting the table of significant U_{diff} values, we see that with any sample over the size of 17, a U_{diff} of .8 has less than a .01 probability of differing this much from zero due to sampling error.

There is a real difference between morning and afternoon children's audiences, and it appears from the size of the afternoon audience that the only way that it can be sold will be in a combination with the more attractive morning children's audience.

Illustration 2. The news department wonders whether the late fringe and early fringe TV news should have different editorial content. They reason that, if the audiences for the two are the same, then the content of the two should be different, so that the later news will have more interest for the audience. On the other hand, if the audience is not the same for both news shows, then the same content in the later show will not seem dull to the new audience.

Again the researcher travels to Beltsville to look at diaries. There are (for illustration purposes) 20 diaries reporting viewing of either or both news programs. Of the 20 households involved, 13 watch early but not late ($a = 13 + s$); 3 watch late but not early ($b = 3 - s$); 4 watch both ($c = 4$ 0s). Therefore:

$$U_{diff} = \frac{15}{20} \text{ or } .75 .$$

Consulting the table, we see that this result is significant at the .05 level. Someone had better get busy and improve the sagging interest values of that late news!

The t test including the special case of the U_{diff} test is the most common form of hypothesis test in radio and television research. While there are other hypothesis test procedures, both more and less complex, none is any more efficient for the research questions for which it is applicable.

Assignment #5—The t Test

1. For several years standardized tests have been given all students completing the basic course in college algebra. The mean score after several years of collecting these scores is 85 percent. During this semester 20 students selected at random received their college algebra course as a tutorial, meeting their instructor in his office weekly. At the end of the semester, all 20 students were administered the standardized tests, receiving the scores below.

.67	.90	.78	.83	.92	.50
.94	.83	.82	.73	.55	.70
.93	.92	.91	.71	.65	.85
		.87	.71		

   a. The instructor involved wants to know whether tutorial instruction made a difference in test scores and asks you to help with a statistical test. You decide to use a t test. What are your null and research hypotheses?
   b. Set the alpha level at .05. Compute the necessary t.
   c. What are the appropriate degrees of freedom?
   d. Refer to your t table. Is this sample mean significant? How will you interpret this result in light of the hypotheses you formulated under 1(a)?

2. Another random sample of 20 students received all instruction via instructional television. Their test scores at the end of the semester follow. Test at the .05 level a research hypothesis that these two groups, tutorial and instructional television, have significantly different mean test scores.

.45	.47	.52	.93	.56	.61
.59	.58	.57	.87	.87	.53
.45	.33	.52	.76	.93	.95
		.66	.53		

Lesson Six: Yes or No—Dichotomous Data

Mean
Variance
Standard deviation
t tests for proportions
Standard deviation of the sampling
   distribution of proportions
Notation—p, q, σ_p

Dichotomous data are those in which responses fall unambiguously into only two categories. Examples include yes or no answers, male or female, viewing or not viewing. In recording dichotomous data, the number one (1) is written when a yes response is to be recorded, a zero (0) when a no response is to be recorded.

In audience research, rating data are dichotomous. The respondent is asked, "What television station are you viewing?" Inferred in this question are questions like these: "Are you watching WKYT?" "Are you watching WLEX?" "Are you watching WBLG?" "Are you watching WKLE?" A "yes" answer to one of these questions implies a "no" response to all the others. When the interviewer asks, "What station are you viewing?" and the respondent answers, "WKLE," the respondent is also answering that WKYT, WLEX and WBLG are not being viewed.

This is a table of responses that might have been collected in a survey of television viewing:

Respondent	X_1 (WKLE)	X_2(WBLG)	X_3(WKYT)	X_4(WLEX)
1	1	0	0	0
2	0	1	0	0
3	0	0	1	0
4	1	0	0	0
5	0	1	0	0
6	0	0	1	0
7	0	1	0	0
8	1	0	0	0
9	0	1	0	0
10	0	1	0	0

To compute the means for X_1, X_2, X_3, X_4, the familiar formula for computation of the mean can be used:

$$\bar{X} = \frac{\Sigma X_i}{N}.$$

For the data tabled above:

X_1	X_2	X_3	X_4	
3	5	2	0	$= \Sigma X_i$
.3	.5	.2	0	$= \Sigma X_i / N = \bar{X}_i$

Computing the means for this dichotomous data was rapidly done. Statisticians prefer to call the mean of a distribution of dichotomous measurements a *proportion,* designated in notation as p. The proportion p can also be considered as the proportion of ones (yes responses). The proportion of zeros (no responses) would then become $1.0 - p$ and designated in notation as q.

Recall that the computational formula for variance is:

$$S^2 = \frac{\Sigma X_i^2}{N} - \left(\frac{\Sigma X_i}{N}\right)^2.$$

A streamlined version of this formula has been developed for dichotomous data:

$$S^2 = pq.$$

It produces exactly the same answer as the first formula, but is simpler because of the ease of computation with dichotomous data.

Illustration: Consider X_2, those who viewed WBLG in the table above:

Computing variance by the usual computational formula for variance:

X_2	X_2^2
0	0
0	0
1	1
0	0
0	0
1	1
0	0
1	1
1	1
1	1

$$\Sigma X_2 = 5 \qquad 5 = \Sigma X_2^2$$
$$N = 10$$

$$S_2^2 = \frac{\Sigma X_2^2}{N} - \left(\frac{\Sigma X_2}{N}\right)^2$$

$$= \frac{5}{10} - \left(\frac{5}{10}\right)^2$$

$$= \frac{50}{100} - \frac{25}{100}$$

$$S_2^2 = .25 .$$

Computing variance by the shortcut formula for dichotomous data:

$$p = \Sigma X_2 / N = 5/10 \text{ or } .5$$
$$q = 1 - p$$
$$q = 1 - .5 \text{ or } .5$$
$$S_2^2 = pq$$
$$= .5(.5)$$
$$S_2^2 = .25 .$$

In the same way the standard deviation of a set of dichotomous data is rapidly computed as:

$$S = \sqrt{pq} .$$

The standard deviation of the sampling distribution of means is somewhat different. Recall that in Lesson Three this value was computed as:

$$\text{est.}\, \sigma_{\bar{X}} = \frac{S}{\sqrt{N-1}} .$$

In the case of dichotomous data this becomes:

$$\sigma_p = \sqrt{\frac{pq}{N}} .$$

This value, σ_p, is called the *standard deviation of proportion,* or standard error of proportion and, for dichotomous data, corresponds to σ_X.

The formula for computing the t from a single sample was introduced earlier:

$$t = \frac{\overline{X} - \mu_o}{\text{est.} \, \sigma_{\overline{X}}} .$$

When dealing with a sample of dichotomous data, the symbols for dichotomous data are merely substituted:

$$t = \frac{p - p_o}{\sigma_p} .$$

The symbol p_o denotes the value for p given in the null hypothesis.

Determining Survey Sample Sizes

In broadcast rating surveys there is some general agreement as to the level of sampling error that is acceptable. The criteria of acceptable accuracy are that the sample be large enough that there will be at least 95 percent likelihood that p will deviate no more than plus or minus .05 (5 rating points) due to sampling error from the true value (p_t). Consider this graphic illustration.

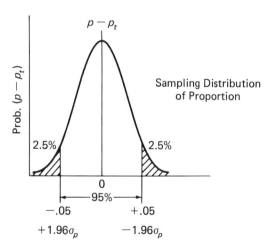

Expressed in terms of this sketch of the sampling distribution of proportion, the criteria are:

$$\text{prob.}(p - p_t = .05) \leqslant .05 .$$

Note that the critical values are $\pm .05$, $\pm 1.96\sigma_p$. Recall that the formula for

$$\sigma_p = \sqrt{\frac{pq}{N}} .$$

If we round 1.96 to 2, then the critical values expressed in measurement units are:

$$\pm 2 \sqrt{\frac{pq}{N}} = \pm .05 \ .$$

Solving for N:

$$\pm 4 \frac{pq}{N} = \pm .0025$$

$$\pm 4pq = \pm .0025N$$

$$N = 4pq \div .0025$$

$$N = 1600\, p(1 - p)\ .$$

This formula is the sample size required to produce the minimum criteria for accuracy when p is known. The statistic p might be known from an earlier study. If it is not, then the researcher must assume that $p = .50$. That is because $p = .50$ will always be the case producing the largest value for σ_p, hence also the case requiring the largest N. This formula has been utilized in preparing the sample size selector at Table IV, Appendix D.

An examination of Table IV also reveals that the smaller the p obtained from a sample, the smaller the sample needed to achieve the criteria for accuracy listed above. Here are several examples of the proper use of Table IV, Appendix D.

Example 1. In Market A ratings are conducted by the commercial rating services only once per year. A local station owner plans a supplementary survey during the Christmas season, to compare the popularity of the station at this peak advertising season. In the past average ratings for the station have ranged between 5 and 60 (NOTE: a rating is 100p; therefore, this range of ratings equals a range of p from .05 to .60). Since this range includes $p = .50$, enter Table IV at $p = .50$ and read down that column to a deviaton $(p - p_t)$ of .05, the criterion of accuracy for our survey. Read horizontally to sample size (N) of 400.

Example 2. In a rating report just released television station A received a rating of 27 $(p = .27)$ for early fringe news-weather-sports. Station B received a rating of 25 $(p = .25)$ for the equivalent program. The program director of station A decides to conduct a survey to determine whether this difference $(p_A - p_B = .02)$ is real or the result of the sampling error inherent in the rating report. To use Table IV, the program director enters the column headed $p = .25$ and reads down to the deviation allowable in this survey (.02), finds the closest value of .019, then reads horizontally to a sample size of 2000 respondents. The survey to meet the requirements for accuracy in this case must include an N of 2000.

It may be apparent from these examples and from the table that the size of the population is not a consideration in selecting the size of the sample. What is important in sample size is the relative difficulty in detecting the size of p with minimum acceptable sampling error.

It should be noted that Table IV, Appendix D represents samples drawn from a *single population.* Typically commercial rating reports are concerned with more than a single population. The report may separate ratings for a metropolitan area and one or more surrounding areas. The total sample size in this case becomes the sum of the sample size required from each of these survey areas.

Assignment #6—Dichotomous Data

1. Following are the results of a telephone coincidental viewer survey conducted in Fayette County during the first week of February for the period, 4:30 to 5:00 P.M.

WKYT	WLEX	WBLG	WKLE
1			
	1		
			1
1			
			1
			1
1			
	1		
		1	1
1			
1			
1			
	1		
			1
		1	
1			
			1
		1	
1			

What are the mean ratings (p) of each station?

2. If the requirement for the design of a survey sample is that there must be a 95 percent likelihood that the mean rating (p) be within $\pm.05$ for any rating (p) between .85 and .15, what sample size (N) is needed?

Lesson Seven: How Things Go Together – Correlation

Correlation coefficient
Product-moment correlation
Coefficient of determination
Notation—r_{XY}, r_{XY}^2, phi_{XY}

Correlation answers the question, how are two measures from the same sample related? The correlation coefficient may tell us that as one measure increases so will the other. Or conversely, it may tell us that as one measure increases, the other will decrease.

This sort of information is important, for it enables us to predict one measure when the other is known. And it helps us understand one sort of behavior when another is known. For example, in the case of audience research, correlation coefficients might help us to know that the audience for "M.A.S.H." one measure, is related to the audience for "Mork and Mindy," another measure.

Correlation Coefficient

The most frequently used sort of correlation coefficient is the product-moment correlation, r_{XY}. It is also the basis for most of the other correlation coefficients with which measurement experts deal. By definition a product-moment correlation is the mean cross product of the standard score equivalents of two measures. In algebraic terms:

$$r_{XY} = \frac{\Sigma Z_X Z_Y}{N}$$

In Lesson Three the usefulness of standard scores in permitting comparisons of measures taken in different measurement units was discussed. With the product-moment correlation, the role of standardized scores is to permit the computation of an index of the association of two measures originally taken in different units.

The range over which correlation coefficients may vary is from $+1.0$ to -1.0. The following graph of standard scores on the variable X, liking for "M.A.S.H.," and the variable Y, liking for "Mork and Mindy," may help to clarify. A correlation coefficient of $+1.0$ means that as measure X increases one standard score unit from $+5.0$ to $+6.0$, so also will measure Y.

A correlation coefficient of -1.0 means that as measure X increases one standard score unit from $+5.0$ to $+6.0$, measure Y will *decrease* from standard score of -5.0 to -6.0.

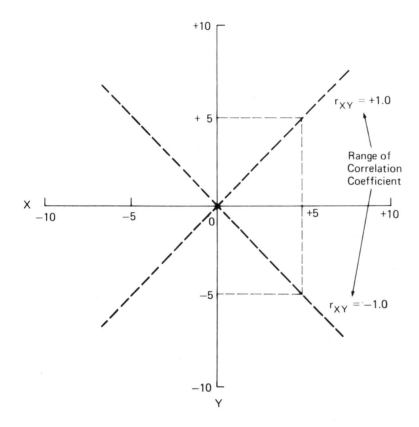

In this graph, variable X is in the horizontal dimension, variable Y in the vertical, and the values plotted are standard scores. The two dotted lines in the graph represent the limits of the possible range of the correlation coefficient, $+1.0$ to -1.0.

On the line, $r_{XY} = +1.0$, a standard score of $+10.0$ on variable X is matched by a standard score of $+10.0$ on variable Y, and vice versa. Similarly on the line, $r_{XY} = -1.0$, $+5.0$ on the X dimension is matched by -5.0 on the Y dimension.

In the graph below a correlation coefficient $r_{XY} = +.50$, has been plotted to illustrate the *bidirectionality* of the correlation coefficient.

All correlation coefficients falling between $+1.0$ to -1.0 actually describe two lines as plotted below for $r_{XY} = +.50$. If this correlation coefficient held for a group of paired scores (two measures from each respondent in a survey, for example), the coefficient could predict that a standard score of $+5.0$ on variable Y would be matched by a standard score of $+2.5$ on variable X *OR* that a standard score of $+5.0$ on variable X would be matched by a standard score of $+2.5$ on Y. Hence, the necessity for two lines to define the correlation coefficient when plotted on the X-Y graph — and the notion of *bidirectionality* in interpreting the correlation coefficient.

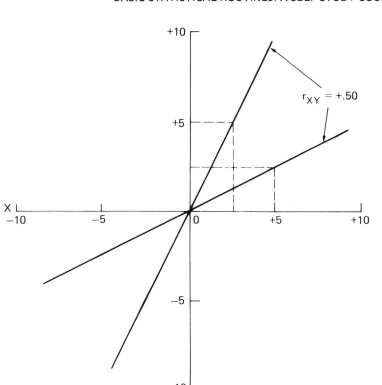

It is common in reporting research results, not only to report the size of a correlation coefficient but to interpret the magnitude of the coefficient in terms of an adjective such as "moderate," "slight," or "high." As an aid to students reading such reports, the following guides to such adjectives are quoted from Frederick Williams.[2]

SIZE OF CORRELATION COEFFICIENT	ADJECTIVE
.20 or less	slight; almost negligible relationship
.20 – .40	low; definite but small relationship
.40 – .70	moderate; substantial relationship
.70 – .90	high; marked relationship
.90 or more	very high; very dependable relationship.

Computational Routine for the Product-Moment Correlaton

The computational formula for the product-moment correlation is:

$$r_{XY} = \frac{\Sigma XY - \dfrac{(\Sigma X)(\Sigma Y)}{N}}{\sqrt{\Sigma X^2 - \dfrac{(\Sigma X)^2}{N}} \sqrt{\Sigma Y^2 - \dfrac{(\Sigma Y)^2}{N}}}$$

Each of these symbols should be familiar with the possible exception of ΣXY which is the sum of cross products of X and Y. Each may be clearer from this numerical illustration. The matrix below (Respondent, X and Y columns) represents the results of a study of five respondents who reported their liking of "M.A.S.H.," X, and their liking of "Mork and Mindy," Y.

Respondent	X	Y
1	7	3
2	5	2
3	4	5
4	3	6
5	1	7

The first step is to develop each of the elements required by the computational formula — ΣX, ΣX^2, ΣXY, ΣY, ΣY^2, N.

Respondent	X^2	X	XY	Y	Y^2
1	49	7	21	3	9
2	25	5	10	2	4
3	16	4	20	5	25
4	9	3	18	6	36
5	1	1	7	7	49
$N = 5$	$\Sigma X^2 = 100$	$\Sigma X = 20$	$\Sigma XY = 76$	$\Sigma Y = 23$	$\Sigma Y^2 = 123$

These values are then substituted for the appropriate symbols in the computational formula.

$$r_{XY} = \frac{\Sigma XY - \dfrac{(\Sigma X)(\Sigma Y)}{N}}{\sqrt{\Sigma X^2 - \dfrac{(\Sigma X)^2}{N}} \ \sqrt{\Sigma Y^2 - \dfrac{(\Sigma Y)^2}{N}}}$$

$$r_{XY} = \frac{76 - \dfrac{(20)(23)}{5}}{\sqrt{100 - \dfrac{(20)^2}{5}} \ \sqrt{123 - \dfrac{(23)^2}{5}}}$$

$$= \frac{76 - 92}{\sqrt{100 - 80} \ \sqrt{123 - 105.8}}$$

$$= \frac{-16}{\sqrt{(20)(17.2)}}$$

$$r_{XY} = \frac{-16}{\sqrt{344}}$$

$$= \frac{-16}{18.54}$$

$$r_{XY} = -.863 \ .$$

Interpretation of the Correlation Coefficient

A correlation coefficient indexes the extent to which one measure varies with another when both measures have been taken from the same sample of respondents. But what proportion of the variability in one measure can be said to have been explained by the variability of the other?

This question is answered by the *coefficient of determination—r_{XY}^2*. In algebraic terms, r_{XY}^2 indexes the proportion of S_X^2, the variance in one measure, which can be explained by S_Y^2, the variance in another measure. This mutual—or bidirectional—shared variance has a value which must be less than the correlation coefficient of the two measures.

The function of the coefficient of determination can be illustrated by this Venn diagram.

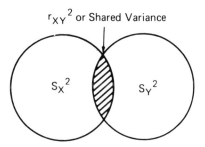

r_{XY}^2 or Shared Variance

S_X^2 S_Y^2

The coefficient of determination is the square of the correlation coefficient. To illustrate, if the correlation between X and Y is +1.0, then the coefficient of determination between the two measures is also 1.0 and we can say that 100 percent of the variance in X is explained by variance in Y. In the same way, if the correlation coefficient is +.70, the coefficient of determination is .49, and we say that 49 percent of the variance in one measure is explained by variance in the other measure. When this relationship is kept in mind, the meaning of the adjectives listed earlier opposite correlation coefficients of various sizes becomes clearer.

The Phi Correlation

The statistics for ordinary numbers also hold for the case of dichotomous numbers, 1 and 0, except that some mathematical shortcuts are possible due to the simplicity of the dichotomous number system. This observation holds true for the case of the correlation coefficient computed from dichotomous data.

The phi coefficient is a product-moment correlation computed from dichotomous data. The first step in computing phi is to construct a two by two contingency table of the form below.

	1	a	b
Y			
	0	c	d
		0	1
			X

Square a represents the number of persons who answered "no" (0) to question X and "yes" (1) to question Y. Square b is the number of respondents answering "yes"

(1) to both questions. Square c is the number answering "no" (0) to both questions. Square d is the number of respondents who answered "yes" (1) to question X and "no" (0) to question Y.

The values from this contingency table are then substituted for the appropriate symbols in the following formula.

$$phi_{XY} = \frac{(bc - ad)}{\sqrt{(a + b)(c + d)(a + c)(b + d)}}$$

In the illustrative distribution below, X represents the question, "Do you watch Captain Kangaroo?" while Y represents the question, "Do you watch the Electric Company?"

X	Y	Respondent
0	1	Jill
0	0	John
1	1	Jorge
1	0	Jacob
0	0	Josie
0	0	Jim
0	0	Jayne
1	1	Joe
1	1	Jack
1	0	Jeri

These data are first distributed as a contingency table:

Substituting the values from the contingency table for those in the formula:

$$phi_{XY} = \frac{(3)(4) - (1)(2)}{\sqrt{(1 + 3)(4 + 2)(1 + 4)(3 + 2)}}$$

$$= \frac{12 - 2}{\sqrt{(4)(6)(5)(5)}}$$

$$= \frac{10}{\sqrt{600}}$$

$$= \frac{10}{24.49490}$$

$$phi_{XY} = .40825 .$$

This result would indicate a *moderate relationship* within the context of this study between viewing "Captain Kangaroo" and viewing "Electric Company."

The great usefulness of correlation coefficients in radio and television research is in their ability to tell us not only that two measures were *significantly* related (something the *t* test for correlated means tells us) but the magnitude of that relationship as well.

Hypothesis Testing with Correlation Coefficients

A test of an hypothesis containing a correlation coefficient may be one or two tailed, directional or nondirectional. Following are some illustrative pairs of null and research hypotheses which might involve correlation coefficients.

$$H_o: r_{XY} = 0 \quad H_R: r_{XY} \neq 0$$

$$H_o: r_{XY} = .5 \quad H_R: r_{XY} < .5$$

$$H_o: r_{XY} = .5 \quad H_R: r_{XY} > .5$$

Any of the above can be tested with a *t* test. The critical value is read for a one or two-tailed test from Table III, Appendix D at $N - 2$ degrees of freedom. The sample *t* is then computed:

$$t = \frac{r_{XY} \sqrt{N - 2}}{\sqrt{1 - r_{XY}^2}} .$$

To return to the example of the respondents who indicated their liking for "M.A.S.H." and "Mork and Mindy," we found the correlation coefficient between these two measures to be – .863 with $N = 5$. Let $H_o: r_{XY} = 0$ and $H_R: r_{XY} \neq 0$. Enter Table III for the critical value for *t* when $df = 3$ $(N - 2)$ and for a two-tailed test and the .05 level. Read a critical *t* of ± 3.132. Now compute the *t* above from the sample data.

$$t = \frac{-.863 \sqrt{5 - 2}}{\sqrt{1 - (-.863)^2}}$$

$$= \frac{-.863 (1.732)}{\sqrt{1 - .745}}$$

$$= \frac{-.1.495}{\sqrt{.255}}$$

$$= \frac{-1.495}{.505}$$

$$t = -2.960, N.S.$$

A test of a null hypothesis of a phi correlation requires a different sampling distribution, that for a statistic dalled chi^2. The critical values for this test are as follows:

	critical chi^2
two-tailed test, .05 level	± .00098
one-tailed test, .05 level	.0039
two-tailed test, .01 level	± .000039
one-tailed test, .01 level	.00016

The *chi*[2] statistic is computed from the sample data according to this formula:

$$chi^2 = N(phi_{XY}) \ .$$

Consider this example based upon the phi_{XY} computed between viewing of "Captain Kangaroo" and viewing of "Electric Company" of + .40825. Let $H_o: phi_{XY} = 0$ and $H_R: phi_{XY} \neq 0$.

$$chi^2 = (10)(.40825)$$

$$chi^2 = +4.0825 \ (prob. \leqslant .01) \ .$$

The correlation coefficient is the basis of many of the more sophisticated methods of analysis called "multivariate statistics." In addition, correlations may show not only that two variables are related but to what extent as well.

Assignment #7–Correlation

Two measures, information retention (X_i) and attention (Y_i) were taken from a random sample of 30 persons who viewed a preview of a new television commercial. Compute the product-moment correlation coefficient for the relationship of these two measures in this sample.

X_i	Y_i
3	8
4	9
7	9
6	8
2	7
3	9
5	8
7	9
4	8
3	8
3	8
4	9
7	9
5	8
3	7
2	8
6	8
4	5
7	6
3	5
7	6
6	8
5	9
4	7
3	8
3	9
4	7
5	8
7	9
6	7

Lesson Eight: How Well Did We Measure?—Reliability and Validity

VALIDITY
  Face validity
  Criterion validity
  Construct validity

RELIABILITY
  Test-Retest reliability
  Internal consistency reliability

NOTATION—r_{XX}, KR –20

Validity

In general, the validity of a measure addresses the question, "Did the investigator in fact measure those attributes he intended to measure?" The varieties of validity differ in the proof offered in answer to this basic question.

Face Validity. This is the sort of validity most frequently raised as an issue by laymen. High face validity implies that the measure looks as though it should be measuring what it purports to measure. The PULSE Audience Surveys consisted of face-to-face interviews with samples of radio listeners. Although the size and coverage of these PULSE surveys was more restricted than those of the PULSE's larger competitors, many station managers believed that due to the face-to-face interviews, from the "face" of things, the PULSE method must have had validity—face validity.

Construct Validity. Construct validity implies a close relationship between a measure and a theoretical notion, or construct. Consider the construct, "good taste in music." One cannot be certain that such a quality exists. But one may theorize that, if "good taste in music" does exist, it should be manifest in attendance at concerts, purchase of certain recordings, and participation in music appreciation efforts. If the measures used to reflect this construct include such theoretically relevant data, then those measures are said to have construct validity.

Criterion Validity. A criterion is an already respected measure against which we may test a candidate measure. Suppose that an investigator in educational television wants a measure of "success in studies at school." After constructing his measure and applying it to a sample of students, he may wish to compare his new measure with grade-point-average, an independent measure of the same attribute—or criterion of "success in studies at school." The appropriate form for such a comparison would be a product-moment correlation of the new measure with grade-point-average. The correlation coefficient that would result would then be called a *validity coefficient.*

Reliability

Reliability as an issue in measurement addresses the question, "How repeatable are the results of this measure?" Or, in other terms, to what extent would these measurements be the same if the measure were applied again under the same circumstances?

The reliability coefficient, r_{XX}, is a theoretic value, the agreement of a set of error-free scores with the corresponding set of actual scores. There are a number of routines for developing reliability coefficients. Two of these routines, test-retest correlation and internal consistency indices, are discussed here.

Test-retest. Test-retest reliability is a reliability coefficient computed as the product-moment correlation between scores of a particular group on the same tests administered on two separate but otherwise comparable occasions. In such a routine we might measure "loyalty to television" among a group of viewers on an evening when sports programs dominate, then readminister the test on another evening of the same sort among the same viewers. Computing a product-moment correlation from these two sets of scores would result in a *test-retest correlation coefficient,* an index of reliability.

Internal consistency. An internal consistency reliability coefficient is computed from a single administration of a measure. It is based on the notion that all elements in a multi-item exam or measure should be related to one another and to total scores. The most familiar routine for computing an internal consistency reliability coefficient is Kuder-Richardson 20, KR-20, a computational routine for the reliability coefficient of a measure made up of dichotomous items. The formula is:

$$ r_{XX} = \frac{k}{k-1} \left(1 - \frac{\Sigma pq}{S_T^2} \right) $$

where r_{XX} = reliability coefficient

k = number of items (questions) in the measure

pq = variance of each item

S_T^2 = variance in total scores.

In the example that follows, a measure of "loyalty to soap operas" consisted of ten dichotomous questions. The instrument was administered to 10 respondents (10 is too small a number for such studies in the real world—only 10 respondents appear to simplify the illustration) to estimate the reliability of the measure.

RESPONDENT NUMBER	1	2	3	4	5	6	7	8	9	10	TOTAL SCORE	SQUARE OF TOTAL TOTAL SCORE
1		1		1	1	1	1		1	1	7	49
2	1	1	1	1	1	1	1		1	1	9	81
3	1	1		1	1		1	1	1		7	49
4	1		1		1		1		1		5	25
5	1	1	1			1	1	1			6	36
6	1								1		2	4
7		1	1	1		1	1		1	1	7	49
8	1	1	1								3	9
9	1									1	2	4
10	1		1				1	1	1		5	25
Σ	8	6	6	4	4	4	7	3	7	4	53	331
$p = \dfrac{\Sigma X}{N}$	.8	.6	.6	.4	.4	.4	.7	.3	.7	.4		
$q = 1 - p$	.2	.4	.4	.6	.6	.6	.3	.7	.3	.6		
pq	.16	.24	.24	.24	.24	.24	.21	.21	.21	.24	$\Sigma pq = 2.23$	

$$ S_T^2 = \frac{\Sigma X_T^2}{N} - \left(\frac{\Sigma X_T}{N} \right)^2 $$

$$ = 33.1 - 28.89 $$

$$ S_T^2 = 5.01 $$

$$r_{XX} = \frac{k}{k-1}\left(1 - \frac{\Sigma pq}{S_T^2}\right)$$

$$= \frac{10}{9}\left(1 - \frac{2.23}{5.01}\right)$$

$$= 1.1111\,(1 - .44110)$$

$$= 1.1111\,(.55490)$$

$$r_{XX} = .61654 .$$

Unfortunately, many in radio and television research do not report the validity or reliability of the measures they employ. The advantages of doing so, however, should be apparent.

Assignment #8—Validity and Reliability

1. A program director believes that whether a person views a television station during the 5:00 P.M. hour will determine whether he will view the 6:00 P.M. hour. He asks you to study the data in 37 viewer diaries reporting viewing during these hours. You designate viewing at 5:00 P.M. as X, viewing at 6:00 P.M. as Y. The following four-fold contingency table results. Compute a validity coefficient appropriate to the program director's notion—that viewing at 5:00 P.M. is a measure of viewing at 6:00 p.m.

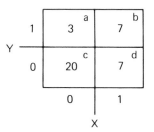

2. You have been asked to check the internal consistency reliability coefficient of an achievement test to be used to evaluate learning produced by an instructional videotape. The following data matrix resulted when you gave the test to a group of 20 students.

STUDENT	1	2	3	4	5	6	7	8	9	10	TOTAL
1	1	1	1			1	1				
2	1	1	1	1		1		1	1		
3		1	1		1	1		1	1	1	
4	1	1	1		1		1		1	1	
5	1		1	1				1			
6		1		1	1		1		1	1	
7	1	1	1		1		1	1	1	1	
8	1	1	1					1	1	1	
9	1		1	1	1	1	1	1	1		
10	1	1		1		1		1		1	
11		1	1	1	1	1					
12	1						1	1	1	1	
13	1	1	1	1	1	1	1		1	1	
14		1			1			1			
15	1		1		1		1		1	1	
16	1		1	1	1	1	1	1			
17	1		1		1						
18	1			1		1		1	1		
19	1	1	1	1	1	1	1	1			
20				1		1	1	1	1	1	

Lesson Nine: What Do They Think?—Likert Scales for Attitude

Attitude Statements
Scale Discrimination

In his book on attitude scale construction, Allen Edwards defined attitude, quoting from psychologist L.L. Thurstone, " 'the degree of positive or negative affect associated with some psychological object.' By a psychological object, Thurstone means any symbol, phrase, slogan, person, institution, ideal or idea toward which people can differ with respect to positive or negative affect."[3] Broadcasters are interested in attitudes of listeners toward broadcasting in general, toward particular stations, toward advertising in general, toward specific sponsors and specific commercials. For measurement purposes attitudes are thought to be tendencies on the part of respondents to formulate verbal statements that are favorable or unfavorable toward the object of the attitude.

Attitude measurement instruments are commonly composed of sets of attitude statements with which the respondent is asked to agree. The set of statements as a whole, rather than any particular statement, are taken as the measure of the respondent's attitude. A relatively simple form of attitude measure is the summated scale, or Likert scale, described in this lesson. It is used frequently, because it is simple and because it does not require the extensive pretesting and analysis of some other attitude measurement tools.

Developing Attitude Statements

An ideal attitude statement will be a simple declarative statement not factual in nature nor answerable by fact. The statement may come from a wide variety of sources—from the imagination of a researcher, from opinion pieces in newspapers and magazines, or from essays written by respondents. A pool of potential attitude statements is then sifted for statements which meet these criteria:

- Simple declarative structure
- Unambiguous—not capable of more than one interpretation
- Relevant to the attitude object
- Not likely to be universally agreed or disagreed to
- Contain no such absolutes as *never, always, all, none,* etc.[4]

The list below are statements used in a scale to measure attitude toward a radio station.

Statement No.
1. I can rely on the accuracy of the news I hear on this station.
2. The editorials broadcast from this station are usually in good taste.
3. The number of commercials on this station is about right.
4. The musical moods of this station are suitable for me.
5. The disc jockeys and announcers on this station are like people I would like to know.
6. The station is considered to be an important participant in community affairs.
7. In a community emergency, this is the station I could rely upon.
8. I can count on this station to show good taste in the material broadcast.
9. The average listener to this station is a person like me.
10. I look forward to the time I spend listening to this station.

Form of the Likert Questionnaire

The questionnaire for Likert attitude measurement will list three, five or seven response alternatives after each attitude statement. The respondent checks the alternative nearest his or her personal position. Five alternative items may look like these:

INSTRUCTIONS. Following each statement below check the one alternative which best describes your feelings about the statement.

1. I can rely upon the accuracy of news I hear on this station.
   ___ Strongly Agree
   _X_ Agree
   ___ Undecided
   ___ Disagree
   ___ Strongly Disagree
2. The editorials broadcast from this station are usually in good taste.
   ___ Strongly Disagree
   ___ Disagree
   ___ Undecided
   _X_ Agree
   ___ Strongly Agree

These responses are scored by the investigator in one of three ways.

Strongly Agree	5		1		+2
Agree	4		2		+1
Undecided	3	or	3	or	0
Disagree	2		4		-1
Strongly Disagree	1		5		-2

Any of these scoring codes works well. The first is probably the most frequently encountered in the "real" world of research. For that reason it will be used in the examples given here.

Reducing Likert Data

Let us assume that the matrix below resulted from administering the instrument for attitude toward a radio station:

Statement	Respondent																			
	1	2	3	4	5	6	7	8	9	10	11	12	13	14	15	16	17	18	19	20
1. Accuracy of news	4	3	2	4	4	4	3	3	4	2	4	3	4	4	5	5	3	4	5	2
2. Editorials in good taste	3	5	3	5	4	3	2	4	5	1	4	5	3	5	5	5	3	4	4	1
3. Number of commercials	2	4	2	4	4	3	3	3	5	1	2	4	2	3	4	4	3	3	3	1
4. Musical moods	4	2	2	5	4	4	3	4	4	2	3	2	2	4	4	4	2	4	4	2
5. Disc jockey and announcers	3	1	1	5	4	3	4	4	4	1	3	2	1	4	5	2	3	4	4	1
6. Participant in community affairs	1	1	1	3	3	2	2	2	3	1	1	1	1	2	3	3	4	2	3	1
7. Use in an emergency	3	1	3	4	2	2	2	3	5	1	3	1	4	3	4	2	4	4	4	2
8. Good taste	4	3	2	4	1	4	3	3	5	2	4	2	2	3	4	2	2	3	5	1
9. Average listener like me	3	3	1	5	1	4	3	4	4	1	4	3	1	4	4	1	2	4	4	2
10. Look forward to listening	4	5	1	5	1	4	4	4	4	1	4	4	1	4	5	1	3	5	4	2
SUM OF RATINGS	31	28	18	44	28	33	29	34	43	13	32	27	21	36	43	29	30	37	40	15
		L	H						H	L			L		H				H	L

The top 20 percent of the respondents—in terms of total scores have been designated "H." The lowest 20 percent in terms of summed rating scores have been designated "L."

The next step is to eliminate from the data responses to those statements that will not discriminate between high (H) and low (L) groups. The test for discrimination used here is the *t* test of independent means discussed in Lesson Five. The example is continued below.

Statement	HIGH GROUP 4	9	15	19	$\bar{X}_H$	LOW GROUP 3	10	13	20	$\bar{X}_L$	crit. $t_{\pm 0.5;\, df=6} = +1.943$
1	4	4	5	5	4.5	2	2	4	2	2.5	+ 3.46100*
2	5	5	5	4	4.75	3	1	3	1	2.0	+ 4.37095*
3	4	5	4	3	4.0	2	1	2	1	1.5	+ 4.99999*
4	5	4	4	4	4.25	2	2	2	2	2.0	+ 8.99999*
5	5	4	5	4	4.5	1	1	1	1	1.0	+12.12435*
6	3	3	3	3	3.0	1	1	1	1	1.0	∞
7	4	5	4	4	4.25	3	1	4	2	2.5	+ 2.52810*
8	4	5	4	5	4.5	2	2	2	1	1.75	+ 7.20119*
9	5	4	4	4	4.25	1	1	1	2	1.25	+ 8.48528*
10	5	4	5	4	4.5	1	1	1	2	1.25	+ 8.51049*

*$p \leqslant .05$

Since from these *t* tests of independent means it appears that all statements significantly discriminate between uppermost and lowest fifths of the sample data, all statements are retained in the analysis. The data for any statement which did not reach significance in this analysis of high versus low quintiles would be removed from further consideration. The score for each respondent over the remaining statements would then be summed to yield that respondent's net attitude score, with higher total scores corresponding to more favorable attitudes.

In Sum

The Likert technique for measuring attitude is a relatively simple one, making attitude relatively accessible to even the beginning researcher.

Assignment #9–Likert Scales

An attitude measurement instrument was constructed along Likert lines to assess attitudes toward local television news programs. The questionnaire was administered to 30 viewers selected at random from the Dallas, Texas market. Results follow. Which attitude statements should be removed from further analysis?

Statement	$\bar{X}$ High Fifth	$\bar{X}$ Low Fifth	t
1	3.0	3.0	0
2	4.0	3.5	+1.75
3	5.0	2.0	+5.0
4	5.0	1.0	+12.0
5	4.0	3.75	+.50
6	4.25	2.75	+2.0
7	3.75	2.5	+1.30
8	4.25	2.5	+1.80
9	3.5	1.0	+9.63
10	3.25	2.75	+1.90

Lesson Ten: Contrasting More Than Two–Analysis of Variance

Factorial ANOVA
Repeated Measure ANOVA
F-statistic
Hotelling's T^2

The *t* tests discussed in Lesson Five provided hypothesis tests between two means of small samples. It may be important upon occasions to compare more than two sets of scores. Upon such occasions it will be necessary to use a statistical routine known as *Analysis of Variance* (ANOVA).

Factorial Designs

A factorial design is one in which groups of equal size experience stimuli which vary along a single dimension. In a laboratory study, for example, Group I consisting of 10 subjects may listen to a commercial for Soft Drink A read by a female announcer; Group II of 10 subjects will hear the same commercial read by a male announcer; Group III will hear the same commercial read by two voices. The dimension along which the commercials differ is the sex of the announcer:

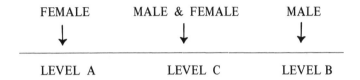

FEMALE	MALE & FEMALE	MALE
↓	↓	↓
LEVEL A	LEVEL C	LEVEL B

The null hypothesis for this *factorial design* would be H_o: $\mu_A = \mu_B = \mu_C$. The mean of each group will be equal to the mean of each other group within the limits of the variability imposed by predictable sampling error.

The research hypothesis could take a number of forms: H_R: $\left. \begin{array}{l} \mu_A \neq \\ \mu_B \neq \\ \mu_C \neq \end{array} \right\} \mu$

This one says that the mean scores of each group of respondents differs from the grand mean μ—all groups considered together—by an amount greater than could be explained as sampling error.

Model of Factorial Analysis of Variance

Statisticians in discussing analysis of variance find it convenient to refer to an algebraic model which incorporates their assumptions about individual scores. Such a model for a simple factorial design might be:

$$X_{ij} = \mu + effect_j + error_{ij}$$

where X_{ij} = the ith individual in the jth treatment group

μ = the mean of the population from which all samples of respondents were drawn

$effect_j$ = the effect produced by treatment j

$error_{ij}$ = the error of measurement involved in measuring individual i in the jth treatment level.

In performing the analysis of variance the $effect_j$ term will be estimated as the difference between the grand mean of all scores and the means of the cells or subject groups. The error term will be taken as the average variability *within* the cells or treatment groups.

Computing the Factorial Analysis of Variance

The analysis of variance computations are based upon squares or squared values. Sums of squares (SS) are computed for each source of variance in the data. Sums of squares are divided by appropriate degrees of freedom to yield mean squares (MS). The mean squares in ratio are the test statistic F for the analysis. These values are summarized for the one-factor factorial design in the table below.

Source of Variance	df	Sum of Squares	MS	F
TOTAL	$aN - 1$	$SS_{tot} = \sum_i^N \sum_j^a X_{ij}^2 - \dfrac{\left(\sum_i^N \sum_j^a X_{ij}\right)^2}{aN}$		
Between Levels	$a - 1$	$SS_A = \sum_j^a \dfrac{\left(\sum_i^N X_{ij}\right)^2}{N} - \dfrac{\left(\sum_i^N \sum_j^a X_{ij}\right)^2}{aN}$	$\dfrac{SS_A}{a-1}$	$\dfrac{MS_A}{MS_{S/A}}$
Within groups	$a(N - 1)$	$SS_{S/A} = \sum_i^N \sum_j^a X_{ij}^2 - \sum_j^a \dfrac{\left(\sum_i^N X_{ij}\right)^2}{N}$	$\dfrac{SS_{S/A}}{a(N-1)}$	

The usefulness of the table above is more apparent when an illustration is given. Three groups of 10 radio listeners each were drawn at random from the Dallas, Texas, audience. Each group listened to one of the three commercials outlined above. They were then asked to rate their liking of the commercial on a scale from 1 (like a little) to 10 (like a lot). In the illustration therefore, N (the number of respondents per group) = 10. The levels of treatment a = 3. The various degrees of freedom called for would be:

Source	df
TOTAL	29
Between levels A	2
Within groups S/A	18

The SS for Total is a familiar equation—that for variance—the variance of all 30 scores collected.

The SS_A is the total variance among means of the three groups of the study.

The $SS_{S/A}$ is the total variance inside the treatment groups. Given the scores below the analysis of variance is computed.

	Group I (Male Voice)		Group II (Female Voice)		Group III (Mixed)	
	X_{i1}	X_{i1}^2	X_{i2}	X_{i2}^2	X_{i3}	X_{i3}^2
	4	16	8	64	6	36
	7	49	7	49	6	36
	3	9	9	81	5	25
	2	4	4	16	3	9
	1	1	3	9	2	4
	4	16	5	25	4	16
	4	16	6	36	5	25
	3	9	7	49	5	25
	2	4	7	49	4	16
	2	4	6	36	4	16
Subtotals	32	128	62	414	44	208
	$\sum_i^N X_{i1}$	$\sum_i^N X_{i1}^2$	$\sum_i^N X_{i2}$	$\sum_i^N X_{i2}^2$	$\sum_i^N X_{i3}$	$\sum_i^N X_{i3}^2$
	$\bar{X}_{i1} = 3.2$		$\bar{X}_{i2} = 6.2$		$\bar{X}_{i3} = 4.4$	

$$SS_{tot} = \sum_i^N \sum_j^a X_{ij}^2 - \frac{\left(\sum_i^N \sum_j^a X_{ij}\right)^2}{aN}$$

$$= \left(\sum_i^N X_{i1}^2 + \sum_i^N X_{i2}^2 + \sum_i^N X_{i3}^2\right) - \frac{\left(\sum_i^N X_{i1} + \sum_i^N X_{i2} + \sum_i^N X_{i3}\right)^2}{3(10)}$$

$$= (128 + 414 + 208) - \frac{(32 + 62 + 44)^2}{30}$$

$$= 750 - \frac{138^2}{30}$$

$$= 750 - \frac{19044}{30}$$

$$= 750 - 634.8$$

$$SS_{tot} = 115.2$$

$$MS_{tot} = \frac{115.2}{29}$$

$$MS_{tot} = 3.94241$$

$$SS_A = \sum_j^a \frac{\left(\sum_i^N X_{ij}\right)^2}{N} - \frac{\left(\sum_i^N \sum_j^a X_{ij}\right)^2}{aN}$$

$$= \left[\frac{\left(\sum_i^N X_{i1}\right)^2}{10} + \frac{\left(\sum_i^N X_{i2}\right)^2}{10} + \frac{\left(\sum_i^N X_{i3}\right)^2}{10}\right] - 634.8$$

$$= \left[\frac{32^2}{10} + \frac{62^2}{10} + \frac{44^2}{10}\right] - 634.8$$

$$= \left[\frac{1024}{10} + \frac{3844}{10} + \frac{1936}{10}\right] - 634.8$$

$$= \frac{6804}{10} - 634.8$$

$$= 680.4 - 634.8$$

$$SS_A = 45.6$$

$$MS_A = \frac{SS_A}{a - 1}$$

$$MS_A = \frac{45.6}{2}$$

$$MS_A = 22.8$$

$$SS_{S/A} = \sum_i^N \sum_j^a X_{ij}^2 - \sum_j^a \frac{\left(\sum_i^N X_{ij}\right)^2}{N}$$

$$= \left(\sum_i^N X_{i1}^2 + \sum_i^N X_{i2}^2 + \sum_i^N X_{i3}^2\right) - 680.4$$

$$= (128 + 414 + 208) - 680.4$$

$$= 750 - 680.4$$

$$SS_{S/A} = 69.6$$

$$MS_{S/A} = \frac{SS_{S/A}}{a(N-1)}$$

$$= \frac{69.6}{27}$$

$$MS_{S/A} = 2.578$$

$$F = \frac{MS_A}{MS_{S/A}}$$

$$= \frac{22.8}{2.578}$$

$$F_{2,27} = 8.84406$$

(Critical F from Table V, Appendix D at .05 level = 3.35)

This analysis of variance would typically be reported in a table like this.

Source of Variance	df	Mean Square	F
TOTAL	29	3.972	
Announcer	2	22.800	8.844 ($p \leqslant .05$)
Within	27	2.578	

The results of this analysis of variance indicate that sex of voices on the commercial did make a difference which reached statistical significance when sampling error was considered. The means of the three groups were distributed:

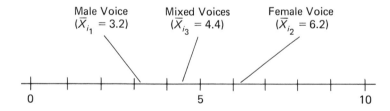

Repeated Measures Analysis of Variance

Sometimes an analysis of variance is performed on data gathered from more than two measurements taken from the same sample of respondents. For example, given the problem of evaluating the same three commercials differing in sex of the announcer, the investigator might have presented all three versions of the commercials to each of the thirty respondents. In this case the liking of one commercial is contrasted with liking by the same individual for the other two commercials. On the whole the *repeated measures* study design would be more efficient in the use of subjects; since each commercial would have been heard by 30 respondents, whereas in the factorial study design each commercial was heard by only 10 respondents.

One important procedural matter in the case of repeated measures studies of response to messages is that the order in which messages are presented will affect the response to each message. Therefore, the careful investigator will present the messages to an equal part of the sample in each possible order. In the case of three messages (A, B, C) the possible orders of presentation are:

(1) ABC
(2) ACB
(3) BAC
(4) BCA
(5) CAB
(6) CBA

Consequently, one-sixth of the sample would hear order (1), another sixth order (2), and so on.

The model of each score for repeated measures analysis of variance is different than that for a factorial analysis of variance:

$$X_{ij} = \mu + effect_j + difference_i + subject\text{-}treatment\ \ interaction_{ij}\ + error_{ij}$$

where

$X_{ij} =$ the score of the ith respondent to the jth message
$\mu =$ grand mean of the parent population
$effect_j =$ influence of the jth message
$difference_i =$ characteristic response set of *individual_i*
subject-treatment
$interaction_{ij} =$ unique interaction of *individual_i* and *message_j*
$error_{ij} =$ error inherent in measuring the response of individual i to the jth message

The computational routine for repeated measures analysis of variance provides for each of the elements in this model.

Source of Variance	df	Sum of Squares	MS	F
TOTAL	$aN - 1$	$SS_{tot} = \dfrac{\sum\limits_{i}^{N}\left(\sum\limits_{j}^{a}X_{ij}\right)^2}{a} - \dfrac{\left(\sum\limits_{i}^{N}\sum\limits_{j}^{a}X_{ij}\right)^2}{aN}$	$\dfrac{SS_{tot}}{aN - 1}$	
Between Levels	$a - 1$	$SS_A = \dfrac{\sum\limits_{j}^{a}\left(\sum\limits_{i}^{N}X_{ij}\right)^2}{N} - \dfrac{\left(\sum\limits_{i}^{N}\sum\limits_{j}^{a}X_{ij}\right)^2}{aN}$	$\dfrac{SS_A}{a - 1}$	$\dfrac{MS_A}{MS_{S/A}}$
Individual Differences and respondent-treatment interaction	$(N - 1)(a - 1)$	$SS_{S/A} = \sum\limits_{i}^{N}\sum\limits_{j}^{a}X_{ij}^2 - \dfrac{\left(\sum\limits_{i}^{N}\sum\limits_{j}^{a}X_{ij}\right)^2}{aN} - SS_{tot} - SS_A$	$\dfrac{SS_{S/A}}{(N - 1)(a - 1)}$	

The procedures that follow from this table are relatively straightforward. In the sum of squares column the only unfamiliar term is the first fraction in the SS_{tot},

$$\frac{\sum\limits_{i}^{N}\left(\sum\limits_{j}^{a}X_{ij}\right)^2}{a}$$

This will require us to create a dummy cell in the analysis composed of the sum of the scores given by each respondent.

In the illustration that follows, the three commercials were played for 12 respondents, 2 respondents hearing the commercials in each of the 6 possible orders of presentation.

Respondent	Heard Order #	X_{i1} Male Voice	$X_{i_1}^2$	X_{i2} Female Voice	X_{i2}^2	X_{i3} Mixed Voices	X_{i3}^2	$\sum\limits_{j}^{a}X_{ij}$ Dummy Cell	$\left(\sum\limits_{j}^{a}X_{ij}\right)^2$
1	(1)	4	16	8	64	6	36	18	324
2	(1)	7	49	7	49	6	36	20	400
3	(2)	3	9	9	81	5	25	17	289
4	(2)	2	4	4	16	3	9	9	81
5	(3)	1	1	3	9	2	4	6	36
6	(3)	4	16	5	25	4	16	13	169
7	(4)	4	16	6	36	5	25	15	225
8	(4)	3	9	7	49	5	25	15	225
9	(5)	2	4	7	49	4	16	13	169
10	(5)	2	4	6	36	4	16	12	144
11	(6)	3	9	5	25	5	25	13	169
12	(6)	2	4	7	49	8	64	17	289
		37	141	74	488	57	297	168	2520
		$\sum\limits_{i}^{N}X_{i1}$	$\sum\limits_{i}^{N}X_{i1}^2$	$\sum\limits_{i}^{N}X_{i2}$	$\sum\limits_{i}^{N}X_{i2}^2$	$\sum\limits_{i}^{N}X_{i3}$	$\sum\limits_{i}^{N}X_{i3}^2$	$\sum\limits_{i}^{N}\sum\limits_{j}^{a}X_{ij}$	$\sum\limits_{i}^{N}\left(\sum\limits_{j}^{a}X_{ij}\right)^2$
		$\bar{X}_{i1}=3.08333$		$\bar{X}_{i2}=6.16667$		$\bar{X}_{i3}=4.75$			

$$SS_{tot} = \frac{2520}{3} - \frac{168^2}{3(12)}$$

$$= 840 - \frac{28224}{36}$$

$$= 840 - 784$$

$$SS_{tot} = 56$$

$$SS_A = \frac{37^2 + 74^2 + 57^2}{12} - 784$$

$$= \frac{1396 + 5476 + 3249}{12} - 784$$

$$= \frac{10094}{12} - 784$$

$$= 841.16667 - 784$$

$$SS_A = 57.16667$$

$$SS_{S/A} = (141 + 488 + 297) - 784 - 56 - 57.16667$$

$$= 926 - 897.16667$$

$$SS_{S/A} = 28.83333$$

$$MS_{tot} = \frac{56}{11}$$

$$MS_{tot} = 5.09091$$

$$MS_A = \frac{57.16667}{2}$$

$$MS_A = 28.58333$$

$$MS_{S/A} = \frac{28.83333}{11(2)}$$

$$MS_{S/A} = 1.31061$$

$$F = \frac{MS_A}{MS_{S/A}}$$

$$= \frac{28.58333}{1.31061}$$

$$F_{2,22} = 21.80918 \ (p \leqslant .05)$$

(Critical F, with $df = 2,22$ at .05 level, $= 3.44$).

This analysis would be reported in a table like this:

Source of Variance	df	Mean Square	F
Total	11	5.09091	
Announcer	2	28.58333	21.80918 ($p \leqslant .05$)
Within Subjects	22	1.31061	

At this point a potential problem of *heterogeneity* of covariance should be mentioned. Ideally respondent-treatment interactions should be of the same degree with each of the three messages presented. If so, this is a situation known as *homogeneity of covariance* and must hold if credence is to be given to the F test above. If the other condition— heterogeneity of covariance holds, then such a degree of bias enters into this F test that it cannot be taken seriously. A simple test for homogeneity of covariance is to test the F computed above against a critical F with degrees of freedom 1 and N-1. In this case that F is $4.84_{1, 11}$. It is justifiable then to have confidence in the F test against a-1 and (N-1) (a-1) degrees of freedom. If the computed F is not significant against 1 and N-1 degrees of freedom, then the data should be analyzed according to a procedure known as Hotelling's T^2. This procedure is too advanced for this discussion but is available at computer centers which deal with statistical analysis.[5]

In Sum

The analysis of variance procedures outlined here are basic in that they envision the effects of programs or messages that vary in only one dimension (such as sex of announcer). More advanced analysis of variance procedures are available which permit study of any number of independent variables in the same study (for example, the effect of musical background and commercial length as well as sex of announcer). Details of these procedures are available in a number of works listed at the end of Appendix C.

Assignment #10—Analysis of Variance

A station manager at a Midwestern television station has become concerned about the portrayal of blacks in a network situation comedy carried by his station. The station conducts a study among blacks, Latin-Americans and among Caucasians under 21 years of age. Each of the three groups is selected by a random procedure which provides 10 respondents in each group. Each respondent is asked to rate the situation comedy as to the favorableness of its portrayal of blacks. The respondents are asked to express their judgment on a scale of 1 (least favorable) to 10 (most favorable). The scores below were the result. Perform an analysis of variance of this data to assess whether portrayal of blacks in this network situation comedy might contribute to cross-racial misunderstanding in the community.

Blacks	Latin-Americans	Caucasians
8	8	2
7	8	3
6	6	2
5	6	4
1	4	9
8	3	1
7	2	2
8	1	3
8	5	1
7	4	2

NOTES—APPENDIX C

1. A. E. Brandt, "A Test for Significance in a Unique Sample," *Journal of the American Statistical Association,* Vol. 28, 1933, 434–7.
2. Frederick Williams, *Reasoning with Statistics* (New York: Holt, Rinehart and Winston, 1968), p. 134.
3. Allen L. Edwards, *Techniques of Attitude Scale Construction* (New York: Appleton-Century-Crofts, 1957), p. 2.
4. *Op. cit.,* pp. 13–14.
5. Jerome L. Myers, *Fundamentals of Experimental Design* (Boston: Allyn and Bacon, 1966), pp. 161–2.

Solution to Assignment #1—Frequency Distributions and Measures of Central Tendency

a. Frequency table

X_i		f
1.00 (.951–1.050)	/	1
.90 (.851– .950)	///	3
.80 (.751– .850)	//	2
.70 (.651– .750)	/////////	9
.60 (.551– .650)	///////	7
.50 (.451– .550)	///	3
.40 (.351– .450)	////////	8
.30 (.251– .350)	/////////	9
.20 (.151– .250)	///	3
.10 (.051– .150)	///	3
.00 (.00 – .050)	//	2

b. Frequency polygon

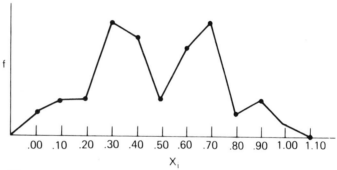

c. Frequency Histogram

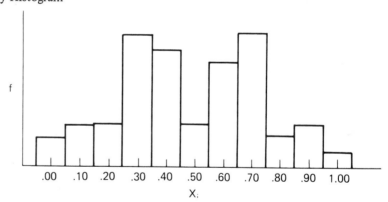

d. Modes—.30, .44, .67
   Median—.445
   Mean:

$$\bar{X} = \frac{\Sigma X_i}{N}$$

$$= \frac{24.68}{50}$$

$$\bar{X} = .4936$$

Solution to Assignment #1 continued

e. Roughly symmetrical, multi-modal.

Solution to Assignment #2—How Typical is Typical?

a. Compare the variance of this distribution of attitude scores using the definitional formula for variance. Show your work:

X_i	X_i^2	$X_i - \bar{X}$	$(X_i - \bar{X})^2$
11	121	3.4	11.56
8	64	.4	.16
3	9	−4.6	21.16
5	25	−2.6	6.76
10	100	2.4	5.76
7	49	− .6	.36
5	25	−2.6	6.76
13	169	5.4	29.16
2	4	−5.6	31.36
6	36	−1.6	2.56
9	81	1.4	1.96
14	196	6.4	40.96
2	4	−5.6	31.36
14	196	6.4	40.96
4	16	−3.6	12.96
12	144	4.4	19.36
7	48	− .6	.36
15	225	7.4	54.76
9	81	1.4	1.96
14	196	6.4	40.98
13	169	5.4	29.16
2	4	−5.6	31.36
1	1	−6.6	43.56
3	9	−4.6	21.16
1	1	−6.6	43.56
190 =	1974 =		530.00 =
ΣX_i	ΣX_i^2		$\Sigma (X_i - \bar{X})^2$

$$\bar{X} = \frac{\Sigma X_i}{N}$$

$$= \frac{190}{25}$$

$$\bar{X} = 7.6$$

Definitional Formula:

$$S^2 = \frac{\Sigma (X_i - \bar{X})^2}{N}$$

$$= \frac{530}{25}$$

$$S^2 = 21.20$$

b. Compute the variance using the computational formula. Show your work.

$$S^2 = \frac{\Sigma X_i^2}{N} - \left(\frac{\Sigma X_i}{N} \right)^2$$

$$= \frac{1974}{25} - \left(\frac{190}{25} \right)^2$$

$$= 78.96 - (7.6)^2$$

$$= 78.96 - 57.76$$

$$S^2 = 21.2$$

c. What is the standard deviation of the distribution of scores?

$$S = \sqrt{S^2} \qquad = \sqrt{21.2} \qquad = 4.60433$$

Solution to Assignment #2 continued

d. How many standard deviations is a score of 10 or above or below the mean of this distribution of attitude scores?

A score of 10 is 2.4 more than a mean of 7.6 (10 - 7.6 = 2.4)

A deviation of 2.4 is .52125 standard deviations below the mean when the standard deviation is -4.60435 (2.4 ÷ 4.60435 = .52125).

Thus we may say that a score of ten is .52125 standard deviations above the mean of this distribution of scores.

e. How many standard deviations is a score of 3 above or below the mean of this distribution of attitude scores?

A score of 3 is 4.6 less than a mean of 7.6 (3 -7.6 = - 4.6).

A deviation of 4.6 is .99906 standard deviations when the standard deviation is 4.60433 (- 4.6 ÷ 4.604333 = - .99906).

Thus we may say that a score of 3 is .99906 standard deviations below the mean of this distribution of scores.

Solution to Assignment #3—Standard Scores and Normal Distributions

1. No, this would not be random selection. Each half of the homes has an equal chance of being selected, but the selection of each home is not independent of the selection of each other home.

2. A standard score is computed by subtracting the mean of the population from the measurement in question and dividing the remainder by the standard deviation.

$$Z_i = \frac{X_i - \mu}{\sigma}$$

$Z_{15} = -.9$ $Z_{18} = -.6$ $Z_{20} = -.4$ $Z_{21} = -.3$ $Z_{24} = 0$

$Z_{25} = +.1$ $Z_{28} = +.4$ $Z_{29.5} = +.55$ $Z_{32.4} = +.84$

$Z_{40} = +1.6$ $Z_{34} = +1.0$

3. In a cumulative normal distribution (see your table) 84 percent of the measurements fall below 1.0 standard deviation above the mean. In problem #2, $Z_{34} = +1.0$, thus is located at the 84th percentile of the distribution.

4.

X_i^2	X_i	f	$f(X_i)$	$f(X_i)^2$
16	4	2	8	32
25	5	3	15	75
36	6	1	6	36
		$6 = N$	$29 = \Sigma X_i$	$143 = \Sigma X_i^2$

$$S^2 = \frac{\Sigma X_i^2}{N} - \left(\frac{\Sigma X_i}{N}\right)^2$$

$$= \frac{143}{6} - \left(\frac{29}{6}\right)^2$$

$$= 23.8333 - (4.83333)^2$$

$$= 23.83333 - 23.36111$$

$$S^2 = .47222$$

$$S = \sqrt{S^2} = .68718$$

Solution to Assignment #3 continued

$$\text{est. } \sigma_{\overline{X}} = \frac{S}{\sqrt{N-1}}$$

$$= \frac{.68718}{\sqrt{5}}$$

$$= \frac{.68718}{2.23607}$$

$$\text{est. } \sigma_{\overline{X}} = .30732$$

Solution to Assignment #4—Hypothesis Testing

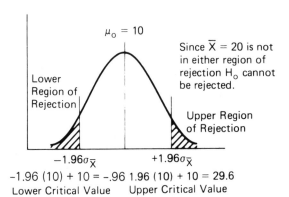

$\mu_o = 10$

Since $\overline{X} = 20$ is not in either region of rejection H_o cannot be rejected.

Lower Region of Rejection

Upper Region of Rejection

$-1.96\sigma_{\overline{X}}$ $+1.96\sigma_{\overline{X}}$

$-1.96 (10) + 10 = -.96$ $1.96 (10) + 10 = 29.6$
Lower Critical Value   Upper Critical Value

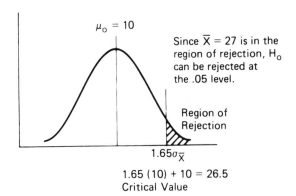

$\mu_o = 10$

Since $\overline{X} = 27$ is in the region of rejection, H_o can be rejected at the .05 level.

Region of Rejection

$1.65\sigma_{\overline{X}}$

$1.65 (10) + 10 = 26.5$
Critical Value

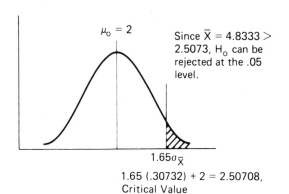

$\mu_o = 2$

Since $\overline{X} = 4.8333 > 2.5073$, H_o can be rejected at the .05 level.

$1.65\sigma_{\overline{X}}$

$1.65 (.30732) + 2 = 2.50708$,
Critical Value

Solution to Assignment #5—The *t* Tests

X_i	X_i^2
.67	.4489
.90	.8100
.78	.6084
.83	.6889
.92	.8464
.50	.2500
.94	.8836
.83	.6889
.82	.6724
.73	.5329
.55	.3025
.70	.4900
.93	.8649
.92	.8464
.91	.8281
.71	.5041
.65	.4225
.85	.7225
.87	.7569
.71	.5041
15.72	12.6724

a. $H_o: \mu = .85; H_R: \mu \neq .85$

b. Step 1—Find S^2

$$S^2 = \frac{\Sigma X_i^2}{N} - \left(\frac{\Sigma X_i}{N}\right)^2$$

$$= \frac{12.6724}{20} - \left(\frac{15.72}{20}\right)^2$$

$$= .63362 - (.786)^2$$

$$= .63362 - .61780$$

$$S^2 = .01582; S = .12579$$

Step 2—Find est.$\sigma_{\overline{X}}$

$$\text{est } \sigma_{\overline{X}} = \frac{S}{\sqrt{N-1}}$$

$$= \frac{.12579}{\sqrt{19}}$$

$$= \frac{.12579}{4.35890}$$

$$\text{est } \sigma_{\overline{X}} = .0286$$

Step 3—Compute *t*

$$t = \frac{\overline{X} - \mu_o}{\text{est } \sigma_{\overline{X}}}$$

$$= \frac{.786 - .85}{.02886}$$

$$= \frac{-.064}{.02886}$$

$$t = -2.218$$

c. Degrees of freedom $= N - 1 = 19$

d. From the table, the critical values of *t* for a two-tailed test at the .05 level with 19 degrees of freedom are $+ 2.093$ and $- 2.093$. Therefore $t = - 2.218$ is in the lower region of rejection and can be said to be significant at the .05 level. The null hypothesis is rejected. Tutorial students scored significantly lower than students taught by the traditional method.

Solution to Assignment #5 continued

2.

X_i	X_i^2
.45	.2025
.47	.2209
.52	.2704
.93	.8649
.56	.3136
.61	.3721
.59	.3481
.58	.3364
.57	.3249
.87	.7569
.87	.7569
.53	.2809
.45	.2025
.33	.1089
.52	.2704
.76	.5776
.93	.8649
.95	.9025
.66	.4356
.53	.2809
12.68	8.6918

Step 1—Compute S^2 and S

$$S^2 = \frac{\Sigma X_i^2}{N} - \left(\frac{\Sigma X_i}{N}\right)^2$$

$$= \frac{8.6918}{20} - \left(\frac{12.68}{20}\right)^2$$

$$= .43459 - (.634)^2$$

$$= .43459 - .40196$$

$$S^2 = .03263; \ S = .18064$$

Step 2—Compute t for two independent means

$$t = \frac{\mu_T - \mu_{ITV}}{\sqrt{\frac{N_T S_T^2 + N_{ITV} S_{ITV}^2}{N_T + N_{ITV} - 2}\left(\frac{1}{N_T} + \frac{1}{N_{ITV}}\right)}}$$

$$= \frac{.786 - .634}{\sqrt{\frac{20(.01582) + 20(.03263)}{20 + 20 - 2}\left(\frac{2}{20}\right)}}$$

$$= \frac{.152}{\sqrt{\frac{.3164 + .6526}{38} \cdot \left(\frac{1}{10}\right)}}$$

$$= \frac{.152}{\sqrt{\frac{.969}{380}}}$$

$$= \frac{.152}{\sqrt{.00255}}$$

$$= \frac{.152}{.05050}$$

$$t = 3.00990$$

Step 3—Find df
$N_T + N_{ITV} - 2 = 38$

Step 4—Formulate hypotheses.
$H_o: \mu_T = \mu_{ITV}$
$H_R: \mu_T \neq \mu_{ITV}$

Step 5—Find critical values for t in table at 38 df, .05 level and two-tailed test.
crit $t_{.05;38} = \pm 2.025$

Step 6—Conclude that prob. ($t = 3.00990$) $\leqslant .05$. The null hypothesis can be rejected.
Tutorial scores are significantly higher than *ITV*.

Solution to Assignment #6–Dichotomous Data

1. Ratings

$$WKYT \quad p = \frac{\Sigma X_i}{N}$$

$$= \frac{8}{20}$$

$$p_{WKYT} = .40$$

$$WBLG \quad p = \frac{3}{20}$$

$$p_{WBLG} = .15$$

$$WLEX \quad p = \frac{3}{20}$$

$$p_{WLEX} = .15$$

$$WKLE \quad p = \frac{6}{20}$$

$$p_{WKLE} = .30$$

2. Use the table for estimating survey sample size. Refer to the .50 column as the range, .85 to .15, includes .50, and this p will always yield the largest sample size. Go down the .50 column until you encounter .05, the acceptable deviation in p, and read this row to the N column. Read out the sample size, $N = 400$.

Solution to Assignment #7– Correlation

X_i^2	X_i	X_iY_i	Y_i	Y_i^2
9	3	24	8	64
16	4	36	9	81
49	7	63	9	81
36	6	48	8	64
4	2	14	7	49
9	3	27	9	81
25	5	40	8	64
49	7	63	9	81
16	4	32	8	64
9	3	24	8	64
9	3	24	8	64
16	4	36	9	81
49	7	63	9	81
25	5	40	8	64
9	3	21	7	49
4	2	16	8	64
36	6	48	8	64
16	4	20	5	25
49	7	42	6	36
9	3	15	5	25
49	7	42	6	36
36	6	48	8	64
25	5	45	9	81
16	4	28	7	49
9	3	24	8	64
9	3	27	9	81
16	4	28	7	49
25	5	40	8	64
49	7	63	9	81
36	6	42	7	49
714	138	1083	234	1864
ΣX_i^2	ΣX_i	ΣX_iY_i	ΣY_i	ΣY_i^2

$$r_{XY} = \frac{\Sigma X_iY_i - \frac{(\Sigma X_i)(\Sigma Y_i)}{N}}{\sqrt{\Sigma X_i^2 - \frac{(\Sigma X_i)^2}{N}}\sqrt{\Sigma Y_i^2 - \frac{(\Sigma Y_i)^2}{N}}}$$

$$= \frac{1083 - \frac{(138)(234)}{30}}{\sqrt{714 - \frac{(138)^2}{30}}\sqrt{1864 - \frac{(234)^2}{30}}}$$

$$= \frac{6.6}{\sqrt{79.2}\sqrt{38.8}}$$

$$= \frac{6.6}{8.89944(6.22896)}$$

$$= \frac{6.6}{55.43430}$$

$$r_{X_iY_i} = +.11906$$

Solution to Assignment #8–Validity and Reliability

1. This problem calls for the computation of a validity coefficient. Since the data is dichotomous, the proper correlation coefficient is phi.

$$phi_{XY} = \frac{(bc - ad)}{\sqrt{(a + b)(c + d)(a + c)(b + d)}}$$

$$= \frac{140 - 21}{\sqrt{(10)(27)(23)(14)}}$$

$$= \frac{119}{\sqrt{86940}}$$

$$= \frac{119}{294.85590}$$

$$phi_{XY} = .40359$$

2.

STUDENT	1	2	3	4	5	6	7	8	9	10	TOTAL SCORE	SQUARED TOTAL SCORE
1	1	1	1			1	1				5	25
2	1	1	1	1		1		1	1		7	49
3		1	1		1	1		1	1	1	7	49
4	1	1	1		1		1		1	1	7	49
5	1		1	1				1			4	16
6		1		1	1		1		1	1	6	36
7	1	1	1		1		1	1	1	1	8	64
8	1	1	1					1	1	1	6	36
9	1		1	1	1	1	1	1	1		8	64
10	1	1		1		1		1		1	6	36
11		1	1	1	1	1					5	25
12	1						1	1	1	1	5	25
13	1	1	1	1	1	1	1		1	1	9	81
14		1			1			1			3	9
15	1		1		1		1		1	1	6	36
16	1		1	1	1	1	1	1	1		8	64
17	1		1		1						3	9
18	1			1		1	1	1	1		6	36
19	1	1	1	1	1	1	1	1			8	64
20			1		1	1	1	1	1	1	6	36
Σ	15	12	14	11	12	11	12	13	13	10	123	809
p	.75	.60	.70	.55	.60	.55	.60	.65	.65	.50		
q	.25	.40	.30	.45	.40	.45	.40	.35	.35	.50		
pq	.1875	.24	.21	.2475	.24	.2475	.24	.2275	.2275	.25	Σpq = 2.3175	

$$S_T^2 = \frac{\Sigma X^2}{N} - \left(\frac{\Sigma X}{N}\right)^2$$

$$= \frac{809}{20} - \left(\frac{123}{20}\right)^2$$

Solution to Assignment #8 continued

$$= 40.45 - (6.15)^2$$

$$= 40.45 - 37.8225$$

$$S_T^2 = 2.6275$$

$$r_{XX} = \frac{k}{k-1}\left(1 - \frac{\Sigma pq}{S_T^2}\right)$$

$$= \frac{10}{9}\left(1 - \frac{2.3175}{2.6275}\right)$$

$$= 1.11111\,(1 - .88202)$$

$$= 1.11111\,(.11798)$$

$$r_{XX} = +.13109$$

Solution to Assignment #9—Likert Scales

Since the t computed from upper and lower quintiles (based on total scores) does not reach significance (crit $t_{.05;df = 10} = +1.812$) for statements #1, 2, 5, 7, and 8, these statements should be eliminated from the questionnaire.

Solution to Assignment #10—Analysis of Variance

Blacks		Latin-Americans		Caucasians	
X_{i1}	X_{i1}^2	X_{i2}	X_{i2}^2	X_{i3}	X_{i3}^2
8	64	8	64	2	4
7	49	8	64	3	9
6	36	6	36	2	4
5	25	6	36	4	16
1	1	4	16	9	81
8	64	3	9	1	1
7	49	2	4	2	4
8	64	1	1	3	9
8	64	5	25	1	1
7	49	4	16	2	4
65	465	47	271	29	133
$\sum_i^N X_{i1}$	$\sum_i^N X_{i1}^2$	$\sum_i^N X_{i2}$	$\sum_i^N X_{i2}^2$	$\sum_i^N X_{i3}$	$\sum_i^N X_{i3}^2$

$$\overline{X}_{i1} = 6.5 \qquad \overline{X}_{i2} = 4.7 \qquad \overline{X}_{i3} = 2.9$$

$$SS_{tot} = \sum_i^N \sum_j^a X_{ij}^2 - \frac{\left(\sum_i^N \sum_j^a X_{ij}\right)^2}{aN}$$

$$= (465 + 271 + 133) - \frac{(65 + 47 + 29)^2}{3(10)}$$

$$= 869 - \frac{(141)^2}{30}$$

Solution to Assignment #9 continued

$$= 869 - \frac{1988}{30}$$

$$= 869 - 662.7$$

$$SS_{tot} = 206.3$$

$$SS_A = \sum_j^a \frac{\left(\sum_i^a X_{ij}\right)^2}{N} - \frac{\left(\sum_i^N \sum_j^a X_{ij}\right)^2}{a - N}$$

$$= \frac{65^2 + 47^2 + 29^2}{10} - 662.7$$

$$= \frac{4225 + 2209 + 841}{10} - 662.7$$

$$SS_A = \frac{7275}{10} - 662.7$$

$$= 727.5 - 662.7$$

$$SS_A = 64.8$$

$$SS_{S/A} = \sum_i^N \sum_j^a X_{ij}^2 - \sum_j^a \frac{\left(\sum_i^N X_{ij}\right)^2}{N}$$

$$= 869 - 727.5$$

$$SS_{S/A} = 141.5$$

$$MS_A = \frac{SS_A}{a - 1}$$

$$= \frac{64.8}{2}$$

$$MS_A = 32.4$$

$$MS_{S/A} = \frac{SS_{S/A}}{a(N - 1)}$$

$$= \frac{141.5}{27}$$

$$MS_{S/A} = 5.25074$$

$$F = \frac{MS_A}{MS_{S/A}}$$

$$= \frac{32.4}{5.24074}$$

Solution to Assignment #9 continued

$$F_{2,27} = 6.18233$$

(Crit $F_{2,27}$ at .05 level from Table V = 3.35)

We can conclude that the perception of the black roles as favorable does differ across these three groups.

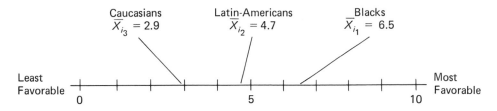

Since blacks in this case seem to consider the portrayals in the situation comedy more favorably than do either Caucasians or Latin-Americans, the program may not be having adverse effects in the market. A second study after more episodes have been broadcast would provide more proof.

Appendix D-
Mathematical
and Statistical Tables

Table I. Squares and Roots

N	N^2	$N^{1/2}$	$(10N)^{1/2}$	$.1N^{1/2}$	$.01N^{1/2}$
1	1	1.0	3.16228	.31623	.10000
2	4	1.41421	4.47214	.47214	.14142
3	9	1.73206	5.47728	.54773	.17321
4	16	2.0	6.32456	.63246	.20000
5	25	2.23607	7.07107	.70711	.22361
6	36	2.44949	7.74597	.77460	.24495
7	49	2.64575	8.36660	.83666	.26458
8	64	2.82843	8.94427	.89443	.28284
9	81	3.0	9.48683	.94868	.30000
10	100	3.16228	10.0	1.00000	.31623
11	121	3.31662	10.48809	1.04881	.33166
12	144	3.46410	10.95445	1.09545	.34641
13	169	3.60555	11.40175	1.14018	.36056
14	196	3.74166	11.83216	1.18322	.37417
15	225	3.87298	12.24745	1.22475	.38730
16	256	4.0	12.64911	1.26491	.40000
17	289	4.12311	13.03840	1.30384	.41231
18	324	4.24264	13.41641	1.34164	.42426
19	361	4.35890	13.78405	1.37841	.43589
20	400	4.47214	14.14213	1.41421	.44721
21	441	4.58258	14.49138	1.44914	.45826
22	484	4.69042	14.83240	1.48324	.46904
23	529	4.79583	15.16575	1.51658	.47958
24	576	4.89898	15.49193	1.54919	.48990
25	625	5.0	15.81139	1.58114	.50000
26	676	5.09902	16.12452	1.61245	.50990
27	729	5.19615	16.43168	1.64317	.51962
28	784	5.29150	16.73320	1.67332	.52915
29	841	5.38516	17.02939	1.70294	.53852
30	900	5.47723	17.32051	1.73205	.54772

Table I. Squares and Roots (continued)

N	N^2	$N^{1/2}$	$(10N)^{1/2}$	$.1N^{1/2}$	$.01N^{1/2}$
31	961	5.56776	17.60682	1.76068	.55678
32	1024	5.65685	17.88854	1.78885	.56569
33	1089	5.74456	18.16590	1.81659	.57446
34	1156	5.83095	18.43909	1.84391	.58310
35	1225	5.91608	18.70829	1.87083	.59161
36	1296	6.0	18.97367	1.89737	.60000
37	1369	6.08276	19.23538	1.92354	.60828
38	1444	6.16441	19.49359	1.94936	.61644
39	1521	6.24500	19.74842	1.97484	.62450
40	1600	6.32456	20.0	2.00000	.63246
41	1681	6.40312	20.24846	2.02485	.64031
42	1764	6.48074	20.49390	2.04939	.64807
43	1849	6.55744	20.73644	2.07364	.65574
44	1936	6.63325	20.97618	2.09762	.66333
45	2025	6.70820	21.21320	2.12132	.67082
46	2116	6.78233	21.44761	2.14476	.67823
47	2209	6.85565	21.67948	2.16795	.68557
48	2304	6.92820	21.90890	2.19089	.69282
49	2401	7.0	22.13594	2.21359	.70000
50	2500	7.07107	22.36068	2.23607	.70711
51	2601	7.14143	22.58318	2.25832	.71414
52	2704	7.21110	22.80351	2.28035	.72111
53	2809	7.28011	23.02173	2.30217	.72801
54	2916	7.34847	23.23790	2.32379	.73485
55	3025	7.41620	23.45208	2.34521	.74162
56	3136	7.48331	23.66432	2.36643	.74833
57	3249	7.54983	23.87467	2.38747	.75498
58	3364	7.61577	24.08319	2.40832	.76158
59	3481	7.68115	24.28992	2.42899	.76812
60	3600	7.74597	24.49490	2.44949	.77460
61	3721	7.81025	24.69818	2.46982	.78103
62	3844	7.87401	24.89980	2.48998	.78740
63	3969	7.93725	25.09980	2.50998	.79373
64	4096	8.0	25.29822	2.52982	.80000
65	4225	8.06226	25.49510	2.54951	.80623
66	4356	8.12404	25.69047	2.56905	.81240
67	4489	8.18535	25.88436	2.58844	.81854
68	4624	8.24621	26.07681	2.60768	.82462
69	4761	8.30662	26.26785	2.62679	.83066
70	4900	8.36660	26.45751	2.64575	.83666
71	5041	8.42615	26.64583	2.66458	.84262
72	5184	8.48528	26.83282	2.68328	.84853
73	5329	8.54400	27.01851	2.70185	.85440
74	5476	8.60233	27.20294	2.72029	.86023
75	5625	8.66025	27.38613	2.73861	.86603
76	5776	8.71780	27.56810	2.75681	.87178
77	5929	8.77496	27.74887	2.77489	.87750
78	6084	8.83176	27.92848	2.79285	.88318
79	6241	8.88819	28.10694	2.81069	.88882
80	6400	8.94427	28.28427	2.82843	.89443
81	6561	9.0	28.46050	2.84605	.90000
82	6724	9.05539	28.63564	2.86356	.90554
83	6889	9.11043	28.80972	2.88097	.91104
84	7056	9.16515	28.98275	2.89828	.91652
85	7225	9.21954	29.15476	2.91548	.92195
86	7396	9.27362	29.32576	2.93258	.92736

Table I. Squares and Roots (continued)

N	N^2	$N^{1/2}$	$(10N)^{1/2}$	$.1N^{1/2}$	$.01N^{1/2}$
87	7569	9.32738	29.49576	2.94958	.93274
88	7744	9.38083	29.66479	2.96648	.93808
89	7921	9.43398	29.83287	2.98329	.94340
90	8100	9.48683	30.0	3.00000	.94868
91	8280	9.53939	30.16621	3.01662	.95394
92	8464	9.59166	30.33150	3.03315	.95917
93	8649	9.64365	30.49490	3.04949	.96437
94	8836	9.69536	30.65942	3.06594	.96954
95	9025	9.74679	30.82207	3.08221	.97468
96	9216	9.79796	30.98387	3.09839	.97980
97	9409	9.34886	31.14482	3.11448	.93489
98	9604	9.89949	31.30495	3.13050	.98995
99	9801	9.94987	31.46427	3.14643	.99499
100	10000	10.0	31.62278	3.16228	1.00000

Table II—The Normal Distribution

Standard Score	Percentile in the Normal Distribution	Standard Score	Percentile in the Normal Distribution
.00	.50	+1.65	.951
+.05	.520	+1.70	.955
+.10	.540	+1.75	.960
+.15	.560	+1.80	.964
+.20	.579	+1.85	.968
+.25	.599	+1.90	.971
+.30	.618	+1.95	.974
+.35	.637	(+1.96)	(.975)
+.40	.656	+2.00	.977
+.45	.674	+2.05	.980
+.50	.691	+2.10	.982
+.55	.709	+2.15	.984
+.60	.726	+2.20	.986
+.65	.742	+2.25	.988
+.70	.758	+2.30	.989
+.75	.773	+2.35	.991
+.80	.788	+2.40	.992
+.85	.802	+2.45	.993
+.90	.816	+2.50	.994
+.95	.829	+2.55	.995
+1.00	.841	+2.60	.995
+1.05	.853	+2.65	.996
+1.10	.864	+2.70	.997
+1.15	.875	+2.75	.997
+1.20	.885	+2.80	.997
+1.25	.894	+2.85	.998
+1.30	.903	+2.90	.998
+1.35	.911	+2.95	.998
+1.40	.919	+3.00	.998
+1.45	.926	+3.05	.999
+1.50	.933	+3.10	.999
+1.55	.939	+3.15	.999
+1.60	.943	+3.20	.999

NOTE: To determine the percentile of a negative standard score, subtract 1.00 from the percentile represented by the positive standard score of the same magnitude. For example, the percentile of a standard score, −.25 would be: .599 (the percentile of a standard score of +.25) − 1.00 = .401.

Table III—Critical Values of the t Test

Degrees of Freedom	1 tail .05	2 tail .05	1 tail .01	2 tail .01	1 tail .001
1	6.314	12.705	31.821	63.657	318.310
2	2.920	4.303	8.965	9.925	22.236
3	2.353	3.132	4.541	5.841	10.213
4	2.132	2.776	3.747	4.604	7.173
5	2.015	2.571	3.365	4.032	5.893
6	1.943	2.447	3.143	3.707	5.208
7	1.895	2.365	2.998	3.499	4.785
8	1.860	2.306	2.896	3.355	4.501
9	1.836	2.262	2.821	3.250	4.297
10	1.812	2.228	2.764	3.169	4.144
11	1.796	2.201	2.718	3.106	4.025
12	1.782	2.179	2.681	3.055	3.930
13	1.771	2.160	2.650	3.012	3.852
14	1.761	2.145	2.624	2.977	3.787
15	1.753	2.131	2.602	2.947	3.733
16	1.746	2.120	2.583	2.921	3.686
17	1.740	2.110	2.567	2.898	3.646
18	1.734	2.101	2.552	2.878	3.610
19	1.729	2.093	2.539	2.861	3.579
20	1.725	2.086	2.528	2.845	3.552
21	1.721	2.080	2.513	2.831	3.527
22	1.717	2.074	2.508	2.319	3.505
23	1.714	2.059	2.500	2.807	3.485
24	1.711	2.084	2.492	2.797	3.467
25	1.708	2.060	2.485	2.787	3.450
26	1.705	2.055	2.479	2.779	3.435
27	1.703	2.052	2.473	2.771	3.421
28	1.701	2.048	2.467	2.763	3.408
29	1.699	2.045	2.462	2.756	3.396
30	1.697	2.042	2.457	2.750	3.385
40	1.664	2.021	2.423	2.704	3.307
60	1.671	2.000	2.390	2.660	3.232
120	1.650	1.980	2.358	2.617	3.160
∞	1.645	1.960	2.326	2.576	3.090

Table IV—95% Likely Deviation in p (Rating ÷ 100) Due to Sampling Error.

When the p rating ÷ 100) is:	.01 or .99	.05 or .95	.10 or .90	.15 or .85	.20 or .80	.25 or .75	.30 or .70	.35 or .65	.40 or .60	.45 or .65	.50	Sample size (N) should be:
Sample size (N) should be:												
25	.040	.087	.120	.143	.160	.173	.183	.191	.196	.198	.200	25
50	.028	.062	.085	.101	.114	.123	.130	.135	.139	.141	.142	50
75	.023	.050	.069	.082	.092	.100	.105	.110	.113	.114	.115	75
100	.020	.044	.060	.071	.080	.087	.092	.095	.098	.099	.100	100
150	.016	.036	.049	.059	.066	.071	.075	.078	.080	.081	.082	150
200	.014	.031	.043	.051	.057	.061	.065	.068	.070	.070	.071	200
250	.012	.027	.038	.045	.050	.055	.058	.060	.062	.062	.063	250
300	.011	.025	.035	.041	.046	.050	.053	.055	.057	.058	.058	300
400	.009	.022	.030	.036	.040	.043	.046	.048	.049	.050	.050	400
500	.009	.020	.027	.032	.036	.039	.041	.043	.044	.045	.045	500
600	.008	.018	.025	.029	.033	.036	.038	.039	.040	.041	.041	600
800	.007	.015	.021	.025	.028	.030	.032	.033	.034	.035	.035	800
1,000	.006	.014	.019	.023	.026	.028	.029	.031	.031	.032	.032	1,000
2,000	.004	.010	.013	.016	.018	.019	.020	.021	.022	.022	.022	2,000

Notes: 1. If a specific deviation must be maintained over p which range above and below values of .50, use the .50 column as this will yield the largest sample size.

2. Should it be necessary to compute a sample size for quantities not reflected in this chart, use the following formula to determine sample size (N) when a 95% likelihood of a deviation in p of no more than plus or minus .05 is desired:

$$N = 1600pq$$

3. These figures deal only with simple random samples and dichotomous measures.

Table V—Critical Values of the F Test at the .05 Level

DEGREE OF FREEDOM MS$_{denominator}$	DEGREES OF FREEDOM MS$_{numerator}$						
	1	2	3	4	5	6	7
1	161.4	199.5	215.7	224.6	230.2	234.0	236.8
2	18.51	19.00	19.16	19.25	19.30	19.33	19.35
3	10.13	9.55	9.28	9.12	9.01	8.94	8.89
4	7.71	6.94	6.59	6.39	6.26	6.16	6.09
5	6.61	5.79	5.41	5.19	5.05	4.95	4.88
6	5.99	5.14	4.76	4.53	4.39	4.28	4.21
7	5.59	4.74	4.35	4.12	3.97	3.87	3.79
8	5.32	4.46	4.07	3.84	3.69	3.58	3.50
9	5.12	4.26	3.86	3.63	3.48	3.37	3.29
10	4.96	4.10	3.71	3.48	3.33	3.22	3.14
11	4.84	3.98	3.59	3.36	3.20	3.09	3.01
12	4.75	3.89	3.49	3.26	3.11	3.00	2.91
13	4.67	3.81	3.41	3.18	3.03	2.92	2.83
14	4.60	3.74	3.34	3.11	2.96	2.85	2.76
15	4.54	3.68	3.29	3.06	2.90	2.79	2.71
16	4.49	3.63	3.24	3.01	2.85	2.74	2.66
17	4.45	3.59	3.20	2.96	2.81	2.70	2.61
18	4.41	3.55	3.16	2.93	2.77	2.66	2.58
19	4.38	3.52	3.13	2.90	2.74	2.63	2.54
20	4.35	3.49	3.10	2.87	2.71	2.60	2.51

Table V—Critical Values of the F Test at the .05 Level

DEGREE OF FREEDOM $MS_{denominator}$	DEGREES OF FREEDOM $MS_{numerator}$						
	1	2	3	4	5	6	7
21	4.32	3.47	3.07	2.84	2.68	2.57	2.49
22	4.30	3.44	3.05	2.82	2.66	2.55	2.46
23	4.28	3.42	3.03	2.80	2.64	2.53	2.44
24	4.26	3.40	3.01	2.78	2.62	2.51	2.42
25	4.24	3.39	2.99	2.76	2.60	2.49	2.40
26	4.23	3.37	2.98	2.74	2.59	2.47	2.39
27	4.21	3.35	2.96	2.73	2.57	2.46	2.37
28	4.20	3.34	2.95	2.71	2.56	2.45	2.36
29	4.18	3.33	2.93	2.70	2.55	2.43	2.35
30	4.17	3.32	2.92	2.69	2.53	2.42	2.33
40	4.08	3.23	2.84	2.61	2.45	2.34	2.25
60	4.00	3.15	2.76	2.53	2.37	2.25	2.17
120	3.92	3.07	2.68	2.45	2.29	2.17	2.01
∞	3.84	3.00	2.60	2.37	2.21	2.10	2.01

Abridged from Table 18 of the Biometrika Tables for Statisticians, Vol. 1, edited by E. S. Pearson and H. O. Hartley. Used with permission.

Table VI—Random Numbers

43477	60830	73687	94649	04709	76408	16075	08774	07971	68860
41429	28832	00128	41279	46525	07645	27143	94052	20034	23726
62058	08809	94329	86703	71253	47185	41832	26329	81486	51958
78368	02590	10219	38009	36018	74406	21715	60630	68351	64431
71428	48688	49271	57434	01171	90110	30131	69786	47553	57236
15444	77536	26221	59499	21012	90577	54359	10955	76502	60417
73985	00157	35073	09029	38521	49869	52521	66306	25148	54133
98466	03606	35437	80165	62063	50889	46769	22611	14742	84952
77033	97631	92489	76251	25101	64343	60192	20273	71808	48393
44084	28966	77036	01530	15846	81309	45250	39714	31036	28784
93387	01265	67102	91231	43474	39757	47278	25851	29606	44979
03423	15722	63524	39655	66210	40363	46287	14457	70155	90821
13531	63793	60988	91786	01828	84886	92871	93247	23641	02622
02960	94167	38365	82681	50806	60703	06966	95465	10106	01444
17713	93284	00293	62190	70508	63341	45472	02759	07303	18988
48202	18322	76110	91767	65614	67773	16117	86738	75380	71634
51381	63576	19028	41979	80628	05957	10086	06902	50641	41726
94590	92009	00739	76344	51425	21447	65855	02117	20001	00953
25712	45700	42792	45451	87575	16398	10208	13665	09119	17730
95306	12273	15873	84785	65859	32083	99768	09861	61250	78755
21278	18872	21730	60536	67646	61053	57503	95540	55718	74438
45166	01058	99854	89612	38983	27384	13454	34267	84516	98698
31549	01005	22084	23462	42018	40957	67575	36843	12874	45662
58108	37688	03154	79733	50019	82512	44902	26805	56711	99024
83747	11261	13839	81686	65571	58246	59335	31797	56772	54455
15785	04614	85622	72207	62644	26003	92220	19297	85798	41120
74535	77131	91967	57625	18046	89644	75453	45925	96470	65494

Table VI—Random Numbers (continued)

24733	58948	31097	56044	56391	33054	96200	71618	63904	38866
58057	98545	68759	25648	35052	79482	61422	53197	66380	19513
19649	42280	76842	80536	91637	24995	25231	26435	31530	51264
23816	81516	74751	14863	16419	64744	40694	61472	02583	62249
50252	41267	95337	00621	45687	68539	00055	83474	00352	50845
01902	53811	05747	50185	49385	44649	23427	21488	80439	89244
11518	65904	91764	57450	18820	95865	05818	72118	80354	33058
75159	53434	44175	84139	07262	86312	52527	38345	57328	98865
77246	73686	46899	18215	87197	59253	70736	91142	10230	41092
54487	57093	52173	99199	25635	61013	35368	63088	60222	93535
19214	73465	67867	46012	65266	77491	77550	67883	09348	45136
86687	13899	03205	94136	35984	68673	88182	11036	72569	36096
63447	55823	63913	81072	11220	17667	25021	11124	41559	49241
21415	85316	19165	47146	10393	38042	34716	65919	83069	05145
83241	53145	69698	39883	12018	13155	70773	06244	00503	46824
76417	37093	34799	74956	36547	44678	39145	32771	44317	70966
26945	22976	95351	65331	33820	14939	85255	77084	95201	77451
07902	50343	30946	32586	17004	08754	99487	18144	13474	17547
84021	46206	21051	10444	73210	45269	12722	68905	98937	73476
50418	41223	93574	90443	00492	88952	29292	75184	87475	48196
01897	77615	48627	93224	21699	91172	51749	89943	73915	34005
38791	26704	11101	26274	57737	09957	40108	51041	45269	12252
66085	86248	22719	60078	86248	22719	60078	56000	95298	67789
49050	84195	63721	24571	73936	22478	69438	14330	61034	37239
74121	09579	90385	56101	23141	33934	95335	66605	41616	50247
26940	09418	14047	99521	70712	28578	35052	53113	03216	41272
18692	40704	75996	89642	53890	16563	14365	37121	93447	26591
18520	71804	64145	38637	54514	79346	85454	98608	22563	47898
84322	74850	90202	67564	93565	53311	77784	86901	21352	45997
83818	88940	79276	75191	37661	49246	56531	95969	67038	38503
27670	19492	67926	32133	81461	99569	64262	89451	58348	45023
45008	64842	83982	20316	66052	13475	86363	96969	04463	54045
84112	18264	52571	51057	33204	39708	39416	79121	19984	07812
67017	31798	87632	39615	49000	37465	83783	65519	39065	44717
16723	97882	36791	07687	87913	58299	58573	26748	33329	59243
55498	99798	99307	97656	92172	74127	15213	24133	07880	30088
09608	86858	34682	26364	46043	38988	19536	66326	22131	35854
15945	72982	94395	09534	07638	60025	91412	08251	26787	86467
77721	88123	29248	82376	31024	44758	89336	33199	95161	72181
76635	10183	71378	36622	77331	34391	10358	52635	22586	61804
67550	49064	86433	77028	84269	12357	15716	83087	57083	94715
54541	74808	57979	74598	25783	83308	67806	57060	32101	79070
85111	01434	39002	21109	75641	63866	02423	39740	16641	42187
03353	40433	12421	10628	51986	16264	29710	31881	23898	56463
23695	34003	90761	38548	14434	39665	08092	91561	76550	35245
22517	17895	04719	67270	61091	61206	17418	53648	65129	07940
61475	97391	31075	09927	79886	89980	20903	15591	05425	92227
04549	97242	42516	79920	96874	61964	99916	41819	51661	33601
36650	17498	75134	93324	83742	62534	21518	66315	04227	28529
33129	42017	53941	45493	87490	15501	05594	94054	13983	37411
89610	55018	42530	60014	77317	23778	46805	66835	79761	77055
44482	73389	40000	79501	17004	86511	66037	17622	11395	09774
56088	48565	86597	82499	15622	51239	66837	39870	37686	39870

Table VI—Random Numbers (continued)

37686	67283	64529	81628	09005	19374	25206	26870	04369	94382
26980	12436	31799	78872	87040	12393	90995	34439	87676	16108
07562	00399	34335	02424	05521	11316	18209	07414	80599	16875
75854	03249	36807	91600	18342	85643	48784	21915	92439	57398
12438	58044	36323	95545	46362	18264	92325	89575	06530	32995

The table above was prepared with the assistance of the University of Georgia Computing Center.

Index